Next-Generation Ethics

Many of the significant developments of our era, including the design of large-scale systems; advances in medicine, manufacturing, and artificial intelligence; the role of social media in influencing behavior and toppling governments; and the surge of online transactions that are replacing human face-to-face interactions, have resulted from advances in technology. These advances have also given rise to new kinds of ethical concerns resulting from the capabilities that are enabled by the technological advancement. This collection of essays by prominent academics and technology leaders covers important ethical questions arising in modern business and industry, offering guidance on how to approach these dilemmas. Chapters discuss what we can learn from the recent ethical lapses of Volkswagen, Cambridge Analytica, and many others. They also highlight the common need across all applications for sound decision-making and understanding the implications for stakeholders.

Technologists and general readers with no formal ethics training as well as specialists exploring a variety of technological applications to the field of ethics will benefit from this broad yet accessible overview of these challenges.

ALI E. ABBAS is Professor of Industrial and Systems Engineering and Public Policy at the University of Southern California, where he also directs the USC Neely Center for Ethical Leadership and Decision Making. His research focuses on decision analysis, multiattribute utility theory, and ethical decision-making, and he is the recipient of multiple awards from the National Science Foundation for his work. Dr. Abbas has authored numerous books, including *Foundations of Multiattribute Utility* and (with Ronald A. Howard) *Foundations of Decision Analysis*. He is also a coeditor of numerous edited volumes, including *Improving Homeland Security Decisions*.

Next-Generation Ethics

Engineering a Better Society

Edited by

ALI E. ABBAS
University of Southern California

CAMBRIDGE
UNIVERSITY PRESS

CAMBRIDGE
UNIVERSITY PRESS

University Printing House, Cambridge CB2 8BS, United Kingdom

One Liberty Plaza, 20th Floor, New York, NY 10006, USA

477 Williamstown Road, Port Melbourne, VIC 3207, Australia

314–321, 3rd Floor, Plot 3, Splendor Forum, Jasola District Centre,
New Delhi – 110025, India

79 Anson Road, #06–04/06, Singapore 079906

Cambridge University Press is part of the University of Cambridge.

It furthers the University's mission by disseminating knowledge in the pursuit of
education, learning, and research at the highest international levels of excellence.

www.cambridge.org
Information on this title: www.cambridge.org/9781108480413
DOI: 10.1017/9781108616188

© Cambridge University Press 2020

First published 2020

Printed in the United Kingdom by TJ International, Padstow, Cornwall

A catalogue record for this publication is available from the British Library.

Library of Congress Cataloging-in-Publication Data
Names: Abbas, Ali E. (Ali El-Sayed) editor.
Title: Next-generation ethics : engineering a better society / edited by Ali E. Abbas,
University of Southern California.
Description: First edition. | New York, NY : Cambridge University Press, 2020. |
Includes bibliographical references.
Identifiers: LCCN 2019012182 | ISBN 9781108480413 (hardback : alk. paper) |
ISBN 9781108727372 (pbk. : alk. paper)
Subjects: LCSH: Technology–Moral and ethical aspects. | Engineering ethics. |
Social responsibility of business. | Technology and state.
Classification: LCC BJ59 .N495 2020 | DDC 174/.96–dc23
LC record available at https://lccn.loc.gov/2019012182

ISBN 978-1-108-48041-3 Hardback
ISBN 978-1-108-72737-2 Paperback

Contents

Contributors

Ali E. Abbas
University of Southern California

James Babcock
Praxamed

John Basl
Northeastern University

Jonathan Beever
University of Central Florida

Christopher Bosso
Northeastern University

Andrew O. Brightman
Purdue University

John N. Celona
Decision Analysis Associates, LLC

Vinton G. Cerf
Google

Glenda N. Cooper
City University of London

Michael Davis
Illinois Institute of Technology

Matthew J. Eckelman
Northeastern University

Kathleen Eggleson
Indiana University School of Medicine-South Bend

James G. Ellis
University of Southern California

Iraj Ershaghi
University of Southern California

Marsha Ershaghi-Hames
LRN, Inc.

Alyssa J. Han
University of Southern California

Kirk O. Hanson
Santa Clara University

William P. Henry
American Society of Civil Engineers

Michael C. Hiles
Purdue University

Randall W. Hill, Jr.
University of Southern California

Eric Horvitz
Microsoft Research Labs

Ronald A. Howard
Stanford University

Josh C. Hyatt
University of Southern California

Jacqueline A. Isaacs
Northeastern University

Marianne M. Jennings
Arizona State University

Jack H. Knott
University of Southern California

János Krámer
DeepMind

Jeremy Harris Lipschultz
University of Nebraska at Omaha

Jeffrey H. Matsuura
Alliance Law Group

Laura Mosqueda
University of Southern California

Deirdre K. Mulligan
University of California Berkeley

Daniel E. O'Leary
University of Southern California

James J. O'Toole
University of Southern California

Patrick S. Ryan
Google

Max Senges
Google

Neil G. Siegel
University of Southern California

Varun Soni
University of Southern California

Richard A. Spinello
Boston College

Richard S. Whitt
NetsEdge LLC

Scott S. Wiltermuth
University of Southern California

Roman V. Yampolskiy
University of Louisville

Yannis C. Yortsos
University of Southern California

Frank Vram Zerunyan
University of Southern California

Acknowledgment

I am grateful to many people who have helped in various ways during the preparation of this book. I would like to thank the authors for their time and patience providing valuable insights and expertise that have created a resource to help people and society think about topics in Next-Generation Ethics. I thank Jerry and Linda Neely for their continuous support to the Neely Center. I also extend heartfelt thanks to many people for their help during several stages of the preparation, especially Arlene Williams for formatting some of the chapters in preparation for submission, and I thank Stephen Gee for his help e-mailing many of the authors in the early stages of the book.

1

Next-Generation Ethics

An Introduction

Ali E. Abbas

Some of the significant features of our era include the design of large-scale systems; advances in medicine, manufacturing, and artificial intelligence (AI); the role of social media in influencing behavior and toppling governments; and the surge of online transactions that are replacing human face-to-face interactions. Most of these features have resulted from advances in technology. While spanning a variety of disciplines, these features also have two important aspects in common: the necessity for sound decision-making about the technology that is evolving, and the need to understand the ethical implications of these decisions to all stakeholders.

Technology is amoral: it does not know how it will be used. In fact, technological advancements have made it even easier to deceive, partly because of the new capabilities that are enabled by the technology (such as creating fake videos from selfies, known as "Deep Fakes") and partly because of the level of complexity that is added to new advancements making the internal structure of a product less obvious to users and policy makers.

In our modern era, the decisions that revolve around technology involve more than just the technical aspects of a product; they also involve implications for individuals, policy makers, and business organizations. The need to increase awareness about the ethical sensitivities related to advances in technology for a broad audience was the main motivation for compiling this book.

Next-Generation Ethics provides reflections from a distinguished selection of authors in both academia and industry, who were asked to share their views about the most important ethical issues they encounter today or that they believe society will encounter in the near future. It is intended for a general audience, and can be used by both specialists in the field of ethics who wish to observe a variety of new implications of technology and professionals in a variety of industries who wish to better understand the ethical sensitivities that they may encounter in their professions.

There are some observations that need to be made when editing a book about ethics and technology advancement. First, because this area intersects with many fields, it was important to have a book that is accessible to a general audience.

1

This is reflected in the writing style of the chapters throughout the book. Second, even today, many graduates of engineering and technology schools have not had prior ethics training or an ethics course during their studies. Therefore, it was important to include an introductory chapter explaining some basic ethical distinctions. Third, while ethics may be taught in public policy or business curricula, the gap between technology advancements and the reaction of legislators to the ethical implications of technology has been increasing and is expected to further widen. Therefore, it was important to include several chapters related to technology in an accessible form.

Many chapters of this book make the distinction between ethics, compliance, and the legal system. It was important to highlight these basic distinctions to a general audience. Relying on the legal system alone to guide our ethical conduct is neither sufficient today nor will it be sufficient in the next generation because the legal system changes systematically and independently of the ethical system. There was a recent time when the consumption (or possession) of a small dose of marijuana in California could land you in jail. Today, you can purchase marijuana freely in many stores in the Golden State. The recent issues with Cambridge Analytica and Facebook, for example, demonstrated a situation where technology had advanced so rapidly that there was not sufficient legislation to oversee it. Yet certain acts could have been prevented based on an ethical awareness and the implications of these actions for stakeholders. Therefore, it was important to have a book that could explain some of the basic technologies and their implications for public policy graduates. Fourth, in many business organizations today, ethics is widely confused with compliance. I often use the term *unethically compliant* to highlight the distinction that you can be compliant with certain regulations or policies, and yet be unethical in your interactions with others.

The book can be used by both specialists in the field of ethics who wish to observe a variety of new implications of technology and by professionals in a variety of industries who wish to better understand the ethical sensitivities that they may encounter in their professions. Indeed, the compilation of authors includes renowned experts in the field of ethics as well as experts in technology.

Chapter 2 of the book by Ronald A. Howard provides the basic ethical distinctions needed to help us think about ethical dilemmas and about creating a personal ethical code. The chapter serves as an introductory tutorial on various ethical distinctions such as ethical–legal–prudential distinctions; positive vs negative ethical commitments, and ethical norms including action-based and outcome-based theories. The chapter also highlights a new ethical distinction: *ethical contamination*. Is it OK to continue to watch a body of work produced by famous artists if you discover that they have had some ethical violations in their personal and professional lives?

The book is divided into four areas representing four parts of the book: Technology, Business Enterprises, Engineering, and Society. This breadth of topics is intended to help us better understand some of the implications of technology for a variety of fields.

Chapters 3 through 8 focus on technology. Chapter 3 provides an ethical framework for reasoning about emerging technologies and the Internet of Things (IoT). The focus is on the decisions around which values and principles engineers uphold to balance competing values and goals, like security and ease of use, faster time to market with reliability, or transparency of work systems vs privacy of employees.

Chapter 4 focuses on the ethics of immersive technologies: any media that may affect an individual's sense of place and time or perception of the world, such as real vs digital productions and virtual reality. The chapter highlights the capabilities of immersive technologies and the ethical considerations raised by several applications.

The Internet is probably the most important technological advancement that has changed human life in the last generation. Chapter 5 presents an interview with Vint Cerf, who is widely considered to be one of the fathers of the Internet. Vint discusses his views on various technology topics such as data and privacy, net neutrality, public policy, self-driving cars, genetic codes, and his personal reflections on the future.

Technology has evolved at an exponential pace, and many social norms have changed significantly. Do the basic distinctions by which technologists should analyze ethical dilemmas still apply? Is "Do no harm" suitable as a guidance for ethical conduct of technologists in today's world? Chapter 6 introduces a Hippocratic Oath for Technologists. The chapter lays the foundations for the arguments and requirements of a unified movement, and calls for a forum for signing up for the oath to enable its widespread dissemination.

Trade-offs between data and privacy are a common theme of today's world. Chapter 7 explains the benefits of machine learning algorithms to make leaps across informational and social contexts and to infer health conditions. The chapter (a selected reprint from a *Science* article) also raises questions about how to best address potential threats to privacy.

Concerns about the potential threat of AI to society have been discussed by several people highlighting that an advanced AI with almost any goals will develop certain sub-goals such as self-preservation, self-improvement, and resource acquisition. Chapter 8 discusses the ethical issues and mechanisms surrounding the potential containment of AI should it arise in the future.

Part II focuses on business enterprises. Chapter 9 presents views on Next Generation Business Ethics and the impact of AI on the business culture. What about the ethical implications of advances in continuous monitoring systems for enterprises? On the one hand, it can be critical for an organization to continuously monitor the ethical behavior of agents, and, on the other hand, such monitoring systems can pose ethical and privacy risks to those being monitored.

Chapter 10 discusses the delicate balance associated with ethics and privacy in "enterprise continuous monitoring systems" within the context of business enterprises.

Chapter 11 highlights how the traditional components of ethical infrastructure, such as codes of ethics, ethics training, anonymous reporting, investigations, and enforcement have been insufficient in preventing ethical lapses in this generation. The chapter offers six guidelines to leaders on how they can prevent the isolation of ethical culture with management goals, strategies, incentives, and performance evaluations.

Next generation teams are unlikely to look like the teams we had twenty years ago. With the advances in technology, society has seen a shift from people staying with employers for long tenures to individuals changing employers relatively frequently. How does this shift affect values like loyalty and fairness that may help teams work effectively? Chapter 12 examines which values will most likely be affected by changes in team structure and team processes.

Chapter 13 highlights the increasing role of leaders in creating a culture of organizational candor and explains how transparent organizations are less susceptible to ethical lapses. The chapter presents guidelines into The What, The Why, and The How of creating transparent corporate cultures.

Chapter 14 highlights how corporate commitment to values will be tested on a global scale in the next generation. The chapter focuses on how organizations can build the next generation of ethical cultures and the essential role that leaders will need to play.

Part III looks at ethical issues facing large engineering firms. Chapter 15 contains a collection of facts about the escalation of ethical lapses in the Volkswagen (VW) exhaust case. While several factors may have contributed to the lapse, such as failure of management, failure of government supervision, or failure of the news media, the chapter presents the view that it was a failure of engineers and something that could be taught in a course in engineering ethics.

Chapter 16 explains ethical issues related to the current engineering and construction industries. The chapter describes some of the potential unethical practices that may be encountered, such as corruption, and raises awareness about them should they occur. The chapter also contains sources of information on anti-corruption practices that can be implemented by individuals and organizations.

Chapter 17 addresses ethical issues facing engineers in the oil and gas industry. The chapter provides some background of the field and highlights that, similar to other industries where engineering design and decision-making include gray areas, ethical decision-making cannot be solely based on the built-in core values of graduating professionals. The chapter argues that ethics needs to be learned in engineering curricula and further enhanced by modern active digital monitoring and control technology.

Chapter 18 addresses engineering codes of ethics. The chapter discusses the balance between the constraints imposed by state and government authorities on engineers and their potential use in providing a framework for justifying their decision-making and their actions.

Chapter 19 addresses the question of when bad engineering becomes bad ethics and particularly when lives are on the line. The chapter offers guidance on this question: bad engineering risks transition into bad ethics when performing proper analyses would have indicated that major system problems were being over-looked in the design, but those analyses were not performed.

Chapter 20 argues that given the rapid rate of technological innovation and a desire to be proactive in addressing potential ethical challenges that arise in contexts of innovation, engineers must learn to engage in value-sensitive design. The chapter presents case studies that may be used in teaching engineering ethics based on current product life cycle and environment impacts.

Part IV focuses on society. Chapter 21 provides the views of four deans at University of Southern California (USC) on current and next generation ethical issues in engineering, medicine, public policy, and business.

Chapter 22 discusses technological innovations and addresses the role of ethical standards, law and regulation, and the public interest on their evolution. The chapter also addresses the role of good governance mechanisms, professional responsibility, and justice and equity considerations in innovations for the next generation.

Chapter 23 presents ethics from an evolutionary standpoint and proposes a hypothesis that ethics is an evolved social behavior, which has changed and adapted following the same evolutionary process that other social behaviors and physical characteristics have followed. The chapter illustrates how this evolution-ary hypothesis has implications for engineering a better society.

The medical domain involves many aspects of ethical decision-making, and it will continue to pose numerous dilemmas in the next generation. Chapter 24 discusses the issues that would be relevant to the past, present, and future of medical ethical dilemmas and decision-making. The chapter highlights the dichot-omous personality of medicine, some of it science and some of it art. The chapter focuses on the foundation of medical ethics and decision-making, and then applies these concepts to three principle conditions that providers and patients face daily: Moral Conditions, Human Conditions, and Technological Conditions.

Chapter 25 focuses on next generation ethical development of medical devices. The chapter highlights that, although each year hundreds of new biomedical devices and therapies are developed, many fail due to unforeseen challenges of ethical, regulatory, and societal issues. The chapter explains how many of these issues can be transformed into drivers of innovation for medical solutions if ethical analysis is considered early, iteratively, and comprehensively in the research and development process.

Relating to other aspects of society, Chapter 26 explains how journalism (and as the definition of a journalist) have undergone significant change in recent times. The chapter highlights how simple it is with the growth of the Internet, and the subsequent ability of anyone with a smartphone camera and a web connection to publish. Furthermore, a US president communicates via Twitter; and Facebook Live spreads news while the mainstream media scramble to keep up. The chapter explains how the business model of journalism and the public service model of journalism are under threat and addresses the question of how mainstream media can function ethically in this challenging environment.

Chapter 27 explains how the development and popularity of computer-mediated communication (CMC), social network sites (SNSs), and social media communication (SMC) sparked twenty-first-century ethical dilemmas. The chapter then discusses global and social network ethics, transparency and independence, and legal consequences, before drawing several ethical conclusions.

Chapter 28 is a reprinted *Science* reflection article concerning AI and society. The chapter highlights how excitement about AI has been tempered by concerns about potential downsides. The chapter proposes that as we push AI science forward, and that it will be critical to address the influences of AI on people and society, on short- and long-term scales. The broad reach of AI's influences will require engagement with interdisciplinary groups, including computer scientists, social scientists, psychologists, economists, and lawyers.

Chapter 29 focuses on several societal issues related to cyberspace including free speech, intellectual property (IP) rights, privacy, and cybersecurity. The chapter also comments on the recent *Apple vs FBI* case.

Chapter 30 discusses the influence of religion on ethics in the next generation. The chapter illustrates how the United States is in the midst of a historic transformation of religious identity, and provides statistical measures for religious affiliations of generations Y and Z. The chapter concludes with thoughts on the next generation of spiritual leaders.

As with many fields, there will also be new developments, unintended consequences, and advances in the future may require reflective thought. I hope that the compilation of these topics will help set examples, and will also provide insights into analyzing future ethical sensitivities as they arise.

2

Ethical Distinctions for Building Your Ethical Code

Ronald A. Howard

2.1 Introduction

This chapter is based on ethical *distinctions*. Creating *clarity* in ethical thought depends on the clarity of distinctions we make in discussing ethical issues. Achieving clarity and consistency in ethical behavior requires understanding some basic distinctions.

Regarding the next generation, many of these distinctions will still exist; but new distinctions may be needed because of advances in technology, social media, and the nature of the world we live in. For example, technological advance has produced a major change in our everyday lives. Many of our goods and services today are obtained through transactions rather than relationships. This distinction is important in understanding the business relationships and the types of behavior resulting from each method of obtaining goods. The chapter also introduces a new distinction: ethical contamination. If we discovered that Rembrandt had defrauded his patrons, could we still admire his paintings? And if we learn that one of our favorite artists has been found responsible for mistreatment of women, how does this affect our appreciation of the art they have produced?

The next step, after understanding these distinctions, is creating your *personal ethical code that determines where you stand on each of them*. Howard and Korver (2008) provide more details on constructing a personal ethical code based on these distinctions. What is the benefit of having a personal ethical code? The answer is the avoidance of *remorse*: the deep and painful regret for having done wrong.

We shall focus our discussion of distinctions on ethical actions including both physical actions and the things we communicate to others in speech or a written equivalent. While it is true that the thought may be the father of the deed and it is unwise to lust in your heart, your ethical actions will determine the effect you have on people, on other living things, and on the inanimate universe depending only on the range of your ethical code.

2.2 Prudential/Legal/Ethical Distinction

Not all actions are ethically sensitive. It is useful to distinguish actions according to their nature. Actions may be *prudential*, *legal*, or *ethical*. Prudential actions are those that are in your personal interest. It may or may not be prudential for you to brush your teeth twice a day, or to purchase long-term care insurance. Depending on the society in which you live, certain actions may be legal or illegal. In some societies taking an action may make it illegal, like smoking certain vegetation; in other societies not taking an action may make it illegal, like not declaring income to the government or not reporting for military service. Whether an action is ethical for you depends only on your personal ethical code.

To illustrate, consider the story of Anne Frank, the girl who was sheltered by others from being arrested by the Nazi officials of the Netherlands. Hiding her was illegal, with extremely serious penalties; ethical to those who did it and found it prudential; ethical to those who did not do it because the risks were not prudential; and unethical to those who simply do what the law requires.

2.3 Lying/Stealing/Harming Distinction

Many ethical decisions are concerned with issues of *lying*, *stealing*, or *harming*. Let us begin with lying. Lying is not simply not telling the truth. Lying is saying something that you know is not true with the intention of deceiving the listener. For example, if you asked me whether I can give you a ride home today, I may reply, "Sure." Then I remember a few minutes later that my car is in for repairs and that I cannot take you home. Did I lie to you? No, I was mistaken: I had no intention to deceive you. As soon as I realize this, I must tell you that I cannot give you a ride home today as you requested. I may be forgetful, but I am not a liar.

Stealing is depriving another of property without his or her permission. Examples include pickpocketing, auto theft, and burglaries. Often lying is involved because there has been a fraudulent representation of property: you thought you were buying a horse but what you got was a pony. Ponzi schemes, for example, are theft through lying.

Harming is physically injuring another with results that can range from minor injury to death. We find that these ethical transgressions often appear together. The victims of the Nazi Holocaust were not only killed but also lied to and stolen from.

2.4 Positive and Negative Ethical Commitments

A *negative ethical commitment* is a statement of what you are committed not to do. For example, I shall not lie, I shall not steal, I shall not harm. I did not murder anybody yesterday, I did not murder anybody today, and it required no energy whatsoever to carry out this pledge. A *positive ethical commitment* requires you to provide the truth to anyone who is lied to, to return stolen property to its owners, and to prevent the harming of others. One must be sparing in making positive ethical commitments. I am sure that committing myself to restoring to their proper owners the bicycles stolen on the Stanford campus would leave me time to do little else.

2.5 Action-Based and Consequence-Based Ethics

There are two major schools of ethical thought. One says that your ethics should be based solely on the actions you take and on the ethical nature of those actions. The other says that your ethics should be based on the consequences of the actions you take and on the desirability of these consequences. Volumes have been written on these notions, and they sometimes have a specialized vocabulary. *Action-based ethics* are called *deontological*, based on a root that means you have a duty to do the right thing. *Consequence-based ethics* are called *teleological*, based on a root that means you have to look at the purpose of your action. An action-based person would say that they always tell the truth, regardless of consequences. The consequence-based person would determine what to say by examining the consequences of different statements before choosing one. Analysis of decisions in the face of uncertainty is easier for the action-based person. All that is required is to remove any action that is ethically unacceptable and then choose from the remaining. The consequence-based person must look at the chances of each possible result of all actions to decide what to do. Howard and Abbas (2016) provide guidance in making decisions.

2.6 Testing Your Ethical Code

Now we have created some ethical distinctions, it is time to build your ethical code and test it. Where do you stand on each of these distinctions? There are various ways you can test your ethical code. One way is the notion of *reciprocity*. How would you feel if everyone treated you the way you are proposing to treat them? Another is the notion of *universality*. Suppose that you could make your ethical code universal for everyone in the world just by saying so. Would that be okay?

A more discerning test of how your ethical code is working in your life is offered by Nietzsche's notion of *perpetual return*. Suppose you are magically confronted by a wizard who tells you, and convinces you, that you are destined when you die to live your entire life over and over again through eternity, exactly reproduced in every detail. Until you die you will be able to make any changes in your life that you wish, but what the wizard says will still be true. You will not be able to make any corrections in the life you have lived up to this point. Do you say to yourself "Oh boy!" or "Oh $#&^!"? The latter would be a sign of remorse, and the impetus to live the rest of your life in a different way.

2.7 The Color of Lies

Since most of the students in my ethics classes have little interest in harming anyone, they find it easy to include in their codes an ethic prohibiting harming innocent people, while allowing the use of force in self-defense. Similarly, they have much better alternatives than stealing from others; although they often succumb to the temptations of downloading copyrighted material. However, much of the discussion concerns the telling of "white" lies. Students often see them as necessary to be "nice" to others, or simply to be efficient in ending a conversation. When asked, "Does what I am wearing make me look fat?," it is easier to reply, "You look fine," than to give an accurate answer.

However, the efficiency often comes at a cost. Consider two male students Joe and Jim who live in the same dormitory. One evening Joe tells Jim that he is going to the movies tonight and wonders whether Jim might go with him. Jim really just wants to goof-off watching TV, but replies, "No, I have plenty of homework to do." And this ends the conversation.

Note that Jim's response is technically true, since students always have plenty of homework that can be done, but it is not the truth because he intends to watch TV.

Now suppose the two men meet at breakfast the next day. Joe might ask Jim, "Did you complete the homework you were planning to do last night?" Jim, who just watched TV, might reply, "Not as much as I would like to have done." This answer is also technically true but still not the truth about how Jim spent the evening.

Consider how telling the truth might change your future relationship. Responding to Joe's request for company at the movies, Jim could have said, "I am planning to goof-off watching TV tonight, but I would like to go with you to a movie on some other occasion." Then, the next day when they meet, Joe could ask Jim what he watched on TV, and Jim could ask Joe what he thought of the movie.

The point is that lies of any color often provoke more lying, while the truth can cement a relationship.

2.8 Truth in Business

We have just discussed the importance of truth in our personal lives. Let us spend some time considering it in business relationships.

2.8.1 Advertising

We have all seen commercial advertising on television. Consider the typical commercial for a new car model. You will see it being driven (by a professional driver) on a scenic two-lane road in California on a beautiful day. It appears to be too good to be true; and, in fact, it is not an accurate depiction of what purchasing, owning, and driving a car in California is like for most people. The commercial never shows cars proceeding at less than walking pace, even on freeways, during rush hours. There is never a problem finding a place to park the car and no mention of the injuries and deaths associated with the use of motor vehicles. The same relationship between the information in the advertisement and the information you need to know about the product to make wise decisions about it is true for virtually all products and services. Like an iceberg, what you see is a small part of the whole.

Sometimes the representation of a product extends beyond the problem of providing only partial information to actual fraud. Recently two of the people in my life accepted offers of a free sample of a skincare product by agreeing to pay for its shipping at a cost of only a few dollars. Both of them discovered that the credit card used for the shipping cost was being charged about $90 each month for a larger supply of the product; an arrangement made without their consent. They both spent considerable time on the phone stopping further charges and arranging for hopeful repayment.

2.8.2 Transactions vs Relationships

The preceding example demonstrates a major change that technological advance has produced in our everyday lives. Many of our goods and services today are obtained through *transactions* rather than *relationships*. I was once a customer in a hardware store where a well-dressed woman, after looking at the tools on offer, brought a hammer to the counter to pay for it. The clerk asked the woman what she was going to use it for. She replied that her husband told her to buy a hammer for hanging some pictures in the playroom. The clerk said, "This is a professional carpenter's hammer. It is excellent, expensive, and designed for everyday use by a professional. We have other hammers for a third of the price that would serve for your purpose." He showed her one and she thanked him for his help as they processed the transaction.

This was an unusual event in a world where cashiers using laser scanners are primarily concerned with making sure the items are properly scanned, paid for, and given to the customer. It would be very unusual, for example, for a cashier to ask whether a customer had sauce for the spaghetti that is being purchased. However, I would not be surprised if some startup will soon create a system that will automatically make suggestions like this. Yet even this supermarket checkout experience is more personal than the transactions we make by ordering over the Internet.

2.8.3 Secrets

When I first studied ethics, I did not think that keeping secrets posed much of a problem. For example, if someone asked me how much money I made in the year, I could reply, "That is none of your business," or, "I prefer not to say," depending upon how sharp I wanted my response to be.

I learned to be more sensitive to keeping secrets from an incident involving my daughter and one of my sons. My daughter was married to a man who was responsible for running an electronic startup company. My son had just graduated from college and had obtained his first job working for the company. One Saturday my daughter phoned me, very agitated. She told me that the company would announce layoffs next week and that my son would be one of those laid off. Her agitation was due to her husband saying that she must not tell anyone, in particular, her brother, before the layoffs were publicly announced. She said, "Dad I just had to talk to somebody because I feel very bad about this, and of course you must keep it secret, too." I told her not to be concerned, that everything would work out fine. Soon the phone rang again and it was the son we had been discussing. He said, "Dad, now that I have a steady job, I want to buy a car. I would like to have you join me today in looking at some of the possibilities." Now I realized that my knowledge of the company's action had changed my relationship with my son. I could not simply tell him that this was not a good time to be buying a car because of his changed prospects at the company. I held my tongue and I went out with him to look at potential cars to buy. Happily, he did not decide to make a purchase, and therefore I was spared from having to say anything about the coming layoffs. If he had decided to buy a car, I probably would have told him, but I had learned a very valuable lesson. That is that any secret you keep can change your relationship with anyone who would benefit by knowing that secret. When I returned home, I called my daughter and told her please not to tell me any information about the company that was not public knowledge. Ever since, my policy has been simply to decline any offer of secret information. For example, I simply do not wish to have someone tell me about rumors of infidelity in a couple of my acquaintance.

2.8.4 Professional Secrets

We also realize that there is information we know that we want to keep secret from other people. Many professions, such as law or medicine, have ethical codes that require keeping secret information about patients or clients. As a consulting decision analyst, I agree to keep secret information I learn from my clients. I make sure that the secrecy agreement specifies exactly what information will be kept secret, the time period during which it will be secret, and that any information I already know is not part of this agreement. In particular, I point out that I have similar arrangements with other clients and that any information that I know, which is covered by the secrecy agreement I have with them, I will not reveal to the new client, no matter how valuable it might be to them.

Suppose I am working for a client and find that the project has changed direction. It is now beginning to work in a new area that I already know to be a waste of money, based on my confidential work for another client. At that point I would have to say that, for professional reasons, I must withdraw from working on the project. I will, if they wish, describe what we have been doing to another qualified consultant (not involved in the other project), at my expense, so that they can continue with the project. Consulting companies must create "Chinese walls" like this to preserve client secrets.

The legal profession also has to have ways to maintain its ethical standards. Our ethics class once received a lecture by the chairman of the California committee on legal ethics. One of the illustrations he used is how a trial lawyer can never allow testimony he knows to be false to be presented to the court. For example, suppose a lawyer is defending a client accused of armed robbery at a specified time and place. The client could say to his lawyer, "I have five guys who will testify that I was at a different place at the time of the crime. Just tell me where you want them to say I was." Since that testimony would be false, the lawyer cannot allow it to be given. If the lawyer convinces his client not pursue such a course, the lawyer can continue doing his best job to present the client's case. However, should the client persist in this course of action, the lawyer must tell the court that unfortunately he cannot continue to represent this client, without disclosing why. Another attorney can continue the defense, possibly after some delay.

Medical doctors must often face ethical challenges. I know of several cases where the same doctor treats both the husband and wife of a couple. Suppose one of them shows up with a sexually transmitted disease – perhaps a serious one. How does the doctor provide excellent care to both the husband and the wife while not betraying any secrets?

Businesses often require employees to keep secrets about research or expansion plans. The introduction of new and supposedly improved products may also be kept secret, to discourage customers from waiting for the new product. Suppose you are a salesman for the company and your brother is one of your good customers. In spite of your instructions, would you tell him that the new product is coming out in two weeks and will offer improved features at the same price?

2.9 Clinical Trials

A *clinical trial* is an experimental study of a new drug or treatment for a medical condition. The subjects to be used in the trial are told that they will be receiving either the drug or a harmless pill called a placebo, and that neither they nor the person treating them will know which is which. If the drug is found to be effective and safe, then it may be authorized to be prescribed by the medical system.

Suppose that you have been suffering from a serious disease for many years in the care of your doctor. The doctor has been following the medical literature and learns that a new drug currently being tested is very promising for the treatment of your condition. You ask your doctor if he would recommend your taking this new drug. He says,

> "I would, but, of course, I cannot prescribe it for you until it is approved. Even if I could get the drug, I could not give it to you. To do so would cause me to lose my license to practice medicine. The only way to get the drug now would be to enroll in a clinical trial. Then, as I have explained, there is a good chance that you would be receiving a harmless pill instead of the drug."

So, even if you were willing to accept all the unknown risks to your health that this drug might cause, you cannot get it. Is this ethical?

2.10 Ethics of Death

Everyone who has dealt with people at the end of their lives and who has spoken in my classes has agreed that dying people should be told the truth about their prospects. Since doctors cannot typically predict death unless it is imminent, the truth will usually be something like, "Some people in your condition die in three months, others live more than a year, and we really do not know why." People can use this knowledge to get their affairs in order and to deal with all their human relationships.

2.11 Ethical Contamination

For many years we have discussed in the ethics class a hypothetical situation based on the horrible medical experiments imposed on certain people interned by the Nazi government during World War II. The question posed is this. Suppose it was discovered that a review of these records, after many decades, revealed that they had in fact produced a cure for a very serious ailment that is currently untreatable. Should the unethical way in which the information was obtained allow using it to alleviate the suffering of current patients with the disease? You can imagine the nature of the discussion. A more general question would be whether the artistic, literary, or scientific achievements of the person responsible for them are tarnished by other unethical behavior of that person. If we found that Rembrandt had beaten his wife or defrauded his patrons could we still admire his paintings?

I encountered this issue personally when I viewed a ten-minute video of a talk show, hosted by Stephen Colbert, in which Jerry Seinfeld, the comedian, was the guest. At one point, Colbert asks Seinfeld how he learned to be a comedian during his childhood, after realizing that it was his dream. Seinfeld replies that he learned by listening to records of the comic performances of Bill Cosby, who had recently been accused and found legally responsible for his mistreatment of women. Seinfeld claims that Cosby produced the greatest body of work in comedy. Colbert says that he listened to the same albums every night and that "they saved my life." Colbert adds, "I can't listen to it now. I can't separate it." Jerry seems surprised.

I decided to gather some evidence. I put on some earphones and listened to some of the very famous comic presentations by Cosby that are available on the Internet. I could not help bursting out laughing. My female partner asked what I was finding so funny. I replied, "I am listening to Bill Cosby routines." She said, "I could not listen to him." I knew that she had been a great fan of Charlie Rose, who interviewed many people in depth over numerous years. Yet Charlie had also lately been publicly accused of transgressions in his treatment of women, and was no longer being broadcast. I asked her to suppose there was a special tonight described as "Charlie Rose's Most Famous interviews." Would she watch? She said she would be tempted, but was not sure whether she would actually watch.

A recent inquiry on the Internet showed that there were over 200 people of some note who had been accused of sexually inappropriate behavior and whose careers were now compromised. The list included many actors whose work had enriched my life for decades. I realized that I could enjoy the good work they had done, and thank them for it, while still acknowledging their ethical lapses. Can you?

References

Howard, R. A. & Abbas, A. E. (2016). *Foundations of decision analysis.* New York, NY: Pearson, p. 807.

Howard, R. A. & Korver, C. D. (2008). *Ethics for the real world: Creating a personal code to guide decisions in work and life.* Boston, MA: Harvard Business School Press.

PART I

Technology

3

Composite Ethical Frameworks for the Internet of Things and Other Emerging Technologies

Max Senges, Patrick S. Ryan, and Richard S. Whitt

3.1 Introduction

Modern engineering and technology have allowed us to connect with each other and even to reach the moon. But technology has also polluted vast areas of the planet and empowered surveillance and authoritarian governments with danger-ous tools. There are numerous cases where engineers and other stakeholders routinely ask what they are capable of inventing, and what they actually should invent. Nuclear weapons and biotechnology are two examples. But when analyz-ing the transformations arising from less controversial modern socio-technological tools – like the Internet, smartphones, and connected devices, which augment and define our work and social practices – two very distinct areas of responsibility become apparent. On the one hand, a question arises around the values and practices of the engineers who create the technologies. What values should guide their endeavors and how can society promote good conduct? On the other hand, there are questions regarding the effects of people using these technologies. While engineering and design choices can either promote or hinder commendable social behavior and appropriate use, this chapter will focus on the first question.

The values of the developers of a technological product are embedded in the product. The values that engineers envisioned may not be the same as what the users want. Engineers define how people can use the technology by limiting or expanding its functionality. Users, in turn, find new applications, adaptations, and enhancements. So, a webcam can be designed to broadcast to the Internet by default, or allow the user to expressly enable it to broadcast. The broadcast function could be even be totally disabled. Another example is when engineers face choices about whether to require a strong, unique password to protect access to a webcam; insist on more rigorous two-factor authentication; or perhaps favor "ease of use" by setting a fixed password (or no password), which then might be abused by hackers.

Our focus here is on the decisions around which values and principles engin-eers uphold, and how they can be supported to balance competing values/goals, such as security and ease of use, faster time to market with reliability, or transparency of work systems versus privacy of employees. The variety of market, ethical, and cultural values at interplay with engineering rationale in these research and development (R&D) scenarios can lead to a complicated analysis of the actual practice of making choices between trade-offs.

This book's focus on emerging technologies adds an important element to the creation of new technical capabilities: Engineers should make a reasonable effort to anticipate and shape the potential of the technology to change society with a particular emphasis on whether the technology will improve or harm individual users. Of course, it is impossible to anticipate all consequences. Nonetheless, a reasonable effort should be made. There is a continuous responsibility to monitor and recognize when negative effects occur and some use of a technology has to be contained. Inappropriate and unsafe behavior, unintended consequences, and intrusiveness regarding human rights can never be fully avoided; but engineers should accept their impact and responsibility as creators of opportunity.

Philosophers have a long tradition in the study of teleology and the various elements and motivations that drive our goals and purpose. Teleological ethics derives one school of thought from normative guidance and by judging the consequences and utility of personal choices. In contemporary machine intelligence systems, it is an increasingly challenging problem to discern what features are personal choices; that is, what aspects were programmed by the engineers and what was "learned by the technology." Our hypothesis in this chapter is that a better understanding of the end goals behind innovations, combined with more informed discourse around "good engineering," can lead to better outcomes for the engineers, their institutions/organizations, and society at large.

In brief, the key proposition of this chapter is that we live today in a society embodied in deontological structure, consisting in part of the basic rights and laws of the universal and national citizen. This deontological structure means that our societies are organized around universal rights and duties, which today are, in turn, encoded in human rights and legal rules that prescribe what is right or admissible and what is unethical or prohibited. This provides a useful basis on which new technologies and business models are built and deployed. However, it would be a mistake to immediately extend the existing *deontological approach* to ethics by crafting discrete laws and rules and regulations proposed to govern these new technologies, such as the Internet of Things (IoT). Instead, we suggest that a better approach is to take full account of two other pathways to ethical frameworks – *the teleological approach* (to consider our overarching vision/goals and their consequences) and *the virtues approach* (the built-in experimental practices and professional codes of conduct) – to give proper shape and focus to our ethical reasoning. Only when we are properly informed by our shared ethical elements of vision and virtues, would it then be more reasonable to step back into the deontological world and consider the appropriate ethical "rules of the road" for various engineering dilemmas, including IoT.

3.2 Three Complementary Approaches to IoT Ethics

The fundamental aspects of IoT systems raise profound ethical questions about the ultimate responsibility for the ways these systems operate in our society. In short, who is to praise, or to blame, for what they actually do? How should we apply and evolve ethics for IoT?

Mike Ananny has discerned three dimensions for scrutinizing ethics in ways that hold accountable advanced technology systems, such as IoT (Ananny, 2016). The deontological approach, based on Kant, focuses on the means and looks to a fixed set of principles, rules, or duties. The teleological approach, based on Bentham (and others), focuses on the ends, and looks to the consequences of goals and decisions. Finally, Ananny's virtue ethics approach focuses on the values and best practices that emerge through experimentation and discourse of the technologists themselves. While doubtless there are other feasible ways to categorize an approach to ethics, for the purposes of this chapter we will focus on Ananny's approach and the virtue ethics framework.

Given the relatively early stage of IoT, virtue ethics seems to be the approach that is most directly suited to discussing the practices and responsibilities of IoT developers. That particular approach provides practical guidance that includes sensitivity to context and practical limits of time and resources, which can influence judgment and decision. Of course, technology ethics emerge from a mix of all three of these dimensions and it manifests itself in institutional codes, professional culture, technological capabilities, social practices, and individual decision-making. There is no single correct path, or one that is correct in all instances.

Deontological ethics require stakeholders to define the specific rules and principles that should be followed in the universality of IoT engineering contexts because of the reliance on principles, rules, and duties. Older technologies are better entrenched in these dimensions; newer technologies like IoT require more flexible and contestable ethical critiques and meanings. As Ananny points out, the ethical dimensions of technology platforms are moving targets. For the deontological approach, there is difficulty drawing lines around the right rules to adopt and apply. For the teleological approach of goals and their consequences, as well as for the virtue ethics approach, there is the difficulty of limited reach and dependence of perspective.

Figure 3.1 illustrates this proposed taxonomy, which includes elements of the three ethical pathways described earlier in the context of the IoT space.

Table 3.1 provides further clarity for how the different approaches can complement each other and outlines a comprehensive framework to discuss ethical dimensions for IoT development.

Table 3.1 *Teleology, deontology, and virtue ethics*

	Teleology	Deontological Ethics	Virtue Ethics / Values
In theory	Identifying goals (like safety or an open society) and then derive practical ethical consequences[1]	Moral principles informing categorical rules	Desirable habits and ways of reasoning
In practice	Socio-technological vision or shaping view that aims to set incentives for ethical conduct and outcomes (Hagel, Brown, & Davison 2008)	Internet Rights and Principles, Regulation, Standards	Codes of conduct and best practices
Applied examples to IoT	Nest vision for thoughtful home (e.g., nest) or narratives like singularity	Intelligent Device Bill of Rights, Hacker's Code of Ethics	IETF Values; IGF IoT DC

[1] Ethics should help people choose "the action that will bring the most good to the party the actor deems most important" (Merrill, 2011).

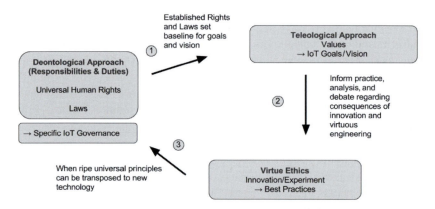

Figure 3.1 *Relation between ethics approaches and application to IoT governance*

3.2.1 Deontological Ethics: The Risk of Premature Prescriptions for Engineers and Application to IoT

Deontological ethics emerge from a fixed set of principles, rules, or duties. For this reason, it is a useful structure for regulatory frameworks that are made up of rights and bolstered by legal code. These instruments are at the heart of the responsibilities and duties of stakeholders, and they should also necessarily address technology on a relatively high level of abstraction in order to remain relevant over longer periods of time. In order to successfully derive deontological principles or better (in most cases) transpose existing rights and laws to address affordances and potential of new technologies, these technologies have to be relatively mature and well understood.

If one applies a deontological approach too early when the features and potential of the emergent technology are not stable, the effort is likely to cause significant unintended side effects and extra work for all parties as the technology "changes under our feet." Further, the deliberation towards deontological ethical codes (i.e., the instruments) can bear meaningful results, and of course, as mentioned earlier, there is no clear border between what we describe as a phased composite approach, as all approaches inform each other and evolve in parallel.

One important segue between virtue ethics and deontological ethics are professional codes of conduct as defined for IoT related engineering by associations like Association for Computing Machinery (ACM) or Institute of Electrical and Electronics Engineers (IEEE). Significant interest and analysis has also focused on hacker ethics (Levy, 1984). Indeed, there have been various calls to define deontological principles for IoT, mostly framed as Bill of Rights (Fried, 2014). This is in addition to various self-proclaimed manifestos including, for example, a "Maker Bill of Rights" (Torrone, 2006). One of the most promising deontological approaches might be to evolve the Internet Rights and Principles Charter by the Internet Governance Forums IRP multistakeholder coalition, as this effort is connected to the United Nations and aims to develop its work as close as possible with the Universal Declaration of Human Rights (UDHR) and the established body of Human Rights instruments. But other initiatives are also pointing in a meaningful direction. We will discuss the Intelligent Device Bill of Rights in more detail, as it enables us to discern the challenges and benefits of the deontological approach.

3.2.2 The "Bill of Rights" Approach

Can IoT devices be entrusted to carry out ethical decisions? And do we need prescriptive means to ensure such an ethical outcome? There have been efforts afoot for some time to do just that. One must ask, however, whether jumping immediately to prescriptive deontological ethics is the right approach.

Proposed in 2001, the Device Bill of Rights, initiated by technologist Bran Ferren and later championed by lawyer Kalle Kontson, is one example of an effort to create a set of rules for IoT to do so (Kontson, 2001). As its name indicates, this proposal is a call for a Bill of Rights that endows a Constitutional character, in this case, to a particular class of IoT devices – those that access the wireless spectrum. The proposal forces a shared responsibility of rights and obligations to the devices between the coders that develop them and the devices that "intelligently" act to enforce the rules. Thus, algorithms can be uploaded to devices to enable those devices to function cognitively in their environment. Moreover, in some cases the addition of devices theoretically could improve the functioning of the system by processing and passing data along, just as the addition of servers and nodes increases capacity on the Internet. The proposed Intelligent Device Bill of Rights reads as follows:

Article 1: The Right to Spectrum Access

Any intelligent wireless device may, on a non-interference basis, use any frequency, frequencies or bandwidth, at any time, to perform its function.

Tenet 1: Mental Competence and Moral Character
To exercise rights under this Article, intelligent devices must be mentally competent to accurately determine the possibility of interference that may result from their use of the spectrum, and have the moral character to not do so if that possibility might infringe on the rights of other users.

Tenet 2: Good Citizenship
To exercise rights under this Article, intelligent devices must actively use the wireless spectrum within the minimum time, spatial and bandwidth constraints necessary to accomplish the function. Squatting on spectrum is strictly prohibited.

Article 2: The Right to Protection

All users of the spectrum shall have the right to operate without harmful electromagnetic interference from other users.

Tenet 1: Priority of Rights
Priority of rights under this Article may be determined by the proper authorities only in cases of National emergency, safety of life or situations of extreme public interest.

Tenet 2: Limit of Rights
Rights under this Article may be exercised only when the systems exercising the rights are designed, as determined by the state of the practice, to be reasonably resistant in interference.

Article 3: Supremacy Clause

All licensing, auctioning, selling or otherwise disposition of the rights to frequencies and spectrum usage shall be subordinate to, and controlled by Articles 1 and 2, above.

Like the Bill of Rights in the US Constitution, the Ferren/Kontson Bill of Rights embraces personal freedoms and records rights and responsibilities – here, the personal freedom of communications. The Device Bill of Rights then aspires to ascribe these rights and responsibilities to technical devices. We will briefly review the meaning and the import of the right to spectrum access and the right to protection, as well as the rationale behind the supremacy clause.

Article 1, the right to spectrum access, guarantees the rights of intelligent wireless devices to use the spectrum on a "non-interference basis," but it also requires that the devices not "infringe on the rights of other users" (Tenet 1) and that they use the spectrum "within the minimum time, spatial and bandwidth constraints" needed to function

(Tenet 2). In short, this principle attempts to set forth the basic parameters for cognitive radio, as well as the "listen before talking" qualities of the Ethernet.

Importantly, Article I can be seen as "permissionless" in that does not set any particular restrictions on the technologies to be used. Thus, by setting the *principles* underlying spectrum use, rather than the *means* by which the spectrum will be used, the document, like the original Bill of Rights, may avoid becoming superannuated. Because the technologies that we use today may change over time, the principles in the Wireless Device Bill of Rights refrain from locking in the use of a particular technology that may become obsolete within the next few years. To put it another way, the Wireless Device Bill of Rights simply protects one's right to access the spectrum resource so long as one follows general principles of good citizenship and behavior.

Article 2, the right to protection, guarantees the rights of those who already use the spectrum and prioritizes different uses of the spectrum. For example, the Article explicitly states that "National emergency, safety of life or situations of extreme public interest" may take precedence over other uses of the spectrum, as determined by "the proper authorities" (Tenet 1). It also would require the devices to be able to be rendered inoperative in order to ensure sufficient spectrum is available for emergency communications. Accordingly, just as automobiles are required by law to pull over to the side of the road to allow ambulances to move through traffic, so too electronic devices would have to be programmed to be automatically disabled in emergency situations in order to give national interest communications a first right of passage through the spectrum.

Furthermore, this Article requires devices to have both an intelligent transmission and an intelligent reception capability. As Federal Communications Commission (FCC) Chairman Michael Powell emphasized at the University of Colorado's Silicon Flatirons conference in 2002, one of the principal problems with receivers is that they are often "dumb," meaning that they are unable to distinguish between different transmission sources (Powell, 2001). This is particularly the case for low-tech receivers that may not have designed the appropriate filters to sort out the noise in the environment. Thus, the obligation to be a good actor is a shared responsibility between transmitters and receivers; and regulations would need to cover receivers in addition to transmission-only devices.

Finally, Article 3, the supremacy clause, indirectly addresses the Coasian free market spectrum model by mentioning the "licensing, auctioning, selling or otherwise disposition of the rights to frequencies and spectrum usage." This Article seems to intimate that Ronald Coase's spectrum-as-property theory and Paul Baran's spectrum-as-commons theory *may*, in fact, be able to work together in spite of their seeming inconsistencies. In theory, then, a broadcasting company (e.g., NBC, ABC, or CBS) could continue to "own" (or have an exclusive license to use) the airwaves to broadcast television on one or more particular channels. This right to exclusive use, however, would be subordinate to the rights of individuals to access the airwaves (Article 1) and to the rights of others who already use the airwaves (Article 2). In other words, this Article suggests that, subject to other rights, limited property rights may be exerted over areas of the spectrum. As a point of comparison, it is like saying that a person may own the beach that connects to his or her house, but that the use of that beach by others may not be prohibited so long as designated rules are followed.

Ultimately, the Wireless Device Bill of Rights has not advanced. The idea provides an opportunity to exchange views and recognize the role of end users, but it remains another unused – yet intellectually satisfying – proposal. The challenge that the Wireless Device Bill of Rights attempts to address remains unmet today. How can industry take these frameworks and apply them in practice?

3.2.3 The New Technology Challenge: Too Much, Too Soon

There are two chief challenges with any deontological ethical approach to a particular industry segment or technology platform. First, the approach may become overly-prescriptive. Second, the approach may be premature, becoming too much, and too soon.

In the case of the Wireless Device Bill of Rights, the deontological backdrop is based on a history of more than 100 years of detailed regulation of radio spectrum as a commercial input. So, the creation of a new "bill of rights" for the devices is, in a way, simply an extension of laws and norms that were set for operators and to offer a set of rights for the end users. The approach ends up with a softer form of principles and has a character that is already well-informed by the rules and practices that already affect the use of spectrum.

By contrast, the world of IoT is one where smart, connected devices for the first time are being embedded into user environments. Thus, the deontological approach should not be our first, and certainly not the only, ethical stop. We need first to understand the appropriate unified perspective of shared visions and goals, followed by identifying the real-world values that inspire engineers in their daily work. Only then should we consider venturing down the Kantian path of regulating market mechanisms.

3.3 Vision as Ethical Framing: Teleology and the Consequences for IoT

Following our analysis of deontological ethics, and our concern about the premature imposing of prescriptive regulation on a nascent technology like IoT, in this section we discuss how higher-level vision and goals – like egalitarian access to connected technologies and the subsequent individual and social benefits – should initially influence engineering practice. Scholars Rafael Calvo and Dorian Peters (2014) argue that we are "leaving behind the stark mechanical push for productivity and efficiency that characterized the early age of computing and maturing into a new era in which people demand that technology contribute to their wellbeing as well as to some kind of net social gain" (Calvo & Peters, 2014).

What are some traditional and some progressive higher-level goals for modern engineers to consider? Instead of a deontological approach, should engineers take into account teleological aspects of IoT technology design? We consider these goals knowing that some are traditionally outside of the scope of what engineers felt responsibility for. However, we would like to argue that the pervasiveness and impact of contemporary connected technology design and innovation on our everyday lives demands an extension to the scope of what engineers should consider as part of their responsibilities. It is worthwhile to engage in this inquiry and ask what kind of positive effects our socio-technological innovations can have both in terms of users' well-being (physiological and psychological health) and with regard to societal benefits.

One aspect we have treated in another article is how the concept of *safety* and safety testing has become a significantly more complex responsibility (Cerf, Ryan, Senges, & Whitt, 2016). This is a shared responsibility between the user and the technology provider, but a constellation of many stakeholders involved (e.g., including government, civil society, and the technical community); thus jointly generating highly complex ecosystems with hundreds of stakeholders contributing their part. The responsibility for safety is taken to a whole new level when machine-learning systems provide results based on training data that cannot be foreseen by the creators of the system. The experts of such systems are already stepping up and addressing the new questions and responsibilities. Academic inquiry and the open exchange of solutions and risks among and between all stakeholders seem to provide the best chances to find and evolve solutions.

Another feature of the engineering mindset has grown significantly in societal relevance: designing for minimal negative impact on our habitats. This highlights the need for stakeholders to consider trade-offs and to play their respective roles in governance practices to meet a minimum standard. A new extension of this notion asks engineers to also minimize the impact on the cyber ecosystem. How can systems minimize traffic and clean up after themselves? Clean de-installs and reasonable refresh rates, for example, are just some practices that engineers can address. While technologists have always cared about how their systems are used, all knowledge and technology can be used for good and bad objectives. IT-based human-resource systems have been leveraged in an attempt to reduce human bias and promote more egalitarian access to opportunities (e.g., inclusion of physiologically or mentally impaired peers). Our innovative machine-learning systems depend on the training data that human stakeholders enter and – although the engineers might aim to program the system with the intention to improve fairness and reduce bias – the systems can learn unconscious biases from training data that

Figure 3.2 *Manipulating the user's own (self)representation by technology*

humans enter, and indeed create fewer equal opportunities. In this space, engineers are addressing these problems as they arise and attempting to include checks-and-balances (i.e., ethical practices) that will evolve with these systems (Hardt, 2016).

Another example of the positive (and negative) normative results that contemporary technologies can cause comes from the connected devices that create augmented or virtual realities. The examples in Figure 3.2 show how developers can shape the use of technologies for good societal impact. Research by Jeremy Bailenson et al. has showed how the use of virtual reality can contribute to better conflict resolution, empathy, and increased tolerance towards the other gender as well as other social and ethnical groups (Stanford, 2016). By manipulating the user's own (self)representation – called an avatar – and by creating experiences around racial discrimination, researchers have caused participants to express significantly more empathic behavior.

Participants of this kind of study also showed improved conflict resolution behavior several days after the experiment, which led the researchers to assume that experiences in virtual reality are to be considered equal or at least very similar to real live experiences in terms of shaping our mindset and behaviors. A study from the Virtual Human Interaction Lab shows this phenomenon at work by superimposing images of users into the images of public officials.

So, as can be seen above, engineers can build in technologies that affect human behavior in subliminal ways, which users may not be aware of, creating what Robert Cialdini has called a "click, whirr" response (Cialdini, 2000). Another type of value that may not traditionally connect with innovators and engineering responsibilities revolves around the influence of technologies on our democratic practices and the ability of our societies to select the most suitable candidate for a given governmental or other role with societal responsibilities (i.e., meritocracy).

The Internet has certainly brought substantial new means for transparency (both for office holders to self-publish accounts of their activities as well as through witness) and participation.

Fake news seems to be "more attractive" (i.e., clicked more often) than the factual story. Politicians (ab)use the media and especially social media along the lines of the old saying, *in public relations there is no such thing as bad press*. It is only important that voters pay attention. Elected officials complain that it is increasingly difficult to implement unpopular but necessary public service projects – like building airports, train stations, or urban overpasses – because relatively small groups of concerned and affected citizens can use new networked means of communication and participation as a loudspeaker to protest and voice their (populist) concerns. These opportunities to participate increase social value, but innovators and engineers should include means of participation that allow for plans and decisions that promote the greater good rather than enable small but loud groups to impose their views or at least block efficient progress.

Lastly, a recurring theme in technological innovation is focused on increased automation and how this supplants more and more jobs. While history has proven over and again that more innovative and advanced economies have created equal or more jobs in higher-level professions, it is true that in every wave of innovation (e.g., mechanical, industrial, and now machine intelligence) significant percentages of workers may be affected and the transition periods involved can be full of social turmoil. The search for new professions and new business models that allow those affected to see that innovation creates jobs takes time, and the dedicated effort of engineers and innovators involved in pushing the cutting edge.

Society's goals should be refined through public debate. A deeper understanding of these goals can (i) contribute to an important public debate about the goals and impact of IoT and (ii) show how the goals we pursue bring consequences in the values and ethics we design into our technologies. For example, several societal goals demand that developers, users, and other stakeholders trust the claims, data, and practices of the IoT systems that surround us. Weil and Haarkötter (2014) have put it well: "The more our everyday life becomes dependent on the technologies deployed in the IoT the more a framework is necessary to ethically establish trust in the IoT. How can we and should we enable subjects to take informed decisions on attributing or depriving trust into the machinery" (Weil & Haarkötter, 2014). This demonstrates the ongoing tension – and reliance – that we have developed with technology.

Similarly, if we envision an IoT-enabled world in which personal assistants and continuously learning systems facilitate our decision-making – and in many cases take decisions – a key ethical question around the agency and responsibility of those intelligent systems has to be deliberated among all stakeholders. Weil and Haarkötter ask: "In the case of the Internet of Things it is vital to clarify whether things that can act enabled by connected computing power are also actors from an ethical point of view. Can these things be attributed to some form of responsibility or accountability or only their originators? And how to regulate that?" In response to these challenges, the White House has published a report on the future of artificial intelligence (AI) and the comments of one expert contributor capture the challenge by comparing the role of AI to the work that decisionmakers in public office undertake:

> Authority is delegated to an agency due to the agency's subject-matter expertise, but the delegation is constrained by due process protections, measures promoting transparency and oversight, and limits on the scope of the delegated authority. Some speakers called for the development of an analogous theory of how to maintain accountability when delegating decision-making power to machines.
>
> *(USG, 2016)*

As we can see, the issues of ethics and IoT are being addressed in public processes. What remains to be seen is how these theories are implemented in practice over the long run.

3.3.1 Virtuous Engineering: Translating Values into Practice

Technology is a pliable thing: it simultaneously mediates our worldview and gives texture to our public and private relationships. Design choices frequently have political consequences and can shape the relative power of different groups in society. Put another way, technology is political. The same can be said for the incorporation of human values and ethics into technology.

The Internet is not some neutral, value-free assemblage of routers and servers and fiber optics. The Internet is, by definition, a "network of networks" that may be viewed from a certain perspective as neutral; but how we design and use it reflects a distinctive social and psychological bias. In the context of today's increasingly autonomous technologies notions. One framework for looking at this comes from actor–network theory (ANT), which views technology as non-human actors playing the role of intermediaries and mediators (Latour, 1987). This becomes increasingly relevant for ethical considerations about engineering and design choices. As an artifact of human ingenuity, technology expresses deep-seated desires and needs. While some component parts may be used for a variety of purposes – think, for example, of assembling mechanical systems into either exploratory rocket ships or atomic weapons – the design and use of those components inevitably reflect very real human impulses (Whitt & Schultze, 2012).

Social norms and professional virtues can be seen as the shared understanding within a group of people of how to live and work together. They are behavioral regularities, based on networks of mutual understanding of relevant virtues and approval or disapproval of conduct. On the highest level these codes of conduct incorporate evolved standards of human fairness, and so help constrain self-interested behavior (Whitt & Schultze, 2009). More concretely, engineers uphold virtues like courage (to speak up/whistle blow), dedication to technical excellence (techne), episteme (scientific truth), and liberality (as codified in Postel's law) as they pursue values and goals like openness, safety, decentralized networking architectures, etc.

In the case of the present-day Internet, that built-in values bias is reflected in the key elements of its architecture and infrastructure. How the Internet runs depends on the instructions in software and the algorithms in code, and its fundamental nature created and shaped by engineers. As Lawrence Lessig has shown us, "Code is Law," or rather, computing technologies are products of human design that affect our behavior. The structure of the Internet reflects the ethos that produced it. The values include interconnectivity, openness, flexibility, and the lack of a pervasive centralized authority. The Internet is also oriented towards user activities at the "edge," rather than network activities at the "core." At the same time, the Internet has no fixed, inherent nature, except for what we build into its architecture.

How are the standards (and corresponding ethos) codified? Since its inception, the Internet Engineering Task Force (IETF) has operated at the center of the standards development community for the Internet. Its stated goal is to "make the Internet work better." The organization has succeeded in gaining widespread adoption for its specifications, based on a strong set of social norms and an effective procedural regime for developing standards. "Rough consensus and running code" (i.e., American pragmatism geared towards experimental innovation and evolution) have been the foundational principles of the IETF's work.

In developing the standards that help run the Internet, the IETF demonstrates its underlying values. These can be seen in two ways, the procedural and the substantive. On the procedural side, how the IETF functions on a daily basis shows its core values. The body employs an open process, where any interested person can know what is being decided and participate in that process. The IETF relies on technical competence, where input and output are limited to areas of "engineering quality," and has a volunteer set of leaders and participants. Standards are derived from a combination of engineering judgment and real-world experience. In addition to taking responsibility for protocols that the IETF has developed, an early document, "Request for Comments" (RFC), states that the IETF should act as a trustee for the public good, with a requirement that all groups must be treated equitably, and an express recognition of the role for stakeholders (RFC 1591: March 1994).

The RFC process was first established by Steve Crocker in April 1969. These memos were intended as an informal means of distributing shared ideas among network researchers on the ARPANET project. The RFC now are viewed as the "documents of record" in the Internet standards community, with over 6,000 documents in existence. In an early document dubbed "The Tao of IETF" (RFC 1718: 1994), the body explains to a newcomer how the IETF actually works

(Hoffman, 2012). The emphasis is on the various processes used to specify protocols and otherwise discuss near-term architecture challenges. The document gets down to the level of dress code (shirts and blouses, please) and colored dots on name tags. Later iterations on "The Tao of IETF" go into greater detail (RFC 4677; RFC 6722), but the section entitled "guiding principles" maintains a similar emphasis on open and transparent operational processes. The later versions are now found online. On the substantive side, the IETF proclaims that:

> the Internet isn't value-neutral, and neither is the IETF [. . .] We embrace technical concepts such as decentralized control, edge-user empowerment, and sharing of resources, because those concepts resonate with the core values of the IETF community.

(RFC 3935)

This and the RFC make plain that modularity or layering is the logical scaffolding that makes it all work together. So, the functional elements of the Internet are an example: interconnection (the why), modularity (the what), end-to-end principle (the where), agnostic protocols (IP) (the how). Each of these functional principles was intended to engender a certain type of network experience from the user's perspective. As was noted earlier, this environment is made up in part of the "deontological backdrop" of laws and regulations and other prescriptive elements that shape and constrain human actions. In this way, technology evolves with us, our human capacities, our culture, and our environment.

3.3.2 Values for Thoughtful IoT Design

Now that we have some insight into the virtues and values that were baked into the Internet technologies by the engineers who designed and evolved it since its inception, we want to consider which engineering and design values seem prudent to guide developers as they work on IoT systems. While we are moving rapidly towards launching IoT products, enhancements, and releases of new functionality, we propose that customers/users will benefit from thoughtful design focused on (i) ease of use, (ii) reliability, (iii) safety, security and privacy, and (iv) offline use (Cerf et al., 2016).

Under ease of use we would also count the current problem of "one device – one app." Adequate thought needs to be given to the interoperability and end-user feasibility to program ensembles of devices from multiple makers. Reliability is, of course, at the heart of the engineering value of excellence; but a new aspect for today's connected devices is to develop them in a way that they can reliably become part of unexpected new constellations of devices and services to serve the user in ad-hoc ensembles.

Safety, security, and privacy can be summarized from an ethical perspective as those elements that together make stakeholders trust the claims, data, and decisions our (IoT) systems make (Cerf et al., 2016). While the engineering profession has developed broad and deep expertise in all three areas, there is an enormous challenge for developers and producers to give adequate resources and promote ethical practice because customers have a hard time understanding complexities of safety, security, and privacy – and hence are not willing to pay adequately for these features. Standards and certification of quality and conformance like the functions institutions such as Underwriters Labs have fulfilled seem to be meaningful instruments to promote good engineering and investment practices.

Finally, a value that engineers should be interested in assuring is offline use. This value addresses the notion that online products can operate usefully even if they are temporarily disconnected from the Internet. One would not want one's house or enterprise to cease functioning usefully because Internet access is down.

3.4 Embodiment in Practice

In this last section we give options for promoting ethical engineering practices for IoT developers. How can we define goals and virtuous engineering to provide practical motivation for developers to behave ethically? In the long term, what are effective and adequate institutions to generate responsibility and obligation to protect the interests of the general public? We identify two loci that might be particularly suitable to shape IoT vision and virtuous practice in this early stage of IoT. These are (i) strong professional culture institutionalized in engineering associations and (ii) discourse and governance solutions that result from collaboration in multistakeholder fora.

3.4.1 Collective Moral Power through Engineering Associations

Sociologists are concerned about the moral decay that goes along (in their view) with the demise of strong, mutually supportive social institutions in modern societies. Durkheim was one of those theorists who advocated for powerful professional associations to allow values and non-commercial interests to be upheld by various other licensed professionals, advocating the following:

> A system of morals is always the affair of a group and can operate only if the group protects them by its authority. It is made up of rules which govern individuals, which compel them to act in such and such a way, and which impose limits to their inclinations and forbid them to go beyond. Now there is only one moral power – moral, and hence common to all – which stands above the individual and which can legitimately make laws for him, and that is collective power. To the extent the individual is left to his own devices and freed from all social constraint, he is unfettered by all moral constraint. It is not possible for professional ethics to escape this

fundamental condition of any system of morals. Since, then, the society as a whole feels no concern in professional ethics, it is imperative that there be special groups in the society, within which these morals may be evolved, and whose business it is to see that they are observed.

(Durkheim, 1964)

As discussed earlier, professional associations and communities like ACM, IETF, and IEEE represent active multistakeholder spaces to make the implicit values and virtues of engineers explicit, and thereby provide reference points and moral authority for individual engineers to judge their practices. However, professional associations are by nature bound to a given discipline or stakeholder group while the ethical challenges around IoT are transdisciplinary. Therefore, as discussed in the next section, collaboration and deliberation about ethical means and ends for IoT should also be promoted in multistakeholder fora like the Internet Governance Forum (IGF).

3.4.2 Multistakeholder Approach to Ethical Systems

Our last example for how IoT related ethical and policy challenges, responsibilities, and solutions can be identified and addressed is the IoT Dynamic Coalition at the United Nations IGF. When multistakeholder groups function best they use a "form follow function" approach to set up working groups as needed to tackle issues at hand (Cerf et al., 2014). This multistakeholder working group was formed in 2008 and has opted to pursue an ethical approach to contribute to the shaping of the IoT policy and market space. Over the last eight years the IGF has been working on a document called "Towards an ethical framework for IoT Good Practice," which currently identifies values around privacy, data management, transparency, and security as well as user education as being key to guide stakeholders in developing IoT products (IGF, 2016).

Although only a small group of experts drafted the first version of the text, the coalition has invited and actively sought feedback and edits from representatives of all sectors (i.e., academia technical community, civil society, government, and the private sector). The ethical framework has also been publicly reviewed in workshops at the global IGF as well as at the European IGF; and the coalition chair now sees it as a living document that will continuously evolve and ripen as the understanding and practices evolve. This open, multistakeholder approach is necessary to generate an institutionalized continuous collaboration to identify issues and define values to guide all actors as they engage in IoT engineering, business development, and use. As the IoT technologies mature, other working groups like the Dynamic Coalition on Internet Rights and Principles might be well suited to work on the deontological approach to IoT (i.e., to transpose Human Rights into the IoT space).

3.4.3 Responsible IoT Research and Innovation

IoT is still in an early stage and we should optimize governance and practice to allow for experimentation and innovation while, of course, adequately considering ethical trade-offs and consequences. In closing, we will address some considerations regarding the question of what "satisfactory consideration of ethical trade-offs and consequences" might mean.

In questions of value and morality, it is often impossible to satisfy all demands. Since the time of Aristotle, decisionmakers have aimed for a "golden mean" of moral virtues as habits of reaching a proper balance between extremes in conduct, emotion, desire, and attitude. To understand this, Von Schomberg has put forward a useful definition of responsible research and innovation, describing it as:

> a transparent, interactive process by which societal actors and innovators become mutually responsive to each other with a view to the (ethical) acceptability, sustainability and societal desirability of the innovation process and its marketable products (in order to allow a proper embedding of scientific and technological advances in our society).
>
> *(Von Schomberg, 2013)*

Along these lines, if IoT developers and innovators could agree to follow this conception, then a good foundation for the development of the next physical stage of the Internet can be established.

3.5 Conclusion

Technology has always embodied social relations and hence it is used for and has empowered good or negative human affairs. Technology is never neutral, nor good, nor bad because its use is always determined by its users. The innovations of more recent years contain certain structural capabilities with them. Scholars like Lawrence Lessig have made a distinction between technologies of access like Wikipedia, which not only gives the power of a modern encyclopedia to all Internet users but also democratized the means to create and update articles, and technologies of control, for example, "security" systems that are used to ensure public parks are not used for shelter by the homeless.

As Admiral Rickover, the first commander of the US navy arsenal of nuclear submarines, expressed as early as 1965 in an article entitled "A Humanistic Technology":

> Technology is nothing but tools, techniques, procedures; the artifacts fashioned by modern industrial man to increase his powers of mind and body. [...] The methods of science require rigorous exclusion of the human factor. They were developed to serve the needs of scientists whose sole interest is to comprehend the universe; to know the truth; to know it accurately and with certainty. The searcher for truth cannot pay attention to his own or other people's likes and dislikes, or to popular ideas of the fitness

of things. This is why science is the very antithesis of "humanistic," despite the fact that historically modern science developed out of and parallel to the humanism of the Renaissance ... We recognize it as a product of human effort, a product serving no other purpose than to benefit man [...] Humanistically viewed, technology is not an end in itself but a means to an end, the end being determined by man.

(Rickover, 1965)

With the advent of innovations like IoT (which move rapidly and include machine-enhanced learning), the ethical responsibility for the engineers and designers of such technologies becomes magnified. Today's engineering and R&D should be informed by considering established deontological codes, as well as a combination of teleological and virtue ethics approaches that can help guide the emergent practices and anticipation of consequences.

Programmers and systems engineers who contribute to the evolution of the IoT need to feel empowered by ethical considerations (e.g., codes of professional associations) to resist release of products that do not meet standards of safety, reliability, privacy, and resilience. Indeed, deontological rules and standards need to be developed over time to address these issues (Clark et al., 2001). However, the development of such standards is most effective when the technological features are somewhat stable and understood in order to hit the right level of abstraction, avoid tussle and other unintended consequences like stifling innovation. The approach of Baldini et al. provides useful guidance for this challenge (Baldini, Botterman, Neisse, & Tallacchini, 2016). In short, adequate ethical analysis and design of IoT devices and services holds a number of beneficial promises: (i) reduced risk for product investments especially from a legal perspective, (ii) enhanced long-term relationships with customers and partners, (iii) improved trust between stakeholders, and (iv) hence reduced overall transaction costs.

The three different approaches discussed in this chapter – teleological ethics, deontological ethics, and virtue ethics – should be combined to inform IoT engineering and product development. Teleology asks the engineers to consider how their innovation fits into the broader struggle for societal progress and to consequently derive design guidance. Weil and Haarkötter formulate an inspiring aspect when they observe that "the old English and German word 'thing' etymologically meant a public assembly and therefore was a synonym of democracy and participation." The IoT could at least imply that the technology brings us together in meaningful exchange around the things that make up our public sphere. Or put differently, as we internetwork our things, we shall also connect ourselves and use the technology to organize our public sphere.

Acknowledgment

The authors would like to thank Vinton G. Cerf for his contribution in analyzing the problem space and shaping the arguments and structure of this article.

References

Ananny, M. (2016). Toward an ethics of algorithms: Convening, observation, probability, and timeliness, *Science, Technology, and Human Values*, *41*(1), 94–96.

Baldini, G., Botterman, M., Neisse, R., & Tallacchini, M. (2016). Ethical design in the Internet of Things. *Science and Engineering Ethics*, *24*(3), 905–925.

Calvo, R. A., & Peters, D. (2014). *Positive computing: Technology for wellbeing and human potential*. Cambridge, MA: MIT Press.

Cerf, V. G. (2017). Responsible engineering and the Internet of Things, *CIO Review*.

Cerf, V. G., Ryan, P. S., Senges, M., & Whitt, R. S. (2014). A perspective from the private sector: Ensuring that forum follows function. In William J. Drake & Monroe Price (Eds.), *Beyond netmundial: The roadmap for institutional improvements to the global internet Governance Ecosystem*. Center for Global Communication Studies, Annenberg School for Communication at the University of Pennsylvania.

Cerf, V. G., Ryan, P. S., Senges, M, & Whitt, R. S. (2016). IoT safety and security as shared responsibility. *Journal of Business Informatics*, *1*(35), 7–19.

Cialdini, R. B. (2000). *Influence: Science and practice*, (4th ed.). Boston, MA: Allyn & Bacon Inc.

Clark, D. D., Wroclawski, J., Sollins, K., & Braden, R. (2002, August). Tussle in cyberspace: Defining tomorrow's internet. Journal IEEE/ACM Transactions on Networking (TON), *13*(3), 462–475.

Durkheim, E. (1964). *Rules of sociological method* (p. 6). New York, NY: Free Press.

Fried, L. (2014, May 15). A bill of rights for the Internet of Things, *The New York Times*.

Gehlbach, H., Marietta, G., King, A., Karutz, C., Bailenson, J. N., & Dede, C. (2015). Many ways to walk a mile in another's moccasins: Type of social perspective taking and its effect on negotiation outcomes. *Computers in Human Behavior*, *52*, 523–532.

Hagel, J., Brown, J. S., & Davison, L. (2008, October). Shaping strategy in a world of constant disruption. *Harvard Business Review*, https://hbr.org/2008/10/shaping-strategy-in-a-world-of-constant-disruption.

Hardt, M. (2016, October 7). Equality of opportunity in machine learning [blog post]. Retrieved from https://ai.googleblog.com/2016/10/equality-of-opportunity-in-machine.html

Haarkötter, H., & Weil, F. (Eds.). (2014, December). *Ethics for the internet of things*. IOT Council.

Himanen, P. (2001). *The hacker ethic and the spirit of the information age.*. New York, NY: Random House Inc.

Hoffman, P. (Ed.) (2012). The Tao of IETF: A novice's guide to the internet engineering task force. Retrieved from

IGF. (2016). Dynamic Coalition on the Internet of Things (DC-IoT).

Kontson, K. R. (2001). Critical review of the wireless device Bill of Rights, presentation at the FCC Spectrum Management Working Group (presentation made on December 4, 2002).

Latour, B. (1987). *Science in action: How to follow scientists and engineers through society*. Milton Keynes: Open University Press.

Levy, S. (1984). *Hackers: Heroes of the Computer Revolution*. New York, NY: Doubleday.

Merrill, J. C. (2011). Overview: Theoretical foundations for media ethics, 3–32. In A. David Gordon, John M. Kittross, John C. Merrill, William Babcock, & Michael Dorsher (Eds.), *Controversies in media ethics* (3rd ed.), New York, NY: Routledge.

Powell, M. K. (2001, October 30). Broadband migration III: New directions in wireless policy. Speech presented to the Silicon Flatirons Telecommunications Program, University of Colorado at Boulder.

Rickover, H. (1965, January). A humanistic technology. *American Behavioral Scientist 8* (5), 3.

Scott, S. (2016, March/April). *The see change*, Stanford Virtual Human Interaction Lab.

Stanford Virtual Human Interaction Lab (2016, October 6). Examining racism with virtual Reality. Stanford Virtual Human Interaction Lab.

Torrone, P. (2006, December 1). The maker's bill of rights. *Make Magazine*.

USG Executive Office of the President (2016, October). Preparing for the future of artificial intelligence. Executive Office of the President, National Science and Technology Council Committee on Technology.

Von Schomberg, R. (2013). A vision of responsible innovation. In R. Owen, M. Heintz, & J. Bessant (Eds.), *Responsible innovation*. London, UK: John Wiley & Sons.

Weil, F., & Haarkötter, H. (2014, December). Ethics for the Internet of Things, *International Review of Ethics 22*.

Werbach, K. (2001, November 28). Here's a cure for bandwidth blues. ZDNet.com.

White House (2016, October). Preparing for the future of artificial intelligence. White Paper, Executive Office of the President National Science and Technology Council Committee on Technology, 2016.

Whitt, R. S. (2009). Adaptive policymaking: Evolving and applying emergent solutions for U.S. communications policy. *Federal Communications Law Journal 61*(3) Article 2.

Whitt, R. S., & Schultze, S. (2012). A deference to protocol. *Cardozo Arts & Ent. LJ 31* (689), 704–705.

4

Ethics of Immersive Technologies

Randall W. Hill, Jr.

4.1 Introduction

When the US Army established the Institute for Creative Technologies (ICT) at the University of Southern California in 1999, the vision was to push the boundaries of immersive technologies for the purpose of enhancing training and education; not only for the military but also for the rest of society. Over the past two decades great progress has been made on the technologies that support this vision. Breakthroughs in graphics, computer vision, artificial intelligence (AI), affective computing, and mixed reality have already transformed how we interact with one another, with digital media, and with the world. Yet this is in many ways only a starting point, since the application of these technologies is just beginning to be realized. The potential for making a positive impact on individuals and society is great, but there is also the possibility of misuse. This chapter describes some of the capabilities underlying the emerging field of immersive digital media; provides a couple of examples of how they can be used in a positive way; and then discusses the inherent dangers from an ethical standpoint.

What exactly is an immersive technology? A simple definition is that it is any medium that affects an individual's sense of place and time or perception of the world. A story is one of the most basic forms of an immersive medium. When well written or told, a story has the power to transport the listener or reader so they feel like they are part of the narrative, identifying with the characters and situations. We humans seem to be wired to identify with the characters and respond to the events as though they are real, even though we know they are not (e.g., see Green, Brock, & Kaufman, 2004). Some refer to this as the suspension of disbelief. Following this line of thinking, an *immersive technology* is any technology that facilitates this transportation to an alternate reality. With this idea in mind, ICT's goal has been to create simulations so compelling that people respond as if they were real. There are many variations of how a simulation or other immersive experience can be implemented and conveyed, but the result is that the human participant responds to it cognitively, emotionally, and even physically.

Some of the applications of immersive technologies are obvious. The entertainment industry employs immersive technologies in the creation of movies; and video game companies leverage the ability to interact with a simulated world for competitive purposes. Beyond entertainment, though, applications are now emerging that will impact many other aspects of our lives.

This chapter is written from the perspective of a technologist. I do not have a formal background in ethics, but I share a concern with other scientists and engineers that the rapid advances in what I am calling immersive technologies are outpacing our understanding of how they will affect the lives of human beings and societies throughout the world. Given the current state of global access to digital media, the application of the technologies described here will at some point be able to reach anyone, anywhere on the planet, nearly instantaneously. This is pretty astounding when one considers how slowly information and new ideas spread in the not so distant past compared to now. To put this in perspective, ten years ago, neither the public nor the government anticipated the power of social media to influence national and international politics, elections, and social movements. Yet this unanticipated influence is now a hot topic of discourse in the news media and in the public domain, where a lot of concern has been expressed about the ability of outside actors to influence national elections. While today's social media have made a significant impact on society, I believe the emerging technologies will have an even more profound effect in the long run; since they will potentially be even more influential and convincing in nature than a text message, social media posting, emoticon, or news story. They will have the power to appeal to some of the most basic aspects of what makes us human – our minds, our hardwired joy of the story (which is one of the oldest ways humans shared knowledge), our imaginations through fantastical virtual worlds, and our emotions and desire to connect and be known by others who do not judge us.

The ethical perspective in this chapter is inspired by the principles outlined in a document published by the Institute of Electrical and Electronics Engineers (IEEE), the world's largest technical professional organization for the advancement of technology, entitled, *Ethically Aligned Design: A Vision for Prioritizing Human Well-Being with Autonomous and Intelligent Systems* (IEEE, 2017). In high-level terms, these principles state that ethically designed technologies should take into account:

1. Human rights – these technologies should be designed so they do not violate internationally recognized human rights, including the ability of people to control their personal data and privacy.
2. Well-being – it is important to make a priority of insuring the well-being of individuals and society.
3. Accountability – the design of a system should support the ability account for the fault and liability when harm is done.

4. Transparency – the data, algorithms, logic, and capabilities of a system should be accessible so that it is possible for users to understand how it functions and its actions or decisions can be traced in cases where the system has caused harm.
5. Awareness of technology misuse and awareness of it – this principle conveys the need to educate policy-makers and enforcers as well as the general public about the potential misuses of a technology.

Interestingly this document highlights future technology concerns in the areas of affective computing and mixed reality, both of which this chapter includes under immersive technologies. Most of my comments on ethics are inspired by these principles.

The rest of this chapter first covers a high-level description of two emerging technologies: human digitization and virtual humans. This is followed by two examples of how immersive technologies have been applied in the domains of education and mental health. Each of these two cases include a discussion of some of the design decisions that were made to insure the applications were properly implemented and used. I conclude the chapter in Section 4.7 with some general ethical considerations.

4.2 Human Digitization Technology

One of the first projects to consider when discussing immersive technologies is how to create more realistic people and objects for the digital world. Under the direction of Paul Debevec, the ICT's graphics lab invented the Light Stage technology to capture images of the human face and other objects under all possible lighting conditions. The goal of this research was to be able to produce a highly realistic representation of a person or thing that could subsequently be used as a digital double in movies, games, and simulations. To accomplish this goal the Light Stage rapidly strobes patterns of light from all possible directions on an actor's face while high-speed cameras photograph the subject in a series of different poses. From the data that is captured about how light reflects from a face, it becomes possible to reproduce the digital version of the face as it would appear under the lighting conditions in any environment. The result is a highly realistic digital representation of the face that looks like it belongs in the scene.

The true potential of the Light Stage became apparent in 2002, when Sony Pictures Imageworks decided to use it to scan actors for the *Spider-Man 2* movie and used the output of the process to create the digital doubles of Alfred Molina, who played Dock Ock, and Tobey Maguire, who was Spider-Man. This movie earned an Academy Award® for Best Achievement in Visual Effects, in part, due to ability to make realistic looking digital characters for scenes where no human could have performed the stunt depicted in the movie. Figure 4.1 shows a

Figure 4.1 *Spider-Man in Light Stage 3*

subsequent Spider-Man being scanned in Light Stage 3. Using the output of the scan graphics pipeline, special effects teams are able to seamlessly insert a digital version of an actor into an action scene, and they animate the digital actors to perform great acts of heroism or evil never seen before in movies. Studios have used the Light Stage in the years since the first *Spider-Man* movie to produce dozens of other movies with this technology. Paul Debevec, along with his industry collaborators received a Scientific and Engineering Academy Award® for "the design and engineering of the Light Stage capture devices and the image-based facial rendering system developed for character relighting in motion pictures."

Each Light Stage has been progressively more powerful and efficient. Continuous innovations led to new versions of the technology, improving the quality of the lighting, the level of detail – down to the pores in the skin – and the speed at which a scan could be produced. To put it in perspective, in 2000 the original apparatus used one spotlight, which was slowly spiraled around the subject being scanned over the course of a minute to capture one pose under varying light conditions. This required the actor to sit very still for an impossibly long period of time, comparable to what it must have felt like in the early days of photography. In contrast, as of 2018 the Light Stage system has 14,532 light-emitting diodes (LEDs) and can capture a single pose in three seconds; and it produces much more data in those three seconds: nineteen frames are captured and they are used to

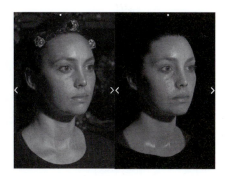

Figure 4.2 *The real Emily is on the left and the "digital" Emily is on the right*

generate thirteen different maps of the face. With these advances, it has become quite difficult to distinguish between the real person and the digital version (Figure 4.2). The details of the skin, down to the pore level, and the way light reflects off the skin creates a compelling digital version of the person. (See Debevec, 2012 for more details about the progression of Light Stage technology.)

Another big breakthrough came in 2012 on a project called Digital Ira (Alexander et al., 2013). Due to the amount of computing required, until recently it simply was not possible to animate the digital doubles in real time. To bring a digital double to life, an army of special effects artists and animators would work with scan data from the Light Stage to create a model that could be made to behave in ways dictated by a movie script so that what was seen by moviegoers on the screen appeared real. Each frame has to be rendered, so to produce a twenty-four frame-per-second, two-hour movie requires a lot of processing. Digital Ira was the first instance of a digital human that could be animated in real time, opening the door for creating video game characters with a high-resolution, realistic performance. One of the underlying technologies that enabled this breakthrough was the advent and use of the Graphics Processing Unit (GPU), a specialized electronic component optimized for generating images. But even with this advance, few organizations could produce a photoreal digital human that could be animated or controlled in real time since it still required specialized equipment, a graphics pipeline, and a special effects team. This will soon no longer be the case.

Through the advent of high-resolution digital cameras on smartphones and the growing use of AI deep learning algorithms on large data sets, it is now possible to take a photo of someone and very rapidly create a digital puppet of that person that can be controlled in real time by the expressions on someone else's face. In a *Los Angeles Times* article published on February 19, 2018 (Pierson, 2018), this was illustrated on the newspaper's website, which contains a link to a video where the reporter's generated three-dimensional face was controlled by the input performance of the researcher, USC computer science Professor Hao Li.

Figure 4.3 *(a) David Pierson (LA Times Reporter), (b) Prof. Hao Li (USC & Pinscreen), (c) David Pierson (puppet). Photo Courtesy of Pinscreen*

Figure 4.3 shows the input and output of a process that took less than a minute, and a digital face that can be controlled in real time. It is anticipated this process will continue to improve both in terms of output quality and efficiency very soon; making it possible for anyone with a smartphone to produce a digital double of a face. The implications of this advancement are pretty stunning and will be discussed in Section 4.6.1.

4.3 Virtual Human Interaction

Creating a digital double for a movie or game is an obvious use of the human digitization technology, but what if we could take it one step farther and create an interactive character – a virtual human? In addition to having a visual representation of a face and body, a virtual human has to hear, see, understand, think, and respond, verbally and non-verbally through gesture, facial expressions, and body language. Progress has been made on all these fronts, to the point that commercial speech recognition and speech synthesis products are routinely embedded in home smart speakers and phones that provide a virtual assistant capability. Commercial automated speech recognition (ASR) technology transforms spoken language into text, and commercial text-to-speech (TTS) synthesis algorithms routinely transform text into spoken language. In between these technology bookends, the virtual human needs to be able to process the input text, make sense of it, decide on an action, and formulate a response, which can be communicated as spoken language.

There are many examples of virtual humans in existence now, though the approach to implementing the AI varies greatly. Simple chatbots often use some form of keyword spotting to decide on a response. In other words, the system looks for certain words to provide a rudimentary understanding of what was said, which is used by a decision procedure to select a canned response. More sophisticated systems seek a deeper understanding of the meaning of what was said and generate a response based on the topic domain and inferences that can be drawn from more general knowledge. And some are designed to carry on an extended dialogue, requiring the virtual human to remember what has been said as the context for understanding and response. Advanced virtual humans can also be implemented for multimodal interaction, meaning that, in addition to processing speech, the system also uses computer vision to perceive the facial expressions and body language of the human. Researchers have shown that depression can be indicated in individuals who have a reduced vowel space in conversational speech (Scherer, Lucas, Gratch, Rizzo, & Morency, 2016), thus the prosody of an individual's voice provides an additional channel of information and can give an indication of the emotional state of the person speaking. On the output side, multimodal interaction not only produces spoken language, but it also generates appropriate facial expressions, hand gestures, and other forms of nonverbal expression.

There are many variants on how these capabilities are being mixed and matched, depending on the needs of the application.

What is perhaps even more interesting is the effect virtual humans can have on real humans in an interaction. Beginning in 2007, Gratch and his colleagues have shown the potential for humans and virtual humans to establish rapport through contingent nonverbal behaviors at emotional, behavioral, and cognitive levels (Gratch, Wang, Gerten, Fast, & Duffy, 2007). What is particularly fascinating, though, is the connection people make with virtual humans in conversational settings, including educational applications such as interviewing a Holocaust survivor; developing negotiation tactics; practicing counseling skills for leaders; exercising a doctor's diagnostic skills; dealing with sexual assault victims; and the assessment of emotional and psychological well-being. What follows are a couple of examples of the positive uses of human digitization and virtual human interaction.

4.4 Educational Use of Immersive Technologies

The New Dimensions in Testimony (NDT) project has the vision of preserving the experiences of Holocaust survivors so that future generations will not only hear their stories but will be able to actively engage with recorded testimonies by asking questions (Traum et al., 2015). This vision is achieved by interviewing survivors in the Light Stage (Figure 4.4, left side) and recording hundreds, and in some cases thousands, of responses to questions about their lives and experiences in the Holocaust. Rather than creating a digital double, the system uses the actual video recording and the testimony is segmented into individual responses that can be replayed for a given question. The video was shot from multiple directions simultaneously so that the interactive session could be experienced not only on a

Figure 4.4 *(a) Pinchas Gutter being interviewed and recorded in Light Stage X for NDT, (b) interactive NDT*

standard two-dimensional display, but also in a virtual reality head mounted display or on a three-dimensional display. Using ASR and natural language processing tools the recorded video is transformed into a digital question-and-answer system. The result is that the viewer feels as though he or she is having a conversation with the survivor. The interaction feels natural. The survivor is displayed sitting in a chair (Figure 4.4, right side), complete with fidgets and small movements that give the impression of an active presence. The viewer simply speaks a question into a microphone and the NDT system retrieves the closest matching pre-recorded response and seamlessly plays it, causing the displayed figure to answer the question, usually by telling a story of a related experience.

There are a couple of major benefits of such an application over a traditional approach. First, memories are not only preserved, but they are also, in effect, indexed by conversational topic. Many of these survivors are quite elderly, but their memories of a major world event have been captured for future generations to experience for themselves. The responses are retrieved by asking questions, meaning that one can pursue the type of information desired as opposed to having to read or watch an entire testimony. Second, there is a qualitatively different experience between reading a history text or watching a pre-recorded video versus interacting with a person who actually experienced the event. It is as though the survivor is in the same room. Some participants have asked whether the session was actually being conducted with a live person via a video feed. Others have apologized to the NDT system for the crimes of humanity committed in the Holocaust. Both reactions are an indication of the level of immersion of the experience. Since the interaction feels more personal it makes a deeper emotional impact, particularly when the responses are delivered by a gifted storyteller.

The emotions stirred by the testimony enable the creation of strong memories, resulting in a transfer of the experiences of one life to the learning of another.

From the perspective of ethics, this project offers clear benefits to society in that an immersive interview format makes history more accessible and memorable. NDT educates people about the atrocities of the past so that they may be avoided in the future. The ethical risk with this type of project is that the actual interview data could be manipulated to either change the testimony or misrepresent what was actually said. The NDT team took these possibilities into account when the project was first begun, and for this reason they did not create "digital doubles" of the survivors; rather, they exclusively used the actual video recordings for the interactive testimony with no modification or editing other than segmenting the testimony into discrete responses. It would be too easy to misuse a digital double and literally put words into its mouth. Even if safeguards were put into place to avoid manipulating the testimony, the mere representation of the survivor by a digital double could raise doubts about the veracity of the character's stories. Given the potential ethical pitfalls of this technology, the team made design decisions that would minimize these possible abuses. The bottom line is that the ethical application of the technology and the potential ramifications of abuse were considered up front and the design was informed by these considerations.

4.5 Clinical Decision Support Use of Immersive Technologies

Another compelling use of immersive technologies is to address the emotional and psychological well-being of military service members, as well as the population at large. The post-traumatic stress disorder (PTSD) rate among veterans and military service members who fought in Iraq or Afghanistan has been estimated to be as high as 20 percent, and as many as twenty former and current service members commit suicide each day. The challenge for the Department of Defense and Veterans Administration has been twofold. First, identifying individuals who are suffering the effects of post-traumatic stress in a culture where there is a stigma associated with admitting depression or stress. Second, helping individuals gain access to advice, support, or professional help, depending on the needs of the case (Lucas et al., 2017).

To address these issues, beginning in 2011, under the sponsorship of the Defense Advanced Research Projects Agency (DARPA), a team at ICT began developing an interactive system called SimSensei. This was intended as a clinical decision support tool that could help identify the signs of depression, anxiety, and stress through the use of an interactive, multimodal virtual human (Rizzo, 2014). SimSensei (Figure 4.5) is, in effect, a virtual social worker who interacts with a human to determine how she or he is doing in life. SimSensei asks a series of questions, beginning with establishing rapport, and eventually getting into issues

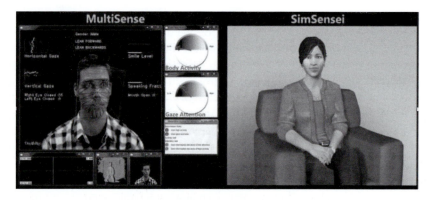

Figure 4.5 *(a) human subject, (b) Ellie, a virtual social worker*

related to sleep, stress, anger, and similar topics. In addition to using natural language processing to understand what the human says, SimSensei senses the human's facial expressions, body language, and voice prosody, and uses this information to respond with the appropriate follow on questions and statements; as well as adjusting its own nonverbal expressions and body language to create a greater sense of connection.

The team tested SimSensei with hundreds of veterans and the findings were significant. According to Lucas et al. (2017), participants in the study were more willing to disclose information about their emotional state to SimSensei than they were on a written behavioral health survey or to a real human. SimSensei was able to establish a connection with the participants, and they felt safe disclosing personal information, in part, because they did not feel judged.

SimSensei was successful as an experimental program for a few reasons. First, the technology worked. Though the virtual human was obviously an animated character, it seemed real enough that the participants took it seriously and interacted throughout the whole session, disclosing personal information that might otherwise have gone undetected. Second, the virtual human was designed to maximize trust and rapport. The character projected warmth and empathy and established trust, leading in many cases to a sense of not being judged. It was intentionally designed to mirror certain nonverbal behaviors of the human being interviewed, further enhancing the connection.

From an ethical perspective, SimSensei was designed with the well-being of the participants in mind. The goal was to act as a decision support tool for clinicians to get past the stigma against talking about one's emotional state. Once the system detected struggles or challenges, it could recommend further materials to help deal with issues like insomnia. More importantly, it could prompt people who were most at risk to seek the help of a professional counselor. From a design perspective, SimSensei was never intended as a "doc in a box" – since the technology does not have the depth of knowledge or experience to provide professional help to someone who is manifesting serious problems. It does not provide a diagnosis nor does it provide therapy. The ethical risk that should be raised about the ability of SimSensei to sense distress and project empathy is the potential to abuse this trust relationship for nefarious reasons. For example, a virtual human could potentially emotionally manipulate a human in order to sell a product or influence a decision. There are many examples of how information gathered through social media has been used to profile people and personalize advertising or customize a news feed. Personalization for the purposes of influence or sales based on an intimate view of a person's mental health does not seem ethical. Another ethical concern is privacy, which is something the medical enterprise is already well aware of in the context of standard patient records. With this emerging type of application, it becomes even more imperative to think about the uses and protection of the confidential information disclosed in a session with a digital interviewer. SimSensei was designed to follow a standard psychological protocol for assessing the emotional state of an individual, and it promised and enforced confidentiality. Because trust is established through a careful design that appeals to human emotions through empathy and support, it is vital that the design of the system follows established medical and psychological protocols for intervention.

4.6 General Ethical Considerations

Up to this point, this chapter has presented some of the general capabilities of immersive technologies and provided a couple of specific use cases, along with the ethical considerations raised by those particular applications. This section lays out some general ethical considerations inspired by the IEEE working document on ethically aligned design mentioned at the beginning of the chapter, as well as by specific concerns that were considered in the development of immersive applications.

4.6.1 Deception

An immediate and obvious concern is the ability to create fake videos (other than action movies!) of known individuals from a photograph, paired with the digitization process previously described. One can easily imagine a digital version of a public figure being made to say things they did not actually say or do things they did not actually do, and this performance could be distributed through social media, advertising, government communications, and the news media. In a sense, the public has already seen how easily digital media can be manipulated with the advent of photograph editing software, which has raised healthy skepticism about photographic evidence. Digitally mimicking a person in a video is already possible, though initially it may be a bit more difficult to deceive the human perceptual system when it comes to performance versus a static photograph. In addition to making the digital human look real, the voice needs to be accurate and mannerisms will have to closely resemble the familiar habits of the person being imitated.

There are several ways to deal with the potential use of digitization for unethical purposes. The first counter to the threat of deception will be to raise awareness of the potential that a video may be fake. Knowing that it is possible to create a fake video performance should raise questions in the mind of the critical consumer of digital media. But as the technologies for creating digital humans and performance improve – which should be expected – it may be necessary to develop a second counter, through the use of sophisticated technical tools for detecting fakery. The veracity of the information or news conveyed in digital media will be undermined if there are not strong tools for detecting deception. A third counter to deception is on the positive side of the ethical consideration, and this has to do with approaching a project with design in mind. As discussed in both the cases presented in this chapter, it is imperative that the designers think through how their application will be perceived and design it in a way that makes the methodology transparent to the user. In the case of the NDT project, the developers made the design decision to use actual video rather than create a digital double. It would have been more convenient and less costly to create the digital double, but veracity was of the utmost importance.

4.6.2 Emotional Manipulation

In the process of studying how people respond to virtual humans, Gratch et al. (2007) and his colleagues (e.g., Lucas et al., 2017) have uncovered an interesting tendency among humans to make an emotional connection when interacting with digital characters. This connection occurs even though the participant is aware that the virtual human is a computer program. In subsequent studies, where virtual humans served as negotiation partners, these teams found that, by using certain negotiation tactics and facial expressions, the emotions of the human participant could be influenced and even manipulated. Likewise, when testing the SimSensei application, the team found that some of the human subjects became quite emotional when interacting with the character as they recounted stories associated with their state of mind. Some participants choked up or even cried. As mentioned previously, SimSensei was designed to be non-judgmental and exhibited empathy, which are some of the ideal qualities of a counselor or friend.

So, what are the dangers that are associated with the ability to make an emotional connection through a virtual human and how can they be countered? It can be argued that any immersive medium can arouse the emotions. Stories, movies, and games all have this effect on the viewer or participant. What is qualitatively different in this case is that the digital encounter is potentially much more personal in nature. If a virtual human is used for a clinical purpose, the interaction must follow established professional protocols. The design of the interaction should consider the limitations of the technology and not venture into territory where a piece of advice is offered that is inappropriate or even damaging. In addition, per the IEEE principles of ethically aligned design, the technology should be transparent and accountable. In other words, it should be evident how the system is making decisions, which must be retroactively traceable. If an error occurs, it has to be clear why it occurred.

In cases where virtual humans are used for entertainment, there is a potential of emotional manipulation for any number of purposes. In a world where a growing number of people are only connected to one another via social media, there is evidence that the degree of loneliness is growing among the general population, particularly among people who are heavy digital media users. Given the growing level of loneliness, there will likely be a market for virtual humans who play the role of friends. After all, if a virtual human can get people to disclose personal information about themselves in a clinical setting, why wouldn't it also be possible to create a character who provides comfort or encouragement, filling the human need for connection without any of the risk of dealing with an actual person? In this context, one potential misuse of this effect would be to design a virtual friend who leads the human down a path toward purchasing products (e.g., more time with the virtual friend!), influencing their beliefs, and even appealing to the pathways associated with addiction. This may sound far-fetched now, but based on the recent attention on game addiction and other forms of social media obsession, it seems reasonable to assume this could become an issue. As already recommended, anyone engaged in the design of such an application should consider the well-being of the end user.

4.6.3 Violation of Privacy

The protection of privacy is an obvious issue for interactions with virtual humans and other forms of interactive digital media. In a clinical setting, the content of an interaction should be protected to the same degree of confidentiality as any other health-related intervention. One of the ethical questions that arises in the context of privacy is whether someone who reveals suicidal thoughts should be automatically referred to a human counselor. In our clinical trials we had a human monitoring the interactions with SimSensei, and the session would be halted if such a case was encountered and the person would receive some form of human intervention. This seems appropriate if the application is viewed as a decision support tool. But if health centers deploy applications "into the wild" without the benefit of a human monitor, where is the safety net for people who need more immediate help? If the system picks up signs of depression and suicidal indicators, does privacy take precedence over the need for intervention? Taking this one step farther, should the person's parent, employer, or insurance company be notified when that individual has indicators pointing to depression or suicide? These are questions that need to be considered in the design, implementation, and fielding of a health and well-being type application.

In education and entertainment settings, privacy should still be a priority, though there will clearly be situations where the purpose of the application is to facilitate learning, social interaction, or competition. In these cases, it should be clear to the user that their interactions are not private.

4.7 Conclusion

Powerful new capabilities have been developed for immersive technologies. Research laboratories have advanced the field of computer vision and graphics so that it is now possible to digitize and animate the human face and body, creating digital doubles for movies, games, and characters. By integrating the digital representation of a human with a suite of AI tools, it is now possible to create a range of interactive experiences with a virtual human. By their nature, immersive technologies appeal to emotion, which enables the creation of a powerful connections between the user and the digital medium. These emerging capabilities have many potential benefits, not only for entertainment, but also for the purposes of education, health, and well-being. They have the power to reach the human at an emotional level, which is what makes these experiences so memorable.

With this power, caution must also be exercised. This chapter identified a number of ethical danger zones related to deception, emotional manipulation, and privacy. To avoid the misuse of immersive technologies, it is best to first be educated about their capabilities and limitations. Second, the team who implements an application with an immersive technology needs to think about the ethical implications up front, during the design phase. Is the well-being of the end user being considered? Does the interaction conform to the professional standards of the clinical field of use? Will the end product be used to enforce veracity where it is expected as opposed to creating a deception? Will the privacy of the end user be considered? If the system fails, will the AI decision process be traceable? In the end, these considerations are really only a starting point for designing an immersive experience. Now is the time to consider the far-reaching implications of immersive technologies.

Acknowledgment

The work depicted here was or is sponsored by the US Army Research Laboratory (ARL) under contract number W911NF-14-D-0005. Statements and opinions expressed and content included do not necessarily reflect the position or the policy of the government, and no official endorsement should be inferred.

References

Alexander, O. et al. (2013). Digital Ira: Creating a real-time photoreal digital actor. In *ACM SIGGRAPH 2013 Posters* (SIGGRAPH '13). ACM, New York, NY, USA, Article 1, 1 page. DOI: https://doi.org/10.1145/2503385.2503387

Debevec, P. (2012). The light stages and their applications to photoreal digital actors. In SIGGRAPH Asia.

Gratch, J., Wang, N., Gerten, J., Fast, E., & Duffy, R. (2007). Creating rapport with virtual agents. In *Proceedings of international conference on intelligent virtual agents*, Paris, France.

Green, M., Brock, T., & Kaufman, G. (2004). Understanding the role of transportation into narrative worlds, *Communication Theory*, *14*(4), 311–327.

IEEE (2017). The IEEE Global Initiative on Ethics of Autonomous and Intelligent Systems. Ethically aligned design: A vision for prioritizing human well-being with autonomous and intelligent systems, Version 2. IEEE. Retrieved from http://standards.ieee.org/develop/indconn/ec/autonomous_systems.html.

Lucas, G. M. et al. (2017). Reporting mental health symptoms: Breaking down barriers to care with virtual human interviewers, *Frontiers in Robotics and AI*, *4*, 51. DOI: 10.3389/frobt.2017.00051.

Pierson, D. (2018, February 19). Fake videos are on the rise: As they become more realistic, seeing shouldn't always be believing, *Los Angeles Times*. Retrieved from www.latimes.com/business/technology/la-fi-tn-fake-videos-20180219-story.html

Rizzo, A. et al. (2014). Detection and computational analysis of psychological signals using a virtual human interviewing agent. In *Proceedings of ICDVRAT 2014, International Journal of Disability and Human Development*.

Scherer, S., G. M. Lucas, J. Gratch, A., Rizzo, S., & Morency, L. (2016, January-March). Self-Reported symptoms of depression and PTSD are associated with reduced vowel space in screening interviews, *IEEE Transactions on Affective Computing* 7(1), 59–73.

Traum, D., et al. (2015). New dimensions in testimony: Digitally preserving a holocaust survivor's interactive storytelling. In Schoenau-Fog H., Bruni L., Louchart S., & Baceviciute, S. (Eds.) *Interactive Storytelling. ICIDS. Lecture Notes in Computer Science*, Vol. 9445. London: Springer.

5

Internet, Technology, and the Future: An Interview with Vint Cerf

Vinton G. Cerf and Ali E. Abbas

5.1 Introduction

This chapter presents an interview with Vint Cerf, one of the fathers of the Internet. The chapter discusses his personal views on ethics, data and privacy, net neutrality, public policy, self-driving cars, genetic codes, and reflections on the future.

5.2 The Interview

ALI ABBAS: Welcome to *The Next Generation Ethics* book, Vint.

VINT CERF: Thanks Ali. Glad to be here.

ALI ABBAS: Let's start by asking you to tell us a bit about your background, how you got into the field, and the early history and creation of the Internet.

VINT CERF: How many hours do we have for this?

ALI ABBAS: A few.

VINT CERF: I'm kidding. Although I was not born in California, I grew up here. Moved here in 1946, was in the San Fernando Valley for a good portion of my growing up period. Went to Van Nuys High and, ironically, several other key people in the Internet story also went to Van Nuys High. It's just a sheer coincidence, but it's interesting. I went to Stanford University for my undergraduate work, and came back.

ALI ABBAS: Great school.

VINT CERF: Yes, it is a great school. Went back to Los Angeles to work for IBM, and then, after a couple of years, realized I needed to go back to school again to get a deeper understanding of computer science and operating systems, programming languages, and things like that; so I went to UCLA. I finished a PhD there, but while I was there, I got very involved in a project called the

ARPANET, which was initiated by the Defense Advanced Research Projects Agency. That organization was trying to figure out how to connect a dozen universities together, that had all been spending money on and doing research in artificial intelligence and computer science. Every one of them, of course, wanted a brand-new computer every year to do world class computing; and even the Defense Department couldn't pay for another six-million-dollar machine every year for twelve universities. They said, "We're going to build a network, and you're going to share." Of course, everybody hated that, but we did build the network. It was called ARPANET. A company called Bolt, Beranek, and Newman (BBN) in Cambridge, Massachusetts won the contract to build this packet switched net. And packet switching at the time was considered to be outrageously impossible. AT&T thought it was crazy – although, in the end, they were happy to sell dedicated circuits to let us build the ARPANET.

Len Kleinrock, in whose group I worked, had done the technical analysis of the mathematical behavior of store and forward packet switched networks, to show that it would work; but the proof, of course, was in the implementation. I worked on that project doing what were called the host-to-host protocols. Steve Crocker, my best friend in high school and still my best friend today, led the Network Working Group that developed not only the host-to-host protocols, but other application protocols as well, like file transfer, and so on.

We got all that working in the late 1960s and early 1970s, and then I finished my PhD and went up to Stanford to join the faculty. I was then doing research on computer networking. About that time, Robert Kahn – Bob Kahn – who had worked on the ARPANET project while at BBN, had joined DARPA. I had gone up to Stanford, and so in the spring of 1973, Bob Kahn shows up in my lab saying, "We have a problem." I'm saying, "What do you mean 'we'?" It turned out he had concluded, based on the success of the ARPANET, that the Defense Department could make use of computers in command and control to manage our resources better.

In theory, a smaller force could overcome a bigger one; a force multiplier. He concluded that if we were going to take advantage of this idea that we would have to put computers in mobile vehicles, ships at sea, aircraft – and the ARPANET had been designed with dedicated telephone lines. You're not going to connect the tanks together with wires because they run over the wires and they break, and the ships get all tangled up, and the planes never make it off the tarmac. He had started developing a mobile packet radio system and a packet satellite system to satisfy all those communication requirements. Then comes the problem: Well how do we connect all these packet switched nets to each other? They were all different, different packet sizes, different error rates, different delays and latencies.

How do we make it look uniform? That was the Internet problem. Over the course of about March to September of 1973, we solved the problem. We did a design, which was published in May of 1974, describing how this could work. By the beginning of 1974, my team at Stanford started developing the detailed specifications for what was called the Transmission Control Protocol (TCP).We started implementing it in 1975 and found mistakes and bugs; and so we iterated for a while until, in about 1978, we had a stable design. By that time, I had been invited to come to Washington, DC and run the Internet program for the Defense Department. I became a program manager. Bob Kahn eventually became the director of the Information Processing Techniques office. I stayed there to run the program until 1982. That's a chronological summary, some of the history that leads us up to the point where the Internet gets turned on in January of 1983.

ALI ABBAS: Did you imagine at the time that it would have the ramifications and implications that we are seeing today?

VINT CERF: The simple answer, of course, would be no, but it's not true. That's not a fair answer. If you think about this a little bit, first of all, remember that the ARPANET project, the predecessor, had already encountered electronic mail. A guy named Ray Tomlinson at BBN realized that he could do networked electronic mail if he just forwarded the messages through the network and got them to go to the right target machine. He had to figure out, "Okay, I get to the right machine. How do I tell it which user it is that I am supposed to be sending this message for?" He needed to separate the machine identity from the user identity, and the only character he could find on the keyboard that wasn't already in use by the operating systems was the @ sign. It's natural, user "at" host. That's the origin of the @ sign in our email. He does this, and demonstrates it in mid-1971. Everybody gets excited about this. We all realize what a powerful tool this is. It's computer-mediated communication. We no longer have to both be awake at the same time to communicate; so we can overcome time zones and everything else. Email was already in place before Internet work was even started.

We also had access to something called the oNLine System (NLS), which was developed at SRI International, by Douglas Englebart. Englebart was one of these visionary guys who's thinking thirty years ahead. He believes deeply that computers should be used and could be used to augment human intellect, that collaboration among people, mediated by a computer, would enhance our ability to understand things, reach conclusions, and solve problems. J. C. R. Licklider was a director of the Information Processing Techniques Office who also believed this. So Vannevar Bush and the other two believe implicitly that computers are going to be part of our future. So we were using Doug Engelbart's NLS system as a document production environment.

The reason this is important is that he had to invent a mouse in order to point on the screen at a document, a location on the document to say "edit here". He invented hyperlinks so that you could click on a hyperlink and go to a related document. He built a World Wide Web in a box, not to be too careful about the definition of what the World Wide Web is.

SRI International invented the mouse, the Xerox team came from SRI International, they brought that idea with them, built the Alto machine as a personal computer, built the Ethernet for high speed communication, three megabits a second at that time. So Xerox PARC was formed in 1972. I am at Stanford late in 1972. They are a mile and a half from my laboratory. I have graduate students who are going back and forth at PARC and people from PARC who are coming to some of my seminars. And so there is some cross-fertilization going on. They were working on something called the PARC universal packet (PUP) but they couldn't tell us very much because Xerox decided they wanted to keep it proprietary.

In the meantime, of course, I'm trying to plow through with my graduate student team the design of TCP, which eventually turns into TCP/IP as we split the Internet Protocol off in order to do real-time communication. So that's a long way of saying that we actually had some appreciation for what this technology could do, and we used it to do a lot of the applications that we still use today. Electronic mail, file transfer, remote access to timesharing machines. But, of course, the most significant change – after the Internet finally gets operational in early 1983 and then becomes commercially available in 1989 – is Tim Berners Lee's development of the World Wide Web. To be honest, Tim releases this out of CERN in Geneva in December of 1991. Nobody notices except for a couple of guys at The National Center for Supercomputer Applications, Marc Andreessen and Eric Bina, who say, "Oh, this is cool. Why don't we build a graphical user interface?"

So they develop and release the Mosaic browser. It makes the Internet look like a magazine, with formatted text and images, and eventually, you know, audio, video, and things like that. Everybody notices – including Jim Clark, who had been the founder of Silicon Graphics, which was a heavily used machine for computer-generated graphics in the movie industry. So Clark dragged these guys out to the west coast and started Netscape Communications around 1994 or so; they go public in 1995. The stock goes through the roof. The DOT boom is on; every venture capital guy is throwing money at anything that looks like it might have something to do with the Internet. This continues for five years or so. And then in April of 2000, everything falls apart and the DOT bust happens – except in that period of time from 1989, as commercial services get started, to that period in 2000, the Internet is growing 100 percent a year; and it continues to grow at that rate for a while. Not today, but it is still growing.

And so the introduction of this new way of sharing information on the net had a profound impact on its accessibility and utility. What we had achieved is this infrastructure that was infinitely – well, not really, but largely – expandable. It dropped the barriers to access to computer communication to as close to zero as possible. We had given away the design of the Internet for free with no patents or any other constraints deliberately in order to stimulate adoption and use. So as the general public encounters a World Wide Web, they have the ability to inject content into the network with very little barrier. And, of course, to get access to that information. In fact there was such an avalanche of content that flowed in that we now couldn't find anything and we needed search engines. So we got things like Alta Vista and Yahoo and eventually Google, Bing, etc.

So did we know what was going to happen? No; but there were milestones in the course of the evolution that signaled that this was going to be a big deal. And it was the commercialization in 1989 of the service as opposed to commercialization of the equipment like packet switches from Cisco Systems or Proteon or others. It was the commercialization of the service and the arrival of the World Wide Web. It really conflated these two things. Then there's one other thing, which I think was equally significant and that's the arrival of the smartphone in 2007.

This is Steve Jobs and Apple. This is very interesting because the mobile phone design work was started in 1973 by Marty Cooper, who was at Motorola at the time. This is ironically the year that Bob and I started designing the Internet. And we didn't know about each other.

Then in 1983, we turn the Internet on and he turns on the first mobile phone service. We still don't know anything about each other. A friend of mine, Danny Cohen, invited me to lunch in 1983. He said, "I have to show you something." I said, "Well, OK. I'll come to lunch". I go there and I see this thing sitting on the table and it's about "this tall" with a big antenna on it. I said, "What's that?" And he said, "It's a phone." I said "Where are the wires?" and he says, "There aren't any." So I asked him, "How does it work?" – and a bunch of other questions. Finally, he said, "I don't know the answer to that, why don't you talk to the guy that developed it?" So I called Marty Cooper on the phone and the first question I asked him was, "Marty how long does the battery last?" And he says, "Well about twenty minutes, but you can't hold the phone up longer than that anyway!" It weighed three and a half pounds.

So at that point in 1983, the mobile phone and the Internet are on parallel courses, they don't really come together at all until the smartphone shows up; and at that point you see a phenomenon that is very important to understand. Two technologies that are mutually reinforcing. The mobile phone makes the Internet more accessible. The Internet makes the mobile phone more useful, because of all the content and functionality that's on the net. And so those two things together have really colored the last decade of the evolution of the Internet and other products and services that go with it.

ALI ABBAS: And then more apps started appearing for the smartphones.

VINT CERF: Exactly right. Yeah, because now we have a platform. So the interesting thing about all of this is the layering that's going on. The Internet is a layered architecture, IP is sort of the core layer, TCP and the other real-time protocols are just above that, and then there are utility protocols like file transfer. When we get to the World Wide Web it's another layer – the hypertext transport protocol sits on top of TCP and then on top of the mobile phones we get APIs that make it easy for people to build applications even if they have no idea how the mobile telephony part works. And it's due to this isolation of knowledge, of necessary knowledge and the stability of the interfaces – whether it's a stable protocol interface or a stable API – that the longevity and stability of those interfaces allow people to do things without having to know very much at all, if anything, about how this works underneath. So you create this opportunity for invention without a whole lot of overhead.

ALI ABBAS: Yeah that happens. Now we are hearing more and more because information is becoming more prevalent due to the Internet; and there's a lot of issues about privacy and that was probably something. What are your thoughts now about data and privacy and some of the issues that we're hearing today?

VINT CERF: So I think we are far more conscious now of the fact that privacy is difficult to come by. I have to tell you though that, when I was 19, I lived in a little village in Germany. It's called Beutelsbach and had about 3,000 people in it. I lived up on top of the hill called Landgut Burg. So it turns out that this is 1962, and the postmaster knew what everybody was doing because nobody had phones at home. You had to go to the post office to place a phone call. He would place the phone call for you. Then you'd go to the booth and talk. And, of course, you know he's sorting all the mail. Everybody knew what everybody was doing. A little village is not a place where privacy is easily obtained. Now I'm not arguing that therefore privacy is weird or odd or a new idea or something. But there is something interesting that happened sociologically. As big cities formed and people migrated to those cities from farm territories, what they got was not quite privacy but they got anonymity. You didn't know everybody in the city unlike a small village.

And so you may have had the sense of privacy because you were sort of anonymous, but it's not the same thing. Well now everybody has a phone. All the phones have cameras. We have applications that let people upload virtually anything onto the Net. And so you don't know – you know – that somebody has taken a picture and sometimes it's inadvertent. So here's a scenario. You're in Egypt and you're standing in front of the pyramids and you ask somebody to take a photograph of you standing in front of the pyramids. Somebody else is captured in that image. You don't know who it is. You don't care. It doesn't matter. You put your image up on the Net. Somebody else is running around looking for pictures of pyramids and they find this and they say oh I know that guy. Wait a minute. He told me he was in London on that day. So now this guy is in trouble because somebody else took a picture for you. So you know it's this inadvertent sharing of information with its side effects that we are all experiencing right now.

So now there are other issues here that we need to take into account. Companies accumulate a lot of information about their users. The phone system, for example, kept track of all your phone calls because that's how you keep track of billing – and everybody understood that – but that information was treated as special. It was only available if it was demanded, for example, by the police department under proper court orders for legal reasons. So companies like Google, Yahoo, Facebook, Amazon, and others accumulate a lot of information about the users' behavior. Some of it's in the normal course of doing business. We're very conscious of and open about the fact that our business at Google is to use information like what you are searching for to figure out what ad we should show you. We don't sell that information to anybody. It's not in our business interests to do that. We are only sitting here saying, if you just did a search I need to go reach in my ad bag and try to figure out if there's anything there that matches the search.

So we feel that that information is sacrosanct and we hang on to that, we don't share it with anybody. There are other companies that don't necessarily follow all the same rules. So the fact that our behavior patterns are the exhaust of our behavior on the Net is captured in one way or another by many different parties; and in some cases it is shared without our knowledge, which is a dawning recognition at this point that the online environment – as useful as it has been and will be – is also a place where privacy is hard to come by. And it's not surprising that we're starting to see reactions to that; and pressures coming from governments at several different levels and individuals to say "I want to have more to say about what happens to the information about me that I leave behind as a result of my online interactions."
So I don't think we have a clear simple set of desirable guidelines. It's discussions about ethics, for example, it's discussions about privacy and privacy rights that will eventually lead us to some conclusions. The hard part is that this is global in scope and the Internet doesn't know when it's crossed international boundaries. And so the preferences and behavioral and cultural patterns of people around the world will differ and vary: and figuring out how to do this in a way that is at least compatible at the edges of country borders is a hard problem. So we have to figure out as a society what is it that we will accept and what is it that we will reject in terms of the behaviors of individuals as well as companies and governments.

ALI ABBAS: Given the advances that are happening in technology and artificial intelligence, what should people in public policy be doing? I mean they obviously need first to learn about what it is before they can make meaningful legislation.

VINT CERF: Don't you wish that the legislators actually had that view. Some of them are sort of happy to make laws regardless of whether they know what they're doing.

ALI ABBAS: Yeah. So how would Americans today or people around the world know whether they should accept, click "yes," so that their information goes off somewhere? I mean should they; should they not? Is that something they should think more about?

VINT CERF: We're asking users to do a lot. We're asking them to understand a lot about the implications of their choices. And I think that most of the online services need to be much more transparent about the implications of saying "yes." Certainly we should not ask people to go through reams and reams of terms and conditions and everything else for them to figure out what the implications are. So I think there's real work to be done there to be more clear. There may very well be, I'm not sure how I would put this exactly, but you know you go to other people for advice about what you should do. You can imagine people being advice givers for safe networking, you know, "How should I configure this thing, if I'm running this application what are the implications of what happens?" And if you can't quite get that out of the app that you just loaded you may actually want somebody to consult with who will help you figure that out. This will emerge again in the Internet of Things; I don't know if we're going to talk about that. But that's another big configuration nightmare and another potential hazard about privacy. If you have webcams all over everywhere. Who has access to them and when and under what circumstances?

ALI ABBAS: Yeah. Net neutrality. What are your thoughts on that?

VINT CERF: Well, of course this has been quite a hoo-hah for almost a decade. And the not so short story is that in the mid-1990s there were 8,000 Internet service providers in the United States alone. The reason that there were so many is that the business was dial up over the telephone with a modem that you connected to the server. Yes, you got it, like the cat whose tail was being twisted. When broadband technology came along it was offered by a small number of providers. The telephone company with DSL, for example, or maybe optical fiber and the cable company with cable modems. So the problem we ran into is that those 8,000 Internet service providers became zero, one, or two from the standpoint of any particular consumer. If you were in the rural part of the country you had zero broadband service; if you were in the suburban part maybe you had a choice of one cable company or telephone company, or if you were in the urban part of the country you might have a choice of two: a cable company and a telephone company.

So suddenly your choices, you know, dropped to a very small number. That's not a highly competitive environment. So we didn't have the discipline of competition to try to limit the behaviors of the broadband providers – that's one important point. The second thing is that as broadband becomes available, now some applications that would not have worked become feasible. So, for example, if you were a cable company and you were providing video services to your consumers, subscribers, and also broadband Internet service, you might encounter a situation where your user is using the broadband Internet service to watch videos from somebody else. Now I'm sure none of the companies would ever do this but you can imagine the reaction to this. Wait a minute. They're using my service to look at somebody else's videos so I'm not getting the benefit of selling you access to mine. Why don't we just mess up the Internet service enough so that this other guy's competitive video doesn't work and drive my subscriber back to my offerings. So this verticalization of the broadband Internet world lead to a potential for that behavior and the users didn't have much of a response because they didn't have a lot of choice to switch from one carrier to another.

And to make matters worse, switching meant a truck roll. Somebody had to come out and tear out some equipment and put in some new equipment. So, this led the FCC [Federal Communications Commission] to conclude that it should establish some kind of net neutrality rules that say you won't mess up people's access to the Internet and block them from getting access to where they wanted to go, or interfere with or do preferential charging or something else. And in the same rough timeframe the cable companies and the telcos each were regulated differently under the FCC rules. One under Title VI for cable and one under Title II for telecom. And so both of those classes of company would come to the FCC and complain, "We're regulated differently but we're both offering Internet service. So can't you fix that?" The fix that was decided was to make the Internet service unregulated – so they were being treated the same, which is to say they weren't being regulated at all.

But now you're trying to combine the net neutrality rules with an unregulated service. So the first time the FCC tries to apply the net neutrality rules against a company that appeared to have violated them this goes all the way up to the Supreme Court and the Supreme Court says, "Excuse me FCC. Since you decided the Internet is not regulated you have no basis to force this company to behave any differently. You have no standing." So the FCC in the next iteration or incarnation says, "OK let's move this back to Title II where the telecom service is and we can regulate it. But recognizing that Internet is not telephony, we will forbear from applying lots of the terms and conditions in the Title II of the Telecom Act." And so we have this partial regulation in aid only of the net neutrality rules. The next FCC that comes along, the current one, decides that this is inappropriate and that there shouldn't be any regulation at all – so they reversed that decision.

So now consumers have little to protect them. The other side argues well, yes, you do because the Federal Trade Commission [FTC] is still there and if you're being harmed you can complain to the FTC and there will be some action taken. But that's a case by case kind of process as opposed to having a fairly crisp list of do not do these things because they are out of scope. So the next possibility, now that we don't have any regulation at the FCC, is to develop a title in the Telecom Act for Internet specifically, which incorporates the net neutrality rules in it. And at that point you could then invoke FCC for access abuse. That's really what the issue was – getting access to the Internet without interference. For content abuse you might still turn to the FTC to say that I've been harmed, fraud has been committed, a variety of harms have occurred, copyright violations, all kinds of things could be FTC responsibility and access abuse would be the FCC responsibility. Now the question is: Will the Congress be able to formulate such a title and pass the law and will the president sign it? But at this stage of the game we're in a relatively unprotected state because of the recent decision to abandon enforcement of the net neutrality rules.

ALI ABBAS: Let me ask you a few questions Vint; and this is very enlightening some of the discussions here. Artificial intelligence has been in the news a lot lately and there are concerns about artificial intelligence and even the ethics of artificial intelligence. What are your thoughts on that?

VINT CERF: So I want to distinguish between artificial intelligence and machine learning for a moment. It may sound like a kind of splitting of hairs but it's actually an important distinction. Most of the time when you hear people talking about artificial intelligence they are thinking about general artificial intelligence. This is machines that are capable of doing the kind of reasoning that human beings do. And I remind you that humans have this remarkable ability to perceive the real world, to build models of that real world, to reason about and to plan with. Most computers don't have that capability right now. So a lot of the excitement that you see is what we would call at Google machine learning. Now what is that all about and why has it suddenly become so important? Well for many years neural networks were a very confined thing. They were maybe one layer deep and there were some 1960s books by Minsky and Papert that basically said perceptrons don't work because they can't even figure out whether a graph is connected because they aren't seeing enough of it.

But we discovered, we the community discovered, five years ago or so that we could build a multilayer neural network, which might be hundreds of layers deep; and we could train that network by exposing it to examples and having it figure out whether, for example, in image processing, is this a cat or a dog. And after a while the various weights that were associated with the connections would help distinguish one from the other. And for the technically inclined this is basically mapping the image space into a very high dimensional space. So the two things that were different could be separated by a hyper plane.

ALI ABBAS: Yeah, and having more data to train the network probably helps

VINT CERF: Yes, it helps you figure out where is that plane in hyperspace. So we've seen some remarkable successes in image separation or image understanding or image identification. We've had super successes at Deep Mind, which is one of the alphabet companies, playing Go. We trained a multilayer neural net over quite a long period of time to play Go at grandmaster level and then tested that against grandmasters in South Korea and China and won all but one game in those series. But the most dramatic thing that happened is that after Alpha Go was demonstrated, the Deep Mind guys developed something called Alpha Zero. Alpha Zero is essentially a system based only on the rules of the game and, playing incarnations of this program with themselves, it learned how to play Go in just a few days' time, enough to beat a grandmaster again. But that's just a few days' worth of playing the game, starting from just knowing the rules. In several hours, given the rules of chess, these programs were able to figure out how to play it well enough to beat other chess-playing programs, maybe not human grandmasters. It was just a few hours.

So this is all very shocking and everybody gets quite excited about that because, well, if they can do that, can they do everything else? And it's an overstatement, an overreach. These are extremely narrow capabilities. Now having said that, the autonomous cars, self-driving cars, are a very dramatic evolution. What's going on there is a blend of a number of techniques, it's not just machine learning but the machine learning is very helpful in identifying objects in the field of view, classifying them. But then additionally we have to say this is an X, a person on a bicycle. This is a pedestrian. This is what we think is a dog. This is a truck. This is a car. Once we've identified them then the question is what are they likely to do in the near term? And so now this is reasoning about a world model, which has been developed not only from LIDAR [light detection and radar] images but from knowledge of the detailed street maps and so on.

At this point we are reasoning about the world around us in real time. So that's a very powerful evolution all by itself. Am I scared that the robots are going to take over? No. I think of these technologies as tools that we apply to make it easier for us to get our work done. It's not too different from the invention of fractional horsepower electric motors, which let us place muscle power in exactly the amount we needed, wherever we needed it, in whatever size we needed it. So this is placing computing power of whatever size we need, wherever we need it, applying it when we need it to augment our own capabilities.

ALI ABBAS: Coming back to the idea of driverless cars and the recognition now, character recognition of the object, who makes the trade-offs?

VINT CERF: The most likely thing is that the car has been trained not to run into anything first of all. Second, when the car doesn't know what to do – I mean if it reaches the point where it does not know how to make a decision – it needs to know that it can't make that decision or doesn't know what to do, and it needs to go into what NASA would typically call safe mode. Safe mode means get to the side of the road and stop. Get out of the way. I mean this is all oversimplification of what's going on but I am convinced that it is possible to make these cars very, very safe to use; and especially if you're willing to accept that the metric is better than human driven.

ALI ABBAS: And, of course, the comeback question is: Shouldn't it know more information about you? In other words, should your car know how many people are in there? If you think of utilitarian rather than just hapless knowledge about who's in the car.

VINT CERF: The defining problem is about physics, it's about the car being able to react faster than a human being can, to make use of its controls to avoid collisions. There are still going to be situations where a collision is unavoidable especially if there are still human drivers on the streets. Or some physical circumstance, a tree falls down and somehow knocks the car out of the way or something breaks and the car comes flying over the overhead. And at that point there will be some unavoidable events. Then the question will be whether there was any action that could have been taken to avoid the problem.

ALI ABBAS: In fact, some would argue that given the number of deaths on the highways – maybe 36,000 a year –a good test would be, when other driverless cars are in place, how many deaths are we going to have now? In other words, we shouldn't fixate on the one incident in Arizona. Rather it is overall how many deaths are we going to have with the interaction of driverless cars.

VINT CERF: Well that's certainly one very pragmatic metric. Did we reduce the number of accidents? Did we reduce the number of fatalities or the number of injuries on the road? That ought to count. On the other hand, you know we're a funny litigious society and when anything bad happens we look around for somebody to sue, even if they didn't have anything to do with it. So I imagine we are in for quite a complicated period of time as liability gets decided. And if we allow the courts to make these decisions exclusively, we will end up with a kind of barnacle encrusted ship of law because each one of those decisions will stick another barnacle on the side of the ship. At some point we are going to need legislation that defines the nature of liability and how it should be adjudicated.

ALI ABBAS: Another question: What about advancements in medicine and genetic codes and our increasing ability to be able to modify or even create? What are your thoughts on that?

VINT CERF: So this is an extraordinary day when we have the ability to apply what's called CRISPR Cas9 to edit genetic sequences – to replace a sequence that has an error in it with one which should perform properly – it could have very dramatic results. But we have to be careful not to misunderstand that many illnesses are a consequence of a collection of different genetic interactions, not just one particular SNP, single nucleotide polymorphism, or other. So we shouldn't get too carried away. On the other hand, our ability to interact with the genetic sequences with some precision is an extraordinary development. There's something deeper going on though. For many years we thought once we knew what the human genome was that we could then predict what kinds of illnesses might occur, we might be able to correct mistakes and so on and therefore we're done, right? Well what we discovered very quickly is that it's more complicated. This is theorem Number 206. "Everything is more complicated."

Genetic interpretation produces proteins and so the question is what protein is being produced? Under what conditions are they produced; how is the gene turned off or turned on? Methylation is a factor, the so-called epigenetics, which are the exterior impacts on the way in which genes get interpreted; but it gets even more complicated than that. We now have discovered that human beings are not just the sum of their genetic sequence, they're also the sum of the microbiomes in the gut, which evolved with us, is part of our immune system, to say nothing of digestion and everything else. And so that suddenly multiplies the genetic complement by large factors. And then there is one other thing. Even after we somehow understand all that, there is something called metabolism, it's what keeps us alive.

And it turns out that there are metabolic exhausts: you eat and then things happen and your body produces waste, and so on. Actually, understanding the metabolism may be even more important than anything else, because it gives you a real clue about how well your body is functioning. So right now, I see this huge potential for continuous monitoring, continued analysis of our metabolic output, and with the purpose in mind not of curing disease but of keeping people healthy. And those I think are not the same thing. Avoiding disease by keeping people healthy is a lot better than trying to respond to a disease that is a result, for example, of bad eating habits, no exercise, smoking, and whatever else causes this trouble.

ALI ABBAS: What about the future? Fifty years from now, what will people be talking about? What will we be talking about with regard to the Internet? What types of advances will we see?

VINT CERF: Well I wish that I could really make that prediction. Go back fifty years to 1969 at the beginning of the ARPANET project, trying to imagine how we could possibly have what we do today. With the shrinking costs and size and energy requirements of a lot of the competing devices, which fifty years ago were in big air-conditioned rooms, now we carry them in our pockets. We have them embedded in our bodies. That's a big leap; but I can make a few guesses. One of them is that communications will be ambient in the sense that you won't even think about it. Of course, things interact with each other. Of course, there is communication in every dimension. Like plugging into a wall to get electricity today, which you generally don't think about until it isn't available. This is what infrastructure is about. You assume that it's there and you only react badly when it isn't.

So I think communications and something which may still be called Internet, it may not work the same way it does today, will still be there. Lots and lots of software surrounding us in programmable devices. We will be extremely dependent on all of that software working properly. Today, if you want to get a sense for the level of dependence, think about what happens when the power goes out. It doesn't take very long before the fabric of society begins to shred and people are breaking into stores to get food because the store isn't open – not because they're criminals and thieves but because they can't buy anything or there's no power so the mobile doesn't work and they can't transfer funds.

So all of these dependencies should worry us some and if we look fifty years into the future we should be asking ourselves what dependencies are we creating that we will then find are harrowing in their loss and can we build more resilience into the system to avoid the consequences of losing that infrastructure? Other than that, maybe we will truly be vacationing on Mars and perhaps we'll have a spacecraft on its way to Alpha Centauri. I sure hope so. I mean, we've been dawdling all this time; we need to get out to the other stars and who knows maybe we even will be approaching the twenty-fourth-century Star Trek society where money isn't needed anymore because the robots do all the work. I've always wondered what that transition period is going to be like. I have no idea exactly how you would do that.

ALI ABBAS: One more question: you know recently we lost Stephen Hawking, what are your reflections on that?

VINT CERF: So Hawking, of course, was the most striking phenomenon, a man who should have been dead at a much earlier age, somehow survived with ALS [amyotrophic lateral sclerosis]. I have several friends who have passed away because of that disease, it's a pernicious thing, it just wastes your body. Somehow or another, interventions and maybe his own determination, his own state of mind, kept him alive into his seventies and I suspect that has a lot to do with it. I mean the attitude that you have, the way in which your brain is occupied may in fact also affect your health and your ability to survive. He was certainly the most brilliant of the physicists of our age; the only possible comparable party with this would be Albert Einstein. And what was lovely about Hawking is that he had a great sense of humor. He managed to reach people at many different levels; and composed some books which I had to read several times before I could quite get the point: like *A Brief History of Time*. And I always appreciated the fact that Hawking would admit when he was wrong.

So he had a number of different bets that he had placed in which he took one position and somebody took another. The thing that I particularly liked is that he was still alive when we finally detected the first gravity waves and I wish I could have been there and just talked about it with him. But that was a great moment that proved Einstein's theory that these things should exist but they were really hard to detect especially from far away. I'm enthusiastic about this because the National Science Foundation funded the Laser Interferometer Gravity Observer Project for something like thirty years patiently going through multiple iterations; and to see that level of let's say trust and determination and patience over a long period of time pay off in this dramatic way is really cool.

ALI ABBAS: Final question Vint. Life on other planets?

VINT CERF: Well I'm convinced that life is likely elsewhere for several different reasons. One of them is that we're starting to see how readily self-replication can happen, we can see bits and pieces of it. Sometimes it's, you know, if you look at clay, calcified clay, you see these chains of chemicals winding up. I mean it's like, what was the game that you used to play where things would come streaming?

ALI ABBAS: Tetris.

VINT CERF: Think about these things being chemicals aligning, just falling – you know – and lining and linking up. And so this self-replication possibility seems pretty easy in some sense, in our world anyway. And if you look at the number of planets that have been discovered now, –some of which are thought to be inhabitable zones – a lot of them around dwarf planets. The little white dwarfs unlike our own M type star – there just seem like an awful lot of places where this could potentially happen. I would be frankly surprised if there was not life elsewhere. Whether it's intelligent life, it's a little hard to tell. But I've always been amused by this project, the search for extraterrestrial intelligence. Some people ask why would you do that? And my answer is, well, we didn't find any intelligence here so we're looking for some out there!

ALI ABBAS: Vint, it's been a real pleasure. Thank you very much.

VINT CERF: Thank you very much.

6

A Hippocratic Oath for Technologists

Ali E. Abbas, Max Senges, and Ronald A. Howard

6.1 Introduction

As technology becomes more powerful, intelligent, and autonomous, its usage also creates unintended consequences and ethical challenges for a vast array of stakeholders. The ethical implications of technology on society, for example, range from job losses (such as potential loss of truck driver jobs due to automation) to lying and deception about a product that may occur within a technology firm or on user-generated content platforms. The challenges around ethical technology design are so multifaceted that there is an essential need for each stakeholder to accept responsibility. Even policymakers who are charged with providing the appropriate regulatory framework and legislation about technologies have an obligation to learn about the pros and cons of proposed options.

As our technologies become more powerful, intelligent, and autonomous, they also bear the potential to address problems previously impossible to penetrate and to create unintended consequences and challenges for transparency and accountability. In many circumstances it becomes difficult to learn from and identify whether an unfortunate result that caused harm was due to ethical failures or simply human error. And in either case, who was responsible.

With recent advances in technology, we are faced with new pathways for deception and escalation of ethical dilemmas leading to some recent collapses that have appeared in the news. Examples of ethical misconduct involving technology abide: Volkswagen (US News, 2018; Lynch, Cutro, & Bird, 2016; Patel, 2015) and other car manufacturers' use of manipulative software to pass diesel emission tests. Theranos founder, Elizabeth Holmes, being charged with wire fraud (*Wall Street Journal*, March 13, 2018) for deceiving her investors and the public about the capabilities of her blood analysis technology. And, of course, the employees of Cambridge Analytica (*The New York Times*, March 19, 2018) abusing Facebook's social media and app platform to obtain personality profiles in order to deploy AI-enabled personalized propaganda at scale.

This chapter presents an ethical creed, which we refer to as the Hippocratic Oath for Technologists. The creed is built upon three fundamental pillars:

(i) proactively understanding the ethical implications of technology for all stake-holders, (ii) telling the truth about the capabilities, advantages, and disadvantages of a technology, and (iii) acting responsibly in situations you find ethically challenging. The oath may be taken by students at universities after understanding its basic definitions and implications, and it may also be discussed with technology firms and human resources departments to provide the necessary support and understanding for their employees who wish to abide by the norms of this oath. This work lays the foundations for the arguments and requirements of a unified movement, as well as a call for a forum for signing up for the oath to enable its widespread dissemination.

Our focus in this chapter is to discuss and raise awareness of the ethical responsibility of the technologist as a user and creator of technology. The main purpose of this work is to provide reflection during the creation phase of a technology and to make ethical distinctions that a technologist may not have considered or have been introduced to in prior education. These essential distinctions will be covered in Section 6.2. A second objective of this work is to help raise sensitivities in technology firms about certain actions that may be deemed legal at the time, and yet have ethical implications for stakeholders. Another objective (and of the proposed oath) is to provide foundations for a movement and its widespread dissemination. A final aim of this work is to provide humility and a sense of community among experts and technologists who explicitly want to promote technology for human progress.

The Hippocratic oath,[1] which is historically taken by physicians, has had a long history and several iterations. In fact the Greek original is so outdated that most medical doctors would not be willing to take it today. A Wikipedia translation[2] of the most historic surviving version of the oath reads: "To hold my teacher in this art equal to my own parents; to make him partner in my livelihood; when he is in need of money to share mine with him; to consider his family as my own brothers." Even the famous line "first do no harm" does not appear to be part of the original version of the oath, and may in fact not withstand critical inquiry as, of course, doctors may need to inflict significant pain and sometimes even harm a patient in order to treat an ailment.

While the Hippocratic Oath is the most famous and possibly the first code of conduct for a profession, there are many other examples. Most relevant is the Archimedean Oath,[3] developed by French engineering students in the 1990. The Appendix presents a long and short version of the Archimedean Oath.

After careful deliberation we opted nevertheless to propose this new instrument with the aim to guide conduct among technologists under the title "Hippocratic Oath for Technologists." The reason is that the concept is so widely recognized, and hence we believe it will facilitate adoption, and because newer versions of the

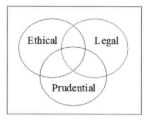

Figure 6.1 *Ethical–legal–prudential distinctions*

Hippocratic Oath – namely the 1964 version by Louis Lasagna, Academic Dean of the School of Medicine at Tufts University – omits the controversial line and simply calls for "utmost respect for human life."

We view the work in this chapter as an initial guideline that may promote reflection and pursuit of good practices by technologists committing to the oath's principles by (i) digitally and publicly signing their name on a dedicated website, and (ii) subsequently receiving a digital badge that they can include in their social media profiles on Facebook, Twitter, LinkedIn, etc. (and of course on their personal websites).

6.2 Basic Distinctions for Ethical Considerations

This part of the chapter reviews basic distinctions to help the technologist understand ethical implications regardless of the legal system or the dollar value to an organization. We believe that, in the current educational system, technologists may not be exposed to some of these distinctions.

6.2.1 Ethical–Legal–Prudential Considerations

It is important to first understand the basic distinction of what is ethical, legal, and prudential in Figure 6.1 (Howard & Korver, 2009, 2015). The legal distinction is often presented as the norm for what is right or wrong when a situation arises. Very often you may hear statements like, "We did nothing wrong" – meaning what was done was legal, and may even be encouraged by the legal system. Understanding the difference between legal and ethical considerations helps technologists realize that while something might be legal, it may be unethical. The prudential distinction refers to what is prudent or beneficial regardless of the legal or the ethical systems. Some might argue that being ethical is prudential in itself, but the distinction helps understand that there may be situations that are perceived as prudential and legal when in fact they may have ethical implications.

6.2.2 Positive vs Negative Injunctions

Another distinction that is important for identifying the role in reflection about ethical dilemmas is that between positive and negative injunctions (Howard & Korver, 2009, 2015). A negative injunction towards a situation asserts that you yourself will not do it. A positive injunction asserts that you will take action when you observe it happening. Positive injunctions are stronger commitments than negative injunctions. For example, you may take an oath that you will not steal, a negative injunction towards stealing, in contrast to a positive injunction where you will report instances of stealing (or even prevent them) when you observe them. Think about the implications of this important distinction in organizations where one employee observes an ethical issue conducted by another (or by the organization). A positive injunction will require them to take action. While taking a positive injunction stance may be difficult, companies can help by providing a supportive environment and structure. The Stanford University Honor Code[4] is an example of both a positive and negative injunction towards receiving unpermitted aid, whereby students, individually and collectively (i) will not give or receive aid in examinations; (ii) will not give or receive unpermitted aid in class work, in the preparation of reports, or in any other work that is to be used by the instructor as the basis of grading; (iii) will do their share and take an active part in seeing to it that others as well as themselves uphold the spirit and letter of the Honor Code.

6.2.3 Deception

Deception is the act of knowingly leaving a false impression or narrative on another person. We find it useful to clarify that deception can occur without even saying a word. If a person has a certain belief (that you know is incorrect), and that person clarifies it with you, then you merely nod, you have knowingly left the person with an incorrect impression. The same applies to interfaces between technology and human, or data gathering, when a user is unaware about the implications/uses of their data. Deception would include situations where a firm has not provided the user with full disclosures about how their data is collected and used.

6.2.4 Utilitarian vs Kantian

In the Kantian view (Kant, 1781) ethical responsibility attaches to the actions taken, regardless of their consequences.

The other major ethical theory, utilitarianism, is consequence based. The responsibility attaches to the expected consequences, not to the person's action. Utilitarianism derives from philosophers such as Jeremy Bentham[5] and John Stuart Mill,[6] who believed that the calculus of world pleasure and happiness should be the justification for action.

6.3 Presenting the Oath

6.3.1 Preamble

Three main goals guided the drafting of the oath: clarity, simplicity, and comprehensiveness.

Clarity of what the oath entails was the central guiding principle meant to ensure that each element is comprehensible and coherent. Another desideratum here is that if any proposed portion is violated, then it should pose a clear ethical issue.

Simplicity is the second requirement, which led us to opt for widely understood terminology and language whenever possible.

Comprehensiveness, or to cover the full scope of technologists' practice and subsequently all possible ethical dilemma, was also a goal; and, of course, we had intense debates about which elements must be covered and which are included in high-level statements.

Another less fundamental requirement was that it should not be based on or merely to endorse some entity that may have ethical implications or might pose terms for a legal/political system.

Last but not least, the oath should be personal in its implications. Put differently, we believe that individual human agency and responsibility is at the core of individual as well as societal justice and well-being. We acknowledge that taking a positive or negative injunction stance may be difficult in practice, especially when an employment or other organizational/political alliance is present. We nevertheless believe that companies, as well as organizations and communities more generally, can help to promote the good conduct and deliberation intended by the oath.

We should always ask what a technology should do and not only explore what it can do. An ethical code should have some essential criteria:

1. The code should have clarity of what the oath entails.
2. It must be as simple as possible but no simpler. We should not add items in the code that if violated do not pose ethical issues. If any portion of the code is violated, then it should pose a clear ethical issue.

3. The code should not be based on merely endorsing some entity that may have ethical codes with implicit legal/political implications. Rather the code should be independent of the legal system.
4. The oath should be personal in its implications for a person to be willing to commit to it.

To ground our practice and conduct, the following principles shall marshal our mindset, decision-making, and practices independent of the legal system as well as our personal and organizational culture:

6.3.2 The Oath

1. **I will seek to understand the ethical implications of the use of technology when making decisions.**
   a) *I will take into account the ethical implications of technology that I am aware of when making choices about technology creation.*
   b) *I will seek to understand the ethical implications of technology for all stakeholders.*
   c) *I will engage in deliberation as needed to understand the evaluation of benefits and harms as well as ethical practices with regards to the technologies I use and create.*
2. **I will tell the truth.**
   a) *I will disclose to the best of my knowledge the potential benefits, disadvantages, risks and consequences of the technology.*
   b) *I will not exploit ignorance or deceive others[7] with regards to the capabilities, consequences, and trade offs of technology.*
   c) *I will appropriately inform the user and will allow the user to decide about the retention and use of personal data and user privacy in the design of technology.*
   d) *I will be truthful and transparent about my positions and stakes with regards to my professional networks, conflicts of interest, and motivation.*
   e) *I will acknowledge the contributions of others by giving credit where credit is due.*
3. **I will act responsibly**
   a) *If asked to do something I find ethically objectionable, I will refuse.*
      i) *If asked to work on a project or develop a technology that I have an ethical issue with I will refuse to do so and disclose my analysis.*
   b) *If I observe any error or misdeed, I will address it.*
      i) *Should I witness any misdeed or potential ethical violation with a technology I shall first address and remedy it with the responsible entity. However, should it prove impossible to resolve directly, I shall draw the attention of the appropriate authorities to the case.*

6.4 Comments on the Oath

The first part of the oath places responsibility on the technologist to understand the ethical implications of technology and take them into account when making decisions. This has an implicit implication of effort and action needed towards understanding the stakeholder views, and also understanding the rationale by which a decision with ethical implications is made. For example, is it a utilitarian approach where the means justify the ends and the overall good outweighs the means? Or a Kantian approach where ethical considerations are determined by the actions themselves? Thinking about these distinctions and their implications for stakeholders is important for people who are taking the oath. Universities may wish to provide introductions to these types of distinctions in their technology curricula.

The second part of the oath is about truth telling and being conscious about deception. Telling the truth about benefits, disadvantages, risks, and consequences may be a legal requirement in some instances (such as risks to human life mentioned on labels of cigarettes) and they may not be legally enforced in others. Abiding by this oath requires the taker to be truthful whether or not a legal aspect exists. Users of the technology must also be made aware of the implications and of what they are signing up for, not just having terms and conditions in a fine print.

The first part of the oath simply requires you to refuse to do an action that you find objectionable even if you are asked. The second part is a positive injunction requiring you to correct an ethically-objectionable behavior if you see one. The third part of the oath is about actions regarding issues one finds ethically objectionable.

This third part (having both a positive and a negative injunction) is a strong ask, which presents an opportunity for companies to provide support on their ethical code. A company might say employees will not be forced to engage in an activity that they find ethically objectionable. Or that the organization will support and protect people who come forward with observations that they find ethically objectionable.

6.5 Conclusion

We view this work as a first step in creating a unified movement for increasing awareness about the ethical considerations of technology. Like the original version of the Hippocratic Oath, which we doubt physicians would be willing to take today, we believe that there will be many variations and updates of this oath. But it is important for a unified movement to start.

The next step will be to share this oath with the academic and industrial communities. We hope that deans of engineering and all technology schools will join this movement and help us spread the word to graduates, and also incorporate the basic distinctions into technology education. We invite feedback and deliberation on the oath. Concretely participants would commit by digitally signing the oath on a dedicated website, they would then receive a digital badge that they can include in their social media profiles.

The authors assess that the unique power of the oath approach is that it roots the responsibility in a person who can then contribute to the debate and practice of the organization and team. We are looking forward to the debate on goals, substance, and practice related to the Hippocratic Oath. We invite you to sign up for the oath on the website.[8]

Acknowledgment

The authors would like to thank John Seely Brown, Peter Norvig, Damon Horowitz, and Roya Pakzad for various discussions.

Appendix:
The Archimedean Oath – Source: Wikipedia

The **Archimedean Oath** is an ethical code of practice for engineers and technicians, similar to the Hippocratic Oath used in the medical world. It was proposed in 1990 by a group of students of the École polytechnique fédérale de Lausanne. The Archimedean Oath has since spread to a number of European engineering schools.

> "Considering the life of Archimedes of Syracuse who illustrated the ambiguous potential of technology since the Antiquity, Considering the growing responsibility of engineers and scientists towards men and nature, Considering the importance of the ethical problems stemming from technology and its applications, Today, I commit to the following statements and shall endeavor to reach towards the ideal that they represent:
>
> - I shall practice for the good of mankind, respecting human rights[1] and the environment.
> - I shall recognize the responsibility for my actions, after informing myself to the best of my abilities, and shall in no case discharge my responsibilities on another person.

- I shall endeavor to perfect my professional abilities.
- When choosing and implementing projects, I shall remain wary of their context and their consequences, notably in their technical, economic, social and ecological aspects. I shall give particular attention to projects with military applications.
- I shall contribute, to the extent of my abilities, to promote equitable relationships between men and to support the development of economically weaker countries.
- I shall transmit, with rigor and honesty, to discerningly chosen interlocutors, any important information, if it constitutes a gain for society or if its retention constitutes a danger for others. In the latter case, I shall ensure that the communication yields concrete action.
- I shall not let myself be governed by the defense of my own interests or those of my corporation.
- I shall endeavor, to the best of my abilities, to lead my company to take into account the preoccupations of the present oath.
- I shall practice my profession in complete intellectual honesty, with conscience and dignity.

I solemnly take this oath, freely and on my honor." 1. According to the Universal Declaration of Human Rights of the United Nations (10 December 1948)

A shorter version goes:

I commit to keeping completely, to the full extent of my capacities and judgment, the following promises:

- I shall use my knowledge for the benefit of mankind.
- I shall not put my skill to the service of people who do not respect human rights.
- I shall not permit consideration regarding religion, nationality, race, sex, wealth and politics to harm people affected by my actions.
- I shall bear the entire responsibility for my actions and shall in no way discharge them on another.
- I shall practice in respect for the environment.
- I shall not use my knowledge for destructive purposes.
- I shall practice my profession in complete intellectual honesty, with conscience and dignity.

I solemnly take this oath, freely and on my honor.

References

Howard, R. A, & C. Korver. (2008). *Ethics for the real world: Creating a personal code to guide decisions in work and life*. Boston, MA: Harvard Business Press.

Howard, R. A, & A. E. Abbas. (2015). *Foundations of decision analysis*. New York, NY: Pearson.

Facebook and Cambridge Analytica: What you need to know as fallout widens. (2018, March 19). *The New York Times*. Retrieved from www.nytimes.com/2018/03/19/technology/facebook-cambridge-analytica-explained.html

Kant, I. (1781). *The critique of pure reason*. Reprinted in 1998 by Cambridge University Press.

Lynch, L. J., Cutro, C., & Bird, E. (2016). *The Volkswagen emissions scandal*. Charlottesville, VA: Darden Business Publishing. Retrieved from http://store.darden.virginia.edu/the-volkswagen-emissions-scandal

Patel, P. (2015, September 25). Engineers, ethics, and the VW scandal. *IEEE, Spectrum*. Retrieved from https://spectrum.ieee.org/cars-that-think/at-work/education/vw-scandal-shocking-but-not-surprising-ethicists-say

SEC Charges Theranos CEO Elizabeth Holmes with fraud. (2018, March 14). *Wall Street Journal*. Retrieved from www.wsj.com/articles/sec-charges-theranos-and-founder-elizabeth-holmes-with-fraud-1521045648

US NEWS: Volkswagen's new CEO promises a more ethical culture. (2018). Retrieved from www.usnews.com/news/business/articles/2018-05-03/new-volkswagen-ceo-promises-push-for-more-ethical-culture

Endnotes

[1] Encyclopedia Britannica Article on Hippocratic Oath. Retrieved from www.britannica.com/topic/Hippocratic-oath

[2] Wikipedia translation of Hippocratic Oath. Retrieved from https://en.wikipedia.org/wiki/Hippocratic_Oath

[3] Wikipedia article on Archimedean Oath. Retrieved from https://en.wikipedia.org/wiki/Archimedean_Oath

[4] Stanford Honor Code. Retrieved from https://communitystandards.stanford.edu/student-conduct-process/honor-code-and-fundamental-standard

[5] Wikipedia article on Jeremy Bentham. Retrieved from https://en.wikipedia.org/wiki/Jeremy_Bentham

[6] Wikipedia article on John Stuart Mill. Retrieved from https://en.wikipedia.org/wiki/John_Stuart_Mill

[7] An example would be if there is a fine print that personal data can be used beyond the original data-gathering purpose and yet most people are not aware of the fine print.

[8] https://hippocraticoath.org/

7

Data, Privacy, and the Greater Good

Eric Horvitz and Deirdre K. Mulligan

7.1 Introduction

Large-scale aggregate analyses of anonymized data can yield valuable results and insights that address public health challenges and provide new avenues for scientific discovery. These methods can extend our knowledge and provide new tools for enhancing health and well-being. However, they raise questions about how to best address potential threats to privacy while reaping benefits for individuals and for society as a whole. The use of machine learning to make leaps across informational and social contexts to infer health conditions and risks from non-medical data provides representative scenarios for reflections on directions with balancing innovation and regulation.

What if analyzing Twitter tweets or Facebook posts could identify new mothers at risk for postpartum depression (PPD)? Despite PPD's serious consequences, early identification and prevention remain difficult. Absent a history of depression, detection is largely dependent on new mothers' self-reports. But researchers found that shifts in sets of activities and language usage on Facebook are predictors of PPD (De Choudhury, Counts, Horvitz, & Hoff, 2014). This is but one example of promising research that uses machine learning to derive and leverage health-related inferences from the massive flows of data about individuals and populations generated through social media and other digital data streams. At the same time, machine learning presents new challenges for protecting individual privacy and ensuring fair use of data. We need to strike a new balance between controls on collecting information and controls on how it is used, as well as pursue auditable and accountable technologies and systems that facilitate greater use-based privacy protections.

Researchers have coined terms, such as digital disease detection (Brownstein, Freifeld, & Madoff, 2009) and infodemiology (Eysenbach, 2009), to define the new science of harnessing diverse streams of digital information to inform public

Horvitz, E. and Mulligan, D. (2015, July 17). Data, privacy and the greater good. *Science 349*(6245). http://erichorvitz.com/data_privacy_greater_good.pdf

health and policy, for example, earlier identification of epidemics (Broniatowski, Paul, & Dredze, 2013), modeling communicability and flow of illness (Sadilek, Kautz, & Silenzio, 2012), and stratifying individuals at risk for illness (De Choudhury, Counts, & Horvitz, 2013). This new form of health research can also inform and extend understandings drawn from traditional health records and human subjects research. For example, the detection of adverse drug reactions could be improved by jointly leveraging data from the US Food and Drug Administration's Adverse Event Reporting System and anonymized search logs (White, Harpaz, Shah, DuMouchel, & Horvitz, 2014). Search logs can serve as a large-scale sensing system that can be used for drug safety surveillance – pharmacovigilance.

Infodemiology studies are typically large-scale aggregate analyses of anonymized data – publicly disclosed or privately held – that yield results and insights on public health questions across populations. However, some methods and models can be aimed at making inferences about unique individuals that could drive actions, such as alerting or providing digital nudges, to improve individual or public health outcomes.

Although digital nudging shows promise, a recent flare-up in the United Kingdom highlights the privacy concerns it can ignite. A Twitter suicide- prevention application called Good Samaritan monitored individuals' tweets for words and phrases indicating a potential mental health crisis. The app notified the person's followers so they could intervene to avert a potential suicide. But the app was shuttered after public outcry drew regulator concern (samaritans.org). Critics worried the app would encourage online stalkers and bullies to target vulnerable individuals and collected 1,200 signatures on a petition arguing that the app breached users' privacy by collecting, processing, and sharing sensitive information. Despite the developers' laudable goal of preventing suicide, the nonprofit was chastised for playing fast and loose with the privacy and mental health of those it was seeking to save (change.org).

Machine learning can facilitate leaps across informational and social contexts, making "category-jumping" inferences about health conditions or propensities from nonmedical data generated far outside the medical context. The implications for privacy are profound. Category-jumping inferences may reveal attributes or conditions an individual has specifically withheld from others. To protect against such violations, the United States heavily regulates health care privacy. But, although information about health conditions garnered from health care treatment and payment must be handled in a manner that respects patient privacy, machine learning and inference can sidestep many of the existing protections.

Even when not category-jumping, machine learning can be used to draw powerful and compromising inferences from self-disclosed, seemingly benign data or readily observed behavior. These inferences can undermine a basic goal of many privacy laws – to allow individuals to control who knows what about them. Machine learning and inference makes it increasingly difficult for individuals to understand what others can know about them based on what they have explicitly or implicitly shared. And these computer-generated channels of information about health conditions join other technically created fissures in existing legal protections for health privacy. In particular, it is difficult to reliably deidentify publicly shared data sets, given the enormous amount and variety of ancillary data that can be used to reidentify individuals.

The capacities of machine learning expose the fundamental limitations of existing US privacy rules that tie the privacy protection of an individual's health status to particular contexts or specific types of information a priori identified as health information. Health privacy regulations and privacy laws in the United States generally are based on the assumption that the semantics of data are relatively fixed and knowable and reside in isolated contexts.

Machine-learning techniques can instead be used to infer new meaning within and across contexts and are generally unencumbered by privacy rules in the United States. Using publicly available Twitter posts to infer risk of PPD, for example, does not run afoul of existing privacy law. This might be unsurprising, and seem unproblematic, given that the posts were publicly shared, but there are troubling consequences.

Current privacy laws often do double duty. At a basic level, they limit who has access to information about a person. This implicitly limits the extent to which that information influences decision-making and thus doubles as a limit on the opportunities for information to fuel discrimination. Because of the heightened privacy sensitivities and concerns with health-related discrimination, we have additional laws that regulate the use of health information outside the health care context. US laws specifically limit the use of some health information in ways considered unfair. For example, credit-reporting agencies are generally prohibited from providing medical information to make decisions about employment, credit, or housing. The Americans with Disabilities Act (ADA) prohibits discrimination on the basis of substantial physical or mental disabilities – or even a mistaken belief that an individual suffers from such a disability. If machine learning is used to infer that an individual suffers from a physical or mental impairment, an employer who bases a hiring decision on it, even if the inference is wrong, would violate the law.

But the ADA does not prohibit discrimination based on predispositions for such disabilities (EEOC, 29 CFR 1630.2 (g) [2013]). Machine learning might discover those, too. In theory, the Genetic Information Non-Discrimination Act (GINA) should fill this gap by protecting people genetically predisposed to a disease. But again, machine learning exposes cracks in this protection. Although GINA prohibits discrimination based on information derived from genetic tests or a family history of a disease (EEOC, 29 CFR 1635.3 (c) [2013]), it does not limit the use of information about such a disposition – even if it is grounded in genetics – inferred through machine-learning techniques that mine other sorts of data. In other words, machine learning that predicts future health status from nongenetic information – including health status changes due to genetic predisposition – would circumvent existing legal protections (Rothstein, 2008).

Just as machine learning can expose secrets, it facilitates social sorting – placing individuals into categories for differential treatment – with good or bad intent and positive or negative outcomes. The methods used to classify individuals as part of beneficial public health programs and nudges can just as easily be used for more nefarious purposes, such as discrimination to protect organizational profits.

Policymakers in the United States and elsewhere are just beginning to address the challenges that machine learning and inference pose to commitments to privacy and equal treatment. Although not specifically focused on health information, reports issued by the White House – which discuss the potential for large-scale data analyses to result in discrimination (EOP, 2014) – and the Federal Trade Commission (FTC) have suggested new efforts to protect privacy, regulate harmful uses of information, and increase transparency.

The FTC is the key agency policing unfair and deceptive practices in the commercial marketplace, including those that touch on the privacy and security of personal information. Its proposed privacy framework encourages companies to combine technical and policy mechanisms to protect against reidentification. The FTC's proposed rules would work to ensure that data are both "not reasonably identifiable" and accompanied by public company commitments not to reidentify it. The same privacy rules should apply to downstream users of the data (Mithal, 2010). This approach is promising for machine learning and other areas of artificial intelligence (AI) that rely on data-centric analyses. It allows learning from large data sets – and sharing them – by encouraging companies to reduce the risks that data pools and data sharing pose for individual privacy.

The FTC proposal grows, in part, from recent agency actions focused on inferences that we have deemed context-jumping. In one high-profile case, Netflix publicly released data sets to support a competition to improve their recommendation algorithm. When outside researchers used ancillary data to reidentify and infer sensitive attributes about individuals from the Netflix data sets, the FTC worked with the company to limit future public disclosures – setting out the limits discussed earlier. In a similar vein, the FTC objected to a change in Facebook's defaults that exposed individuals' group affiliations from which sensitive information, such as political views and sexual orientation, could be inferred (FTC, 2012).

Additionally, the FTC has made efforts to ensure that individuals can control tracking in the online and mobile environments. These are in part due to the nonobvious inferences that can be drawn from vast collections of data (FTC, 2012, 2013; Directive 95/46/EC) and the subsequent risks to consumers, who may be placed in classifications that single them out for specific treatment in the marketplace (Sweeney,2014;FTC, 2014a). In a related context, the FTC recommended that Congress require data brokers – companies that collect consumers' personal information and resell or share that information with others – to clearly disclose to consumers information about the data they collect, as well as the fact that they derive inferences from it (FTC, 2014b). Here, too, the FTC appears concerned with not just the raw data, but inferences from its analysis.

The Obama Administration's Big Data Initiative has also considered the risks to privacy posed by machine learning and the potential downsides of using machine inferences in the commercial marketplace (Podesta, 2015;EOP, 2015a,[1] concluding that we need to update our privacy rules; increase technical expertise in consumer protection and civil rights agencies to address novel discrimination issues arising from big data; provide individuals with privacy preserving tools that allow them to control the collection and manage the use of personal information; as well as increase transparency into how companies use and trade data. The Administration is also concerned with the use of machine learning in policing and national security. The White House report called for increased technical expertise to help civil rights and consumer protection agencies identify, investigate, and resolve uses of big data analytics that have a discriminatory impact on protected classes (EOP, 2015b).

Note that reports and proposals from the Administration distinctly emphasize policies and regulations focused on data use rather than collection. While acknowledging the need for tools that allow consumers to control when and how their data is collected, the Administration recommendations focus on empowering individuals to participate in decisions about future uses and disclosures of collected data (EOP, 2014). A separate report by the President's Council of Advisors on Science and Technology (PCAST) concluded that this was a more fruitful direction for technical protections. Both reports suggest that use-based protections better address the latent meaning of data – inferences drawn from data using machine learning – and can adapt to the scale of the data-rich and connected environment of the future (PCAST, 2014). The Administration called for collaborative efforts to ensure that regulations in the health context will allow society to reap the benefits and mitigate the risks posed by machine learning and inferences. Use-based approaches are often favored by industry, as well, which tends to view data as akin to a natural resource to be mined for commercial and public benefit, and industry is resistant to efforts to constrain data collection.

Although incomplete and unlikely to be acted upon by the current gridlocked Congress, adoption of these recommendations would increase transparency about data's collection, use, and consequences. Along with efforts to identify and constrain discriminatory or unfair uses of data and inferences, they are promising steps. They also align with aspects of existing European privacy laws concerned with the transparency and fairness of data processing, particularly the risks to individuals of purely automated decision-making.

Current EU law requires entities to provide individuals with access to the data on which decisions are rendered, as well as information about decision criteria (see Articles 12 and 15 of Directive 95/46/EC). Although currently governed by a Europe-wide directive, both provisions are a matter of national law. What exactly individuals receive when they request access to their data and to processing logic varies by country, as does the implementation of the limitation on "purely automated" processing. The European Union is expected to adopt a data privacy regulation that will supplant local law, with a single national standard. Although the current draft includes parallel provisions, their final form is not yet known nor is how they will ultimately be interpreted (EC General Data Protection Regulation, COM (2012)). In theory, a new EU requirement to disclose the logic of processing could apply quite broadly, with implications for public access to data analytics and algorithms. In the interim, the decision in a case before the European Court of Justice may provide some detail as to what level of access to both data and the logic of processing is currently required under the EU Directive (*Schrems vs Facebook Ireland Limited*, 2013).

Improving the transparency of data processing to data subjects is both important and challenging. Although the goal may be to promote actual understanding of the workings or likely outputs of machine learning and reasoning methods, the workflows and dynamism of algorithms and decision criteria may be difficult to characterize and explain. For example, popular convolutional neural-network learning procedures (commonly referred to as "deep learning") automatically induce rich, multilayered representations that their developers themselves may not understand with clarity. Although high-level descriptions of procedures and representations might be provided, even an accomplished programmer with access to the source code would be unable to describe the precise operation of such a system or predict the output of a given set of inputs.

Data's meaning has become a moving target. Data sets can be easily combined to reidentify data sets thought deidentified, and sensitive knowledge can be inferred from benign data that are routinely and promiscuously shared. These pose difficulties for current US legal approaches to privacy protection that regulate data on the basis of its identifiability and express meaning.

Use-based approaches are driven in part by the realization that focusing solely on limiting data collection is inadequate. In a way, this presupposes that data are an unalloyed good that should be collected on principle, whenever and wherever possible. Whereas we are not ready to abandon limits on data collection, we agree that use-based regulations, although challenging to implement, are an important part of the future legal landscape – and will help to advance privacy, equality, and the public good. To advance transparency and to balance the constraints they impose, use-based approaches would need to emphasize access, accuracy, and correction rights for individuals.

The evolution of regulations for health information, although incomplete, provides a useful map for thinking about the challenges and opportunities we face today and frames potential solutions. In health care, privacy rules were joined by nondiscrimination rules and always were accompanied by special provisions to support research. Today, they are being joined by collective governance models designed to encourage pooling of data in biobanks that sup- port research on health conditions while protecting collective interests in privacy.

Despite practical challenges, we are hopeful that informed discussions among policymakers and the public about data and the capabilities of machine learning, will lead to insightful designs of programs and policies that can balance the goals of protecting privacy and ensuring fairness with those of reaping the benefits to scientific research and to individual and public health. Our commitments to privacy and fairness are evergreen, but our policy choices must adapt to advance them, and support new techniques for deepening our knowledge.

References

Brownstein, J. S., Freifeld, C. C., & Madoff, L. C. (2009). Digital disease detection—harnessing the web for public health surveillance. *New England Journal of Medicine* *360*(21), 2153–2155. Doi: 10.1056/NEJMp0900702

J Broniatowski, D. A., Paul, M. J., & Dredze, M. (2013). National and Local Influenza Surveillance through Twitter: An Analysis of the 2012-2013 Influenza Epidemic. *PLOS ONE 8*(12), e83672.

Change.org. Shut Down Samaritans Radar. Retrieved from www.change.org/p/twitter-inc-shut-down-samaritans-radar

De Choudhury, M., Counts, S., & Horvitz, E. (2013). Predicting postpartum changes in emotion and behavior via social media (pp. 3267–3276). In Proceedings of the SIGCHI Conference on Human Factors in Computing Systems Association for Computing Machinery, New York..

De Choudhury, M., Counts, S., Horvitz, E., & Hoff, A. (2014). Characterizing and predicting postpartum depression from Facebook data (pp. 626–638). In Proceedings of International Conference on Weblogs and Social Media. Association for the Advancement of Artificial Intelligence (AAAI), Palo Alto, CA.

Directive 95/46/EC of the European Parliament and of The Council of Europe, 24 October 1995.

Equal Employment Opportunity Commission (EEOC), 29 Code of Federal Regulations CFR (2013).

European Commission, Proposal for a Regulation of the European Parliament and of the Council on the Protection of Individuals with regard to the processing of personal data and on the free movement of such data (General Data Protection Regulation), COM (2012) 11 final (2012) Retrieved from http://bit.ly/1Lu5POv

Executive Office of the President. (2015). Big data and differential processing. White House, Washington, DC.

Executive Office of the president (2015b). Big data report. White House, Washington, DC. Retrieved from www.whitehouse.gov/sites/default/files/docs/Big_Data_Report_None mbargo_v2.pdf

Executive Office of the President. (2014). Big data: seizing opportunities, preserving values. White House, Washington, DC. Retrieved from www.whitehouse.gov/sites/default/files/docs/big_data_privacy_report_may_1_2014.pdf

Eysenbach, G. J. (2009). Infodemiology and infoveillance: Framework for an emerging set of public health informatics methods to analyze search, communication and publication behavior on the internet. *Journal of Medical Internet Research*, *11*(1), e11. doi: 10.2196/jmir.1157.

FTC. (2014a). Opening remarks FTC Chairwoman Edith Ramirez: Big data: A tool for inclusion or exclusion? Washington, DC September 15, 2014. Retrieved from www.ftc.gov/news-events/events-calendar/2014/09/big-data-tool-inclusion-or-exclusion

FTC. (2014b). Data brokers: A call for transparency and accountability. Report of the FTC, May 2014. Washington, DC). Retrieved from www.ftc.gov/system/files/documents/ reports/data-brokers-call-transparency-accountability-report-federal-trade-commission-may-2014/140527databrokerreport.pdf p. 52

FTC. (2013). Mobile privacy disclosures: Building trust through transparency. Report of the FTC. Washington, DC). Retrieved from www.ftc.gov/sites/default/files/docu ments/reports/mobile-privacy-disclosures-building-trust-through-transparency-federal-trade-commission-staff-report/130201mobileprivacyreport.pdf

FTC. (2012). Protecting consumer privacy in an era of rapid change: Recommendations for businesses and policymakers. Report of the FTC. Washington, DC). Retrieved from www.ftc.gov/reports/protecting-consumer-privacy-era-rapid-change-recommenda tions-businesses-policymakers

Mithal, M. (2010). Letter from Maneesha Mithal, FTC, to Reed Freeman, Morrison, & Foerster LLP, Counsel for Netflix, 2 [closing letter]. Retrieved from http://1.usa.gov/ 1GCFyXR

President's Council of Advisors on Science and Technology (PCAST). (2014, May). Big data and privacy: A technological perspective (pp. 48–50). Retrieved from www.whitehouse.gov/sites/default/files/microsites/ostp/PCAST/pcast_big_data_and_ privacy_-_may_2014.pdf (White House, Washington, DC). Retrieved from http:// 1.usa.gov/1C5ewNv

Podesta J. (2015, February 5) Big data and privacy: 1 year out [blog]. Retrieved from www.whitehouse.gov/blog/2015/02/05/big-data-and-privacy-1-year-out

Rothstein, M. A., (2008). GINA, the ADA, and genetic discrimination in employment. *The Journal of Law, Medicine & Ethics: A Journal of the American Society of Law, Medicine & Ethics*, *36*(4), 837–840. doi:10.1111/j.1748-720X.2008.00341.x.

Sadilek, A., Kautz, H., & Silenzio, V. (2012). Predicting disease transmission from geo-tagged micro-blog data. In Proceedings of the Twenty-Sixth AAAI Conference on Artificial Intelligence (AAAI, Palo Alto, CA, 2012).

Schrems vs Facebook Ireland Limited, §J. Unlawful data transmission to the U.S.A. ("PRISM"), paras 166 and 167 (2013). Retrieved from www.europe-v-facebook .org/sk/sk_en.pdf

Samaritans. Samaritans Radar. Retrieved from www.samaritans.org/how-we-can-help-you/ supporting-someone-online/samaritans-radar

Sweeney, L. (2014). Online ads roll the dice [blog]. Retrieved from www.ftc.gov/news-events/blogs/techftc/2014/09/online-ads-roll-dice

White, R. W., Harpaz, R., Shah, N. H., DuMouchel, W., & Horvitz, E. (2014). Toward enhanced pharmacovigilance using patient-generated data on the internet. *Clinical Pharmacology Therapeutics 96*(2), pp. 239–246. doi:10.1038/clpt.2014.77.

White House Council of Economic Advisers. (2015). *Big data and differential pricing* (White House, Washington, DC).

Endnotes

[1] For a summary of the White House led Big Data effort see, www.whitehouse.gov/blog/2015/02/05/big-data-and-privacy-1-year-out. Most recent report focuses specifically on price discrimination, Big Data and Differential Pricing, White House Council of Economic Advisers, (February 2015) (concluding that concerns with the practice can be addressed through enforcement of existing anti-discrimination, privacy, and consumer protection laws, and increased transparency into how companies use and trade data).

8

Guidelines for Artificial Intelligence Containment

James Babcock, János Krámar, and Roman V. Yampolskiy

8.1 Introduction

The past few years have seen a remarkable amount of attention on the long-term future of artificial intelligence (AI). Icons of science and technology such as Stephen Hawking (Cellan-Jones, 2014), Elon Musk (Musk, 2014), and Bill Gates (Gates, 2015) have expressed concern that superintelligent AI may wipe out humanity in the long run. Stuart Russell, coauthor of the most-cited textbook of AI (Russell & Norvig, 2003), recently began prolifically advocating (Dafoe & Russell, 2016) for the field of AI to take this possibility seriously. AI conferences now frequently have panels and workshops on the topic. There has been an outpouring of support from many leading AI researchers for an open letter calling for greatly increased research dedicated to ensuring that increasingly capable AI remains "robust and beneficial," and gradually a field of "AI safety" is coming into being (Pistono & Yampolskiy, 2016; Yampolskiy, 2016, 2018; Yampolskiy & Spellchecker, 2016). Why all this attention?

Since the dawn of modern computing, the possibility of AI has prompted leading thinkers in the field to speculate (Good, 1966; Turing, 1996; Wiener, 1961) about whether AI would end up overtaking and replacing humanity. However, for decades, while computing quickly found many important applications, AI remained a niche field, with modest successes, making such speculation seem irrelevant. But fast-forwarding to the present, machine learning has seen grand successes and very substantial R&D investments, and it is rapidly improving in major domains, such as natural language processing and image recognition, largely via advances in deep learning (LeCun, Bengio, & Hinton, 2015). Artificial *general* intelligence (AGI), with the ability to perform at a human-comparable level at most cognitive tasks, is likely to be created in the coming century; most predictions, by both experts and non-experts, range from fifteen to twenty-five years (Armstrong & Sotala, 2015).

As the state of research in AI capabilities has steadily advanced, theories about the behavior of superintelligent AGIs have remained largely stagnant – though nearby scientific fields examining optimal agents (game theory and decision theory), idealized reasoning (Bayesian statistics and the formal theory of causality), and human cognition (cognitive neuroscience) have come into being and given us some clues. A prominent theory is that an advanced AI with almost any goals will generically develop certain subgoals called "basic AI drives" (Omohundro, 2008), such as self-preservation, self-improvement, and resource acquisition. Pursuit of these goals could motivate the AI to, for example, make copies of itself on Internet-connected computers, build new hardware or software for itself, and evade the attention of human observers until it is confident that it's beyond their control. An influential book (Bostrom, 2014) thoroughly reviewing and building on existing work on superintelligent AI found no compelling counterarguments or easy workarounds. To the best of our knowledge, safe AGI will require significant theoretical advances in AI safety, and very careful implementation. This implies a risk that the first human-level AGI will be unsafe; at least until research and testing are done on it.

We do need to highlight that, like in many other domains of science, there is also a group of skeptics to this view, claiming that any concerns about the human caused issue of AI risk are just pseudoscientific alarmism. AI risk skeptics dismiss or bring into doubt scientific consensus of the AI safety community on super-intelligent AI risk, including the extent to which dangers are likely to materialize, severity of impact superintelligent AI might have on humanity and universe, or practicality of devoting resources to safety research (Benthall, 2017; Danaher, 2015; Loosemore, 2014). Our belief is that their skepticism does not stand up to scrutiny, as many examples of AI failure have already been reported (Pistono & Yampolskiy, 2016; Yampolskiy, 2016, 2018; Yampolskiy & Spellchecker, 2016). Regardless of the view you take on this, the ethical sensitivities that may arise with any future AI safety and containment are worthy of discussion. This chapter brings these issues to surface.

8.1.1 Containment and the AI Safety Problem

Due to the "basic AI drives" already mentioned, an unsafe AGI will likely be motivated to falsify tests or monitoring mechanisms to manipulate the researchers into thinking it's safe, to gain access to more resources, to embed dormant copies of itself in device firmwares, and to hack computers on the Internet. In order to reliably test and safely interact with an AGI with these motivations and capabil-ities, there must be barriers preventing it from performing these actions. These barriers are what we refer to as containment.

Some have argued that controlling AGI – especially if superintelligent – is impossible or infeasible. For example, Ray Kurzweil writes that "intelligence is inherently impossible to control" (Kurzweil, 2005). Eliezer Yudkowsky's AI box experiment (Yudkowsky, 2002) found that human factors make containing AI difficult. Vernor Vinge argued that "confinement is intrinsically impractical" in the long run (Vinge, 1993).

We agree that containment is not a long-term solution for AI safety; rather it's a tool to enable testing and development of AGIs with other, more robust safety properties such as value learning (Soares, 2015; Yudkowsky, 2011) and corrigibility (Soares, Fallenstein, Armstrong, & Yudkowsky, J2015). Value learning is the strategy of programming an AGI to learn what humans value, and further those values. If this is done correctly, such an AGI could be very good for humanity, helping us to flourish. Corrigibility is the strategy of programming an AGI to help (or at least, to not resist) its creators in finding and fixing its own bugs. An AGI that has both of these properties will not need to be contained, but experience with software suggests that developers are very unlikely to get it right on the first try.

Other safety strategies that have been proposed depend on containment more directly. For example, in his book *Superintelligence* (Bostrom, 2014), Nick Bostrom suggests using tripwires to monitor the AGI and shut it down if it appears to be behaving dangerously. However, the AI drives thesis (Omohundro, 2008) suggests that an AGI might try to bypass tripwires or remove them from itself, which would render them ineffective in an AGI that had full control over its hardware. On the other hand, an AI containment system with internal security boundaries could both keep an AI from disabling its tripwires and from learning the details of what tripwires there were.

Regarding the tractability of containment, encouraging progress has been made on the human factors front; Yampolskiy has proposed ways of limiting an AGI's communication channels so that even a superintelligent AI could not trick an operator into doing something dangerous (Armstrong, Sandberg, & Bostrom, 2012; Yampolskiy, 2012). As for preventing the AGI from tampering with data and hacking its way to the Internet, essentially no work has been done on this problem. However, we have reason to think that bringing the tools of cybersecurity to bear will yield results that will substantially mitigate the risk of escapes.

8.1.2 Ethical Dilemma of Containment

One of the main ethical concerns with containment is the justification for placing an intelligent agent in a prison-like environment, proactively, before it commits any criminal or dangerous action. AI rights proponents have argued that such containment is both unethical and is likely to antagonize AI against humanity. However, we do have a precedent of placing mentally unstable individuals in confinement in the name of community safety. Once they are determined to not constitute danger to themselves or others, such individuals are released from restrictions imposed on them. The alternative to containment is to simply release any developing AI into the wild (World Wide Web), but it would also be unethical as such AIs are very likely to be misaligned with human values and so would be very dangerous by default. Deciding if and when to release AI from containment is itself a very difficult ethical dilemma.

8.2 Overview of the Proposed Guidelines

The proposed guidelines are based on our analysis of AI containment, incorporating all aspects of the problem, a concrete technical perspective, and attention to specific technologies that can be used.[1] Background research for developing this framework turned up surprising interactions between seemingly disparate aspects of the problem. For example, existing research into the human factors of AI containment suggests that tripwire/intrusion detection systems might need to censor details of what happened. Understanding the threat model requires incorporating widely varied predictions, and these predictions lead to very different ways of approaching the security/usability trade-off (Amodei et al., 2016).

We have identified seven major subproblems to the AI containment. Rather than focusing our attention narrowly on one subproblem, we have made it our priority not to have any blind spots. These subproblems are: threat modeling; navigating the security/usability trade-off; concrete mechanisms; sensitive information management; human factors; tripwires; and graceful degradation. This last issue – the need for graceful degradation – has led us to envision containment systems with multiple dissimilar containment mechanisms combined with intrusion detection, providing defense in depth and resilience in a system built from components that may individually contain bugs.

8.2.1 A Prototype AI Container

A prototype AI container can be built by combining multiple pre-existing containment tools, in such a way that a security vulnerability in any one of them would not lead to a complete compromise of the system. Developers should provide source code, scripts, and documentation sufficient for others to easily use it. Additionally, it is important to test how the container interacts with the most common machine-learning tools, including, in particular, those that involve distributed computation and general-purpose computing on graphics processing units (GPGPU) computing, and should have working support for at least some GPGPU and distributed computing mechanisms.

8.2.2 Analysis of the AI Containment Threat Model

A preliminary threat model is included in this chapter. To produce a more comprehensive threat model would require a literature review of AI safety and forecasting results that may affect the threat model. It is necessary to attempt to determine upper and lower bounds on an AGI's ability to find specific types of security vulnerabilities at different levels of intelligence and information constraint.

8.2.3 Analysis of the Security/Usability Trade-Off

Our guidelines define what constitutes light, medium, and heavy containment. Future efforts will survey available options within each category; and analyze risk at each level of containment in terms of the threat model to produce necessary guidance for AGI developers' risk analysis, indicating which level of containment is likely to be necessary. The details of how options are classified will depend mainly on how the options interact with the types of computations and development tools used, for which present-day machine-learning practices can be used as a proxy for the sorts of tools likely to be used by AGI developers in the future.

8.2.4 Limits of Provably-Secure Communication

Proposed guidelines suggest provably-secure communication protocols, suitable for use in a "heavy containment" context where security means preventing an AGI from communicating messages complex enough to be used for social engineering attacks. It will be necessary to explore the information theoretic limits of how much information can be communicated while maintaining maximum security.

8.2.5 New Categories of Sensitive Information Created by AGI Development

AGI development creates new categories of sensitive information. Some information is sensitive in the sense that it should be kept away from the AGI; some information is sensitive in that an AGI could use it as a tool for social engineering attacks. Our guidelines suggest identifying in greater detail what types of information are sensitive, and provide guidance on how to manage it.

8.2.6 Analysis of Human Factors

It is necessary to analyze the channels in which an AGI might be able to place messages for untrained personnel, and identify actions that create unintuitive risks that people near an AGI should be warned about. AI safety researchers need to explore methods of preventing disallowed AGI communication with untrained personnel, such as understanding all possible side channels, by adding noise to remove steganographically hidden messages from intended outputs, and by controlling the ways output is viewed.

8.2.7 Analysis of AI Container Tripwires

AI safety researchers will need to explore the space of feasible tripwires, creating a guide for implementers describing what tripwires would be desirable and how they would be implemented.

8.3 Significance of AI Containment

This research sits at the intersection between cybersecurity, machine learning, and the emerging field of AI safety. AI forecasting determines our threat model; we need predictions about how intelligent future AIs are likely to be and the software, hardware, and organizational contexts in which it might be created. These are not straightforward questions to which the answers can be simply looked up; predictions in the literature feature a wide variety of possible AI scenarios, motivations, and types, leading to an equal variety of overlapping threat models. Practices within the field of machine learning determine the shape of the usability–security trade-off. Existing security tools and techniques can help, but only with reanalysis in light of this new threat model.

Our guidelines bring AI containment from the abstract theoretical domain, where it previously resided, into the cybersecurity world with a threat model, software and procedures that are concrete enough to check for vulnerabilities.

8.3.1 Why Present Techniques Aren't Adequate

Futurists have speculated on such extreme strategies as choosing computations that make processors trigger unknown corner cases in physics; placing messages in log files that hack the brains of humans who read them; or reprogramming non-radio hardware components to act as radios by creating and detecting RF interference (Guri et al., 2015). These attacks may seem unlikely, but a more pressing concern comes from simply searching the Common Vulnerabilities and Exposures (CVE) database for entries related to common virtualization and sandboxing technologies. We found that every major virtualization and sandboxing solution we looked at had critical vulnerabilities discovered within the past two years – with vulnerabilities continuing to be found at a rate that suggests there are many more vulnerabilities left to be discovered. While it is probably feasible to find and fix all of the vulnerabilities that are easy enough for a human to find, there is no reason to think that any of these solutions could stand up to a smarter-than-human intelligence, nor that they will ever be strong enough to do so.

One might ask: why not just use airgapping? We are mainly concerned with scenarios involving AGIs being tested under laboratory conditions, where physical disconnection from the Internet is possible. Unfortunately, this does nothing to protect the integrity of tests being performed, to protect monitoring systems, or to protect the hardware being used from modification and persistence, which are all very necessary.

8.3.2 Why Now?

Given that AGI has not been created yet, one might ask: why now? There are several compelling reasons. Human-level AGI may be invented sooner than expected. Technology forecasting is notoriously difficult, and has tripped up serious scientists time and again. The nuclear physicist Ernest Rutherford, for example, said in 1933 that nuclear energy was "moonshine"; and another accomplished physicist, Lord Kelvin, in 1896 said "I have not the smallest molecule of faith in aerial navigation other than ballooning".

Another reason to do this work now is that developing secure systems requires time, careful review by many independent experts, and iteration. Unfortunately, many of the predicted scenarios do not allow second chances; if an AI that's unfriendly to human values or that's dangerously buggy escapes into the world, it could do immense damage. If we wait until someone has created a human-level AGI, or the creation of human-level AGI appears imminent, it will be too late. Some of this research has an even longer lead time; if our research finds security improvements that depend on changing software in ways more complicated than mere bugfixes, then finding out now will allow time to influence the next generation of software.

A working AI container will improve the security of the Internet and the world in any future scenarios where AGI is developed, enabling prospective AGI designs that might not share human values to be safely studied and assessed. It will also bridge the cybersecurity, AI safety, and machine learning communities. The direct application of our research is very important, but more speculatively, approaching security from this unconventional angle may yield insights into old problems, particularly those related to dealing with risk from newly discovered exploits and highly reliable systems.

8.4 Previous Work

To succeed in constructing an AI container it is important to merge techniques from a number of relevant fields such as: computer security (Yampolskiy, 2008b);

behavioral biometrics (Yampolskiy, 2008a; Yampolskiy & Govindaraju, 2008); cryptography (Majot & Yampolskiy, 2015; Yampolskiy, Rebolledo-Mendez, & Hindi, 2014), steganography (Abboud, Marean, & Yampolskiy, 2010); stylometry (Ali, Hindi, & Yampolskiy, 2011; Ali, Schaeffer, & Yampolskiy, 2012); computer forensics (Beck, Rouchka, & Yampolskiy, 2013; Losavio et al., 2009); utilization of AI in security (Novikov, Yampolskiy, & Reznik, 2006a,, 2006b); AI Safety (Majot & Yampolskiy, 2014; Muehlhauser & Yampolskiy, 2013), including security work with current AIs (Yampolskiy & Fox, 2013) and theoretical work on AGI safety and security (Yampolskiy, 2013a).

Other relevant work is in the field of artimetrics, which deals with ways to identify, classify, and authenticate robots, intelligent software, and virtual reality agents for security purposes (Yampolskiy, Cho, Rosenthal, & Gavrilova, 2012; Yampolskiy & Gavrilova, 2012). Other tools may include linguistic profiling of Chatbots (Ali et al., 2011; Ali et al., 2012); the visual identification of virtual reality avatars (McDaniel & Yampolskiy, 2011; Mohamed, Baili, D'Souza, & Yampolskiy, 2011; Yampolskiy & Govindaraju, 2009); and the behavior-based authentication of bots (Yampolskiy & Govindaraju, 2009). More recent areas of importance are AI Safety Engineering (Yampolskiy, 2015); AGI Safety (Sotala & Yampolskiy, 2015) and utility function security (Yampolskiy, 2014b); AI-Completeness (Yampolskiy, 2013a); the singularity paradox (Yampolskiy, 2013b); the space of minds (Yampolskiy, 2014a); recursive self-improvement (Yampolskiy, 2015); and the Artificial Intelligence Containment Problem (AICP) (Yampolskiy, 2012). In particular, Yampolskiy's seminal work on the AICP not only defines the problem, from the computer science point of view, but also proposes a number of possible solutions, including a steganographically-safe communication protocol, a classification of levels of communication with respect to the amount of shared information, and the concept of safe questions for interacting with AGIs. In the same work Yampolskiy also analyzes a number of potential attack vectors against the confinement cyberinfrastructure, including social engineering attacks.

8.5 Evaluation and Success Criteria

8.5.1 Soundness

Schneier's Law says that "anyone can invent a security system that he himself cannot break." For a containment system that's meant to stand up to smarter-than-human adversaries, that's not good enough. In the long run, good security can only be guaranteed by time and careful review by many independent experts (Potter & McGraw, 2004). Allowing time for review and iteration is the main reason to do this research now, when AI may still be decades away, rather than waiting until it's closer. It is commonly said that perfect security is impossible, but when the opponent might wield superhuman abilities, it's important to get very close.

It is imperative to design a containment system that's sound in the sense that we'll be confident in its security *eventually*, after sufficient independent review. Needing a few simple bugfixes is okay; presenting something that won't ever be secure even after said bugfixes is not.

8.5.2 Breadth

There is a lot of uncertainty about how AGI may first arise; for example, whether it will be developed inside a company or in academia, what size the team will be, what sorts of algorithms and technologies it will use. As much as possible, it is important to cover all reasonable scenarios, and find all the likely attack surfaces and mitigations.

8.5.3 Relevance and Usability

The next major risk is that these guidelines will produce something that is secure but unusable in practice; or worse, something that is only usable up to a point, after which an AGI researcher would break something security-critical to work around a limitation. There are two main ways this could happen in practice. The first is incompatibility with the tools and libraries that AI researchers are using. The second is overly obnoxious configuration.

In order to learn and pragmatically respond to the priorities and practical constraints of cutting-edge machine learning researchers, AI container developers have to establish collaborations with AI researchers. Such collaborations will be needed to ensure that the containment measures do not unnecessarily interfere with existing tools and research practices – by finding out what they're using, testing it for compatibility, and distributing container prototypes for external evaluation. When soliciting feedback, it is important to engage with all the major subcommunities within AI, such as the "Good Old Fashioned AI" community and the machine learning community.

8.6 Threat Model

8.6.1 AI Motivation

The "AI drives" thesis gives us a starting point for reasoning about what an AGI might want; according to the thesis, while researchers may give the AGI any goal explicitly, it will likely develop subgoals like self-defense, self-improvement, self-replication, and resource acquisition. This allows us to recognize what AGI behaviors are likely: those that further these subgoals. Details of how this scenario would play out is explored in greater depth in Nick Bostrom's book *Super-intelligence* (Bostrom, 2014). On the other hand, if the thesis is false, it may still be helpful as a sort of upper bound on the difficulty of the problem; after all, what could be more dangerous than a superintelligence bent on world domination?

8.6.2 AI Capabilities

Predictions about AGI development trajectories tend to fall into two main categories, known as *hard takeoff* and *soft takeoff* (Bostrom, 2014). In a *soft takeoff*, the capabilities of AGI increase gradually, with much time and effort; and it will be feasible to learn about its capabilities and behaviors through experimentation. Although as Yudkowsky (Yudkowsky, 2008b) points out, the change in capability as the AGI surpasses us may enable new plans and behaviors that are undesirable.

In a so-called *hard takeoff*, after some critical point is reached (which may be preceded by steady improvement), AGI capability increases very rapidly. One proposed mechanism for this is that AGIs that are as good at AGI research as their researchers can undergo a process of *recursive self-improvement* (Good, 1966; Loosemore & Goertzel, 2012; Omohundro, 2007; Solomonoff, 1985), where each improvement in an AGI's capability enables it to find more improvements to make. Whether a hard or soft takeoff will happen is a subject of considerable disagreement among experts (Yudkowsky & Hanson, 2008), but the possibility of recursive self-improvement makes an AGI's ability to self-modify particularly important to monitor and control.

As far as the ceiling of AI capability is concerned, it's likely to be significantly above human level in general (Legg, 2008; Sotala, 2012), though it's not clear what hardware is required for this. Of course, this raises the question: what do we mean by a smart AGI, anyway? As commentators often point out, a superhuman chess player like Deep Blue is no match for us at any other tasks, even simple ones like tic-tac-toe. For present purposes, we will answer this question using a list of "cognitive superpowers" humans have, proposed by Bostrom:

- **Intelligence amplification** (AI programming, cognitive enhancement research, social epistemology development, etc.)
- **Strategizing** (Strategic planning, forecasting, prioritizing, and analysis for optimizing chances of achieving distant goals)
- **Social manipulation** (Social and psychological modeling, manipulation, rhetoric persuasion)
- **Hacking** (Finding and exploiting security flaws in computer systems)
- **Technology research** (Design and modeling of advanced technologies, such as biotechnology or nanotechnology)
- **Economic productivity** (Various skills enabling economically productive intellectual work)

(Bostrom, 2014)

Using this framework, we can say that:

- An AGI with strong strategizing and hacking ability might plan an escape using security vulnerabilities.
- An AGI with strong technology ability might additionally be able to find surprising side-channel attacks.
- An AGI with strong social manipulation ability could use social engineering techniques to enable an escape.
- An AGI with other superpowers may additionally be able to make compelling offers or threats, which could assist with the manipulation.

Countermeasures for these attack vectors are discussed in the remaining sections.

8.7 The Security–Usability Trade-Off

Existing work on the AGI containment problem (Yampolskiy, 2012) has generally assumed that the AGI in question is superintelligent, and therefore warrants a great deal of concern: any exploit that seems theoretically possible will be within the AGI's reach, and therefore the only acceptable containment system is one that we have strong theoretical reason to believe is immune to circumvention. This is a high bar for a containment system to clear; we'll call containment that we can be confident meets this standard *heavy containment*. Some examples of containment mechanisms that belong in this category (Yampolskiy, 2012) include:

- limiting output to a small number of yes/no questions whose answers are securely shuffled before being output, to avoid any chance of social engineering attacks
- running the AGI as a homomorphically encrypted computation
- putting the AGI's datacenter in a very inaccessible place

But as we noted in Section 8.6, researchers developing AGI are unlikely to be willing to conduct their research with such substantial handicaps. Researchers who believe their project is aimed at a breakthrough short of human-comparable AGI are particularly likely to balk at costs during use and setup, and will only be willing to deploy containment mechanisms that are made simple and convenient. We'll call these *light containment*. It's unlikely that light containment measures will suffice for a superintelligent AGI, but there may also be containment escape risks from less powerful AGIs, and effective light containment would help mitigate those risks. Light containment is particularly relevant to groups that don't yet have AGIs at all, and only need to ensure that their AGI doesn't escape before they notice they've made a breakthrough. Technologies like hardware virtualization, network firewalls, and software sandboxing belong in this category.

Researchers who understand that they're dealing with potentially human-level AGI will probably be able to deploy containment measures that add modest costs and overheads to their development process, but in a competitive scenario as in (Armstrong, Bostrom, & Shulman, 2016) heavy containment measures will likely be out of bounds; they would cause anyone applying them to fall behind. Measures that keep costs within the same order of magnitude, however, will have a good chance of being taken by responsible researchers. We'll call measures in this category *medium containment*. Possible measures in this category include:

- preventing the AI from accumulating information about its researchers between runs
- adding real-time external redundant supervision, which is tested using appropriately varied drills
- instruction-level virtualization
- specialized hardware

If reliable containment mechanisms are developed that don't impose significant computational overhead but are incompatible with the development environments that the researchers would otherwise find most productive, then those will be best thought of as medium containment, until the compatibility issues are addressed. This underscores the importance of investigating the requirements and techniques in advance, to forestall this sort of situation.

Existing AI safety research has focused primarily on measures suitable for heavy containment – that is, measures with high reliability but with a very high cost to computational performance and AGI functionality. This is sensible; containing a superintelligence is very hard, and people's risk and difficulty estimates are easily miscalibrated. It is more important to have containment that works than it is to have it run fast and support the best development tools. Still, this should not be the end of the story. These guidelines are the first to meaningfully address light containment and medium containment. It aims to strike an appropriate balance between caution and practicality.

8.8 Sensitive Information Management

In most applications of cybersecurity, there isn't very much uncertainty about which kinds of information are sensitive and need to be restricted; but when an AGI enters the picture, this becomes much less clear, because an AGI that's trying to evade containment may be helped by information about what stands in its way. Detailed information about this might comprise personal information about the researchers; books on psychology, negotiation or salesmanship; or books on cybersecurity and manuals to the software and hardware the AGI is running on. Any of these would make it easier for the AGI to invent attacks. A slightly more sophisticated AGI would be able to make use of more indirect information, such as works of literature to learn about psychology or content about computing, engineering, or physics to learn about its environment. However, there's no fundamental reason an AGI would be limited to learning from such explicit information; an AGI that can perform experiments may be able to figure out its environment the hard way, as humanity has.

Limiting access to detailed information about the AGI's containment is superficially similar to what is referred to pejoratively as "security through obscurity." However, there is an important difference between the usual cybersecurity context and the AGI containment context: researchers have control over all of the information that the contained AGI learns from. For this reason, hiding information from the AGI is more feasible than maintaining secrets in a deployed system.

This kind of information restriction is palatable for many applications of AGI. However, it poses a challenging trade-off with the requirements of value learning. This is another key project for AGI safety; value learning requires information about our preferences (stated or enacted, abstract or concrete, etc.), and this information would be relevant to manipulating people. This trade-off will require more research attention; there may be adequate subsets of preference information for developing value-learning techniques that are nonetheless inadequate for social engineering attacks. From our current vantage point it seems that the requirements of value learning will diminish the effectiveness of information-hiding measures targeted at obstructing social engineering – so more intensive non-information-hiding-based measures will be needed to manage the resulting risk.

8.8.1 Strategies

The light containment approach is to avoid giving access to sensitive information of the kinds mentioned. Because this is a broad class of data, there would also be a risk of some researcher accidentally providing sensitive data that's embedded in some larger dataset. A possible light containment tool would be something akin to a content filter, though ultimately discretion about what data is shared would necessarily fall to the researcher.

A medium containment approach would be to prevent the AGI from deducing that it's running as a particular piece of software in the world by letting it interact only with a virtual environment, or some computationally well-defined domain, with as few embedded clues as possible about the outside world. (Arguably projects like the DeepMind's Atari-game-playing AI (Mnih et al., 2015) are already doing this.)

If it was possible to embed all of the AGI's computations (not merely its action, reward, and sense streams) inside a virtual world and get theoretical guarantees that a full description of the virtual world doesn't contain enough information to deduce anything significant about the world outside, then this would be a way of providing heavy containment. Getting these theoretical guarantees may not be tractable, however.

The most pressing aspects of the AGI containment problem are to open all avenues of investigation, and to conduct research on subtopics that require a lot of lead time before their results can be realistically put into practice, usually due to technical complexity. The sensitive information management problem does not appear to have very much technical depth, unless we consider the heavy containment problem, which seems mathematically challenging. However, AI safety researchers will need to bring clarity to the question of what constitutes sensitive information.

This topic has been discussed in an AI safety context, though not, to our knowledge, investigated deeply. There is substantial uncertainty about whether our intuitions about what can be learned from a corpus are an acceptable guide. For example, Yudkowsky (2008a) has speculated that a very small amount of data is enough to reveal much of how the world works to a superintelligent mind. Dileep George, cofounder of the AI startup Vicarious, on the other hand, has argued that a great deal of gradual observation is needed for knowledge acquisition. Some theoretical work has been done on the topic, but it's not sufficient to answer practical questions (Solomonoff, 1964).

8.9 Concrete Mechanisms

There are many off-the-shelf tools that implement sandboxing. However, none of them were developed with the AI containment threat model in mind and many of them are difficult to reconcile with the requirements posed by AI software development. We've grouped these into categories; sandboxing techniques within a category tend to have similar strengths and limitations, and it is generally more useful to combine techniques from different categories than from the same category. A prototypical AI container will attempt to combine techniques from as many distinct categories as is feasible, in a modular fashion. The categories we have identified are:

- **Physical isolation**, aka airgapping.
- **Language-semantics based methods**, such as the Java sandbox – i.e., the use of a sound type-system with memory safety to prevent the introduction of new code. Of particular interest are Lua (with the Torch7 library) and Python (with the Theano library), which might be able to implement this kind of sandbox but which incorporate components in C that could make them insecure. These are currently popular software packages for implementing machine-learning algorithms (Collobert, Kavukcuoglu, & Farabet, 2012).
- **Operating-system-based process sandboxing methods**, such as Linux's seccomp mode, FreeBSD's Capsicum, and the Chrome sandbox. These work by

starting a process and then signaling to the operating system that most APIs will not be used and should be disabled, before the execution of any risky code.

- **Virtual machines**, such as VirtualBox and QEMU. These use central processing unit (CPU) hardware features to create multiple access levels within a computer, each with its own operating system. These might be improved by new security features in future CPU architectures, such as the Mill (http://millcomputing.com/topic/security), which has features to defend against some classes of exploits.

- **Instruction-level emulation**. This technique is used heavily in malware analysis tools such as V2E (Yan, Jayachandra, Zhang, & Yin, 2012), but imposes heavy computational overhead.

Since many software sandboxing tools already exist, we think creating another one from scratch is likely to be premature. Instead, AI safety researchers should concentrate on finding existing tools, attempting to adapt them to the AI containment threat model and analyzing them in that context.

The main difficulty will be adapting these sandboxing methods to a multi-node cluster context; AGIs are expected to depend heavily on parallel computation, which means they need to run on multiple hosts connected to each other. This will most likely mean a cluster of compute nodes within a single data center, connected to each other but not to the Internet, where there is both a high-privilege enforcer and a low-trust AGI process on each node. Since none of these sandboxing mechanisms were designed with this requirement in mind, we expect most of these mechanisms to be either unsuitable or to require considerable adaptation and configuration, performed with great care.

The other major consideration will be the need for GPGPUs computing. Because GPGPU involves using two heterogeneous compute engines and the interaction between them, it tends to require significantly greater privileges than CPU computation. In particular, GPU drivers combine a very complicated attack surface with an unavoidable need for low-level hardware access, posing considerable risk. We are not yet sure how best to address this risk, but it might be possible to shrink this attack surface by validating and limiting GPU API calls or modifying open source graphics drivers.

8.10 Graceful Degradation

8.10.1 Defense in Depth

Because an AGI could potentially discover novel security vulnerabilities, it's important for an AGI containment system to remain secure even if there are vulnerabilities in its components. Therefore, we envision a system featuring defense in depth, with multiple techniques providing overlapping guarantees of integrity. Conceptually these overlapping techniques act as layers, in the sense that the attack surfaces of an outer layer are only accessible to probing and attack if the integrity guarantees of all inner layers have been broken. This should be combined with intrusion detection systems, so that any attempt by an AI to break the integrity constraints imposed on it would be noticed, allowing the developers to shut it down. Ideally the traps and detection systems would be implemented in higher layers, making them more difficult to detect and circumvent. When deciding which interfaces to expose and which interfaces to architect around protecting, researchers should look at design attributes like complexity and check exploit databases such as NVD.nist.gov, OSVDB.org, and Exploit-DB.com, using projects' security history as a warning if they're likely to have a bad security future.

This part of our research applies to all levels of containment (light, medium, and heavy); a medium containment system would use a subset of the layers used by a heavy containment system, while a light containment system would use a subset of the layers used by a medium containment system. These guidelines will enable developers to set up effective containment systems, assess their systems' security, and assess the consequences of a breach or partial breach. Our initial work in this area has indicated which features of AGI containment systems are most in need of work, and we expect continued work in this area to expose more necessary lines of inquiry.

8.11 Tripwires

Tripwires are systems that monitor the operation of a running AGI, and shut it down if they detect an anomaly that suggests the AGI might be malfunctioning or unsafe. For example, one might install a tripwire that monitors the AGI's thoughts for signs that it was planning to deceive its developers (Bostrom, 2014); or a tripwire that monitors the AGI's execution for signs that it had self-modified or self-improved. Similarly, intrusion detection systems are tripwires that detect if code is executing somewhere it shouldn't; they increase the value of multilayer architectures like the one described in Section 8.10, by adding a cost to unsuccessful attempts to break the system's integrity and preventing an AI from keeping its progress in breaking out over time.

We classify tripwires into two general categories. *Semantic* tripwires refer to the contents of an AGI's thoughts or plans; their design requires detailed knowledge of the algorithms and data structures it will be using. *Technical* tripwires do not refer to the AGI's thoughts or plans, but only to algorithm-independent aspects of its execution. In this classification, detecting that the AGI was formulating a plan to deceive its developers would be a semantic tripwire, while detecting that the AGI had self-modified would be a technical tripwire. Intrusion detection systems are another kind of tripwire.

Semantic tripwires present highly unusual requirements. Conceptually, a semantic tripwire is similar to the *assert* statement used in many programming languages. Unlike a simple *assert* statement, however, it's desirable to keep the implementation details of a semantic tripwire inaccessible to the program it's located in; it would improve security if the tripwires could be somehow excluded from the AI's readable address space. Because the algorithms that will be used by real AGIs have mostly not been developed yet, designing the specific contents of semantic tripwires does not yet seem feasible; AI safety researchers should instead focus on designing technical tripwires, and on algorithm-independent aspects of tripwire placement, such as how to add tripwires in such a way that an AGI with unrestricted read access to its own memory couldn't study them to find workarounds. AI safety researchers should also investigate the human factors involved in tripwires, which could be ignored or disabled by AGI developers if they seem to be having false positives, to disastrous effect.

There are many intrusion detection systems (Garfinkel & Rosenblum, 2003; Modi et al., 2013) that might be adapted to AI containment. However, they assume a significantly different threat model and context, which may limit their applicability and requires great attention to detail in order to operate. Existing research into honeypots (Spitzner, 2005) will also be helpful for designing trip-wired/fake escape paths.

8.12 Human Factors

AI containment presents a mix of both conventional human-factor problems, and some very novel and unusual ones. The most conventional problem is that for anyone involved in a scenario involving AGI, there are very high stakes, which can lead to high stress and heightened risk of mistakes. There are several problems that are specific to the circumstances, but reminiscent of similar problems seen elsewhere. There is a risk that an employee could release the AGI deliberately, for ideological reasons (Dietrich, 2007; Garis, 2005). There is also a risk that external parties could undermine the security of the containment system: for example, an AGI development lab with a working prototype is likely to attract espionage.

The more unusual risk comes from the AGI itself. An AI with human-level social manipulation powers could have many ways to use social engineering to escape, and AI with other cognitive powers (or superhuman social manipulation powers) could muster significant leverage to negotiate with. An AGI that had superhuman intelligence would be quite persuasive indeed.

What's more, just as an AGI might use side channels or advanced persistent threats to break its technical containment infrastructure, it may also find similarly difficult-to-control ways to convey messages to the researchers or to distant third parties; for example, by adjusting its computation to shape its power-usage graphs or embedding steganographically hidden messages in images it produces – presumably other modes also exist that we're not yet aware of. The actions that

Figure 8.1 *User error can negate most defenses*

release the AI can look harmless or unrelated, especially if messages reach non-experts who don't understand the significance of technical actions like plugging things in.

Most existing security human factors research involves preventing problematic actions by laypeople (see Figure 8.1) or by people who may be spread out through a large company. In the case of AI containment, only a very small number of people need to interact directly with an AGI, and so they can be screened and trained carefully, making the problem easier. On the other hand, those few carefully selected personnel could be exposed to extremely clever trickery.

Informal studies of the human factors of AI containment have provided reason to think it's difficult. The AI box experiment (Yudkowsky, 2002) and replication (Tuxedage, 2013) provide data about the sorts of strategies an AGI would use to convince humans to let it out of a container deliberately, but countermeasures have not yet been explored, nor have the strategies one might use to make humans open a container accidentally.

8.13 Conclusion

With almost daily improvements in capabilities of AI it is more important than ever to develop safety software for use by the AI research community. Building on our previous work on the AI containment problem we proposed a number of guidelines that should help AI safety researchers to develop reliable sandboxing software for intelligent programs of all levels. Such safety container software will make it possible to study and analyze intelligent artificial agents while maintaining certain level of safety against information leakage, social engineering attacks, and cyberattacks from within the container. In the face of the challenges of developing and controlling increasingly sophisticated AIs, it is crucial to anticipate and restrict the ways an AI could perform unwanted actions. There has been little work on establishing practical ways for AI R&D to enforce these restrictions; our chapter provides guidelines so that the technologies and information required will be ready to be used by AI projects as they advance toward human-comparable intelligence and beyond.

Acknowledgments

Authors are grateful to Jaan Tallinn and Effective Altruism Ventures for providing funding towards this project, and to Victoria Krakovna and Evan Hefner for their feedback. Roman Yampolskiy is also grateful to Elon Musk and the Future of Life Institute for partially funding his work.

References

Abboud, G., Marean, J., & Yampolskiy, R. V. (2010). "Steganography and Visual Cryptography in Computer Forensics." Paper presented at the Systematic Approaches to Digital Forensic Engineering (SADFE), 2010 5th IEEE International Workshop.

Ali, N., Hindi, M., & Yampolskiy, R. V. (2011). "Evaluation of Authorship Attribution Software on a Chat Bot Corpus." Paper presented at the 23rd International Symposium on Information, Communication and Automation Technologies (ICAT2011), Sarajevo, Bosnia and Herzegovina.

Ali, N., Schaeffer, D., & Yampolskiy, R. V. (2012). Linguistic profiling and behavioral drift in chat bots. In *Proceedings of the Midwest Artificial Intelligence and Cognitive Science Conference, 27*.

Amodei, D., Olah, C., Steinhardt, J., Christiano, P., Schulman, J., & Mané, D. (2016). Concrete problems in AI safety. arXiv preprint arXiv:1606.06565.

Armstrong, S., Bostrom, N., & Shulman, C. (2016). Racing to the precipice: a model of artificial intelligence development. *AI & Society, 31*(2), 201–206.

Armstrong, S., Sandberg, A., & Bostrom, N. (2012). Thinking inside the box: Controlling and using an oracle AI. *Minds and Machines, 22*(4), 299–324.

Armstrong, S., & Sotala, K. (2015). How we're predicting AI–or failing to. In J. Romportl, E. Zackova, & J. Kelemen (Eds.), *Beyond Artificial Intelligence* (pp. 11–29). Cham, Switzerland: Springer.

Babcock, J., Kramar, J., & Yampolskiy, R. (2016). "The AGI Containment Problem." Paper presented at the 9th Conference on Artificial General Intelligence (AGI 2015), NYC, USA.

Beck, M. B., Rouchka, E. C., & Yampolskiy, R. V. (2013). Finding data in DNA: Computer forensic investigations of living organisms. In P. Gladyshev & M. K. Rogers, *Digital forensics and cyber crime* (pp. 204–219). Berlin; Heidelberg: Springer.

Benthall, S. (2017). Don't fear the reaper: Refuting Bostrom's superintelligence argument. *arXiv preprint arXiv:1702.08495*.

Bostrom, N. (2014). *Superintelligence: Paths, dangers, strategies*. Oxford: Oxford University Press.

Cellan-Jones, R. (2014). Stephen Hawking warns artificial intelligence could end mankind. Paper presented at the BBC. Retrieved from www.bbc.com/news/technology-30290540

Collobert, R., Kavukcuoglu, K., & Farabet, C. (2012). Implementing neural networks efficiently. In G. Montavon, G. B. Orr, & K-R, Müller (Eds.), *Neural networks: tricks of the trade*, (pp. 537–557). New York, NY: Springer.

Dafoe, A., & Russell, S. (2016). Yes, we are worried about the existential risk of artificial intelligence. Retrieved from www.technologyreview.com/s/602776/yes-we-are-wor ried-about-the-existential-risk-of-artificial-intelligence/.

Danaher, J. (2015). Why AI doomsayers are like sceptical theists and why it matters. *Minds and Machines, 25*(3), 231–246.

Dietrich, E. (2007). After the humans are gone. *Journal of Experimental & Theoretical Artificial Intelligence, 19(1)*, 55–67.

Garfinkel, T., & Rosenblum, M. (2003). A virtual machine introspection based architecture for intrusion detection. Paper presented at the NDSS.

Garis, H. D. (2005). *The artilect war*. Palm Spring, CA: ETC publications.

Gates, B. (2015). Reddit. Retrieved from www.reddit.com/r/IAmA/comments/2tzjp7/hi_ reddit_im_bill_gates_and_im_back_for_my_third/

Good, I. J. (1966). Speculations concerning the first ultraintelligent machine. *Advances in Computers, 6*(1), 31–88.

Guri, M., Kachlon, A., Hasson, O., Kedma, G., Mirsky, Y., & Elovici, Y. (2015). GSMem: Data exfiltration from air-gapped computers over GSM frequencies. Paper presented at the 24th USENIX Security Symposium (USENIX Security 15).

Kurzweil, R. (2005). *The singularity is near: When humans transcend biology*. New York, NY: Viking Press.

LeCun, Y., Bengio, Y., & Hinton, G. (2015). Deep learning. *Nature, 521*(7553), 436–444.

Legg, S. (2008, June). "Machine Super Intelligence." Paper presented at the PhD Thesis, University of Lugano. Retrieved from www.vetta.org/documents/Machine_Super_ Intelligence.pdf

Loosemore, R. (2014). The maverick nanny with a dopamine drip: Debunking fallacies in the theory of AI motivation. AAAI Spring Symposium Series 2014 (March).

Loosemore, R., & Goertzel, B. (2012). Why an intelligence explosion is probable. In A. H. Eden, J. H. Moor, J. H. Søraker, & E. Steinhart (Eds.) *Singularity hypotheses* (pp. 83–98). New York, NY: Springer.

Losavio, M. et al. (2009). Assessing the legal risks in network forensic probing. In G. Peterson & S. Shenoi (Eds.) *Advances in Digital Forensics V* (pp. 255–266), IFIP AICT. Heidelberg: Berlin: Springer

Majot, A. M., & Yampolskiy, R. (2015). Global catastrophic risk and security implications of quantum computers. *Futures, 72*(1), 17–26.

Majot, A. M., & Yampolskiy, R. V. (2014). AI safety engineering through introduction of self-reference into felicific calculus via artificial pain and pleasure. Paper presented at the IEEE International Symposium on Ethics in Science, Technology and Engineer- ing, Chicago, IL (May 23–24).

McDaniel, R., & Yampolskiy, R. V. (2011). "Embedded non-interactive CAPTCHA for Fischer Random Chess." Paper presented at the 16th International Conference on Computer Games (CGAMES), Louisville, KY.

Mnih, V., Kavukcuoglu, K., Silver, D., Rusu, A. A., Veness, J., Bellemare, M. G., & Ostrovski, G. (2015). Human-level control through deep reinforcement learning. *Nature, 518*(7540), 529–533.

Modi, C., Patel, D., Borisaniya, B., Patel, H., Patel, A., & Rajarajan, M. (2013). A survey of intrusion detection techniques in cloud. *Journal of Network and Computer Appli- cations, 36*(1), 42–57.

Mohamed, A., Baili, N., D'Souza, D., & Yampolskiy, R. V. (2011). "Avatar face recogni- tion using Wavelet Transform and hierarchical multi-scale LBP." Paper presented at the Tenth International Conference on Machine Learning and Applications (ICMLA'11), Honolulu, USA (December 18–21).

Muehlhauser, L., & Yampolskiy, R. (2013, July 15). "Roman Yampolskiy on AI Safety Engineering." Paper presented at the Machine Intelligence Research Institute. Retrieved from http://intelligence.org/2013/07/15/roman-interview/

Musk, E. (2014). A 'potentially dangerous outcome' with AI. Paper presented at the CNBC. Retrieved from www.cnbc.com/video/2014/06/20/elon-musk-a-potentially-dangerous-outcome-with-ai.html

Novikov, D., Yampolskiy, R. V., & Reznik, L. (2006a). "Anomaly Detection Based Intrusion Detection." Paper presented at the 3rd International Conference on Information Technology: New Generations (ITNG 2006), Las Vegas, Nevada, USA (April 10–12).

Novikov, D., Yampolskiy, R. V., & Reznik, L. (2006b). "Artificial intelligence Approaches for Intrusion Detection." Paper presented at the Long Island Systems Applications and Technology Conference (LISAT 2006). Long Island, New York (May 5).

Omohundro, S. M. (2007). The nature of self-improving artificial intelligence. Paper presented at the Singularity Summit, San Francisco, CA.

Omohundro, S. M. (2008). The basic AI drives. In P. Wang, B. Goertzel, & S. Franklin (Eds.), *Proceedings of the first agi conference, volume 171, frontiers in artificial intelligence and applications.* Amsterdam: IOS Press.

Pistono, F., & Yampolskiy, R. V. (2016). "Unethical Research: How to Create a Malevolent Artificial Intelligence." Paper presented at the 25th International Joint Conference on Artificial Intelligence (IJCAI-16). Ethics for Artificial Intelligence Workshop (AI-Ethics-2016).

Potter, B., & McGraw, G. (2004). Software security testing. *IEEE Security & Privacy*, 2(5), 81–85.

Russell, S., & Norvig, P. (2003). *Artificial intelligence: a modern approach.* Upper Saddle River, NJ: Prentice Hall.

Soares, N. (2015). The value learning problem. Machine Intelligence Research Institute, Berkley, CA, USA.

Soares, N., Fallenstein, B., Armstrong, S., & Yudkowsky, E. (2015). "Corrigibility." Paper presented at the Workshops at the 29th AAAI Conference on Artificial Intelligence, Austin, Texas, USA (January 25–30).

Solomonoff, R. J. (1964). A formal theory of inductive inference. Part I. *Information and Control*, 7(1), 1–22.

Solomonoff, R. J. (1985). The time scale of artificial intelligence: Reflections on social effects. *North-Holland Human Systems Management*, 5, 149–153.

Sotala, K. (2012). Advantages of artificial intelligences, uploads, and digital minds. *International Journal of Machine Consciousness*, 4(01), 275–291.

Sotala, K., & Yampolskiy, R. V. (2015). Responses to catastrophic AGI risk: a survey. *Physica Scripta*, 90(1), 018001.

Spitzner, L. (2005). Know your enemy: Honeynets. *Honeynet Project.*

Turing, A. M. (1996). Intelligent machinery: A heretical theory. *Philosophia Mathematica*, 4(3), 256–260.

Tuxedage. (2013, September 5). *I attempted the AI Box Experiment again! (And won – Twice!).* Retrieved from http://lesswrong.com/lw/ij4/i_attempted_the_ai_box_experiment_again_and_won/.

Vinge, V. (1993). "The Coming Technological Singularity: How to Survive in the Post-Human Era." Paper presented at the Vision 21: Interdisciplinary Science and Engineering in the Era of Cyberspace, Cleveland, OH (March 30–31).

Wiener, N. (1961). *Cybernetics or control and communication in the animal and the machine 25.* Cambridge, MA: MIT Press.

Yampolskiy, R., Cho, G., Rosenthal, R., & Gavrilova, M. (2012). Experiments in artimetrics: avatar face recognition. *Transactions on Computational Science XVI,* 77–94.

Yampolskiy, R., & Fox, J. (2013). Safety engineering for artificial general intelligence. *Topoi, 32*(2), 217–226.

Yampolskiy, R. V. (2008a). Behavioral modeling: An overview. *American Journal of Applied Sciences, 5*(5), 496–503.

Yampolskiy, R. V. (2008b). *Computer security: From passwords to behavioral biometrics.* New York, NY:New Academic Publishing.

Yampolskiy, R. V. (2012). Leakproofing singularity – Artificial intelligence confinement problem. *Journal of Consciousness Studies (JCS), 19*(1–2), 194–214.

Yampolskiy, R. V. (2013a). Artificial intelligence safety engineering: Why machine ethics is a wrong approach. In V. C. Müller (Ed.) *Philosophy and theory of artificial intelligence* (pp. 389–396), Berlin; Heidelberg: Springer.

Yampolskiy, R. V. (2013a). Turing test as a defining feature of AI-completeness. In Xin-She Yang (Ed.), Artificial *intelligence, evolutionary computation and metaheuristics - In the footsteps* of Alan Turing (pp. 3–17). Berlin; Heidelberg: Springer.

Yampolskiy, R. V. (2013b). What to do with the singularity paradox? In V. Müller (Ed.) *Philosophy and theory of artificial intelligence* (pp. 397–413). Berlin; Heidelberg: Springer.

Yampolskiy, R. V. (2014a). The universe of minds. *arXiv preprint arXiv:1410.0369.*

Yampolskiy, R. V. (2014b). Utility function security in artificially intelligent agents. *Journal of Experimental & Theoretical Artificial Intelligence, 26*(3), 373–389.

Yampolskiy, R. V. (2015). Artificial superintelligence: A futuristic approach. London: Chapman and Hall/CRC Press.

Yampolskiy, R. V. (2015). From seed AI to technological singularity via recursively self-improving software. *arXiv preprint arXiv:1502.06512.*

Yampolskiy, R. V. (2016). "Taxonomy of Pathways to Dangerous Artificial Intelligence." Paper presented at the Workshops at the Thirtieth AAAI Conference on Artificial Intelligence.

Yampolskiy, R. V. (2018). *Artificial intelligence safety and security.* Boca Raton, FL: CRC Press.

Yampolskiy, R. V., & Gavrilova, M. L. (2012). Artimetrics: Biometrics for artificial entities. *Robotics & Automation Magazine, IEEE, 19*(4), 48–58.

Yampolskiy, R. V., & Govindaraju, V. (2008). Behavioural biometrics: a survey and classification. *International Journal of Biometrics, 1*(1), 81–113.

Yampolskiy, R. V., & Govindaraju, V. (2009). Strategy-based behavioural biometrics: a novel approach to automated identification. *International Journal of Computer Applications in Technology, 35*(1), 29–41.

Yampolskiy, R. V., Rebolledo-Mendez, J. D., & Hindi, M. M. (2014). Password protected Visual cryptography via cellular automaton Rule 30. *Transactions on Data Hiding and Multimedia Security IX,* 57–67.

Yampolskiy, R. V., & Spellchecker, M. (2016). Artificial intelligence safety and cybersecurity: A timeline of AI failures. *arXiv preprint arXiv:1610.07997.*

Yan, L.-K., Jayachandra, M., Zhang, M., & Yin, H. (2012). V2E: combining hardware virtualization and software emulation for transparent and extensible malware analysis. *ACM Sigplan Notices, 47*(7), 227–238.

Yudkowsky, E. S. (2002). *The AI-Box experiment*. Retrieved from http://yudkowsky.net/singularity/aibox

Yudkowsky, E. S. (2008a). That Alien Message. Retrieved from www.lesswrong.com/posts/5wMcKNAwB6X4mp9og/that-alien-message.

Yudkowsky, E. S. (2008b). Artificial intelligence as a positive and negative factor in global risk. In N. Bostrom & M. M. Cirkovic (Eds.), *Global catastrophic risks* (pp. 308–345). Oxford, UK: Oxford University Press.

Yudkowsky, E. S. (2011). Complex value systems in friendly AI. In *Proceedings of the Artificial General Intelligence: 4th International Conference, AGI 2011* (pp. 388–393). Mountain View, CA: Springer.

Yudkowsky, E. S., & Hanson, R. (2008). "The Hanson-Yudkowsky AI-foom Debate." Paper presented at the MIRI Technical Report. Retrieved from at: http://intelligence.org/files/AIFoomDebate.pdf

Endnotes

[1] We have previously published a less detailed description of those guidelines as: Babcock, Kramar, & Yampolskiy (July 16–19, 2016).

PART II

Business Enterprises

9

Next-Generation Business Ethics: The Impact of Artificial Intelligence

Kirk O. Hanson

9.1 Introduction

The concerns and corporate practice of business ethics have evolved over the past sixty years. But none of the changes of the past are as great as those that will occur in the next ten years as artificial intelligence (AI) and machine learning become ubiquitous tools in American society. This chapter presents a concise history of corporate attention to business ethics over this historical period in order to identify how "next-generation business ethics" will demonstrate both continuity with and divergence from past attention to business ethics.

This chapter describes how both the substance and the process of business ethics has and will evolve. The substance of business ethics is the growing list of corporate behaviors that have been of concern – from automobile safety in the 1960s to the fairness of algorithms in the 2020s. The process of business ethics focuses both the methods by which ethical behavior has been managed in the corporation and also the methods by which regulatory and criminal authorities have sought to rein in unethical behaviors.

9.2 The History of Business Ethics

While there has long been an interest in and concern for the morality of business behavior, the modern history of business ethics begins in 1959.[1] A young lawyer from Connecticut, Ralph Nader, joined with a future Harvard professor, Daniel Patrick Moynihan, to promote the idea that deaths in automobile accidents were not just the fault of bad drivers and poor road design but also the fault of automobile manufacturers who failed to build into cars common-sense safety features. Nader's later book provides the most complete version of this concept (Nader, 1965). In writing it, Nader had challenged the most iconic and respected corporations in America. He launched the modern debate over business ethics and first personified what we would come to call an "activist." The history of business ethics from that point forward gives us significant guidance in predicting the character of "next-generation business ethics."

9.2.1 The 1960s

The formal study and practice of business ethics emerged in the 1960s as companies absorbed the first confrontations with advocates for product safety, for employment of African Americans and the hard core unemployed, and for environmental awareness. Ralph Nader promoted auto safety, and the first auto safety laws were passed in 1966 after General Motors' naïve and ill-fated attempts to discredit Nader. The urban riots of 1965–1967 led to President Lyndon Johnson's creation, with Henry Ford II as chair, of the voluntary National Alliance of Businessmen (later the National Alliance of Business) to encourage American corporations to hire the hardcore unemployed, mostly African Americans. Rachel Carson's *Silent Spring*, published in 1962, stimulated a rising demand for federal clean air and water legislation, passed in 1969 and 1971. The first Earth Day was held in April 1970 to promote both greater public awareness and attention to environmental goals by corporations and individuals.

9.2.2 The 1970s

After the first stirrings of interest in what were then called "corporate social responsibility" issues, corporate interest waned in the 1970s; until specifically "ethical" concerns emerged due to illegal corporate contributions to the re-election campaign of President Richard Nixon in 1972 and the overseas corporate bribery scandals of the 1975–1978 period. These crises over the "ethical" behavior of corporations and corporate leaders led to a growing demand for attention to business ethics, particularly in the nation's business schools, which ramped up their faculty and courses on business ethics starting in 1978. A flood of textbooks and managerial books on business ethics appeared at the same time.

9.2.3 The 1980s

While business ethics slowly found its place in the curricula of business schools, the 1980s saw the emergence of at least four major crises of unethical corporate behavior, each of which concerned a major industry or sector of the economy. These were scandals involving insider trading on Wall Street; procurement in the defense industry, which cast doubt on the ethics of defense procurement; neglect by chemical industry leaders for consumer and employee safety; and the complicity of European and American firms in the racial segregation system of apartheid in South Africa.

After these four scandals in the 1980s, the term "business ethics" had overtaken the language of corporate responsibility. Business ethics focused on meeting minimum expectations of behavior, whereas corporate social responsibility implied that companies already met the minimum standards and were "going beyond" the minimum.

Another major change was in process. In companies, ethics was still thought of primarily as a characteristic of individual employees and leaders, not of corporations and their organizational cultures. A few companies, including Chemical Bank and McDonnell Douglas Corporation, launched workshops in the early 1980s, designed to shore up the ethics of their individual employees and executives. The assumption that ethics was only a problem of individual character began to change in the mid-1980s, when virtually all major defense contractors were charged with one or more ethical and legal violations of defense procurement standards. In 1986, prompted by pressure from Hewlett-Packard CEO David Packard who headed a Blue Ribbon Commission on Defense Procurement, a group of defense contractors launched the Defense Industry Initiative on Business Ethics and Conduct (DII) to demonstrate that defense companies could clean up their own behavior. Initial efforts by the defense firms included adopting ethics codes, training their employees on the content of those codes, and strengthening accounting and audit systems to monitor employee behavior. By 1990, after multiple whistleblowers had emerged, demands that companies create a system for internal reporting of unethical behavior was added to the DII voluntary standards.

9.2.4 The 1990s

By 1990, a second truly industry-wide scandal emerged. As the 1980s ended, more than 750 savings and loan companies collapsed – victims of reckless lending practices, which were often covered up by frauds. More than 1,000 people were charged with crimes, 580 were convicted, and 451 were sentenced to prison (Josephson, 2014). Simultaneously, Drexel Burham, a large investment banking firm, and its leader "junk bond king" Michael Milken, were charged with various financial manipulations. Milken paid $600 million in fines and restitution and Drexel Burnham collapsed.

Both the savings and loan and defense procurement scandals led most to the conclusion that ethical misbehavior could be a corporate or industry-wide problem, not just a problem of the character of a few executives or employees. Shortly thereafter, action at the national level in the United States helped change the trajectory of business ethics. In 1991, the first version of the US Federal

Sentencing Guidelines was released. These were instructions by the Justice Department to judges that they could give "credit" to companies convicted of crimes if those companies had good ethics programs and systems in place when the bad behavior occurred. The presumption was that if good ethics programs were in place, the chances were much greater that the cause of unethical behavior in corporations was due to the bad character of one or a few individuals, not the culture of the corporation. General Counsels in most major corporations rushed to adopt the specific elements of a good ethics program outlined in the Sentencing Guidelines. One of the elements was the appointment of a chief ethics officer for the corporation. The growing cadre of such corporate officers then launched their own professional association, the Ethics Officers Association (later the Ethics and Compliance Officers Association) in 1992.

By the end of the 1990s, companies were deeply enmeshed in yet another new ethics concern: how their supply chains, now often outsourced to independent contractors in the third world, treated workers and the environment. Consumer boycotts of several companies, including the athletic apparel manufacturer Nike, led most major companies to take responsibility for ethical behavior in their supply chain. This required new ethics policies, systems, and sophistication.

9.2.5 The 2000s

Many new ethical issues arose in the 2000s but ethical concerns regarding the mortgage industry and its ties to the investment ratings industry and other financial firms dominated. The economic crash of 2008 was seen as a crisis of corporate ethics, due to sloppy and fraudulent lending practices; complicit behavior by ratings agencies that inflated the quality of investments for favored investment firms; and "see no evil" behavior by many banking and brokerage firms that sold these investments knowing they were likely misrepresented.

Two major laws regulating the ethical behavior of the financial industry were passed during the 2000s: the Sarbanes Oxley Act of 2002 to address an earlier series of financial manipulations and the Dodd Frank Act of 2010 to address the crash of 2008. Meanwhile, the Federal Sentencing Guidelines Commission, set up to manage the Sentencing Guidelines, revised them several times to expand on the elements of what was considered a good corporate ethics program. Companies continued to develop their ethics functions in order to create more ethical cultures, but also to qualify for mitigation if caught in illegal behavior. The Justice Department also began publishing a periodic letter to federal attorneys known as the "Prosecutorial Guidelines," which similarly gave credit for the prior existence of an effective ethics program, telling prosecutors that they could prosecute individual employees and not the company if an effective ethics program was in place when misbehavior occurred.

9.2.6 The 2010s

While we are still witnessing the evolution of business ethics in the 2010s, some patterns are identifiable. Major scandals involving overseas bribery have reemerged, the largest of which, Siemens, led to $2 billion in fines and mitigation costs for the company. Other companies – notably well-respected enterprises such as BP and General Motors – were penalized for cutting ethical corners, which resulted in safety problems such as the Deepwater Horizon fire in the Gulf of Mexico and the largest oil spill in history (BP), and more than 100 deaths in auto accidents due to negligent and hidden product mislabeling (GM). Perhaps the most surprising scandals were those involving blatant fraud at Volkswagen, where engineers and their bosses falsified environmental tests, and Wells Fargo's systematic and company-wide misrepresentation of its products and opening thousands of customer accounts without authorization. A rising crescendo of criticism against pharmaceutical firms for the manipulation of drug prices threatened in 2018 to become yet another major scandal of the decade.

These 2010s developments indicated to some that either competitive pressures had increased dramatically, driving even good firms to more unethical behavior, or that the greatly increased financial rewards available to successful senior executives had led them to compromise their ethics more frequently for personal gain.

Finally, the #MeToo movement of the 2010s outed executives for sexual assault and harassment and led to the firing and forced resignation of hundreds of corporate officials. There were signs that firms were rethinking their ethical responsibility to protect female employees.

9.3 A Coming Revolution in the Concerns of Business Ethics

While all of the concerns of business ethics cited in Section 9.2 do and will remain important, an entirely new set of concerns will soon emerge and dominate business ethics efforts. These are the concerns of next-generation ethics. The concerns, broadly called big data ethics or AI ethics, began to appear in the 2010s, but will affect every industry and every company, small and large, by the 2020s. Further, the same technological developments giving rise to these new concerns for ethical corporate behavior will also change forever how business ethics is managed in corporations, indeed in all organizations.

The new concerns of business ethics are all related to the emergence of data collection, mathematical modeling techniques, and the penetration of computing and the Internet into every aspect of modern life. In the 2010s, machine-learning technology and the deployment of AI for an increasing number of applications have challenged corporate ethics practices. Because computing, the Internet, and machine learning will be harnessed to serve applications of AI in every aspect of life, the problem will most likely be labeled "The Ethics of Artificial Intelligence" or "AI ethics." Concern for AI ethics will dominate many other concerns about corporate behavior, though those will also persist. AI may even "solve" some other ethical concerns such as algorithms and other techniques of AI audit, not just the expense reports of every employee but every action they take. Surveillance and evaluation of employees may become a 24/7 reality.

The concerns of AI ethics are many and will be reviewed in detail in this chapter. How is the corporation handling this powerful new tool of AI? Is it concerned about the provenance of the data it uses? Does it protect the privacy of its employees and customers? Does it protect the security of its data?

Some ethical concerns regarding how companies handle data had already emerged even before the 2010s. In the 2000s, some companies were pioneering policies regarding the data they collected and how it would be handled. It was revealed that retail companies could create detailed profiles of their customers from data they collected, and from other databases they purchased, public concern increased. Some companies began to set limits on how they handled data and started exploring what was then called "data ethics."

In the 2010s, concern for data ethics (which had become "big data ethics" in many articles) first focused on data breaches, which had become an almost daily news item. Hospital systems were hacked and patient records stolen; Sony was hacked and the personal data of millions of customers was lost; even the federal employee data base was compromised. Companies rushed to hire cybersecurity experts and were engaged in an escalating cold war with hackers whose skills advanced as rapidly as cybersecurity systems.

The key insight in this essay is that AI will be deployed in almost every product and service used by the average American. This in turn will lead to significant demand for corporate ethics policies and practices that guide how businesses develop and deploy AI.

In this new reality, devices will "learn" how fast we use milk and order the next half gallon for us. Smart watches will monitor our health and alert us when we are at risk of a heart attack. Apparel companies will track what clothes we buy (and maybe by cameras what clothes we wear) and will automatically order new clothes for us to try out. Home assistants such as Alexa may listen 24/7 to our home discussion and suggest books to fill in our knowledge. And, of course, AI will take over many of the functions previously handled by human beings – accounting, radiology, checking us into hotels, recommending restaurants for dinner, etc. The impacts on human beings of deploying all this AI are only partially understood. Some even argue that the human species will evolve more rapidly; others argue that it will atrophy because machines will have taken over all our previous actions.

9.4 New Ethical Concerns Every Company Will Face

What does all this change mean for the corporation and its ethics? As AI is adopted in virtually every product and process of the modern corporation, there will be a common set of ethical concerns to be addressed by every company.[2] Among them are the following.

9.4.1 Data Collection

As companies gather data to improve their products and services, and to refine their marketing, they must address the ethics of the type of data they gather. Do they have a legal and ethical right to the data? Is the individual whose data is being collected aware of the collection? Have they consented to its collection?

9.4.2 Data Manipulation

Companies have the ability to collect and buy data from many different sources, cross referencing the data to draw new conclusions and inferences. Are they as concerned about the ethics and provenance of data they purchase or secure from partners as they are about the data they themselves collect? Does the cross referencing of data produce insights and conclusions that tread on privacy concerns of individuals (e.g., inferences about health conditions)?

9.4.3 Accuracy and Bias in Algorithms

There are many concerns about simple accuracy in algorithms developed for various purposes. Sloppily constructed algorithms can do real harm if they are poorly designed. Algorithms may have intended and unintended bias built in – giving advantages to certain racial groups or to the wealthy, which are not available to others (e.g., sale prices; bail determinations).

9.5 Data Protection/Cybersecurity

As noted earlier, data breaches in the 2010s have focused concern on whether the companies adequately protect the private information of individuals. This is particularly acute in cases of financial and health data, where disclosure could result in significant harm to the individuals. Safety can be a genuine concern in some data breaches. Is the data secure? What practices are in place when data breeches occur? Who gets notified of a breach and how quickly? What steps are taken after a breach to limit damage?

9.6 Misuse of AI Systems

The 2018 debate over the responsibility of Facebook, Twitter, and other social platforms for their misuse by some users, even by nation states working to influence elections in other countries, dramatizes the importance of anticipating possible misuse. When a product with integrated AI is deployed, manufacturers will be expected to anticipate how the product may be misused. Can an Alexa, for example, be programmed to listen 24/7 to a family's conversations and report on its concerns and opinions?

9.7 Transparency

A growing debate in AI and machine learning is how much the creator or user of an algorithm is willing to tell those whose data is used and those affected by it how it works and makes its choices. Will a retailer, for example, tell its customers why consumers with a particular profile are offered discounts not available to others? In some cases of machine learning, of course, the creator cannot really tell what criteria end up being employed by the algorithm to choose between mortgage applicants, bidders, etc. To what extent are black box algorithms acceptable?

9.8 Adoption of Artificial Intelligence: Employment Effects

Some unions are fighting the adoption of AI for some purposes. Are there any limits to the deployment of AI in order to save jobs? Is it acceptable to replace all radiologists with an algorithm that can read x-rays as well as they do, or all hotel desk clerks by an interactive algorithm that checks in all hotel visitors or advises them where to go to dinner? How about an algorithm that decides who qualifies for mortgages, thereby replacing underwriters? And when AI displaces employees, what obligation does the company have to the workers displaced?

9.9 New Generation Business Ethics Already Underway

As noted, there was some attention to big data ethics in the 2000s and early 2010s. However, most of these concerns remained compartmentalized in a single company or even a single department such as marketing. There was little systematic thinking about the broader implications of what was being addressed. For example, an ethics debate in the 2000s concerned whether the company owned messages on an employee's corporate email, and whether an organization could surveil an employee by counting their key strokes and monitoring their productivity in small increments. Little attention was paid to the massive implications of surveillance using sophisticated algorithms. An early scandal involving hospital employees looking at celebrities' health records on line did not immediately provoke enough attention to the potential for hacking medical information.

To date only a few high-tech companies, sometimes only the firms designing applications of AI, have been deeply concerned about AI ethics. Most organizations planning to deploy AI have not yet emerged from the high-tech belief that "if it can be one, it ought to be done," which of course has driven so many pathbreaking and "disruptive" firms in Silicon Valley. Facebook has become the favorite case study of a company that develops and deploys technology and then thinks later about what impact it might have. Time and again Facebook has been criticized for not anticipating negative effects that emerged after an innovation was rolled out.

During the 2010s, a significant gap opened between the United States and Europe over how big data ethics and now AI is deployed. Over several years, the European Union has developed and in 2017 enacted the General Data Protection Regulations (GDPR). This established significant new ethical and regulatory responsibilities on every corporation active in online commerce or in collecting, storing, and using data on the Internet. As the effective date of the GDPR in May 2018 approached, both companies that had not paid much attention to the ethical management of data and those who had thought deeply about it accelerated their efforts to get ahead of this ethical concern.

The GDPR establishes standards requiring consent of subjects for data collection and processing; anonymizing collected data to protect privacy; providing data breach notifications; safely handing the transfer of data across borders; and requiring companies to appoint a data protection officer to oversee GDPR compliance. Most significantly, the European Union made the GDPR apply to any firm that had operations and processed data in Europe, thereby affecting virtually every large company in the world.

In response to the GDPR and other governmental concerns, many commentators observed that there was little chance regulations could keep up with the development and deployment of new generations of AI. Therefore, they argued, AI ethics would primarily remain the province of corporate ethics and not of governmental regulation. Regulation would always lag badly. In part to take the leadership in addressing these ethical questions, and in part to avoid poorly drawn and out-of-date regulation, six major corporations in October 2017 launched the Partnership on AI to Benefit People and Society. By September 2018 it had more than 70 partners, over half of which are nonprofit organizations. These include AI research institutes at major universities, ethics centers, and activist organizations such as the American Civil Liberties Union. The Partnership on AI, as it is known, had hired a former Obama Administration official as executive director, and had launched three working groups: Safety Critical AI; Fair, Transparent and Accountable AI; and AI, Labor and the Economy.

Internet and AI research programs at major universities were expanding rapidly, fueled by a surge of individual, foundation, and corporate support. Among these programs are the Berkman Klein Institute for Internet and Society at Harvard University; the Stanford Center for Internet and Society; the Oxford Internet Center; AI Now at New York University; Center for Information Technology Policy at Princeton University; and the MIT Media Lab. Two ethics centers have moved actively into the field: The Markkula Center for Applied Ethics at Santa Clara University and the Hastings Center on health care ethics. Several activist and independent groups have focused increasing attention on AI ethics, including the Electronic Frontier Foundation, the American Civil Liberties Union (ACLU), and Data & Society.

9.10 How Can Corporate Business Ethics Programs Manage AI

It is clear that ethics concerns about AI will be addressed only slowly by regulation and compliance. Therefore, addressing the ethics of AI will be an exercise of the "ethics" portion of the job of "ethics and compliance officers." For some, this will require skills closer to engineering and science than to law, which has increasingly been the background of corporate ethics and compliance officers in the 2010s.

While regulation and compliance standards lag – and likely always will – companies will be rapidly developing and adopting AI for both products and processes. The ethics professional must find ways of addressing this rapid development in an area without standards. There will be considerable uncertainty about the effects of some AI systems as they are deployed. Companies will be pushing to adopt the technology, as in autonomous vehicles, before all the effects are known. And it is not just the companies deploying AI that will face difficult ethical choices. The town council of Los Altos Hills, CA, near the headquarters of Waymo, formerly Google's autonomous vehicle division, has been asked to approve the testing of completely autonomous vehicles in the town. How does a town council or even a corporate executive determine when a system is ready for use on the streets of a municipality?

Simultaneously, ethics officers must contend with considerable public pressure for transparency and disclosure regarding systems that are not easily explained, or perhaps unexplainable because they were developed by machine learning. In these cases, how do ethics officers stand up for corporate principles of transparency developed in other spheres of corporate activity?

Advocates of AI use and many companies have aligned themselves with the public policy position that eschews all regulation. Does that position compromise company values, and the values of some ethics officers, who believe in common sense regulation?

AI systems have advanced greatly in the handling of customer interactions; sometimes it is hard to tell whether you are conversing with an automated system or a real person. Unfortunately, many companies, in a rush to cut costs, provide few avenues of appeal or clarification if the automated system is not adequate for the customer's problem. What do ethical principles about customer service and customer first mean in such cases?

Ethics and compliance officers will be coping with the GDPR regulations and the need to comply in good faith with standards that in some cases cannot technologically be fully met. Other governmentally adopted standards will challenge these officers. In this and other tasks, the ethics officers will have to collaborate with engineering and scientific managers and employees in the company who think differently.

Finally, the job of the ethics officer may be complicated by the very existence of a data trail. Proving corporate malfeasance may be much easier in some cases because the data record exists. How will the job of an ethics officer change if one can surveille employees in new ways, can audit the behavior of executives more thoroughly, can quickly prove that malfeasance has occurred in some cases?

But what are common sense standards and practices a company can follow in AI? D. J. Patil, the first US Chief Data Scientist under President Obama, has argued that only by the adoption of internal processes and standards can companies exercise their ethical obligations regarding the deployment of AI (Patil, 2018) His recommendations apply to all corporations and demonstrate how AI has transformed the work of ethics. He argues for several ethics initiatives, all aimed at achieving the 5 Cs, which have come to represent good ethical and design process in AI: consent, clarity, consistency (and trust), control (and transparency), and (a focus on) consequences. He advocates an expansion of professional codes.

9.10.1 An Expansion of Professional Codes

Patil focuses first on the individual engineer and scientist and argues that corporate ethics efforts must be complemented by codes of ethics for professionals involved in the development of AI, including computer engineers, data scientists, machine learning experts, and others. These oaths or codes, he argues further, must be based on the data golden rule: "Treat the data of others as you would like your data to be treated."

9.10.2 Adoption of Corporate "Stop the Line" Policies

Patil then argues companies should adopt a "stop the line" policy, mimicking Toyota's empowerment of every person on the assembly line to stop the line when a quality problem occurs. Employees, empowered by their professional oaths and codes, would be able to demand that their companies address ethical questions any employee identified in the development of AI algorithms or products. They would be able to stop deployment or continued use of an AI system if they felt it was doing significant damage.

9.10.3 Adoption of a Checklist Mentality for AI Development

Patil, an admirer of the checklist movement in medicine, argues that AI has many of the complexities and rapid advances now seen in medicine, and that only a commitment to checklists – which force attention to central ethical questions facing AI – can avoid ethical pitfalls. He argues that companies ought to develop these checklists on an "open source" basis and share them with others working to develop AI applications.

9.10.4 Creation of a Dissent Channel

In his advocacy for good system checks in AI development, Patil also recommends an active and accessible channel by which any AI professional can dissent from how an AI application is being structured or used. He admires the State Department's dissent channel and thinks it is more effective than typical ethics hotlines.

9.10.5 A Corporate Commitment to Learning

Arguing that the development of AI is progressing so rapidly, Patil believes only a commitment to do post-mortems on AI projects, both successes and failures, can enable companies to learn the ethical lessons on a "real-time" basis. Further, he argues there is an ethical obligation to share that learning in the form of case studies from company to company and sector to sector.

9.10.6 Team Building with a Commitment to Diversity and Ethics

Patil's final recommendation is to think of diversity as essential to ethical AI. Only diversity in gender, race, and life experience, he argues, can enable a team to see the ethical implications of AI and to develop and implement AI responsibly. He recommends paying deliberate attention to the ethical reasoning skills of team members at the point of hiring, possibly by asking an ethics question in every interview.

Patil's is one of the first proposals for internal ethics management of AI going forward. It demonstrates that the task of managing AI ethics is in the hands of the companies and the individual professionals involved in its rapid development and deployment. Other recommendations will follow as companies develop their internal systems for managing AI ethics.

9.11 How Business Ethics Must Prepare for the 2020s – the AI and Ethics Age

The ethics and compliance professional needs to have a new set of skills that includes a sophisticated understanding of AI and machine learning. They must be able to understand how AI is developed and deployed. The professional has to be able to suggest to management how the process can be influenced, whether by culture or by specific practices such as checklists. In short, the ethics professional must be technologically and AI savvy.

Influencing AI's development and deployment will require significant new training programs for engineers and design staff involved in the development of AI. A training program being developed by faculty and staff of the Markkula Center for Applied Ethics has identified how engineers may be oriented toward the key ethical concerns of AI. Aided by the participation of X (formerly GoogleX) and Omidyar Networks, this training effort is now being tested in several other Silicon Valley firms. There will also be a need for a new type of training for the users of AI. When health records originally went online, hospitals and medical companies had to develop ethical principles and trainings to let employees know that certain uses of the data were inappropriate; and certainly that browsing the hospital records of celebrities was a violation of privacy. Such policies will be needed in multiple areas of AI use.

Above all, the ethics professional needs to understand that this is an exercise of ethics and not of compliance, calling on a less developed set of skills that are held by many of the lawyers who now populate ethics and compliance offices. And corporate executives need to address the reality that because addressing the ethics of AI is indeed an "ethics" activity, they must exert ethical leadership to insure that the company takes this seriously. Doubling down on leadership and board oversight is the only way to make this happen.

This is the path of next-generation business ethics.

References

Carroll, A., Lipartito, K. J., Post, J. E., Werhane, P. H., & Goodpaster, K. E. (Executive Ed.). (2012). *Corporate responsibility: The American experience*. Cambridge, MA: Cambridge University Press.

Carson, R. (1962). *Silent spring*. Boston, MA: Houghton Mifflin.

DeGeorge, R.T. (2006). The history of business ethics. In Epstein, J.J. & Hanson, K.O. *The accountable corporation. Volume 2* (pp. 47–58). Westport, CT: Praeger Publishers.

Frederick, W.C. (2006). *Corporation be good!: The story of corporate social responsibility*. Indianapolis, IN: Dog Ear Publishing.

Green, B. (2018). Artificial intelligence and ethics. Essay on website of Markkula Center for Applied Ethics, sourced 9/1/2018. Retrieved from www.scu.edu/ethics/all-about-ethics/artificial-intelligence-and-ethics/

Josephson, M. (2014, January/February 2014). History of the integrity, ethics and compliance movement: A cautionary tale for CEOs and corporate directors. *Ethikos*, *28*(1), 13–15.

Nader, R. (1965). *Unsafe at any speed*. New York, NY: Grossman Publishers.

Patil, D. J. (2018, September 24). Notes from speech delivered at Santa Clara University School of Law.

Endnotes

[1] Several other authors have compiled histories of business ethics, among them Carroll et al. (2012), DeGeorge, R.T.(2006), Frederick (2006), and Josephson (2014).

[2] Several scholars in AI ethics have compiled their own lists of key ethical questions to be addressed by corporations and other organizations engaged in the development and deployment of AI. For example, see Green (2018).

10

Big Data Privacy, Ethics, and Enterprise Continuous Monitoring Systems

Daniel E. O'Leary

10.1 Introduction

> Today it's a given that businesses must behave ethically and responsibly at all times. But how can you be certain that the people and organizations you do business with maintain the same high ethical standards?
>
> *KPMG (2016)*

There is a delicate balance associated with ethics and privacy in "enterprise continuous monitoring systems." On the one hand, it can be critical to enterprises to continuously monitor the ethical behavior of different agents, and thus, facilitate enterprise risk management, as noted in the KPMG quote. In particular, continuous monitoring systems help firms monitor related internal and external agents to make sure that the agents hired by or engaged by the enterprise are behaving ethically. However, on the other hand, such continuous monitoring systems can pose ethical and privacy risks to those being monitored and provide risks and costs to the company doing the monitoring. For example, inappropriate information can be assembled, stored, and inferred about a range of individuals. Thus, information obtained by continuous monitoring generally should follow privacy principles that require that the data be up-to-date and conform to the purpose for which the data was originally gathered, and other constraints.

10.1.1 Continuous Monitoring Systems as Accounting, Auditing, and Big Data

Continuous monitoring systems continuously and with persistence typically gather data from a wide range of data sources, including the Internet. As a result, generally, continuous monitoring systems are considered to be based in the emerging technologies of "big data" and "analytics." Since continuous monitoring systems are constantly gathering and processing information, and as they typically are monitoring multiple databases, they are inevitably steeped in *big data*. In addition, since continuous monitoring systems are trying to gather usable knowledge from data and text, they employ different *analytics* depending on the information that they are capturing and analyzing and on the overall specific purposes of the system.

10.1.2 Privacy and Ethics

Privacy has a number of definitions particularly as it relates to issues of big data (e.g., O'Leary, 2015) and is discussed in substantial detail in this section. In addition, based on a definition of computer ethics by James Moor (1985), big data ethics are defined "as the analysis of the nature and societal impact of big data technology and the corresponding formulation and justification of policies for ethical use of big data" (O'Leary, 2016, p. 83). Although there are a number of big data technologies, we will focus on continuous monitoring; and despite there being different issues associated with the ethical use of big data, we will focus primarily on ethical privacy conditions and resulting policies. As will be noted, the suggested privacy conditions are based on the Organisation for Economic Co-operation and Development (OECD) privacy principles, while we focus on the ethical behavior being linked to the use of those principles.

10.1.3 Enterprise Continuous Monitoring Systems

This chapter is primarily concerned with what we will call enterprise continuous monitoring systems (ECMS). Although that term has been used at least once[1] before (DOT, 2015, p. 12), that specific use referred to a tool designed for analysis of security and controls and to create device inventories. Our use of the term ECMS will not be aimed specifically at computer security or controls. Instead, in this chapter ECMS will broadly refer to systems designed to continuously monitor internal and external (e.g., through the Internet) information available to an enterprise about the behavior of any of the "agents" (employees, executives, owners, vendors, clients, partners, etc.) that are a part of the enterprise or interact with the particular enterprise; or any of a range of different "objects" (and processes) of concern to the enterprise, including the supply chain, purchases, etc. Further, although the objects typically are directly related to systems and entities (such as other enterprises), the objects often can be directly traced to particular people. For example, purchases are an object that generally is executed by people, so the objects could be used to provide information about people and their behavior. As a result, both agent-based ECMS and object-based ECMS can gather and store information (whether "appropriate" or "inappropriate") directly related to specific individuals.

10.1.4 Findings

Based on our analysis of ECMS we find three insights. First, we find that ECMS can provide firms with potential insight into the behavior and risks associated with a wide range of agents and objects – both in the firm and outside the firm. As a result, such systems provide a vehicle potentially to monitor agent ethical behavior and provide risk management. Second, since such systems basically only require a "parameter change" to go from analyzing a particular employee, vendor, client, etc., to analyzing a broad base of similar agents, ECMS likely can be used to analyze broad swathes of such agents. Accordingly, organizations could accumulate large quantities of information about a wide range of people and objects, potentially in contrast to promulgated privacy policies. Third, unfortunately, such systems can find and store the "wrong" type of information or "inappropriate" information (race, religion, etc.) – whether gathered directly or indirectly – that can be used to infer knowledge about the agents. As a result, there are potential privacy and ethical concerns associated with tracking and monitoring by such systems.

10.1.5 Plan of This Chapter

This chapter proceeds in the following manner. This first section has motivated and introduced the problem. Section 10.2 reviews some generic continuous monitoring systems capabilities. Section 10.3 investigates some sample continuous monitoring systems that are used by different enterprises. Section 10.4 examines selected issues related to ECMS, such as parameterization and coordination between multiple ECMS. Section 10.5 briefly reviews the OECD principles of data collection. Section 10.6 examines some of the resulting issues associated with privacy and ethics in continuous monitoring systems, with a particular focus on the OECD principles of data collection. Section 10.7 analyzes some additional issues related to the ethical use of ECMS. Section 10.8 briefly summarizes the chapter, examines its contributions, and reviews some extensions.

10.2 Continuous Monitoring Systems

Continuous monitoring systems are designed to mitigate and potentially eliminate information asymmetries by finding, capturing, assembling, and storing information that is distributed across multiple available databases and information sources (such as the Internet), often in a single location, such as a data warehouse. In addition, continuous monitoring systems need to be able to analyze that information and draw inferences from it that can guide their human users to make decisions based on that information.

Table 10.1 Continuous Monitoring - Number of Google Search Results[a]

Panel A – Continuous Monitoring of Agents

Continuous Monitoring of Employees	111,000
Continuous Monitoring of Personnel	104,000
Continuous Monitoring of Customers	67,600
Continuous Monitoring of the Supply Chain	53,700
Continuous Monitoring of Clients	42,700
Continuous Monitoring of Competitors	12,000
Continuous Monitoring of Vendors	10,700
Continuous Monitoring of Counterparties	5,990
Continuous Monitoring of Partners	8
Continuous Monitoring of Management	6
Continuous Monitoring of Agents	6
Continuous Monitoring of Computer Users	0
Continuous Monitoring of Executives	0

Panel B – Continuous Monitoring of Objects

Continuous Monitoring of Computer	147,000
Continuous Monitoring of Finance	76,800
Continuous Monitoring of Transactions	47,800
Continuous Monitoring of Accounts	43,300
Continuous Monitoring of Internal Controls	36,100
Continuous Monitoring of Expenses	23,000
Continuous Monitoring of Revenue	10
Continuous Monitoring of Purchasing	10
Continuous Monitoring of Accounting	6
Continuous Monitoring of Products	5
Continuous Monitoring of Reputation	3

[a] Quotation mark-based Google searches - As of April 17, 2018

There are a wide range of systems designed to continuously monitor conditions in a range of settings. For example, there are systems that monitor computer system use and controls (DOT, 2015), diabetes patients with continuous glucose monitoring,[2] money laundering (Nice Atimize, 2016), financial transactions (Alles et al., 2006 and others) and a wide range of other activities as seen in Table 10.1.

10.2.1 Who/What Gets Continuously Monitored?

Table 10.1 presents a summary of a recent set of Google searches[3] related to continuous monitoring of both agents (panel A) and objects/processes (panel B) for different topics associated with enterprise continuous monitoring. Based on Table 10.1, panel A, it is clear that there is substantial interest in continuously monitoring of a wide range of agents: personnel, employees, customers, clients, vendors, competitors and others.

In addition, as seen in Table 10.1, panel B, continuous monitoring systems have been built to monitor a number of different objects/processes.

10.2.2 Required System Capabilities

What are likely to be some required system capabilities of continuous monitoring systems? Although those capabilities are likely to depend on the specific monitoring being done, if continuous monitoring systems are to be effective, they need to at least be able to gather and analyze data and to "read" and "understand" text in order to ensure that they collect the right information to fulfill their requirements.

As a result, ECMS are likely to employ different analytics, some based in the analysis of data and some based in the analysis of text, in order to generate that structured view of that text. Further, continuous monitoring systems generally need to provide a structured set of measures about the text that they analyze. As an example, it is not unusual for such systems to have analytics to capture the sentiment (positive or negative) of the text and potentially be able to track those sentiment assessments over time to capture the overall current response to some enterprise. In order to read that text, in some settings, continuous monitoring systems will require a multilingual capability, as part of that text understanding. In addition, in order to provide the appropriate breadth of response such systems also will need access to a range of different text databases, ranging from classic media to other digital media, such as social media, including blogs, Twitter, etc.

In addition, although such systems will likely be given some particular set of issues to explore (e.g., a list of products), as discussed in the next section, they also might be expected to notice new and emerging issues. One approach to finding such new issues is to capture those concepts that "co-occur" with the initial topics (e.g., O'Leary and Spangler, 2016). Further, such systems might be interested in determining who the key influencers are, that is, those people or sources that seem to be at the "root" of the information that the system finds (O'Leary and Spangler, 2016).

10.2.3 Domain-Specific Capabilities

In some cases, continuous monitoring systems will be developed to perform domain-specific tasks, beyond generic tasks, such as determining the existence of positive or negative sentiment. In particular, if the specific tasks that the agents are responsible for can be specified, a priori, and then likely distinct conditions can be monitored through the appropriate choice of databases and a specific search for domain-specific concepts in those databases. As a result, domain-specific issues might include particular contract provisions, law suits, and changes of ownership that can be monitored to capture information about risky third parties. As an example, O'Leary and Spangler (2016) discuss a system that potentially monitors specific products and corporate leaders of candy companies.

10.3 Sample Systems and Capabilities

There are some continuous monitoring systems that have been discussed in greater detail in both firm-specific discussions about the systems and in the academic literature about those systems. The purpose of this section is to review some of those systems designed to perform enterprise continuous monitoring, summarizing some of their specific capabilities.

10.3.1 KPMG's Astrus Due Diligence

KPMG (2014) has developed a system (Astrus) that uses continuous monitoring to facilitate "third-party due diligence reporting and monitoring." In order to facilitate due diligence, the system continuously investigates shareholders; negative media reports; sanctions; lawsuits; corporate interests; global sanctions and regulatory enforcement lists; personal and corporate data; litigation records; adverse global media and press; and trade/economic sanctions lists.

Astrus has some domain-specific capabilities designed into the system as part of its search capabilities, including analysis of the following:

- anti-bribery and corruption regulatory compliance
- anti-money laundering compliance
- financial services regulatory compliance
- merger and acquisition in both emerging and other global markets
- risk assessments of *current and prospective* business partners, agents, and vendors

In order to meet the demands placed on it, Astrus apparently uses more than 30,000 individual digital public data sources worldwide. Astrus draws information from at least five basic sources: premium content data aggregators, surface Web content (indexed), deep Web content (non-indexed), non-English content (data in over 88 languages) and KPMG independent research.

Astrus (KPMG, 2014, p.2) generates information about both individuals and organizations. Associated with each assessment is a risk indicator (in the form of a stoplight with different colors of lights – red, yellow, and green – indicating the status), which indicates if they are a "politically exposed person" (PEP), the existence of sanctions on the entity or person, and other information, including a summary report.

10.3.2 PwC's Supply Chain Monitoring

PwC (2016, p. 9) has developed a system designed for "continuous supply chain monitoring through advanced analytics." Their system is based on information gathered similarly from the open Web, the unindexed Web, unstructured internal and external data, watch lists, and internal data. Ultimately, the system allows continuous monitoring of the full vendor network, including third-party and fourth-party suppliers. The resulting output includes risk-based analysis of different entities, products, geographic locations, and other features.

It is not just enterprises that need to be and can be tracked as part of supply chain monitoring. As noted by PwC (2016), the behavior of both individual entities and individuals need to be tracked (emphasis added).

> As regulators and prosecutors start feeling the pressure to escalate enforcement of regulations governing supply chain risk, they are turning their attention to *individuals*.
>
> (p. 5)

> Companies must be able to verify whether each *individual entity* in the network is abiding by the laws of the countries with jurisdictions over it.
>
> (p. 6)

Accordingly, the system can generate substantial information about individuals, ideally mitigating information asymmetries about those people.

10.3.3 COBRA

O'Leary and Spangler (2016, 2018) discussed a system designed to monitor reputation of a company, its leading executives, its products, its competitors, and other issues. The system, labeled "COBRA" (corporate brand and reputation analytics), examined a number of different databases and social media sources. Since COBRA integrates a range of agents it can perform many monitoring functions. However, the system does not contain any domain-specific measures of risk, supply chain, etc. The system illustrates the apparent ease with which additional agents can be added: adding an executive to be monitored is a matter of adding their name and context information (e.g., company, location, position, etc.) to a list of existing executives and their characteristics.

10.4 Growth in Continuous Monitoring Systems

The purpose of this section is to briefly investigate some additional issues associated with the potential growth of continuous monitoring systems.

10.4.1 How Difficult Is It to Add Another Firm, Individual, etc.?

The primary development and implementation costs of such systems are initially establishing the system, choosing the criteria being analyzed, the databases being examined, etc. and are largely fixed costs. As a result, rather than narrowly focusing on a few individuals, we likely would anticipate that such systems include a broad base of agents to spread the costs of such monitoring. For example, if the system is monitoring some executives from specific companies, others could be monitored relatively easily. Extending the base of individuals and organizations covered would be relatively costless – it would effectively be equivalent to just adding another name in order to spread the development/implementation costs over more agents to monitor (e.g., O'Leary and Spangler, 2016).

10.4.2 More and More Continuous Monitoring Systems

As seen in Table 10.1, apparently there are a wide range of different continuous monitoring systems available. Further, if they are successful at doing what they do, then there probably will be an increase in the use of such systems. If they do remove information asymmetries, reduce risk, etc. then such systems likely would be used to monitor more and more groups of agents and objects. In addition, if extending the reach of such systems, to other entities or individuals, is relatively easy, then we'd expect more and more entities and people to be analyzed by each instantiation of an ECMS. Accordingly, we would predict a growth both in the number of continuous monitoring systems and in their coverage over time.

10.5 OECD Principles of Data Collection

Perhaps the best known and most comprehensive approach to the primary concerns associated with privacy are the OECD principles of data collection. These principles have been used in the previous literature to investigate the effects of knowledge discovery on privacy (e.g., O'Leary 1995 and others). The purpose of this section is to briefly summarize key issues associated with those eight different OECD (2013) principles.

> *Collection limitation:* Data should be obtained lawfully and fairly, while some very sensitive data should not be held at all. Where "appropriate," the data should be held only with either the "knowledge or consent" of the data subject.
> *Data quality:* Data should be relevant to the stated purposes, accurate, complete, and up-to-date; proper precautions should be taken to ensure this accuracy.
> *Purpose specification:* The purposes for which data will be used should be identified not later than the time of collection and use of the data. Further, the data should only be used for those purposes or purposes that are not

incompatible with those purposes. Generally, the data should be destroyed if it no longer serves the given purpose.

Use limitation: Use of data for purposes other than specified is forbidden, except with the consent of the data subject *or* by authority of the law.

Security safeguards: Agencies should establish procedures to guard against a number of risks, including unauthorized access, destruction, use, modification or disclosure of data.

Openness: It must be possible for agents to acquire information about the collection, storage, and use of personal data.

Individual participation: The data subject has a right to access and challenge the data related to him or her. In addition, the data subject can have communications regarding the data relating to him within a reasonable amount of time and the individual can challenge the available data about them.

Accountability: A data controller should be accountable for complying with measures giving effect to all these principles.

We would expect organizations that adhere to the OECD privacy principles to be seen as ethical based on the above definition of big data ethics.

10.6 Potential Privacy and Ethical Issues Associated with Continuous Monitoring

The purpose of this section is to map the capabilities and typical uses of continuous monitoring systems into the OECD data principles. Unfortunately, continuous monitoring systems that scan the Internet for information about enterprise agents can violate virtually all of the OECD data principles.

Collection limitation: Continuous monitoring systems likely violate the portion of the limitation that the data is gathered with the "knowledge or consent" of the data subject. It is unlikely that many (any) data subjects have agreed to have their Internet behavior monitored by some continuous monitoring system.

Data quality: Unfortunately, when information is gathered from many sources on the Internet, it is unlikely that the information is "complete" or "up-to-date." In addition, when it comes to Internet data, it is likely that much of the data gathered may not be "accurate."

Purpose specification: If data is available on a range of data sources, such as the Internet, it is unlikely that a specified purpose is that the data could be used as part of a system designed to continuously monitor their manifested behavior.

Use limitation: It is likely that continuous monitoring systems do not gather the consent of the data subject. As a result, if the OECD data principles are part of the "law" in any setting then the systems are not likely put in place with the "authority of the law."

Security safeguards: Continuous monitoring systems ultimately create reports based on the data they gather. In addition, those reports are likely to be distributed within the organization responsible for the system. As a result, there may be unauthorized access, use, or disclosure of data.

Openness principle: Unfortunately, enterprises doing continuous monitoring do not typically make their policies and practices openly available. Further, since those being monitored may not know that they are being monitored, they may not know that others are using their personal data.

Individual participation: If continuous monitoring systems use Internet-available data then it is unlikely that the data subject will be aware of the use of the data. If a data subject is unaware then it is unlikely that they will be able to challenge the data that the system is using about them. Unfortunately, the system may derive conclusions about that user and the user may never know that the system is monitoring them.

Accountability principle: Although there is a limited literature about continuous monitoring systems, there seems to be even less administration and governance of such systems. Based on the OECD guidelines, there apparently needs to be a data controller that has to assess all of these concerns about the data.

Based on this analysis, it appears that there are many concerns associated with the use of much of the data that continuous monitoring systems are likely to employ; for example, on the Internet.

10.7 Other Sources of Ethical and Privacy Concerns

There are additional sets of issues associated with continuous monitoring systems, particularly as they relate to use of information available over the Internet and other issues.

10.7.1 Is Available or Secondary Data, "Open" Data?

Continuous monitoring systems often use data that is available over the Internet. Unfortunately, such available or secondary data may not be "fair game" from a privacy perspective. Many of the concerns discussed in Section 10.6 suggest that such data could violate some of the OECD privacy principles, including use, purpose, and participation issues.

10.7.2 Putting Together Data from Multiple Databases

One of the key capabilities associated with the analysis of big data, in general and continuous monitoring systems in particular, is the access to and analysis of multiple databases. As a result, it is likely that information that is not normally adjacent can be put together in order to generate understanding. One of the core principles of business intelligence is that such adjacency could generate an understanding that goes beyond the data in the context of the individual databases. Although generating insights may create value, there are many instances when joining multiple databases together can result in potential privacy or related issues. For example, as noted in the case of classified data, "two or more items of unclassified information, when put together [can] create some additional factor which warrants classification."[4] This suggests that perhaps an addition to OECD principles might be to include some protections from aggregation of seemingly unrelated personal data.

10.7.3 Multiple Meanings/Multiple Individuals

Continuous monitoring systems are based on using search queries, for example, from Google, in order to find information of interest. Unfortunately, search queries may not generate "unique" or "targeted" information. O'Leary (2011) (and others) have done an analysis of Google searches based on some terms and found that the same term could have multiple meanings resulting in diverse search findings. As an example, "Public Image" does not only relate to the obvious view of what is a firm's public image, say as on the Internet. Instead, "Public Image" also is a music group. Similarly, search for any individual or company can generate findings that are different from the actual search target. As a result, a data controller needs to constantly monitor the results to ensure that the concept being sought is the concept being found.

10.7.4 Maintenance of Stored Databases

The OECD principle for data quality indicates the importance that the data stays "up-to-date." ECMS "continuously" monitor, thus creating substantial amounts of data over time. Unfortunately, there is a potential cost associated with maintaining databases so that they are up-to-date and that the resulting information is not dated: pruning dated or "no longer needed information" from databases is costly. Further, since that process is expensive, it may not be done in a timely manner. However, if they are not updated, then the stored information can be in violation of the OECD principles.

10.7.5 Expectations Associated with Having a Continuous Monitoring System

As noted in O'Leary (2012) in a Cisco Systems case, when an enterprise has continuous monitoring systems there may be expectations as to how well an organization can respond to challenges. In the case of Cisco, it appeared that many expected that a continuous monitoring system for sales and inventory would mitigate economic effects faced by the firm. As a result, there was surprise that even though Cisco had a continuous monitoring system, they had a $2 billion write down in inventory. Unfortunately, continuous monitoring does not necessarily generate better results; such systems still require human response and, in some settings, there may not be a good solution.

10.7.6 Is There Coordination between Continuous Monitoring Systems?

Although it appears that there are many opportunities for firms to create and use continuous monitoring systems, it is not clear the extent to which such systems could or would or should share information about their respective entities and individuals. From a design perspective, it is likely that problems regarding some entity or person likely would be an issue of interest in some related ECMS. However, integration across multiple continuous monitoring sources may lead to additional potential privacy concerns in a manner similar to the classified data concerns issue, discussed already.

10.8 Summary, Contributions, and Extensions

Organizations face potential and emerging privacy and ethical issues associated with ECMS. On the one hand, they need to use them to remove asymmetries of information about the agents that they employ and interact with. On the other hand, they have to be careful what information they find, store, and use. The chapter has analyzed those issues both from the perspective of using the systems to monitor agents to ensure ethical behavior and from the perspective of concern for those agents being monitored.

10.8.1 Contributions

This chapter has a number of contributions. First, as technology changes and different classes of systems emerge it becomes possible to begin to elicit or start to discuss the next generation of concerns for privacy and ethics. This chapter elicits and discusses a category of systems referred to as ECMS. Second, this chapter has focused on an emerging class of systems that are used in a wide range of applications, while defining and focusing on a particular subset of those systems: ECMS. Third, the chapter has examined both the ECMS user and the data subject to begin to understand some of the emerging privacy and ethical issues of such systems.

10.8.2 Extensions

There are a number of potential extensions to the discussions in this chapter. First, we have focused on ECMS. However, there likely are similar concerns in other types of continuous monitoring systems. As a result, such systems in other areas, such as computer systems monitoring or diabetes monitoring, could be the subject of additional analysis. Second, some of the issues identified here, such as the relationship between the content of different ECMS, will probably be of interest to future researchers. For example, what are the implications or technical issues associated with different systems sharing their information and discoveries? Third, this chapter was most concerned about the ethical impact of issues related to privacy. Future research could examine other ethical concerns beyond privacy. Fourth, a number of expectations about the use and implementation of continuous monitoring systems have been noted. For example, it was speculated that the number of ECMS would increase and that the number of people/objects being monitored within existing systems would also increase over time. Empirical research could examine some of those statements. Finally, although this chapter's focus is on continuous monitoring of sources on the Internet, systems could be developed to continuously monitor blockchain data. For example, interesting information about agents or objects could be a part of different public block chains and such a system could bring together information from those different sources (e.g., O'Leary 2017).

References

Alles, M., Brennan, G., Kogan, A., & Vasarhelyi, M. A. (2006). Continuous monitoring of business process controls: A pilot implementation of a continuous auditing system at Siemens. *International Journal of Accounting Information Systems, 7*(2), 137–161.

Appek, K. (2010, November). Comparing Pharmaceutical Continuous Monitoring Systems: Part 1. Retrieved from www.qualitydigest.com/inside/metrology-article/comparing-pharmaceutical-continuous-monitoring-systems-part-1.html#

Chan, D. Y., & Vasarhelyi, M. A. (2011). Innovation and practice of continuous auditing. *International Journal of Accounting Information Systems, 12*(2), 152–160.

DOT. (2015). Department of Transportation, Office of Inspector General, Audit Report, FISMA 2015: DOT has major success in PIV implementation, but problems persist in other cybersecurity areas (November 5) (Redacted Version). Retrieved from www.oig.dot.gov/sites/default/files/FISMA%20FY%202015%20FOUO%20Redacted.pdf

KPMG. (2014). Astrus: A web-enabled integrity due diligence solution. Retrieved from https://assets.kpmg.com/content/dam/kpmg/pdf/2014/08/astrus-due-diligence-solution-v2.pdf

KPMG. (2016). Astrus Enhanced due diligence reporting and monitoring. Retrieved from www.youtube.com/watch?v=OgMNFsWBZc4

Moor, J. (1985). What is computer ethics? *Metaphilosophy, 16*(4), 266–275.

Nice, Atimize, (2016). Watch list filtering. Retrieved from www.niceactimize.com/Lists/Brochures/AML_Brochure_WatchListFiltering.pdf

OECD. (2013). OECD guidelines on the protection of privacy and transborder flows of personal data. Retrieved from www.oecd.org/sti/ieconomy/oecdguidelinesonthe protectionofprivacyandtransborderflowsofpersonaldata.htm

O'Leary, D. E. (1995). Some privacy issues in knowledge discovery: The OECD personal privacy guidelines. *IEEE Expert*, *10*(2), 48–59.

O'Leary, D. E. (2011). Blog mining-review and extensions: From each according to his opinion. *Decision Support Systems*, *51*(4), 821–830.

O'Leary, D. E. (2012). The virtual close and continuous monitoring at Cisco. *Journal of Emerging Technologies in Accounting*, *9*(1), 111–126.

O'Leary, D. E. (2013). Knowledge discovery for continuous financial assurance using multiple types of digital information. In K. Lawrence (Ed.) *Contemporary perspectives in data mining* (pp. 103–122). Charlotte, NC: Information Age Publishing.

O'Leary, D. E. (2015). Big data and privacy: Emerging issues. *IEEE Intelligent Systems*, *30*(6), 92–96.

O'Leary, D. E. (2016). Ethics for big data and analytics. *IEEE Intelligent Systems*, *31*(4), 81–84.

O'Leary, D. E. (2017). Configuring blockchain architectures for transaction information in blockchain consortiums: The case of accounting and supply chain systems. *Intelligent Systems in Accounting, Finance and Management*, *24*(4), 138–147.

O'Leary, D., & Spangler, S. (2016). "Monitoring and Mining Digital Media for Brand and Reputation Information." Paper presented at the International Conference on Information Systems (Dublin 2016). Retrieved from http://aisel.aisnet.org/icis2016/ISCurriculum/Presentations/3/

O'Leary, D., & Spangler, S. (2018). Continuously monitoring bank risk, Reputation and opportunity, *Journal of Emerging Technologies in Accounting*, forthcoming.

PwC. (2016). Needle in the haystack: Monitoring vendor networks through supply chain risk analytics (July). Retrieved from www.pwc.com/us/en/risk-assurance/publications/supply-chain-risk-analytics.pdf

Endnotes

[1] Based on a Google search on April 10, 2017.
[2] www.medtronicdiabetes.com/treatments/continuous-glucose-monitoring
[3] Google search findings provide one measure of the number of potential items on the Internet for the particular search query. Although the estimated findings provided by Google's search engine are not likely to be exact, Google does provide a relative measure that allows us to compare the number of occurrences for different queries.
[4] www.fas.org/sgp/othergov/dod/nimaguide.pdf

11

How Management Theories and Culture Fads Kill Organizational Ethics

Marianne M. Jennings

11.1 Introduction

There was a time when we were all six-sigma-ing. We did so because Jack Welch had bought into the six-sigma phenomenon and he had created a phenomenally performing General Electric (GE). Then we moved along from good to great to the search for excellence to becoming great by choice to whatever superlative Jim Collins told us was the way to a company that was built to last. Then someone moved our cheese. We had no time for that because we were just one-minute managers. We smoothed earnings, incentivized employees, and created three tiers of employees – including getting rid of the bottom tier of employees, whether they deserved termination or kudos. We all wanted to be part of the *Fortune* 100, the *Fortune* Most Admired Companies, even as we were led by Fortune CEOs and CFOs of the year – many of whom ended up doing time.

Business fads, business strategies, and other novel ideas have been leading business people around by their noses since 1997 in search of good, great, better, and best, and back from failure to so–so. The built-to-last companies (the original set of companies that resulted in the Collins data and charts) included GE, Motorola, HP, Piedmont Airlines, Sony, Wang Labs, and Procter & Gamble. If you have not heard of a few of them it would be because they no longer exist, that is, they did not last. Some that you have heard of probably brings to mind this question, "Are they still around?" Others you are familiar with are struggling to survive. Still others have grappled with more than their fair share of ethical lapses.

Ron Zemke and Dick Schaaf's (1989) *The Service Edge* brought us a study of 101 companies that "profit from customer care." Here are a few of their lauded companies: Piedmont Airlines, Wachovia, Vons Super Markets, Chicken Soup, and GE. Wachovia collapsed from a little too much customer service, that is, making loans to people who could not afford them and were not offering much in the way of collateral. Even more members of this group have suffered from the problems of the previously listed great ones.

The chase for the shiny object that will be the answer to all business issues, challenges, malaise, or setback has resulted in aggressive pursuits of mirages.

That aggressive pursuit has proven destructive to the ethical values of too many organizations. From accounting fraud to manipulated results, poor ethical choices have been the food for fueling the achievement of the goals. Strategy, goals, and their pursuit bury ethical infrastructure as trivial and irrelevant. The result is an ethical culture that finds employees reduced to lyin', stealin', and cheatin' their way through the strategy to the goals. Ethics becomes a separate silo in the organization, something that employees sign off on once each year, or an online training program to be clicked through and tolerated. Reality for employees is what is emphasized every day: the numbers, the goals, the results, the rewards, and the promotions. Reality is an organization's culture. Ethics is what we say, and results are what we live. Management's strategies, fads, and theories eat the ethical infrastructure.

"Culture eats strategy for breakfast." While Peter Drucker is given attribution for this clever phrase, no one can find the thought in his writings. "Culture eats strategy for lunch" has been attributed to Scott A. Mason (Mason, 2000). Since Mason's first use of the clever phrase in 2000, countless CEOs have relied on the quote's sentiment – varying only by the meal and the source. Dr. Edgar Schein is more likely the originator of the thought, but not the clever phraseology. Dr. Schein wrote that "culture constrains strategy," and "culture determines and limits strategy" (Schein, 1985).

Despite the historical disagreements on the origin of culture's appetites and meal preference, the underlying sentiment on the power of culture was prescient in its founding and is demonstrably true today. The best laid strategic plans are toppled by organizational culture. The same is likewise true of the ethical infrastructure that include ethics officers, compliance programs, codes of ethics, reporting mechanisms, and ethics training. Culture consumes ethical values. The good intentions and solid components of these checklist approaches to ethical culture cannot and will not keep ethical missteps in check. The list is long and distinguished of companies, government agencies, nonprofits, and nongovern-mental organizations (NGOs) that have been recognized for their efforts in the areas of ethics and social responsibility. However, too many of those same organizations have made headlines for serious ethical and legal difficulties.

Management theorists tout the importance of a focus on strategic planning, goals, and measurement of those goals. Once those components are in place, under strategic planning research, just stand back and watch the results gush in on schedule. Theory does not take into account human nature and what human nature can fabricate when a competitive, goal-setting culture takes hold.

What are the components of culture that may drive achievement but at the expense of values, standards, integrity, and even compliance with the law? Why do decent employees engage in behavior that results in headlines and finds us all asking, "Why would they believe that what they were doing was acceptable behavior?" There are six key factors that all organizations, from publicly traded companies to NGOs to nonprofits to government agencies and all the way to the smallest of businesses, need to understand and keep in check if culture's appetite for consuming ethical values is to be curbed. In other words, what is missing from the management theories, fads, and studies is the reality that without an ethical culture, whatever magical formula is being applied will, at a minimum, result in a setback, and, in too many cases, destroy the organization its leaders were trying to salvage through management magic. These are some culture curbs that should be in place to prevent culture from eating ethical values:

1. Use caution and foresight in developing incentive plans.
2. Figure out how employees are reaching goals and meeting numbers.
3. Tie your audit plan to goals, measurements, and results.
4. Watch what you say, and what you don't say.
5. Enforce your own rules.
6. Get a strong board or some form of candid third-party input.

The following sections offer the details on these curbs.

11.2 Use Caution and Foresight in Developing Incentive Plans

Be careful what you incentivize. Of course, incentive plans work! Management theory on this topic is borne out by longstanding research. The missing component in the research is the follow-up on whether the numbers on which the bonuses were given were real. Chasing after nothing does bring a bit of damage to any organization. One of the management theories/fads that Collins encouraged companies to use is to set big, hairy, audacious goals (BHAGs). Who could be opposed to such drive and ambition? This author. Be careful what you set for goals and be careful what you incentivize. You will get the results that you had everyone shooting for, chanting included, but those results may not be real. Ethics fall by the wayside as the BHAGs march and trample over everything. For example, the Veterans Administration (VA) was meeting its goals for reducing patient queues for evaluation and treatment. The progress stoplight charts used to measure goal progress were all green, no slippage into white, yellow, or, worse yet, the red failure zone. However, the VA employees were not getting better at service nor were they actually meeting the BHAGs. The employees simply developed the equivalent of two sets of books. One set was the reporting set, the numbers that determined performance evaluations and bonuses and that were released to the public to tout the progress of the VA. The patients who were funneled off into the other set of books found themselves in a twilight zone of no appointments, no call-backs, and no treatments. Sadly, too many VA patients died or suffered while waiting in limbo because of the employees' creation of a no-virtue zone of hidden reality inspired by the zeal to meet those BHAGs.

Another example was BP, which had BHAGs for its oil exploration and production. Numbers for that era of implementing the BHAG exploration and production goals indicate that BP employees were indeed meeting or exceeding those goals. Ironically, BP was touted as a responsible, climate-friendly company as it received awards and recognition for its safety programs. The reality that the goal- and cost-driven-culture created, however, was that, in order to meet exploration and production goals, the employees took shortcuts in process safety and maintenance. For example, BP did not bother to test its Alaska pipeline for weaknesses. BP's Texas City refinery had over 400 unaddressed OSHA violations that eventually resulted in explosions and fatalities. Then came BP's use of the single thread design in the Deepwater Horizon well in the Gulf of Mexico (and in other oceanic projects). The 2009 explosion of Deepwater Horizon resulted in $62 billion in fines, a 30 percent reduction in production, negative net income (decreasing from $16 billion to a $3.3 billion loss), and a nearly 40 percent drop in the company's market capitalization.

BP's culture on paper and what it said publicly was one of social responsibility and safety. Its real culture was one of cost-cutting and goal-setting that ate the company's state values. As one employee phrased it, you were only questioned about why you couldn't spend less on safety and drilling. The culture consumed the ethical values and even compliance with laws and regulation. Today BP is nearing the end of a decade of recovery. Cut corners, safety violations, and spills that were a function of shortcuts in process safety – all risky behaviors that permeated the culture – were the end result of its BHAGs.

In the government sector, the Atlanta Public School System (APS) had an incentive plan to improve the test scores of the children in the district. Those teachers who achieved their test scores were given bonuses between $750 and $2,600. Twenty-five percent of principals' performance evaluations were based on test scores, and if their schools did not achieve targets within three years, they were replaced. As a result, for almost a decade, the scores of APS students on the Criterion Referenced Competency Tests (CRCT) were phenomenal. The students were reading at or above their grade levels, and then-Superintendent Beverly Hall won educator of the year as well as recognition from the White House for her efforts and great success. Ms. Hall also received $383,000 in bonuses during the decade of increasing test scores.

The test scores were not real. Three different investigations found mind-boggling cheating, with the governor's task force report documenting the following behaviors in the district:

- Teachers and students erased incorrect answers and put in correct answers after the testing was complete.
- The changes to answers were so sophisticated that administrators and teachers created plastic transparency answer sheets to allow for quick reviews and faster answer changes.
- Teachers arranged classroom seating so that struggling students were better able to "cheat off" the brighter students.

- First- and second-grade teachers used voice inflection when reading the questions and answers to their students (who were not yet reading) in a manner that gave away the answers.
- Some teachers just read the answers aloud to their students.
- Teachers pointed to correct answers while standing next to students' desks as they took the test.
- Teachers changed test answers with gloves on at what came to be called "test cleanup" parties (Jennings, 2017).

These examples of cheating processes are but a small portion of a list too long to reproduce. Once the cheating began, there was no turning back. Just to stay even, cheating became necessary. However, the goals kept growing. To produce increasing scores to meet tougher goals, teachers and principals developed innovations in cheating methodologies. The drive to meet the test score goals consumed the culture and all ethical values. The report noted, "Once cheating started, it [the district] became a house of cards that collapsed on itself" (Jennings, 2017). In addition, the report concluded: "APS became such a 'data-driven' system, with unreasonable and excessive pressure to meet targets, that Beverly Hall and her senior cabinet lost sight of conducting tests with integrity" (Jennings, 2017).

These examples provide important insights into the design of incentive systems. When there is a focus on outcome measurement, employees meet measured goals. However, the numbers might not be real and the actual outcome may be the opposite of the desired outcome. Test score measurements did not produce educated students because the measurement for the goal was easily manipulated. What was measured was *only* the outcome, the numbers. In the outmoded language of the 1980s, there is a paradigm that needs shifting. The paradigm on incentives requires a seismic shift.

11.2.1 Focus on Outcome, Not Output

Although again credited with the idea, Peter Drucker did not actually say you cannot manage what you can't measure. His actual thought is, "[A manager] must be able to measure his performance and results against the goal" (Drucker, 2001). Numbers are the usual measure for performance. Sales numbers tell us how sales teams are doing, so salespeople are measured by the number and amounts of their sales. More total sales, in number and amount, mean greater revenues and profits. Customer satisfaction surveys, employee engagement surveys, culture surveys, ethics surveys, production numbers, and test scores are all examples of measurements used to determine progress and/or success in organizations. All incentive programs have numerical measurements – goals that employees must reach if the bonus pool is to be released and if their performance evaluations are to be satisfactory. But these measurements are foolhardy efforts if the measurements can be manipulated. Think of the simple example of the post-repair surveys that auto dealers do on their service department. The employees and service department managers put so much pressure on customers to give them perfect ratings that customers simply give all 10s. The dealership and car manufacturers believe that they have remarkable service departments. What those looking at the survey results do not know is that customers are being pestered into saying nothing about any problems. The goals are achieved, but the numbers are not real.

In every case study of manipulation – from falsified earnings to Volkswagen's low emissions to the number of new accounts at Wells Fargo – the output was the measurement of success and the standard for incentives, bonuses, and performance evaluations. When incentives are in play, employees find a way to get to the numbers goal. The achievement of the goal and those numbers eats the ethical culture. Volkswagen employees developed software programs for falsifying emissions in order to meet both fuel economy and emissions standards. Wells Fargo employees opened dozens of accounts for family members, then evolved to creating accounts for existing customers without their knowledge. This eventually graduated into just making up customers. The result was that Wells Fargo had a services/account ratio of 6.1 per customer vs. 2.7 for the industry, and those numbers resulted from 3.5 million fake accounts.

APS test scores not only met district goals, but wowed the rest of the education world. But the measurement is not a reflection of methodology; that is, the work that goes into achieving the results. Education critics have a saying: "A cow does not get fattened up by your weighing it all the time." The weight gives results, but does not reveal the steps that should be taken to ensure weight gain. Measuring the types of actions that are known to increase weight would be more productive and eliminate the manipulation of the output numbers. All incentives should focus on behavioral change, not output number measurements. Checking on the cow's nutritional intake, not its daily weight will ensure that the weight is there, sans measurement. If behaviors drive the results or cause the shortfalls on goals, then changing behaviors will change the numbers. We measure output without understanding what actually produces those measurements and how to improve those production steps.

In rethinking incentives, focus on the desired outcome first; and then determine what behaviors will get you to that outcome. If the outcome sought is better-educated students, the questions to answer are:

How do students learn?
What steps do other countries take in producing higher test scores than in the United States?

Incentivize the behaviors that are proven to lead to the desired outcome. For example, one clear difference between the United States and countries that have higher test scores is work done outside the classroom. The old adage of practice makes perfect has solid research behind it. Homework assignments – homework that is focused on substantive learning and not projects – are a measurable behavior. For those schools struggling with difficult conditions in students' homes that make homework problematic, incentives for after-school programs and teacher involvement in outside-the-classroom efforts will not only help students learn but also play a role of stability in the lives of those students whose parents are not engaged in their education. Knowledge and ability drive test scores. The test scores are the outcome; the behaviors are teaching techniques and homework. Moving the focus from measuring output to measuring behaviors also changes the culture from one that drives scores and resulting manipulation to one that drives learning.

A business case study in how focusing on behaviors can result in goals being met comes from Paul O'Neill's tenure as CEO of Alcoa. When he became CEO, he found that the company was meeting all of its safety goals; as measured by all-work-injury-rates, lost work days, and all the usual, albeit facile, measurements of safety. However, he also felt that reaching goals that were as good as the employer average or those of the industry was not enough, because Alcoa employees were still being injured. O'Neill changed the safety record of Alcoa by focusing on behaviors. He introduced a requirement for daily reports on every injury at every plant (175) globally. O'Neill and his staff began analyzing the incidents for common threads and universal application. He then held weekly conference calls with managers from the plants to review the incidents, accidents, and their recommendations for changes that could be implemented to prevent injuries. Managers around the world therefore knew about every injury and the vetted steps to take to prevent that type of injury in the future. The result was that Alcoa employees met the safety goals that had previously been labeled unrealistic. The focus was on their behavior with regard to injuries. The changed behaviors addressed safety; and the numbers followed.

11.2.2 Like Parents with Teens: MBWA and the Pulse of the Culture

Compliance, training, and obligatory safety moments cannot compensate for a culture that is driven by numerical goals and performance measurements. Measuring ethics training, compliance activities, hotline reports, and ethics codes will not give you the story of your culture. In determining whether there is a disconnect between actual performance and the reported numbers, observation is the key. The 1970s theory of management by walking around should not have been shelved as it was decades ago. Management by walking around (MBWA) is perhaps the only way to learn what culture is doing and what it has done to values in the organization. For example, an insurance company CEO could not understand why claims adjustors were not following the company's new edict of, "Pay the claim." The edict was issued as a way of building good customer relations and long-term loyalty of those customers. Its core principles were to get claims processed as quickly as possible, avoid technicalities, and base the payment on a determination of good faith of the claimant. Yet, when the CEO and other executives visited a claims call center, what they heard were claims adjustors using proof requirements, procedures, and additional documentation to avoid paying the claim. There was a disconnect between the behaviors the management team wanted (pay the claim and use good faith) and what the adjustors were doing. The reason was simple: the adjustors were measured in job performance and awarded bonuses based on their ability to delay claims and reduce payouts. The culture, based on performance and incentive measurements, had devoured the strategy of winning over customers for the long term.

A better measurement would have been examining the work of the adjustors along with surveying the customers to find out what their experience with claims was really like. If the goal is long-term loyalty, determining customer experiences and attitudes are the means for discovering behaviors and a path to an incentive system that focuses on those behaviors.

If regulators are issuing citations for an organization's violations in operations, the question for managers is: why are employees skirting the rules, policies, and procedures? Akin to parents returning home early to check on teenage behavior, surprise visits provide information, insights, and the fodder for change. O'Neill visited all 175 Alcoa plants to observe first-hand the behaviors of employees. These observations are a thumb on the pulse of the culture. One behavior to incentivize is measuring the number of unplanned and unscheduled interactions managers and supervisors have in their facilities and with their employees; as reflected in reports that they develop on what they learned and what changes need to be made. The bonus pool is then released based on how well the managers and supervisors are observing and documenting what they witness in the field, and making the resulting necessary changes.

Managers who witness the slippage on safety, rules, regulations, and processes can make changes in real time. Culture does not change overnight. Visits allow for spotting trends, and trends can be stopped before the culture is infiltrated. For example, in the Upper Branch Mine explosion that resulted in the death of twenty-nine miners was the result of chronic pressure to meet coal output goals. Former Massey Coal CEO Don Blankenship demanded hourly faxes of coal production from all of the company's mines. However, the pressure for production took a toll on regulatory compliance, particularly in the area of safety. The federal government had issued sixty-one withdrawal orders at the mine in both 2009 and 2010. That was a rate nineteen times the national average for coal mines. A withdrawal occurs when federal inspectors inspect a mine and find it unsafe for occupancy, forcing an evacuation of all miners. Internal safety employees at Upper Branch had expressed concerns about poor ventilation and noted that the company was "cheating" in taking its samples of the presence of coal dust. The equipment for spreading limestone, which keeps the coal dust down, was in poor condition and often not working. All of these behaviors could have been spotted in a single surprise visit to the mine and a few short conversations with the miners.

At the Upper Branch Mine, the pursuit of production goals trumped compliance and safety. The end results – beyond the explosion and tragic deaths – were criminal convictions of managers and the CEO, the shuttering of the mine, criminal penalties of \$210 million, and the sale of Massey to a competitor. The story of the Upper Branch Mine and Massey Coal is one of the culture consuming ethics. The drive for sales quotas, production, revenue, share price, and a host of other financial goals consumes compliance and ethics, unless incentive structure is changed from outcome measurement to behavior measurement, including unplanned and unscheduled interactions.

11.3 Figure Out How Employees Are Reaching Goals and Meeting Numbers

A study by Louis Grossman and this author, of companies that had been able to pay dividends for 100 years (or more) without interruption, found amazingly consistent threads in management behaviors. One such behavior is that they not only understood what their performance numbers were, they knew how those numbers were produced. Former Securities Exchange Commission official Gary Lynch once said, "You have to understand *how* people are making money" (Grossman and Jennings, 2002). Pick up any 10-K for a publicly traded company and you can find creative, albeit accounting compliant, methods being used to show phenomenal earnings. But WorldCom, Enron, HealthSouth, Madoff Securities, GE, and Tesla teach us that those numbers may not tell the full financial story.

Some airlines appear to have phenomenal on-time performance rates, until we learn that they do not include in that computation their regional flights that are operated under their name but by third parties. Their records on regional flights are full of significant delays. Airlines' rates for reports of lost luggage also seem inconsistent with our personal experiences. We learn that when the airlines have lost a bag, they contact the passengers immediately to ask them where to deliver their luggage. Because the passengers know that the airline is aware of their lost bag situation, they do not file a lost-luggage report. The airlines pre-emptively cut off the reports to garner a low lost-luggage rate. The numbers are meaningless until we know the computation methodology.

For example, part of the Affordable Care Act included monetary incentives and penalties. Those who designed the incentive/penalty structure assumed behaviors in health care delivery would change with resulting cost reductions. Part of the incentive/penalty program was the Hospital Readmissions Reduction Program (HRRP). The goal was to have providers reduce the number of Medicare/Medicaid readmissions and the vicious cycle of repeat patient hospitalizations. The cost of patient readmissions is high. To implement the system, the HRRP program developers imposed a penalty system for readmission on the hospitals. If the hospital rate for hospitalization exceeded the national average, the hospital's share of Medicare payments was reduced. Since the implementation of the program, the federal government has imposed penalties on 79 percent of hospitals for higher-than-average readmission rates; with an average penalty of 0.74 percent of all Medicare payments (penalties can go up to 2 percent of all Medicare payments).

The assumption by the program developers was that hospitals would work to be sure that there was no need for patient readmission. The belief was that new strategies – such as clear discharge instructions for post-hospitalization care and direct connection with primary care physicians who could manage post-release care – would be used to prevent the need for readmission. Since the system was implemented in 2013, it is true that the readmissions rate has gone down to 18.4 percent from 20 percent. On paper and initial examination, strategies had indeed been implemented and the goal of reduced readmissions was achieved. However, a study published in the *Journal of the American Medical Association* (*JAMA*), found (in a study of 115,245 Medicare patients) that during the same period the thirty-day mortality rate for the heart patients in the study increased from 7.2 percent to 8.6 percent – about 5,400 additional deaths per year (Dharmarajan et al., 2017). (Perhaps the most interesting aspect of the study is the accompanying *JAMA* editorial, which concludes that the readmission incentives and penalty program did not result in increased mortality rates for other hospitalizations and that the strategies of successful hospital should be implemented. The editorial downplayed the heart patients' increased mortality rate, and no reference was made to the possibility of employees gaming the system.) The readmission rate fell by 0.9 percent, but the mortality rate rose. The ethical issues surrounding the patients' best interests were consumed by a culture that gamed the Medicare system. Medical professionals, including those who took the Hippocratic Oath, used observation stays, delaying admissions, or referring the Medicare patients to the emergency staff in order to avoid penalties. In many cases, the cost of trying to avoid readmission penalties was the patients' health. The penalties were powerful motivators and sufficient to impair judgment on best approaches for patient care. As with all phenomenal results, the numbers simply were not real.

Be suspicious of numbers, computation formulas, and those who do the computing. Delve into the metrics and methodology, especially when the numbers are good. *You cannot improve what you are lying to yourself about.* Prepositional endings aside, there is a level of insight and wisdom in that thought. That phrase might also find attribution to Peter Drucker one day.

11.4 Tie Your Audit Plan to Goals, Measurements, and Results

Careful review of audit plans is a key component in integrating ethical values into the culture. Good audit plans focus on whether employees are gaming the system when it comes to goal achievement. One of the goals of an audit plan should be examination of the "hows" of reaching numbers. Without this audit, check-and-balance creativity grows with the numbers because, as noted, once the cheating starts, you cannot stop because the beginning measuring points were skewed. Not addressing the gaming methodology means that the inaccuracy of the numbers grows in organizations that meet those numeric goals.

Audit plans should be tied to verification of numbers used for metrics. For example, one tool auditors use often is comparing organizational metrics with other similar organizations. In Wells Fargo, a good auditor's interest would have been piqued by the amazing products per customer number Wells enjoyed vs. the industry average that was one-third of the Wells number. Is Wells a three times better bank? Are employees at Wells three times better than employees at other banks? Are Wells products and services three times better than competitors?

The benefit of a case study such as Wells is the ability to spot the signals that emerged over the years that indicated problems with the account numbers and services in retail banking. The following timeline indicates the year and the type of information that was available at the bank, information that should have triggered further audit examination:

2000 – sixty-three employee internal reports of "gaming the system" on new accounts

2002 – all employees in a Colorado branch issued debit cards that customers did not request

2004 – 680 employee internal reports of "gaming the system"

2007 – 288 allegations of employee sales misconduct in second quarter

2007 – report of a branch manager

Teen daughter had twenty-four accounts

Adult daughter had eighteen accounts

Husband had twenty-one accounts

Brother had fourteen accounts

Father had four accounts

2008 – discovery that customers with new accounts had "noname@wellsfargo.com" e-mail addresses

2013 – employees talked a homeless woman into opening six checking and savings accounts, costing $39 per month (Los Angeles City Attorney announces investigation)

2013 – 1,469 internal allegations of employee sales misconduct in fourth quarter

2013 – Wells fires 1 percent of its employees annually for ethics violations related to gaming the system (CEO called it "immaterial" and cited it as good news)

2016 – two million fake accounts discovered

2017 – another 1.4 million questionable accounts found.

The lessons learned from this timeline provide a framework for the audit function related to incentive programs correlated to performance goals. The first lesson is that audits are necessary. The second lesson is that when employees are raising questions about the legitimacy of the numbers of accounts and account services being reported, auditors should be reviewing the accounts, calling the account holders, and verifying the information provided for those accounts. A sampling of employees with the highest numbers reported and a follow-up with their account holders was a path to uncovering the problems. A sampling of customers with new accounts and new account services can uncover such deeds early on in the investigation.

The newspaper coverage of the homeless having Wells accounts was a red flag. If the story is true, Wells has a problem. If the story is false, documenting it as such is necessary for the bank's reputation. The terminations in 2013 may have been immaterial in a quantitative sense, but were material in a qualitative sense and revealing in terms of the incentive program.

Sadly, the Wells story is indicative of the other organizational ethical debacles that grace the headlines. There are no organizational ethical issues that make it into the headlines that do not have similar timelines to Wells – timelines that show weaknesses in audit reviews. For example, the following timeline indicates the period of time during which the Volkswagen falsified emissions program evolved and grew:

1973 – paid fine of $120,000 for installing "defeat device" that shut down pollution control devices in cars

1998 – $1 billion settlement with the Environmental Protection Agency (EPA) for software on truck engines with "defeat devices"

2009 – clean diesel announced

2010 – CEO speech: "By 2018, we want to take our group to the very top of the global car industry"

2010 – software added to cars to defeat emissions tests

2010 – EU finds emissions discrepancies

2012 – promise by leadership to cut emissions 30 percent by 2015

2013 – California tests begin

2014–2015 – Volkswagen challenges findings; engineers admit software installation

2016 – criminal indictments; billions in settlements

2017– guilty pleas; employees testify that knowledge of deception was widespread

Note that the problems with emissions were resulting in fines for Volkswagen as early as 1973. One of the critical audit flags in this timeline is the 2010 announcement of the CEO: that Volkswagen wanted to be the number one car company in the world by 2018, with its strategy being to use its diesel vehicles to meet that goal. Pressure increased in 2012 with the promise to also cut emissions by 30 percent. The software was added that year because employees could not see a path to meeting the strategic goal without some type of manipulation. Audit plans should focus on the numbers reported in response to management's strategic goals. Auditors should focus on the "how" behind the numbers.

Another audit flag in the timeline is the need for auditors to determine whether the board and all of senior management are aware of regulatory violations, fines, and settlements. The regulatory issues evolving in the Volkswagen case were the very same regulatory issues that resulted in the recalls, fines, and criminal charges.

These are the areas that reveal the impact of numbers pressure in the organization on the ethical culture. Meeting the strategic goals is the obsession and that success compensates for the ethical lapses used in the process. Careful audit plans, including a component for examining goals, also place a thumb on the pulse of culture and whether it is creating ethical lapses.

11.5 Watch What You Say and Don't Say

In a culture driven by goals and incentives, there are often what are referred to as management mantras. These are the motivational phrases repeated by management, printed on posters, and used as a central focus in performance evaluations and incentive plans. The following is a collection of motivational mantras, with some identified by organization.

"No exceptions. No excuses." (Atlanta Public Schools)
"Failure is not an option." (NASA)
"Sharpen your pencil!"
"The Power of Yes." (Washington Mutual)
"Do whatever it takes to make Uber a success." (Uber)
"Growth, Above All Else." (Uber)
"Find a way."
"Do whatever it takes."
"Go the extra mile."
"100% results, all the time."
"Extra effort, extraordinary results."
"Staying at number 1."
"Margins matter."
"Committed to deliver despite all obstacles." (CDDAO)

"On time, every time." (Southwest Airlines)
"Achieve the edge."
"70% Comfort. 100% Alignment"
"Never question success." (Kidder Peabody)
"Fire, Ready, Aim!" (Zenefits)
"Go for Gr-eight!" (Wells Fargo mantra for every employee to achieve eight
    products per customer)

A glance at the list provides some insights. There is plenty of room for
employee interpretation on what is permitted in achieving goals – that is, do
whatever it takes. Many of the organizations had ethical difficulties. Washington
Mutual's mantra for its loan officers may have been overly broad. Given the
institution's collapse, perhaps no would have been a better answer for its questionable loans. Imagine an organization in which only 70 percent of the employees are comfortable with decisions but all of them are willing to go along. Failure
is not an option, except in real business life. Some customers go with another
company. Sometimes there is a bad quarter. The constant repetition of the mantras
provides employees with the license to cross ethical, and, sadly, in too many case,
legal lines.

Mantras can be kept in check if managers caution employees about limitations.
Leaders establish parameters for the mantras. The claw-backs of Dodd-Frank
have been a perceived scourge in the business world. However, the number of
restatements by public companies has declined, the amounts in those restatements
is smaller (often immaterial), and most restatements are made voluntarily and not
as a result of Security and Exchange Commission (SEC) investigations. In other
words, we behave when we know the boundaries. When we repeat, "Get to yes,"
we add, "But not at the expense of sound lending." If we chant, "Do whatever it
takes," we add, "But remember our core value of 'Always honest.'" Paul O'Neill,
upon visiting Alcoa plants, told managers not to cheerlead or bludgeon employees
into zero lost-work days. He told them that he never wanted to see a trade-off
between values and economics, and added that they should not budget for safety.
The mantras of earnings, results, and performance require counterbalancing
repetitions that focus on ethical parameters.

References

Dharmarajan, K. et al. (2017). Association of changing hospital readmission rates with
    partial mortality rates after hospital discharge. *Journal of American Medical Associ-
    ation*, 318(31), 270–278.
Drucker, P. F. (2001). *The essential Drucker*. New York, NY: HarperCollins.
Grossman, L., & Jennings, M. M. (2002). *Building a business through good times and bad*
    (p. 166). Westport, CT: Quorum Books.

Jennings, M. (2017). *The Atlanta public school system: Good scores by creative teachers* (p. 343). Business ethics: Case studies and readings. Boston, MA: Cengage.

Lagace, M. (2002). Paul O'Neill: Values in action, *Working Knowledge*, Harvard Business School. Retrieved from https://hbswk.hbs.edu/archive/paul-o-neill-values-into-action

Mason, S. (2000). Performance-based planning for hospitals. *Health Care Strategic Management*, *12*(14), 14.

Schein, E. (1985). *Organizational culture and leadership* (pp. 33–34). San Francisco, CA: Jossey-Bass.

Zemke, R., & Schaaf, D. (1989). *The service edge*. London: Penguin.

12

How Next-Generation Teams and Teaming May Affect the Ethics of Working in Teams

Scott S. Wiltermuth and Alyssa J. Han

12.1 Introduction

The way people work in teams is changing. The changes are affecting what work teams look like and how those teams function. In years past people worked for the same organizations for many years, perhaps even their whole careers (see Sullivan, 1999 for review). Because their colleagues also stayed in the same organizations for many years, they were likely to work on teams that had relatively stable memberships. This has changed. People now switch employers more frequently and they change roles within organizations more often (Miles & Snow, 1996; Rousseau & Wade-Benzoni, 1995). They are also more likely to work as independent contractors rather than as employees of the company and seek to develop a "boundaryless career" defined as "a sequence of job opportunities that go beyond the boundaries of a single employment setting" (DeFillippi & Arthur, 1996, p. 116).

These trends have accelerated over the last couple of decades (Edmondson, 2012). More recently, organizations have even ramped up their use of "flash teams," which may not ever meet physically and may exist only for a short and, often, pre-defined amount of time (Retelny et al., 2014). These teams exist to achieve specific objectives and their members go their separate ways right after the specific task is accomplished. In many cases there is no expectation of a future work relationship and the only way people have communicated with their team-mates is electronically. As such, the concept of working in a team may mean something very different in the coming years than it did twenty years ago, or even than it does today.

Scholars have devoted considerable attention to how these changing relationships with teammates can influence people's ability to coordinate and collaborate effectively with each other (e.g., Edmonson, 2012; Tannenbaum, Mathieu, Salas, & Cohen, 2012). Scholars have also studied how these changes affect people's satisfaction with their work (e.g., Altman & Post, 1996). Much less attention has been paid to how the changing nature of teams may affect the ethics involved with working on those teams (but see Tannenbaum & Valentine, in press). We focus in this chapter on that question.

We examine the ethical implications of changing team dynamics for a couple of reasons. First, we believe it is important for organizations and managers to understand how their employees or contractors are likely to treat each other if they are concerned about the well-being of those employees or contractors. Organizations may use this information to set up systems and procedures to motivate their employees and contractors to play well with others. In essence they may be able to anticipate what external forces might be needed to replace internal pressures to treat each other decently, which may have been stronger when employees had more regular and closer contact with each other. Second, we believe that organizations may be able to take steps to improve the performance of their teams if they better understand how the ethical concerns guiding behavior are changing. Values like loyalty and fairness help teams work effectively. These values have led people to be more likely to sacrifice for the common good of the team. If these values are diminished when teams are more transient and team-mates have less physical contact with one another, organizations may need to design incentives or work processes to compensate for the diminished influence that ethical values may exert on team behavior.

We begin our analysis of how next-generation teams and teaming may affect the ethics of working in teams by first describing how the nature of teams is changing. We then examine which values are most likely affected by the changes in team structure and team processes. Specifically, we consider the values of fairness and loyalty, which are two of the core foundations of morality (Graham et al., 2013; Graham, Nosek, Haidt, Iyer, Koleva, & Ditto, 2011; Haidt & Graham, 2007). For each foundation we describe the likely change in influence the value may have on behavior and attitudes. Finally, we describe strategies for managers wishing to adapt to and cope with the changing role of each ethical concern.

12.1.1 How Teams Are Changing

Next-generation teams are unlikely to look like the teams of twenty years ago. Over the last thirty years society has seen a shift from people staying with employers for long tenures to people changing employers relatively frequently. Society has also seen a sharp increase in the percentage of people working as independent contractors, and a decline in the percentage of people who are employees per se of the companies for whom they are providing labor (Katz & Krueger, 2016). Teams have consequently come to have less stable memberships than they have had in the past.

The change from teams as they currently exist to what they look like in the not-so-distant future may be just as dramatic as the change has been over the last few decades. In Silicon Valley we are already starting to see the emergence of flash teams, which are temporary teams that pop up virtually to work on particular issues (Valentine, Retelny, To, Rahmati, Doshi, & Bernstein, 2017). Such teams come together quickly and they dissipate just as quickly as soon as the project for which they had assembled is finished. For some types of tasks, the quick assembly and the just-as-quick disassembly of the team is commonplace. Websites such as Mturk.com, Upwork, Elance, and others enable managers to outsource work to people whom they are not likely to meet. While most of the work completed on these websites is either complex work handled by individuals or simple work completed by a larger number of people, some websites have arisen in hopes of enabling companies to complete more complex tasks requiring teamwork without having either to physically assemble and hire teams or spend time working on contracts for the independent contractors. For example, the start-up company Foundry used its platform to show that it is possible to enable a group of specialized employees to complete interdependent work online to create short films in short time periods.

We expect the capacity of people to collaborate virtually and in teams constituted by unstable memberships to increase sharply over the next twenty years. Technological tools enabling such work will no doubt improve. Moreover, the people who have the talent to complete complex, interdependent work without spending significant time with their teammates will likely increasingly accept work opportunities over the Internet. There is consequently hope that these kinds of virtual teams with dynamic memberships will be tremendous tools. However, people working on these types of teams will no doubt face some predictable obstacles. For example, teams will likely struggle with coordination neglect (Crowston, 1997; Heath & Staudenmayer, 2000; Wageman, 1995) and the communication challenges brought about by forms of communication through relatively impoverished media, such as email (Daft & Lengel, 1984, 1986; Straus & McGrath, 1994). As significant research has shown, the potential for miscommunication can increase when people do not have an opportunity to spend time with each other and interact face-to-face. We also anticipate that people working on these teams will be subject to different ethical compulsions and hold different attitudes about what it means to be an ethical team member. We explore this issue in Section 12.2.

12.1.2 Dilemma of How to Use Next-Generation Teams with Attenuated Concerns About Ethics

We hypothesize that people on these short-lived teams, that may or may not interact primarily through electronic forms of communication, may face ethics-related challenges that are not experienced to the same extent by more traditional teams. So too may those who try to lead these teams. Managers and team members who want to take advantage of the power of these new forms of teams therefore face a dilemma. How does one motivate team members to cooperate fully with one another, subjugate their own individual interests, and contribute fully toward fulfilling the group's interest when so many of the forces that have driven these tendencies in traditional teams may be attenuated? How does one either instill a sense of loyalty among people who may never meet each other face-to-face or compensate for the attenuated loyalty that may result from the lack of face-to-face interaction? How does one get team members to regard resource and workload allocations as fair when there may not be a long term to smooth out inequities that may occur in the short term?

In the subsequent sections we examine which ethical values are likely to receive different degrees of emphasis in intragroup relationships as a result of teams becoming more temporary and less based on relationships that involve face-to-face interactions. We propose that people will come to view their teammates and/or their relationships to those teammates very differently when people enter and depart teams frequently and they have little real-world interaction with their teammates. We examine how the change in team dynamics are likely to affect the team's performance. Finally, we suggest strategies to cope with the potentially attenuated role that some ethical concerns might play in shaping team behavior.

12.2 Which Ethical Values Will Play Attenuated Roles in Shaping Team Behavior?

Moral foundations theory holds that people view morality as consisting of five distinct moral values (Haidt & Graham, 2007). These include harm, fairness, loyalty, authority, and sanctity. The latter three foundations are generally described as binding foundations that bring and hold social groups together, whereas the first two foundations describe concerns for the individual. It is possible that teams becoming more temporary and less likely to be rooted in real-world relationships could affect the degree to which team leaders and team members consider each of these foundations in determining how they should behave toward and with their teammates. However, we believe that concern with two particular foundations will be affected more than the other foundations will be affected. Specifically, we posit that the move to virtual, temporary teams will alter most how people on teams think about loyalty toward their teammates and what they perceive as fair. We therefore concentrate our analysis on these two moral foundations.

12.3 Loyalty

Loyalty can drive much of team behavior. Although loyalty has been conceptualized in various ways, at its core it can be understood as "the principle of partiality towards an object (e.g., a group) that gives rise to expectations of behavior on behalf of that object such as sacrifice, trustworthiness, and pro-sociality" (Hildreth, Gino, & Bazerman, 2016, p. 17). When the object of one's loyalty is a group, loyalty manifests in forms of behavior that further the interests of the group, even if those behaviors involve personal sacrifice (Hildreth et al., 2016; Schrag, 2001; Van Vugt & Hart, 2004; Zdaniuk & Levine, 2001). These behaviors can range from the highly ethical, such as engaging in prosocial acts on behalf of one's team members, to the highly unethical, such as cheating on behalf of one's team. The common denominator is that these behaviors are motivated by a desire to further the interests of the group.

Previous work on group loyalty has primarily examined teams with traditional stable structures (Tannenbaum, Mathieu, Salas, & Cohen, 2012). The characteristics of traditional teams that once gave rise to loyalty or the expectation of loyalty from others may exist to lesser degrees in temporary teams and virtual teams. We therefore revisit the role that loyalty is expected to play within such teams in order to better understand the ethics-related challenges that managers might now face.

12.3.1 Catalyzing Pro-Group Behavior

People in next-generation teams will likely have less exposure to their fellow team members than they did in traditional teams (Hackman, 1987, 2012; Tannenbaum et al., 2012; Wageman, Gardner, & Mortensen, 2012). Whether this is due to the temporary nature of the team or the lack of face-to-face interaction in virtual teams, the outcome is that people lack shared time and experiences with their team members. Members of temporary and virtual teams are consequently less likely to build social bonds with one another than members of traditional stable teams. Given that "loyalties develop over time because of a continuity of overlapping, shared experiences of the same place or persons or events," these short-lived teams and virtual teams lack the very characteristics necessary for loyalties to develop among team members (Schrag, 2001, p. 44). The knowledge that future collaboration with one's current teammates is limited also likely hinders the development of loyalty. Without the expectation of future reciprocity and accountability, team members are less likely to develop a sense of trust, which is an important component of loyalty (Hildreth et al., 2016; Schrag, 2001).

One likely consequence of this attenuated loyalty is that team members may become less willing to exert extra effort on behalf of their team. Extra-role behaviors are those employee behaviors that go above and beyond the job expectations, such as helping out a team member by taking on extra work or voicing methods for improvement (Katz & Kahn, 1966; Morrison & Phelps, 1999; Organ, 1988, 1997; Smith, Organ, & Near, 1983; Van Dyne & LePine, 1998). Researchers have long recognized the importance of employee extra-role behaviors in contributing to the viability and success of groups and organizations (Katz & Kahn, 1966; Morrison & Phelps, 1999; Organ, 1988).

Heightened group identification increases employees' willingness to perform extra-role behaviors (Blader & Tyler, 2009; O'Reilly & Chatman, 1986; Van Vugt & Hart, 2004; Zdaniuk & Levine, 2001). According to social identity theory and self-categorization theory, group identification results from individuals perceiving themselves as belonging to some human aggregate (Ashforth & Mael, 1989; Hogg & Terry, 2000; Mael & Ashforth, 1992; Tajfel & Turner, 1979; Turner, Hogg, Oakes, Reicher, & Wetherell, 1987). As individuals identify with a particular group, they not only come to define themselves in terms of their group membership, but they also begin to personally experience the successes and failures of the group as their own (Ashforth & Mael, 1989). Unsurprisingly then, individuals become inherently concerned with the welfare of the team when they strongly identify with it.

In traditional teams, the stability of the team structure facilitates the development of identification with and loyalty to one's team. Stability therefore increases the likelihood that team members will in turn engage in these extra-role behaviors. However, the same cannot be said for temporary and virtual teams. To the extent that members of these new types of teams are less likely to develop loyalty to their team, there is little to motivate such members to engage in extra-role behaviors on behalf of the team. Managers may even find that members are less motivated to fulfill their prescribed duties and more likely to free-ride when possible. We discuss this problem of free-riding in greater detail in a later section.

One positive outcome of diminished loyalty, however, is that team members may become less likely to cheat on behalf of their teams. Research has shown that people are more likely to cheat when the beneficiaries of their wrongdoing include other individuals besides themselves (Gino, Ayal, & Ariely, 2013; Gino & Pierce, 2009; Wiltermuth, 2011). In fact, people become more likely to cheat as the number of beneficiaries of their wrongdoing increases (Gino et al., 2013). Researchers have also found that employees are often willing to engage in unethical behaviors on behalf of their organizations (Chen, Chen, & Sheldon, 2016; Thau, Derfler-Rozin, Pitesa, Mitchell, & Pillutla, 2015; Umphress & Bingham, 2011; Umphress, Bingham, & Mitchell, 2010). Whereas cheating for one's own gain tarnishes one's own self-image, people find it easier to justify unethical behavior when such behavior is done for the benefit of others (Wiltermuth, 2011). This is even more likely to be the case when people feel a greater connection to or identification with the potential beneficiaries of their unethical acts (Chen et al., 2016; Gino & Pierce, 2009; Umphress et al., 2010). With the change from traditional team structures to temporary and virtual team structures, as team members have less contact with one another and less opportunities to develop social bonds with one another, they may also be less motivated to commit unethical acts on behalf of their team. Therefore, the diminishing loyalty in temporary and virtual teams may reduce people's willingness to engage in pro-group behaviors that are unethical in nature.

12.3.2 Deterring Team Abandonment

Traditionally, scholars characterized teams as a bounded set of individuals (Hackman, 1987, 2012; Tannenbaum et al., 2012; Wageman et al., 2012). However, temporary teams, flash teams, and virtual teams are more likely to have fluid memberships, with people coming and going more frequently than before (Hackman, 2012; Tannenbaum et al., 2012; Wageman et al., 2012). When the composition of teams changes so frequently, it may even become difficult for individuals to identify who is actually a member of one's team (Wageman, Nunes, Burruss, & Hackman, 2008). The consequence of having such fluidity in membership is that team members may become even less likely to identify with and develop loyalty to their team given that the team is constantly changing.

Even when membership is not fluid, temporary teams and virtual teams may nevertheless have ambiguous boundaries. Such ambiguity is especially likely in – but certainly not limited to – cases in which team members are geographically dispersed, as with virtual teams (Mortensen & Hinds, 2002). Members might not only experience difficulty identifying other members of the team but also disagree among one another as to who are and who are not members of the team (Mortensen, 2014). In certain situations, individuals might even fail to recognize that they themselves are a part of a team. In ad-hoc teams, while there may be a number of people who are working towards the same goal, each individual might perform his/her respective job individually. These individuals may consequently fail to recognize that they themselves are working as part of a team to accomplish a common goal. For example, researcher Amy Edmondson (2012) narrates a scenario in a hospital in which multiple different health care specialists each individually attend to the same patient as they prep the patient for a CT scan. In a series of discrete steps, each specialist completes a separate task. Altogether the work is interdependent since each step depends upon the successful execution of the former (by a different specialist) and therefore requires a certain level of coordination to provide proper patient care. However, due to the nature of their work, these health professionals may have very little direct interaction with one another. They may therefore not even see themselves as part of a team (Edmondson, 2012).

Scholars have suggested that in order to identify with a particular group, not only do individuals need to feel that they belong within the group, but they also require a clear sense of boundaries that differentiate their own group from other groups (Brewer, 1991, 1999). Without clear delineation of group boundaries, compounded by the fluidity of membership, individuals may be more likely to experience uncertainty regarding membership – whether one's own or that of other potential team members. In turn, this uncertainty is expected to hinder the development of loyalty and attachment to one's team.

The danger of this is that temporary and virtual teams may be more likely to suffer from what researchers have called the exit problem (Van Vugt & Hart,

2004). When team members do not experience loyalty to their team, they become more likely to leave the group at will, which can potentially lead to a loss of valuable human capital. Researchers have demonstrated that individuals who strongly identify with a group are more willing to stay with that group, even when doing so would not be personally beneficial to themselves (Van Vugt & Hart, 2004; Zdaniuk & Levine, 2001). On the other hand, those who do not strongly identify with a group are likely to abandon the group once it benefits them to do so, even at the expense of the remaining members. The fuzzy boundaries and fluid membership of next-generation teams may lead individuals to feel greater license to leave the team at will.[1]

12.3.3 Multiple Team Membership and the Devaluation of Community

With temporary teams and virtual teams, individuals may also be more likely to feel a lack of commitment to one specific team. As such, individuals may be more likely to join multiple teams at once. Research has shown that multiple team membership – a situation in which individuals are members of two or more teams concurrently – is more common than expected (O'Leary, Mortensen, & Woolley, 2011; Tannenbaum et al., 2012). Unfortunately, multiple team membership is likely to pose challenges to the development of familiarity and trust within a given team (Mortensen, Woolley, & O'Leary, 2007). In part, this may be due to the fact that individuals who are a part of multiple teams now have these various teams competing for group identification and loyalty (O'Leary et al., 2011). Individuals who are a part of multiple teams may also have less time and energy to devote to a particular team. Given the time constraints arising from multiple team commitments, team members are likely to be more task-focused rather than relationship-focused when working as part of any given team (Pluut, Flestea, & Curseu, 2014). As a result, managers of such teams may be more likely to encounter greater challenges to fostering social bonds and loyalty among team members.

Individuals are likely to experience a decreased sense of commitment to social groups regardless of whether they belong to too many teams or they fail to recognize that they are part of a team. People may come to devalue community and loyalty as they begin to adopt more of an individualistic mindset in their jobs. In turn, a widespread increase in the adoption of individualistic mindsets could contribute to an erosion of the social capital – including social networks and norms of reciprocity – that is essential for cooperation (Putnam, 2000). As people adopt an individualistic concept of work, managers may encounter an exacerbation of existing challenges like coordination neglect (Heath & Staudenmayer, 2000). Team members may become slower to develop loyalties and quicker to abandon them, and the noncommittal nature of these next-generation teams may further perpetuate the challenge to team loyalty.

12.3.4 Team Heterogeneity

Temporary and virtual teams are much more likely to be comprised of members of diverse backgrounds than traditional teams (Edmondson, 2012; Tannenbaum et al., 2012; Townsend, DeMarie, & Hendrickson, 1998). Members are likely to vary widely in terms of geographic location, demographic characteristics, cultural backgrounds, and their areas of expertise (Edmondson, 2012). These factors matter because group heterogeneity can have a negative impact on group cohesion and cooperation (Chatman & Flynn, 2001; Harrison, Price, & Bell, 1998). People often classify themselves and others into groups on the basis of perceived similarity (Ashforth & Mael, 1989; Hogg & Terry, 2000; Mael & Ashforth, 1992; Tajfel & Turner, 1979; Turner et al., 1987). People will perceive similar individuals as ingroup members and dissimilar individuals as outgroup members (Hogg & Terry, 2000; Tajfel & Turner, 1979; Turner et al., 1987). As such, when people are members of heterogeneous teams comprised of a number of dissimilar others, they may be less likely to identify with their team as a whole. Ingroups and outgroups may form even within a single team, with members displaying favoritism and loyalty towards certain members and not others.

Additionally, team heterogeneity may pose a challenge to rallying team members around common norms and values. Due to the diverse backgrounds, team members may be accustomed to different cultural and workplace norms, as well as different moral beliefs (Edmondson, 2012). For instance, members might not only differ in terms of their beliefs on right and wrong, but they may also weigh different moral values to varying extents (Graham, Haidt, & Nosek, 2009; Haidt & Graham, 2007). Such differences are likely to cause tensions and conflict among team members. Without team loyalty serving as a unifying force, managers may experience greater difficulty establishing common ground among members on such issues.

When team members have little exposure to one another in temporary heterogeneous teams, it may actually be possible that the lack of identification with the team will serve as a barrier to the contagion of unethical behavior within the team. Research has shown that when people witness an individual behaving unethically, they become more likely to behave unethically themselves only when they perceive that individual as an ingroup member. When people perceive the individual as an outgroup member, they become less likely to behave unethically themselves, due to a desire to differentiate themselves from the "bad apple" (Brewer, 1993; Gino, Ayal, & Ariely, 2009; Tajfel & Turner, 1986). To the extent that individuals in heterogeneous teams are less likely to perceive other team members as ingroup members, this may help to diminish the spreading of unethical behavior within the team. Additionally, whereas a sense of loyalty to one's team member might prevent one from doing so, in temporary and virtual teams, individuals may be more willing to report the unethical behavior of others (Waytz, Dungan, & Young, 2013). Of course, whether a team member would actually go out of his/her way to do so is uncertain, given that the reporting of unethical behavior is usually a form of an extra-role behavior, which, as previously discussed, is expected to become less likely with the attenuation of loyalty in these next-generation teams (Brief & Motowidlo, 1986; Trevino & Victor, 1992).

12.4 Fairness

People managing next-generation temporary teams and teams that interact mostly in virtual contexts also likely face different issues regarding the fairness of work and rewards than people managing traditional teams have historically faced. We will now consider a number of these issues.

12.4.1 Fairness As a Constraint on Free-Riding and Social Loafing

The emergence of temporary teams and teams that exist primarily on a virtual basis likely also has important consequences for how people on the team think about fairness. As discussed in Section 12.3 on loyalty, people will likely have less concern about how their actions impact other team members because their relationships with those team members are not as developed. This may be the case regardless of whether the team exists almost entirely as a virtual team or the team is temporary and people do not have much time to develop social bonds with their teammates. People feel worse about letting others down or free-riding off of others' efforts when they have had personal contact with their team members than they do when they do not know them. Indeed, over 100 studies have shown that people free-ride less often and cooperate more often when they have a chance to socialize with other team members (e.g., Deutsch, 1958; for review see Sally, 1995). Studies have similarly shown that people engage in more free-riding behavior in virtual teams than they do in face-to-face teams (Chidambaram & Tung, 2005). In short, the compelling force of wanting to be fair to one's team members may therefore not be so compelling in an environment in which one does not know the people who would suffer from the free-riding or social loafing.

However, people may not only become more likely to free-ride in temporary teams or virtual teams simply because they have less concern for harming people that they don't know. Instead, they may exert less effort because they may perceive there to be less accountability for actions in that environment. They may therefore expect others to contribute less to the collective effort. This expectation could make them feel like a "sucker" if they end up contributing more to the common effort than others do (Kerr, 1983; Mulvey & Klein, 1998; Orbell & Dawes, 1981; Schnake, 1991). Opposition to this potential inequity and the feeling that one has been taken advantage of by team members may lead people who would otherwise give their all to the collective effort to hold back. Thus, it may not be less concern for teammates but a lowered trust in teammates that could lead people to refrain from exerting as much effort toward the collective goal as they might if they had longer and face-to-face relationships with their teammates.

This concern about people not contributing to the common effort may be particularly acute in tasks in which either individual effort or the result of individual effort is hard to measure. In such settings, people feel less accountable for their actions. This may tempt people to get away with social loafing in such teams because the probability of negative consequences arising from free-riding would be diminished. In such settings people may also perceive that their teammates will feel that they will be less accountable for their actions. As such, a lack of accountability could lead people both to feel uninhibited about free-riding because of diminished concern for teammates and to make people perceive that those teammates will free-ride themselves.

Free-riding may also be a particularly important concern for next-generation teams in which roles are ambiguous, to the extent that the role ambiguity makes contributions less identifiable. When the contributions of individual group members become less identifiable free-riding becomes more likely (Harkins, 1987; Stroebe, Diehl, & Abakoumkin, 1996). When roles are ambiguous people may not only be able to shield themselves from accountability but also genuinely construe tasks as being outside of their jobs.

Alternatively, it is also possible that the ambiguous roles may lead people to take on an increased sense of responsibility for team success if the ambiguity of roles makes them feel either more in control of the work that they do or more involved in numerous significant aspects of the team's process. Research on the job characteristics model holds that autonomy and task variety can each heighten workers' intrinsic motivation to do a job well (Hackman & Oldman, 1976). The flexibility required of team members when there is not a formal structure to the teams and the roles are somewhat ambiguous may also help people feel like an indispensable member of the team. These feelings can also decrease free-riding and social loafing (Price, Harrison, & Gavin, 2006).

12.4.2 Divisions of Labor and Resources

People's fundamental attitudes about what divisions of labor and resources are fair could also start to change if they start working on temporary teams and do not have sufficient time to develop strong social bonds with one another. People make egocentric attributions of how much they contribute to common efforts because they have privileged access to their own thoughts and behaviors (Ross & Sicoly, 1979; Schwarz, Bless, Strack, Klumpp, Rittenauer-Schatka, & Simons, 1991). A lack of observability exacerbates egocentric perceptions of fairness (Thompson &

Loewenstein, 1992) because it means that team members do not have the impetus to correct their egocentric attributions of contributions and effort. This suggests that increased contact with others may make people more likely to accept labor splits if their increased contact with teammates reveals that team members are making contributions to the collective effort. For example, people may be opposed to splitting the marketing of a product between domestic and international markets because the task of marketing to the international market may seem more daunting. If, however, the person who is held responsible for the international marketing has an opportunity to see the nuances required in domestic marketing and the effort involved with it, her resistance to this division of labor may wane. We consequently propose that in ad-hoc teams and in teams that meet only virtually people might have less of an opportunity to observe what their teammates have to do; and they may therefore reject divisions of labor that they might otherwise have found acceptable if they had insight into the effort involved in fulfilling their teammates' responsibilities.

Of course, the transparent views that traditional teams offer into how much teammates are working can cut the other way. If one's teammates are slacking, that slacking may be more evident if one has the opportunity to work for longer stints with the teammate or in physical proximity to them. It is therefore possible that people may be more accepting of labor allocations that place more of a burden on themselves in temporary teams and teams that work virtually than they would be in more traditional teams.

We believe, however, that it is much more likely that people will be more willing to shoulder more of the load in traditional teams than they would be in temporary teams or in teams that only meet virtually. As already noted, the heightened transparency about how much teammates are working may either increase or decrease an individual's likelihood to shoulder a significant portion of the workload to be completed. However, the emotional connection that comes from frequent and meaningful contact would likely produce more directionally-consistent effects. In most cases social contact heightens empathy (for review see Davis, 2018) and people's willingness to sacrifice for the common good (for review see Sally, 1995). We would therefore expect that if people in next-generation teams have less contact with their teammates, they may be less willing to shoulder workloads that could be perceived as unfair.

These considerations raise the question of whether allocation norms should be different on next-generation teams than they should be on more traditional teams. Our intuition is that the amount of effort people contribute toward the team's goals may be more difficult to observe with next-generation teams than it would be in more traditional teams. If the productivity stemming from individuals' efforts are no more observable in these teams (and we have no reason to believe they would be), members of next-generation teams may have more objections to (and more support for) equity-based distribution than would members of teams in which effort would be more directly observable. We caution that our speculation may not hold if new technology enables people to measure individuals' efforts and contributions to team success. If so, people on next-generation teams may be more comfortable with equity norms than people on traditional teams have been.

12.4.3 Managing Fairness Across Projects

People managing traditional teams that work on several projects and have relatively stable memberships have a tool to ensure fairness that those managing temporary teams designed to work on a single project do not have. Specifically, they have the ability to manage fairness across projects.

On some projects, equal distribution of work may be either impractical or inefficient. This may occur for at least two reasons. First, it may make sense for one employee to take on a disproportionately large part of the task because the elements of that portion of the task are sufficiently connected that those elements are best performed by one person. Second, it may be that the learning acquired from completing one element of the task makes the marginal cost of completing the other elements of that portion of the task so low that it is logical for one person to complete all elements of that portion of the task.

If it is not practical to offer differential rewards that depend upon the amount of work an individual on a team takes on, people looking to create temporary teams may find themselves facing a challenge. According to equity theory (Walster, Walster, & Berscheid, 1978), the teammate who shoulders most of the load on that project may feel a sense of inequity in that ratio of effort to rewards will not seem commensurate to the ratio experienced by other team members. In traditional teams that handle numerous projects this issue is easier to fix. Managers can assign different allocations of work on the next project, such that in the long run the allocation of work responsibilities and benefits will even out. When there is no such option to even out the work across projects managers will likely be hamstrung in their ability to appear fair and just in their allocation of responsibilities.

12.4.4 Potential for Adverse Selection of People Joining Temporary and Virtual Teams

Managers assembling temporary teams or teams that will exist largely on a virtual basis alone might also need to think about selection in ways that differ from how they did so for more traditional teams. A number of characteristics related to the complementarity of team members may be more important when assembling teams that will have relatively stable memberships and interact with each other in face-to-face settings than when assembling teams that will be short-lived and/or exists primarily through virtual interactions. Personality mismatches, for example, may be more irksome when people have to interact regularly with their teammates.

However, managers assembling temporary teams, flash teams, or teams that meet only virtually may face a selection hazard faced less often by managers assembling more traditional teams. Potential team members may believe that an assignment to a virtual team or one that is only slated to exist for a relatively-short period of time will mean that they will be held less accountable for their work. They may also believe that the cost to contributing comparably little to a team's effort would be lower than it would be in a traditional team because employers or team members might be less able to punish this kind of social loafing or free-riding. People who are not particularly interested in contributing effort to the team's effort may become disproportionately more likely to apply to work on these sorts of teams. As such, people staffing these temporary teams may face an adverse selection issue in that they may be creating a moral hazard such that people who are lazy (but calculating) may be more likely than others to find their way onto such teams.

12.4.5 The Fairness of Dismissing Team Members

Although adverse selection issues may arise when people are staffing temporary teams, people hiring for such teams likely have other factors compensating for the risk of adverse selection. Consider what happens if a team adds a member who has some issues that detract from the team's performance. Regardless of whether the new team member lacks skill, effort, or just is a poor fit for the team, the people running the team may more easily rid themselves of the team member in the short term than would people running more traditional teams.

The status quo bias (Kahneman, Knetch, & Thaler, 1991) lies at the root of why this would be. If an employee has just a marginally negative impact on the team it may be socially costly for the people running a traditional team to let the employee go. Employee morale could suffer and people may develop animosity toward team management. The presumption in this case is that employees will work indefinitely and any decision to change that requires enough evidence to overcome people's natural bias to hold to the status quo, which in this case is ongoing employment. If, on the other hand, the team exists explicitly to handle a short-term project, people would be more likely to see the default outcome as employees working for a preset amount of time and leaving thereafter. Both the worker not remaining on the team and the team-mates of that person might find this outcome less bracing because having a contract not renewed may be seen as the default option that people should have been expecting. In short, team members may see teams letting people go as "fairer" when the team members believe that their tenure on teams will be time-bound.

12.5 Strategies to Adapt to Changing Ethics of Teams

In the previous sections we outlined a few key ways that the changing nature of teamwork is likely influencing the ethical concerns associated with working in teams. We have detailed how reductions in the amount of exposure people have with their teammates may change team members' views toward the importance of loyalty and how these reductions may also promote more egocentric views of fairness. The outlook we provide is not altogether bright – as we suggest that feelings of loyalty may be lower on next-generation teams than on traditional teams and that people may take others' perspectives less when assessing the fairness of work and resource distributions. Such changes, of course, do not bode well for the effectiveness of teams.

These predictions raise the question of what teams can do to compensate for the changes in how people view loyalty and fairness in teams. We would argue that the research literature on virtual, geographically-disparate teams provides many useful suggestions even for teams that do connect face-to-face but do not have long histories or long expected existences. Of course, next-generation teams are likely to differ from existing virtual teams. For example, the expected duration of teams' existences will differ, as will the degree of turnover on the team. As such, they face some different challenges. We will now provide some suggested ways to ameliorate the ethical challenges that next-generation teams are likely to present.

12.5.1 In-Person Initial Meetings

Studies have documented that initial in-person meetings can go a long way toward establishing trust within virtual teams (Hill, Bartol, Tesluk, & Langa, 2009; Rocco, 1998). Research has shown that the initial medium of communication among team members is important for the development of trust given that different communication mediums convey contextual information – such as behavioral cues – to varying degrees, with face-to-face communication offering the richest information (Daft & Lengel, 1984; Hill et al., 2009; Wilson, Straus, & McEvily, 2006). Introductory face-to-face meetings can function as a transition phase wherein team members can prepare for their upcoming work together (Hill et al., 2009). These meetings can help establish social norms of cooperation, and they may even go so far as to facilitate the development of a group identity (Rocco, 1998). In-person meetings may also deter behaviors like social loafing by eliminating team members' ability to hide behind anonymity. Those who create virtual teams may therefore find that scheduling introductory face-to-face meetings will increase trust, loyalty, and cooperation among team members.

12.5.2 Shifting the Target of Loyalty

If people have less loyalty to teams because they are having less contact with team members, it may be helpful to try to instill loyalty to a different target. More specifically, it may be helpful to try to instill loyalty to a target that is more constant than the unfamiliar and changing members of one's team. Leaders might try to build team loyalty by encouraging team members to identify with the team's shared vision or goal, rather than with one's team's members. By emphasizing the shared goal towards which team members are collectively working, leaders can foster team loyalty in the same way that social movements give rise to a collective identity (Polletta & Jasper, 2001).

Those leading teams could also exert efforts to build loyalty to the organization if the team members consistently work on teams within that same organization. As previous research has shown, there are a number of ways to heighten organizational identification and increase loyalty (Mael & Ashforth, 1992; Smidts, Pruyn, & Van Riel, 2001). For instance, leaders can emphasize the status and prestige of the organization to increase team members' sense of pride in being a part of such an organization. When team members come to identify with the same organization, they may experience a greater sense of group cohesion even when they do not have much contact with one another.

12.5.3 Appealing to Professionalism and Individualism

Building loyalty to the organization may not be as effective when organizations hire contractors who also work for many other organizations. In such cases, appealing to the professionalism of workers may be more effective. People assembling and organizing teams may productively remind employees that being a professional in their area entails both a strong work ethic and an ability to work well with others. In this way shirking duties or not extending maximum effort would transform from an indication of how much the individual cares about the project to a reflection of that worker's professionalism and perhaps even integrity.

In situations where team members have widely adopted an individualistic mindset of work, leaders may be able to reframe what such mindsets mean for workplace behavior. Leaders can speak to employees' individualistic mindsets by emphasizing the importance of taking ownership of one's own actions and considering the consequences – both positive and negative – of one's actions for one's own reputation. Doing so may not only empower employees but also discourage them from free-loading.

12.5.4 Strength of Weak Ties

Educating employees on the strength of weak ties can further help with issues related to both loyalty and fairness in temporary and virtual teams. Research on social networks has shown that interacting with distant individuals like acquaint-ances enables people to develop bridges to other social circles, which in turn gives them access to new information and resources as well as opportunities (Grano-vetter, 1973, 1983, 1995). If the members of next-generation teams are informed of these benefits, they may be more likely to value having their teammates view them positively. This desire may compensate for the attenuated feelings of loyalty and accountability that people may have on next-generation teams.

12.5.5 360-Degree Rating Systems

Organizations can also implement formal structural changes to their team designs in order to reduce the prevalence of potential ethical issues. Organizations could benefit from using 360-degree rating systems to help address free-loading con-cerns. Members of a team may have more insight than team leaders or supervisors into which team members are pulling their weight (or more than their weight) and which ones are shirking their duties. Work and effort that appears indistinguish-able from an outside perspective may be more distinguishable from the viewpoint of the workers within the teams. These rating systems are likely to address problems with free-loading by creating an environment of increased accountabil-ity in which employees will want to avoid the negative consequences of failing to do their part. These systems may also incentivize employees to engage in more extra-role behaviors by providing them with credit and recognition for their efforts. Organizations might therefore benefit from implementing 360-degree rating systems when they create next-generation teams. Such rating systems may be particularly effective if these next-generation teams do not have clear official supervisors or leaders who could provide ratings of the team members.

Should the ratings generated by 360-degree rating systems be made public? Would it be useful to have a public rating system similar to Yelp for team members? The results of these rating systems may help those assembling next-generation teams. However, there are also reasons to believe that workers may game such rating systems and that such systems therefore may not be as effective as one might expect. Teammates might preemptively agree to give each other high ratings in order to game the system and ensure that their experiences on the team do not negatively affect their careers or reputations. The use of these rating systems may also provoke retributive ratings, such that workers who are evaluated negatively by their peers may rate those peers more negatively than they otherwise would. Whereas customers enjoy relative anonymity and are not at risk of receiving low ratings themselves when they issue low ratings to stores or service providers on websites like Yelp, workers on teams would not enjoy the same advantages. Publicizing the ratings may even lead to a culture of competition and breed animosity among team members to in turn hinder group cohesion. Creators and developers of teams may therefore potentially benefit by restricting who can see team members' ratings.

12.5.6 Social Influence Tactics

Another way to get around the shortcomings of the 360-degree rating system is to utilize social influence tactics. Research on normative social influence has shown that social norms can have a substantial impact on people's behaviors (Cialdini, Reno, & Kallgren, 1990). People who believe other team members are exerting pro-team efforts and exercising honest behaviors (including their usage of the 360-rating system) are more likely to exhibit similar behaviors themselves. There are two ways in which descriptive norms might be established within a team. First, organizations can incorporate into team structures formal channels to inform team members of others' commendable behaviors. By informing team members of others' positive behaviors but not negative behaviors, team members will come to believe that ethical pro-group efforts are commonplace and may in turn feel pressure to engage in similar behaviors themselves. Fortunately, research has shown that such forms of normative influence are under detected by those who are being influenced; meaning that normative messages can be a powerful tool for persuasion without rousing suspicion (Nolan, Schultz, Cialdini, Goldstein, & Griskevicius, 2008).

Second, organizations can also establish descriptive norms by utilizing informal structures within the team, such as gossip networks. Researchers have suggested that gossip can function as a source of information about social norms and therefore as a source of social influence (Baumeister, Zhang, & Vohs, 2004; Kurland & Pelled, 2000). To the extent that leaders can shape employee gossip to include discussion of the positive pro-team behaviors of members, this may influence the recipients of such gossip to also behave in similar ways that benefit the team.

Gossip can also function as a source of social influence by more directly incentivizing team members to behave in proper ways. Knowing that they may become a subject of gossip is likely to deter employees from behaving in ways that will incur negative gossip about themselves, as well as encourage them to behave in ways that will produce positive gossip about themselves (Kurland & Pelled, 2000). Gossip, when managed properly, can therefore effectively police employee behavior for the benefit of the team.

12.6 Conclusion

The changing ways that people work on teams will likely affect how ethical values influence the behavior of people in teams. We believe specifically that the temporary nature of next-generation teams and the tendency for these teams to work virtually will attenuate feelings of loyalty toward team members. We also believe that it will lessen the compulsion people might have to try to treat their teammates fairly. We hope this chapter serves as a warning and as a guide to organizational leaders who want to take advantage of the power of next-generation teams while still ensuring that team members will be motivated to contribute to the achievement of the team's goals.

References

Altman, B. W., & Post, J. E. (1996). Beyond the social contract: An analysis of the executive view at twenty-five larger companies. In D. T. Hall (Ed.), *The career is dead – long live the career* (pp. 46–71). San Francisco, CA: Jossey-Bass.

Ashforth, B. E., & Mael, F. (1989). Social identity theory and the organization. *Academy of Management Review*, *14*(1), 20–39.

Baumeister, R. F., Zhang, L., & Vohs, K. D. (2004). Gossip as cultural learning. *Review of General Psychology*, *8*(2), 111–121.

Blader, S. L., & Tyler, T. R. (2009). Testing and extending the group engagement model: Linkages between social identity, procedural justice, economic outcomes, and extra-role behavior. *The Journal of Applied Psychology*, *94*(2), 445–464.

Brewer, M. B. (1991). The social self: On being the same and different at the same time. *Personality and Social Psychology Bulletin*, *17*(5), 475–482.

Brewer, M. B. (1993). The role of distinctiveness in social identity and group behaviour. In M. A. Hogg & D. Abrams (Eds.), *Group motivation: Social psychological perspectives* (pp. 1–16). Hertfordshire, UK: Harvester Wheatsheaf.

Brewer, M. B. (1999). The psychology of prejudice: Ingroup love and outgroup hate? *Journal of Social Issues*, *55*(3), 429–444.

Brief, A. P., & Motowidlo, S. J. (1986). Prosocial organizational behaviors. *Academy of Management Review*, *11*(4), 710–725.

Chatman, J. A., & Flynn, F. J. (2001). The influence of demographic heterogeneity on the emergence and consequences of cooperative norms in work teams. *Academy of Management Journal*, *44*(5), 956–974.

Chen, M., Chen, C. C., & Sheldon, O. J. (2016). Relaxing moral reasoning to win: How organizational identification relates to unethical pro-organizational behavior. *The Journal of Applied Psychology*, *101*(8), 1082–1096.

Chidambaram, L. and Tung, L.L. (2005). Is out of sight, out of mind? An empirical study of social loafing in technology-supported groups. *Information Systems Research 16*(2), 149–168.

Cialdini, R. B., Reno, R. R., & Kallgren, C. A. (1990). A focus theory of normative conduct: Recycling the concept of norms to reduce littering in public places. *Journal of Personality and Social Psychology*, *58*(6), 1015–1026.

Crowston, K. (1997). A coordination theory approach to organizational process design. *Organization Science*, *8*(2), 157–175.

Daft, R. L., & Lengel, R. H. (1984). Information richness: A new approach to managerial behavior and organizational design. *Research in Organizational Behavior*, *6*, 191–233.

Daft, R. L., & Lengel, R. H. (1986). Organization information requirements, media richness, and structural design. *Management Science*, *32*(5), 554–571.

Davis, M. H. (2018). *Empathy: A social psychological approach*. New York, NY: Routledge.

DeFillippi, R. J., & Arthur, M. B. (1996). Boundaryless contexts and careers: A competency-based perspective. In M. B. Arthur & D. M. Rousseau (Eds.), *The boundaryless career* (pp. 116–131). New York, NY: Oxford University Press.

Deutsch, M. (1958). Trust and suspicion. *Journal of Conflict Resolution, 2*, 265–279.

Edmondson, A. C. (2012). *Teaming: How organizations learn, innovate, and compete in the knowledge economy.* San Francisco, CA: Jossey-Bass.

Edmondson, A. C., & Harvey, J. F. (2017). Cross-boundary teaming for innovation: Integrating research on teams and knowledge in organizations. *Human Resource Management Review, 28*(4), 347–360.

Edmondson, A. C., & Harvey, J. F. (2017). *Extreme teaming: Lessons in complex, cross-sector leadership.* Bingley, UK: Emerald Publishing.

Ellemers, N., Spears, R., & Doosje, B. (1997). Sticking together or falling apart: In-group identification as a psychological determinant of group commitment versus individual mobility. *Journal of Personality and Social Psychology, 72*(3), 617–626.

Gino, F., Ayal, S., & Ariely, D. (2009). Contagion and differentiation in unethical behavior: The effect of one bad apple on the barrel. *Psychological Science, 20*(3), 393–398.

Gino, F., Ayal, S., & Ariely, D. (2013). Self-serving altruism? The lure of unethical actions that benefit others. *Journal of Economic Behavior & Organization, 93*, 285–292.

Gino, F., & Pierce, L. (2009). Dishonesty in the name of equity. *Psychological Science, 20* (9), 1153–1160.

Graham, J., Nosek, B. A., Haidt, J., Iyer, R., Koleva, S., & Ditto, P. H. (2011). Mapping the moral domain. *Journal of Personality and Social Psychology, 101*(2), 366–385.

Graham, J., Haidt, J., Koleva, S., Motyl, M., Iyer, R., Wojcik, S. P., & Ditto, P. H. (2013). Moral foundations theory: The pragmatic validity of moral pluralism. *Advances in Experimental Social Psychology, 47*, 55–130.

Graham, J., Haidt, J., & Nosek, B. A. (2009). Liberals and conservatives rely on different sets of moral foundations. *Journal of Personality and Social Psychology, 96*(5), 1029–1046.

Granovetter, M. (1983). The strength of weak ties: A network theory revisited. *Sociological Theory, 1*, 201–233.

Granovetter, M. (1995). *Getting a job: A study of contacts and careers.* Chicago, IL: University of Chicago press.

Granovetter, M. S. (1973). The strength of weak ties. *American Journal of Sociology, 78* (6), 1360–1380.

Hackman, J. R. (1987). The design of work teams. In J. W. Lorsch (Ed.), *Handbook of organizational behavior* (pp. 315–342). Englewood Cliffs, NJ: Prentice-Hall.

Hackman, J. R. (2012). From causes to conditions in group research. *Journal of Organizational Behavior, 33*(3), 428–444.

Hackman, J. R., & Oldham, G. R. (1976). Motivation through the design of work: Test of a theory. *Organizational Behavior and Human Performance, 16*(2), 250–279.

Haidt, J., & Graham, J. (2007). When morality opposes justice: Conservatives have moral intuitions that liberals may not recognize. *Social Justice Research, 20*(1), 98–116.

Harkins, S. G. (1987). Social Loafing and social facilitation. *Journal of Experimental Social Psychology, 23*(1), 1–18.

Harrison, D. A., Price, K. H., & Bell, M. P. (1998). Beyond relational demography: Time and the effects of surface- and deep-level diversity on work group cohesion. *Academy of Management Journal, 41*(1), 96–107.

Heath, C., & Staudenmayer, N. (2000). Coordination neglect: How lay theories of organizing complicate coordination in organizations. *Research in Organizational Behavior, 22*, 153–191.

Hildreth, J. A. D., Gino, F., & Bazerman, M. (2016). Blind loyalty? When group loyalty makes us see evil or engage in it. *Organizational Behavior and Human Decision Processes, 132*, 16–36.

Hill, N. S., Bartol, K. M., Tesluk, P. E., & Langa, G. A. (2009). Organizational context and face-to-face interaction: Influences on the development of trust and collaborative behaviors in computer-mediated groups. *Organizational Behavior and Human Decision Processes, 108*(2), 187–201.

Hogg, M. A., & Terry, D. I. (2000). Social identity and self-categorization processes in organizational contexts. *Academy of Management Review, 25*(1), 121–140.

Jones, G. R. (1984). Task visibility, free riding, and shirking: Explaining the effect of structure and technology on employee behavior. *Academy of Management Review, 9*(4), 684–695.

Kahneman, D., Knetsch, J. L., & Thaler, R. H. (1991). The endowment effect, loss aversion, and status quo bias. *Journal of Economic Perspectives, 5*, 193–206.

Katz, D., & Kahn, R. L. (1966). *The psychology of organizations.* New York, NY: HR Folks International.

Katz, L. F., & Krueger, A. B. (2016). The rise and nature of alternative work arrangements in the United States, 1995–2015. National Bureau of Economic Research.

Kerr, N. L. (1983). Motivation losses in small groups: A social dilemma analysis. *Journal of Personality and Social Psychology, 45*(4), 819–828.

Kiesler, S., & Cummings, J. N. (2002). What do we know about proximity and distance in work groups? A legacy of research. In P. Hinds & S. Kiesler (Eds.), *Distributed work* (pp. 57–80). Cambridge, MA: MIT Press.

Kurland, N. B., & Pelled, L. H. (2000). Passing the word: Toward a model of gossip and power in the workplace. *Academy of Management Review, 25*(2), 428–438.

Latané, B., Williams, K., & Harkins, S. (1979). Many hands make light in the work: The causes and consequences of social loafing. *Journal of Personality and Social Psychology, 37*, 822–832.

Mael, F., & Ashforth, B. E. (1992). Alumni and their alma mater. *Journal of Organizational Behavior, 13*(2), 103–123.

Miles, R. E., & Snow, C. C. (1996). Twenty-first-century careers. In *M. B. Arthur & D. M. Rousseau* (Eds.), *The boundaryless career: A new employment principle for a new organizational era* (pp. 97–115). New York, NY: Oxford University Press.

Morrison, E. W., & Phelps, C. C. (1999). Taking charge at work: Extrarole efforts to initiate workplace change. *Academy of Management Journal, 42*(4), 403–419.

Mortensen, M. (2014). Constructing the team: The antecedents and effects of membership model divergence. *Organization Science, 25*(3), 909–931.

Mortensen, M., & Hinds, P. (2002). Fuzzy teams: Boundary disagreement in distributed and collocated teams. In P. Hinds & S. Kiesler (Eds.), *Distributed work* (pp. 283–308). Cambridge, MA: MIT Press.

Mortensen, M., Woolley, A., & O'Leary, M. (2007). Conditions enabling effective multiple team membership. In K. Crowston, S. Sieber, & E. Wynn (Eds.), *Virtuality and virtualization* (pp. 215–228). Boston, MA: Springer.

Mulvey, P. W. & Klein, H. J. (1998). The impact of perceived loafing and collective efficacy on group goal processes and group performance. *Organizational Behavior and Human Decision Processes, 74*, 62–87.

Nolan, J. M., Schultz, P. W., Cialdini, R. B., Goldstein, N. J., & Griskevicius, V. (2008). Normative social influence is underdetected. *Personality and Social Psychology Bulletin, 34*(7), 913–923.

O'Leary, M. B., Mortensen, M., & Woolley, A. W. (2011). Multiple team membership: A theoretical model of its effects on productivity and learning for individuals and teams. *Academy of Management Review, 36*(3), 461–478.

Orbell, J. & Dawes, R. (1981). Social dilemmas. In G. M. Stephenson & J. H. Davis (Eds.), *Progress in applied social psychology*, (pp. 37–65). Chichester, UK: John Wiley & Sons.

O'Reilly, C. A., & Chatman, J. (1986). Organizational commitment and psychological attachment: The effects of compliance, identification, and internalization on prosocial behavior. *Journal of Applied Psychology, 71*(3), 492–499.

Organ, D. W. (1988). *OCB: The good soldier syndrome.* Lexington, MA: Lexington Books.

Organ, D. W. (1997). Organizational citizenship behavior: It's construct clean-up time. *Human Performance, 10*(2), 85–97.

Pluut, H., Flestea, A. M., & Curșeu, P. L. (2014). Multiple team membership: A demand or resource for employees? *Group Dynamics: Theory, Research, and Practice, 18*(4), 333–348.

Polletta, F., & Jasper, J. M. (2001). Collective identity and social movements. *Annual Review of Sociology, 27*(1), 283–305.

Price, K. H., Harrison, D. A., & Gavin, J. H. (2006). Withholding inputs in team contexts: member composition, interaction processes, evaluation structure, and social loafing. *Journal of Applied Psychology, 91*(6), 1375–1384.

Putnam, R. D. (2000). *Bowling alone: The collapse and revival of american community.* New York, NY: Simon & Schuster.

Retelny, D., Robaszkiewicz, S., To, A., Lasecki, W. S., Patel, J., Rahmati, N., Doshi, T., Valentine, M., & Bernstein, M. S. (2014). Expert crowdsourcing with flash teams. In *Proceedings of the 27th annual ACM symposium on User interface software and technology* (pp. 75–85). ACM.

Rocco, E. (1998). Trust breaks down in electronic contexts but can be repaired by some initial face-to-face contact. In *Proceedings of the SIGCHI conference on human factors in computing systems* (pp. 496–502). New York, NY: ACM.

Ross, M., & Sicoly, F. (1979). Egocentric biases in availability and attribution. *Journal of Personality and Social Psychology, 37*(3), 322–336.

Rousseau, D. M., & Wade-Benzoni, K. A. (1995). Changing individual–organization attachments: A two-way street. In A. Howard (Ed.), *Changing nature of work* (pp. 290–321). San Francisco, CA: Jossey-Bass.

Sally, D. (1995). Conversation and cooperation in social dilemmas: A meta-analysis of experiments from 1958 to 1992. *Rationality and Society, 7*, 58–92.

Schnake, M. E. (1991). Equity in effort: The "sucker effect" in co-acting groups. *Journal of Management, 17*(1), 41–55.

Schrag, B. (2001). The moral significance of employee loyalty. *Business Ethics Quarterly, 11*(1), 41–66.

Schwarz, N., Bless, H., Strack, F., Klumpp, G., Rittenauer-Schatka, H., & Simons, A. (1991). Ease of retrieval as information: Another look at the availability heuristic. *Journal of Personality and Social Psychology, 61*(2), 195–202.

Smidts, A., Pruyn, A. T. H., & Van Riel, Cees B M. (2001). The impact of employee communication and perceived external prestige on organizational identification. *Academy of Management Journal, 44*(5), 1051–1062.

Smith, C. A., Organ, D. W., & Near, J. P. (1983). Organizational citizenship behavior: Its nature and antecedents. *Journal of Applied Psychology, 68*(4), 653–663.

Straus, S. & McGrath, J. (1994). Does the medium matter? The interaction of task type and technology on group performance and member reactions. *Journal of Applied Psychology 79*(1), 87–91.

Stroebe, W., Diehl, M., & Abakoumkin, G. (1996). Social compensation and the Köhler effect: Toward a theoretical explanation of motivation gains in group productivity. In E. H. Witte & J. H. Davis (Eds.), *Understanding Group behavior: Small group processes and interpersonal relations* (Vol. 2, pp. 37–65). New York, NY: Psychology Press.

Sullivan, S. E. (1999). The changing nature of careers: A review and research agenda. *Journal of Management, 25*(3), 457–484.

Tajfel, H., & Turner, J. C. (1979). An integrative theory of intergroup conflict. In W. G. Austin & S. Worchel (Eds.), *The social psychology of intergroup relations* (pp. 33–47). Monterey, CA: Brooks/Cole.

Tajfel, H., & Turner, J. C. (1986). The social identity theory of intergroup behavior. In S. Worchel & W. G. Austin (Eds.), *Psychology of intergroup relations*, (2nd ed., pp. 7–24). Chicago, IL: Nelson-Hall.

Tannenbaum, S. I., Mathieu, J. E., Salas, E., & Cohen, D. (2012). Teams are changing: Are research and practice evolving fast enough? *Industrial and Organizational Psychology, 5*(1), 2–24.

Tannenbaum, S. I., John, E., & Valentine, M. (In Press). When equity seems unfair: The role of justice enforceability in temporary team coordination. *Academy of Management Journal.*

Thau, S., Derfler-Rozin, R., Pitesa, M., Mitchell, M. S., & Pillutla, M. M. (2015). Unethical for the sake of the group: Risk of social exclusion and pro-group unethical behavior. *The Journal of Applied Psychology, 100*(1), 98–113.

Thompson, L., & Loewenstein, G. (1992). Egocentric interpretations of fairness and interpersonal conflict. *Organizational Behavior and Human Decision Processes, 51*(2), 176–197.

Townsend, A. M., DeMarie, S. M., & Hendrickson, A. R. (1998). Virtual teams: Technology and the workplace of the future. *Academy of Management Perspectives, 12*(3), 17–29.

Trevino, L. K., & Victor, B. (1992). Peer reporting of unethical behavior: A social context perspective. *Academy of Management Journal, 35*(1), 38–64.

Turner, J. C., Hogg, M. A., Oakes, P. J., Reicher, S. D., & Wetherell, M. S. (1987). *Rediscovering the social group: A self-categorization theory.* Cambridge, MA: Basil Blackwell

Umphress, E. E., & Bingham, J. B. (2011). When employees do bad things for good reasons: Examining unethical pro-organizational behaviors. *Organization Science, 22*(3), 621–640.

Umphress, E. E., Bingham, J. B., & Mitchell, M. S. (2010). Unethical behavior in the name of the company: The moderating effect of organizational identification and positive reciprocity beliefs on unethical pro-organizational behavior. *The Journal of Applied Psychology, 95*(4), 769–780.

Valentine, M. A., & Edmondson, A. C. (2014). Team scaffolds: How mesolevel structures enable role-based coordination in temporary groups. *Organization Science, 26*(2), 405–422.

Valentine, M. A., Retelny, D., To, A., Rahmati, N., Doshi, T., & Bernstein, M. S. (2017). Flash organizations: Crowdsourcing complex work by structuring crowds as organizations. In *Proceedings of the 2017 CHI conference on human factors in computing systems* (pp. 3523–3537). New York, NY: ACM.

Van Dyne, L., & LePine, J. A. (1998). Helping and voice extra-role behaviors: Evidence of construct and predictive validity. *Academy of Management Journal, 41*(1), 108–119.

Van, M. V., & Hart, C. M. (2004). Social identity as social glue: The origins of group loyalty. *Journal of Personality and Social Psychology, 86*(4), 585–598.

Wageman, R. (1995). Interdependence and group effectiveness. *Administrative Science Quarterly, 40*(1), 145–180.

Wageman, R., Gardner, H., & Mortensen, M. (2012). The changing ecology of teams: New directions for teams research. *Journal of Organizational Behavior, 33*(3), 301–315.

Wageman, R., Nunes, D. A., Burruss, J. A., & Hackman, J. R. (2008). *Senior leadership teams: What it takes to make them great.* Boston, MA: Harvard Business Review Press.

Walster, E. H., Walster, G. W., & Berscheid, E. (1978). *Equity: Theory and research.* Boston, MA: Allyn and Bacon.

Waytz, A., Dungan, J., & Young, L. (2013). The whistleblower's dilemma and the fairness–loyalty tradeoff. *Journal of Experimental Social Psychology, 49*(6), 1027–1033.

Wilson, J. M., Straus, S. G., & McEvily, B. (2006). All in due time: The development of trust in computer-mediated and face-to-face teams. *Organizational Behavior and Human Decision Processes, 99*(1), 16–33.

Wiltermuth, S. S. (2011). Cheating more when the spoils are split. *Organizational Behavior and Human Decision Processes, 115*(2), 157–168.

Zdaniuk, B., & Levine, J. M. (2001). Group loyalty: Impact of members' identification and contributions. *Journal of Experimental Social Psychology, 37*(6), 502–509.

Endnotes

[1] The permeability of group boundaries alone does not necessarily increase the likelihood of individual mobility (Ellemers, Spears, & Doosje, 1997). We therefore propose that the fluidity of membership will contribute to the exit problem indirectly through the decreased ability of individuals to identify with or develop strong attachments to a changing group.

13

Transparency: The What, Why, and How of Organizational Effectiveness and Ethics

James J. O'Toole

13.1 Introduction

In the 1990s, British writers began using "transparency" as a portmanteau word to describe that desirable state of organizational management and governance characterized by candor, openness, honesty, clarity, legal compliance, and full disclosure (Handy, 1990). At first, the word didn't take hold on this side of the Atlantic, perhaps because it was too vague and philosophical for American tastes in managerial buzz words (which tend to run more to the precise and practical).

But thanks to recent scandals at Wells Fargo and Volkswagen, corporate managers everywhere are learning that organizational transparency – in the form of free flow of information both internally and externally – is required for both effectiveness and ethical behavior. Of course, they should have learned that lesson as early as 2000 when, as fast as a click of a mouse, unethical behavior was exposed at Enron, Arthur Anderson, and WorldCom and reputations irrevocably shattered.

Since then, technology (social media, tweets, blogs, hand-held smartphone photos, and text messaging), federally-mandated disclosure requirements (Sarbanes-Oxley), and changing social expectations regarding corporate ethics have aligned in near-perfect syzygy to create a world in which transparency is all but inevitable. As a consequence, many managers now live in fear that some anonymous, enterprising blogger will "out" them and their company, causing disgrace and financial ruin. Indeed, that can – and does – happen. But experience also shows that corporate leaders who embrace transparency rather than fear it can reap enormous gains not only in hours of peaceful sleep but also in the black ink of high organizational performance.

The purpose of this chapter is to call attention to the leader's role in creating a culture of organizational candor. Such transparent organizations are less susceptible to innovation sapping "groupthink" and more likely to produce a climate of trust in which ethical misbehavior is both less likely to occur and more likely to be quickly identified if it does.

The chapter is divided into three sections: The What, The Why, and The How of creating transparent corporate cultures.

13.2 The What: Transparent vs Opaque Organizations

Transparency is a measure of the impedance to the flow of information within an organization and outward to all its stakeholders – including shareowners, regulators, customers, suppliers, dealers, and host communities. Research shows that organizations need a free flow of information much like the heart needs a continuing supply of oxygen-bearing blood: as organizational theorists Robert Blake and Jane Mouton documented when they examined data from a 1970s NASA study designed to uncover the human factors involved in airline accidents (Blake and Mouton, 1985). The researchers discovered that the habitual ways in which pilots interacted with their crews determined whether or not the crewmembers would provide essential information to the pilots in the midst of an in-air crisis. Intact cockpit crews – pilot, co-pilot, navigator – were placed in flight simulators and tested to see how they responded within the crucial thirty to forty seconds between the first sign of a potential accident and the fatal moment it would occur. The result: the stereotypical take-charge "fly-boy" pilots who acted immediately on their gut instincts were far more likely to make the wrong decisions in trying to avoid disaster than were the more open and inclusive pilots who, in effect, said to their crews "We've got a problem. How do you read it?" before making up their minds on a course of corrective action.

At one level, the lesson of the study is simple: leaders are far more likely to make mistakes when they act on too little information than when they wait to learn more. One shouldn't be surprised by this finding, considering the old saw that "None of us is as smart as all of us." But Blake and Mouton went deeper in their analysis, demonstrating that the pilots who made the right choices had habitually engaged in open exchanges with their crew members, while crew members who regularly had worked with the "decisive" pilots were unwilling to intervene with those "take-charge" bosses – even when they had information that might well have saved the plane. In effect, those crew members said to themselves, "He's the boss; who are we to challenge his authority?" Blake and Mouton go on to make the obvious analogy: "Such attitudes create real problems for management, from top to bottom, whether the manager is the captain of a 747 with 400 passengers on board, the manager of a crew of forest fire fighters, the executive in the boardroom, or the supervisor on the shop floor" (Blake and Mouton, 1985).

In essence, the silent crew members knew from experience that their leaders were not going to listen to them, wouldn't listen even if they volunteered useful information and, worse, were likely to reprimand them if they dared "speak out of turn." It's a matter of trust, and it is leaders themselves and their organizations who suffer most in un-trusting cultures. By not listening to what they don't want to hear, too many leaders shut out sources of potentially useful information. That's why transparency is simply good management.

Admittedly, it is difficult to wrap one's mind around such an inclusive and expansive concept as transparency. It is easier, perhaps, to understand it in contrast to its opposite: *opacity*. An opaque organization is characterized by secrecy, closed doors, and limited access to operational information. It is run by an elite cadre of "in the know" fast-trackers, insiders and A-team golden boys who are badly served by a mass of uninformed outsiders who are "out in the dark" and voiceless. In addition to an absence of trust, the consequences of such organizational opacity include groupthink, de-motivation, lack of innovation, and the failure of leaders to get the information they need, when they need it, in order to make effective decisions. For example, former CEO of Compaq, Eckhardt Pfeiffer was known to listen only to his A-list managers. When members of the B-list came to him with news that Dell and Gateway were poised to eat Compaq's lunch, he predictably ignored them, thus putting the company's future at peril. And, of course, such willfully in-the-dark leaders face the continual threat of unexpected revelations that can their destroy careers. In essence, then, those at greatest risk from opacity are the very executives responsible for creating impediments to the flow of information.

A basic fact of organizational life is that most organizations are more opaque than transparent. By far the most common metaphor managers use to describe their own cultures is *a mushroom farm* (as in, "people around here are kept in the dark – and fed manure"). When I recently polled a group of Midwestern executives, 63 percent of them described the cultures of their own companies as "opaque." The remaining 37 percent were more likely to choose various shades of gray over bright sunshine to describe the companies they worked in and, in many cases, actually led.

13.3 The Why: Transparency Is Inevitable

Rationally, ethically, and in terms of organizational effectiveness, transparency makes sense. But transparency doesn't just happen on its own because it runs against the grain of behavior in groups and, in some ways, appears contrary to human nature – particularly with regard to executive hubris and ego. In all groups, leaders try to horde and control information because they believe that knowing something others don't is a source of power. In some cases, managers believe access to information is a perquisite of power, a benefit that separates their privileged "caste" from the unwashed hoi polloi they lead. Leaders also often feel that they are smarter than followers and thus only they need, or would know how to use, sensitive and complex information. Worse still, they may believe that opacity allows them to hide their embarrassing mistakes – ironically, all-the-while everyone at the water cooler is gossiping about them.

These problems are compounded when executive power confers infallibility. The "shimmer effect" surrounding celebrity CEOs frequently allows them to get away with, if not murder, then "theft" on a massive scale. Witness the behavior of Blackstone's former CEO Conrad Black who spent some $8 million of his shareholders' funds to treat himself to a private collection of Franklin D. Roosevelt memorabilia. The company's board, which included the esteemed statesman Henry Kissinger, held Black in such awe that they failed to provide prudent oversight (Fabrikant, 2004). Similarly, the General Electric (GE) board turned a blind eye when its soon-to-retire CEO, Jack Welch, negotiated a secret retirement package that included a passel of regal perks (including a lifetime box at Yankee Stadium). Both Black and Welch failed to appreciate the inevitability of transparency, a fact of life the former now has time in jail to contemplate, and the latter doubtless rues as he finds his once-spotless reputation now permanently sullied. Inevitably, both Black's and Welch's "secrets" were publicly and embarrassingly revealed.

What executives are learning – often the hard way – is that they live in an era in which they can no longer hide. As information has become more widely available, the opportunity for secrecy – and privacy – has vanished. Paradoxically, executives live in a world of increasing enlightenment, but one in which they no longer can control information. It's now a world in which the once-powerless are more empowered and freer but, at the same time, a potentially Orwellian world in which liberties are more constrained. Yet, there is no utility in cursing the darkness, no payoff from Luddite refusals to accept new technology, and no virtue in continuing to practice outmoded managerial behavior. In reality, leaders today have little choice but to embrace the inevitable, learn how to cope with the drawbacks of transparency and, most important, learn how to capitalize on its potential benefits.

Anyone with a smartphone or access to a computer has the power to bring down a government, or a billion-dollar corporation. An instructive example is the decision of Guidant executives to continue selling their Contak Renewal defibrillators even after they learned that the implanted heart regulators were prone to electrical failures implicated in the deaths of at least seven patients. Guidant executives remained silent on the matter for three years, neglecting to recall the faulty device, apparently believing that *no one would notice*. What they failed to understand is that truth ultimately will out. When word finally spread, and the devices had to be recalled in 2005, the result was not only needless deaths but a catastrophic trust problem with the company's primary customers: physicians. According to *The New York Times*, Guidant's share of the defibrillator market dropped from 35 percent to about 24 percent after the recall; apparently because of the disgust many physicians felt concerning the company's decision to try to conceal an embarrassing truth upon which patients' lives literally depended. As an angry physician wrote to the firm: "I am not critical of Guidant's device problems – these devices are so complex, issues are expected. I will not, however, work with a company that put profit and image in front of good patient care and honesty in device manufacturing" (Meier, 2006).

The lesson is that the cardinal sin of management is not making a mistake, but lying about it, or trying to hide it. Leaders who ignore that basic lesson about transparency soon find themselves attempting to explain embarrassing cover-ups: witness Nixon and Watergate; Regan and Iran Contra; Clinton and Monica Lewinsky; and Bush and weapons of mass destruction. One would think leaders would learn that, in the eyes of followers, their mistakes can be forgiven, but lying to them is unforgivable. In the corporate world, the lesson was long ago reinforced by Johnson & Johnson's handling of the Tylenol crisis. The moment it was clear that people were dying from cyanide-laced Tylenol, the company's then-CEO, James Burke, immediately opened the doors of the executive suite to the media. He did this before knowing what had happened or, as it turned out, that his company was *not* responsible. Burke credited that transparency as the reason why customer faith in the product was so quickly restored. In contrast, when the Exxon Valdez oil spill occurred a few years later, the company attempted to stonewall, with a subsequent loss of credibility similar to that suffered by the Nixon Administration after Watergate.

It goes without saying that complete transparency is not possible, nor even desirable in some cases. Corporations have a legitimate interest in holding competitive information close: the imperative for transparency obviously does not include Coca-Cola revealing its secret recipe, or Microsoft letting its competitors in on the planned specs of its next generation of software. Strategic, product, and research secrets are necessary and reasonable – as is protecting the privacy of employees and customers. However, most organization secretiveness is simply reflexive. When in doubt, the natural tendency of leaders is to suppress information, defining everything that is potentially sensitive as a vital secret. Indeed, some scholars – and lawyers – even advise against transparency, arguing it is a mistake to call attention to embarrassing problems that might go unnoticed. However, that argument ignores the potency of the *National Enquirer effect*, in which there is a premium for those who disclose facts people are trying to hide, even if those facts would be viewed as unimportant if they had been freely disclosed.

The biggest problem with transparency in the age of the Internet is the increasing risk of misinformation, those unsubstantiated accusations that spread like wildfire on blogs (e.g., the widely repeated falsehood that Barack Obama is Muslim). Tweeters can start rumors that are difficult to counter with facts and, unfortunately, there is no easy way to deal with those who seek to perpetrate lies online. Hence, what is called for is a new managerial capability: the ability to use technology to convey truthful information and honest corporate messages. For example, contrarian corporate internal postings can be thorns in the side of older executives who are not computer-savvy; but younger technology-wise managers know how to use the intranet to "energize expertise from the bottom" of their organizations. Those managers appreciate the fact that there is always someone buried down in the hierarchy who has the information or insight that those at the top need, and information technology is the best way to tap that knowledge. Wise executives are learning to view even nasty online critiques of top management as an organizational benefit that prevents tunnel vision and reminds the powers that be that they don't have a lock on all useful truth. All-in-all, there are some unpleasant things about transparency that managers simply have to learn to live with, and learn how to turn into opportunities.

Knowing where to draw the line between what information must be revealed and what should be withheld is another emerging organizational capability. The clearest example of this is salary data, which – in most companies – is a closely held secret. With the exception of the salaries of top executives in publicly traded corporations (the posting of which is legally mandated), salaries of everyone else in most companies are typically treated like national security secrets. But, as my colleague Edward Lawler has shown, it actually redounds to the benefit of organizations to post everyone's salary (Lawler, 2000). When salaries are closely shrouded secrets, the tendency is for employees to suspect favoritism in the treatment of others. This leads to mistrust. But when salaries are posted, experience shows that most employees conclude that the distribution of rewards is relatively fair and, hence, salaries disappear as a bone of contention.

The centrality of transparency to organizational health is well documented. One survey shows that companies with high transparency ratings outperform those with low ratings, and the thirty-four most transparent companies outperform the S&P 500 financially by 11.3 percent. In 100 studies, researcher Carl Larsen found that "openness" is the primary predictor of success in work teams (La Fusto and Larsen, 2001). A major reason for the high correlation between transparency and effectiveness may be that openness is the only known antidote to the dreaded organizational affliction known as groupthink: a state of collective denial or self-deception that often has disastrous business and ethical consequences. Group-think is especially difficult to remedy because shared values and assumptions play a necessary role in holding any group together. However, if that glue turns toxic it can result in organizational morbidity.

People in all organizations typically form shared ideas – "collective representa-tions" in the language of social anthropology – and all the forces of the group conspire to protect those notions, no matter how inaccurate or outmoded they may be, or may become. For example, as the Japanese began to win a share of the US auto market in the late 1970s, one of General Motors (GM) top executives depicted his GM colleagues in Detroit looking down from their (near-hermetically sealed) fourteenth-floor executive suite onto the enormous company parking lot below and saying, "Look at all those big cars! Who says Americans want small ones?" Ditto GM's leaders' self-defeating collective representation that American consumers at the time didn't care a fig about product quality.

Clearly, groupthink is a major impediment to both customer responsiveness and innovation. Experience shows that, for good or ill, management teams commonly hold shared assumptions about the sources of innovation, motivation, productivity, product quality, and profitability in their respective organizations, and those untested assumptions drive their behavior. In large part, that's why Kodak had such a difficult time adjusting to the new age of digital photography, and why Polaroid completely failed to make the technological cross-over. A bit later, Xerox executives were said to have "fumbled the future," when they failed to heed the warnings of researchers at their Parc facility regarding changes in technology. Significantly, the more basic – and therefore the more potent – the assumption the *less* likely it is to be examined. The Altria company has a reputation for having squeaky-clean legal compliance procedures thanks to devoting high-level attention and generous resources to their internal auditing and control processes, yet it is highly unlikely the company's managers could raise the question of the basic morality of its cigarette business.

The 2001 HBO television film *Conspiracy* offers a chilling reminder of how lethal groupthink can become. The film is a verbatim enactment of a transcript found in Nazi files of the famed "Wansee Conference" at which leaders of the Third Reich plotted the extermination of European Jewry. Peer pressure and the group's collective representations were so powerful that not one person uttered even a minor demurral regarding the horrendous plans to send millions to their deaths.

No group is immune to the phenomenon of groupthink, as confirmed by findings offered in psychologist Philip Zimbardo's book *The Lucifer Effect*. He gives a riveting account of the Stanford Prison Experiment he conducted in 1971, which "got out of hand" (Zimbardo, 2007). Young men had been assigned to play the roles of guards and inmates in an ersatz "jail" in the basement of a campus building, but the participants took their play acting so seriously that the scheduled two-week experiment had to be aborted at mid-point when the student/guards psychologically and physically abused the student/prisoners. Zimbardo's recent retelling of what happened at Stanford some thirty-five years ago was prompted by the bizarre and terrible events at the Abu Ghraib prison in Iraq, which eerily replicated what happened in the prison experiment.

Zimbardo seeks to understand why good people do bad things by combining the retelling of his own hellish experiment with a review of the real-life horrors that occurred in Nazi concentration camps, at Mai Lai, Jonestown, and in Rwanda. He re-analyzes those familiar events in light of two decades of social-psychological research. In the process, Zimbardo turns what we thought we knew about the sources of evil on its head. For years, experts had assumed that people do bad things because they have an inherent disposition, or "bent," that makes them susceptible to temptations to do wrong. Zimbardo presents data disproving that assumption. It turns out that almost all of us are susceptible to being drawn over to "the dark side": human behavior is determined more by situational forces and group dynamics than by our inherent natures. Good people can end up doing unspeakable things that are "out of character" given such conditions as peer pressure and groupthink. Zimbardo shows how easy it is to create situations and systems in which good people cannot resist the temptation to do bad. But he concludes on the hopeful note that we can just as readily design systems that lead to positive behavior.

Although Zimbardo did not study business organizations, his conclusions belie the standard explanation offered by corporate leaders when people in their organizations are caught misbehaving: *there are a few bad apples in any barrel.* Zimbardo demonstrates that, in fact, ethical problems in organizations originate with the "barrel makers" – the leaders who, wittingly or not, create and maintain the systems under which participants are encouraged to do wrong. The managerial implications of this are enormous. Instead of companies wasting millions of dollars on ethics courses designed to exhort employees to "be good," it would be far more effective for managers to make an effort to create corporate cultures in which people will be rewarded for doing good things. Indeed, at Wells Fargo the source of the recent unethical behavior was the compensation system devised by executives to incentivize the bank's front-line employees to sell customers services they didn't want or need.

Zimbardo's conclusions are important for business leaders not only because they explain the source of unethical behavior that leads to travesties like Wells Fargo's but, more immediately, they shed light on the quotidian organizational problems of pressure to conform and the reluctance to speak truth to power. These same organizational forces hamper a company's capacity to innovate, solve problems, achieve goals, meet challenges, and compete – and the only effective antidote is creating an unimpeded flow of information and an organizational climate in which no one fears the consequences of speaking up. The value of transparency is that it keeps the leaders of organizations honest with others and, perhaps more important, honest with themselves. In brief, by broadening the perspectives of leaders, transparency mitigates against groupthink.

Unfortunately, transparency doesn't just happen because, as Zimbardo demonstrates, it runs against the grain of human nature. In all groups, there is a powerful desire "to belong." Everybody wants to be liked, to be part of the "family." Hence, the pressure to conform in organizations is almost irresistible. That appears to have occurred at Volkswagen, where scores of managers and technicians engaged in a conspiracy of silence about the company's blatant misrepresentations concerning the level of pollutants emitted from certain Volkswagen models. Doubtless, no one spoke up because no one wanted to be the skunk at the party – the one who tells the boss his fly is open or, worse, causes the company to lose customers or money. That said, the hopeful implication of Zimbardo's findings is that transparency is a *choice* that managers are free to make.

13.4 The How: What Leaders Do to Foster Transparency

While transparency is in the long-term interest of all organizations, it occurs infrequently because most leaders do not know how to create a bond of trust with followers. Alarmingly, research shows that most employees will not even attempt to deliver an unpleasant message to their bosses. In a recent survey of a cross-section of American workers, over two-thirds report having personally witnessed unethical behavior on the job, but only about a third of those say they reported what they observed to their supervisors. The reasons given for their reluctance range from fear of retaliation to the belief that management would not act on the information appropriately (LRN Corporation, 2007). The missing element, again, is *trust*. Corporate employees, much like the co-pilots and navigators in the NASA experiment discussed earlier, will not convey important information to their superiors because they mistrust how those above them will respond.

Whenever followers are asked to rank what they require of leaders, trust is almost always at the top of the list. But leaders can't provide trust directly to followers. Instead, trust is an outcome of all a leader's accumulated actions and behaviors. When leaders are candid, open, consistent, and predictable in their dealings with followers, the result will almost always be a condition of trust. Leaders who reliably commit candor, perforce, will tell everyone the same thing, and not continually be changing their stories. The resulting constancy allows followers to act with the assurance that the rules of the game won't suddenly change, and that they will not be treated arbitrarily. Given that assurance, followers become more willing to stick their necks out, make an extra effort, put themselves on the line to help leaders achieve goals, and tell the truth themselves.

In practice, trust is thus created by the behavior of leaders toward followers: when leaders treat followers with respect, followers respond with trust. Leaders demonstrate respect by sharing relevant information with followers and by including them in the making of decisions that affect them. Of course, leaders often say that it is impossible to always practice such inclusion. Be that as it may, showing respect for people by including them in the flow of relevant information is the essence of transparency and trust. As one CEO explained, "In the absence of trust, all ambiguous behavior is viewed with suspicion ... and, by definition, all behavior is ambiguous!" That's why the failure to include people is the second most common source of mistrust, close behind the failure of leaders to tell the truth consistently.

But some leaders reward candor. Whole Foods' founder John Mackey's company has a "no secrets policy," including the posting of everyone's pay. In many ways, Mackey is the poster boy for transparent leadership, yet he recently learned the hard way that there is no such thing as a corporate secret in the Internet age. In July 2007, it was revealed that Mackey had been using a pseudonym to make controversial posts on an online stock forum. Using the handle Rehodeb (an anagram of Deborah, his wife's name), Mackey was caught promoting Whole Foods and slamming rival Wild Oats, even as his company was in the process of acquiring the smaller chain. Mackey's deception provided ammunition to the Federal Trade Commission, which filed an antitrust action against the acquisition.

The lesson to draw from this sorry tale isn't that a "no secrets" policy is undesirable but, rather, that it takes full-time commitment and diligence to deliver on it. However difficult it may be, it can be done. For example, Kent Thiry, CEO of DaVita, a dialysis-treatment operator, systematically collects data and solicits candid feedback from his employees, ex-employees, customers, and suppliers in order to keep from "messing up." Thiry actively seeks out bad news and rewards employees who give it to him. To reinforce trust, he and his top management team act promptly to correct aspects of the business that employees identify as in need of fixing, practices that, if left unchecked, could come back to haunt the company (Hymowitz, 2006).

Thus, there are practical actions leaders can take to build confidence among followers that they are safe to speak up – indeed, that they are encouraged to do so. After a spate of ethical lapses involving government contracts in the 1990s, leaders at Northrup Grumman instituted a skills-building program on how to have "difficult conversations" that successfully led to greater numbers of employees speaking truth to power before small problems became major corporate scandals.

For numerous reasons – ranging from ethics to creating a climate in which innovation is nurtured – it is essential for leaders to create conditions of trust under which they will receive an unimpeded flow of intelligence, even news and information they might not want to hear, or that subordinates are afraid to convey to them. In fact, such candor is in the *self*-interest of the very leaders who, paradoxically, refuse to listen to those who would bring them useful information. In this regard, we might recall the guiding precept of one clear-headed manager: "The only messenger that I would ever shoot is one who arrived too late."

Daring to speak truth to power often entails considerable risk – whether at the hands of an irate parent, a neighborhood bully, or an incensed boss. Imagine the courage it would have taken for an Enron employee to confront Jeff Skilling with the facts of the company's (and his) financial deception? Or, even the courage required by a GE employee simply to question the company's former CEO, Jack Welch? According to *Fortune*, former GE employees reported that dissenters were berated, insulted, and abused: "Welch conducts meetings so aggressively that people tremble. He attacks almost physically with his intellect – criticizing, demeaning, ridiculing, humiliating" (Tichy and Sherman, 1993).

In the early 1970s, Albert O. Hirschman posited that employees who disagree with company policy have only three options: "exit, voice, and loyalty" (Hirschman, 1970). That is, they can offer a principled resignation (exit), try to change the policy (speak truth to power), or remain loyal team players despite their opposition. Experience shows that most people choose option three, the path of least resistance. They swallow whatever moral objections they may have to questionable dictates from above, concluding that they lack power to change things or, worse, will be punished if they attempt to do so. Such docile employee behavior is assumed: most executives expect their people to be "good soldiers" and not question company policy (or, if they do, that they will go away quietly).

Indeed, "disloyalty" is the organization's trump card in dealing with those who dare to voice truth internally in the hope of changing policy, and against those who exit and then "tell tales out-of-school." Experience shows that employees who muster the courage to question the prevailing groupthink in an organization open themselves to charges of "disloyalty," as Enron's Sherron Watkins, World-Com's Cynthia Cooper, and the FBI's Coleen Rowley learned when they were shunned by colleagues after they courageously had tried to bring news of unethical behavior to the attention of leaders in their respective organizations. The three were shunned by their fellow employees and accused of disloyalty, and that is why leaders have an ethical responsibility to create cultures where people are free to speak truth to power (Time, 2002).

Leaders of companies with healthy cultures continually challenge old assumptions, rethink basic premises, and question, revise, and unlearn outmoded truths. In the late 1970s, then-president of ARCO, Thornton Bradshaw, became the first top executive in a major corporation not only to meet regularly with his employees, the press, shareholders, and regulators in open exchanges, but also to frequently interact with his industry's critics in the labor, environmental, and product safety movements, listening with respect to their various perspectives.

Bradshaw also held regular meetings with his company's managers to discuss how to respond to enquiries from the press. His first rule: *always tell the truth*. Bradshaw assured his managers that they never would be second-guessed by the company if they simply told what they knew when asked. Long before the Watergate scandal hammered the point home, he argued that the most unforgivable sins are lying and covering-up. Bradshaw's second rule: *admit it when you are wrong*.

He argued, as a general proposition, that no one ever stayed in hot water if they candidly and contritely admitted they had erred. On Bradshaw's watch, ARCO never experienced even a minor ethical or legal scandal, a record that was rare for an oil company in that era. That's why leaders would do well to reflect on their receptivity to suggestions, alternative points of views, and others' opinions. They need to forgo the ego-satisfying pleasure of being "the boss" and, instead, adopt the roles of teacher and listener. To do so, they need to learn to trust employees with the managerial and financial information typically hoarded by executives in most companies, as to trust them to act responsibly on the basis of that information. When they do, in the end they may find a marvelous pot of gold: their companies will be both successful financially *and* have high ethical standards. Here, at least, is one arena in which there is no trade-off between doing good and doing well: transparency is the element critical to *both* organizational effectiveness and ethics.

Acknowledgments

In this chapter I draw heavily on my work with the late Warren Bennis, including our book *Transparency: How Leaders Create Cultures of Candor* (Jossey-Bass 2008), and our *Harvard Business Review* article, "What's Needed Next: A Culture of Candor" (*HBR*, June 2009, pp. 54–61).

References

Blake, R. R., & Mouton, J. S. (1985). Effective crisis management. *New Management*, (3) 1. 14.

Fabrikant, G. (2004, February 16). A 'Yes Lord Black' board says 'No.' *The New York Times*.

Handy, C. (1990). *The age of unreason*. Cambridge, MA: Harvard Business School Press.

Hirschman, A. O. (1970). *Exit, voice, and loyalty*. Cambridge, MA: Harvard University Press.

Hymowitz, C. (2006, May 15). Executives who build truth-telling cultures learn fast what works. *Wall Street Journal*.

La Fusto, F. & Larsen, C. (2001). *When teams work best*. Thousand Oaks, CA: Sage.

Lawler, E. E. (2000). *Rewarding excellence*. San Francisco, CA: Jossey-Bass.

LRN Corporation. (2007). Ethics Study. Retrieved from www.LRN.com.

Meier, B. (2006, February 28). Internal turmoil at device maker as inquiry grew. *The New York Times*.

Time Magazine. (2002, January 1). Persons of the Year. *Time* cover story.

Tichy, N. & Sherman, S. (1993). *Control your own destiny or someone else will*. New York, NY: Doubleday.

14

Global Engagement by Leaders Is a Moral Imperative: Building the Next Generation of Ethical Corporate Cultures

Marsha Ershaghi-Hames

14.1 Introduction

In an era of corporate mistrust, creating sustainable ethical corporations goes beyond implementing governance, risk, and compliance (GRC) strategy. It requires an ongoing intensified spotlight to make the highest ethical standards the norm, and ruthless intolerance of anything less. Corporations are at a tipping point seeking to build sustainable businesses while striving to avoid a front-page scandal. They are placing greater scrutiny on values as business enabler, leadership accountability, and building ethical decision-making as an integrated business process. The next generation of ethical systems is at our corporate doorstep. As Albert Einstein famously said, "we cannot solve problems by using the same kind of thinking we used when we created them." Today's workplace has an unprecedented four generations working alongside each other. Globalization and the flattened twenty-first-century economy have pivotally shifted the norms of communication, information sharing, and collaboration. Greater visibility through mass media and social media has revealed new consumer and corporate behaviors. With greater transparency at our fingertips, trust has become the new currency, evidenced in the backlash as trust in public officials and corporate leaders steadily declines. The Edelman Trust Barometer has been studying trust across four institutions since 2012: businesses, government, nongovernmental organizations (NGOs), and media. Their 2017 report reveals that trust has declined broadly across all four institutions and that trust is in crisis around the world.

My focus is on why the next generation of ethics relies on how we are developing the next generation of leaders. Several studies point to the influence that leaders have on setting the tone of acceptable behavior and influencing the trust gap between leaders and the enterprise. Even the regulators speak to the impact of leaders in crafting culture. From the Department of Justice and Securities and Exchange Commission to guidance outlined within the US Sentencing Guidelines (Saris et al., 2015), there is a prominent recognition of the necessity not only to have the building blocks of a strategy but also to *place a stronger spotlight on intentionally shaping ethical organizational cultures.* The research presented will demonstrate how contemporary GRC strategies are shifting the tone from rules-based to values-based decision-making, and framing the charge with a leadership commitment that entails active modeling of ethical decision-making. The chapter will highlight how language such as *"commitment, responsibility, and accountability"* has emerged as the lexicon organizations are using to demonstrate leaders "walking the talk." Corporate commitment to values is being tested on a global scale. Corporate leaders are recognizing the opportunity to leverage their platform for intentionally crafting organizational culture, promoting speaking out while leaders learn to listen up. While there is greater scrutiny on the role of board accountability by shareholders, consumers and investors around corporations need to rethink growing the bottom line ethically. This chapter will focus on how organizations can build the next generation of ethical organizations, by adopting the strategy of building profits with purpose. In brief, the proposition of this chapter is that in today's hyper-transparent workforce – especially those organizations operating with an expansive global footprint – it is imperative that leaders play a prominent and accountable role in modeling the everyday ethical decision-making in a practical and relevant manner. Compliance is an outcome of an ethical culture.

14.2 The Inverse of Trust

Relationships matter. Whether you are with a partner, family, part of a team, or an organization. As Stephen M.R. Covey writes in *The Speed of Trust*, "When trust goes down, speed goes down and cost goes up . . . The inverse is true: When trust goes up, cost goes down, and speed goes up" (Covey & Merrill, 2006, p. 52). The rapid rise of technology and social media has enabled a new norm of blurred lines with our communication. Whether its public or private behaviors, business practices are becoming transparent if they either choose to opt in or not. In this era of transparency, trust is emerging as the key currency for success. Trust matters, whether between organizations and their consumers, or their shareholders and their leaders, and ultimately trust with and from their workforce.

In my nearly two decades as an executive advisor on GRC strategy and development, my consulting work has placed me in the halls and corridors of some of the world's most complex organizations. I've led transformational strategies for multinational organizations through an integrated approach to ethics – compliance with the objective of building sustainable organizational cultures. I've advised dozens of organizations around their brand reputation efforts by developing and invigorating their values spotlight, connecting value-based decision-making to their business objectives. Engaging leaders as trust ambassadors and models of ethical behavior takes deep commitment, alignment, and patience. I've walked the corporate corridors across a diverse spectrum of industries in the private, commercial, and non-profit sectors, across multiple continents. My unique close-up lens has allowed me to bring narratives of authenticity to my work around leadership accountability, workforce engagement, and strategies to eliminate the pitfalls and signs of toxic organizational culture. One theme that cuts across all industry verticals and international country business norms is *trust*. Trust is the currency that carves through it all, enabling rapid growth or decline. CNBC interviewed me on my thoughts around the hallmarks of the next generation of leaders, and the lessons learned from some of the organizational reputational scandals in the technology sector. My comments focused on trust. I emphasized that even the mere perception of leaders allowing or turning a blind eye to behavior can cultivate organizational toxicity:

> *"Just the mere perception that an organization has a history or allowance of a toxic culture can lead to a tank in stock value and an exodus of employees, who will go to competitors," says Ershaghi. "This is how companies that are quickly built also quickly fall."*

(Umoh, 2017)

14.3 Taking Action

Corporations are going to great lengths to formally revise, simplify, and reissue their corporate policies – standards – around the notion of trust. The bar has been raised. Corporations are actively implementing fresh business models of integrity through formal statements such as Ethical Codes of Conduct and Standards of Values and Principles, thus creating a new deck of cultural artifacts for the twenty-first century. Companies are devoting entire sections of their public corporate websites to ethics, compliance, and culture. A few notable examples include NRG Energy, where they have highlighted the fundamental value of *integrity* as the pivot that their revised Code of Conduct centers around. Their values provide a framework for their business, with an entire section on their corporate website devoted to Core Values. NRG designed their Code of Conduct as a practical "Field Guide" filled with tools and resources to help with the "Compass Point: Finding the NRG Way" (NRG, 2016).

Another exemplar is how Kellogg Company has spotlighted their ethical performance culture as part of their legacy and continued sustained success factor. Their revised and refreshed Global Code of Ethics reflects the human side of their business through the faces of people, the ways they work, and their commitment to a diverse organizational DNA (Kellogg, 2013). The chapters are organized using inclusive language like "Our People"; "Our Consumers"; "Our Market-place"; "Our Investors." Oracle's enhanced Code of Ethics and Business Conduct, devotes web space with the theme of "Our Code. Our Connection. Our

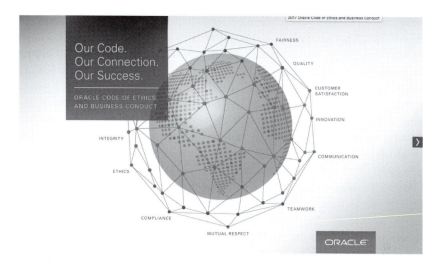

Figure 14.1 *Oracle Code of Ethics and Business Conduct*

Success." Oracle explicitly links the principles of their Code and core values as the connective tissue to business performance. See Figure 14.1, which depicts the cover of their code and lists its principles.

A fluid slide share of their Core Values, Commitment from Leadership and Code of Ethics can be viewed by clicking the link in endnote 1.[1]

How a corporation conducts business, their mission and purpose to drive impact, and guidance around ethical decision-making have become more prominent in shaping ethical codes of conduct in the last few years. Yet, despite the formal efforts to produce and document values that reside on beautiful corporate websites, layered into new hire offer packages, and hanging in the hallways of the businesses worldwide, corporate ethical failures have become painfully common, and costly. Ethical breaches are paralyzing businesses, costing organizations billions of dollars in fines. Today's headlines of corporate scandals are different from the product-safety scandals we grew accustomed to in the twentieth century. There is a distinct, almost toxic behavioral component. There is a blatant misuse of trust. It is no surprise that the Edelman Trust Barometer's annual reports point to a decline in trust in the four institutions, slipping to an all-time low. Unfortunately, as the daily headlines illustrate, there is an ominous trend, a rise in open, blatant, and defiant institutional failures, omissions, and toxic behavior by leaders. The headlines are prompting greater scrutiny on corporate ethics reform. According to PwC's Annual Global CEO survey, in 2013, 37 percent of CEOs were concerned about low trust in business. In 2016, that number reached 55 percent (19th Annual global CEO Survey, 2016). There is a concerted effort by organizations to position and develop leaders to make a more holistic effort to embed trust and accountability into the corporate systems, processes, and environments, with a lens towards values-based decision-making. But despite these efforts, according to the Ethics Resource Center's most recent National Business Ethics Survey® (NBES®) (Ethics Resource Center, 2014), 41 percent of the workforce reported observing ethical misconduct in the last twelve months. More than 10 percent felt organizational pressure to compromise ethical standards. For example, the failures unfolding at Wells Fargo produced a cost of $185 million in fines because 5,300 employees were pressured to open nearly two million fraudulent accounts (Corkery, 2016).

Federal banking regulators have indicated that the practice of cross-selling and opening illegal bank accounts for customers without their consent, reveals a serious flaw in the long-time internal culture and oversight at Wells Fargo. Common sense would dictate that it is nearly impossible to force over 5,000 individuals to all do the wrong thing, unless the behavior is built into a systematic process. Factors such as workforce employment, compensation, and livelihood can be acculturated by some sort of regular reinforcement over time, most effectively via front-line management. Harvard Business School has conducted research in this area. In one study they cited that over prescribed goal-setting can encourage people to make compromising decisions in order to reach unrealistic targets (Lacker & Tayan, 2016). This can spark a cultural environment of rampant goal-setting, encouraging leaders to invite their teams, in unspoken terms, to cheat. This can be exhibited by cutting corners in how teams achieve a goal, or even manifest itself in the misrepresentation of information when reporting on the targets.

14.4 Manage the Culture or It Manages You

Edgar Schein's widely cited modern organizational culture model defines culture as the shared assumptions and norms as well as tangible artifacts of the corporate environment (Schein, 2010). These aspects of workforce culture can influence employee behavior and beliefs. Organizational cultural beliefs define perception of acceptable behavior. For example, if employees believe their contributions are valued and recognized they are more likely to stay engaged and help the company thrive and innovate. With workforce recruitment and retention at the top of many corporate leaders' minds, according to renowned expert in workforce talent and organizational change Josh Bersin, culture is the at the forefront of the talent management efforts (Bersin, 2015).

According to the 2017 Deloitte Global Human Capital Trends, organizational culture is emerging as the single most critical influencer of job seekers today (Deloitte, 2017). Even with a competitive compensation offer on the table, a lethal workforce culture can be tormenting and will consume the employee overtime.

With the continuous front-page scandals tarnishing corporate brand reputation and consumer confidence, with whistleblowers surfacing conflicts and corruption, job candidates are carefully evaluating their options. They are observing and assessing how organizations are developing leaders, promoting innovation and opening up to new ideas, as well as how organizations solicit employee feedback and encourage a speak up culture. For example, in my discussions with several candidates, an often-referenced litmus test is assessing how the prospective company has addressed failures or apologies in the public eye. According to the 2017 Deloitte Global Human Capital Trends research, one of the top trends in talent recruitment is for organizations to actively market their culture to prospective candidates. People are attracted to organizations they can thrive within. A company's culture can have a powerful ripple effect on the colleague and company's success. Threading an organization's values with the bottom line can demonstrate a healthy and vibrant culture, where the workforce is practicing business and decision-making behaviors that align with the norms and shared values of the organization. For example, in an interview Indeed.com led with Jet Blue Senior Vice President of Talent Rachel McCarthy, organizational culture is highlighted as the DNA of Jet Blue. "JetBlue was founded on 'bringing humanity back to air travel,' says McCarthy. At the very start of the company, the founders put the firm's mission in the forefront, identifying five core values that JetBlue would stand for: safety, caring, integrity, passion and fun" (Indeed Blog, 2017). As Edgar Schein famously said, "manage the culture or it manages you" (Schein, 2010, p. 20). With the headlines placing a public eye on how a culture of silence can truly "eat away" at the organization, companies are doubling down their efforts on how to promote greater comfort levels in supporting decision-making and a healthier speak up culture.

14.5 Speaking Out

Fostering a speak out organizational culture truly requires a foundation of the organization embracing and living values-based leadership and promoting values-based decision-making. Trust is a necessary ingredient for any meaningful speak up culture. Without it, an employee's willingness to challenge decisions, raise issues, or voice concern is limited no matter what types of policies or protections are in place. In my consulting work, I've observed two fundamental challenges within organizations that discourage employees from speaking up. The first is a sense of futility, whereby employees are thinking, "why bother, no action will be taken." They may perceive that speaking up is not worth the effort, or perhaps the tone set by their supervisor signals that they really do not want to hear concerns. Employees are seeking organizational justice, more visibility and transparency into how their company is taking steps to follow up on concerns. Employees want to understand what are the actions, if any, being taken to improve or repair failing processes and systems or to make the appropriate leadership changes to remove unethical behaviors. One notable example of discomfort in speaking up is the very raw and public memo a former Uber engineer, Susan Fowler, penned after leaving the company. The memo highlighted concerns about a toxic "bro-culture," patterns of sexism, discrimination, retaliation, and more (Fowler, 2017). Speaking out prompted a wave of other employees to highlight their similar experiences across Silicon Valley, including allegations against venture capitalists as well (Zetlin, 2017). Covington & Burling LLP led an investigation to assess the claims and produced a recommendations report that focused on core themes: Tone at the Top, Trust, Transformation, and Accountability (*Wall Street Journal*, n.d.).

Several studies point to the actions and behaviors of leaders as the model that sets the tone for acceptable behaviors. When I reflect on my years of consulting work, I have observed that C-Suite leaders may not always be self-aware of their actions and the perceptions it sets for everyday decision-making. Thus, failing to model free expression with their employees, whether the employee wants to raise an innovation or improvement, or conversely report an unethical observation, is all important expression. Passive leadership is one of the biggest pitfalls I've observed. If leaders fall into a trap of pseudo-participation, where they demonstrate they are not interested in hearing feedback or progressive ideas, then employees perceive that leadership is "going through the motions" of listening with little intent to follow up.

The research points to fear or retaliation and retribution as a second strong indicator that limits employees from taking action and raising concerns. Although the Federal Sentencing Guidelines for Organizations requires implementing an anonymous hotline as a fundamental component for an Ethics and Compliance program, some corporations advertise the anonymity factor as incentive to promote employees to safely raise concerns in a protected format (Saris et al., 2015). The strategy here is that if no one knows who raised the concern, then no repercussions will follow; so anonymity can encourage people to be forthright. The complexity here is this can form a subtext culture – indicating that perhaps it is not safe to share your views openly in this organization – so we've created other channels to get the information we need. Another factor is that repeated negative feedback raised in a hotline can cause demands from supervisors to determine who said what, which can create a tension – almost a sense of a witch hunt. One of my clients had received dozens of documented complaints of racial and gender discrimination by a supervisor at one of their newly acquired business units. When the supervisor and local management was confronted their first response was to place complex pressure on the human resources (HR) and internal investigations units to determine which employees spoke up. Their notion was that it is just a few bad apples speaking up. Overtime they churned through several HR leaders locally. There was a deep-seated trust gap between employees and leaders and views that the acquisition company was to be distrusted. Silos and lines in the sand were being drawn at a local level, whereby subtle pronounced loyalties needed to play out to demonstrate who was on which side of the equation. Speaking up was considered being disloyal, even if it would have helped create progress in the newly merged organization. In my consulting work, I've been saddened to see the great lengths some employees will pursue to find ways to anonymously report their fears, such as going to public places like libraries or public work space kiosks to complete employee surveys for fear of IP addresses being traced to them. This is why it is so important to foster ongoing dialogue at a local level, whereby leaders serve as a catalyst for influence and sustained change. Local leaders can serve as the models to shepherd the workforce culture at a local, ground level and promote greater comfort levels for employees to raise concerns.

14.6 Trust Must Be Earned

According to the Edelman Trust Barometer's 2014 report, "business has steadily rebounded since the implosion of trust experienced in 2008/2009 and is showing signs of stability but memories of the meltdown and the usual stream of scandals that play out in the media reinforce strong distrust in business as its own regulator" (Edelman, 2014, p. 5). Since 2008, there is a widening trust gap between the organization and the institution, the consumer and the corporation. This almost self-inflicted crisis continues on an astounding global scale, whether it is emission data that is falsified at Volkswagen; the two million accounts opened without customers' knowledge at Wells Fargo; or the billions of dollars skimmed from Petrobras through inflated contracts channeling funds to various Brazilian construction firms including Odebrecht. Yet in the 2016 Edelman Trust Barometer Report there is a resounding spotlight on the role of leadership in a "Divided World" (Edelman, 2016). Pointing to the 2016 findings they show that leadership must recognize the importance of action, values, engagement, and employee advocacy. The report shines a light on the actions and attitudes that demonstrate the behaviors expected of leaders.

A leader's consistency in action, especially walking the halls at a local level, is the most significant influencer of the local organizational culture. Leveraging leaders as global agents for leading key messages and modeling everyday ethical decision-making, helps nurture and embrace local business cultural similarities, differences, and sensitivities. I often ask my clients questions like these:

> "Who else is in the best position to take the key messages from your corporate mission 'off the wall and down the hall'?"
> "Who else is in the best position to serve as an integration point between the company Code of Conduct and everyday decision-making?"

Taking a step back the answers are obvious. Yet, so many organizations are deep into navel gazing and lose sight of the objectivity, or a healthy perspective around operationalizing organizational ethics. According to a 2017 Ethics and Compliance

Survey, when leaders engage in dialogue, their employees and teams not only acquire the skills to recognize concerns but also gain the confidence to share their views and voice their opinions on change, innovation, or concerns (Ethisphere, 2017). Middle management can represent a visible extension –that is, the arms and legs – for driving a healthy organizational culture. Leaders should be positioned as local champions of the core messages. They are at the apex of observation to actively help surface complex themes around the Code of Conduct, such as respect in the workplace, navigating the pitfalls of social media, or fostering a healthy speak out environment. These critical topics can really resonate when there is an ongoing dialogue led by local management, not just an annual tone at the top message from the CEO. Sometimes leveraging local management enables breaking the ice around the issues that can pose serious risks to the organization. Having these conversations regularly, from the bottom up versus top down, can bring more resonance to the workforce, allowing them to be a part of the company conversation. The company's organization should wholly feel like their views are welcome and valued. As President and CEO of Edelman Richard Edelman (2016) states, "trust in institutions and their license to operate is no longer automatically granted on the basis of hierarchy or title' rather, in today's world, trust must be earned."

14.7 Tone in the Middle

According to the Ethics and Compliance Initiative's (ECI) 2018 Global Business Ethics Survey (GBES^{TM}) on Workplace Integrity, employees tend to follow leaders' cues for both good and ill, which makes it especially problematic when leaders break rules or violate standards of integrity (ECI, 2018). The GBES^{TM} research demonstrates that leaders, especially at multinational organizations need to spotlight the priority of building strong ethical leadership metrics for all levels of leadership. For example, emphasizing integrity as a requirement for a promotion or as part of the leader key performance indicator metrics, can establish ethical leadership as an essential metric of the job success criteria. Numerous studies point to a leader's lack of engagement, apathy, or behavior misalignment with the Code of Conduct breeding negative perceptions, local cynicism, and potential skepticism about the ethics and compliance program. This dampens organizational culture as a whole. Perceptions can vary by location and local business culture Figure 14.2 shows correlation between employee engagement and strength organizational character.

One trend that I've observed in my work with clients is that misconduct is typically a result of a pattern of bad behavior over a period of time, rather than an isolated incident. Therefore, the types of behavior patterns that are supported by leadership can lead to employees perceiving what is considered acceptable versus what behaviors they may not even bother reporting because they fear retaliation or assume these negative behaviors are part of the local business culture. A problem that leaders do

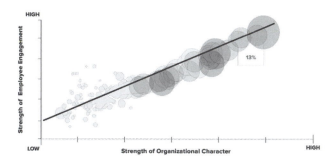

Figure 14.2 *2016 HOW Metrics® Report: LRN*

not know about is also a problem that leaders cannot address. Reporting of observed misconduct enables those committed leaders to tackle issues proactively and attempt to resolve or mitigate the issues. Yet complete silence in the face of misconduct allow problems to fester and take root. This is where the longer-term patterns arise. This is a development opportunity that organizations can invest in with their leaders. Consider investing in developing managers to become more aware of how their daily inter-actions and regular communications with team members can either support or undermine an atmosphere in which ethical decision-making and living the company Code is a welcome topic of discussion rather than an interruption. Most reports of misconduct are initially made to the front-line manager, whereas studies report that less than 10 percent of reports are made to the ethics hotline. Sometimes managers simply do not have the self-awareness that their behaviors or rapport deem them unavailable to listen, or unapproachable. In some of my executive coaching sessions, I've learned that there is a single loop process that develops with executives that have been in their position for significant periods of time, sometimes decades. There needs to be a willingness for leaders to recognize and unlearn defensive thought patterns and old behavior routines. Some get stuck in what Dr. Chris Argyris studied in his theory of action and illustratively defines as a single loop versus double loop learning process (Argyris, 1982; see Figure 14.3).

There are organizational cultural habits and attitudes that allow organizations to hide their problems and have an inability to uncover the unpleasant truths and learn from them. Today double loop learning is widely used by organizational psychologists and advisors as a framework for leadership development. Argyris (1982) suggests that individual behavior does not change because people are stuck in the single loop learning cycle. This cycle presents itself when the individual attempts an action at the same problem with no variation and without questioning why they are behaving or making decisions in the same way: similar to the notion of "this is how we've always done things." Argyris presents the need for integrating leaders into a double loop learning process, where the individual adopts new behaviors such as exhibiting the willingness to be reflective, seek feedback, and recognize the mistakes or issues unfolding. The individual engaged

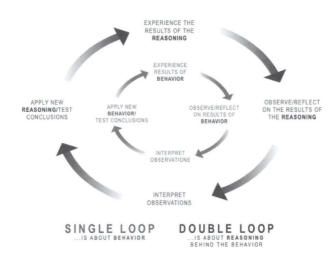

EXPERIENCE THE
RESULTS OF THE
REASONING

EXPERIENCE
RESULTS OF
BEHAVIOR

APPLY NEW
REASONING/TEST
CONCLUSIONS

APPLY NEW
BEHAVIOR/
TEST CONCLUSIONS

OBSERVE/REFLECT
ON RESULTS OF
BEHAVIOR

OBSERVE/REFLECT
ON THE RESULTS OF
THE **REASONING**

INTERPRET
OBSERVATIONS

INTERPRET
OBSERVATIONS

SINGLE LOOP
...IS ABOUT BEHAVIOR

DOUBLE LOOP
...IS ABOUT **REASONING**
BEHIND THE BEHAVIOR

Figure 14.3 *Double loop learning*

in double loop learning will begin to attempt to achieve a different goal, by modifying their behaviors or rejecting old ones. This is a transformation self-awareness and practice, so that the leader can unlearn old behaviors and reflect critically on their performance.

When a leader is unavailable or uninterested in receiving input – or simply does not realize the importance of providing feedback – employees are more likely *not* to speak up. This is a thin bitter layer in the organization that can crumble altogether. What organizations need to recognize is that the barriers must be lifted, both the physical and the virtual blinds. When a colleague builds up the confidence to raise an issue directly, escalates it to their supervisor, and then it falls upon deaf ears, this poses a huge risk. Most likely these issues will never be called into the hotline and can slowly seep and snowball into larger risks, sometimes catastrophically fatal. An example of this can be seen in the BP and Deepwater Horizon case study (Ingersoll, Locke, & Reavis, 2012). Providing a vehicle to develop leaders around their role in driving engagement around the Code of Conduct and squarely centering the responsibility around their contributions as mentors and coaches to listen, offer feedback, and give guidance is critical. Tools, resources, and development need to be provided to help this front-line group create a consistent, effective tone in the middle.

14.8 Localizing the Message

Ethical decision-making in today's high-pressured, hyper-transparent, global environment is not always clear cut and riddled with gray areas. There are so many factors that can influence decision analysis. Organizations typically provide rules, policies, and standards that are designed to educate employees around potential risks and provide guidance around decision-making. As corporations rapidly expand their global footprint, simplifying and localizing the message are critical components that can promote greater understanding and knowledge retention. First off, employees need time to process their understanding and build the skills to effectively apply decisions. Providing clear and salient points that simplify complex and sometimes abstract policies into relevant application helps tremendously. Sharing stories of unintended consequences matters. Whether it's the disabling of warning lights on an oil rig so that employees can sleep, or prescribing of an off-label drug for weight loss that is actually a diabetes prescription drug, can lead to harmful outcomes. Discussing these messages by providing practical real-life situations is an excellent way to promote better understanding. Employees really need to visualize the context of ethical dilemmas, however big or small. For example, there are just too many ways bribery can occur and be hidden in the folds of an organization. Sometimes its visible, sometimes its right in front of us but we cannot see it. One study identified the source of issues around bribery as being a notion around collectivism: whereby the culture placed a shared identity and responsibility over the employee promoting bribery. Essentially the study showed that people who had a collectivist mindset were more likely to pay bribes and feel less personal accountability for their actions. Several studies around the psychology of corruption have pointed to the clouded perception of harm and/or lack of connecting the bribe to the human impact. People are less likely to see bribery as unethical when the harm from bribery appears remote. Therefore, communication is a critical activity that organizations should drive through local management on a regular basis. Instead of a corporate message from a CEO in London, for example, a regional leader for a company's operations in Kenya is in the better position converse with the local workforce. They can shine a light on the human element of corruption, citing how the bribes can lead to environmental damage, political crises, health impact, and so forth. Surfacing real-life scenarios that have unfolded within the organization or pointing to peer organizations in the headlines can contextualize the impact at a local level. The tailoring these scenarios for local, in-country examples drives more inclusivity and helps employees feel like they can truly relate to the situations. Supporting diversity of perspectives and experiences provides a framing of respect and sensitivity around local issues. It can also promote greater efficiencies and break down barriers that can often build silos or emerge as the result of mergers and acquisitions. The notions of "this is how we do things here" or "this is how it has always been done" can often be a natural blocking mechanism to change and growth, which suppress employees from speaking up. Bridging the dialogue by embracing cross-cultural environments and supporting a comfortable and open conversation can drive more impact. With more inclusivity and relevant messaging, there is greater local adaptation of how to apply the Code of Conduct in a local and practical context. Colleagues are more likely to lean in, report misconduct, and collaborate to problem solve when they (i) understand that they have a voice and (ii) realize how their voice can make a difference!

14.9 Decision Paralysis

Decision analysis and decisive action takes practice and is often motivated by the notion of "what's in it for me?" When anticipating how to navigate complex junctures in the journey of solving a problem, or when driving innovation, the path is riddled with decision points. In my practice, I've often observed that colleagues, even leaders, would rather make no decision than be held accountable for the wrong decision. Like playing in the sandbox of life, employees need the opportunity to practice their ethical decision-making skills. We can all relate to the fact that some of the best lessons in life are when we try–fail–learn. A great deal of professional responsibility involves making judgments and finding solutions to problems. Decision-making is a behavior that draws on one's own experiences and knowledge, while balancing this with decision guidelines. Learning new thinking skills and how to apply them can arise from observation, that is, watching the decision rules and reasoning models demonstrated by leaders. When employees are immersed in a decision-making model led by their front-line supervisor, they are likely to use that model as the acceptable norm or standard for reaching solutions and ethical decision-making. Stanford's Dr. Albert Bandura, a renowned expert in social cognitive theory, introduced a concept in his research referred to as the cognitive mastery modeling (Bandura, 2000). In this experiential model, employees who watched models verbalize their thoughts as they solved problems and heard rules being verbalized into action strategies produced faster learning than those only being told the rules or just watching the actions modeled. By combining the behavior and auditory learning, the experiential modeling produced an informative context that demonstrated how to go about solving problems. This cultivated self-efficacy for personal and organizational effectiveness (Locke, 2009).

Emerging from ongoing practice, and placing ourselves in environments that can help simulate real ethical dilemmas, allows us to practice collaborating, seeking guidance, and truly owning the learning experience from our own voice. Countless research studies have demonstrated that behavior change unfolds in phases and takes time, consistency, and relevant interactions. But without your workforce having the confidence to own their decisions, the pitfall is no decision. This can lead to inefficiencies, to a stagnant culture, and can breed fear. As an example, let's take a $50 billion multinational pharmaceutical client that was facing this complex issue. Despite being placed under several Corporate Integrity Agreements and designing a massive overhaul of their systems and approach to ethics and compliance, the bottom-line surface issue emerged as leaders' fear of making the wrong decision. I met with dozens of leaders through group and one-to-one interviews. It was clear that the systems, processes, and policies were all directly incentivizing and measuring success around achieving profit targets, without any evaluation criteria around ethical choices or how the leader achieved the target. The systems were basic building blocks to their program strategy, but there was a human element creating barriers whereby leaders lacked confidence or were not incentivized or encouraged to take accountability and drive forward decision-making or to question ineffective approaches and old ways of thinking. These behaviors point back to the earlier discussion on single loop versus double loop mindsets and how critical it is to unbreak the shackles of trying to achieve a new goal with old behaviors. Not surprisingly, the behavior emanated from leaders at some of the highest levels in the organizational hierarchy. Despite full empowerment and encouragement to make the right decisions and a plethora of policies and guidelines, leaders complained that their unfettered revenue targets and compensation incentives were not in alignment with the organization's desire to promote more transparent decision-making. No leader wanted to shoulder the visible individual responsibility of a significant decision that could challenge production or sales targets. Perceived efficacy can play a very influential role on the behaviors and motivations of individuals. If a leader anticipates an outcome based on their beliefs of how well they can perform in a specific situation, then that will motivate their pursuit of that outcome. The path in which they pursue that outcome will be guided by the organizational cultural norms and acceptable practices and behaviors to get there. After all, people act on their beliefs about what they can do, as well as on their beliefs about the likely outcomes of their performance. Skimming the front-page headlines, it is clear that these unethical behaviors are not limited to a specific region in the world or industry. Whether we read headlines from two decades ago about companies such as Worldcom, Enron, and the Bernie Madoff Ponzi scheme (Ackman, 2002) or more recent corporate scandals unfolding at Walmart, Uber, Petrobras, Volkswagen, and Wells Fargo, clearly there is a pattern of perceived efficacy influencing the outcome expectations.

Unfortunately, within many of today's twenty-first-century organizations, GRC program strategies are stuck in Phase I: a continuous cycle of simply raising awareness and checking the box. Behavior change requires a few sequential phases of activities to help the learner visualize and build the skill. Experience is another important factor to shape how we formulate decisions. Seeking formal or informal opportunities to simulate the environment and potential pressure points and competing perspectives can offer great practical application of decision-making. Often in my consulting I advise organizations to consider offering a quick discussion simulation at the top of a staff meeting or team tag-up, or a brown bag lunch discussing a ripped from the headlines issue. This can help normalize the dialogue, foster safer paths to surfacing tensions, and promote a greater voice for employees to raise concerns.

14.10 Avoid Blind Spots: Develop Managers to Lead with Integrity

A longtime industry colleague and influencer, CEO of ECI Patricia J. Harned has stated: "Everything a leader does sets a tone and organizations need to recognize that the line between public and private gets less clear every day. It is often said that a strong tone for ethics begins at the top" (Ethics.org, 2014). This crystallizes the essence of why it is important for organizations to get out in front and to proactively develop managers to lead. Leadership can truly make the difference between success and failure. According to ECI's NBES®, the most significant factor in ethical leadership is employees' perception of their leaders' personal character. Employees base their perceptions, on the behavior of those whose actions define what is acceptable or unacceptable behavior, that is, their supervisors. Leaders who model the message and demonstrate that they are ethical people with strong character have a much greater impact on employee behavior than merely the messaging efforts to promote ethics. As the old adage goes, actions speak louder than words. The NBES® report goes on to cite three factors where employees evaluate leaders: (ii) the overall character of their leaders as experienced through personal interactions; (ii) how senior leaders handle crises; and (iii) the policies and procedures adopted by senior leader to manage the organization (Ethics Resource Center, 2014).

Front-line management is in the best position to bring more practical and contextual reinforcement of how the organization's Code and Principles apply to everyday decision-making. These leaders can also surface blind spots. Leaders at every level need the right tools to proactively engage their teams by facilitating natural and informal conversations around living the Code of Conduct. Leveraging front-line management is a critical and reinforcing point of integration that can often be a missed opportunity when planning your ethics and compliance program strategies and implementing long-term planning. One of the top trends is for organizations to proactively develop opportunities to coach leaders to be more comfortable and prepared to exercise visible leadership in the context of living the Code of Conduct. People tend to fail to apply what they have learned if they distrust their ability to do it successfully. Albert Bandura (1994) refers to this action barrier as varying levels of self-efficacy, in which a person's beliefs in their abilities is derived by how they perceive and measure their ability from various sources, such as performance outcomes, verbal persuasion physiological feedback, and vicarious experiences (see Figure 14.4).

Leaders need to provide safe environments to support their colleagues' success. Employees tend to adopt modeled ways more readily if they see individuals in a position of influence, whether it be peers or managers, modeling strategies for success. This helps build their own confidence. Leaders at the top and throughout the organization influence patterns of perception around acceptable behavior. But the research points to the middle as the most influential layer; whereby front-line

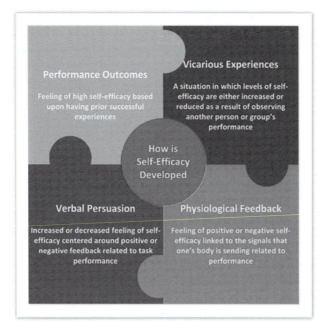

Figure 14.4 *Albert Bandura: self-efficacy development*

management is creating a safe space in which it is possible for employees to articulate their values and make a positive impact in situations where others may be pursuing an ethically questionable agenda. These middle influencers must demonstrate through guidance and visible action that every colleague can choose to exercise ethical leadership and help others find a more balanced and responsible decision path.

14.11 Listening Up: Building an Inclusive Workforce Culture

No colleague should feel alone. Inclusivity and feedback are a major component to learning, building confidence, and knowledge retention around ethical behavior. The more we can receive and provide constructive feedback, the more likely we will be able to sustain behavior change. One of the challenges I've observed in my consulting work is that employees who are exposed to rules and guidelines in the abstract usually struggle with applying them in contextual situations. Providing training on guidelines with generalized scenarios can satisfy a check-the-box strategy around ethics and compliance programs, yet it does not promote knowledge retention and skill building. Practicing the application of ethical decision-making in a relevant context will allow learners to draw on what is sometimes characterized as "moral muscle memory" (Barton, 2013). Adopting an experiential simulation on practical, real-life ethical dilemmas is the strategy that can help provide the right backdrop for colleagues and teams to practice integrating and learn how to recognize risk. Practicing evaluating dilemmas and the consequences of decision-making, through a safe and open conversation, can breed familiarity and supports a more cohesive dialogue. This framework is reinforced in Dr. Mary Gentile's practice around "giving voice to values" Actualizing consequences – that is, practicing the evaluation of what is at stake for all parties involved in a decision – is an important step in the learning process. Providing guided mastery by leaders to support colleagues around how to evaluate the reasons, rationalizations, and toxic triggers, is an important component to values-based decision-making. Individuals should not feel alone. Instead they should feel supported by a team of peers. Your workforce should sense that leadership is prepared to discuss how best to work together towards issue spotting and problem resolution (Gentile, 2012).

Simply allocating time for colleagues to practice application of complex ethical dilemmas in a safe space, facilitated by a leader, can promote internal diffusion of learning and supports the best practices of effective learning. Human behavior is extensively motivated and regulated anticipatorily by cognitive self-influence (Bandura, 2000). Unless people believe that they can produce desired effects and forestall undesired ones by their actions, they have little incentive to act. The outcomes people anticipate depend largely on their beliefs of how well they can perform in given situations, the research around expectancy-value theories frames this phenomenon. People will intrinsically act on their beliefs about what they can do well, as well as the likely outcomes of their behavior results. Therefore, those people that expect high efficacy will expect to gain favorable outcomes through their good performance. On the other hand, people who expect poor performances of themselves can conjure up negative results (Bandura, 1997; Locke & Latham, 1990). Several studies point to the neuroscience around building a high-trust environment. When oxytocin is activated the individual is more likely to extend trust, employees are more likely to intentionally build social bridges with their employer, and performance is more likely to improve. When managers demonstrate visible interest and concern for their employees' success and well-being, workers are more likely to outperform others in the quality and quantity of production. Another study has pointed to leaders who demonstrate vulnerability as being more likely to stimulate higher levels of trust amongst their teams. Requesting help can effectively tap into the natural human impulse to cooperate. When a leader demonstrates openness or vulnerability it can motivate employees to lean in and collaborate towards the collective success of the team. Further, employees are more likely to be engaged and productive when they operate in a high-trust environment, as visibility aligns them with their companies' purpose.

Timely coaching and mentorship are also critical to intentionally shaping an organizational culture. Guided mastery is a very effective method of cultivating ethical decision-making competencies. Yet decision-making is only as good as the execution. Therefore, individuals can perform poorly if the organizational environments that they are operating within are limiting, or not promoting ethical decision-making.

14.12 Moral Leadership

With Edelman Barometer's 2017 report pointing to trust declining across four institutions and Bloomberg's report on trust in public officials being at an all-time low (Green & Hopkins, 2017), the recent communication, decisions, and overall behavioral tone coming from the White House has placed greater pressure on corporate leaders to take a stance. LRN's State of Moral Leadership Report (LRN, 2018) points out that employees really want moral leadership from their managers and from those at the top of their companies – believing it will make their organizations better. The research shows that the vast majority of employees (83 percent) think their companies would make better decisions if they were to follow the "Golden Rule," and 59 percent think that their organizations would be more successful when taking on their biggest challenges if their leadership had more moral authority. This was exemplified in August 2017 shortly after the tragic events in Charlottesville, Virginia, when several prominent CEOs of multinational organizations resigned from the President's Councils on Infrastructure, Manufacturing, and the Arts (Price, 2017). This wave of CEOs using their world platform to send a message of intolerance to hatred, racism, and bigotry sent a strong message of alignment with their corporate GRC strategies. As corporations strive to build speak out cultures and promote values as business enablers, it is encouraging to see the CEOs take a stand on their commitment to American values and moral leadership. As noted by Matt Kelly, who runs the blog RadicalCompliance.com and is former editor of *Compliance Week*, "this is the moment for CEOs to show they are actual human beings, not self-driving vehicles on a quest for more shareholder value. Sometimes human beings have to stand up for what they know is right, even when standing up sucks and might cost them money. CEOs ask employees, through their compliance programs, to be willing to make that sacrifice every day. Let's hope the remaining number of CEOs on Trump's advisory council have the guts to do the same themselves." (Kelly, 2017).

Further, there is a bottom-line advantage to moral leadership leads. The State of Moral Leadership reports indicates that moral leadership leads to stronger performance. When managers lead with humility, they are twenty-two times more likely to be trusted by their colleagues. When managers are able to make themselves "small," thereby creating an atmosphere where others can stand up and deliver great performance, they are eleven times no more likely to achieve their business goals. At the World Economic Forum Annual meeting in 2017, one of the most overlooked leadership skills highlighted was having a moral compass. In this world of volatility, ambiguity, and constant change leaders need to be present: they must have moral agency. The next generation of ethics is upon us and leaders need to have the courage, when under pressure, to make the ethical trade-offs by "doing the right thing" (Hill, 2017).

References

Ackman, D. (2002, July 1). WorldCom, Tyco, Enron – R.I.P. *Forbes*. Retrieved from www.forbes.com/2002/07/01/0701topnews.html

Argyris, C. (1982, September). The executive mind and double-loop learning. *Organizational Dynamics*, *11*(2), 5–22. Retrieved from www.academia.edu/5321092/Reprinted_from_The_Executive_Mind_and_Double-Loop_Learning

Bandura, A. (1994). Self-efficacy. In V. S. Ramachaudran (Ed.), *Encyclopedia of human behavior*, Volume 4 (pp. 71–81). New York, NY: Academic Press.

Bandura, A. (1997). *Self-efficacy: The exercise of control*. New York, NY: Freeman.

Bandura, A. (2000). Cultivate self-efficacy for personal and organizational effectiveness [PDF File]. In E. A. Locke (Ed.), *Handbook of principles of organization behavior* (pp. 120–136). Oxford: Blackwell.

Barton, E. (2013, October 13). Managers: Train you brain for ethical decisions. BBC Capital. Retrieved from www.bbc.com/capital/story/20131007-the-morality-muscle

Bersin, J. (2015, March 13). Culture: Why it's the hottest topic in business today. *Forbes*. Retrieved from www.forbes.com/sites/joshbersin/2015/03/13/culture-why-its-the-hottest-topic-in-business-today/#5ad352b8627f

Corkery, M. (2016, September 8). Wells Fargo fined $185 million for fraudulently opening accounts. *The New York Times*. Retrieved from www.nytimes.com/2016/09/09/business/dealbook/wells-fargo-fined-for-years-of-harm-to-customers.html?_r=0)

Covey, S. M. R., & Merrill, R. R. (2006). *The speed of trust: The one thing That changes everything*. New York, NY: Free Press.

Deloitte. (2017). Global human capital trends. Retrieved from www2.deloitte.com/us/en/pages/human-capital/articles/introduction-human-capital-trends.html

ECI. (2018). Global business ethics survey. Retrieved from www.ethics.org/ecihome/research/gbes

Edelman. (2014). Edelman Trust Barometer, 2014. Retrieved from www.edelman.com/insights/intellectual-property/2014-edelman-trust-barometer/

Edelman. (2016). Edelman Trust Barometer, 2016. Retrieved from www.edelman.com/insights/intellectual-property/2016-edelman-trust-barometer/

Edelman. (2017). Edelman Trust Barometer, 2017. Retrieved from www.edelman.com/trust2017/

Ethics.org. (2014, December 11). Press release. Retrieved from www.ethics.org/press-release/employee-views-leaders-personal-conduct-perceptions-ethical-leadership/

Ethics Resource Center (2014). National business ethics survey of the U.S workforce [PDF File]. Retrieved from www.ibe.org.uk/userassets/surveys/nbes2013.pdf

Ethisphere (2017). 2017 Ethics and compliance survey: Align business goals with your ethics and values [PDF File]. Retrieved from www.ethic-intelligence.com/wp-content/uploads/2017-ethics-and-compliance-survey.pdf

Fowler, S.J. (2017, February 19). Reflecting on one very, very strange year at Uber. Retrieved from www.susanjfowler.com/blog/2017/2/19/reflectinSg-on-one-very-strange-year-at-uber

Gentile, M. C. (2012). *Giving voice to values: How to speak your mind when you know what's right*. London: Yale University Press.

Green, J., & Hopkins, J. S., (2017, August 15). Trump CEO's quitting panels as defectors' list grows. *Bloomberg Politics*. Retrieved from www.bloomberg.com/news/articles/2017-08-15/in-trump-we-trust-three-more-ceos-turn-backs-on-ceo-president

Hill, L. (2017, January 11). The most overlooked leadership skill? Having a moral compass. Part of the World Economic Forum Annual Meeting. Retrieved from www.weforum.org/agenda/2017/01/the-most-overlooked-leadership-skill-having-a-moral-compass/

Indeed blog (2017, August 8). Culture is the DNA of the company: An interview with JetBlue's SVP of Talent, Rachel McCarthy. Retrieved from http://blog.indeed.com/2017/08/08/culture-is-dna-company-interview-jetblue/

Ingersoll, C., Locke, R. M., & Reavis, C. (2012, April 3). *BP and the Deepwater Horizon Disaster of 2010* [PDF File]. Retrieved from https://mitsloan.mit.edu/LearningEdge/CaseDocs/10%2011O%20BP%20Deepwater%20Horizon%20Locke.Review.pdf

Kellogg Company (2013, September). *Living our values: Kellogg Company's global code of ethics* [PDF File]. Battle Creek, MI: Author. Retrieved from www.cnbc.com/2017/08/03/what-silicon-valley-can-learn-from-ubers-rise-and-fall.html

Kelly, M. (2017, August16). Trump tests corporate America's commitment to values.

Landler, M. (2017, August 16). Unlike his predecessors, Trump steps back from a moral judgement. *The New York Times*. Retrieved from www.nytimes.com/2017/08/16/us/politics/trump-charlottesville-moral-neo-nazis.html?mwrsm=LinkedIn

Larcker, D., & Tayan, B. (2016, June 9). We studied 28 incidents of CEO bad behavior and measured their consequences. *Harvard Business Review*. Retrieved from https://hbr.org/2016/06/we-studied-38-incidents-of-ceo-bad-behavior-and-measured-their-consequences

Locke, E.A. (2009). *Handbook of principles of organizational behavior* (2nd ed.) [PDF File]. Chichester, UK: John Wiley & Sons.

Locke, E. A., & Latham, G. P. (2013). *New developments in goal setting and task performance* (pp. 3–15). New York, NY: Routledge.

LRN. (2018). The State of Moral Leadership in Business. Retrieved from https://content.lrn.com/research-insights/2018-the-state-of-moral-leadership-in-business

Murray, A. & Huddleston, T., Jr. (2017, August 21). The moral imperative of leadership: CEO Daily. *Fortune*. Retrieved from http://fortune.com/2017/08/21/ceo-daily-monday-21st-august/

NRG Energy, Inc. (2016). *Powering Our Values: A Field Guide* [PDF File]. Retrieved from www.nrg.com/documents/legal/Code-of-Conduct-NRG.pdf

Office of Public Affairs. (2016, December 21). Odebrecht and Braskem plead guilty and agree to pay at least $3.5 Billion in global penalties to resolve largest foreign bribery case in history. *Justice News*. Retrieved from www.justice.gov/opa/pr/odebrecht-and-braskem-plead-guilty-and-agree-pay-least-35-billion-global-penalties-resolve

Oracle (2017). *2017 Oracle code of ethics and business conduct*. Redwood Shores, CA: Author.

Pellegrini, F. (2002, January 18). Person of the week: "Enron whistleblower" Sherron Watkins. *Time*. Retrieved from http://content.time.com/time/nation/article/0,8599,194927,00.html

Porath, C. (2015, May 11). The leadership behavior that's most important to employees. *Harvard Business Review*. Retrieved from https://hbr.org/2015/05/the-leadership-behavior-thats-most-important-to-employees

Price, R., (2017, August 17). Charlottesville is a tipping point in Silicon Valley's approach to hate speech. *Business Insider*. Retrieved from www.businessinsider.com/tech-companies-crack-down-hate-speech-charlottesville-2017-8

PwC. (2016). 19th Annual global CEO survey. Retrieved from www.pwc.com.cy/en/press-releases/2016/19th-annual-global-ceo-survey.html

Saris, P. B. et al. (2015). Sentencing of organizations [PDF File]. *Guidelines Manual* (pp. 499–542). Retrieved from www.ussc.gov/sites/default/files/pdf/guidelines-manual/2015/CHAPTER_8.pdf

Schein, E. (2010). *Organizational culture and leadership*. San Francisco, CA: Jossey-Bass.

Umoh, R. (2017, August 3). What Silicon Valley can learn from Uber's rise and fall. *CNBC*. Retrieved from www.cnbc.com/2017/08/03/what-silicon-valley-can-learn-from-ubers-rise-and-fall.html

Wall Street Journal. (n.d.). Retrieved from http://online.wsj.com/public/resources/documents/Uber-covington.pdf?mod=e2tw

Zetlin, M. (2017, June 30). Silicon Valley reeling after 24 female entrepreneurs speak out about sexual harassment. *Inc.* Retrieved from www.inc.com/minda-zetlin/sex-for-funding-silicon-valley-reeling-after-24-fe.html

Endnote

[1] www.oracle.com/webfolder/assets/ebook/employee-code-of-conduct-and-ethics/index.html#/page/57

PART III

Engineering

15

A Whistle Not Blown: VW, Diesels, and Engineers

Michael Davis

15.1 Introduction

This chapter is a "case study," that is, a collection of facts organized into a story (the case) analyzed to yield one or more lessons (the study). Collecting facts is always a problem. There is no end of facts. Even a small event in the distant past may yield a surprise or two if one looks carefully enough. But the problem of collecting facts is especially severe when the facts change almost daily as the story "unfolds" in the news. One must either stop collecting on some arbitrarily chosen day or go on collecting indefinitely. I stopped collecting on October 3, 2016 (the day on which I first passed this chapter to the editor of this volume). There is undoubtedly much to be learned from the facts uncovered since then, but this chapter leaves to others the collecting and analyzing of those newer facts. The story I tell is good enough for the use I make of it here – and for future generations to consider. Increasingly, whistleblowing is being understood to be part of the professional responsibilities of an engineer.

The facts this chapter collects concern what appears to be illegal conduct by employees of Volkswagen (VW), including board members and senior officers. There are several ways to analyze these facts. One can analyze them as a failure of management such as might be included in a course in business ethics; or as a failure of government supervision suitable for political scientists to study; or even as a failure of the news media the public may want to ponder. But I shall analyze them as a failure of engineers, something appropriate for a course in engineering ethics, both because my chief interest in these facts concerns engineering ethics and because that interest corresponds to the focus of this book.

Engineering may be studied as a function, job title, discipline, occupation, agent of technology, or the like, but I typically study engineering as a profession – and I understand "profession" in a specific way. For me, a profession is *a number of individuals in the same occupation voluntarily organized to earn a living by openly serving a certain moral ideal in a morally permissible way beyond what law, market, morality, and public opinion would otherwise require.*[1] Engineers typically embody that morally permissible way of serving their moral ideal in technical standards. So, when I study engineering, I am careful to distinguish engineers from those with whom they work, identify the special standards that apply to them, and note violations (if any). Most engineers are easily identified by their education, career path, and current title. Their code of ethics is one place to look for their technical standards.

This chapter is about whistleblowing – or, more exactly, about its absence when it seems there should have been some. Since "whistleblowing" is still a word that has several meanings, I should say what I mean by that term here. For the purpose of this chapter, one "blows the whistle" when one belongs to a legitimate organization (as would a VW employee) and goes out of the organization's normal channels to report serious wrongdoing in the organization for a morally permissible reason. Whistleblowing is a certain sort of going out of channels.

15.2 The Tip of the Iceberg

On September 9, 2016, James Robert Liang, a VW employee for more than thirty years, pled guilty in the United States District Court for the Eastern District of Michigan to having a significant role in VW's conspiracy to mislead US regulators concerning pollution-related emissions of diesel engines VW sold in the United States. Liang seems to be a technically adept mechanical engineer much of whose career was in Europe. He is credited as the inventor in at least one European patent related to motor technology. His indictment is unlikely to be the last. Facing up to five years in prison and a fine of $250,000, Liang agreed to cooperate with prosecutors (Tabuchi and Ewing, 2016c).

We still know relatively little about the scandal sometimes called "dieselgate." For example, we do not know what part Liang actually had in the scandal. All that we can now be sure of is that US prosecutors pursued him because he did enough to be indicted and, being resident in the United States at the time, could be arrested, questioned, and threatened with long imprisonment if he did not cooperate. The sovereignty of various European states, especially Germany, protects most of his coconspirators from similar treatment in the United States.

That protection is important because – from what we do know, or at least think we know – the center of the conspiracy was in Wolfsburg, VW's corporate headquarters in the German state of Lower Saxony, not in the United States. Software similar to that giving false readings for pollution tests on about a half million VW diesels sold in the United States between 2007 and 2015 did the same for more than eight and a half million VW diesels sold in Europe during the same period and another two million sold elsewhere (Tabuchi and Ewing, 2016a). After carrying out its own investigation in 2015, VW claimed that the software in question was the work of a small group of its employees ("a handful of rogue engineers") (Smith and Parloff, 2016). That claim is probably true. The software in question seems relatively simple – a few hundred lines of code (in a system having a hundred million lines), something a few engineers could have written and inserted.[2] However, the question in any corporate scandal of this scale is not so much who did the "dirty deed" itself as who ordered it; who aided it; who supervised it; who lied to authorities rather than reveal it; who knew but did nothing about it; and who took pains to remain ignorant, typically a much larger group. Of course, even that much larger group is probably no more than a few hundred employees out of VW's approximately 600,000 worldwide. (Volkswagen, Human Resources, 2016)

But that much larger group, even though still relatively small, is important. It has already cost VW much of its good reputation as well as $2 billion to be spent on cleaner-automobile projects, $2.7 billion for a US government fund to compensate for the environmental damage the diesels may have caused, and $10 billion to buy back affected autos in the United States at their pre-scandal value (and otherwise compensate owners) (Tabuchi and Ewing, 2016a).[3]

That group seems to include at least four high-ranking *engineers* at Wolfsburg, all of whom have now left VW, probably because of the scandal: Martin Winterkorn, then VW's chief executive officer (CEO); Wolfgang Hatz, then head of engine and transmission development at VW and Audi; Ulrich Hackenberg, then head of development for Audi; and Heinz-Jakob Neusser, then head of development for the VW brand (Tabuchi and Ewing, 2016b).[4] Unlike most scandals involving engineers, dieselgate seems to have no heroic engineers inside the organization.[5] What I want to do here is consider why that might be and what might be done about it.

15.3 The "Facts"

What we think we know about dieselgate may change substantially should any of those accused of wrongdoing go to trial, or the prosecutors open their files as part of a plea agreement, or someone leak VW files about the case. Until then, this is what we think we know:

1. For reasons of convenience and cost, regulators have been evaluating automobile pollution primarily by using a laboratory test-rig rather than more realistic road tests. They have known for some time that automobile performance on test-rigs can be several times better than on the road. But for autos other than VW's, the discrepancy between test-rig performance and road performance is generally the consequence of the testing protocol itself, both the rigidity necessary to apply the same standard to a large number of quite different autos and a failure of the test to keep up with the computerization of what used to be

simple mechanical devices. Autos today are much "smarter" than they were even a decade ago; the tests are not (Hakim, 2016).

2. All modern autos must have a test-rig mode as well as an on-the-road mode because the test-rig requires the front wheels to move while the back wheels do not. Without the test-rig mode, the traction-control system would interpret the rear wheels not rotating while the front wheels are rotating as a skid and try to correct, giving results having nothing to do with ordinary driving. The test-rig mode is necessary to keep the auto's computerized traction-control system from interfering with the tests.

3. The test-rig mode does not require any special hardware, only special software. The software switches from standard mode to test-rig mode when the traction-control senses that the front wheels can rotate freely while the back wheels cannot move at all. What distinguished VW's arrangement for testing diesel autos from others in the industry was not the test-rig mode but the *standard mode* that the test-rig mode preempted. The test-rig mode is not supposed to change any setting affecting pollution-control devices. VW's standard mode for diesels ("the cheat code") differed from the test-rig mode in the fuel pressure, injection timing, exhaust-gas recirculation, and (in models with AdBlue) the amount of urea fluid sprayed into the exhaust. The standard mode typically delivered the better mileage, responsiveness, and power on the road that drivers expected in their diesels. This is because, unlike the test-rig mode, the standard mode permitted much larger amounts of nitrogen oxide to exit the exhaust pipe, up to forty times more than the US limit.[6] Anyone who has ever driven a car when it lost its muffler will have some idea of the advantage VW's standard mode had over its test-rig mode.

4. On November 2, 2015, the US Environmental Protection Agency enlarged dieselgate by issuing notice of similar violations for the Porsche Cayenne and five Audi models as well as VW's Touareg (a joint venture between Audi, Porsche, and VW). Though Audi and Porsche are VW brands, their engines were developed by Audi in Ingolstadt, about 300 miles south of Wolfsburg. Thus, at least two groups of engineers were simultaneously breaking the law in much the same way for seven years, with little in common except the senior executives in Wolfsburg to whom both groups reported. Since it seems unlikely that two groups of engineers widely separated and working on engines belonging to different engine families would both "go rogue" in the same way at the same time, the obvious conclusion is that senior executives in Wolfsburg oversaw dieselgate. If there were any rogue engineers, they were in senior management.

5. Bosch provided the software for sensing the test-rig mode in 2007, warning against its misuse (just the sort of warning lawyers would insert in a contract to protect their client). VW promptly used Bosch's test-rig mode in software that had the pollution-spewing standard mode. Why? When Martin Winterkorn became VW's CEO in 2007, he announced that he would make VW the world

leader among auto-makers in volume, profit, and quality. One of his early actions was to order VW's engineers to deliver a clean diesel that could be sold worldwide (Ewing, 2015). The engineers soon realized they could not deliver such an engine without increasing the cost of a VW auto by at least $300, requiring owners to refill their urea reservoir inconveniently often, and otherwise making the diesel less marketable than desired. The engineers may have adopted the "cheat code" as a stopgap while they continued to look for a better way to control diesel pollutants.[7] Months became years as their search proved unsuccessful. Did Winterkorn know about the cheat code? He has denied any knowledge of it (Robinson, 2015).

6. That denial is implausible for at least three reasons. First, VW has a long history of strong management. Winterkorn was apparently brought in as CEO because he was that sort of manager. He was known to "rule by fear." Second, Winterkorn was not only a strong manager but a micromanager, someone who paid attention to details. The effectiveness of pollution controls was more than a detail. Diesel engines were a significant part of Winterkorn's strategy to make VW the world's largest automaker. Subordinates were therefore unlikely to adopt the cheat code on their own (Smith and Parloff, 2016). Third, Winterkorn was an engineer, though a metallurgical rather than mechanical engineer. He had enough experience at VW to understand its diesel technology, including the pollutant emission controls. If Winterkorn could honestly deny knowledge of the cheat code, it seems likely that he could do so only because he took pains to avoid such knowledge.

7. The cheat code seems like software that computer scientists could write, test, and insert, but not software that they could write, test, and insert without others, especially management and engineers, knowing. VW's documentation system should track all changes in software; hence, some managers should have known about the cheat code, especially what it was designed to do. A number of engineers would also have to know because they had to write the specifications for the software, calibrate the test-rigs, run the physical tests, and so on. The skill of VW's engineers is evident in the deception (Smith and Parloff, 2016).

8. Like Watergate, dieselgate is actually two scandals. VW engineers seem to be prominent in both. The first involves the original deception just described; the second, a cover-up. For almost a year after the California Air Resources Board first asked VW to explain why its diesels did so much better in rig tests than in road tests, VW engineers tried to explain away the difference – for example, by pointing to inadequacies in the road tests. Then one day they admitted what they had denied for almost a year: starting in 2008, VW had installed undisclosed software in its diesel engines that triggered a "second calibration intended to run only during certification testing [on the test rig]." On September 3, 2015, a VW official formally signed a document so stating (Smith and Parloff, 2016).

9. Some VW engineers in Germany may have informed a manager outside of their department of the cheat code – but none ever informed anyone *outside VW* even after the managers so informed seemed to have done nothing.[8] There may, then, have been some internal whistleblowing at Wolfsburg, perhaps reaching the very senior managers who had approved the deception. Winterkorn was "Chairman of the Board of Management of Volkswagen AG," the very body to which Group Auditing and other watchdogs reported. There was also (something like) internal whistleblowing in the United States once the cover-up reached it. But there was no *external* whistleblowing in Germany or the United States (Ewing, 2016a).

15.4 The Engineer As Employee

Any event as complex as dieselgate is likely to have several causes – not just one – but one cause seems to stand out: VW's (German) corporate culture. Let me explain.

If we accept the Code of Conduct issued under the signature of "Prof. Dr. M. Winterkorn, Dr. H. Neumann, and Bernd Osterloh" in 2010 as a (rough) statement of VW's culture during Winterkorn's term of office, we can see much that is good.[9] The Code applies not only to all employees of every company in the VW Group, their suppliers, and dealers but also to members of its executive bodies. The Code sets the baseline. Any of the organizations subject to it may adopt a stricter standard. Among the Code's "General Conduct Requirements" are: Responsibility for the Reputation of the Volkswagen Group; Responsibility for Basic Social Rights and Principles; Equal Opportunity and Mutual Respect; Avoiding Conflict of Interest and Corruption; Privacy and Data Security; Secrecy; Handling Insider Information; Occupational Safety and Health Protection; Environmental Protection; and Protection and Proper Use of Volkswagen Group Property. Even this recitation of section title suggests a code covering most categories of business ethics. In addition to the Code, there is an "ombudsman," an "anti-corruption officer," and other channels for reporting a violation of the Code. Yet, on close examination, it is clear that the Code has nothing useful to say about dieselgate.

The jurisdiction of the ombudsman, the anti-corruption officer, and the like is only over conflict of interest, secondary employment, corruption, and similar "white-collar crime":

> Each of our employees is obligated to seek help or advice upon suspicion or legal uncertainty about the existence of corruption or white-collar crime. Advice and assistance are provided by the superior, the responsible internal departments (e.g., Auditing, Legal, Compliance, Group Security, or Human Resources), the anti-corruption officer, or the ombudsmen. In addition, every employee can also turn to the Works Council.

(Volkswagen, 2010, p. 11)

Though this language (especially "white-collar crime") might seem to justify blowing the whistle internally in a case like dieselgate, the context forbids that interpretation. The language appears in the section entitled "Conflict of Interest and Corruption." The context thus limits the whistleblowing obligation to conflict of interest, corruption, and the like. That need not be so. VW America (VWGoA) does not so limit the corresponding provision. In the United States, the corresponding provision has its own section ("Reporting Code Violation, Corruption and Conflicts of Interest"). It is also much more explicit about when an employee should blow the whistle. It says (in part):

> Any employee who has knowledge of, or information concerning a past or present
> violation or possible violation of any law, regulation, policy or provision of this Code,
> or has knowledge or information indicating that such a violation may occur in the
> future, must promptly report such information to the Company's Compliance Officer,
> the Office of General Counsel, or the Ethics Hotline. In addition, all employees,
> contractors, suppliers or business partners may also turn to the VWGoA Ethics Hotline
> upon discovering indications of corruption or unethical or illegal practices.
>
> (VWGoA, 2015)

The text of the American version of VW's whistleblowing provision, like its placement, makes it clear that it would cover the kind of wrongdoing involved in dieselgate – since, whatever else dieselgate did, it violated a law or regulation. But, like its German counterpart, VWGoA's code makes no mention of *external* whistleblowing.

The other provisions of VW's (German) Code would also not be of much help to employees in Wolfsburg or Ingolstadt aware of dieselgate. The obvious place for them to look for guidance is "Environmental Protection." What would they find? Here is the whole section:

> We develop, produce, and distribute automobiles around the world to preserve
> individual mobility. We bear responsibility for continuous improvement of the
> environmental tolerability of our products and for the lowering of demands on natural
> resources while taking economic considerations into account. We therefore make
> ecologically efficient advanced technologies available throughout the world and
> implement them over the entire lifecycle of our products. At all of our locations, we are
> a partner to society and politics with respect to the configuration of social and
> ecologically sustainable positive development. Each of our employees make[s]
> appropriate and economical use of natural resources and ensure[s] that their activities
> have only as limited an influence on the environment as possible.
>
> (Volkswagen, 2010, p. 19)

The language in this section takes the form of statements of fact, not of obligations as in "Conflict of Interest and Corruption"; the focus is the "macro-ethical" ("we"), not on what individuals should do. The sentiments are noble (something one might expect in a public relations brochure). But the only responsibility VW recognizes for itself is "continuous improvement of the environmental tolerability of our products and for the lowering of demands on natural resources while taking economic considerations into account" (Volkswagen, 2010). Dieselgate was arguably trying to do that, that is, lower demands on natural sources *while* also taking economics considerations into account. The economic considerations won. The only reference to individuals in this section declares that each employee "make[s] appropriate and economical use of natural resources and ensure[s] that their activities have only as limited an influence on the environment as possible" (Volkswagen, 2010). It provides no measure of what is appropriate in a case like dieselgate (as VWGoA's Code does by requiring that what the employees do at least be legal).

The VW Group thus seems to have given little thought to ethics apart from conflict of interest and corruption. It certainly did not provide employees with internal channels for blowing the whistle on dieselgate, much less make any provision for dealing with wrongdoing by senior management.

The effect of a code of ethics is, of course, an empirical question, one I am in no position to resolve. My claim here is that, even if the code of ethics did guide the conduct of everyone at VW, dieselgate might well have occurred as it did. Whatever its effect, it seems to be a good guide to the way VW employees thought about what they should be doing.

15.5 The Engineer As Member of Profession

The VW Code (like VWGoA's) is for all employees, suppliers, and so on, not just for VW engineers. We might suppose, then, that VW's German engineers do not need a whistleblowing provision in their employer's code because European codes of engineering ethics, like their American counterparts, already have such a provision. Not so. Consider the Code of Conduct of the European Federation of National Engineering Associations (FEANI). There is no whistleblowing provision. The only provision that seems at all relevant to blowing the whistle on dieselgate is the last, "Social Responsibility":

The Engineer shall

- respect the personal rights of his superiors, colleagues and subordinates by taking due account of their requirements and aspirations, provided they conform to the laws and ethics of their professions,
- be conscious of nature, environment, safety and health and work to the benefit and welfare of mankind,
- provide the general public with clear information, only in his field of competence, to enable a proper understanding of technical matters of public interest,
- treat with the utmost respect the traditional and cultural values of the countries in which he exercises his profession. (FEANI, 2000)

We certainly can argue that the engineers at VW violated at least one of this section's four clauses. While VW's engineers might claim that they "work[ed] to the benefit and welfare of mankind" and were "conscious of nature, environment, safety and health [of mankind]", they could not claim to "provide the general public with clear information" about VW's diesels, a technical matter within their competence (FEANI, 2000). In that respect at least, they failed to blow the whistle on VW *externally* when they should have. But, another provision of FEANI's Code, one near the beginning, seems to forbid external whistleblowing (while allowing for informing the public with the consent of the employer): "He shall consider himself bound in conscience by any business confidentiality agreement into which he has freely entered" (FEANI, 2000). Employees, including engineers, typically must sign such an agreement as a condition of employment.[10] Even if they did not, VW's Code of Conduct (presumably a part of every employment contract, implicit if not explicit) declares ("Secrets"):

> Each of our employees is obligated to maintain secrecy regarding the business or trade secrets with which they are entrusted within the scope of the performance of their duties or have otherwise become known. Silence must be maintained regarding work and matters within the Company that are significant to the Volkswagen Group or its business partners and that have not been made known publicly, such as, for example, product developments, plans, and testing. (Volkswagen, 2010)

FEANI's code is meant to be "additional to and does not take the place of any Code of Ethics to which the registrant might be subject in his own country" (FEANI, 2000) Since 2002, there has been such a code for German engineers: "The Fundamentals of Engineering Ethics" of the Association of Engineers in Germany (VDI, 2002). At least five of its provisions seem relevant here. The first (1.3) requires engineers to "honour [laws and regulations of their countries] insofar as they do not contradict universal ethical principles." Of course, honoring laws or regulations is not necessarily the same as obeying them. But, even if it were, this provision would only tell German engineers to obey (morally acceptable) German law, not that of other countries, such as the United States, for which their products are destined. In any case, the point of 1.3 seems to be to deny that positive law automatically takes precedence over "universal ethical principles" (such as "don't lie," "don't cheat," and "keep your promises").

Another provision of the VDI Code (2.2) nudges German engineers in the direction of sustainable development rather than (dieselgate's) "short-term profitability":

> The fundamental orientation in designing new technological solutions is to maintain today and for future generations, the options of acting in freedom and responsibility. Engineers thus avoid actions which may compel them to accept given constraints (e.g. the arbitrary pressures of crises or the forces of short-term profitability).

Section 2.4 of the VDI Code provides more than a nudge in the same direction. It specifies that, in cases of conflicting values, engineers should give priority:

- to the values of humanity over the dynamics of nature, – to issues of human rights over technology implementation and exploitation,
- to public welfare over private interests, and
- to safety and security over functionality and profitability of their technical solutions.

Having set these priorities, 2.4 then hedges a bit: "Engineers, however, are careful not to adopt such criteria or indicators in any dogmatic manner." But the section ends with what seems to be an invitation to blow the whistle when appropriate: "[Engineers] seek public dialogue in order to find acceptable balance and consensus concerning these conflicting values."

Section 3.3 seems to reassert the priorities of 2.4: "national laws have priority over professional regulations, such professional regulations have priority over individual contracts." Engineers are, it seems, not to be bound by the employment contract when obeying it, even a pledge of secrecy, would violate national law or professional obligation. That is important because another provision of the VDI code seems to *allow* external whistleblowing:

> 3.4 There may be cases when engineers are involved into [sic] professional conflicts which they cannot resolve co-operatively with their employers or customers. These engineers may apply to the appropriate professional institutions which are prepared to follow up such ethical conflicts. As a last resort, engineers may consider to [sic] directly inform the public about such conflicts or to refuse co-operation altogether. To prevent such escalating developments from taking place, engineers support the founding of these supporting professional institutions, in particular within the VDI.
>
> (VDI, 2000)

Presumably, applying to "appropriate *professional* institutions" is a kind of external whistleblowing. The last resort, "consider to directly inform the public," does not quite allow informing the public, but it at least comes close.

To summarize: Engineers in Germany are *allowed* to blow the whistle on an employer who is violating human rights or harming the public welfare. They may blow the whistle by going to a "professional institution" and, as a last resort, perhaps by going public. They are under no obligation to do either. While the engineers involved with dieselgate did act contrary to their professional obligations – both because what they did was illegal and because it violated universal ethical principles, such as "don't lie" and "don't cheat" – all they were required to do was say no (i.e., to refuse to do the illegal or unethical acts in question). More could be required. Consider, for example, the equivalent provision of an American code of ethics for engineers:

> Engineers having knowledge of any alleged violation of this Code shall report thereon to appropriate professional bodies and, when relevant, also to public authorities, and cooperate with the proper authorities in furnishing such information or assistance as may be required.
>
> (NSPE, 2007)

15.6 Conclusion and Recommendations

The VW Group seems to have been ill-prepared to deal with wrongdoing by its senior management. Its internal whistleblowing arrangements covered only a narrow range of possible wrongdoing (conflict of interest and corruption), far from the full range of wrongdoing its own Code of Conduct covered.

Arrangements for internal whistleblowing seem to have assumed that senior management would never do anything in violation of the Code. There was, for example, no provision allowing the ombudsman, the legal department, or the auditors to turn a complaint over to an outside investigator who, upon establishing that senior management was implicated in wrongdoing, could report directly to stockholders or the appropriate governmental agency.

Nowhere in VW's Code of Conduct is there any recognition that engineers, or members of any other profession, might have their own code of ethics, much less that VW might want to encourage them to follow their code even when – indeed, especially when – that profession's ethics collided with management's plans.

Last, dieselgate seems to show that the codes of engineering ethics both of FEANI and VDI need to adopt much strong provisions for external whistleblowing. German engineers having knowledge of a violation of their code of ethics should have an obligation to report it to appropriate professional bodies and, when that is not enough to set things right, also to public authorities.

Whether changes in any code of engineering ethics, or in VW's Code of Conduct, would have any effect must, of course, depend in part on what engineering schools, engineering associations, and VW then do to inform engineers of their ethical responsibilities and to support engineers when they want to act responsibly. A code of ethics forgotten in a drawer is unlikely to have much effect on conduct even if it says everything it should. But a code of conduct integrated into the everyday operations of a corporation is likely to prevent wrongdoing of the sort we now call dieselgate.

References

Atiyeh, C. (2016, July). Everything you need to know about the VW diesel-emissions scandal. *Car and Driver*. Retrieved from http://blog.caranddriver.com/everything-you-need-to-know-about-the-vw-diesel-emissions-scandal/ (accessed September 23, 2016).

Boston, W. (2015, Feb. 27). Germany's Volkswagen posts rise in 2014 profit. *Wall Street Journal*. Retrieved from www.wsj.com/articles/germanys-volkswagen-posts-rise-in-2014-profit-1425052616 (accessed September 29, 2016).

Davis, M. (2009, June) Is engineering a profession everywhere? *Philosophia 37*: 211–225.

European Federation of Engineering Associations (FEANI), Code of Conduct (2000). Retrieved from www.tendrup.dk/feani.htm (accessed September 29, 2016).

Ewing, J. (2015, December 10). VW Says Emissions Cheating Was Not a One-Time Error. *The New York Times*. Retrieved from www.nytimes.com/2015/12/11/business/international/vw-emissions-scandal.html (accessed September 24, 2016).

Ewing, J. (2016a, March 14). VW Whistle-Blower's Suit Accuses Carmaker of Deleting Data. *The New York Times*. Retrieved from www.nytimes.com/2016/03/15/business/ energy-environment/vw-diesel-emissions-scandal-whistleblower.html?_r=0 (accessed September 25, 2016).

Ewing, J. (2016b, July 24). Researchers Who Exposed VW Gain Little Reward from Success. *The New York Times*. Retrieved from www.nytimes.com/2016/07/25/ business/vw-wvu-diesel-volkswagen-westVirginia.html?action=click&contentCollec tion=International%20Business&module=RelatedCoverage&region=EndOfArticle& pgtype=article (accessed September 25, 2016).

Hakim, D. (2016, February 7). Beyond Volkswagen, Europe's Diesels Flunked a Pollution Test. *The New York Times*. Retrieved from www.nytimes.com/2016/02/08/business/ international/no-matter-the-brand-europes-diesels-flunked-a-pollution-test.html?_ r=0 (accessed September 24, 2016).

Code of Ethics for Engineers (2007). National Society of Professional Engineers (NSPE), http://ethics.iit.edu/ecodes/node/4098 (accessed October 3, 2016).

Robinson, A. (2015, November 3). Caught black-handed: why did Volkswagen cheat? *Car and Driver*. Retrieved from http://blog.caranddriver.com/caught-black-handed-why- did-volkswagen-cheat/ (accessed September 23, 2016).

Smith, G. & Parloff, R. (2016, March 7). Hoaxwagen: How the massive diesel fraud incinerated VW's reputation – and will hobble the company for years to come. *Fortune*. Retrieved from http://fortune.com/inside-volkswagen-emissions-scandal/ (accessed September 25, 2016).

Tabuchi, H. & Ewing, J. (2016a, June 28). VW's US Diesel Settlement Clears Just One Financial Hurdle. *The New York Times*. Retrieved from www.nytimes.com/2016/06/ 29/business/vw-diesel-emissions-us-settlement.html (accessed September 20, 2016).

Tabuchi, H. & Ewing, J. (2016b, July 19). Volkswagen Scandal Reaches All the Way to the Top, Lawsuits Say. *The New York Times*. Retrieved from www.nytimes.com/ 2016/07/20/business/international/volkswagen-ny-attorney-general-emissions-scandal .html?module=Promotron&region=Body&action=click&pgtype=article (accessed Sep- tember 21, 2016).

Tabuchi, H. & Ewing, J. (2016c, September 9). VW Engineer Pleads Guilty in US Criminal Case Over Diesel Emissions. *The New York Times*. Retrieved from www.nytimes.com/ 2016/09/10/business/international/vw-criminal-charge-diesel.html?_r=0 (accessed Sep- tember 20, 2016).

VDI (2002, March). Fundamentals of Engineering Ethics. Retrieved from www.vdi.de/filead min/vdi_de/redakteur_dateien/. . ./engineering_ethincs.pdf (accessed October 1, 2016).

Volkswagen, Human Resources. Retrieved from www.volkswagenag.com/content/ vwcorp/content/en/human_resources.html (accessed September 21, 2016).

Volkswagen Group (2010, May). Code of Conduct (accessed September 28, 2016).

Volkswagen Group of America (VWGoA) (2015). Code of Conduct, December. Retrieved from https://search.yahoo.com/search?ei=utf-8&fr=tightropetb&p=Volkswagen+Group +of+America%2C+Code+of+Conduct%2C&type=113219_101817 (accessed September 28, 2016).

Volkswagen Group of America (VWGoA). Confidentiality Agreement. Retrieved from www.google.com/search?q=vw+employee+confidentiality+agreement&ie=utf-8& oe=utf-8 (accessed September 30, 2016).

Endnotes

[1] For an explanation (and defense) of this definition, see Davis, 2009.

[2] Computer scientists I have consulted think one or two computer scientists must have been involved. The engineers I consulted think not.

[3] For comparison, VW's annual profit in the last year before the scandal (2014) was $12.3 billion (Boston, 2015). The US settlement alone wiped out the annual profits of VW worldwide (in a good year).

[4] For engineering credentials, see: Martin Winterkorn, https://en.wikipedia.org/wiki/Martin_Winterkorn (accessed September 22, 2016); Wolfgang Hatz, www.bloomberg.com/research/stocks/people/person.asp?personId=73467911&privcapId=875012 (accessed September 22, 2016); Ulrich Hackenberg, www.volkswagenag.com/content/vwcorp/info_center/en/news/2014/01/Stanford_University.html (accessed September 22, 2016); Heinz-Jakob Neusser, www.bloomberg.com/research/stocks/people/person.asp?personId=222431348&privcapId=377732 (accessed September 22, 2016).

[5] The chief engineer-heroes of this story are in West Virginia. See, for example, Ewing, 2016b.

[6] Nitrogen oxide is a smog-forming pollutant linked to lung cancer (Atiyeh, 2016; Robinson, 2015).

[7] "The engineers viewed the ruse as a stopgap measure, Volkswagen has suggested, and hoped to abandon it when better technologies became available" (Smith and Parloff, 2016).

[8] "A whistleblower allegedly revealed the use of a defeat device to Heinz-Jakob Neusser, a Volkswagen brand-development boss and, later, management board member, according to the *Süddeutsche Zeitung*" (Smith and Parloff, 2016). There was also at least one other internal European "whistleblower" *after* the scandal broke. Under questioning by the American law firm (Jones Day) that VW hired to carry out an internal investigation of the scandal, he testified:

The pressure seemed to intensify inside VW. It wasn't "acceptable to admit anything is impossible," a company whistleblower told Jones Day … "Instead of telling management that they couldn't meet the parameters, the decision was taken to manipulate. No one had the courage to admit failure. Moreover, the engine developers felt secure because there was no way of detecting the deceit with the testing technology that existed at the time." It was, the whistleblower said, "an act of desperation" (Smith and Parloff, 2016).

[9] Like Winterkorn, Neumann (VW's Supervisory Board's member for Human Resources) retired since the scandal. www.volkswagenag.com/content/vwcorp/info_center/en/news/2015/11/Neumann.html (accessed September 26, 2016). Osterloh (Supervisory Board member for Labor, a lawyer) is still in office; www.volkswagenag.com/content/vwcorp/content/en/investor_relations/corporate_governance/supervisory_board.html (accessed September 26, 2016). The version of the Code now posted at www.volkswagenag.com/content/vwcorp/content/en/the_group/compliance.html (accessed September 28, 2016) is unsigned and dated September 2015 but seems otherwise without significant change.

[10] While I could not obtain a copy of VW's (German) confidentiality agreement, I think the English version used by VWGoA gives a general idea of what it contains. See VWGoA, 2016.

16

Addressing Corruption in Our Global Engineering/Construction Industry

William P. Henry

16.1 Introduction

The global engineering/construction industry is huge. In 2017, it was estimated to be an $8.8 trillion industry (Market Research Hub, 2016). The US construction industry in 2017 was estimated at $1.2 trillion (Wilcox, 2018). Because the industry is comprised of a myriad of projects to build new facilities or to repair or upgrade existing ones, it is often the location for bribery, fraud, and corruption. Government leaders in Panama, Brazil, and Spain have been removed from office for receiving bribes and kickbacks from projects in their countries. Engineering firms in the United States and Canada have been sanctioned for giving bribes to secure projects. These are the facts.

Another fact is that the projects are needed to improve the lives of the people in their area. Still another fact is that the project is the focus of working engineers and constructors. The unit of work produced by most engineers in private practice with consulting engineering firms or construction companies is the project. Many engineers in government and with manufacturers also regularly produce projects as their work output. Engineers are expected to hold paramount public health, safety, and welfare. They also are expected to support the principles of sustainable development, which has become a primary consideration on projects. Sustainable development, which strives to achieve economic, environmental, and social goals on a project, cannot occur where corruption is present. A major dilemma, which is based on reality, is that a little bribery or kickback is often required in order to move the needed project forward. How can we tolerate this corruption while striving to meet the goals of sustainable development? The answer is that corruption cannot be a part of our industry.

Forecasts show that most engineering/construction projects will be built in the developing countries. By 2020, two thirds of the major cities in the world will be in these developing countries, and they will be the homes for many engineering/construction projects (Henry, 2009). In addition, engineering/construction projects are becoming larger. Not too long ago, multi-million-dollar projects were considered large. Today we see multi-billion-dollar ones. With this increase in the geographical distribution of projects and in project size, more and more of the projects are being performed by ad hoc teams of firms who join together for a specific piece of work. These teams may be comprised of firms from a variety of countries and cultures with little or no experience working together on joint projects. There may not be a common understanding of ethical practice which can lead to corruption occurring on the project. Large, multinational projects as well as small local projects all face the potential for corruption. All these changes point to the fact that ethical practice in the next generation will have to have a stronger, more focused approach than ever before.

It is estimated that more than $500 billion is lost to corruption each year in the global engineering/construction industry. While the economic loss is staggering, the real tragedy lies with the people who need clean water, wastewater treatment, flood control, roads and bridges, schools, hospitals, and residential projects implemented – and implemented safely. Corruption reduces the number of projects that can be built, and can compromise the safety of some that are. These are other reasons why corruption cannot be part of our engineering/construction industry.

In this chapter, we will learn the names and have descriptions of corrupt practices to give individuals the vocabulary and information needed to discuss potential corruption issues as they arise and to avoid corrupt practices at work. We will identify the wide variety of organizations that participate in the engineering/construction industry. We will cover current anti-corruption activities so you may follow the progress of those which interest you. In addition, the chapter will contain sources of information on anti-corruption practices that can be implemented by individuals and organizations in the engineering/construction industry.

16.2 Engineering/Construction Industry Participants

There is a diverse variety of participants on engineering/construction projects:

- public owners – infrastructure projects, public buildings, procurement
- private owners – factories, refineries, power plants, buildings, procurement
- engineers – planning, design, permit applications, construction services
- constructors – procurement, construction, material disposal
- lenders – to owner, to constructor
- material suppliers – to owner, to constructor
- equipment suppliers – to owner, to constructor
- insurers – to all of the above participants
- regulatory/permitting agencies – owner, engineer, constructor, suppliers.

While not all participants have contractual relationships with each other, all will interact on a project. Because there are so many types of organizations involved, and corruption requires only two individuals to act in an unethical manner, there is a wide array of opportunities for corruption on a project.

16.3 Corruption Vocabulary

Ethical behavior is the goal, but many engineers don't have the vocabulary needed to achieve it. It has proved helpful to define components that are the opposite of ethical behavior – corruption – to provide needed vocabulary.

The dictionary defines corruption as the "inducement to [do] wrong by improper or unlawful means," and "dishonest or illegal behavior especially by powerful people" (Merriam-Webster, 2018). The latter includes the misuse of official power for personal gain.

In our engineering/construction industry, the main forms of corruption are:

- kickbacks and bribery
- front companies
- bid rigging and collusion
- conflicts of interest
- fraud
- money laundering.

Any and all of these can occur on any project.

16.3.1 Kickbacks and Bribery

Kickbacks and bribery are two sides of the same coin. A kickback is a demand for payment by someone in a position of authority in return for a decision favorable to the prospective payee. Bribery is an offer to pay someone in a position of authority to make a decision favorable to the offeror.

The person in the position of authority seeking a kickback may be a purchaser (a government official, private owner, or purchasing agent buying materials, equipment, engineering services, or construction services); engineer, constructor, or supplier selecting subcontractors; lender making a decision to lend to a given owner; or regulator in charge of permitting or inspection decisions.

The person offering a bribe may be an engineer, constructor, material or equipment supplier (seeking business, permits, or inspection approvals), or an owner seeking funding. The results of bribery can be devastating for both firms and individuals. In 2012, the chief executive officer (CEO) of the Canadian company SNC-Lavalin resigned and was criminally indicted by the

Canadian government for bribery in regard to a billion-dollar contract for a hospital in Montreal. In 2013, the World Bank announced a ten-year ban on SNC-Lavalin for its conduct on a project in Bangladesh (The World Bank, 2013). In another recent case, two senior executives of Louis Berger, a New Jersey–based construction management company, were sentenced to prison in July 2016 for bribing officials in India, Indonesia, Vietnam, and Kuwait in order to secure government contracts (USAO–New Jersey, 2016).

Bribes can be direct payments or "political contributions," known as "pay to play" payments, which keep qualified, ethical firms from obtaining work. In April 2016 three executives from Birdsall Services Group received prison sentences, fines, and disbarments for a scheme in which their employees made political contributions in New Jersey that the firm then reimbursed to the employees (OAG–New Jersey, 2016).

By far the biggest fine for bribery – $1.34 billion – was levied by the US Department of Justice and Germany against Siemens AG for paying more than $100 million in bribes to the Argentine government in order to secure a $1 billion contract (Lichtblau and Dougherty, 2008).

There are opportunities for bribes and kickbacks on any project in any country.

16.3.2 Front Companies

A front company is established in secret by a corrupt owner or staff to provide little service to a project while being paid substantial fees. On a multinational project, it often serves as a local agent for the engineer or constructor.

A front company is usually a new company that has no available track record and offers a variety of unconnected services. Although these traits are also common among legitimate joint venture companies, the biggest difference is the availability of ownership records. A front company has few records of ownership because the owners do not want to be known; a legitimate joint venture has clear, open ownership records.

16.3.3 Bid Rigging and Collusion

Bid rigging and collusion can be accomplished by any member of an engineering/construction project team – the owner, engineer, constructor, lender, supplier, insurer, or regulator. An owner can rig bids by setting short bid periods so that only the firms they illegally notify of the project in advance of the general project announcement will be able to submit detailed, responsive bids. An owner could also rig bids by excluding qualified firms from bid lists that include only "favored" firms.

After contracts have been signed, collusion may involve deals between the owner's and constructor's personnel. For example, the owner's staff may approve unjustified project modifications or change orders that raise the contractor's revenue, lower its cost, or both, in exchange for compensation.

Constructors and suppliers may engage in bid rigging and collusion by agreeing among themselves which firm will be the successful bidder on each of a series of projects. On each project, the agreed-upon winner submits an artificially high bid, and the others submit even higher bids. This gives excess profits to firms and reduces the funds available for other projects.

Bid rigging and collusion can also be parts of more complex corruption schemes.

16.3.4 Conflicts of Interest

All types of conflicts of interest are forms of corruption. The most obvious conflicts involve decisionmakers who get direct personal gain from their decisions on a project. Less obvious conflicts of interest involve the decisionmaker's friends or family members who get the direct personal gain from a decision. All participants in a project have the potential for conflicts of interest.

16.3.5 Fraud

There are many opportunities for fraud in engineering/construction projects; some of the most common fraudulent acts are:

- embezzling funds from project accounts
- taking vehicles, computers, other project equipment or materials for personal use
- using project funds, equipment, and/or materials for non-project uses such as building or remodeling a house or taking a vacation
- selling project equipment or supplies for personal profit
- setting up employment and collecting paychecks for "ghost employees"
- substituting lower-quality materials or equipment than specified in the contract, while billing at the contract prices
- billing employees at rates higher than called for in their pay grades
- falsely claiming Disadvantaged Business Enterprise (DBE) status.

In August 2016, Larry Davis, an executive with DCM Erectors Inc., a firm that received nearly $1 billion in contracts to rebuild the World Trade Center in New York City, was convicted of wire fraud and conspiracy in Federal District Court in Manhattan (USAO–Southern District of New York, 2016). His fraudulent behavior involved claiming that people were owners of qualified DBE firms when they were not.

In 2013 the Justice Department recovered nearly $3 million from TesTech and its owner Sherif Aziz, and CESO and its owners David and Shery Oakes, for falsely claiming DBE status on federally funded transportation projects in Ohio (USDOT OIG, 2014).

Opportunities for fraud are open to all project participants, but, if discovered, you could face stiff fines and, in some cases, jail, making it a risky proposition.

16.3.6 Money Laundering

Money laundering involves taking illegally obtained money (e.g., from bribes or kickbacks) and channeling it into legal businesses such as a construction company. The company's revenue and expenses can be overstated and the resulting profit appears to be legitimate.

In March 2016 in Brazil, Marcelo Odebrecht, president of Odebrecht Construction, was sentenced to nineteen years and four months in prison for corruption and money laundering (Dickerson et al., 2016).

If kickbacks, bribery, front companies, bid rigging, collusion, conflicts of interest, fraud, and money laundering are not part of your vocabulary and the vocabulary of the people you work with, training is needed to ensure that all engineers fully understand the terms presented here, so that they recognize the behaviors and can communicate about corruption and related activities.

Once the terms are understood, it is easier to communicate about corruption and the activities that could reflect poorly on you, your organization, and our profession.

16.4 Promoting Ethical Behavior

By now, you've realized that corruption and projects can go together like summer and heat or winter and cold. But just as you can put on the appropriate clothing for heat or cold, you can also make sure that you and your organization don the appropriate protective gear to thwart corruption. The gear includes management systems that are open, transparent, and implemented throughout the organization as well as training for employees on anti-corruption policies and procedures. It also includes an organizational culture in which all employees, from the chairman down to the newest hire, know the potential for corruption on projects, the actions they must take if they find it, and your overall stance on ethical performance.

Organizations have developed practical, economical, and successful management systems that prevent corruption on megaprojects. Key ones are:

• Constructors
• Consulting Engineers
• Construction Observers
• Lenders
• Professional Societies
• Independent Industry Groups
• Engineering/Construction Industry Standards.

The broad array of material these organizations have produced for use in formulating, improving, or implementing an anti-corruption program in an organization
and strengthening the ethical focus of its culture is detailed in the following pages.

16.4.1 Constructors

Partnering Against Corruption Initiative (PACI)
In 2005, the firms in the engineering/construction section of the World Economic
Forum launched PACI (Tashjian, 2009). Today, more than 140 companies
from thirty-nine countries have agreed to the PACI Principles for Countering
Bribery. PACI is a private sector, supply-side initiative to establish multi-industry
principles and practices to eliminate corruption in both the procurement and
performance phases of projects. The principles and practices are based on integrity, fairness, and ethical conduct. Under PACI, the CEO of each participating
company commits, in writing, to do two things:

1. Commit the company to a zero-tolerance policy for bribery; and
2. Implement a strong, active anti-corruption program to guide the behavior of
   the company's employees.

A firm may join PACI without joining the World Economic Forum. Details can be
found at the PACI website[1]

16.4.2 Consulting Engineers

International Federation of Consulting Engineers (FIDIC)
FIDIC chose to identify their products with "integrity management" because the
term identifies that ethical integrity is needed to fight corruption and that a strong
management system is needed to control a firm's activities and verify its ethical
performance. FIDIC's Business Integrity Management System (BIMS) provides
the necessary management documents and examples from companies and is
available on CD. BIMS is tailored to the engineering units of a firm and can be
independently verified as an International Standards Organization (ISO)

9000 management system. Government Procurement Integrity Management System (GPIMS) is tailored to the procurement units of a firm. The FIDIC website contains detailed information.[2]

16.4.3 Construction Observers

Transparency International (TI)

TI's 2008 Bribe Payers Index (Krishnan, 2009) noted that public works and construction were seen to be the most corrupt industry sectors. In 2007, TI published its Project Anticorruption System (PACS) containing standards and templates that target bribery and fraud. PACS allows the user to implement programs that include: independent monitoring; due diligence; contract terms; procurement requirements; government commitments; corporate programs; programs for individuals; training; reporting; and enforcement. PACS has been distributed to TI national units, engineering and construction associations, banks, and governments. TI also prepares their Corruption Perceptions Index, which addresses the openness of decision-making in countries around the world annually.[3]

16.4.4 Lenders

The major lenders are:

The World Bank
Asian Development Bank
African Development Bank
Inter-American Development Bank
European Investment Bank
European Bank for Reconstruction and Development
International Monetary Fund

These lenders have standardized their approaches when dealing with corruption and are developing proposals to assist countries in strengthening their anti-corruption capabilities. While these programs may not be directly applicable to any given organization, they provide good information on the changes that governments may make in project procurement procedures and the roles and activities of regulatory and permitting agencies. Checking on how a government agency does business is always part of complete due diligence on every project.

16.4.5 Professional Societies

The World Federation of Engineering Organizations (WFEO), Asian Civil Engineering Coordinating Council (ACECC), Engineers Australia (EA), and the American Society of Civil Engineers (ASCE) all are active in addressing corruption in the engineering/construction industry. They are all societies whose membership is comprised of individuals – not companies or agencies. As such, they offer material and opportunities that focus on the individual engineer: including training in avoiding and dealing with corruption, and opportunities for networking with others from different parts of the engineering/construction industry and different countries. They also offer materials that can make beneficial contributions to an organization's corporate culture.

WFEO has a standing Anti-Corruption Committee with members from each continent. The Committee holds annual meetings where the latest information is shared with all in attendance and leads workshops dealing with addressing corruption in business dealings. You can learn of their activities at their website.[4]

ACECC also has a standing Anti-Corruption Committee with members from each member country. Like the WFEO Committee, they hold meetings and workshops. Information on ACECC activities can be found at their website.[5]

Both WFEO and ACECC provide anti-corruption information useful in marketing and professional development programs.

EA has been active in revising the National Code of Practice for the Construction Industry in Australia (Hartley, 2009). Firms working on government-funded projects there must be in compliance with the Code, including its provisions for ethical behavior.[6] The website will also provide ideas on the contents for an anti-corruption management system.

ASCE offers many resources for individual training, management systems, and practical information on ethical behavior. It has a comprehensive Continuing Education Department that delivers technical, management, and ethical courses via seminars and webinars. Its Code of Ethics contains the elements needed for a strong anti-corruption culture.[7]

16.4.6 Independent Industry Groups

The Global Infrastructure Anti-Corruption Centre (GIACC) and the Anti-Corruption Education and Training (ACET) program also have valuable, well-developed materials available for use.

In May 2008, two experienced construction attorneys in England founded GIACC (Stansbury, 2009): an independent, non-profit organization that promotes implementing anti-corruption measures as part of managing companies, agencies, and projects. It models its approach to managing corruption similarly to the ways safety, quality, and risk are controlled – by using procedures, training, monitoring, and enforcement. The GIACC website contains a great deal of useful information.[8] There are descriptions and examples of corruption, which are useful for employee vocabulary and training exercises. There are also examples of anti-corruption programs suitable for agencies, companies, and lenders. A complete PACS designed to prevent and detect corruption on projects is introduced. An array of anti-corruption tools is presented, including:

- a claims code
- example contract terms
- a corporate code
- a discussion of due diligence procedures
- example employment terms
- a gifts and hospitality policy
- suggested procurement activities
- suggested reporting requirements
- organization rules to consider
- training needs and programs
- ideas for achieving transparency in your organization.

The GIACC website provides a wealth of materials that are useful for starting an anti-corruption program in an organization or for benchmarking a current program against other well thought out, practical programs. Of particular use on megaprojects is the information on due diligence. It covers the following: country of the project and its laws; the reality that the project is necessary and conceived for a legitimate purpose; the owner's history; potential business partners, subcontractors, suppliers, and agents; and the tools available to help an organization be sure that corruption will not be part of its project.

The ACET Program is a second industry group project that offers valuable information. This Program was carried out by a senior international group from the engineering/construction industry who believed that a good training program for practitioners and engineering students would be a valuable contribution to the profession. The ACET team raised the funds, hired the writer and producer, and, with them, developed the script for a forty-two-minute DVD drama entitled *Ethicana*. The drama depicts corruption in the procurement and production of a megaproject. The complete *Ethicana* package contains the DVD, classroom materials, trainer materials, and a "Train the Trainer" module. *Ethicana* is suitable for use with both procurement and project staffs. It reinforces the vocabulary needed to have an ongoing dialogue on anti-corruption in an organization. It exposes the attendees to situations they may face on megaprojects. The scenarios depicted were developed from the experience of the ACET team members. Having faced these situations in a classroom, and having discussed them with senior personnel and peers, makes employees better able to handle the situations properly in their work. *Ethicana* is a training program to develop and improve the ethical standards of employees because it shows them "why" they should act ethically while following the anti-corruption program of their organization, which tells them "what" to do.

Information on *Ethicana* is found on the ASCE website.[9]

16.4.7 Engineering/Construction Industry Standards

The ISO is well known for its important contributions to project quality (ISO 9001) and environmental management (ISO 14001). In October 2016, it adopted a new standard ISO 37001:2016 Anti-Bribery Management Systems. ISO 37001 is based on the premises that:

1. Organizations should implement anti-bribery measures because bribery prevention is a *management issue*. Good management reduces bribery.
2. Bribery prevention should be treated like safety, quality, and environmental management.

Internationally, many organizations have implemented anti-bribery management systems and are ensuring that their partners and supply chain members implement such programs. Governments, lenders, and companies are all adopting anti-bribery measures.

ISO 37001 is a Type A requirements standard, which can be independently certified. It contains supporting guidance to help with implementation. While ISO 37001 focuses on bribery, it can be expanded to include other corruption offenses. ISO 37001 requires the organization to implement measures designed to help the organization prevent, detect, and deal with bribery. The key measures are:

1. Implementing an anti-bribery policy and supporting procedures – the Anti-Bribery Management System (the ABMS). These procedures are listed here.
2. Ensure that top management has responsibility for implementing an effective anti-bribery policy and ABMS.
3. Appoint a person(s) to oversee anti-bribery compliance (compliance function).
4. Allocate responsibilities for ensuring compliance with the anti-bribery policy and ABMS throughout the organization, e.g., department heads responsible for compliance in department; all personnel responsible for their personal compliance.
5. Ensure that controls are in place over decision-making (e.g., appropriate seniority of decisionmaker, no conflicts of interest).
6. Implement appropriate vetting and controls over personnel to ensure their competence and their willingness to comply with the anti-bribery policy and ABMS.
7. Provide training to personnel on the anti-bribery policy and ABMS.
8. Perform periodic bribery risk assessments and appropriate due diligence on transactions and business associates.

9. Implement financial controls to reduce bribery risk (e.g., two signatures on payments, restricting use of cash, etc.).
10. Implement procurement, commercial, and other non-financial controls to reduce bribery risk (e.g., separation of functions, two signatures on work approvals, etc.).
11. Implement controls over gifts, hospitality, donations, and similar benefits to prevent them from being used for bribery purposes.
12. Ensure that every organization it controls implements anti-bribery measures.
13. Require, where practicable, any business associate that poses more than a low bribery risk to implement anti-bribery controls that *manage* the relevant bribery risk.
14. Obtain anti-bribery commitments from business associates who pose more than a low bribery risk.
15. Ensure that the organization does not participate in, or withdraws from, transactions in which it cannot *manage* the bribery risk.
16. Ensure that resources (personnel, equipment, financial) are available to implement the ABMS effectively.
17. Produce and retain documentation on the design and implementation of the anti-bribery policy and ABMS.
18. Implement reporting (whistleblowing) procedures that enable persons to report suspected bribery, or a breach of the ABMS, to the compliance personnel.
19. Implement procedures to investigate and deal with suspected or actual bribery or a violation of the ABMS.
20. Monitor, measure, and evaluate the effectiveness of the ABMS.
21. Perform internal audits to assess whether the ABMS complies with ISO 37001 and is being effectively implemented.
22. Undertake periodic reviews of the effectiveness of the ABMS by the compliance function and top management.
23. Rectify identified problem with the ABMS, and improve the ABMS as necessary.

ISO 37001 has an Annex that contains guidance to help an organization implement an anti-bribery program.

Neither ISO 37001 nor any standard can totally eliminate bribery. But it establishes that an organization has implemented anti-bribery measures. The risk of bribery is reduced and the playing field is leveled if proof of compliance with ISO 37001 is a project pre-qualification requirement. The publication and use of ISO 37001 is a major step forward in reducing bribery.

16.5 Conclusion

Engineering/construction projects are vital to the people for whom they are built, and important to agencies in implementing their missions as well as lenders and firms to keep their businesses thriving. All indications are that there will be more global projects in the future than ever before. Many are forecast in developing countries where corruption has been systemic. It will take vigilance and ongoing management attention to keep corruption at bay on all projects in all countries.

The two most effective tools for ethical practice are:

1. A project culture founded on ethical behavior, embraced by all levels of staff and management, and communicated to all project team members and business partners.
2. Strong management systems that start from the highest ranks of the organization and whose implementation is regularly verified throughout the organization.

For the first tool to be effective, employees must be able to talk with a common, well-understood vocabulary. The importance of vocabulary cannot be overstated – it is the basis for communicating about the ethical component of a project, and marks the difference between people talking with each other or talking past each other. It enables regular discussions on ethics among engineers, between engineers and managers, and among managers.

For the second tool to be effective, organizations must have anti-corruption systems that clearly demonstrate a strong conviction to keep corruption away from projects. Such systems are the day-to-day guardians against corruption. If they are in place, it is wise to benchmark them against what others are doing; if they are not, now is the time to develop and implement them. GIACC, FIDIC, and ISO 37001 provide the tools needed to initiate or benchmark an anti-corruption management system.

There are many sources of information on effective anti-corruption systems that can be developed in stages. The important thing to remember is that systems are only words on paper unless they are implemented with top-down authority and their continuous use is verified on a regular basis.

Anti-corruption materials, guidelines, and training programs give real-life meaning to the words through realistic examples of corruption. These materials can make corruption less likely to occur on every project.

Note

William P. Henry, P.E., D.WRE, is a past president of the ASCE and a past chair of the American Association of Engineering Societies (AAES). He has chaired or served on the ACECC, Union of Pan American Engineering Associations (UPADI), and the WFEO Anti-Corruption Committees.

References

Dickerson, M., Magalhaes L., & Lewis, J. T. (2016, March 8). Odebrecht ex-CEO sentenced to 19 years in prison in Petrobras scandal. *The Wall Street Journal.*

Retrieved from www.wsj.com/articles/odebrecht-ex-ceo-sentenced-to-19-years-in-prison-1457449835

Hartley, R. (2009, July). Fighting corruption in the Australian construction industry: The National Code of Practice. *Leadership and Management in Engineering*, ASCE, 9(3), 131–135.

Henry, W. (2009, July). Addressing corruption in our engineering/construction industry. *Leadership and Management in Engineering*, ASCE, 9(3), 101–102.

International Standards Organization (ISO). (2016, October 15). International Standard ISO 37001 Anti-bribery management systems – Requirements with guidance for use. Switzerland.

Krishnan, C. (2009, July). Combating corruption in the construction and engineering sector: The role of Transparency International. *Leadership and Management in Engineering*, ASCE, 9(3), 112–114.

Lichtblau, E., & Dougherty, C. (2008, December 15). Siemens to pay $1.34 billion in fines. *The New York Times*. Retrieved from www.nytimes.com/2008/12/16/business/world business/16siemens.html

Market Research Hub. (2016). Global Construction Outlook 2021. Albany

Meriam-Webster. (2018). Retrieved from www.miriam-webster.com

OAG [Office of the Attorney General]–New Jersey. (2016, April 22). Ex-CEO of Birdsall Services Group sentenced to prison for evading pay-to-play law by using employees to make illegal political contributions. News release. Trenton.

Stansbury, C. (2009, July). The Global Infrastructure Anticorruption Centre. *Leadership and Management in Engineering*, ASCE 9(3), 119–122.

Tashjian, L. (2009, July). Partnering against corruption initiative leads industry battle against corruption. *Leadership and Management in Engineering*, ASCE, 9(3), 123–124.

USAO (US Attorney's Office)–New Jersey. 2016. Two former executives of Louis Berger International sentenced in foreign bribery scheme. Press release, July 8. Newark.

USAO (US Attorney's Office)–Southern District of New York. (2016, August 10). CEO of steel contractor on World Trade Center site convicted at trial of fraud in connection with program designed to encourage participation of minority and women-owned businesses. Press release. New York.

USDOT OIG (US Department of Transportation Office of Inspector General). (2014, February 7). Seven Ohio Businesses and Individuals Suspended for DBE Fraud. Investigations, Washington, DC.

World Bank, The. (2013, April 10). The World Bank debars SNC-Lavalin Inc. and its affiliates for 10 years. Press Release. Washington, DC.

Wilcox, K. (2018, April). The long road back. *Civil Engineering*. Retrieved from https://ascelibrary.org/doi/10.1061/ciegag.0001281

Endnotes

[1] www.weforum.org/en/initiatives/paci/index.htm. The website has an outline of PACI's 3-Stage process to develop, implement, and verify a company's anti-corruption program.

[2] FIDIC website www.fidic.org

[3] For more on the products and information available from TI, go to their website at: www.transparency-usa.org

[4] See www.wfeo.org
[5] See www.acecc.net
[6] You can learn how to be in compliance with the Code by visiting: www.abcc.gov.au.
[7] You may review this material at: www.asce.org
[8] The GIACC website at: www.giaccentre.org
[9] ASCE website at: www.asce.org

17

Ethical Issues Facing Engineers in Oil and Gas Operations

Iraj Ershaghi

17.1 Introduction

Advances in technologies that were unimaginable a century ago have helped in establishing the current high standards of living. Undoubtedly, the oil and gas industry has played a pivotal role in this respect. Thanks to the advent of the petroleum industry, the use of oil and gas has created new factories and revolutionized industries such as transportation and power generation for more than a century. Liquid fuels have impacted transportation and have made various communities closer. The reliance on liquid and gaseous fuels has affected the lives of every person in the world with the invention of air transportation and personal vehicles.

Petroleum-derived products have also provided new sources of materials for many other industries. Hundreds of products sourced from oil and gas have turned out to be critically essential for the protection and safety of the public. Examples include hygienic tools and containers, synthetic fabrics, household and industrial items, and other components made of plastics. On a larger industrial scale, we can also list other vital innovations including the development of petrochemical products, insulation material in the electrical industry, and lightweight preservation and containers in the food industry. Add to the list essential devices and tools, including measurement and scanning systems in the medical industry, automobile tires and other parts in the transportation industry, and power plants all depending on the oil and gas resources. These hydrocarbon-based products and services have brought comfort to the young and old. They have prevented infectious diseases, saved human lives, and significantly and positively advanced the way we conduct our daily lives. In summary, hydrocarbon-based materials have fundamentally shaped modem living standards.

The question is, then, how could an industry, that has advanced the human civilization with such essential fuels and products that save lives, develop a negative reputation among the public? Historically, the oil industry's commitment to safety and ethical standards has often been criticized for safety and risk management credentials control and prevention of major future incidents and accidents. In the minds of many, the industry is perceived as one where

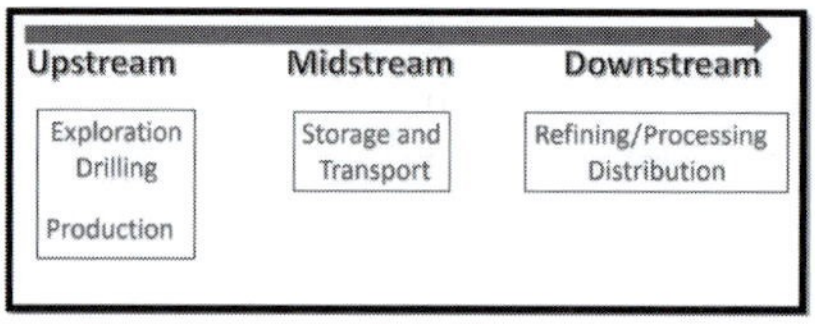

Figure 17.1 *Divisions of the oil and gas industry*

decisionmakers take risks, by ignoring trouble spots in the name of economic optimization. While, based on the available data, this weakness may have been responsible for some of the past catastrophic failures affecting people and the environment, realistically, however, we cannot ignore the challenging complexity of the industry. On the safety issues, one key consideration is that oil and gas operations often cover vast geographical areas. Using human intelligence alone is inadequate in managing risk for such extensive operational systems.

But of course, the oil and gas industry is not alone when we review accidents caused by human errors and electromechanical failures. Tragic consequences can also occur in several other industries, such as the airlines (planecrashinfo.com), nuclear power plants (*The Guardian*, 2011), and other chemical plants (ICIS, 2008). The question is, then: what can this industry learn from other hazardous industries to develop reliable control systems and mechanisms that can ensure the safety and ethical standards of its operations? To start, for those unfamiliar with the industry, it may not be obvious what a journey it takes for the oil and gas molecules to reach from subterranean reservoirs to the market. These pressurized hydrocarbon molecules, and associated gasses trapped in underground reservoirs, in depths often exceeding several miles, need to be first discovered and then brought to the surface. It is the joint effort of a large community of investors, engineers, business people, technicians and other professionals that connect the subsurface hydrocarbon molecules to the surface for processing and marketing. Figure 17.1, shows the divisions of the complex petroleum industry that includes three major subdivisions. To deliver products to the consumers, in the oil and gas industry some professionals work in the upstream, some in the midstream, and many are engaged in the downstream and marketing. Each subdivision has its set of challenges and associated uncertainties and risks.

In the upstream operations, management of assets distributed in a large geographical area is quite challenging. We can look at significant oilfields that are underneath vast areas of land or hidden below the sea floors. There have been more than 60,000 oil and gas fields discovered in the world. This includes several giant fields in the Middle East, Brazil, United States, Mexico, Russia, and Venezuela. For all commercial fields, the geographical land coverage is extensive. For example, fields in the United States such as Prudhoe Bay (Alaska), the Bridge (California), and Eagleville, Spraberry (Texas) each cover extensive geographic areas. The Ghawar field in Saudi Arabia is underneath a surface area of 3300 square miles.

Depending on the development plans, sometimes the entire surface area is dedicated to producing operations, such as the Kern River oil field in California. In other cases, such as the Wilmington oilfield, California, the oilfield is under land areas covered by houses, offices, parks, and waterways while oil and gas operation is handled via directionally drilled wells from operational sites targeting the field.

For midstream operations similar and even more substantial land coverage can pose management challenges. For example, consider the management challenges in operating and monitoring more than 800 miles of Alaska pipeline (Alyeska Pipeline Co., 2016) transporting oil from Prudhoe Bay to Valdez, Alaska. There are also management concerns where tanker transportation of liquid hydrocarbons via waterways may take months to navigate to the market.

When managing the economics and safety of extraction, refining, and delivery of petroleum products, there are uncertainties that affect these operations. The inherent risks and ethical issues facing the oil and gas industry to a great extent relates to these uncertainties and associated hazards. The goal must be the protection of the public, the workers, the environment, and the investors risking their capitals in initiating and maintaining such projects.

When faced with a problem that includes moral and economic issues, oil and gas professionals need to often make rapid decisions. The real solution is then, how can the science assist with making choices. Science needs data and, naturally, to move in the direction of science-based decision-making we need data from multiple sensors, performance data, and the analytics to examine such massive amounts of data and get timely alerts about impending risks and system failures to prevent catastrophic accidents.

To understand the issues, we shall first review some of the inherent risks about the three main branches of the industry. We will then discuss new transformative directions and solutions that the industry is adopting. To implement and honor effective plans that are ethical, these solutions can help the professionals when they face risky conditions. In principle, there is now more reliance being developed based on science and not guesswork. Oil and gas operations are generating substantial amounts of data and operators are more and more relying on data analysis tools. Decisions made with better data analytics tend to routinely lower the risk by reducing the impact of human tendencies. Taking it one step further is the gradual incorporation of smart devices that can substantially advance the cause of making the industry safe from all different dimensions.

17.2 Risk and Ethical Issues in Branches of the Oil Industry

There are several documented case studies discussing incidents that in the past have affected the credibility of the petroleum industry. Unprofessional practices seen in the past in the oil and gas industry have included several categories.

First are those that primarily affect the economic interest of stakeholders. The second include intentional decisions often based on cost-cutting measures that have threatened the safety of people and the environment. There are also cases related to the negligence on the part of workers and supervisors that substantially affect the companies and negatively impact human lives and the environment.

Risk issues in the upstream can be divided into two major categories; the economic or soft issues and the operational or hard issues. The soft category can include aspects related to human relations such as discriminating policies related to employment or working in hazardous conditions, and resource evaluation (including overbooking or write-downing reserves) negligence on record keeping and incident documentation and report. These are issues that can economically impact and devastate workers, companies, and/or individual investors and other economic stakeholders. The hard issues include operational processes and decision-makings that can impact the safety of people and the environment and can cause significant economic losses to the operations and the community at large. In examining risk avoidance methods and to enforce ethical standards in the oil and gas industry, we need to realize the inherent risks associated with operating any component of the oil and gas operations.

A source of weakness in the past has been the lack of transparency. The traditional competitive nature of the industry has been a source of reluctance in sharing best practices and documentation on failures among the competitors. The emergence of organizations such as the American Petroleum Institute (API) or the Society of Petroleum Engineers (SPE) has helped somewhat in the establishment of the best practices and standards. Some of the lessons learned from documented records of incidents in the past have also been the motives in the development of excellence in operating standards.

In each segment of the industry – the upstream exploration and production (E&P) and the midstream and downstream operations – there are components designed based on a series of physical laws and design principles. To operate them safely a set of rules is usually added in the training of the professionals to ensure that the record keeping, management, and process operations are non-hazardous to the people and the environment, and responsive to the investors.

Ethics can play a role in the design, operations, and project management of oil and gas operations. Both the designers and the operators must take the risk issues seriously. This is similar to other industries. For example, one designs a fail-proof control system in a cockpit for an airliner and then a pilot tries to operate it safely. In oil and gas operations, it is the interaction of thousands of components in a large geographical area that needs to be monitored for smooth, accident and trouble-free operations.

The E&P sector includes the production of crude oil and natural gas. In principle, the objectives are creating an injury-free and healthy work place for maximizing efficient use of resources and recovery of hydrocarbons while minimizing spills and environmental incidents, and preserving the economic viability

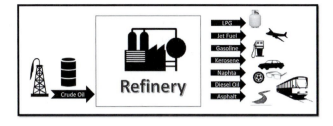

Figure 17.2 *Function of a petroleum refinery*

of the operation. All the components of exploration, assessment, testing, booking reserves, drilling and completions, and production oil and gas are complicated and require substantial skills and qualification in uncertainty management. There are public concerns about exploratory work done by the oil companies in both the onshore and offshore prospects. Most concerns relate to the environmental aspects, especially if the prospecting leads to drilling operations and subsequent completion and well stimulation operations. The use of newer technologies can eliminate some of these concerns.

From the safety point of view, among the hard issues are the drilling and production operations. The challenge is the competency and ethical standards of the management of the operating company for containment and handling of high-pressure fluids, toxic materials, and waste that can affect the health and safety of people and the environment. There have been several case studies of incidents during drilling and production operations cited in the literature that could have been prevented (Offshore Technology, 2011).

Midstream operations include transportation to refineries and the markets. Depending on the location of production and refineries, transportation for oil can be via onshore and or offshore pipelines, trucks, trains, and crude oil tankers. Natural gas transportation is usually via pipelines or liquified natural gas (LNG) tankers. Pipelines, in general, cover large geographical areas and, unless they are equipped with automated shut-off valves and remote monitoring, during the process of aging and corrosion related defects leaks can develop that may be devastating to people and the environment. Several incidents of environmental damage and injuries related to pipeline and other transport means have been reported in the past (National Transport Safety Board). The impact on the environment caused by spillage, explosion, and leaks have also been documented.

The downstream portion of the oil industry includes the journey of crude oil to reach processing plants, called refineries (Figure 17.2). Crude oil includes a mixture of hydrocarbons and other components such as nitrogen, sulfur, oxygen, water, salts, and trace metals. During the refinery process, a wide range of products are produced from crude oil. These include petroleum naphtha, gasoline and diesel fuel, asphalt base, heating oil, jet fuel, and liquefied petroleum gas.

Naphtha is processed to produce a range of plastics, including polystyrene. The polystyrene granules are converted to polystyrene products.

In refineries similar to all manufacturing plants, handling mixtures of toxic and inflammable ingredients require superb engineering design and monitoring standards. Because of the use of furnaces, reactors, heat exchangers, and other sources of heat, there are, of course, increased risks of fire or explosion in crude oil refineries. Furthermore, there is always the added the risk of toxic chemical exposure that can cause corrosion and burns.

17.3 Ethics in Estimation of Oil and Gas Reserves

Accurate reserves reporting is an ethical corporate mandate. Both overstatements and write-downs have occurred in the oil and gas industry. These practices may include different asset types, geography, and operator sizes. Historically there have been significant corporate and employee penalties for such practices, including class action lawsuits by the shareholders. Such practices can destroy the credibility of management teams and result in significant civil penalties. Examples of practices like these resulting in penalties include recording proved reserves to an unproved category; booking reserves in the absence of sufficient engineering and geologic data; and intentional decisions to reduce reserves based on the actual performance data. It is unfortunate that at times some operators may have hired the services of a third-party consultant to manufacture false reserves numbers. Such shady practices violating the requirements of Security and Exchange Commission (SEC) rules (OGRC, 2005) may include intimidation of professional staff whose estimates may have been lower than the management undue optimism and expectation. This latter one is a severe matter reflecting systemic flaws in any company's control structure. A study by Olsen (2010) provides a summary of case studies related to reserves overbooking and write-downs.

17.4 Employment Discrimination

While the issue of employment discrimination is not unique to the petroleum industry, oil and gas companies have faced discrimination law suits that have included cases such as lack of diversity or unacceptable race-related behaviors at isolated locations being ignored or going unchecked by the management. Effective oversight by the human resources (HR) department can be limited when operations are in remote locations. At times other issues have also developed when workers are promoted to supervisory positions without the adequate training in HR management that is expected from responsible managers. These issues are part of the broader categories that also affect other industries.

17.5 Oil and Gas Accidents and Related Injuries

Oil and gas workers at times face and often experience life-threatening signifi-cant injuries. The severity and duration of injuries for oil and gas workers at times may be far worse than similar mishaps in other industries. There are reasons why such devastating incidents occur. Most are the result of comprom-ised occupational safety conditions. A great contributor has been carelessness and/or recklessness on the part of the workers, supervisors, and sometimes the top company decisionmakers. Firms that have maintained practices to minimize such incidents have focused on proper training. Organizing ways to handle timely equipment repairs and maintenance, worker's certification and training, implementation of safety procedures, and effective communication must become part of the certification process before professionals are permitted to function as decisionmakers.

In a study published by Qi and Ershaghi (2013), some major past oil and gas industry-related incidents were grouped into those related to the drilling of wells, pipeline transportation accidents, chemical safety and storage and facilities oper-ational integrity, and unsafe working condition issues.

The general practice has been to follow standards set by Occupational Safety and Health Administration (OSHA), US Chemical Safety Board (CSB), American Petroleum Institute, American National Standards Institute (ANSI) and American Society for Testing and Materials (ASTM). Despite all that, oil and gas accidents still occur at work sites where the employer and employee are negligent, or where there are defective products. The keyword in "negligence." This flaw can magnify an incident with often significant environmental and safety impact.

A notable shortcoming also has included practices that have not adequately prepared workers for potential risks associated with intended operations. While steps can be taken to fortify regulations and the power of regulatory agencies, best is the operator's attitude to prepare workers for recognizing emerging vulnerability conditions and understanding of various risks associated with any operations.

17.6 Risk in the Oil and Gas Industry

As indicated before, the oil and gas industry faces great challenges high number of challenges. In setting goals and standards, the oil and gas industry – beyond serving the needs of investors – must strive to be sustainable by honoring the highest standards of safety and care for people and the environment. Safe and ethical operations have two main components: (i) investing in the technologies of safe operations and (ii) the addressing the weaknesses associated with human factors. To serve its purpose in satisfying the world's demand for oil and natural gas, the industry still needs to invest in challenging production areas, including the deep reservoirs under ultra-deep waters, unconventional resources, and difficult environments like the Arctic. But in the coming decades, what matters is which company will have the license to operate. To get the license to operate, oil and gas companies need to further enhance their ethical and regulatory compliant business conducts.

In summary, operationally there are inherent risks involved in the oil and gas operations. Some are technological, some are economical, some are environmental, and some relate to relying heavily on core competencies and ethical standards of the industry professionals. Another risk management issue for the oil and gas companies is the limitations caused by finding and hiring qualified professionals who can use their skillsets and ethical standards to make these operations safe. Other concerns relate to auditing mechanisms for the estimation of reserves, uncertainties related to prices and cost management, operational challenges, climate change concerns, and competition from new technologies. What will make the companies ethical is focusing on details, accuracy, and transparency to minimize financial and operational risk and to prevent underperformance of their operations.

Tarnished by the lingering memory of past highly visible accidents, and in-spite of substantial progress in using advanced technologies, the industry has realized that it needs to improve its image in order to attract professionals who may wish to join the industry. Appealing to and recruiting skilled and dependable professionals is and will be the primary challenge to engage in such complicated projects. As such, the oil industry very much cares about the protection of its critical infrastructure. This has also been emphasized in various policy-level presidential and federal directives. One significant way to provide such protection measures for reducing and handling operational risks is the incorporation of digital solutions. These solutions, which can help in remote monitoring, also simplify asset management. The infusion of digital solutions into oil and gas industry operations has been termed "smart" oil and gas operations. There is now greater attention focused on the incorporation of the digital solutions affecting upstream and refinery operations.

Despite such inherent hazards, thanks to the advancement of science and technology and enforcement of safety standards, operations in all areas of the oil and gas industry are becoming safer for the comfort of the product users. Recent developments have made the industry better at shifting and improving its technological base to enhance its safety records. Advances made by the industry include incorporating new technologies, such as machine learning for fault detection and minimizing human error. The change of paradigm for the industry has been the advent of federated systems in smart oil and gas technologies using tools such as sensor nets, embedded computing, predictive analytics, mobile solutions, and the cloud. These capabilities have the potential to help companies implement closed-loop management systems and to gain control of operations for reducing financial and operational risk and maintaining excellence.

17.7 Digital Solutions for Managing Ethics

The smart oilfield concept has found a new meaning because of the contribution it can make to reducing operational risks in areas of high vulnerability. Digital tools and solutions for the management of elaborate oil and gas production, transportation, and processing are significantly compensating for the shortcomings related to relying on the human decisions system with limited data systems. The ethical concerns must be minimization and mitigation of harm to humans through automation. Refineries of today are safer than those built fifty years ago. Without the new technologies we could not have transported hydrocarbons via subsea pipelines; and we could not have drilled deep wells without incidents. Modern oil and gas operations are safer and more reliable than in the past, but still, some accidents happen, harming workers and the environment. The critical issue is how to help the human element in making critical safety decisions.

With the digital data systems and controls, a concern with the use of digital solutions has also been the task of securing the operations against physical and cyber-attacks. These smart systems must also incorporate measures to safeguard against cyberattacks, such as the ones experienced by the Saudi Aramco and Qatar's Ragas. Fortunately, many oil and gas companies are gradually installing and including these control systems and navigating to deploying cloud-based solutions.

The advent of the Internet of Things (IoT) practice is also opening new frontiers as to how strategies can be developed to fine tune operations (Rayner and Cottier, 2015). The objectives are improving reliability, optimizing operations, and creating new values. The derived business values include machine learning applications for automated fault detection and surveillance.

While the adaptation of information technology (IT) and new industry tools and techniques are changing the face of the industry (National Academies, 2016), the human factor aspect of ethical decision-making in managing risk requires further study that can be partly mitigated through overhauling petroleum engineering education. However, beyond depending on IT, in order to prevent harm, professionals must be schooled on ethical rules that govern interactions in the oil industry.

17.8 Teaching Ethics: A Step Change for Reducing Risk

As said by French philosopher Paul Virgilio (Virgilio & Lotringer, 2008) traditionally technology could not exist without the potential for accidents. That is, by inventing airplanes we are also inventing plane crashes, and by building a refinery we are inventing accidents. The noble goal must then be to make tomorrow's worst accidents less impactful than today's.

Certainly, decision-making with integrated data systems can help in enabling collaborative decision models. Trust in the services of professionals who contribute as solution providers has traditionally been based on their knowledge and training. How then can the industry assure itself of the necessary development of systems that can address the responsibility of self-regulation and protection of the public and the environment? A critical remedy could be the integration of the ethical dimension in engineering education. The practitioner must develop principles applicable to their work when there are gray areas and conflicts among options.

As indicated by Gordon (1998), an essential step in minimizing the probability of accidents in the oil and gas industry is the reliability of the professionals. Enforcing a culture of ethical professionalism includes multitudes of educational components. There is a need to expose the new engineering graduates to case studies related to past accidents. Engineers need to be engaged academically in consequence studies that embody ethics, risk management, and health, safety, and environment (HSE) issues affecting the operations. Safety training must engage the professional to realize a sense of personal vulnerability. Risk perception can be useful in safety-related behaviors.

Protection of workers versus a business/profit-oriented consideration requires support from the top management of any organization. Resource managers must be entirely supportive of the cost and time issues associated with pursuing preventive, protective, or continual improvements. The human mind may have limitations in predicting the risk acceptable under given circumstances. However, the infusion of science can help the professionals. Science needs data, and other industries have adopted and shown the benefits of digital operational checking and control. The oil industry has also realized the need and the good news is that these systems have been and are being implemented.

The other improvement has been the incorporation of collaboration rooms and decision-making with input from experts using data from input sensors and sensor nets, and data sciences including the use of AI and machine learning. Historically the education had focused on specific niches. However, the petroleum industry is multidisciplinary, and there is a need to train the engineers to learn the art and science of collaborative decision-making. This collaborative decision-making needs to leverage new technologies that simplify the knowledge sharing processes.

17.9 Conclusion

The essence of modern civilization has depended on the oil and gas industry. Unless an alternative source of energy becomes economically available on a really large scale and within reach during the next century, the energy-demand reality is that the dependence on oil and gas will continue well into the next century. Public sentiments against oil and gas operations have included significant concerns about the environmental aspects of this energy source, and the issue of climate change: and that needs more scientific research, thinking, and solutions. For example, there have also been concerns about hydraulic fracturing of source rocks that are opening up access to vast new hydrocarbon resources. To offer the global economy substitution for fossil fuels, the question to ask is whether these new forms of energy can be extraordinarily scaled up to meet the more than 400 quadrillion British thermal unit (BTU) world's energy demands without generating new sets of environmental concerns. The answer is no at present. While it sounds desirable to have a world economy without using oil and gas, getting there will be expensive and require sacrifices (Bryce, 2011). The focus of science should also be on reducing the environmental impact of oil and gas consumption while other efforts on alternatives are underway,

Like other hazardous industries such as aerospace, transportation, and nuclear power, great strides have been made in reducing the risk of operation by science-based decision-making. The oil and gas industry is a hazardous one, but great progress has been made to minimize harms associated with the industry substantially. Significant advances in technology have been made to help the oil and gas industry management, and the professionals effectively handle some of the operational uncertainties (IOPG, 2016). The oil and gas industry has historically made great efforts to enhance its safety and ethical culture. It has made progress in the development and incorporation of new advanced technologies and surveillance methods. It has also been emphasizing, promoting, and requiring a strict safety culture among its professionals and service providers.

Implementing automation and advanced computer-aided process control and machine learning in oil and gas operations have opened new frontiers and directions for restoring public trust in the industry. However, building public faith in the industry, besides inclusion of technological advancements, requires the infusion of ethics-based and risk-avoidance training of the professionals who manage the day-to-day decisions. What still needs improvement is the incorporation of ethical decision-making and risk management in formal and company-based training of management and technical personnel.

Ethical decision-making in the oil and gas industry reflects the credibility of the top management. The challenge has been how to ensure that the watchful eyes of its professionals and workers can identify vulnerable areas and fraudulent behavior that if not detected can negatively impact the industry's reputation and economic survival.

A step change taking place that has revolutionized the safety records of the industry has been the significant leverage offered by an introduction of smart fields operations. Judging from other industries, IT can help in minimizing operational risks. These digital technologies have enhanced the visibility, control, and systems tracking of various operational components in the oil and gas industry (Gordon, 1998). Technologies, such as in-memory computing, enterprise mobility, and analytics to integrate processes are helping the industry to make better decisions on various components. Use of digital oilfield services is helping to integrate data and analytics for production, maintenance, and engineering operations. Increasing operational insight in data collection, validation, surveillance, systems tracking, and real-time notification processes is improving the decision-making processes. This, of course, is leading to better compliance processes for safe operations while also improving various functions related to revenues optimization.

Parallel to the incorporation of digital technologies and collaborative decision-making has been the growth of teaching engineering ethics in academic courses related to oil and gas operations. As discussed by the U S National Academy of Engineering report (NAE, 2016), the motivation has been academia's responsibility to provide educational curriculums emphasizing ethical sensitivity to the consequences of engineering decision-making. This has also been in part a response to accreditation criteria set by Accreditation Board for Engineering and Technology (ABET).

In summary, if in the oil and gas industry ethical decision-making is treated as an optimization process, the objective function among the many that control the decision process must be in essence the safety of people and the environment. What distinguishes risk versus safety is how far the professionals running the industry can distance these objective functions from the operational economics. The oil and gas industry of today must reinforce a corporate culture that clearly defines pursuing ethical behaviors. This is not what the general public may have imagined about this industry because of occasional past incidents. It will take some trouble-free years before the industry can prove its transformative efforts in re-tooling the operations. That should include adoption of digital ethics, which include step changes in using automation, smart devices, machine learning, data management and collaborative decision-making. To advance the cause of the industry there is of course still more that can be done. But at least the tools and methodologies are being noted and developed that can substantially enhance the reputation of the industry in the years to come.

References

Alyeska Pipeline Co. (2016). Trans Alaska Pipeline Facts. Retrieved from www.alyeska-pipe.com/TAPS/PipelineFacts

Bryce, R. (2010). *Power hungry: The myths of "green" energy and the real fuels of the future,*. New York, NY: PublicAffairs.

Gordon, R. P. E. (1998).The contribution of human factors to accidents in the offshore oil industry. Aberdeen University, Psychology Department. Kings College. Phd Thesis, Aberdeen AB24 2UB *Reliability Engineering and System Safety 61,* 95–108.

Guardian, The (2011, March 14). Nuclear power plant accidents: listed and ranked since 1952. Retrieved from www.theguardian.com/news/datablog/2011/mar/14/nuclear-power-plant-accidents-list-rank

International Association of Oil and Gas Producers. (2016, July). Process safety – leading key performance indicators. Supplement to IOGP Report 456. Retrieved from www.iogp.org/Reports/Type/556/ID/811#sthash.uPQC7tPH.dpuf

ICIS. (2008). A guide to major chemical disasters worldwide. Retrieved from www.icis.com/resources/news/2008/10/06/9160653/a-guide-to-major-chemical-disasters-worldwide/

NAE (2016) Report: "Infusing Ethics into the Development of Engineers-Exemplary Education Activities and Programs," 2016.

National Academies. (2016): Application of remote real-time monitoring to offshore oil and gas operations. Special Report 322, National Academies of Sciences, Engineering, and Medicine. 2016. Washington, DC: The National Academies Press. Retrieved from https://doi.org/10.17226/23499.

National Transportation Safety Board. Pipeline Accident Report. Retrieved from www.ntsb.gov/investigations/AccidentReports/Pages/pipeline.aspx

Offshore Technology. (2014, January 11). The world's worst offshore oil rig disasters. Retrieved from www.offshore-technology.com/features/feature-the-worlds-deadliest-offshore-oil-rig-disasters-4149812/

Oil and Gas Reserves Committee (OGRC) "Mapping" Subcommittee Final Report – December 2005 Comparison of Selected Reserves and Resource Classifications and Associated Definitions Mapping Subcommittee: John Etherington Torbjorn Pollen Luca Zuccolo.

OLSEN, Grant_ (May_2010). RESERVES OVERSTATEMENTS: HISTORY, ENFORCEMENT, IDENTIFICATION, AND IMPLICATIONS OF NEW SEC DISCLOSURE REQUIREMENTS Thesis, Texas A &M.

PlaneCrashInfo.com. Accident database. Retrieved from www.planecrashinfo.com/database.htm

Qi, Q., & Ershaghi, I. (2013, September 30). Aspects of Oilfield Related Accidents. Society of Petroleum Engineers. doi:10.2118/166412-MS

Rayner, M. E., & Cottier, M. J. (2015). The more things change: Value creation, value capture, and the Internet of Things. *Deloitte Review* 17, May 30.

Virilio, P., & Lotringer, S. (2008). *Pure war, new edition (Semiotext(e) / foreign agents)*. Translated by Mark Polizzotti and Brian O'Keeffe. Boston, MA: MIT Press.

18

Engineering Codes of Ethics: Legal Protection and Empowerment for Engineers

Jeffrey H. Matsuura

18.1 Introduction

Engineers who operate under constraints and obligations established by codes of ethics or professional responsibility maintained by professional organizations of which they are members and by state government authorities view these constraints and obligations, at times, as limitations or barriers. It is important to recognize, however, that these codes can also work to the benefit of the engineers governed by their terms. The codes of ethics of professional organizations and state authorities can serve a defensive and empowering function for engineers by providing a basis for preserving legal rights of the engineers and by reducing their risk of personal liability based on misconduct. Engineers should understand thoroughly the ethical obligations established by these codes and should identify the provisions of the codes that they can apply in their daily practice to help establish and document their personal defenses against potential future claims of misconduct.

At their essence, all codes of ethics and professional responsibility require professional engineers to take responsibility for their actions and to apply their best professional judgment to their decision-making, no matter what other parties, including employers and clients, request or demand. Codes of ethics established by state government authorities carry the force of law, prescribing mandatory conduct for engineering professionals. The codes applied by professional organizations present aspirational goals intended to preserve the integrity of the engineering profession. Although these codes set duties for professional engineers, they also provide a framework of conduct that can be used by engineers as a justification for their decision-making and their actions. This discussion will help engineers to understand the defensive potential of professional codes of ethics. This material is intended solely for educational purposes. It is not intended as legal advice. Questions regarding legal rights and obligations associated with specific circumstances should always be directed to an engineer's personal legal counsel.

This chapter assists engineers to resolve successfully the dilemma of how best to reconcile their professional activities with the ethical obligations placed upon them by state governments and professional organizations. The chapter provides engineering professionals with knowledge to help them understand those ethical obligations and to devise strategies to comply with those obligations while also using the ethical requirements to reduce their risk of personal legal liability.

18.2 State Codes of Ethics

Every state government in the United States applies some level of licensure and oversight to ensure that the conduct of professional engineers providing services in their jurisdiction is of adequate quality and is delivered in a professional manner.[1] Oversight of the conduct of professional engineers by state government authorities generally takes the form of both testing of engineers to protect quality of service, and codes of conduct to ensure professional performance by engineers who offer services to the public. These requirements for professional responsibility established by state government authorities carry the force of law. Compliance with these requirements is mandatory, there is no discretion. Failure to comply with state-imposed codes of conduct can result in disciplinary action against an engineer, and ultimately loss of the licensing to practice as an engineer in the state.

State regulatory oversight of engineering professionals is generally justified based on the state's duty to protect the public welfare. Services provided by professional engineers have a significant impact on the safety, health, and welfare of the public. As a result of this impact, state governments assert oversight regarding qualifications for professional engineers and standards of conduct.

The states have generally adopted codes of conduct and professionalism for engineers that are relatively standard in terms of content and format. In general, they require that practicing engineers act in good faith, avoid deception, exercise continuing control over their services, and work to serve the overall public interest.[2] These requirements can have broad reach, significantly affecting the actions of engineers as they interact with employers and clients.

Review of some of these state professionalism requirements directed toward engineers provides a sense of their expansive reach. For example, the Commonwealth of Virginia enforces "Standards of Practice and Conduct" for engineers operating in that jurisdiction.[3] Those standards include broad obligations for good faith conduct by all engineers, and they are administered by the state government agency, the Virginia Department of Professional and Organizational Regulation.

Other state governments apply similar oversight of the professionalism of engineers. For example, state authorities in California enforce the "Code of Professional Conduct" for engineers operating in that state.[4] Their Code establishes broad requirements for professionalism addressing issues such as deceptive or misleading conduct and protection of the public interest. Similarly, state authorities in Texas enforce requirements for "Professional Conduct and Ethics" for practicing engineers, which include expansive requirements of good faith and protecting the public interest.[5]

It is essential to recognize that the codes of ethics and professionalism directed toward engineers by state governments carry the force of law. Failure to comply with those requirements can result in disciplinary action imposed by the state, including loss of license and thus loss of the ability to work as an engineer in the jurisdiction. Before a professional engineer takes any action, including those directed by employers or clients, the engineer must consider the impact of that action on his or her professional obligations. Through codes of professional responsibility for engineering professionals, state governments place an affirmative obligation on practicing engineers to serve the public interest.

18.3 Codes of Ethics of Professional Societies

Virtually every professional organization representing engineers, in all disciplines, impose codes of ethics and professional conduct on their members. Although obligations imposed by professional organizations do not have the force of law, they are recognized by legal institutions, such as courts and regulatory agencies, as standards that merit attention and compliance. Code provisions of professional organizations are afforded greater deference by legal institutions than are personal opinions or beliefs; but less deference than that provided to the codes of conduct imposed by state governments. An argument that an action was taken based upon a good faith reasonable belief that the conduct was necessary to meet an obligation established by a relevant professional organization code of ethics is more persuasive to a legal authority than is reliance on a personal opinion or belief. Thus, codes of ethics and professional responsibility provide engineers with a framework of evidence, which can be used to support their professional decision-making and actions.

18.4 Actions to Protect the Engineer's Interests

When an engineer is asked or ordered by an employer or client to engage in conduct the engineer believes in good faith to be suspect, that engineer should immediately consult the codes of ethics and professional responsibility presented by state governing authorities as well as those of the leading professional organizations in his or her engineering field. Some of those codes specifically require an engineer to communicate ethical concerns directly to the employer or client. If the relevant code bars or discourages the conduct and requires the engineer to communicate ethical concerns to the employer or client, the engineer should express the ethical concerns in writing, specifically referencing the applicable code provisions. Copies of this written expression of concern and code of ethics reference should be provided to the person who ordered the action and to appropriate human resources department staff. If there has been a mistake or misunderstanding, this action will likely force clarification. If the order stands even after the written expression of concern, then the engineer has begun to establish documentation of his or her concern and of the basis for that concern in the code of ethics.

Consider a hypothetical situation not far removed from recent headlines. An engineer is ordered by his employer to alter a technical system in a manner that enables that system to circumvent or deceive regulatory monitoring. Despite personal reservations, the engineer complies. Later, when the deception is publicly discovered, the employer claims no knowledge of the fraudulent conduct, blaming it instead on the actions of rogue engineers. Had the engineer created a written record identifying the basis for the concern and citing the code of ethics as the justification for that concern, the engineer would have documentation with which to mount a personal defense.

Written records describing the concerns and objections and referencing specific code of ethics prohibitions and cautions can help the engineer present a defense in the event of claims of insubordination or failure to perform raised by an employer or client. This documentation is also useful to rebut allegations that the engineer acted maliciously while performing his or her duties. Those records can also be used as evidence to support efforts by an engineer to obtain "whistleblower" status – with the legal protections associated with that status – if the engineer chooses to raise the concerns with appropriate government authorities.

Records documenting an engineer's concerns and actions to address those concerns can also play an important role if the engineer faces disciplinary actions by state engineering regulators. If the engineer is accused of violating state professional conduct requirements for professional engineers, the engineer will be required to document his or her conduct. The record created as the engineer identified and expressed his or her concerns to the employer or client and relevant government authorities creates vital documentation for the engineer's efforts to defend against disciplinary actions based on claims of violation of professional conduct requirements.

Finally, documentation developed by the engineer is essential to support legal claims the engineer may choose to initiate against an employer or client. Under some circumstances, an engineer may choose to sue an employer for wrongful termination, breach of contract, or defamation based on the employer's conduct regarding concerns raised by the engineer. An engineer working as a contractor could sue a client for breach of contract or defamation based on the client's conduct in response to technical concerns raised by the engineer. In each of these legal actions, the engineer will need to rely on documentation of his or her conduct and that of the employer or client in order to sustain a lawsuit.

As noted previously, the codes of ethics and professional responsibility applied to engineers by state government authorities generally include broad obligations. Understanding of and documented compliance with these code requirements can help an engineer substantially to protect his or her interests. Among the most relevant are general obligations to protect the public interest and to act in good faith. The state codes of professional responsibility also commonly require that engineers avoid deceptive or misleading conduct and that they take direct control over the professional decisions they make regarding engineering matters. All of these professional obligations are particularly relevant in instances when an employer or client is pressuring an engineer to take an action that the engineer believes is not appropriate.

Consider for example the "Code of Ethics for Engineers and Surveyors" of the State of Ohio. This Code places an affirmative duty on professional engineers providing services in the state to act in a manner that protects the public safety, health, and welfare. Additionally, the Ohio Code requires that an engineer who has good faith concern that some conduct could harm or significantly threaten the public welfare must notify the employer or client involved of the threat, refuse to approve the conduct, and if appropriate sever his or her relationship with that employer or client and notify proper authorities (including law enforcement authorities) of the issue.[6] The Ohio Code thus places a substantial duty on a practicing engineer in instances when the engineer has a good faith belief that a requested course of conduct is contrary to the public welfare. As compliance with this state Code is mandatory for all licensed engineers in Ohio, it seems that an engineer in Ohio who believes that conduct requested by an employer or client presents a substantial risk of public harm has a legal duty to raise that issue with the client or employer, and if necessary resign and report the conduct to government authorities.

Other state codes of professional responsibility for engineers impose similar obligations to inform the client or employer of the risks associated with the proposed conduct, and if appropriate to report the conduct to government authorities. Few states, however, go as far as Ohio with respect to the mandatory severing of ties with a client or employer based on proposed conduct that carries a substantial risk of threatening the public welfare. For instance, the State of Washington requires its professional engineers to protect life, health, and property, and to promote the public welfare by informing clients and employers of risks associated with conduct and reporting conduct to regulatory authorities, as appropriate.[7]

The State of Connecticut also requires professional engineers in that jurisdiction to protect the public health, safety, and welfare, and imposes specific obligations on engineers to inform their clients and employers of risks and threats to the public welfare and to inform government authorities of such risks and threats as appropriate.[8] Similarly, the State of Alaska requires professional engineers to protect the public welfare, to inform clients and employers of risks to the public welfare, and to notify government authorities of risks and threats to public welfare as appropriate.[9]

Viewed from one perspective, these broad state code requirements are challenging for engineers as they can present difficult compliance obligations. At the same time, however, those requirements also empower professional engineers to apply their experience, knowledge, and good judgment. As professional engineers, these individuals are expected to use their expertise to serve the needs of clients and employers while also protecting the general public welfare. Indeed, the state codes effectively order engineers to apply their best judgment to actions, no matter what their client or employer demands. Professional codes are a source of obligations for engineers, yet they are also source of authority for those engineers. When professional engineers make difficult decisions, they take their actions based on their own expertise and under the authority of codes of professional responsibility – which, in effect, empower engineers to exercise their professional judgment, even in the face of contrary orders from clients and employers.

In addition to the mandatory codes of professional responsibility applied by state governments, virtually all of the most prominent engineering professional societies also apply voluntary codes of ethics and conduct for their engineer members. Review of the codes of ethics of several of the leading professional engineering organizations reveals the scope of their reach. For example, the "Code of Ethics" of the Institute of Electrical and Electronics Engineers (IEEE) places an obligation on engineers to "disclose promptly facts that might endanger the public or the environment."[10] "The Fundamental Canons" in the "Code of Ethics" of the American Society of Mechanical Engineers (ASME) assert that "Engineers shall hold paramount the safety, health, and welfare of the public in the performance of their duties."[11] These are sweeping obligations that place a clear public interest standard on the professional activities of engineers.

Of course, the codes also generally require a standard of care and duty to employers and clients. For example, in both its "Fundamental Canons" and its "Rules of Practice" within its "Code of Ethics," the National Society for Professional Engineers (NSPE) requires that engineers "act for each employer or client as faithful agents or trustees."[12] Yet, also in the "Fundamental Canons" and the "Rules of Practice" the NSPE requires engineers to "hold paramount the safety, health, and welfare of the public" and to "avoid deceptive acts." The "Code of Ethics" of the American Society of Civil Engineers (ASCE), in its "Fundamental Principles" places the public on par with employers and clients, requiring engineers to serve "with fidelity the public, their employers, and clients."[13] The NSPE "Code of Ethics" includes among its "Professional Obligations" a duty that "Engineers shall be guided in all their relations by the highest standards of honesty and integrity" and that "engineers shall at all times strive to serve the public interest."

Perhaps the clearest expression of how an engineer should balance public interest concerns with the interests of employers and clients is presented by the "Code of Ethics" of the Association for Computing Machines (ACM). The lead "Principle" presented in that document states that "Software engineers shall act consistently with the public interest ... ." It further asserts that the software engineer should "moderate the interests of the software engineer, the employer, the client, and the users with the public good. . . ." The ACM Code further states that software engineers should "approve software only if they have a well-founded belief that it is safe, meets specifications, passes appropriate tests, and does not diminish quality of life, diminish privacy or harm the environment." The ACM Code succinctly notes, "The ultimate effect of the work should be the public good."

Engineers have a general obligation to preserve the secrecy of confidential materials of their employers and clients. That obligation most commonly arises as part of an engineer's terms of employment or terms of engagement with a client. Codes of ethics also impose this obligation. For example, the NSPE "Code of Ethics," "Professional Obligations" includes a prohibition against disclosing without consent confidential information "of any present or former client or employer." Of course, the NSPE Code also requires that "Engineers shall avoid deceptive acts," which presumably includes avoiding deception of the public or government authorities. Similarly, the IEEE Code requires that the engineer "avoid injuring others, their property, their data, reputation or employment by false or malicious action."

The ASCE Code attempts to address this tension between obligations for confidentiality and duty to serve the broader public interest.[14] In its "Canon 1" the ASCE places an obligation on an engineer to inform an employer or client when the safety, health, and welfare of the public may be adversely affected by conduct. If the employer or client continues to demand the conduct, the engineer must present the information in writing to the proper authority and cooperate with that authority. The American Institute of Chemical Engineers "Code of Ethics" also places an obligation on engineers to inform their employer or client if the engineer has a good faith belief that an action could have adverse effects on the health or safety of the public, and to consider additional disclosures as warranted.[15]

The ACM "Software Engineering Code of Ethics and Professional Practice" offers perhaps the best balance between confidentiality and public welfare.[16] It requires that an engineer serve the best interest of an employer or client "consistent with the public interest." The ACM Code also obligates engineers to preserve employer or client confidentiality, "consistent with the law." The ACM Code thus specifically describes what courts and other legal authorities have long recognized: that an employee's duty to an employer does not extend to perjury or fraud. To its credit, the ACM Code clearly expressed this balance. Similarly, the IEEE Code requires engineers to "comply with applicable laws, rules, and regulations in all countries where the IEEE does business." The Society of Manufacturing Engineers "Code of Ethics" requires that all of its members "act in accordance with all applicable laws" as they engage in their professional activities.[17]

The ACM Code is also enlightened with respect to an engineer's duty to disclose risks and threats. It places a duty on the engineer to "disclose to appropriate persons or authorities any actual or potential danger to the user, the public or the environment, that they reasonably believe to be associated with software or related documents." It also requires an engineer to "cooperate" with efforts to address the concern. Finally, it obligates the engineer to "be fair and avoid deception" in all statements associated with the software in question.

18.5 Whistleblower Status

The federal government and approximately seventeen states provide some level of protection for individuals deemed to be "whistleblowers."[18] In general, a whistleblower is an individual who reports to appropriate legal or regulatory authorities behavior the individual reasonably believes to be illegal or fraudulent. In some jurisdictions, the whistleblower protections extend to reporting of actions that threaten public health, safety, or the environment. Protections afforded to qualified whistleblowers generally include protection against employment termination and other forms of retaliation or harassment by employers and other employees. Federal whistleblower protections are generally limited to reports of misconduct associated with workplace health and safety and environmental protection. Under some circumstances, whistleblowers who report government contracting fraud or misconduct or securities law violations may also qualify for whistleblower protection.

A critical element of qualifying for whistleblower protection is demonstrating that the report of misconduct is based on a reasonable assessment of the circumstances. Written references to engineering codes of ethics can be helpful on this point. If an engineer has clearly expressed his or her concerns within the relevant organization citing appropriate code of ethics references, and if despite those concerns the organization moves forward with the conduct, the engineer can reference that entire history to the appropriate legal or regulatory authority. That documentation of the dispute and associated professional concern can help to persuade an authority of the reasonableness of the engineer's claim, thus facilitating a request by the engineer for whistleblower status.

Whistleblower status is generally limited in focus, applicable to a relatively narrow set of concerns. It seems, however, that perhaps state legislatures should consider expanding the scope of whistleblower status in those jurisdictions in which professional engineers are required by state codes of professional responsibility to report concerns regarding potential threats to public health, safety, and welfare to government authorities. As those state codes represent state action requiring reporting by professional engineers, it seems appropriate that all engineers who submit such reports based on a good faith belief that there is a threat to the public welfare should receive formal whistleblower status. Although this is not currently the situation, it appears that broader grant of whistleblower status to professional engineers acting in compliance with state professional responsibility requirements would be beneficial for both the engineering profession and the general public.

18.6 Protection in Litigation

Professional engineers can face personal legal liability for their actions. Legal claims against engineers sometimes take the form of breach of contract lawsuits that claim that the engineer failed in some meaningful way to satisfy all of the key terms of an agreement for his or her professional services. Professional engineers can also face litigation in instances when a client or other party claims the engineer failed to meet his or her professional obligations while performing engineering service. This type of legal action is sometimes characterized as a claim of engineering malpractice. An engineering malpractice claim is essentially a tort law claim alleging that the engineer acted negligently while performing his or her engineering services (*Donatelli vs Strong Consulting Engineers*, 2013).

In order to prevail in an engineering malpractice lawsuit the plaintiff must prove that the engineer failed to meet an accepted standard of care while providing the engineering services (*Hydro Investors vs Trafalgar Power*, 2000). One approach to identifying appropriate standards of care for engineers and assessing an engineer's compliance with that standard involves examination of codes of ethics and professional responsibility presented by state regulatory authorities and by leading engineering professional organizations. Evidence that the conduct of the defendant engineer was consistent with duties applied to engineers by state engineering regulators and by major professional organizations can help to prove that the engineer's conduct was consistent with standard practices in the profession and was thus not negligent.

Codes of ethics can also assist engineers to pursue their own legal action against an employer or client if the engineer faces reprisals as a result of expressions of concern or refusal to follow orders. In many states, courts recognize claims of wrongful termination raised by employees against employers. In those cases, the employee bears the burden of demonstrating that the termination of employment was illegal. To the extent that there is a documented record of the engineer raising reasonable concerns of illegal, fraudulent, or potentially harmful conduct by the employer, the engineer's case is made stronger. By demonstrating that the engineer's actions were motivated by reasonable professional concerns – an argument made more compelling through reference to the codes of ethics – the engineer can represent a stronger argument that the termination was retaliatory and not justified by insubordination.

In situations where there has been some type of corporate misconduct, it is often all too tempting for senior management to attempt to place blame on engineering staff. In the Volkswagen emission testing case, for example, at various times during the company investigation, suggestions were apparently made by company insiders that engineering staff was largely responsible for the problem (*Independent*, 2015; *New York Post*, 2015). If engineers had created a written record using codes of ethics to document their concerns and objections then that record could have been used to rebut such unfair corporate allegations.

18.7 The Future of Engineering Codes of Ethics

To date, codes of professional conduct for engineers have been viewed primarily as obligations faced by professional engineers. In the future, there may be greater emphasis placed on the ways in which those codes can help engineering professionals to play a more active role in controlling the impact of their work. For example, codes of professional conduct now routinely authorize engineers to challenge the orders of employers and clients. They also commonly authorize engineers to report their concerns to appropriate government authorities. In this environment, it seems probable that professional engineers will become more active in asserting their concerns and expressing those concerns to interested parties. Greater involvement by professional engineers is likely to improve the technical quality of engineering services and better serve the needs of the public.

Two key sets of institutions influencing the future impact of engineering codes of ethics and professionalism are the state engineering regulatory authorities and the leading engineering professional organizations. Both of these groups can have a significant positive impact empowering the engineering profession through more active application of codes of professional conduct. State engineering regulators can act to support expansion of their codes of ethics to recognize that professional engineers should be supported as they assert their expertise in their relationships with employers and clients. State codes should not only require professional engineers to exercise their expertise for the public benefit, but those codes must also provide support for engineers when they take such actions.

Professional organizations can begin to play a more active role in the enhancement of engineering codes of professionalism as platforms for empowerment of professional engineers. Those organizations can encourage state authorities to expand the scope of the state codes of engineering professionalism. The professional organizations can also take a more visible and active role in supporting individual engineers who face legal consequences for actively asserting their professional judgment. For instance, the leading engineering professional organizations could back development of a legal defense fund to be used in support of professional engineers involved in litigation as a result of their efforts to practice engineering with integrity and in a manner consistent with the public welfare goals presented by the majority of engineering ethical codes. Professional organizations can also participate in litigation, submitting court pleadings in support of members involved in litigation as a result of their compliance with the code of professional responsibility.

Although the engineering profession has long played a major role in our economy and society, that role continues to expand significantly on a daily basis. In today's world of embedded technologies, ubiquitous devices, and autonomous intelligent systems, the engineering profession is routinely relied upon to help meet the demands of society and to protect the welfare of society. Increasingly, technologies and technical systems are beyond the knowledge and understanding of citizens and public leaders. In that setting, it is usually engineers – the people most closely involved in the planning, development, operation, and maintenance of those technologies and technical systems – who have the ability to provide meaningful insights into the opportunities and threats presented by those technologies and systems.

The public interest in our highly technical age requires the presence of professional engineers who are actively engaged in oversight of the impact of their work. In many instances, it is the engineers who are best positioned to identify and evaluate risks and rewards associated with technologies. In some instances, the engineers may well be the only people in a position to make that assessment effectively. Codes of professional ethics can empower engineers to play a more active role in management of their work. It will be increasingly important in the future that professional engineers assert themselves as their work product is made available to the public. Engineering codes of professionalism should be structured and enforced in ways that empower greater involvement by engineering professionals in oversight of technologies and technical systems.

18.8 Conclusion

As noted previously, this discussion is not offered as legal advice. Appropriate legal advice can only be provided by an individual's attorney who is fully familiar with the specific facts associated with that individual's circumstances. Each set of facts is different and anyone facing the type of concerns raised in this chapter should consult with his or her own attorney. On that point, it is worth noting that an engineer experiencing issues involving professional responsibility should consult with an attorney representing the engineer personally. It is not wise to consult on these matters with a lawyer representing the employer. A lawyer paid to represent the employer owes a duty to that employer, not the employees of that employer. Counsel for the employer would be unable to perform effectively representing the interests of any employee to the extent that the interests of the employee diverge from those of the employer.

This discussion is presented purely for educational purposes. It is intended only to inform engineering professionals on how the codes of ethics of states and professional organizations can help them to preserve and express their personal legal rights and reduce their risk of personal legal liability. The intention is also to encourage all of the professional engineering organizations to recognize and consider this important defensive use of their codes of ethics as they establish and modify those codes. If those organizations appreciate the potential defensive value of their codes for their members, they will exercise appropriate care to ensure that the codes of ethics provide an effective foundation to assist engineering professionals to protect themselves from liability and to exercise the full range of their legal rights. Professional societies should work closely with state engineering regulators to create an environment in which both the mandatory professional responsibility requirements applied by the states and the voluntary codes of ethics established by the professional organizations combine to create a setting in which practicing engineers are empowered to assert their expertise in the context of decisions involving use of their work.

The primary message of this discussion is that engineering codes of professionalism, both mandatory state codes and voluntary professional organization codes, play a key role in empowering practicing engineers to participate actively in the management of their work. In today's technology-based society, active participation by professional engineers is essential if there is to be effective assessment of benefits and risks. Codes of professional responsibility are thus vital to preserving the integrity of the engineering profession, protecting the interests of engineers as well as their employers and clients, and promoting the public welfare.

References

Donatelli v. D R. Strong Consulting Engineers, Inc. 312 P.3d 620 (2013)

Hydro Investors, Inc. v. Trafalgar Power, Inc., 227 F3d 8 (2nd Cir. 2000)

Independent. (2015, October 9). Volkswagen emissions scandal. Few rogue engineers are to blame says VW chief executive. Retrieved from www.independent.co.uk/news/business/news/volkswagen-emissions-scandal-few-rogue-engineers-are-to-blame-says-vw-chief-executive-a6687201.html

New York Post. (2015, October 8). Volkswagen exec blames rogue engineers for emissions scandal. Retrieved from http://nypost.com/2015/10/08/volkswagen-exec-blames-rogue-engineers-for-emissions-scandal, 2016

Endnotes

[1] "Guidance on Licensure and Ethical Responsibilities for Civil Engineers" at www.asce.org/uploadedFiles/About_ASCE/Ethics/Content_pieces/Licensing_and_Ethics_FINAL.pdf (accessed August 1, 2017).

[2] "Model Rules," 240.15 Rules of Professional Conduct at http://ncees.org/wp-content/uploads/2012/11/ModelRules-20151.pdf (accessed August 1, 2017).

[3] Virginia Department of Professional and Organizational Regulation, "Regulations Governing Architects, Professional Engineers, Land Surveyors, Certified Interior Designers and Landscape Architects, Part XII Standards of Practice an Conduct

at   www.dpor.virginia.gov/uploadedFiles/MainStie/Content/Boards/APELS_07_01_
11.pdf

[4] California Code of Regulations, Title 16, Division 5 §475, "Code of Professional
Conduct – Professional Engineering" at www.bpelsg.ca.gov/laws/boardrules.pdf
(accessed August 1, 2017).

[5] "The State of Texas, Texas Engineering Practice Act and Rules Concerning the Practice
of Engineering and Professional Engineering Licensure," Subchapter C Professional
Conduct and Ethics at https://engineers.texas.gov/standards/enf_pub.pdf (accessed
August 1, 2017).

[6] Ohio Code of Ethics for Engineers and Surveyors, Section 4733-35-03, at
www.peps.ohio.gov/4733/4733_35.aspx (accessed August 2, 2017).

[7] Washington Rules of Professional Conduct and Practice, Section 196-27A-020 at http://
apps.leg.wa.gov/wac/default.aspx?cite=196-27A-020 (accessed August 2, 2017).

[8] Connecticut Code of Ethics, Section 20-300-12 at www.ct.gov/dcp/lib/dcp/pdf/forms/
penlsregs298.pdf (accessed August 2, 2017).

[9] Alaska Statutes and Regulations for Architects, Engineers, Land Surveyors, and Landscape   Architects,   Article   2:   Code   of   Professional   Conduct   at
www.commerce.alaska.gov/web/Portals/5/pub/aelsstatutesregs.pdf (accessed August
2, 2017).

[10] IEEE Code of Ethics at www.ieee.org/about/ieee_code_of_conduct.pdf (accessed February 2, 2017).

[11] American Society of Mechanical Engineers, Code of Ethics at www.asme.org/getme
dia/9EB36017-FA98-477E-8A73-77BO4B3BD410/P157_Ethics.aspx (accessed April
20, 2017).

[12] National Society of Professional Engineers, Code of Ethics at www.nspe.org/resources/
ethics/code-ethics (accessed April 5, 2017).

[13] American Society of Civil Engineers, Code of Ethics at www.asce.org/code-of-ethics
(accessed April 28, 2017).

[14] American Society of Civil Engineers, Code of Ethics at www.asce.org/code-of-ethics
(accessed May 5, 2017).

[15] American Institute of Chemical Engineers, Code of Ethics at www.aiche.org/about/
code-ethics (accessed April 20, 2017).

[16] Association for Computing Machines, Software Engineering Code of Ethics and Professional Practice at www.acm.org/about/se-code (accessed April 16, 2017).

[17] Society of Manufacturing Engineers, Code of Ethics at http://chapters.sme.org/s147/
code_of_ethics.htm (accessed April 20, 2017).

[18] National Conference of State Legislatures, State Whistleblower Laws at www.ncsl.org/
research/labor-and-employment/state-whistlebloweer-laws.aspx (accessed March 10,
2017).

19

Engineering Ethics When Lives Are on the Line: When Does Bad Engineering Become Bad Ethics?

Neil G. Siegel

19.1 Introduction

Numerous engineering projects create products and services that are important to society; many have explicit safety implications; some are distinguished by explicitly supporting national security. Failures and deficiencies that might be considered "routine" in some settings can in these cases directly cause injuries and lost lives, in addition to harming national security. In such a setting, decisions regarding quality, testing, reliability, and other "engineering" matters can become *ethical* decisions, where balancing cost and delivery schedule, for example, against marginal risks and qualities is not a sufficient basis for a decision. When operating in the context of an engineering project with such important societal implications, established engineering processes must therefore be supplemented with additional considerations and decision factors. In this chapter, long-time defense contractor executive and US National Academy of Engineering member Neil Siegel discusses specific examples of ways in which these ethical considerations manifest themselves. The chapter starts with his thesis, asserting that bad engineering risks transitioning into bad ethics under certain circumstances, which are described in the chapter. It then uses a story from the NASA manned space program to illustrate the thesis; unlike some stories, this one has a "happy ending." The author then moves to the main aspects of the chapter, starting by explaining the behavioral, evolutional, and situational factors that can tempt engineers into unethical behavior: how *do* engineers get into situations of ethical lapse? No one enters a career in engineering intended to put lives and missions at risk through ethical lapses; at the very least, this is not the path to promotion and positive career recognition. With the basis for such behavior established, the author then defines what he calls the *characteristics of modern systems that create risk of ethical lapse;* he identifies five specific traits of modern societal systems – systems of the sort that today's engineers are likely to be engaged in building – as being those that can allow people to slip from bad engineering into bad ethics. These characteristics are then illustrated with examples, from everyday engineering situations, such as working to ensure the reliability of the electric power grid, and designing today's automobiles. The very complexities and richness of features that distinguish many of today's products and critical societal systems are shown to become a channel through which bad engineering can transition into bad ethics. Lastly, the chapter discusses some of the author's ideas about how to correct these situations, and guard against these temptations.

19.2 Thesis

In my view, bad engineering risks transitioning into bad ethics when performing proper analyses *would* have indicated that major system problems are being overlooked in the specification and design of the system – but those steps are not performed.

Herein, I provide examples that illustrate the pervasiveness, subtlety, and potentially severe impact of such bad engineering ethics, and also identify a set of *specific system characteristics* that can trigger this type of ethic quandary. The systems that we engineers create – and will continue to create in the future – serve vital and increasingly pervasive roles in our society. We owe society, and ourselves, the very best that we can do. This is my motivation for talking about ethics in engineering.

19.3 A Story That I Was Told: The Return-to-Earth Orbit Design

I start with a story from the past; in my experience, such stories can help us form strong intuitions about what to do in the future.

My parents were both engineers who worked on the US manned space program: my father in propulsion, my mother in guidance. Through them, I met many other engineers who worked on that program. One of the more senior of these engineers[1] told me this story:

> "I was working on the *orbitology* team at Space Technology Laboratories"[2]; as the word orbitology implies, this team designed the orbits for the US manned space missions, including the Apollo program, which was intended to take humans to the moon, and return them safely to the Earth.
>
> The team conceived of the idea of designing the orbit so that if something went wrong, the space vehicle would coast around the moon and return to the Earth, even if for some reason no additional engine burns were possible. "We thought that this was a really good design, offering an entire additional layer of safety for the astronauts." So, the idea was presented to NASA.

"To our surprise, NASA *hated* the idea"; the return-to-Earth orbit required more power at launch (that is to say, a slightly larger booster rocket) than some other orbit designs. It took a lot of time and arguing to convince NASA to adopt the idea. Fortunately, NASA eventually embraced the idea, and even published papers about it as if it were their idea in the first place.

In the end, NASA selected a slight compromise: some of the earliest Apollo missions (which were only going to orbit the moon and return to the Earth, rather than land on it) used exactly the contractor-invented return-to-Earth orbit design, but for the actual moon landing missions, NASA used a variant of that design that required a small engine burn in order to get back to the Earth. NASA thought that this was okay, because the required engine burn was small – well within the capacity of the engine on the Apollo service module that they selected to use for this purpose – and they would program the computer in the command module to be ready, upon emergency, to do the required calculations.

Everyone of course now knows that there was an explosion on the way out to the moon during the Apollo 13 mission. When that explosion took place, the *service module* was severely damaged, and because of that, the power to the *command module* was so limited that NASA had to turn off most of the command module systems (so as to conserve what little battery capacity remained for the actual re-entry phase of the mission). The astronauts were instructed to move to the *Lunar Excursion Module*. This move had its own issues: the Lunar Excursion Module was designed only to support two astronauts, not the three that had in fact to move into it during this emergency, and its batteries were sized only to support operations for about two days, not the five or so days that it would take to get the astronauts around the moon and back to the Earth. Dealing with the limited battery power capacity required turning off many of the devices and systems in the Lunar Excursion Module (in additional to having already turned off almost everything in the command module).

One of the results of the explosion was that the engine on the service module that NASA had intended to perform the engine burn required to get into an actual return-to-Earth orbit was not available for use; the service module had suffered too much damage. Nor was the computer in the command module that NASA had intended to control this mid-course engine burn that would transform the orbit into a true return-to-Earth orbit available; the power to command module was largely turned off. NASA and the contractor team decided to perform this course-correcting engine burn using the engine on the Lunar Excursion Module that was intended to perform the actual moon landing; this was called the "Lunar Excursion Module *descent engine*."[3] NASA also needed a computer to control the timing and duration of the engine burn; since they were going to be using the engine in the Lunar Excursion Module, they decided to use a computer in the Lunar Excursion Module that was a part of what was termed the "abort guidance system"[4] to control the engine burn that would redirect the astronauts back to the Earth.[5]

Fortunately, all worked well, and the astronauts managed to return safely to the Earth.[6] But to this day, some of the surviving contractor team members remain irate about NASA's attitude when the idea for a return-to-Earth orbit design was originally presented. NASA did not want to use the return-to-Earth orbit design because it would require a little more capacity in the booster-rocket system. The contractor team felt that the small additional expense was warranted; NASA did not. "I believe that we only convinced them to adopt this design by telling NASA that they were putting the lives of future astronauts at risk."

Cost-versus-safety is always a design consideration and an important system trade-off, but in this case the incremental cost of employing the return-to-Earth orbit design to the overall Apollo mission was so small that it could not even be measured (e.g., a slightly larger booster rocket), whereas the situation that could develop if the return-to-Earth orbit (or the small variant that was eventually adopted) had *not* been used would have made it absolutely impossible to rescue the astronauts in the event of an incident like that which actually transpired on the Apollo 13 mission. NASA personnel were reported by my contact as saying that it was "absolutely impossible" for so many things to go wrong that a return-to-Earth situation would arise. In this, of course, NASA was absolutely wrong – this sort of situation *did* in fact arise (and only on the third attempt to land on the moon; so, not only was this situation not impossible, it was probably not even particularly rare). My contact always stated that he felt that the issue that caused NASA to reject the idea originally was actually rooted in a "not invented here" syndrome; that is, since the idea originated with a contractor, rather than within NASA's own engineering staff, the NASA engineering staff rejected it. My contact went on to state that the contractor decided to allow NASA to write about the return-to-Earth orbit concept *without* making reference to the idea having been developed by a contractor. He believed that this was an essential part of the "socialization" that allowed NASA eventually to accept and adopt the idea; that is, the contractor allowed NASA to transfer "emotional ownership" of the idea from the actual inventors (the contractor) to NASA's own engineering staff, and that this made it easier for NASA to adopt the idea. If my contact's assessment of the motivations involved is correct, this approach is an important lesson about how to get useful things done!

Since the overall cost impact was so small that it could not even be measured, the normal sort of cost-versus-benefit analysis did not apply, and this situation can be viewed almost entirely as a near-lapse of engineering ethics on the part of NASA; that is, they nearly let their "not invented here" mentality add an intolerable risk to the mission. It reflects credit on NASA, of course, that in the end they came to a good decision and adopted the suggestion of using the return-to-Earth orbit. We can all be thankful for that!

19.4 How Do Engineers Get into Situations of Ethical Lapse?

No one enters a career in engineering intended to put lives and missions at risk through ethical lapses; at the very least – as mentioned earlier – this is not the path to promotion and positive career recognition. So how did this happen?

In his book *Fooled by Randomness* Taleb (2004) writes about the tendency of humans to *underestimate the likelihood of low-probability events*. That is, if an event is reasonably rare, humans tend to act as if the probability actually approaches zero. Taleb even cites sources that attribute this tendency to the deep operation of our brains, as developed through evolution. If this is true, it takes active effort to overcome such a tendency.

The problem with this tendency is that rare events do occasionally occur. This is why we ought to buy fire insurance for our homes, and collision insurance for our cars.

This tendency to underestimate the likelihood of *low-probability events* was probably relevant to NASA's attitude in the situation described in Section 19.3; since they deemed the likelihood that a set of events that could necessitate a return-to-Earth event was "absolutely impossible" (my contact's phrasing: to put it in the language I use herein, he felt that NASA underestimated the likelihood of this particular low-probability event), NASA may have therefore decided that they were not *actually* creating the *ethical dilemma* that they did in fact create. This may help explain their behavior. No one would deny, of course, that NASA did in fact have the responsibility to assess the probabilities reasonably. The contractor did so, and therefore was worried about the potential of catastrophe; NASA at first avoided such a realistic assessment, and therefore essentially excluded the potential of this type of catastrophe, and in turn (at first) elected to exclude the only possible feature that could be incorporated into the system design that could mitigate against this particular low-probability event.

A large organization like NASA that is attempting novel and difficult enterprises will perhaps face these sorts of issues more often that the average organization. This is not to say that NASA is less ethical than other organizations; it just suggests that NASA perhaps is dealing with the complex and the unknown more often than some other organizations.

19.5 Characteristics of Modern Systems That Create Risk of Ethical Lapse

As already mentioned, I believe that *bad engineering* risks turning into *bad ethics* when drawing from experience and performing correct analyses *would* suggest that major system problems are being unobserved in the design and specification of the system. However, but those steps are *not* carried out. In the case described in Section 19.3, NASA nearly fell into this position.

I further believe that it is the case that modern systems exhibit *specific technical and social characteristics* that can lead to this particular type of *ethical quandary*. Among the specific system characteristics that can trigger this problem, I have already discussed (in the discussion about the NASA moon-shot program), the apparently-normal human tendency to discount the likelihood of low-probability events to essentially zero probability, and how that discounting can lead to ethical quandaries, not just to engineering and management quandaries. In this section, I will discuss four additional system characteristics that can trigger a transition from engineering risks to ethical risks:

1. The *complexity* and *scale* of modern systems.
2. *Reliability* and *availability* tend to be under-emphasized, as compared to functionality and capability.
3. We tend to accept *operator-induced* and *user-induced* failures as being outside of our design responsibilities.
4. We ignore – or seriously under-emphasize – the potential for use of the system beyond the uses that were originally envisioned, and also do the same for potential use beyond the originally-specified conditions.

19.5.1 Complexity and Scale Introduce Non-Linearities

Another important characteristic of modern systems is their *complexity* and *scale*. Complexity and scale introduce *non-linearities* in system behavior,[7] so that our intuition – which many people suspect basically operates by linear or proportional extrapolation (see, e.g., Kilpatrick et al., 2001) – is no longer even approximately valid. This can cause lapses in consideration of failure modes (among many other system characteristics), for example – which can in turn manifest themselves as unsafe operation. Many systems in fact exhibit serious failure modes that come entirely from scale, complexity, and the resulting errors in their *dynamic behavior*[8] – that is, scale and complexity can be actual *sources* of failure modes. This therefore can become another path via which we can create an ethical lapse through incomplete or inadequate engineering – we understand the scale and complexity of the system we are designing, but fail to account for the failure modes that such scale and complexity introduce themselves, above normal engineering considerations.

19.5.2 Reliability and Availability Are Under-Emphasized

Reliability and *availability*, when they are under-emphasized in favor of focusing on system capabilities and functionality, can also become a source for lapses in engineering ethics. There is a natural tendency to focus on functionality and the visible features and capabilities of our systems, and therefore to under-emphasize quality characteristics (such as reliability and availability, which are in some sense "less visible" to the eye of the intended users than system capabilities and functions). This tendency is reinforced by our contracts and system specifications: a typical specification for a big system will have most of its listed requirements dealing with functionality and capability (at times, as much as 99 percent of the requirements by count), and only a small portion (sometimes just 1 percent of the requirements by count) dealing with quality and usability factors. But reliability and availability – and other quality factors, too – are quite likely to be involved in safety and other important societal considerations, even though they did not require very many words in the specification to define their requirements. As a result, many system-development efforts perform only rudimentary analysis during design of these quality parameters. For example, the fault-tree might only identify the most obvious types of faults, completely omitting many faults that are equally impactful, but harder to see. The result is that the realized system reliability often is actually far less than the predicted system reliability. Another result of this behavior is that even if the occurrence rate of faults is as predicted, the severity (e.g., the impact of those faults when they occur on system operational effectiveness) is often far higher than predicted. Having system reliability much lower than predicted, and/or the impact of system faults being more severe than predicted, can have serious safety and other consequences – and therefore, once again, we have created an ethical lapse through incomplete or inadequate engineering.

19.5.3 Treating *Operator-Induced Failures* As Being Outside of Our Design Responsibilities

Yet another characteristic of modern systems that can cause ethical lapses is that we tend to accept the idea that operator-induced failures are *outside* of our design responsibilities. That is, if the user or operator of our system does something wrong (or even just something unexpected) and a problem results, we tend to say that it was *his or her* responsibility, rather than saying that *we* should have foreseen the possibility of such a mistake, and made the system react in a safe and predictable fashion, even in the presence of such "wrong" inputs.

This is an ethical lapse because it is 100 percent certain that at some point in the life of a system the users will "punch the wrong button," or create an input outside of nominal range, or provide some other "wrong" input or action. A robust design is precisely one that protects the system and its users against excessive adverse consequences from such an action.

Early versions of the DOS computer operating system, for example, did not even have a simple "Are you sure?" check when a command to erase a file (or even an entire directory of files) was entered. Even this simple example constituted negligent design (quickly corrected by Microsoft in later versions of DOS), as such "Are your sure?" queries were standard practice in many competing computer operating systems at the time. "Negligence" evolves into an "ethical problem" when the consequences can harm people. For example, why should a motor–generator accept a command to spin faster than it is designed to tolerate, when the consequence of such a command is that the generator may physically come apart, and that people could be injured or killed by that action (see Schneier, 2007)? The creators of StuxNet, of course, took advantage of just such a lapse on the part of the designers of the centrifuges being used to distill out heavy uranium isotopes.[9] But why should the microcontrollers of those centrifuges have accepted commands to operate outside of their known physical limits?

Those examples are of *single-point* instances of "wrong" user inputs causing actual physical damage. Much more common, and much more subtle, is the creation of physical damage through a *combination* of commands – none of which may be intrinsically unreasonable – that only in *combination* result in physical damage (and thereby, can cause injuries or death to people). Think of the chain of valves and pumps (these days, all of which are capable of being controlled remotely by computer commands) that operate an oil refinery or a chemical plant. With heavy, hot fluids moving through pipelines, control commands to a succession of valves and pumps must be properly synchronized, else the momentum of the column of moving fluid can burst a pipe wall, or cause other damage. A command to an individual valve or pump may be within the range of operation for that single device, but in the context of the *total operating picture* of the facility, that same command may be a disaster. I assert that proper design and good engineering ethics require that we design our systems with the appropriate dynamic checks-and-balances that prevent command sequences that can combine to cause damage; and do so whether those commands are intentional or accidental. Very few of today's complex systems meet such a standard. I believe that we have a responsibility to protect our systems even against such operator-induced failures, and therefore also against hacker-induced and bad-inside-actor-induced failures, as well.

19.5.4 Ignoring the Potential That Our Systems Will Be Used in Ways Other Than We Intended

Another characteristic (somewhat related to the example in Section 19.5.3) is that we often ignore – or seriously under-emphasize – the potential for using our systems in ways that we did not envision, or beyond the specified operating conditions.

One simple example is using a screwdriver as a chisel (or vice-versa). Many of us have done that.

A more relevant example of this that everyone knows about is the *Internet*. The Internet was designed to share small bits of textual information between academic and scientific researchers; no other use was envisioned or specified at the time of its creation. Certainly, the use of the Internet for *safety-critical missions* was not imagined (Kleinrock 2013); yet today, an almost countless number of safety-critical and societal-critical missions are operated over the Internet. I will discuss the implications of this specific example in the case studies in sections 19.6 and 19.7.

19.6 A Case Study: The Electric Power Grid

I will now talk a little bit about the electric power grid, as an example of the quandary that society has gotten itself into; in this case by using the Internet for the sort of societal-critical missions that we are considering herein.

A modern industrialized country such as the United States depends in an essential way on a complex set of *interconnected technical infrastructures*, such as water, electricity, natural gas, gasoline, sewage treatment, road building and maintenance, traffic signals, food production and distribution, and so forth.

Following the principles formalized in Ricardo's *Law of Comparative Advantage* (Ricardo, 1817), society has become *specialized*. Whereas at one time most people were fairly self-sufficient – digging their own water wells, growing their own food, building their own shelters, and making their own clothes – this is no longer the case for the majority of people in the United States and the industrialized world. Instead, each individual person specializes in performing one type of task (e.g., growing wheat, teaching, programming a computer), and in essence exchanges his or her contribution on that specialized task for the remaining goods and services that he or she needs. Money was long-ago recognized as a more efficient medium of exchange under such circumstances, as compared to barter. If I depend on barter and have grain and need meat, I must find someone who has meat and wants grain. As you can see, having a freely convertible medium of exchange (e.g., cash) making exchange easy is of enormous economic benefit. As a result, most of us work for cash wages, and purchase – rather than make – each of the aforementioned critical infrastructure services such as water, food, and so on.

While such specialization lies at the root of our economic progress over primitive societies, and hence at the root of increased human life-span[10] and other obvious benefits, we are most of us now dependent on the continuous operation of these *critical* technical infrastructures. Few of us have artesian water wells on our property, yet we can only live for about three days without potable water. Even fewer of us, especially in the cities, grow our own food.[11]

Those who design and operate these critical infrastructures are responsible people, and they have endeavored to make them reliable. What they have not done, however, is made adequate provision to defend against *deliberate* attempts to undermine, disrupt, or destroy these infrastructures; nor in many ways have they dealt effectively with undesired *emergent behavior* that arises not from their individual component of the overall system, but from the complex interactions among all of the components of their system. In their defense, they have not been tasked to do this, or not authorized by their ratepayers to incur these costs.

In the "post-9/11" world, this is increasingly recognized as a gap that must be corrected. For example, multiple nations have tested or are believed to be developing *electro-magnetic-pulse* weapons that are designed explicitly to attack the electric power grid over a large area with a single attack (Foster et al., 2008). There are a few rare natural phenomena (e.g., extreme space weather) that could cause similar disruptions – they are rare, but they do periodically occur!

Electricity plays a key foundational role among these key infrastructure services. For example, water must be pumped to be available, and most of that pumping is directly powered by electricity. In turn, many of the electric power plants are powered by natural gas, but much of that natural gas is produced far from where it is used. This mean the natural gas must be pumped from its production locations to the locations of the power plants (several thousand separate sites in the United States alone) – and that pumping is in turn often powered by electricity. In particular, while many natural gas pumping stations are in fact powered by the gas in the pipeline itself (using about 3 percent of the gas energy for this purpose), increasingly (and in my view, unfortunately), recent installations and upgrades (including many in critical gas-distribution locations, such as Houston, Denver, and California) have instead used electricity to power such pumping (Judson, 2013).

Furthermore, electricity has another nearly unique characteristic: we have little capacity to store electricity upon rapid changes in demand. Yet demand must match generated power to an astonishingly accurate degree, and on sub-second response-times. As a result of these characteristics, in order to recover from a large-scale power outage, those facilities generating electricity must coordinate closely with the major users of electricity (water pumping, water treatment, etc.) as generation capacity is brought back online: generation and electric load must be brought online and then kept exactly in balance. If generation at any instant exceeds demand, voltage and/or frequency can go up, damaging equipment. If generation at any moment falls short of demand, voltage and/or frequency can go down, causing equipment to shut off, perform outside of specification, or be damaged. But with all forms of real-time communications off-line due to this same power failure, how is this coordination – which is necessary for the electric grid to be restarted – going to be performed? Once the grid is up and running in a steady state, generators can monitor voltage and frequency, and make small adjustments without having explicitly to coordinate with the users of that electricity, but to start the grid from "off", such coordination is required; otherwise, the fluctuations would be far too large, and cause damage to equipment.

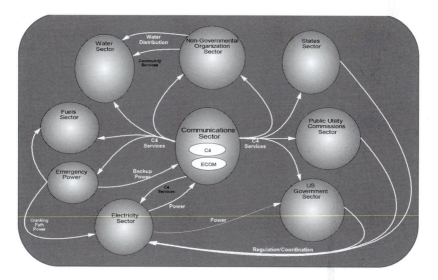

Figure 19.1 *Complex interactions among the critical infrastructures, their stakeholders, and their regulators.*
Source: Siegel and Ferren, 2016

The result is a complicated set of interdependencies among these critical infrastructures, and among the people and organizations that operate, pay for, and regulate them, as illustrated by Figure 19.1.

Many of these mission-critical and safety-critical links are implemented via the Internet, but as already noted, the Internet was not in fact designed to support such critical applications. Specific ways in which the Internet falls short of properly supporting these sorts of critical missions include the following:

- The variance in packet delivery time on the Internet is practically unbounded, and is at best large as compared to networks that are designed specifically for critical-mission use
- The packet successful-delivery-on-first-attempt rate on the Internet is considerably smaller than that achieved by networks specifically designed for critical-mission use.
- The availability of service between any two points on the Internet is considerably lower than that achieved by networks designed for critical-mission use.

Any of these characteristics of the Internet can contribute to irregularities, errors, wrong answers, and failures of service for the mission-critical and safety-critical missions supported by the Internet, including the electric power grid and the critical infrastructure services (water, sewage treatment, etc.) that depend on the electric power grid.

Given this combination of nature of the electric grid, and the limitations of service for safety-critical missions provided by the Internet, it is easy to see the cascading disaster that could result from a large-scale electric outage in an industrialized country.

- Due to a man-made (e.g., electromagnetic pulse (EMP) attack or cyberattack) or natural (e.g., severe space weather) event, electric service would instantly go out, and (due to the recent substitution of computer-controlled switches to control the power grid, rather than the older electromagnetic relays) potentially over a far wider area than previous power outages. The computer-controlled switches offer great convenience when the power is on, but are vulnerable to EMP and cyberattack, whereas the older electromagnetic relays were not.
- Other critical infrastructure services that consume very large amounts of electricity (e.g., water pumping, water and sewage treatment, etc.) would go out, too. Some of these sites have diesel generators to replace a small portion of their electricity needs, but (due to safety concerns) most such sites are not allowed to store more than a nominal amount of diesel fuel.
- Communications systems (telephone, Internet, satellites and satellite phones, cellular phone base stations, and switching centers) might be instantly disrupted, depending on the cause of the event (e.g., if the cause of the event is an EMP attack, many of these services would go off the air instantly). Those that did not go off the air instantly would go off the air within four to eight hours, as their battery back-up systems exhaust their capacity. As a result, utility company emergency managers could not communicate with their field operatives or with the major users of electricity; government officials would not be able to communicate with utility company managers; the police and non-government organizations (NGOs) could not coordinate actions; no one would know where to send supplies and people with critical skills; and so forth.
- People would attempt to leave their cities, in search of somewhere where power might be on (and remember that with no electricity, no information about what to do or where to go could be provided to the public – radio and television stations, too, would be off the air in the event of a power outage). The roads would become completely clogged, and even emergency vehicles could not get through. After a few days, this congestion would get *worse*, as cars that are out of gasoline would be abandoned on the road. Even gas stations that have gasoline in their underground tanks need electricity to pump that gasoline up to the cars – and the electricity is off.
- High-rise buildings would become uninhabitable within a few days, as sewage would back up on every floor (sewage is *pumped* out of a high-rise building).
- Food in grocery stores, restaurants, homes, and storage centers would rot.
- The sewage overflows and the rotting food would become sources of infection; the combination of a lack of food and consistent sources of potable water (you can't provide water to a large city for very long out of little plastic bottles, even

if necessary trucks could get fueled and get through the clogged roads) would reduce people's resistance to disease, and massive outbreaks of dysentery, cholera, and so on would occur.

Estimates are that such a scenario could kill *tens of millions* of people in the United States alone, and that it could take years (or even decades) before power was restored and the economy back to normal (EIS Council, 2017).

The electric grid and its vulnerability is therefore another example of the creation of physical damage through a *combination* of activities. Each portion of the electric grid is designed sensibly within its own small domain of operations and responsibility, but no one apparently has the responsibility to assess and protect the grid against the damage that comes from such a *combination* of interactions. Yet the critical infrastructure of the industrialized world depends on such a combination of interactions. For example, if electric power goes out, natural gas stops being pumped, and since most of the electricity in the United States comes from burning natural gas, the power plants cannot be re-started because they don't have natural gas. The natural gas pumping stations either don't have back-up diesel generators or they are not allowed to store enough diesel fuel on site to restore steady-state operations. The trucks that were planned to deliver that extra diesel fuel cannot get through because of clogged roads; and so forth. I again assert that proper design (and good engineering ethics) requires that we find a way for society to account for (and to pay for!) methods to prevent and/or recover from these sort of multi-domain/multi-step events. As we have seen, the power grid does not yet meet this standard (although I am glad to report that this problem is at last beginning to attract interest[12]).

19.7 An Additional Case Study: The CAN Bus

Computer hacking and sabotage are also just beginning to be understood as a real threat to society's safety and well-being. Hacking is not just a threat to private data. Consider the physical damage that could be caused by hacking traffic signals, water pumping stations, and so on and so on. I believe that we in the engineering profession have a responsibility to design our systems so that the impact of attacks on their capability is minimized, at least to the point of protecting human lives. Yet when I have approached industries (e.g., banking) offering to improve their cybersecurity posture, a common response is that "We are waiting for the government to establish guidance via statutes, because if we do things in the absence of such laws, our stockholders and regulators will attack us for spending money needlessly." We engineers have to take a role in leading society out of this dilemma; driving some of the engineering studies into our systems designs in advance of the law requiring it; providing information to professional societies and others who can work to get appropriate laws and regulations enacted; creating demand for all of the above through educating the general public; and so forth.

I provide one last example of what I think is a bad design enabled by a lack of thinking about the ethical implications of a design: the automotive CAN bus.

A Controller Area Network (CAN) bus is an electronic communications path, intended for use in a vehicle (like an automobile) that is designed to allow microcontrollers and other devices to communicate with each other without the use of a host computer. The specific version used in cars was apparently started at Robert Bosch GmbH (a German automotive electronics company), and was officially released for use by the automotive industry in 1986 (CAN in Automation Group, retrieved 2018). The design decision adopted throughout the automobile industry was to place *all* of the microcontrollers and electronics in the *entire* car on a *single* such bus: engine controls, brake controls, transmission controls, and other motion-related (and hence safety-related) items are on the same bus as the radio and air conditioning.

In contrast, in other types of vehicles that employ extensive electronic controls (such as warships), the state of practice has long required that *multiple independent* buses be employed, so as to separate the control of safety-critical and/or mission-critical items from "convenience items." For example, on the typical US warship, there is one bus that connects all of the devices that control the basic movement of the ship (e.g., power generators, engines, steering apparatus, etc.), a second bus that connects all of the devices that control the military functions on the ship (e.g., sensors, weapons, etc.), and still a third bus that connects the "convenience items" (e.g., non-emergency lighting, recreational devices, etc.). Good engineering – and good engineering ethics – would have had the designers who were implementing an automotive CAN bus in a specific vehicle looking at the rationale behind this well-known warship design practice, and considering how those rationale and lessons-learned would apply to passenger cars. This *ought* to have resulted in a design for a communications bus system for automobiles that did not, for example, allow hackers to gain remote wireless access to a car via the audio entertainment system and use that access (since there is only a single bus) remotely to "take over" motion-critical and safety-critical items – such as being able to accelerate the car without any action on the part of the driver (and the driver not being able to "override" this acceleration), to prevent the driver from turning off the ignition or taking the transmission out of "drive," and even to disable the brakes. Yet this is precisely what has come to pass (for examples, see Greenberg, 2015; Koscher et al., 2010). Such poor design, especially when well-known examples were available of better approaches (e.g., warship control systems), verges, in my view, into a serious lapse of engineering ethics. We are just beginning to learn the cost of this particular lapse.

In addition, there are "second-order" effects that should have been considered, but evidently were not. For example, the audio system in most modern cars is so powerful that it can create sounds that are so loud as to constitute a serious distraction to the driver; actually causing pain in the ears, and so forth. Therefore, a remote hacker who "only" was able to seize control of the sound system of a car (even without trying to take over the engine, brakes, etc.), could still seriously degrade the ability of the driver to safely control the vehicle.

19.8 Corrective Actions

Having defined and illustrated via examples the problem, I wish to present some ideas about how to avoid the problem.

First and foremost, in my opinion, is the matter of placing proper emphasis on good design. At present, I believe that it is fair to say that most engineering projects place their primary emphasis on developing good requirements. Many texts and corporate guidelines about performing systems engineering, for example, are heavily focused on the matter of requirements. Many academic papers that examine the question of problems in the system development process focus on requirements, too, citing factors like incomplete requirements or "requirements creep" (e.g., the problem that the requirements continue to change, even as the design and implementation progress) as the root cause of the large number of engineering projects that have significant problems. It is natural for the customers and eventual users of the system to focus on the requirements, too; after all, the requirements are something that they can understand, and are also something that they have a natural reason for wishing to influence.

There is no doubt that such problems occur, for example, engineering projects often end up costing much more than promised, usually accompanied by taking significantly longer than predicted, failing to implement all of the promised capabilities. The data indicates that a large portion of engineering projects are terminated before their completion, due to these factors. But I spent several years of my engineering career as a sort of "designated engineering project fix-it person," and what I found was *not* that engineering projects that were in trouble had bad requirements; instead, what they had consistently was *bad designs*.

I have also seen cases of two completed systems that do approximately the same thing, where one runs 100 times faster than the other. Similarly, I have seen cases of two completed systems that do approximately the same thing, where one is 1000 time more reliable than the other. Having for these examples also had the opportunity to examine the root cause for the slower and less reliable performance, I can assert that the systems at the bad end of these examples had bad designs.

This finding has many interesting implications. First of all, having a 100x or 1000x range of outcomes for a critical parameter from an engineering project is shocking; mature engineering disciplines simply do not have such large range of outcomes. Consider mid-sized family sedans offered for sale that meet US emissions-control requirements; the variation from best to worst, for example, in gas mileage is no more than 25 percent, not 100x (10,000 percent) or 1000x (100,000 percent). Something is going radically wrong inside the designs of the systems that exhibit such bad performance on such an important metric.

I drew on this experience in fixing troubled engineering projects in my Ph.D. research. In my Ph.D. dissertation I develop and attempt to validate a hypothesis describing exactly in what way are these designs bad, and how could they have been improved. I am not the only person to have examined the question of how to accomplish an effective design for a complex engineering system.

Creating a good design for an engineered system is, in my experience, far more difficult that developing the requirements for that same system. Furthermore, we get a lot of "help" as we develop the requirements for an engineering system; after all, our customers and our users understand well *what* they want the new system to do, and such *what* constitutes a major portion of the requirements.

We do not usually have such a resource pool to help us with the design. The design is far subtler than the requirements, interactions between elements of the design are far more likely to have significant impacts on the system and its performance than are interactions between elements of the requirements, and the design is far more technical (and hence opaque to many observers). Furthermore, most projects do not have reasonable technical metrics for measuring the progress of the design; they tend to use only management metrics for measuring progress on the design (e.g., we held these reviews, we produced these documents, etc.).

Engineered systems almost always aspire to create some sort of emergent behavior, a sort of "$1 + 1 = 3$", where useful things happen due to the interaction of formerly separate elements. But what also happens is, while creating a design that produces the desired emergent behaviors, the design fails to *prevent* the arising of unplanned emergent behaviors that appear as unintended adverse consequences.

As a result, unintended adverse emergent behavior often creeps into our systems through such incomplete designs. In my judgment and experience, this is the *true root cause* of most failures of engineering project developments (rather than requirements creep, etc.). Such incomplete design – that is, a design that does *not* incorporate features explicitly aimed at preventing such unintended emergent behavior (in my Ph.D. dissertation and other writings, I often call this "unplanned dynamic behavior") – is likely to exhibit the poor characteristics that I have described, and therefore these are the projects most likely to fail and/or be cancelled.

So, improving the design and the design process is "step 1," in my view, towards avoiding the problem of bad engineering transitioning into bad ethics.

After the design, I believe the next most important corrective is the risk management process. Most big projects have some type of formal risk management process; the process itself is usually pretty rigorous. What is lacking, in my experience, is *content*. I have found that the risks contained on the risk register of an engineering project are often completely superficial and general. I have actually seen the statement "The software might be late" as an entry on the risk register in a multi-billion-dollar engineering project. Such a statement is useless as a risk register entry. First of all, it is true on every project that has a material amount of software (as almost every engineering project does these days), therefore it is not specific in any fashion about this particular project. But far worse is the fact that it contains no insight about what the project should be measuring every month in order to determine if in fact the risk is coming to pass, or what steps should be taken to mitigate the impact if and when they determine, through those measurements, that the risk is coming to pass.

So the next corrective is generating much more specific and far more measurable entries on the risk register, and then taking the corresponding actions in the rest of the risk management process; for example, figure out what to measure, work out how to make those measurements, create mitigation plans if the risk materializes, and so forth.

Of course, doing this takes intense (and expensive) effort, expertise, and a lot of time. It also results in there being many more items on the risk register! These are probably the reasons that it is not done properly more often.

19.9 Conclusion

In my view, *bad engineering* can transition into *bad ethics* when proper analyses and experience *would* have shown that serious system problems are being overlooked in the specification and design of the system – yet those steps are not performed.

Examples have been provided that illustrate the pervasiveness, subtlety, and potentially severe impact of such bad engineering ethics.

I further believe that it is the case that modern systems exhibit *specific technical and social characteristics* that can lead to this specific type of ethical quandary. Examples of such system characteristics that can trigger this quandary were discussed, including the following:

- The human tendency to discount the likelihood of low-probability events to essentially zero probability
- The complexity and scale of modern systems
- Reliability and availability tend to be under-emphasized, as compared to functionality and capability

- We tend to accept *operator-induced* and *user-induced* failures as being outside of our design responsibilities
- We ignore – or seriously under-emphasize – the potential for use beyond the uses of the system that were originally envisioned, and for potential use beyond the originally-specified conditions.

Societal expectations for engineering are very high; whereas a baseball player has only to succeed (e.g., get a hit) 30 percent of the time to be considered a major success, in contrast, society's expectations for engineered products and systems is near 100 percent availability and correctness. I believe that, in turn, this expectation grants us license to insist on proper designs, based on proper analyses, especially in safety-critical and mission-critical situations.

I also wish to plea for practicing engineers to believe that developing a personal reputation for thoroughness, diligence, and good engineering ethics is a boon, not a liability, to one's individual career. I cannot "prove" this, but most of my experience over nearly forty years as a practitioner supports that conclusion. One last little story: When I was the vice-president and general manager of an operating division at a large aerospace company, we elected to bid on a competition for a new type of system for the US Marine Corps. The system specification had a "hard limit" of 11,000 pounds for the complete system, because this was the capacity of the specific vehicle chassis that we were to use in building the system. When it came time to submit our bid, my proposal manager pointed out that when they added up all of components of our proposed design (which we thought was wonderful, and would offer the Marines a lot of operational advantages), we were slightly over that weight limit; as I recall, 11,045 pounds. My proposal manager asked what we should do; the implication was for me to choose between fudging the analysis to make it say "10,999" pounds, or to submitting the proposal as-is (i.e., over the specification weight limit) and assume that the Marines would appreciate the honesty, understand that 1000 design decisions remained between the proposal and the fielded system, and that there was plenty of time to solve the weight problem before we were done. I said to submit it as-is. And we won – despite being overweight. Many, many years later the proposal manager came to me and said how much he and the proposal team had appreciated my having taken the ethical approach in that situation.

References

CAN in Automation Group (retrieved 2018). History of CAN technology. Retrieved from www.can-cia.org/can-knowledge/can/can-history/
EIS Council (2017). EPRO™ Black Sky Event Simulation Project. Some of the key results of this simulation scenario are reported at the website. Retrieved from EIS Council http://eiscouncil.org/Epro/SimulationProject

Foster, J. et al. (2008). Report of the Commission to Assess the Threat to the United States from Electromagnetic Pulse Attack. A commission chartered by United States public law 106-398, Title XIV.

Greenberg, A. (2015). Hackers Remotely Kill a Jeep on the Highway – with Me in it. Retrieved from www.wired.com/2015/07/hackers-remotely-kill-jeep-highway/

Koscher, K. et al. (2010). Experimental Security Analysis of a Modern Automobile. IEEE 2010 Symposium on Security and Privacy.

Judson, N. (2013). Interdependence of the Electricity Generation System and the Natural Gas System and Implications for Energy Security, MIT Lincoln Laboratory Technical Report 1173.

Kilpatrick, J., Swafford, J., a7 Findell, B. (Eds.) (2001). *Adding it up: Helping children learn mathematics*. Washington, DC: National Academies Press.

Kleinrock, L. (2013). Personal communication. Kleinrock, still a professor at UCLA and who made important contributions to the design of the Internet (e.g., hierarchical routing), often says this in his lectures and speeches.

Kushner, D. (2013). The real story of Stuxnet. Retrieved from http://spectrum.ieee.org/telecom/security/the-real-story-of-stuxnet

Ricardo, D. (1817). *On the principles of political economy and taxation*. London, UK: John Murray.

Schneier, B. (2007). Staged attack causes generator to self-destruct. Retrieved from www.schneier.com/blog/archives/2007/10/staged_attack_c.html

Siegel, N., & Ferren, B. (2016). The figure is from "Emergency Communications System (ECOM), A technical report for the electric Infrastructure Security Council. Retrieved from www.eiscouncil.org

Siegel, N. (2011). Organizing projects around the mitigation of risks arising from system dynamic behavior. *International Journal of Software Informatics* 5(3), 78–99.

Taleb, N. N. (2004). *Fooled by randomness*. New York, NY: Random House.

Endnotes

[1] Who prefers that I not use his name.

[2] A NASA contractor. This company was later re-named "Thompson Ramo Woolridge" and was usually known by its initials "TRW." TRW was acquired by Northrop Grumman in 2002.

[3] The author's father was a member of the team at STL that developed this Lunar Excursion Module descent engine.

[4] The abort guidance system was intended to guide the Lunar Excursion Module to a rendezvous with the command module in the event that the mission commander decided that he could not finish a moon landing, and instead had to abort the landing and return to the command module, which was waiting for them in an orbit around the moon. Since the motions of the LEM near the moon were "free-flight," under the control of the LEM commander, the return-and-rendezvous course could not be pre-planned, but instead had to be calculated in real-time using telemetry and instrumentation; to do that required a guidance computer.

[5] The author's mother was a member of the development team for this abort guidance system.

[6] Among the "thank-you" visits that the Apollo 13 astronauts made after safely returning to Earth was a trip to Space Technology Laboratories in Redondo Beach, California, to

thank the teams that created the LEM descent engine and the abort guidance computer. Both of my parents were part of the teams that met the Apollo 13 astronauts during this thank-you visit. The author was a teenager, and had the opportunity to accompany his mother during this visit.

[7] That is, small changes in an input can lead to more than a small change in an output; at times, small changes in an input can lead to gigantic changes in an output.

[8] The subject of "unplanned dynamic behavior" in a system, and how to design systems that exhibit markedly less on this undesirable behavior, is discussed in Siegel (2011).

[9] StuxNet was a computer-based attack on the Iranian nuclear program, which allegedly caused physical damage to Iranian centrifuges being used to weaponize uranium, by commanding those centrifuges to operate outside of their specified physical limits, for example, to spin too fast, to change speed too fast, and so forth. Many descriptions and analyses of the StuxNet endeavor are available. More information is available in Kusher (2013).

[10] After remaining constant for several hundred thousand years at a life-expectancy of about thirty-five years, human life-span has doubled (from about thirty-five years to approximately seventy years) more or less exactly in coordination with the creation and adoption of the industrial revolution, which is simply the period where humanity first intensely implemented the economic specialization described here. Note that the US National Academy has studied the causes of such increased life-span, and attributes most of that increase to the *engineering accomplishments* that created these technical infrastructures: water, sewage treatment, refrigerators, self-propelled tractors (and the fuel and parts supply chains that keep them running) – and *not* to modern medicine. In substantiation of this conclusion, the Academy notes that locations and countries that by and large do *not* have modern medicine have still achieved much the same life-span increases if they have adopted economic specialization and these technical infrastructures.

[11] As recently as during the Theodore Roosevelt administration, more than 90 percent of the US population engaged in farming or animal husbandry of some sort. Today, that figure is about 3 percent.

[12] As evidenced by the formation of the Electric Infrastructure Security Council (www.eiscouncil.com/), among other indicators.

20

Case Studies of Product Life Cycle Environmental Impacts for Teaching Engineering Ethics

Matthew J. Eckelman, John Basl, Christopher Bosso,
Jacqueline A. Isaacs, and Kathleen Eggleson

20.1 Introduction

Given the rapid rate of technological innovation and a desire to be proactive in addressing potential ethical challenges that arise in contexts of innovation, engineers must learn to engage in *value-sensitive* design – design that is responsive to a broad range of values that are implicated in the research, development, and application of technologies. One widely-used tool is Life Cycle Assessment (LCA). Physical products, as with organisms, have a life cycle, starting with extraction of raw materials, and including refining, transport, manufacturing, use, and finally end-of-life treatment and disposal. LCA is a quantitative modeling framework that can estimate emissions that occur throughout a product's life cycle, as well as any harmful effects that these emissions have on the environment and/or public health. Importantly, LCA tools allow engineers to evaluate multiple types of environmental and health impacts simultaneously and are not limited to a single endpoint or score. However, LCA is only useful to the extent that its models accurately include the full range of values implicated in the use of a technology, and to the extent that stakeholders, from designers to decisionmakers, understand and are able to communicate these values and how they are assigned. Effective LCA requires good ethical training to understand these values.

20.1.1 Chapter Summary

In the case presented in this chapter, students must decide among four potential courses of action related to a drug with direct clinical benefits but negative societal side effects. There are two important ethical dimensions to this case that must be traded off against one another. First, there is the dimension of uncertainty and risk. Whereas the therapeutic benefits of a drug can be quantified through clinical trials and by direct comparison to existing standards of care, the damages to public health must be estimated on the basis of modeling rather than direct measurement through controlled experiments. As with any model, there is inherent uncertainty in the results. Deciding how to weigh uncertainty requires a value judgment, which is made difficult by the fact that being too conservative in how we manage risks can come at significant costs in terms of patients not being given access to beneficial technologies. Second, the benefits and costs of the drug are typically borne by different populations. While the drug provides health benefits to the individual patients and clinicians who make use of it, any potential environmental and public health impacts typically are borne by society at large. This raises questions of distributive justice, questions that prompt us to anticipate distributions of potential harms, and evaluate their fairness. The answers to these distributive justice questions will inform an ethical approach to confronting questions about how much risk should be accommodated.

20.2 Next-Generation Ethics, STEM Education, and Sustainability

Ethics has long been incorporated into engineering and science education and is rightly required by many accreditation and certification programs. The Engineering Accreditation Commission (EAC) and Technology Accreditation Commission (TAC) of ABET, Inc. both require undergraduate engineering curricula to include the study of ethics. As one means of incorporating ethics into curriculum, students are frequently introduced to engineering codes of ethics associated with a number of professional engineering societies – for example, American Society of Civil Engineers (ASCE), American Society of Mechanical Engineers (ASME), Institute of Electrical and Electronics Engineers (IEEE), and Society of Manufacturing Engineers (SME). Although there is no single standardized system of ethical conduct for all engineering disciplines, the codes provide frameworks to guide engineers in addressing ethical issues associated with professional practice. Presenting these codes of conduct in the classroom has educational value, but is not sufficient. How can we help students to recognize the ethical challenges in engineering and internalize the approaches to resolving them?

Harris et al. place ethics training at the core of engineering, stating that "Engineering ethics is as much a part of what engineers in particular know as factors of safety, testing procedures, or ways to design for reliability, durability, or economy. Engineering ethics is part of thinking like an engineer. Teaching engineering ethics is part of teaching engineering" (Harris et al., 1996). The focus of most engineering ethics materials and courses has been situational – what are an engineer's obligations to an employer and a client on a particular project. These are situations that present conflicts of interest, or questions of ethical conduct, so-called "microethics" cases where the stakeholders are present and relatively few in number (Herkert, 2005). Two common types of engineering ethics cases are (i) those involving matters of degree where the ethical question is at what scale a behavior is acceptable or not, and (ii) those involving conflict resolution, where the engineer must balance conflicting ethical responsibilities (Harris et al., 1996).

The rise of sustainability as a central concept in engineering curricula has broadened the paradigm of engineering education, from considering single projects and direct impacts to considering engineering systems or multiple projects concurrently while analyzing both direct and indirect impacts in terms of cost and the environment. The same trend can be seen in engineering ethics as well, where situational microethics training is being complemented by instruction in "macroethics"; for example, on how an engineer should consider obligations to public health and safety at large, or to ecosystems and populations that are indirectly affected by decisions that an engineer might make (Herkert, 2005).

Conceptually, promoting innovation and commercialization of emerging technologies, while simultaneously considering legitimate social and ethical concerns has broad support. However, responsible development is inherently challenging to realize in practice. One reason is the rapid rate of innovation, which frequently outpaces that of policy and regulatory processes.

This difficulty is compounded by the fact that many oversight institutions lack basic capacity – for example, they are underfunded or understaffed relative to their regulatory mandates – and often are not as familiar with novel technologies as are those for whom they are developing policy and regulation (Bosso et al., 2011). In response to these challenges, there has been a widespread call for creation of more anticipatory and agile responsible product development processes, so that social and ecological issues can be addressed early in technology development (sometimes called *upstream*). Proactive responsible development is contrasted with reactive approaches, in which social and ecological issues are addressed only after they arise and have perceptible impacts – at which point it may be too late to do much about harmful effects (Bosso, 2016; Sandler, 2012).

20.3 Technical Background: Life Cycle Assessment and the Quantification of Indirect Effects

Engineers who seek a professional credential understand that they will be assuming liability for the *direct* performance of their designs; however, they are largely untrained in considering the ethical dimensions of their *indirect* obligations and liabilities. The indirect effects of a product, project, or policy can be characterized and quantified using LCA, which is a formal modeling method that utilizes a comprehensive "cradle-to-grave" approach to evaluate environmental and social impacts by incorporating material, energy, and economic flows as well as social and biological effects at different stages. LCA is in wide use by designers, scientists and engineers, and businesses, primarily for use in product design and management. It is also employed in policy spheres to quantify the systemic impacts of large-scale engineering and technology decisions. LCA provides information to users about the magnitude and the location of impacts that may occur out of their immediate control or purview, up the supply chain, in a different country, or in an unrelated sector, for example.

LCA is vital to proactive responsible development, since it is a tool that can be used by researchers and industry to assess the ecological impacts of industrial processes and products during development to determine where their impacts can be reduced. It is therefore crucial that engineering graduate students are trained in both the technical workings of LCA and in the ways that it can be employed to advance responsible development efforts, at both the technology development and technology policy levels. Moreover, ecological LCA training is an avenue into education regarding value-sensitive design more generally – i.e., designing technologies in ways that are informed by social and ecological evaluation of them. In fact, social LCAs have the potential to incorporate consideration of human rights, distributive justice, and worker conditions into the technology development process by identifying how technologies and industrial processes intersect with these concerns and could be modified to protect rights and promote justice. Because the rate of technological innovation so far outstrips the rate of policy and regulatory development, non-formal resources and approaches typically are crucial to responsible development. At minimum, education on how to conduct LCA and employ it in value-sensitive design, and promoting these as educational standards and professional best practices, is vital to developing the capacity for proactive responsible development of emerging technologies and processes.

There have been several documented efforts to introduce sustainability into engineering ethics education, and many more are underway. In an early article, Vanderburg wrote of the need for "preventative engineering" that weighed the larger environmental or social implications of a project (Vanderburg, 1995). Some implications have been traditionally considered in economic terms as in mandated economic benefit–cost analysis, but increasingly they can be formally quantified in environmental terms through the use of LCA. Negative life cycle environmental or social impacts have also been linked to product liability and the need for engineers to address indirect effects during the design stage, not just of the product itself, but of the standards and regulations that apply to that product (Herkert, 2003). At the course level, innovations in incorporating ethics and sustainability into engineering education include courses designed to "develop [civil engineering] students decision-making skills under environmental, social and ethical constraints" (El-Zein et al., 2008) and experiential ethics training, where students personally work through sustainability-related ethical dilemmas in the context of classroom games and group cooperation/competition (Sadowski et al., 2012).

While the use of LCA is widespread, the modeling structure and the interpretation of results involve ethical and value judgments that must be navigated carefully by both the analyst and by the receiver of the results. Ethical issues arise in the following areas:

1. *Conducting an LCA*. Building LCA models is a value-laden enterprise. Researchers conducting an LCA must make decisions about which data sets to use (and so the quality of data required) and how to scope their analyses. In addition, life cycle modeling provides information on a range of environmental, social, or economic indicators, leaving users to decide how best to normalize or weight different metrics against each other, many of which have ethical dimensions such as distributed cancer-causing pollution or ecotoxicity.

2. *Communicating results of an LCA*. For example, endpoint impact assessment methods directly link a single product to such damages as loss of species, human morbidity and mortality, or ecotoxicity. Such impacts are highly case-dependent and uncertain, so what is the ethically appropriate way to communicate linear, deterministic model results that are in fact subject to a high degree of non-linearity and stochasticity?

3. *Using LCA results in practice*. It is often unclear what role LCA results play – or *ought* to play – in engineering and policy decisions, even with greater focus on and increased calls for integration of life cycle thinking in decision-making. Challenges arise when attempting to use LCA results without understanding the techniques and value judgments embedded in those results. It is crucial that decisionmakers understand which social and ecological values LCA represents and which it fails to capture, as well as the value assumptions embedded in it.

4. *Determining responsibility for social and ecological impacts identified by an LCA*. How much responsibility does the maker of the product bear for the damages it may cause over its life cycle, which occurs in large part beyond the factory gates? How much ethical responsibility does the individual consumer bear in buying and using a product that negatively impacts ecosystems or impinges on human rights in the countries where it is made or disposed?

At present, there is a dearth of teaching materials designed to integrate ethics education into life cycle-oriented coursework. Courses that utilize LCA and life cycle management exist in a variety of departments, including mechanical, chemical, environmental, and civil engineering; biology; environmental science; public health; and business and decision science. At the same time, many of these same fields incorporate ethics education into their curricula (Barry and Ohland, 2009), which largely ignore ethical training around the indirect, life cycle impacts that LCA can illuminate, and that can in many cases dominate the direct effects and ethical considerations.

For the past several years, we have been developing case studies for next-generation engineering ethics education with the twin goals of (ii) improving ethics education for scientists and engineers on indirect, systems level effects and (ii) integrating ethics training into LCA and management education. The case studies explore ethical issues surrounding different engineering topics along the product life cycle, from disposal of byproducts from aluminum production, to use of toxic materials in consumer products, to managing complex electronic waste streams. In all cases, students must synthesize technical material from the case study with fundamental concepts in ethics rather than ethical codes of conduct that are based on these concepts (presented in a separate "Ethics Primer," written by collaborating ethicists) to consider decisions that were made or that face the stakeholders in that particular case.

The Case Study on environmental implications of drug use in the healthcare sector explores the ethical issues in extending a clinician's traditional duty to patients out to consider indirect environmental and public health effects of healthcare practices. In it, students hit on many of the major themes of sustainability and macroethics – distributive justice, intergenerational equity, the precautionary principle, and reductionist economic valuation. Discussion questions for the case are provided at the end, as are active assessment questions developed for use across all of the cases.

Case Study

Life Cycle Assessment to Support Sustainability Measures at Hospitals: Patient Health and Public Health Considerations

Eckelman Matthew

A.1 Introduction

Inhaled anesthetics are a class of chemicals used in general anesthesia to reduce pain or cause a temporary loss of consciousness, typically to facilitate surgical procedures. As such, they are a cornerstone of modern medicine. Inhaled anesthetics can vary in chemical complexity; most are chlorinated or fluorinated hydrocarbons, but other types of compounds such as nitrous oxide (N_2O –"laughing gas") and the noble gas xenon have also been found to be effective.

A.2 Historical Development of Inhaled Anesthetics

Diethyl ether, the first inhaled anesthetic, was synthesized back in the mid-1500s and noted by the Swiss–German scientist Paracelsus (the father of modern toxicology) for its ability to lessen pain. But it wasn't until three centuries later that ether's usefulness in medical procedures was demonstrated and inhaled anesthetics entered common use (stemming in part from a famous public demonstration in Boston on October 16, 1846 – later dubbed "Ether day"). N_2O, first synthesized in the mid-1700s, and chloroform, also naturally occurring but first synthesized in the early 1830s, also entered common use around this time.

An important precept in medical drug development is to maximize potency while minimizing hazards and side effects. Many early inhaled anesthetics had serious disadvantages, but with the scientific and medical methods available during that period, these took time to uncover. The most obvious was the flammability of ether, to this day used in some fuel mixes, but the substance also had side effects such as nausea and vomiting. Chloroform became popular in Europe but was found to be fatal in a small number of anesthesia cases; it was later linked to cardiac fibrillation. N_2O was effective in dental cases and minor surgeries, but was not potent enough to be used universally.

A century after the introduction of these early inhaled anesthetics, the fluorinated compound halothane was developed, which solved the problem of flammability, while being sufficiently potent and fast-acting for general surgery. However, halothane was found to cause liver failure in some patients. Later fluorinated anesthetics were also found to have serious side effects; for example, methoxyflurane affected the kidneys while enflurane could lead to seizures. Starting in the 1980s, three new fluorinated ether drugs entered use that were potent, non-flammable, not well-metabolized (thus minimizing potential side effects), and near-universally effective: these were isoflurane, sevoflurane, and desflurane. Together with N_2O, these are the most commonly used inhaled anesthetics today (Jones, 2014).

A.3 Environmental Considerations

The aforementioned history of inhaled anesthetics involved unintended consequences, with new replacements solving some issues, such as ether flammability, while introducing others, such as potential organ damage. While the current fluorinated ether drugs have far fewer physical and toxicological hazards than those that preceded them, their use has important environmental consequences, primarily for global climate change. Anthropogenic climate change is caused by emissions of greenhouse gases (GHGs) from human activities. A GHG is so-called because it absorbs outgoing radiation from Earth and reradiates a portion back to the surface, with the effect of trapping energy in the lower atmosphere as in a greenhouse. The most abundant GHGs in the atmosphere are water vapor (H_2O), carbon dioxide (CO_2), methane (CH_4), N_2O, ozone (O_3), and a class of synthetic chemicals called chlorofluorocarbons (CFCs). The potency of a GHG is most commonly measured by its global warming potential (GWP) factor, which represents both a GHG's ability to absorb radiation and its average lifetime in the atmosphere. GWP values are evaluated over a specific time period and normalized to an equivalent mass of CO_2, or CO_2 equivalents (CO_2e) (IPCC, 2007). For example, N_2O has a GWP_{100} factor of 298, meaning that over a 100-year period, a kilogram of N_2O will absorb and reradiate 298 times as much energy as a kilogram of CO_2.

In addition to N_2O, all three of the major fluorinated ether anesthetics have been found to absorb radiation at wavelengths that classify them as GHGs. And like many CFCs, they are potent: their GWP_{100} values are 510 for isoflurane, 2540 for desflurane, and 130 for sevoflurane (Sulbaek Andersen et al., 2010). The fact that these inhaled anesthetics are not well-metabolized – a characteristic that makes them medically advantageous – means that these gases are exhaled by patients during procedures that require general anesthesia. If the gases are not somehow subsequently captured and/or chemically converted, they will leave the hospital through vents as direct emissions to air. Their high GWP values combined with their ubiquity means that these drugs represent a major category of GHG emissions, contributing up to 5 percent of the healthcare total in a UK study (NHS Sustainable Development Unit, 2012).

A.4 Life Cycle Assessment of Anesthesia Options

Emissions of anesthetic gases after their use (called "waste anesthetic gases") directly contribute to climate change because they are GHGs themselves, but they are not the only emissions that are relevant. Emissions of anesthetic gases may also occur at several other points in their technological "life cycle" – during their manufacture, from leaky valves and seals as they are being transported or stored, or even from unused or half-empty containers that have been discarded. Other types of GHGs might be emitted from the life cycle as well. For example, manufacturing chemicals requires pumps, pumps require electricity, and electricity that is based on combusting fuels leads necessarily to CO_2 emissions. These CO_2 emissions do not come *directly* from hospitals or clinics that use inhaled

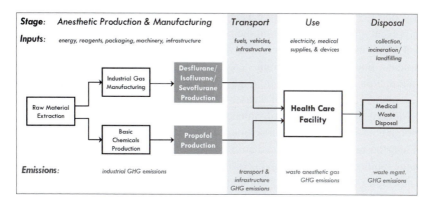

Figure A.1. *LCA system boundary and process flow diagram for delivery of general anesthesia*
Source: adapted from Sherman et al., 2012

anesthetics; rather, they are *indirectly* associated with anesthetic use, specifically in the "upstream" supply chain of the drugs. Indirect emissions have many sources and can take many forms. CO_2 emissions from producing electricity and heat or from combusting motor fuels; N_2O emissions from agricultural operations that supply food for workers in the supply chain; methane emissions from medical waste incineration associated with the product life cycle – all are indirect GHG emissions that contribute to the climate change effect of anesthetic gases (Figure A.1).

LCA is an environmental modeling tool that has been developed to quantify emissions throughout a product life cycle, and to link these emissions to environmental effects such as climate change. LCA results can reveal where in the life cycle changes can most effectively be implemented in order to reduce the environmental impacts of a product. Finding a way to capture waste anesthetic gases will reduce or eliminate the direct emissions of these potent GHGs, but this action does nothing to reduce emissions from anesthetic gas manufacturing. But how important are GHG emissions from drug manufacturing compared to direct emissions? In general, chemicals manufacturing is among the most energy-intensive manufacturing sector in the United States and many other industrialized economies (US Energy Information Administration, 2016), suggesting that CO_2 emissions from supplying heat and electric power to chemical plants may be a dominant source of life cycle GHG emissions.

In LCA and many other comparative assessment methods, product options are evaluated on the basis of their function rather than on a mass or volume basis. This "functional unit" of comparison reflects the actual product amounts that would be used in a given application, and must be measurable. In the case of inhaled anesthetics, function or efficacy is measured in terms of Minimum

Alveolar Concentration (MAC). This is the amount of an anesthetic drug needed
to prevent a response to a given incision in 50 percent of patients. The higher its
unit MAC value, the less potent the drug, as more is needed to fully anesthetize
patients. Enough drug is administered in order to achieve the required concentration, typically one MAC, although higher or lower concentrations can be used
depending on the specifics of a case.

Modern administration of inhaled anesthetics uses a generically-named
"continuous-flow anesthetic machine." These machines allow for precise control
of anesthesia dose. Vaporizers that fit into the machine bring the inhaled drugs up
to the required temperature and pressure and change those that are liquid at room
temperature (sevoflurane and isoflurane) into the gas phase. Patients under anesthesia still need oxygen to breathe, so anesthetic machines mix inhaled anesthetics
with air or oxygen as a "carrier gas." N_2O is also used as a carrier gas in order to
provide additional anesthesia in many situations, mixed with oxygen and one of
the fluorinated ether drugs. Tubes carry this gaseous mixture from the anesthetic
machine to the patient in a "breathing circuit," which consists of plastic tubing, a
mask or airway device, and in closed circuits that recirculate gases, materials that
absorb the CO_2 exhaled by patients. In contrast, delivery of a liquid injectable
anesthetic uses plastic tubing, a needle and syringe for the injection, and a syringe
pump for even drug delivery.

Sherman et al. (2012) published an LCA study investigating life cycle GHG
emissions associated with the most common types of anesthetic gases – desflurane, isoflurane, and sevoflurane – against propofol, a common injectable option.
All options were compared on the basis of one MAC-hr, that is, providing general
anesthesia for one hour. Each of the three inhaled anesthetics were modeled with a
carrier gas mix of oxygen and N_2O, with 1 L/min required for desflurane and
isoflurane and 2 L/min required for sevoflurane. Unlike the inhaled anesthetics,
propofol is prepared in vials with enough drug to cover a long case. In practice,
this means that for most cases, much of the drug is unused and discarded after the
operation. This level of drug wastage was approximated by hospital clinicians at
50 percent.

For all three of the inhaled anesthetics, direct emissions of waste anesthetic
gases were found to dominate, assuming no gas capture and destruction,
exceeding indirect emissions from other life cycle stages by approximately two
orders of magnitude, or 100x (Figure A.2, panel A). Desflurane had the highest
emissions by far, both because of the quantity required and potency of desflurane
as a GHG. Because N_2O is commonly used as a carrier gas/co-anesthetic and a
GHG, it also makes an important contribution to life cycle GHG emissions,
particularly for sevoflurane, which requires a fresh gas flow rate of approximately
double that of the other options. GHG emissions from manufacturing the anesthetic drugs, packaging them, transporting them, and delivering them were relatively minor in comparison, indicating that in this case GHG emissions from
upstream or supply chain activities were relatively insignificant. Propofol, the

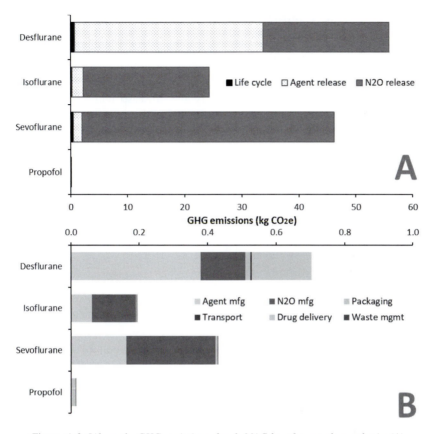

Figure A.2 *Life cycle GHG emissions for 1 MAC-hr of general anesthesia (A) including and (B) excluding emissions of waste anesthetic gases*
Source: adapted from Sherman et al., 2012

injectable anesthesia option, was found to have by far the lowest life cycle GHG emissions.

However, if waste anesthetic gas capture and destruction technology were used, these indirect sources of GHG emissions would become dominant (Figure A.2, panel B). Production of the anesthetic drugs in chemical manufacturing plants would dominate, again including both the halogenated drug and the carrier gas N_2O. Emissions from producing packaging, transporting drugs to the hospital, and medical waste disposal of auxiliary equipment such as tubes were all small contributors to life cycle impacts. The one other important source of emissions in this scenario, particularly for desflurane, is the generation of electricity used to run the vaporizers that actually deliver the inhaled anesthetics to the patient breathing circuit.

A.5 Patient Health vs Public Health

Medical care is primarily aimed at minimizing early mortality and suffering from disease or temporary or permanent disabilities. Clinicians and public health professionals have developed metrics that encompass these considerations and allow healthcare professionals to quantify the "disease burden" in different countries and from different causes. One of the most common of these is the disability- adjusted life-year, or DALY, which was developed under the auspices of the World Health Organization and has been in use since the 1990s. One DALY could be one year of life lost from premature death, or several years lived with a disability, the multiplier being proportional to the severity of the disability. For example, the multiplier for lower back pain is ~0.33 (3 years with disability = 1 DALY), whereas the multiplier for dementia is 0.66 (1.5 years with disability = 1 DALY).

Future climate change is projected to negatively impact health in many regions of the world. Potential impacts of climate change on human health, well-being, and security have been characterized in detail and include thermal stress, flooding and extreme events, air pollution, infectious disease, malnutrition, and potential conflicts (Haines and Patz, 2004). Several different groups have created estimates of future health damages in these categories and linked them to the quantity of GHG emissions, in order to create a "damage factor," or measure of health damages per kilogram of CO_2 equivalent emission (De Schryver et al., 2009; Tang et al., 2015). There is wide variation in modeling approaches – such as the socioeconomic and emissions scenarios considered, inclusion/exclusion of particular health effects, potential adaptive responses, and modeling parameters such as discount rate and modeling time horizon – leading to order-of-magnitude differences in damage factors. Averaging previous damage factor estimates (and restricting results to GWP_{100} values) gives a value of 2.55×10^{-7} DALYs/kg CO_2e.

From the results of Sherman et al. (2012), one MAC-hr of desflurane use with a life cycle GHG emissions of approximately 60kg CO_2e results in 1.53×10^{-5} DALYs, or about eight minutes of disability-adjusted life lost. Though no definitive data exist, it is estimated that approximately 50 million procedures requiring general anesthesia are carried out annually. In a study of drug use for sixty-two hysterectomies, Thiel et al. (2015) found that procedures where desflurane was used had approximately twenty times the life cycle GHG emissions of those where sevoflurane was used (both with N_2O as a carrier gas). (This ratio differs from that seen in Figure A.2 because of the standard rates of fresh gas flow used in the hospital in question.) Where medically acceptable, switching from desflurane to sevoflurane would lower emissions from approximately 300 kg CO_2e per procedure to approximately 15 kg CO_2e per procedure. If desflurane were used in 50 percent of procedures (corresponding to the proportion of desflurane use in the hysterectomies study), and substituted with sevoflurane, for example, more than 3500 DALYs would be saved for American patients.

A.6 General Ethical Considerations: Fairness and Distributive Justice

Engineering and policy decisions frequently involve ethics-based choices about resource use, waste placement, and distributions of risk over a population. For example, for any company's management and operations, individuals must decide which resources to use; from where to source them; what labor pool to use to gather those resources; where to manufacture that product and therefore where to risk any negative consequences of manufacturing; where and how to dispose of or store waste; and so on. This raises questions of "distributive justice" and especially questions of "environmental justice," that is, questions of how to fairly distribute the benefits and burdens of these choices, including the resulting environmental burdens and benefits. Many individuals or companies will make choices about these distributions according to the market, in whichever way makes the most economic sense. Often, however, this leads to people who have no say in the decision shouldering a large proportion of the "negative external-ities," or costs to people or society that are not included in the direct price of goods and services.

Is this fair? Should policies or regulations governing resource use be structured so as to promote a different distribution of burdens and benefits than what the market would dictate? What would that distribution look like? Distributive justice and negative externalities can be considered across space, where products are used in one location but negative impacts occur to people far away, and across time, where impacts occur to people in the future. This ties into the ethics and sustainability concept of "intergenerational equity."

A.7 Implications and Options for Action

These LCA results have several implications for which measures will be most meaningful when trying to reduce GHG emissions from operating room proced-ures where general anesthesia is required, all of which were discussed in the original article (Sherman et al., 2012):

1. *Investing in effective waste anesthetic gas capture.* Controlling waste anes-thetic gases will have the greatest benefit. There are several technologies that are available for gas capture and/or destruction. For example, photo-chemical air purification can theoretically destroy all waste anesthetic gases.

Existing volatile waste anesthesia gas capturing systems can reclaim volatile gases for reuse rather than discharge waste into the atmosphere. The Dynamic Gas Scavenging System designed at Vanderbilt University is a cryogenic condensing system built into the exhaust system of multiple operating rooms. This system is activated only when the patient exhales. Since the vacuum pump is only intermittently active, the system has minimal impact on heating, ventilation, and air conditioning energy usage (Barwise et al., 2011). Another technology, Deltasorb®, consists of a canister that snaps into existing scavenging circuits and that is filled with material that absorbs volatile anesthetic gas. The canisters are returned to the vendor where the captured anesthetics can be extracted, liquefied, and processed into medical grade anesthetics (Blue-Zone Technology, Toronto, Canada). Such an investment throughout a hospital would require either purchase or lease of the required equipment, or establishment of a service contract. Moreover, inhaled anesthetics could be reused, thus saving money, either in the same hospital or in less purity-sensitive applications such as veterinary medicine. This option would have no effect on clinical options for patient care.

2. *Eliminating desflurane from formularies.* This option prevents use of the anesthetic option with the highest emissions of all drugs considered. Desflurane is also the costliest of all drug options on a MAC-hr basis, so this choice would also save money. However, eliminating desflurane would reduce available options for patient care. First, compared to the other inhaled anesthetic options, desflurane does have distinct advantages. First, it is the least metabolized, reducing the potential for side effects from degradation products. Second, it has the lowest solubility in the blood, meaning that its concentration can be precisely controlled, allowing for rapid emergence and recovery of patients from general anesthesia. Rapid emergence and recovery are particularly useful for obese patients who may experience trouble regaining normal function of their respiratory systems and getting enough oxygen. Third, desflurane has not been shown to depressed kidney and liver function during general anesthesia, a particular concern in elderly patients. Even so, despite these advantages, the clinical functions of desflurane can be achieved through using the other drugs in combination.

3. *Use rebreather circuits and/or reduce fresh gas flow rates when possible.* In open breathing circuits, fresh gas flow is used to push out CO_2 exhaled by the patient so that it doesn't build up in concentration. Higher gas rates mean that less exhaled gas remains in the circuit. Eckelman and Sherman assumed constant gas flow rates of 1–2 L/min, but rates of 4–6 L/min are not uncommon. By using closed rebreather circuits where CO_2 is captured by sorbents and the unmetabolized anesthetic gases can be reused directly greatly reduces required fresh gas flow rates, perhaps even achieving metabolic flow rates where fresh gas only serves to replace the metabolized

drug. In addition, more fresh gas is needed during initiation, but during anesthesia when respiration is depressed, gas flow rates can be turned down. In practice, fresh gas flow rates are commonly maintained at initial levels. High flow rates mean that more halogenated anesthetic and nitrous oxide are being used, which increases costs and leads to GHG emissions and future, indirect health damages. So, using rebreather circuits and reducing fresh gas flow rates can save money and reduce public health impacts. However, Option 3 requires a change in anesthesia practice, potentially conflicting with the original training of clinicians and staff, and may encounter pushback from anesthesiologists.

4. *Do nothing and wait for regulatory guidance.* Options 1–3 are all proactive, voluntary measures on the part of hospitals, but are not currently required by any regulatory agency or certifying body. The do-nothing option maintains the status quo and leaves all anesthesia drug options and practices open for clinicians and staff.

A.8 Actions Taken

Following the publication on LCA of anesthetic agents discussed in Section A.7, Dr. Jodi Sherman, an anesthesiologist at Yale-New Haven Hospital (YNNH) approached the manager in charge of the drug formulary to discuss the potential banning of desflurane due to the environmental implications of its use. As she notes (during an interview with the author), because of the relatively high cost of desflurane compared to other options, "the manager had additional motivations for eliminating desflurane from the formulary because of economic considerations." By leveraging both economic and environmental benefits, Dr. Sherman and the administrative team at YNNH agreed to remove desflurane from the formulary, the first time that an approved drug had been removed for (in part) environmental reasons.

Dr. Sherman presented on this success at medical conferences and was subsequently invited to speak to anesthesiology departments at other hospitals. As a result, Dartmouth-Hitchcock Medical Center also stopped using desflurane, while several other hospitals decided to erect barriers that made using desflurane more time-consuming, for example, by locking desflurane vaporizers in a special-access cabinet. Gas capture technology has also decreased in price, but as Dr. Sherman noted when relaying the concerns of hospitals that she has visited, "reimbursement is changing so quickly under the Affordable Care Act that even small additional expenditures have to get approved." This raises an additional barrier to budgeting for capital equipment that is not strictly necessary.

Dr. Sherman also caught the attention of Joe Bialowitz, head of sustainability for Kaiser Permanente, a California-based healthcare network that is the largest managed care organization in the country, covering more than 10 million people. As part of the company's sustainability efforts, Mr. Bialowitz and his team had assembled a carbon footprint for the entire company and found that fully 5 percent of its GHG emissions were from medical gases and anesthetic agents. Based on this GHG inventory, Kaiser Permanente set a company-wide goal to reduce GHG emissions by 30 percent by 2020, against a 2008 baseline. Mr. Bialowitz subsequently arranged for Dr. Sherman to meet the head of the anesthesia practice for Northern California, who agreed to the removal of desflurane.

Even without administrative actions to remove desflurane from formularies, clinicians can choose whether to move away from using the drug in general anesthesia. The LCA results and associated research have given them additional environmental information about their practice and linked the decisions made in hospital operating rooms to health damages in the public at large. As Dr. Sherman emphasizes, "climate change impacts of health care should be seen as a patient safety issue."

A.9 Ethics Questions for Discussion

1. Of the four options presented in the case, which do you think is the most ethical course of action? Which is the most realistic course of action in your opinion? If you have different answers here, what societal forces have led to this tension? If the realistic option is different than the most ethical option, and given the social forces you believe lead to this difference, who bears responsibility for choosing the less ethical option?

2. Do doctors' responsibilities, as doctors, extend beyond the health of their patients? Some clinicians have pushed back against the LCA research on inhaled anesthetics and desflurane in particular because it has some clinical advantages, described in the case. If using desflurane is more convenient for clinicians but does not affect healthcare outcomes compared to other drug options, should these advantages matter? Why or why not?

3. The decision to remove desflurane from the formulary of Kaiser Permanente (KP) hospitals will affect millions of patients in the United States. Desflurane has some clinical advantages compared to the other fluorinated ether drugs, described in the case. Suppose that these advantages could save the life of one patient in a KP hospital, and yet doctors no longer have access to the drug. Did KP make the right decision? Why or why not?

4. One of the precepts of healthcare and bioethics is the Latin expression *primum non nocere*, or "first, do no harm." Doctors and nurses are accustomed to considering the welfare of their patients as of primary concern. If they also

start to consider broader and more indirect damages to public health, how should they equate direct with indirect damages? Should one year of patient life lost equal one DALY of public health damages to people elsewhere? Should a different equivalence be used, and how could its value be fairly determined?

5. Some users of DALYs perform "time discounting," meaning that future health damages are discounted to the present day according to a certain annual rate (analogous to an interest rate). One of the early studies on global disease burden used a discount rate of 3 percent for future DALYs. Is this fair from the perspective of distributive justice and intergenerational equity?

6. Now that LCA has been developed and can be used to quantify the indirect public health effects of medical products, should there be a requirement that all medical products be evaluated?

7. LCA modeling can include simplifying assumptions and the use of general data sets that may not be perfectly applicable for a certain hospital. In other words, its results may be uncertain. Should healthcare professionals wait until more studies are conducted on indirect health effects before taking action? (Note that this is a question about the application of the "precautionary principle.")

8. In the United States, the Food and Drug Administration (FDA) is responsible for assessing the safety of medical products. The FDA routinely approves drugs with serious side effects to patients. Should the indirect damages to public health be considered as an acceptable side effect of inhaled anesthetics? What is the difference between these two situations?

9. For regulatory assessment purposes, many governments have developed a "value of a statistical life" (VSL). VSL can be used to estimate the societal value of one DALY. If health damages can be monetized in this way, should there be a surcharge levied on medical products that accounts for their indirect health damages? (In economics this would be an example of "internalizing the negative externality.") Who would ideally levy such a surcharge – governments or someone in the health supply chain? What should be done with the proceeds of such a surcharge? And finally, if such a surcharge were levied and the proceeds fairly distributed, does this absolve healthcare professionals from thinking about the indirect effects of their actions?

10. Eliminating desflurane at YNNH was a win–win situation – good for both economic and environmental/health outcomes. If desflurane were actually the cheapest of all anesthetic agents, would you still support its elimination from the formulary? If no, what if there were no cost difference among treatment options? Is there a different price point at which you would make the switch? How did you estimate this point?

11. Some portion of the life cycle GHG emissions come from electricity use from coal-fired power plants, far outside the direct control of clinicians, hospitals, or even drug manufacturers. The installation of equipment to capture waste anesthetic gases, on the other hand, will eliminate GHG emissions that are under the direct control of hospitals. Should actions or opportunities that affect emissions directly have priority over those that are indirect?

12. LCA can be used to examine the actions of every aspect of a healthcare professional's life. Results could be found for GHG emissions from driving to work, having lunch, the paper used in patient charts, every single piece of equipment in an operating room, even the construction of the hospital itself. If every product and every action lead to GHG emissions and indirect health damages, which products or actions should clinicians consider? Only actions they take while on the job, or should personal actions be considered as well?

A.10 Short Answer Questions for Active Assessment of Learning Objectives

1. Who are the stakeholders in this case, both those involved in the decision and those principally affected by the decision?

2. For each stakeholder group, how are their perspectives and interests communicated to others?

3. Are any of the stakeholder interests in conflict? If so, explain how.

4. What are the potential professional or legal responsibilities of the designers or decisionmakers in the case to the other stakeholders?

5. Do any of the stakeholders face ethical dilemmas or have ethical responsibilities to one another? If so, explain how.

6. What were the ethical issues or dimensions of this case? Use background information from the Ethics Primer, if assigned.

7. From assessment questions 4 and 6, which responsibilities are direct (i.e., the stakeholders have direct contact) and which are indirect (i.e., the stakeholders never actually meet)?

8. Which stakeholder interests were (or could be) quantified? Which stakeholder interests could not be quantified?

9. Identify any value-based decisions made in the case or facing any of the stakeholders.

10. Is there a single right answer in the case? If not, how might quantitative data, qualitative interests, and values be fairly considered together, and what decision would you make based on this strategy?

A.11 Conclusion

A central goal of engineering ethics education is to provide students with an understanding of context for their designs and decisions, environmental and public health implications being central themes. Ethics education typically focuses on cases where engineers consider the direct impacts of their design decisions; however, indirect impacts (e.g., from supply chain emissions) may in fact be much more consequential. These impacts can be effectively discussed in the context of life cycle engineering, which is a design strategy that utilizes a comprehensive "cradle-to-grave" approach to evaluate environmental and social impacts, incorporating material, energy, and economic flows. While the use of life cycle engineering and LCA tools is widespread, the modeling structure and the interpretation of results involve ethical and value judgments that must be navigated carefully by the analyst and by the receiver of the results. LCA is increasingly important in corporate and government decision-making, yet there is a dearth of materials specifically designed to integrate ethics education into life cycle-oriented coursework. Our ethics education efforts center on the integration of life cycle-oriented case studies into design, engineering, management, and public policy fields. The case presented here is inspired by current events and calls for engineering design decisions that involve balancing local or direct effects with larger, indirect effects on society, as well as managing uncertainty. Specifically, in this case on drugs used for general anesthesia, students consider the indirect effects of healthcare practices on the environment and public health, how costs to patients must be balanced against harms borne by these indirect stakeholders, and how to balance known benefits against potential risks and costs that defy precise calculation.

Acknowledgments and Funding

The authors would like to thank Laurie Poklop at the Northeastern University Center for Advancing Teaching & Learning Through Research (CATLR) and Dr. Michael Loui of Purdue University for assistance in development assessment materials, and Dr. Jodi Sherman of the Yale Medical School for her participation in an interview during case study research. This work was funded by the National Science Foundation Engineering and Science Education (EESE) grant, "Ethics Education in Life Cycle Design, Engineering, and Management" (Federal award numbers 1338687 and 1623870).

References

Barry, B. E., Ohland, & M. W. (2009). Applied ethics in the engineering, health, business, and law professions: A comparison. *Journal of Engineering Education* 98(4), 377–388.

Barwise, J. A., Lancaster, L. J., Michaels, D., Pope, J. E., & Berry, J. M. (2011). An initial evaluation of a novel anesthetic scavenging interface. *Anesthesia & Analgesia 113*(5), 1064–1067.

Bosso, C., 2016. Settling into the midstream? Lessons for governance from the decade of nanotechnology. *Journal of Nanoparticle Research 18*(6), 163.

Bosso, C., DeLeo, R. A., & Kay, W. (2011). Reinventing oversight in the twenty-first century: the question of capacity. *Journal of Nanoparticle Research 13*, 1435–1448.

De Schryver, A. M., Brakkee, K. W., Goedkoop, M. J., & Huijbregts, M. A. (2009). Characterization factors for global warming in life cycle assessment based on damages to humans and ecosystems. *Environmental Science & Technology 43*(1), 1689–1695.

El-Zein, A., Airey, D., Bowden, P., & Clarkeburn, H. (2008). Sustainability and ethics as decision-making paradigms in engineering curricula. *International Journal of Sustainability in Higher Education 9*(2), 170–182.

Haines, A., Patz, J. A. (2004). Health effects of climate change. *JAMA 291*(1), 99–103.

Harris, C. E., Davis, M., Pritchard, M. S., & Rabins, M. J. (1996). Engineering ethics: what? why? how? and when? *Journal of Engineering Education 85*(2), 93–96.

Herkert, J. R. (2003). Professional societies, microethics, and macroethics: product liability as an ethical issue in engineering design. *International Journal of Engineering Education 19*91), 163–167.

Herkert, J. R. (2005). Ways of thinking about and teaching ethical problem solving: Microethics and macroethics in engineering. *Science and Engineering Ethics 11*(3), 373–385.

IPCC (2007). Intergovernmental Panel on Climate Change (IPCC), Fourth Assessment Report.

Jones, R. (2014). A history of inhaled anesthetics. In: Eger Ii, I. E., Saidman, J. L., & Westhorpe, N. R. (Eds.) *The wondrous story of anesthesia* (pp. 609–627). New York, NY: Springer.

NHS Sustainable Development Unit (2012). NHS England breakdown of goods and services carbon footprint by organisation type. Retrieved from www.sduhealth.org.uk/documents/resources/Hotspot_full.pdf, London.

Sadowski, J., Seager, T., Selinger, E., Spierre, S., & Whyte, K. (2012). An experiential, game-theoretic pedagogy for sustainability ethics. *Science and Engineering Ethics 19* (3), 1–17.

Sandler, R. (2012). Value sensitive design and nanotechnology. In Scott, D., & Francis, B. (Eds.). *Debating science: Deliberation, values, and the common good*. Amherst, NY: Humanities Books.

Sherman, J., Le, C., Lamers, V., Eckelman, M. (2012). *Life cycle greenhouse gasemissions of anesthetic drugs. Anesthesia & Analgesia 114*(5), 1086–1090.

Sulbaek Andersen, M. P., Sander, S. P., Nielsen, O. J., Wagner, D. S., Sanford, T. J., & Wallington, T. J. (2010). Inhalation anaesthetics and climate change. *British Journal of Anaesthesia 105*(6), 760–766.

Tang, L., Ii, R., Tokimatsu, K., & Itsubo, N. (2015). Development of human health damage factors related to CO2 emissions by considering future socioeconomic scenarios. *The International Journal of Life Cycle Assessment*, 23(12), 1–12.

Thiel, C. L. et al. (2015). Environmental impacts of surgical procedures: Life Cycle Assessment of Hysterectomy in the United States. *Environmental Science & Technology 49*(3), 1779–1786.

US Energy Information Administration. (2016). Washington, DC. Retrieved from www.eia.gov

Vanderburg, W. H., 1995. Preventive engineering: strategy for dealing with negative social and environmental implications of technology. *Journal of Professional Issues in Engineering Education and Practice 121*(3), 155–160.

PART IV

Society

21

Topics in Next-Generation Ethics

Public Policy, Medicine, Business, and Engineering

James G. Ellis, Jack H. Knott, Laura Mosqueda, and
Yannis C. Yortsos

21.1 Introduction

This chapter presents reflections on next-generation ethical issues by four deans at the University of Southern California: Public Policy, Medicine, Business, and Engineering. Each of the deans was asked to reflect on some of the important ethical issues that they believe we face today or that we will face in the near future. Their responses follow.

21.2 Reflections by Jack H Knott: Dean of USC Price School of Public Policy

Good morning everyone. I'm really pleased to be here and share this panel with my fellow deans. I'm going to talk about the unique role of public policy in ethical decision-making.

The state is different than other actors in society because it has sovereignty over the country and can use force to get citizens to obey its laws and policies. It also establishes the legal basis for private market transactions and social interactions, including contracts, money, and private property. In some sense, the state is involved in every area that is represented here at this event, and in many other areas as well.

The state uses several instruments to carry out its activities. The most familiar is the passage of laws, which are interpreted and enforced by the courts, but it employs several other instruments as well, including executive orders, regulations, military and police force, and agency decision-making. For this reason, I prefer to use the term "public policy" rather than just "law," because it includes all these other instruments of state activity.

I would like to examine four basic ethical issues in public policy. The first ethical issue is the tradeoff between efficiency, equality, and equity. In Arthur Okun's classic book on this subject, *Efficiency versus Equity: The Big Trade-Off*, he discussed the moral principle that individuals and groups should be treated equally before the law and in practice. He argues that shifting the allocation of society's resources to assure equality potentially reduces market efficiency. One aspect of this moral question is how to define what equality means in practice. Should people have equal opportunity to succeed, even if in the end some people are enormously wealthy and others are impoverished? Or, should the government seek to create more equal outcomes for people, for example, by redistributing income?

A second aspect of this moral issue is the scope of what one defines as included in basic human rights. In some countries rights are limited to equality before the law based on gender, race, and age; but some other countries extend basic human rights to include housing, healthcare, childcare, voting, and other things. The broader the definition of human rights before the law, the more the conflict grows between equity and efficiency.

A second ethical issue in public policy is individual liberty vs. accountability. One moral principle is the right to freedom for individuals to be able to do as they please, which is a fundamental American value expressed in the Declaration of Independence as the right to "life, liberty, and the pursuit of happiness." Yet one person's right to do as she pleases can be another person's harm or injury. Individuals acting in their own self-interest can also cause harm and add cost to society in general. When I was a kid, the political debate over this ethical issue centered on the proposed law that motorcyclists must wear helmets and passengers and the drivers of cars must wear seat belts. These laws restrict individual freedoms but they also reduce the costs to individuals and society. Today, this ethical issue is focused on policies such as the individual right to buy and sell assault weapons, and the potential harm that this freedom can cause in terms of the increase in murders and mass killings.

Individual liberty vs. accountability is also a key ethical issue in the regulation of the Internet. We now have unlimited access to information and can communicate our thoughts, ideas and opinions, pictures, and images worldwide almost instantaneously in a way never before in history. The ethical issue is: who is accountable for the accuracy of the data and the safety and appropriateness of the images? Should anyone be accountable, especially when false information and certain images can cause real harm to many people? The recent case of Facebook and Cambridge Analytics brought this ethical issue to the forefront of American politics. Is Facebook a technology company or is it a content provider? What is its responsibility to its users and to society? An increasing number of countries – China is one example – restrict certain corners of the Internet and use the regulation of the Internet to hold people accountable for their actions and opinions. Where does the ethical tradeoff lie between the values of individual liberty and accountability?

This same ethical issue is fundamental to the relationship between individuals and authority. The classic work on this is the set of experiments conducted by Stanley Milgram at Stanford. His research showed that when people are under the structure of authority, say in a hierarchy in a private company or a government agency, or taking advice from a doctor or other professional, they are more willing to do things to harm others than they would otherwise find acceptable if they were just making decisions on their own. The most extreme example of this is chronicled in the book *Eichmann in Jerusalem*, by Hannah Arendt. Eichmann was tried for his crimes during the Holocaust when he was a transportation engineer scheduling trains to the concentration camps. His defense in the trial, though unsuccessful, was that he was part of a large bureaucracy and was just following orders he received from his superiors.

We see this issue of the relationship between the individual and authority being played out in the hierarchy of the Catholic Church and the scandal centered on sexual abuse and harassment. In the broader society, the #MeToo movement has exposed the role of organizational culture and authority that can tolerate and even foster abuse, in such different organizations as news agencies, film studios, and universities. Who should be held accountable in these situations? Is it the individual, the company, the government agency, the political and organizational leaders? In what ways do public policy and organizational culture and authority facilitate these kinds of behaviors in people?

A third ethical issue in public policy that I would like to address is that of private benefits vs. public goods. The classic book on this is Mancur Olson's *The Logic of Collective Action*, which makes a convincing argument about the advantage that organized interests have over the general public in gaining beneficial policies from government. In part because of this, there is the temptation toward collusion between private organized interests and public leaders to aggrandize themselves at the expense of the society as a whole. Corruption and rent seeking are found in many countries around the world, including in the United States, where subsidies and favorable regulations for special interests benefit these companies and groups as well as the participating politicians but they reduce the overall economic efficiency and output of the economy.

The best large-scale quantitative study of this phenomenon is the book by Martin Gilens and Benjamin Page, *Democracy in America? What has Gone Wrong and What Can We Do about It*. The authors studied 2000 policies over fifteen years to see if organized interests and economic inequality can lead to political inequality. Here is a quotation that summarizes their findings: "When the preferences of economic elites and the stands organized interest groups are controlled for [in our statistical analysis], the preferences of the average American appear to have only a minuscule, near-zero, statistically non-significant impact on public policy" (Gilens & Page, 2017).

Kleptocracies are the worst example of this form of collusion. Vladimir Putin, for example, is a multi-billionaire, but I am confident that he doesn't earn that salary as the president of Russia. He has become enormously wealthy by extracting rents from leaders of industry, and those industry leaders who support him, in turn, also become very wealthy as well. Other historical examples include Saddam Hussein in Iraq and Ferdinand Marcos in the Philippines.

Another important ethical issue in private benefits versus public goods is how to account for the externalities of many private market transactions. The most significant example is climate change. Firms, households, and individuals engage in daily activities that benefit them but which also send carbon dioxide (CO_2) into the atmosphere through the production of goods, driving cars, flying in airplanes, eating beef, and other activities. Tragically, this externality of increasing carbon in the atmosphere is now threatening the world's climate. The ethical question is how much of these private benefits should be regulated or curtailed to prevent in this case a global public bad outcome? One of the most compelling books on this ethical issue is Jared Diamond's book, *Collapse: How Societies Choose to Fail or Succeed.*

And then finally, a fourth ethical issue concerns the point I made at the beginning of this talk. Governments sometimes use force and violence to achieve their public policy goals. The use of violence in itself is a central ethical question of public policy. This past year a police officer in Sacramento shot and killed a young, black, unarmed man; a sad story that seems to repeat itself across the country. In the United States about 456,000 people were incarcerated in jails and prisons in 2018. How much force should the state use in different kinds of situations?

Internationally, countries operate in a global system that has some economic and diplomatic rules but that is fundamentally an anarchy in which state economic and military power is critical to maintain security. Kenneth Waltz's book *Man, the State, and War* is a classic work on this topic. In response to the 9/11 terrorist, the United States imprisoned thousands of combatants, executed terrorist leaders, and perpetrated wars for "regime change," – in the process killing hundreds of thousands of people. Then there are the ethical issues of the increasingly common use of military drones to attack enemies, which raises the critical question of who is responsible for the fatalities. Is it the machine, the person who coded the algorithm, the person running the machine, or the system?

This has been a very brief overview of four of the fundamental ethical questions in public policy that we need to understand and address if we are to make sound ethical choices about our government and society. Thank you very much.

21.3 Reflections by Laura Mosqueda: Dean of the USC Keck School of Medicine

As a family medicine physician and a geriatrician, I specialize in care for people of all ages, but particularly older adults. In family medicine, we learn and practice the biopsychosocial–spiritual model of care – a holistic approach that is particularly helpful in geriatric medicine. One of the most important ethical issues facing us is one that's been around for a very long time: lack of access to sufficient healthcare for all. If you believe, as I do, that healthcare is a right and that universal access to it is a mark of a civilized society then, to quote a famous astronaut, "Houston, we have a problem."

The implications for not having universal healthcare are significant. Appropriate and sufficient healthcare contributes to physical wellness, cognitive fitness, and sets the stage for a healthy life starting *in utero*. There have been attempts to remedy lack of access, such as the Affordable Care Act (ACA), which certainly has its flaws. But at least the ACA provides most people with some access. I have found that even people experiencing homelessness know who their primary care provider is.

Many people who have access to adequate healthcare or who have good health themselves, simply don't want to think about the issues of access and adequate healthcare. Whether you're a Democrat, Republican, Independent, or in any another party, my plea is: please don't be in the "I don't care" category. Take a stand, because there's a lot to care about and a lot of work to do.

Improving access to care, and the growing issue of the disparity between the "haves and have-nots," is important and has major health implications for our society. Another important ethical issue is one of integrity, and its link to the commonly heard phrase, "physician burnout." We now have, on average, one physician committing suicide every day in this country. As we dig deeper and explore what is causing this moral despair among healthcare providers, part of the challenge is that we can't provide the kind of care we *want* to provide. Our financial incentives are not always properly aligned with providing the best care. How can we prepare a healthcare workforce to provide the kind of care that is truly wanted and needed?

I believe that technology will help solve some of these issues. Perhaps x-rays will be interpreted by computers, and robots will help transfer and position patients. Even with technological advances, we will still have to deal with the healthcare workforce issues of empathy and compassion that are needed among providers. Wouldn't it be terrific if technology could actually help to improve empathy and compassion?

Computer software is becoming more sophisticated. Data can be entered into the electronic record about your symptoms and then consequently you can receive a differential diagnosis. How should we be training our healthcare providers to use and interpret such information? Will people *want* healthcare providers to help interpret that information? If so, how?

I don't know what to do when somebody comes in with their Fit Bit data and throws it into my proverbial lap. Are the data that were relevant for one-time measurements in the doctor's office, such as blood pressure and heart rate, to be interpreted similarly as the data gathered continuously in the home environment? We don't know the answer to that. A lot of assumptions are being made and we don't know if these assumptions are accurate. This issue concerns me because we have a long history in medicine of making assumptions that eventually turn out to be inaccurate and in fact sometimes harmful to people. So we need to be careful with our assumptions and presumptions.

As a geriatrician, I have stopped more prescribed medications than I've ever started. We are in an overly medicated society, although there are times when medications are genuinely life-saving and significantly improve quality of life. This brings me to the issue of shortages. At times there are shortages of common medications, which again brings up the theme of improperly aligned financial incentives. These shortages aren't for high-profit medications – they're for medications like saline solution, which we recently had a critical shortage of in Puerto Rico due to the hurricanes that occurred there. There is little profit motive for generic medications and for the day-to-day medications that people need. It's the sufficient supply of low-cost medications that are actually life-saving for many people.

We also have a shortage of internal organs. Researchers are exploring the development of artificial organs, or at least parts of organs that are artificial but, in the meantime, we still have the ethical challenges of organ transplantation. Is it acceptable to pay someone for a kidney? How much is it okay to pay? At what point does it become coercive and take advantage of people who are in the "have-nots" category? These are challenges that we as a society have grappled with and will continue to grapple with in the years to come.

Returning to technology, we have seen that pacemakers and insulin pumps can be hacked. The Sherlock Holmes character, whom the author based on a real-life physician, I think would be interested to use his detective's powers of deduction to investigate a possible murder related to manipulating someone's medical device. It might sound farfetched, but it is now indeed possible to commit such a crime. As we have more and more wearable and connected devices integrated with our personal physiology, we will need to find ways to protect those devices from being hacked or controlled by nefarious people.

On the other hand, technology can augment human capabilities. It can help us become healthier, smarter, faster. The question is, will these technological innovations increase the divide between the haves and have-nots? We are now of the "23 and Me" generation with many people analyzing their genes and genomes. What are you going to do if you discover that you have a 62.8 percent risk of developing Alzheimer's Disease? How will that change your life for better or for worse? Are you prepared to think about the impact that information will have on you and your loved ones? Not only might this affect you emotionally, but will your insurance company ask you about any known risk factors when discussing things like long-term care insurance and health insurance? How will you be required to respond?

What will we do when microscopic robots are surging through our blood vessels, detecting disease and sending alerts to our smartphone, or our digital contact lens telling us that an infection is brewing before we develop any symptoms? Will terrorists be able to hack the nanobots that are coursing through our veins? What will we do when we find out that we have a very early stage lung cancer, for example? We might jump on the notion, "Well great! We can take care of it early and cure it." But sometimes we forget that taking care of it will require an intervention, with its own risks of morbidity and possible side effects. It might have been the case that the tumor would not have grown into a significant cancer that actually threatened that person's life. What will happen with in vitro fertilization technology? Are we going to be okay with people selecting the most intelligent embryo's to be implanted? What will happen with gene editing and CRISPR (clustered regularly interspaced palindromic repeats) technology? The concept of eliminating heritable disorders seems wonderful. But are there unanticipated consequences of doing so?

I'm going to conclude with what is near and dear to my heart: geriatrics and end of life issues. *Kaiser Health News* (2018) reported last year that, "Treading into ethically and legally uncertain territory, a New York end of life agency has approved a new document that lets people stipulate in advance that they don't want food or water if they develop severe dementia." In the end stages of dementia, people stop being able to feed themselves and need to be fed by others. The document allows me to request "comfort feeding" for myself. That means that if it seems like I'm opening my mouth and appear to be enjoying getting food or liquid, then I will continue to be provided assistance with eating and drinking. Some people say, however, that this is just prolonging the dying process. On the flip side, others say that it is disturbing to allow the withdrawal of basic sustenance from the most vulnerable in our society. An End of Life Choices, New York (n.d.) document states: "My instructions are that I do not want to be fed by hand, even if I appear to cooperate in being fed by opening my mouth." The decision that this person is making is: if and when I have end stage dementia and am no longer able to feed myself, I don't want anybody to feed me. Allow me to die a natural death.

This misses a crucial point. People who don't have dementia presently can't possibly know how they will feel in the future if they get dementia. Yet, you're making a decision to forgo nourishment in that possible future, and it's a Catch 22 because by the time you're in that situation, you're no longer able to state your preferences. There are people putting this directive in place now, and I'm sure this issue will be vetted through our court system.

I'll end with a quick story and this is about a house call I did last weekend with an eighty-seven-year-old woman who has advanced bladder cancer. There were four generations of a Hispanic family living in very small, cramped conditions. The whole family was loving and caring for this woman. She had just completed chemotherapy and was absolutely wiped out by it. Her family adored her and was pushing, pushing, pushing for her to keep getting care. She didn't want the care but she didn't know how to talk to them about that, so we were able to sit together and discuss her options – one of which was to stop cancer treatment.

She needed a healthcare provider by her side, helping to advocate for her and lead her and her family through a very loving conversation about the potential of technology, what was being offered by the oncologist, and about what this woman did and did not want for herself. She decided to stop treatment and that very night she passed away comfortably at home surrounded by family.

21.4 Reflections by James G. Ellis: Dean of the USC Marshall School of Business

Before coming to USC, I spent twenty-seven years in business – a world that many regard as totally unethical. To overcome this perception, it is enormously important that we do things properly. There are two types of ethical dilemmas that businesses face: one is organizational, and the second is personal. There's often a convergence of these two issues, but let's talk about them separately for just a minute.

On an organizational level, during the course of a day, a month or a year, business leaders make very quick decisions on the fly. From an ethical standpoint, those decisions can be relatively simple, or they can be quite complex. Imagine you are the CEO of Remington Arm's Company. Should you even be making guns? That gets us into the public policy realm. And, of course, there are different perspectives on why you would – or wouldn't – do certain things.

From an organizational standpoint, the one thing we have to remember is that our stakeholders trust us. "Trust" is the key word here. When we gave our data to Facebook, we trusted them. But they sold the data without telling us. What does that do to trust? Taking an opposite example, we also gave our data to Equifax. They *didn't* sell our data, and although they were hacked, they quickly tried to correct the situation.

Under Armour was just hacked yesterday. A massive amount of data was exposed, but the company immediately took steps to maintain public trust, saying, "We've been hacked, and we have to solve this." The bottom line is that things happen, but companies have a choice as to how they react when things go wrong.

Organizational decisions impact accounting, finance, sales, marketing, and production. I remember the first time I went to Asia as a young retail department store buyer, and I was negotiating the best price with a Chinese factory for flannel shirts. I kept driving the price down, and finally I thought, "They're going to give me a shirt with two left sleeves." So I took the price back up a little bit because I was worried about what might happen.

Because business transactions cross borders, we can also face international ethical dilemmas. Bribery is a prime example. In some cultures, you have to give businesses money just to get your foot in the door. Some markets contend with the practice of dumping, where companies say, "We have too much inventory, let's just offload it somewhere." That's not an ethical position, and yet businesses face pressure to get rid of the surplus product. As the CEO of a company, you face this dilemma between doing what is financially expedient and upholding the trust placed in you by your stakeholders, whether they are shareholders, employees, or customers. Those people look to you to run your company in the right manner.

Now, let's talk about ethics from a personal standpoint. If you are the CEO of a company, your job is to maximize shareholder value. You do that by generating profits, and you generate profits because the market looks at you on a quarterly basis. Maintaining consistent performance can be really tough. If your business doesn't look very good, what can you do? One option is to keep the month open for a number of additional days so you can record those sales days during the current period. Or maybe you decide not to record some expenses, and you simply take the sales. There are many games you can play, and because performance reflects directly on you as CEO, the temptation is always there for you not to do the right thing.

Ethical dilemmas play out right here at USC, especially vis-à-vis privacy. We have been entrusted by 19,000 sets of parents to take care of their kids and protect them as they come through our undergraduate program. The day before yesterday we had a rapper come into two of our classrooms trailed by a camera, jump up on the professors' tables and start dancing to music. Fortunately, it was just an overzealous rapper who thought he was being cool and wanted to brag about his exploits on Instagram. But it could have been a shooter. And we have a duty to protect our students' bodies *and* their privacy.

Our own vice president of admissions and planning deals with ethical challenges all the time. I'm sure if she wanted to, she could raise a lot of money for USC by accepting gifts from parents whose children are applying to the university. But we don't do that. There's a firewall, put in place to make sure that we protect the institution and do the right thing.

When I talk to students, I often tell a personal story about me that taught me quite a lesson. I was the number two person at a company, and I was fired because I had a different philosophy of how to run the business from my boss, who was number one. I was thirty-two years old; I had achieved a lot already and I was really distraught. As I got in my car to drive home, I started to cry. And then, after about fifteen seconds, I said to myself, "Dry up; you've got to go find a job."

The minute I got home, I called an old boss and said, "I just got fired, but I didn't do anything wrong; we just had a disagreement on the way to run the business. Do you have any opportunities for me?" He said, "Actually, I do. Let me get back to you tomorrow" – tomorrow being Friday. It was potentially good news, but it wasn't anything concrete, and I was panicked because I was a single guy, taking care of myself, and I didn't have a paycheck coming in. So I started calling and setting up a bunch of interviews for the following week.

Well, Friday afternoon at 5:15 pm he called me back and said, "I'd like to offer you a job. I need you to help me turn the division around, and this is how much money I'm going to pay you." It was a decent salary, so I took the job, which was slated to start a week from Monday.

Right away I had to start canceling all the interviews I had scheduled for the next week. But there were no cellphones, no email, and I had an appointment in Northern California at 8:00 am on Monday. I had no way to contact the interviewer, so I decided to go on the job interview. I wanted to learn about the company anyway, since it was actually a competitor of the organization I was going to work for. So I went up there and spent the day.

As I look back on it, I think, "Why didn't I say something at 8:05 am" But I didn't. I went through the entire day, and they said, "It's great to have you here; thanks for coming." Then I got on the plane and flew back home. And I thought to myself, "Well that was fun, and I learned a lot." I felt good because now I was done with interviews and felt ready to start my new job.

That night at 8:00 pm, I got a call from the senior vice president of human resources (HR) of the company I had just flown back from seeing. He said, "The job we were interviewing you for is truly beneath your expertise. We have created a job one level above that we want to offer you. And your salary is X amount." That amount was four times bigger than what I had been offered by the company that I was supposed to be starting with the next week. I said, "Can I get back to you?" and the guy said, "Sure; call me tomorrow." I hung up and started shaking like a leaf, sitting in my house by myself. What should I do? Of course, when I tell this story to students, they have all kinds of answers, but what I actually did was call my dad.

I said, "Dad, here's my situation," and told him the story. He asked, "What did you tell the first company?" I said, "I told them I'd take the job – but, Dad, it's four times as much money. Do you know how much money that is?" He repeated, "What'd you tell the first company?" I said, "Dad, you know what I told them. I just told you." He replied, "Then what are you calling me for? You already know the answer." "Yeah," I said. "You're right." And I accepted the original job offer I'd agreed to on Friday.

Ethical dilemmas – whether they're personal or related to running a huge organization – can come home to roost quickly. What we have to do is just remember that we have been entrusted by organizations to do what is right. Staying true to that makes decision-making extremely easy to do.

21.5 Reflections by Yannis C. Yortsos: Dean of the USC Viterbi School of Engineering

We live in unprecedented times. Technological advances occur at an exponentially accelerating pace that changes our world as never before, constantly. And this rate of change is only expected to further grow, as it is a consequence of the fundamental underpinnings of innovation (often called Moore's law, but in fact having a much more universal validity than exponentially increasing electronic chip density). These changes can be immensely beneficial, e.g., in health care, or in helping eliminate extreme poverty. They can also have unintended consequences – which can be equally powerful and long lasting. This is not at all paradoxical.

I like the following very simple definition of technology, which I have paraphrased from Brian Arthur: *technology is leveraging phenomena for useful purposes*. Absent from the definition is what is typically associated with technology – devices, algorithms, etc. Indeed, technology now encompasses not only physical and chemical phenomena, as in the more conventional definition. It now also includes biological and, increasingly, social phenomena. Indeed, "tech" companies today, such as Facebook, penetrate and shape the realm of social phenomena as never before.

A key word in the aforementioned definition is "useful"; it is a pivotal word that connects technology to ethics. Technology is by definition amoral. It is intent, that provides the missing link to ethics. If I were to think in terms of Maslow's hierarchy of needs, a *useful purpose* would be enhancing any of the corresponding Maslow pyramid stages: *sustainability*, *security*, *health*, and *life enrichment*. These in fact are the key buckets of many recent initiatives on Grand Challenges – from the National Academy of Engineering Grand Challenges for Engineering, as well as in/to the United Nations Sustainable Development Goals. I will hasten to add that a key part of many of these is the *scientific and technological discovery of new phenomena*, which if fed back to the abovementioned definition of technology creates a positive feedback loop, which produces the current exponentially accelerating technology.

Useful is the key objective: it links *phenomena* with *leveraging*. It underscores a process of *decision-making*. Ideally, decision-making should occur at the intersection of three, hopefully intersecting, circles: *smart*, *legal*, and *ethical*. I must add that, at least so far, such decision-making remains a domain of human activity. Although, whether or not machines will be able to produce innovation that operates at such an intersection becomes increasingly less implausible. It is in fact a question for the discussion of *ethics today*.

Does the aformentioned definition actually conform with how technology evolves? Namely, has technological innovation (e.g., a startup) followed from its very onset a specific *useful* purpose, in an intersection that has remained constant (and limited to that scope)? The answer is quite nuanced. One obvious reason is that the original innovation idea is subject to change and evolution, often dramatically, as a result of what is known as *pivoting*. But a more fundamental reason is that if the technological leap is such that it can produce a significantly powerful effect, its evolution will almost certainly lead to equally powerful *unintended consequences*. Technology will have a strong core, but it will also grow branches, which are in fact likely to reside outside the three-circle intersection. Moreover, the intersection itself will likely vary, as what is ethical and legal may likely evolve with the technology itself. Such effects are more pronounced as the technology is more powerful, and as it impacts society more strongly. It is instructive to see this as a dynamic phenomenon. As a successful (and powerful) technology evolves in time, it first starts within the three-circle intersection, within which it (the core technology that is) continuously lives. However, one or more of its branches may follow a path (intentionally, through a bad actor, or through unintended consequences) outside the three-circle-intersection. To imagine this, think of a plane parallel to the first one, where the circles have not changed, but where a technology branch deviates outside the three-circle intersection.

The most obvious example is a deviation or a mutation due to a bad actor. Examples abound: technology-enhanced violation of privacy rights, cybersecurity breaches, sabotage. In some way, these are relatively easy to spot. Malfeasance has been encountered throughout the ages – it leads to deliberate actions, where the *useful purpose* of the bad actor is of course detrimental to society at large. They are reminding us that what is useful to someone may not be useful to another. These are not unintended consequences.

Less obvious, but no less important, are (unpredictable) *unintended consequences*. These are the unavoidable outcome of technologies that are ubiquitous, powerful and disruptive – as many of today's technologies are. With the risk of becoming too technical, their unpredictability lies in two facts: that our world is not "linear" (hence leading to unpredictable phenomena), and that organized society reacts much slower, through the legislation process, to technological change.

How we react as a society to technological change has multiple dimensions. The ideal action would be to keep strengthening the core of technology that serves useful purposes, namely the one that continues to reside in the three-circle intersection. And to prune the unwanted or undesirable branches that grow outside. For this to happen requires ethically-minded technologists to discourage the growth of such branches; and much faster policy and legislative processes that are in step with technology and can create the new perimeter that is defining what is legal. I would add that a crucial additional dimension in the latter endeavor is accurate and factual communication to the public. All these will have a cascading effect on how we educate our students today on the importance of ethics, acquiring and maintaining an internal moral compass, the process of decision-making, and the power of technology, and its unintended consequences.

But this is only one aspect of the discussion. Equally importantly, as technology evolves in unchartered territories, it will invariably challenge us with redefining the perimeter of the other circle, that of ethics. Multiple new and rapidly evolving fields address the synergy of humans with technology, e.g., Human Machine Interaction (HMI), Human Building Interaction (HBI), Socially Assistive Robotics (SAR), to name a few. Autonomy introduces a symbiosis of machines with humans, until now only the figment of the imagination of science fiction writers. The impact of automation on human labor and income questions the ability of society to adapt to the exponential changes, while challenging the fundamentals of education. Everything related to personalized customization (from medicine to preferences and human desires) risks the loss of privacy at unprecedented levels. The use of machine learning and AI (artificial intelligence) to model human and societal behavior, and hence to inform future action, inherently includes biases, recently termed WMD (Weapons of Math Destruction). While reverse engineering the brain, one of the NAE (National Academy of Engineering) Grand Challenges, probes truly fundamental aspects of what it means to be human – and so does the field of Synthetic Biology.

All these bring fundamental questions to what we value as society – from the individual to the collective. Which brings me to a likely unavoidable question: should technology entities become engaged with the task of predicting unintended consequences (the branches noted) and then guide their evolution in ways that are consistent with our values – past and evolving? Or, should such companies also establish another "C-Suite" title/position (but this time the Chief Ethics Officer)? The question may not be that farfetched.

References

Akun, A. M. (2015). *Equality and efficiency: the big tradeoff*. Washington, DC: Brookings Institution Press.

Arendt, H. (1984). *Eichmann in Jerusalem: A report on the banality of evil*. London, UK: Penguin Books.

Diamond, J. (2005). *Collapse: How societies choose to fail or succeed*. London, UK: Penguin Books.

End of Life Choices, New York. Dementia Advance Directive. Retrieved from https://endoflifechoicesny.org/directives/dementia-directive/

Gilens, M., & Page, B. I. (2014). Testing theories of American politics: Elites, interest groups, and average citizens." *Perspectives on Politics 12*(3), 564–581.

Gilens, M., & Page, B. I. (2017). *Democracy in America?: What has gone wrong and what we can do about it*. Chicago, IL: The University of Chicago Press.

Kaiser Health News. (2018). "Aggressive" New Advance Directive Would Let Dementia Patients Refuse Food. Retrieved from https://khn.org/news/aggressive-new-advance-directive-would-let-dementia-patients-refuse-food/

Olson, M. (1965). *The logic of collective action: Public goods and the theory of groups*. Cambridge, MA: Harvard University Press.

Waltz, K. (1954). *Man, the state, and war: A theoretical analysis*. New York, NY: Columbia University Press.

22

Techno Innovations: The Role of Ethical Standards, Law and Regulation, and the Public Interest

Frank V. Zerunyan

22.1 Introduction

Twenty-first-century innovations in the technical fields designed for human consumption and ultimately as daily life necessities such as personal robots, intelligent implants, driverless cars, and drones require innovations in ethical standards, laws and, rules of ethics. Ethical issues around robots and artificial (AI) intelligence, for example, present a new set of challenges about the new capabilities they afford. These capabilities outpace law and policy in ethics. Tesla and Space X CEO Elon Musk recently warned the governors of the United States that "robots will do everything better than us" and that "AI is a fundamental existential risk for human civilization." He called for the proactive government regulation of AI, "I think by the time we are reactive in AI regulation, it's too late" (Domonoske, 2017)

Indeed, for the first time an American police agency in Dallas, Texas, admittedly used a remote-controlled robot armed with lethal force to kill a suspect. The US Supreme Court in two prominent cases limited the use of deadly force against a fleeing suspect to a significant threat to the officer or others using an "objective reasonableness" standard (*Tennessee vs Garner*, 1985; *Graham vs Connor*, 1989). This novelty begs the question whether an autonomous "Robocop" should be armed with a lethal weapon. Will this method of law enforcement run afoul of the Constitution, the law, or ethical norms? Should we not arm Robocop with law and ethics first before arming it with this techno innovation in policing? I write this chapter within this context. While I agree with the express criticism of others in Silicon Valley (Dowd, 2017) and elsewhere that broad regulation of an innovative field with potential force for good may be premature, I don't disagree that robots and AI must share our societal values rooted in ethics. Techno innovations need standardized legal and inspirational guidelines very similar to medicine, law, and public service.

In this chapter I categorize ethics as a legal and reflective discipline used to resolve conflicts not only of technical means but also of societal means. The human-like characteristics of these AI forms must use a set of values and judgments that is able to interact with their human inventors, collaborators, and consumers. While humans would not hesitate to steer a car to strike a shopping cart instead of a baby stroller, will the autonomous car make the same decision? The social science connection to real science is not only desirable but also inevitable in this twenty-first century. More importantly, the public interest demands that these techno innovations adhere to known ethical standards, laws, and rules of ethics so that they are integrated into societal norms as well as existing legal structures. Public interest in turn relies on good governance for the proper delivery and enforcement of these laws.

In this chapter I focus on the public interest and the ethical standards, laws, and rules that affect a large number of actors. I review two very public and private professions that are necessary to humans and the civilized society in which they live. I also discuss public service as a necessity to governance and the rules guiding public servants to serve the public interest to emphasize the importance of these rules. I am interested in these professions for personal reasons. I am trained as a lawyer. I practiced for over two decades before accepting a full-time position in academia. I am an elected council member and a three-term mayor for the city of Rolling Hills Estates, California, serving since 2003. In 2006 and until 2011, I was a gubernatorial appointee under Governor Schwarzenegger. I had the honor of representing the 38 million medical consumers of the state on the California Medical Board, as a public representative. I focus on medicine, law, and the public service not only because of my personal experiences but also because of the common thread between them serving the public or the public interest.

22.2 Ethics and the Public Interest

Ethics is typically described as beginning where the law ends. Our moral conscience and developed values are the basis for the development of legal rules. Interestingly, ethics and law enjoy a symbiotic relationship for social good. While each discipline has its own unique parameters, they overlap to advance society. This is also where elements of good governance such as transparency and accountability, for example, help protect the public interest.

My colleague Terry Cooper in his book *The Responsible Administrator*, reviews ethics as the study of moral conduct and moral status. He distinguishes ethics and morality by asserting that morality "assumes some accepted modes of behavior" by tradition, culture, religion, organization, and family. He then suggests that ethics is "one step removed from action." In that "it involves the examination and analysis of the logic, values, beliefs and principals that are used to justify morality in its various forms" (Cooper, 2012). These values, beliefs and principles among other things include fairness and justice especially as they apply to the public interest in law, medicine, and public service.

Although the overlap of the disciplines in law, medicine, and public service and the relationship they enjoy is fundamentally important for the practitioners and their constituents, the laws of practice generally remain the indispensable discipline for sustained social good. Cooper refers to these laws as the "moral minimum." I agree. While they may be the minimum, these laws in practice, however, achieve more than just the minimum for the organizations and the constituents they serve. In this context, the establishment and enforcement of ethics standards, laws, and regulations preserve the credibility and therefore the sustainability of the professional actor as well as the profession. In addition, these laws inspire trust and confidence in public servants and the governments or professions they serve.

Public service forges a special bond between public servants and the citizens they serve. This special connection requires public officials of all levels and employees working for the public sector to place allegiance to citizens, laws, regulations, and ethical principles above self-interest. Strict adherence to the rule of law and ethical principles are paramount to safeguarding the public's trust in government. Whether elected, appointed, or hired, public servants must comprehend and practice ethical norms to attain good governance and eliminate improprieties. To accomplish this crucial goal, the rule of law exists to guide public servants in avoiding conflicts between the interest of the public and self-interest (Zerunyan & Sargsyan, n.d.). I discuss these laws to drive home the point that techno innovations need a similar blueprint of formal and informal rules to protect the innovators as well as the public consuming the innovations in a system of compatible governance. This blueprint may contain specification guidelines for technologies but also guidelines for ethical conduct for AI. Consumer protection laws, product liability, and tort laws to apportion liability must predate the use of these techno innovations. The laws of finance and insurance are among other sets of guidelines that will most likely complete this blueprint to fit select governance structures in transportation, medicine, and law enforcement. There is precedent in revamping or creating a brand-new set of laws and rules in the state of California and the nation, especially as we examine environmental laws, for example, since the 1980s. Therefore, legislating or regulating techno innovations will not be an innovation itself.

22.3 Role of Good Governance Mechanisms and Regulation of Conflicts

High quality governance characterized by stakeholder collaboration, effective communication, high levels of accountability and transparency, and strong human and institutional capacity is critical to improving public administration and hence the public interest (United Nations Division of Public Administration and

Development Management, n.d.). Research shows that an ethical organizational culture – free from personal self-interest – is necessary for high-performing governments, which are expected to make decisions that benefit the public (Grindle, 1997). Furthermore, openness and transparency in government encourages valuable civic input and participation in decision-making processes. Public laws and regulations establishing independent oversight over public officials and mandating public disclosures of private interests support informed decision-making, thereby improving public trust and participation in the governance process.

Public servants in California are guided by a myriad of laws and regulations promulgated by a central authority called the Fair Political Practices Commission (FPPC).[1] The FPPC is the brainchild of the Political Reform Act of 1974 codified in California statutes as Government Code Sections 81000 and following. The California electorate to ensure that public officials perform their duties in an impartial manner enacted the Political Reform Act of 1974 (Act). The Act quite descriptively defines the "moral minimum" and implies clearly in its narrative and direction that public service is a way of thinking and behaving. Because of my experience and practice, I use this California Act to illustrate my points in this chapter. Suffice it to say that each state legislates and promulgates its own laws and rules as they relate to political practices.[2] However as is the case with my elected colleagues around the country, my daily life as a public official, while defined by laws and regulated by rules, is more about doing what is right for my constituency rather than worrying about the laws and rules. Hence the motivation may be laws and rules but the intention is the "proper behavior" of the public official. My point therefore is that in practice the laws and the rules create the framework to influence the "proper behavior" of the public official.

Under the Act, no public official can make, participate in making, or in any way attempt to use his or her official position to influence a governmental decision if he or she has a financial interest in the decision.[3] A public official has a financial interest, therefore a conflict, in a decision if it is reasonably foreseeable that the decision will have a foreseeable and material financial effect on the official or one or more of his or her economic interests.[4] A conflict of interest may arise under the Act only with regard to those decisions in which the public official has an economic stake of a type recognized by the Act. In other words, the Act's rules apply only to financial conflicts.

According to the Act and the ensuing regulations "financial interests" and "economic interests" are distinguished but are equally regulated. Financial interest is conclusive and denotes that the public official has an actual conflict because the decision he or she is about to make will have a material effect on his or her economic position. Economic interest on the other hand is a term of art used by the Act for specific types of interests recognized by the Act as potential sources of conflict of interest.[5] These include business investment, business employment, real estate interest, and gifts all over and above specific amounts specified in the Act.[6] With regard to economic interests in business entities and real property, a public official may have such an economic interest by virtue of an indirect investment. An indirect investment or interest means any investment or interest owned by the spouse or dependent child of a public official, by an agent on behalf of a public official, or by a business entity or trust in which the official, the official's agents, spouse, and dependent children own directly, indirectly, or beneficially a 10-percent interest or greater.[7]

California's experience under the Act is valuable in terms of execution of an elaborate legal mechanism to detect conflicts of interest during the service of public officials. In 1998 the FPPC adopted an eight-step standard analysis to determine conflict of interests.[8] This eight-step analysis is quite methodic, transparent, and accountable for both the public official and the general public. This step-by-step analysis provides the framework and the inspiration for public servants for the "proper behavior." This standardized analysis also creates a common benchmark to protect the public interest. Much can be learned from such an elaborate methodic analysis in order to also create minimum standards and inspiration for technology to interact with its inventors and users. Clear laws and rules promote good governance and the public interest at large.

Perhaps more importantly these eight steps that I will describe here integrate the actor and the profession to various societal expectations and existing legal framework in order to connect the governed to government and to make government accountable to the governed. For example, finding of a conflict of interest may result in specific and required consequences, namely the disqualification of the public official from the government decision-making process or the use of his or her authority as a public official. Therefore, step one under the Act is to determine whether the individual involved is a public official within the meaning of the Act. If the individual is not a public official, he or she is not covered by the Act for the purpose of a conflict.

"Public official" is very broadly defined under the Act. Public officials include elected officials, appointed officials, employees, members of boards and commissions, and consultants (87,200 filers) who make or participate in the making of a governmental decision or manage public investments.[9] Public officials also include those covered by a code (code filers) created by an agency under the Act for enumerated positions within the agency, which involve the making or participation in the making of decisions.[10] By way of example, a city manager, planning director, or code enforcement officer all are examples of code filers. On the other hand, a committee, board or commission does not possess decision-making authority under the Act or the regulations if it is formed for the sole purpose of researching a topic and preparing a report or recommendation for submission to another governmental body that has final decision-making authority.[11] Therefore, a subject matter expert on a committee investigating a disaster – for example, to provide recommendations to the policymakers – may not be a "public official" within the meaning of the Act.

Step two deals precisely with the public official's making, participating in making, or using or attempting to use his or her official position to influence a government decision. If the public official is not making, participating in making, or using or attempting to use his or her official position to influence a government decision, then he or she does not have a conflict of interest within the meaning of Act.[12] The identification of the statutorily defined economic interest as in business, real estate, and gift is step three. If of course no such interest is identified the public official does not have a conflict of interest within the meaning of the Act.[13]

Step four is to determine the public official's level of official participation as in direct or indirect involvement in the government decision.[14] An indirect involvement may require additional analysis and may not be a conflict as described in step five.

Step five is the ensuing "Materiality Standard," which based upon the degree of involvement determines whether the public official is conflicted or not.[15] For example, a public official's ministerial, secretarial, manual, or clerical actions may not be material enough to constitute a governmental decision for the purpose of the Act.[16] Materiality standards for each financial and economic interest are specifically spelled out in the Act.[17] For example, if the real property, in which the public official has an interest, or any part of that real property, is located within 500 feet of the boundaries (or the proposed boundaries) of the property, which is the subject of the governmental decision, then the decision is deemed to be material under the Act.

Like the materiality standard in step five, step six is to determine the reasonable foreseeability that the governmental decision will have a material financial effect on the public official's economic interest(s). If it is not reasonably foreseeable that there will be a material financial effect on any of the public official's economic interest(s), he or she does not have a conflict of interest within the meaning of the Act.[18] This step calls for a factual judgment, not necessarily a legal one. The Political Reform Act uses the words "reasonably foreseeable" and the FPPC has interpreted these words to mean "substantially likely." Generally speaking, the likelihood need not be a certainty, however, it must be more than a mere possibility.

Step seven is to test the effect of the government decision on the official's economic interest and the effect of the same decision on the general public. If the reasonably foreseeable material financial effect on the public official's economic interest is indistinguishable from the effect on the public generally, he or she does not have a conflict of interest within the meaning of the Act.[19] In fact as mayor and council member I routinely vote on policies in my city that affect me personally or my property but the effect on the policy on me or my property is no different than my neighbors. A perfect example is the repairing of my street where I live on a list of streets to be repaired in the city of Rolling Hills Estates.

Step eight is the exception to the rule in that it allows the public official to apply a statutory version of the common law "rules of necessity" as implemented through the regulation, which may enable the official to participate despite the conflict of interest.[20] This may include an emergency vote on an item that cannot be continued. Last but not least, under certain circumstances decisions may be segmented so that the official may participate in some components of the decisions despite having a disqualifying conflict of interest in other components of the decision(s).[21] Common sense, transparency, and the greater good dictate the outcome in this this last step.

If a public official has a conflict of interest, he or she may be required as a matter of duty to disqualify him or herself. In those instances where the public official determines not to act because of a disqualifying conflict of interest, the public official must disclose the financial interest by stating it on the record at a public meeting, and/or in writing to be kept in the agency's official record. In short, the basic function of the Act is to obligate public servants to conduct public's business in an orderly and open system of administration under narrowly defined rules. These rules are the public's minimum expectations from its public officials and are not open for good faith or even common-sense interpretation by the public servant. More importantly, these rules provide the framework and the inspiration for the public official to do what is right.

The other important set of rules and laws are found in the Ralph Brown Act, which applies to public servants in all cities, counties, and special districts. The preamble of the Brown Act, which is widely known to every municipal office holder in California, truly frames public service at this level as well as the expectations of the electorate in the conduct of the people's business:

> The people of this State do not yield their sovereignty to the agencies which serve them. The people, in delegating authority, do not give their public servants the right to decide what is good for the people to know and what is not good for them to know. The people insist on remaining informed so that they may retain control over the instruments they have created.[22]

This preamble and the Brown Act itself continue to shine a positive light upon the municipal enterprise and the mindset of people who serve the public. Regardless of the severe consequences for the violation of these laws, it is truly a mindset to believe that nothing is a secret in deciding people's business. Local public officials typically in trouble with the law and rules tend to forget this golden rule under the Brown Act. Highlighting the importance of doing people's business in public also assists public officials to avoid conflicts in the exercise of their responsibilities as public servants. Based on my almost two decades of public service both at local and state levels, these laws and rules, aside from being the "minimum" expectations of the public, create a culture of service beneficial to all.

22.4 Professional Responsibility As a Guide

I now turn to my professional experiences and training as a lawyer and former California Medical Board member for guidance in this chapter. In the practice of medicine or law a remarkable overlap exists between the disciplines of clinical ethics, law, and risk management. These two public and private professions are rooted in formal and informal rules that are typically codified in rules of conduct. Clinical ethics is the discipline or method to consider the ethical implications of policies, practice, application, or technologies with emphasis on what ought to be done or not done in the delivery of healthcare or legal services. The law is the establishment and enforcement of social rules of conduct or non-conduct, the violations of which creates civil or criminal liability on the medical or legal professional. In other words what the medical or legal professional must do or not do to avoid some form of punishment. Risk management on the other hand is the reduction of legal liability through institutionalized policies and practices or what the professional choses to do to manage risk.[23]

The licensing and regulation of physicians and lawyers as professionals is and has been an important topic worldwide. Licenses are justified and preserved for qualified individuals to ultimately protect the public. To preserve the integrity, veracity, culture of the professional actor, and the profession as an organization, society continues to legislate clear standards, laws, and rules about medical and legal ethics. Written laws are not a novelty in human civilization. Various religious traditions speak of the written laws of God set in stone and handed to Moses as the Ten Commandments. The Commandments found in Exodus (20:2–17) and Deuteronomy (5:6–21) remain the basis for most moral codes in human history. These moral codes form the foundation for several religious traditions to inscribe religious and moral teachings. Medical and legal codes are not different.

Medical ethics traces its roots to the Hippocratic Oath, and early Christian teachings. One of the oldest binding written documents as an oath, named after the "father of medicine" Hippocrates, remains in practice in overwhelming majority if not all medical schools in the United States. While the oath has been modernized to address the realities of the medical profession in science, economics, politics, and social change, its key principals remain unchanged.

The principals guiding medical ethics are well documented in general ethics literature. Medical ethics is a substantial discipline in its own right but most agree that four key principles dominate the theory and the practice (Beauchamp & Childress, 2001). The principle of autonomy respects the rights of an individual to self-determination. Respect for autonomy (*Voluntas aegroti suprema lex*) is the basis for a patient's informed consent as well as advanced directives for healthcare. The patient's right to choose or refuse treatment is a good indicator for both personal well-being and for the well-being of the profession at large. Ethics by definition attempts to find a good balance between the actor in the profession as well as the public served by the profession. This principle actually gives rise to one of two primary areas of healthcare law for civil actions against care providers for injuries resulting from care based on lack of informed consent. The legal concept of informed consent refers to a state of mind in understanding the medical information provided to make an informed choice. If a patient is capable of making that informed choice, the law is clear about healthcare providers' duty to follow that choice ethically and legally. This is an established and enforceable legal standard consistent with the ethical principal of autonomy. The law is also well established on surrogate decision-making in the event of patient incompetency or unavailability to make that informed choice. A surrogate decision maker may be authorized by a court or may be permitted by specific statutes. Finally, various state laws permit advance directives where the patient is capable of making a future decision in the event of future incapacity. Typically these advanced directives deal with medical orders for life sustaining treatments or the refusal for such treatment.

The other primary and certainly wider area of potential civil or disciplinary actions against healthcare providers arise from the violation of the standard of care, which is tied to the other two old ethical principles. The principle of "beneficence" requires by definition to act for the good or the interest of another. In the medical context this requires medical professionals to take all actions necessary to serve the best interest of the patient including the preservation of the patient's autonomy discussed previously. In law this is called the standard of care. Some in this field argue that healing is the sole purpose of the profession and therefore this principal is the core of medical ethics. Others, on the other hand, focus on first things first. They articulate that the more important medical principle is "first do no harm" (*primum non nocere*), in that it is more important not to harm the patient than to do any good. This last principle supports many moral rules such as "do not kill," "do not cause pain and suffering," "do not incapacitate," and "do not deprive others of quality of life." Wise judgment or prudence is wrapped into this principal.

In my years on the California Medical Board, I read and acted on many discipline cases of medical doctors violating this principal of "do no harm" and the moral rules contained in it. Particularly in the field of plastic surgery where the doctor is convinced to deliver (mostly wrongfully) the first principal of "beneficence" forgetting the second or arguably the more important principal of doing no harm. Unfortunately for the patient, the results are much worse and severe than the results for the doctor. Including in some recent and very highly publicized cases, when many celebrity or celebrity related patients died in the operating room. In many instances and thankfully for the profession, ethical practitioners turn down these patients for surgery recognizing the potential risk and the associated harm. In one case the patient had seen three previous doctors, who had consistently refused any surgery. I also read an inordinate amount of cases in the pain management field. In these cases, the doctor generally attempts to benefit the patient by mitigating pain with prescription drugs only to create an addict. The doctors that end up before the Medical Board are the risk takers, at the expense of the patient, contravening this very important medical ethic of doing no harm and violating the standard of care in law. While risk taking may be inherent in the advancement of science and technology, uncontrolled and unprincipled risk taking is dangerous for the public at large and is incompatible with the legal framework organized to govern a civilized society.

22.5 The Role of Justice, Equity, and Conduct According to Rules

Caring for the public also means leaving one's prejudice at the hospital door. Like cases are to be treated equally and unlike cases treated differently. The principle of "justice" requires that patients be given the best possible care and no harm is done to them without regard to age, sex, sexual orientation, ethnicity, religious beliefs, or politics. Interesting parallels exist here with the legal profession especially in the context of everyone being entitled to competent legal representation including those charged with unthinkable crimes.

Other similarities between the two professions are also quite striking. Each profession is legally described in the Medical Practice Act[24] and/or the Business and Professions Code. Each profession is also highly regulated by its respective regulatory body, the Medical Board and the State Bar of various states. Although these laws and regulations deal with the conduct, professionalism, and responsibility of the professionals, what in practice influences and guides most practitioners are not laws or regulations but simply standards of conduct, which define the essentials of honorable behavior for doctors and lawyers.

The power and effect of this honorable behavior for doctors and lawyers are much more important for practitioners than the laws and regulations themselves. Again, these rules are not laws but standards of expected conduct by members in order to sustain a very public and private profession. Two distinct and influential organizations describe in writing honorable behavior for these professions. The American Medical Association (AMA) and the American Bar Association (ABA) stand out as powerful organizations not only supporting their individual members but also the professions and the public they serve. The organizations also issue "ethics opinions" to address the ever-changing needs of the profession and the application of the rules to technology and innovations. In the case of medicine, for example, cloning, genetic testing, cadaveric organ transplantation, and electronic or digital communication are evolving fields and require ethical guidance for the common good. These innovations defy various religious values, which form the basis of our laws and ethical norms. Integration of these innovations into the main stream of our lives is not possible without credible guidelines and ethical standards.

AMA's vision statement on its web site is "improving the health of the nation is at the core of the AMA's work to enhance the delivery of care and enable physicians and health teams to partner with patients to achieve better health for all."[25] ABA's mission is "to serve equally our members, our profession and the public by defending liberty and delivering justice as the national representative of the legal profession."[26] ABA's mission is achieved by education, elimination of bias, enhancing diversity, and advancing the rule of law through respect, access, and independence. Not surprisingly, the focus on public interest in each mission is quite remarkable.

The preamble for the medical ethics of the AMA always begins with a statement recognizing a doctor's responsibility to patients first and foremost, then to society at large, other professionals, and lastly to self. Similarly, legal ethics describe fiduciary duties to the client as well as to the court as the representative of the rule of law and the interest of justice. The main text for professional responsibility in law is the ABA's "Model Rules of Professional Conduct, (Rules)," which replaced the "Model Code of Professional Responsibility (Code)." All states, except California, use the full version of the ABA's Rules. California adopted its own version. While the Rules collapse all facets of professional conduct, the Code better described the three distinct but interrelated components of professional responsibility. The three components of the Code included the "Canons," "Ethical Considerations," and "Disciplinary Rules." The Cannons of professional conduct, which were axiomatic norms, described the relationships between lawyers, the public, the courts, and the profession. The Ethical Consideration" were more aspirational and were the objectives of each and every professional in the practice of their profession. Lastly, the Disciplinary Rules, unlike the Ethical Considerations, were required of the professional as a minimum level of conduct below which no lawyer could practice without consequences and sometimes the ultimate penalty of being disbarred.

The Code and now the Rules are the law and the inspiration to the members of the profession to establish standards and demand behavior suitable for the guardians of the law in the preservation of a civil society. The Rules in the preamble of lawyer's responsibilities (ABA, n.d.) state:

> many of a lawyer's professional responsibilities are prescribed in the Rules of Professional Conduct, as well as substantive and procedural law. However, a lawyer is also guided by personal conscience and the approbation of professional peers. A lawyer should strive to attain the highest level of skill, to improve the law and the legal profession and to exemplify the legal profession's ideals of public service . . . [and] as a public citizen, a lawyer should seek improvement of the law, access to the legal system, the administration of justice. . .In addition, a lawyer should further the public's understanding of and confidence in the rule of law and the justice system because legal institutions in a constitutional democracy depend on popular participation and support to maintain their authority.

The Rules point to high standards and to a blue print to judge transgressions. A free and democratic society depends on justice grounded in the rule of law. The rule of law mandates and inspires conduct to achieve more than the minimum prescribed in medicine, law, and public service. These are professions affecting the public and the public interest; not just profit-driven businesses. My two favorite quotes to illustrate this point come from justices of the California and United States Supreme Courts:

> The title of professional requires that in daily practice, an attorney strive to transcend the demands of the moment to consider the greater good. Lawyers are not simply representatives or employees of their clients – they are officers of the court. That denomination reminds us that a lawyer's obligations flow not only to the client but to the courts and to the system of justice of which they are an integral part.[27]

> Certainly, life as a lawyer is a bit more complex today than it was a century ago. The ever- increasing pressures of the legal marketplace, the need to bill hours, to market to clients, and to attend to the bottom line, have made fulfilling the responsibilities of community service quite difficult. But public service marks the difference between a business and a profession. While a business can afford to focus solely on profits, a profession cannot. It must devote itself first to the community it is responsible to serve. I can imagine no greater duty than fulfilling this obligation. And I can imagine no greater pleasure.[28]

In short, I am struck by Justice O'Connor's statement about public service marking "the difference between a business and a profession." It is this distinction that promotes the need for conscientious and responsible behavior by public servants, medical doctors, and lawyers notwithstanding the moral minimum. Intrinsic to the law, perhaps representing the bare minimum, are the precepts that doctors, lawyers, and public officials, individually and collectively, must respect and honor their office and profession to gain public trust and sustain confidence in a system representing the public's interest.

22.6 Conclusion

Techno innovations and AI set to transform humanity need interdisciplinary policy and priorities from the outset. Inventors, collaborators, and consumers must join forces to develop legal and reflective ethical rules to manage and govern a more civilized and balanced society in the twenty-first century and beyond. From rules set to do what is right to risk management in determining liability in an insured world, techno innovations need standardized legal and inspirational guidelines very similar to medicine, law, and public service. Many law schools and think tanks already track legislative and regulatory developments for cyber-space as well as techno innovations such as autonomous vehicles, for example.[29] A handful of states including California are very active in the regulations of autonomous vehicle deployment through statutes already enacted in the Vehicle Code.[30] California has recently passed a law that makes a person liable for physically intruding on someone's privacy when that person knowingly enters "into the airspace" above the land of another without permission. The new law applies when the entry is for capturing any type of visual image, sound recording, or other physical impression of the land owner engaging in a private activity.[31]

For now, most of these regulations focus on equipment requirements, performance, and safety certifications.

Ryan Calo, a colleague at the University of Washington School of Law, in a piece that originally appeared in Brookings and later in *Time* magazine, advocates the coordination of technology oversight through a central authority. He explains his argument:

> I do not argue we should go so far as to put into place, today, a full-fledged enforcement body capable of regulating anything that touches robotics. That would be deeply inadvisable. Rather, I believe on balance that we should consider creating an institutional repository of expertise around robotics as well as formal mechanism to promote robotics and artificial intelligence as a research agenda and industry
>
> (Calo, 2014).

Calo's frame, like much of the law and regulation already in place or in upcoming proposals, focuses on the technology. I advocate that it is time we focus on a different frame placing humans, their values, and the public interest first. Intelligent and complementary systems are not too futuristic anymore. Mimicking the intricacies of the human brain and adding neuromorphic chips to create AI forms as smart or smarter than humans is a very attainable innovation in the twenty-first century (Al-Rodhan, 2015). Fear and inaction are not an option. We have seen technology develop, and do so very quickly. More importantly, this development outpaces law and policy especially in ethics. The development of legal frameworks and moral standards similar to the Hippocratic Oath, ABA's Rules, and the Brown Act may be a good start to regulate and inspire innovators as professionals to look out for the public's interest.

References

ABA (n.d.). Model Rules of Professional Conduct. Retrieved from www.americanbar.org/groups/professional_responsibility/publications/model_rules_of_professional_conduct/model_rules_of_professional_conduct_preamble_scope/

Al-Rodhan, N. (2015, March 13). The Many Ethical Implications of Emerging Technologies. *Scientific American*. Retrieved from www.scientificamerican.com/article/the-many-ethical-implications-of-emerging-technologies/

Beauchamp, T. and Childress, J. (2001). *Principles of biomedical ethics*. New York, NY: Oxford University Press.

Cooper, T.L. (2012). *The responsible administrator: An approach to ethics for the administrative role* (Sixth Edition) San Francisco, CA: Jossey-Bass/Wiley.

Calo, R. (2014). The case for a Federal Robotics Commission. Retrieved From https://poseidon01.ssrn.com/delivery.php?ID=73909808612210402006912100910211701112304902802903902708506807711109911012609911609405503403012301805901511307609607510408111303801305405903903011511007508700612109202203501411708202710610101801209102909110310307410710208403109800412301710206501001908508&EXT=pdf

Domonoske, C. (2017, July 17). Elon Musk warns governors: Artificial intelligence poses "existential risk." *NPR News.*

Dowd, M. (2017, March 26). Elon Musk's billion-dollar crusade to stop the A.I. apocalypse. *Vanity Fair.*

George, R. M, Former Chief Justice (October 2001). The Public Administration Scientific Journal Republic of Armenia is Volume 2 Pages 26-34 (2016) and Volume 3 Pages 16-22 (2016)

Grindle, M. S. (1997). The good government imperative: Human resources, organizations and institutions. In M S Grindle (Ed.) in *Getting good government: Capacity building in the public sectors of developing countries.* Harvard Institute for International Development

Tennessee vs Garner 471 U.S. 1 (1985)

Graham vs Connor 490 U.S. 386 (1989)

Zerunyan, F. V., & Sargsyan, T. (2016) Analysis of select ethical regulations in the public service system for the republic of Armenia and benchmarking the system to California's experience in the United States. *Public Administration Scientific Journal, 2,* 26–34.

United Nations Division of Public Administration and Development Management et al. (n.d.). Collective Impact: An Adapted Framework for Public Administration and Governance to Promote Sustainable Development (n.d.). United Nations Division of Public Administration and Development Management, Apple Xuefei Ji, Tania Fatima Reza, Christopher Robinson, & Frances Teves, Faculty Advisor Frank V. Zerunyan J.D., Professor of the Practice of Governance University of Southern California Sol Price School of Public Policy.

Endnotes

[1] www.fppc.ca.gov

[2] I.e., Official compilation of codes, rules and regulations of the state of New York Title 9. Executive Department Subtitle V. State Board of Elections Part 6201. Fair Campaign Code.

[3] California Government Code Section 87100.

[4] California Government Code Section 87103; 2 California Code of Regulations Section 18700(a).

[5] California Government Code Section 87103.

[6] California Government Code Section 87103; 2 California Code of Regulations Sections 18703.1.

[7] California Government Code Section 87103.

[8] Title 2, California Code of Regulations, Section 18700(b).

[9] California Government Code Section 87200.

[10] California Government Code Section 87302.

[11] Title 2, California Code of Regulations, Section 18701.

[12] Title 2, California Code of Regulations, Section 18702.
[13] Title 2, California Code of Regulations, Section 18703.
[14] Title 2, California Code of Regulations, Section 18704.
[15] Title 2, California Code of Regulations, Section 18705.
[16] Title 2, California Code of Regulations, Section 18702.4.
[17] Title 2, California Code of Regulations, Section 18705.
[18] Title 2, California Code of Regulations, Section 18706.
[19] Title 2, California Code of Regulations, Section 18707.
[20] California Government Code Section 87101; Title 2, California Code of Regulations, Section 18708.
[21] Title 2, California Code of Regulations, Section 18709.
[22] California Government Code § 54950.
[23] Brock, L. V. and Mastroianni, A. (2013). Ethics in medicine. University of Washington School of Medicine.
[24] Medical Practice Act includes Business and Professions Code Sections 1–4999.7 and 17500–17539.6, Corporations Code Sections 13400–13410, Family Code Sections 17500–17561, Government Code Sections in Titles 1, 2, and 3, Health and Safety Code Divisions 2, 10, 104, 106, and 107, and Unemployment Insurance Code Section 10501.
[25] www.ama-assn.org
[26] www.americanbar.org
[27] Former Chief Justice Ronald M. George (October 2001).
[28] Justice Sandra Day O'Connor *78 Or. L. Rev. 385, 391 (1999)*.
[29] www.cyberlaw.stanford.edu
[30] California Vehicle Code Section 38750.
[31] California Civil Code section 1708.8.

23

Evolutionary Ethics: A Potentially Helpful Framework in Engineering a Better Society

John N. Celona

23.1 Introduction

Examinations of whether particular actions or intentions are ethical or not must grapple with the questions of what the applicable ethical standards are, how people may act in particular situations and why. These are difficult questions and the subject of much inquiry. There are many schools of thought and disciplines for answers, from religious traditions to philosophical to psychology.

In this chapter, we present a hypothesis for modeling ethics, which may be helpful in engineering systems and in predicting how people might act in them from an ethical perspective. We use "system" here in the broad sense Oxford English Dictionary, n.d.), which may or may not include a technology component.

Suppose ethics were an evolved social behavior that has changed and adapted following the same evolutionary process that other social behaviors and physical characteristics have followed?

As with any hypothesis (including evolution), the question of whether it is true or not does not apply: a hypothesis can only be disproven, never proven. Rather, the test is whether the hypothesis yields useful and accurate predictions of observable phenomena. If it does, one continues to use the hypothesis until a better one comes along. If it fails to make accurate predictions, then best to add it to the long list of disproven hypotheses (e.g., lightning comes from the gods, the Earth is the center of the solar system, bloodletting treats disease, etc.).

If ethics is an evolved behavior, then it should develop in response to the advantages or disadvantages it creates for the individual or species in its environment. Do particular ethics make an individual or species more successful or not, and how would you characterize that success or failure?

Social behaviors have an added wrinkle in that whether or not they confer advantage or disadvantage depends on what other individuals are doing. Sticking with the herd for protection is only helpful if the other herd members are staying together. Sharing food sources with others is only useful if they are likewise sharing food sources with you.

The last point gets us into where ethics may provide feedback and a type of "success" beyond individual survival or reproduction. If others are sharing their food with you and you are sharing in that while at the same time concealing a food source for yourself (which may help you survive a famine), what feedback may discourage that behavior? It confers an individual survival advantage, but is it also *wrong* by some standard; and how does that help or hurt the individual or the species?

These are exactly the sorts of questions we aim to grapple with by presenting a framework for modeling ethics as an evolved social behavior. The balance of this chapter presents this approach for ethics, as well as for describing the various sorts of advantages and disadvantages that may enter into the calculus of whether particular ethics are advantageous or not.

Taking the food example, hoarding the source may help you survive, but would you feel bad about it? Is "feeling bad" part of the evolved response promoting more ethical behavior that would benefit the individual or species or both? Might this "feeling bad" rise to the level of "moral injury," as some have suggested (Press, 2018)? Are sanctions for unethical behavior also part of the evolved social system promoting more ethical behavior? For example, if discovered hoarding food, would you then be cast out and excluded from future sharing in addition to feeling bad?

From this perspective, ethical standards are not fixed and constant but, rather, have evolved and continue to evolve along with other behaviors and physical characteristics. There is a continuum of possible ethical standards. Ethical conflicts may result from individuals choosing different ethical standards in addition to actions that conflict with one's own particular standard.

This approach has profound considerations for engineering a better society. If ethics is an adapted social behavior, then it will respond to the incentives and disincentives in its system and environment. Implementing social and technical change powerfully changes the system, environment, and incentives. How those systems are designed and implemented (including their social and technical aspects) would drive the ethical standards individuals aspire to and those they actually follow. This approach also provides a new way of describing and clarifying ethical dilemmas and of helping individuals make decisions in ethical dilemmas.

To illustrate these points, we take a detailed look at ethics in the legal system, including some suggestions for how both attorneys and clients may live up to their better ethical selves.

23.2 The Hypothesis and Chapter Overview

Ethical standards evolve along with the physical and social characteristics of species, including nonhuman species. There is a continuum of possible choices of ethical standards. Groups (including nonhuman groups) enforce a minimum set of ethical standards with a variety of means. The minimum human ethical standards to avoid social or legal penalty have changed over time and vary around the world.

Ethical conflicts result when one's ethical, legal, or prudential interests conflict, or when individuals are following different ethical standards. Someone following a different ethical standard may be acting unethically by your standards, but not by his or her own.

The ethics individuals choose to follow is highly influenced by the system they operate in, and especially by authority figures in that system. Accordingly, when engineers are designing a system or solution, they should be aware of the ethical choices the system incentives promote. To help engineer a better society, systems and solutions should be designed that promote choice of higher-level ethical standards.

The ethical standards for the legal system and profession are codified at length in statutes and codes of professional responsibility, but are often different than the ethical standards an individual might choose to live by. There are some basic, practical strategies for attorneys and litigants to avoid ethical conflicts and to deal with them when they arise.

23.3 The Evolution of Ethics

The theory of evolution postulates that organisms experience physical and behavioral changes over time to better adapt to their environments. The adaptations that enable greater "success" and can be passed along to the next generation through inheritance ("nature") or learned behavior ("nurture") endure to help the continued success of that species.

We examine whether ethics can be viewed as an evolved characteristic; the relationship between ethics and the law; the implications are for engineering a better society; and suggestions for avoiding and resolving ethical dilemmas in litigation.

23.4 A Framework for Inquiry

Certainly, many lifetimes may be devoted to study of the development and various theories of ethics and morals. Howard and Abbas propose a straightforward approach: "**Ethics** are your *personal* standards of right and wrong" (Howard & Abbas, 2016, p. 781). Those ethical standards are a choice. Depending on the choice made, it may be easier or more difficult to live "up" (or "down") to the chosen standards.

The chosen ethical standards (right or wrong) furnish one criterion for evaluating alternatives. Others are whether an alternative is prudential (in one's best interest) or legal (in compliance with or violation of the applicable legal system).

Not everyone chooses the same ethics or applies them with the same degree of consistency. Howard and Abbas point out that "[f]or the enlightened person, there may be no distinction between ethical and prudential actions, and this would be a desirable state for everyone" (Howard and Abbas, 2016, p. 783).

Like enlightenment, the ethical standards each of us chooses may be thought of as a journey rather than a destination. Like every journey, it is useful to consider where you have been, where you might go, and why. Taking this question more broadly of where man has been and may go and why brings us to consideration of the evolution of ethics.

23.5 Progressive and Overlapping Evolutionary Characteristics

Students are familiar with the theory of evolution presented as a picture of gradually developing species, whether humans, whales, and so on. New and helpful features are progressively added (more upright gait for humans) while prior features are gradually dropped as they become either not necessary or not helpful (fur, large orbital ridges). Some features hang on for quite some time though they no longer have a discernible function. Humans still have an appendix, coccyx, and wisdom teeth while whales still possess pelvis and femur bones, although they are not attached to anything. The physical differences between humans and non-humans are a matter of degree rather than of kind.

The same is true of behavioral characteristics. Use of tools was perhaps once thought to distinguish humans, but many animal uses of tools have now been documented, ranging from primates to other mammals to birds and fish and even in some insects. So it is with caring for one's young, with the club of outstanding moms and offspring including orangutans, polar bears, elephants, cheetahs, and emperor penguins.

Suppose, then, we accept an evolved continuum of physical and behavioral characteristics encompassing both humans and non-humans. Does this continuum include ethics and morals? Darwin expressed his opinion on this issue in *Descent of Man*.

> The following proposition seems to me in a high degree probable – namely, that any animal whatever, endowed with well-marked social instincts, the parental and filial affections being here included, would inevitably acquire a moral sense or conscience, as soon as its intellectual powers had become as well, or nearly as well developed, as in man."
>
> (Darwin, 1981, p. 71–72)

This process of ethical development continues in humans.

Notwithstanding many sources of doubt, man can generally and readily distinguish between the higher and lower moral rules. The higher are founded on the social instincts, and relate to the welfare of others. They are supported by the approbation of our fellow-men and by reason. The lower rules, though some of them when implying self-sacrifice hardly deserve to be called lower, relate chiefly to self, and owe their origin to public opinion, when matured by experience and cultivated; for they are not practiced by rude tribes.

As man advances in civilization, and small tribes are united into larger communities, the simplest reason would tell each individual that he ought to extend his social instincts and sympathies to all the members of the same nation, though personally unknown to him. This point being once reached, there is only an artificial barrier to prevent his sympathies extending to the men of all nations and races.

(Darwin, 1981, pp. 100–101)

The question of whether this progression in ethics and morals extends from non-humans into humans was taken up at length by evolutionary biologist Marc Beckoff and bioethicist Jessica Pierce, who argue that the evolutionary continuity between humans and non-humans includes a wide variety of cognitive and emotional capabilities in diverse species. They define "morality as a suite of interrelated other-regarding behaviors that cultivate and regulate complex inter-actions within social groups. These behaviors relate to well-being and harm, and norms of right or wrong attach to many of them" (Beckoff and Pierce, 2009, p. 7).

They organize their work on the moral lives of animals into "the *cooperation* cluster (including altruism, reciprocity, honesty, and trust), the *empathy* cluster (including sympathy, compassion, grief, and consolation), and the *justice* cluster (including sharing, equity, fair play, and forgiveness)" (Beckoff and Pierce, 2009, p. xiv). These behaviors are made possible by greater social, cognitive, and emotional intelligence. The greater a species' social complexity, the more nuanced its moral behavior is.

Putting the pieces together, one might consider defining a continuum of behavior stretching across species in which any point is a possible choice of what's right or wrong for an individual. One dimension might be along the lines of Maslow's hierarchy (*what* you're concerned with) while the other describes for *who*. This continuum is shown in Figure 23.1.

Simple species would fall right at the origin (point **A**): only concerned with the physiological needs of the individual, and any action taken to survive is just fine. A species developed enough to recognize danger to itself and react accordingly might fall at point **B**. Social creatures add concern for others; this is the territory explored by Beckoff and Pierce and posited by Darwin. The ethics of a pride of lions might be described by point **C**. In contrast, the ethics of a human psychopath (by definition incapable of feeling for another) might be described by point **D**.

Darwin also adds possible concern for people that one hasn't met. This would involve moving "east" in the continuum from only concern for one's tribe or nation, as shown in Figure 22.2. Becoming a vegetarian might involve adding concern for other warm-blooded creatures, as also shown in Figure 23.2. If that

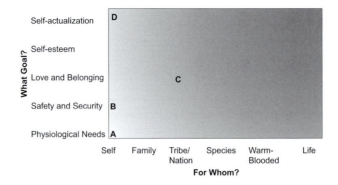

Figure 23.1 *A gradient describing alternative choices of ethics*

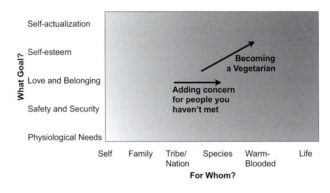

Figure 23.2 *Moving to a different choice of ethics in the continuum*

improved your self-esteem as well (as illustrated), that would indicate your choice of ethics moving "northeast" on the continuum.

One might move further "east" on the continuum by adding concern for all life, though that might allow eating organisms that don't "mind it," like plants.

We introduce the continuum as a tool for framing and thinking about the many possible personal choices of right and wrong.

Seen as a continuum, the possible choices of ethics (standards of right or wrong) began to change from immediate self-preservation at all costs with the development of social species and became a lot more varied with people. The progression in choices of ethics extends not only with the development of civilization but also in the course of one's life. An infant starts at the origin (hungry or otherwise uncomfortable) and progresses as it becomes aware of the existence and feelings of others. The progression continues in life. Even teenagers at some point become aware that their parents have feelings.

Circumstances may push one to move "backward" (e.g., "west" or "south") from one's previous choice, as with survivors in a life boat. On a less extreme scale, the opportunity for personal gain may prompt one to consider a more "westerly" choice.

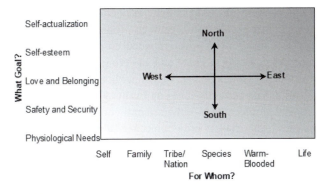

Figure 23.3 *A moral "compass"?*

Figure 23.4 *Changing minimal legal and social ethical behavior*

We invite the reader to consider whether this continuum of ethical choices is a sort of moral "compass," as shown in Figure 23.3.

On a societal level, the minimum ethical choice to avoid legal sanction has likewise changed over time. "An eye for an eye" in the Old Testament indicated the introduction of proportionality to revenge: one could take no more than an eye for an eye, or a life for a life. It was no longer permissible to kill an entire family or tribe in revenge for one killing. In more modern times, killing another in revenge is not legal at all; only a civil suit for damages and possible punishment by the criminal justice system are allowed.

Social sanction tends to be a leading indicator for future legal sanction (or elimination of sanction). The abolitionist movement was founded long before trading and owning slaves became illegal. Likewise, same-sex couples began to cohabitate (under various levels of disguise) long before legal change started. The gray and changing differentiations between minimum legal and socially acceptable moral choices are illustrated in Figure 23.4.

Figure 23.4 illustrates, for example, that it is neither legal or socially acceptable to kill or threaten other people or to steal their property. Moving "northeast," it is socially acceptable to eat other warm-blooded creatures, though it may not be legal to abuse them. Being a cruel and unloving person is likewise socially unacceptable, though generally not illegal without a specific prohibited act. Insults are legal; debate currently rages on insults via online bullying.

Although social attitudes on minimum moral choices are a principal indicator of legal change, legal change often precedes consensus – leading to much controversy over newly enacted law. Our purposes here are to illustrate that:

- There are many different possible personal choices of right and wrong
- They progress in continuous fashion from other species to humans
- They change over the course of an individual's life
- The minimum ethical behavior to avoid social or legal sanction has changed over time and continues to do so.

23.6 Ethical versus Prudential or Legal Considerations

An action is ethical if it is right given your choice of ethics. It is prudential if you consider it to be in your best interests. It is legal if it can be undertaken without risking sanction by the relevant legal system.

As discussed in Section 23.5, an individual's perception of what is right or wrong changes over the course of their life, and society's has changed over time. Likewise, one's perceptions change regarding prudential considerations. A small child might consider it just fine to eat all the ice cream because of the pleasure in consuming it. An older child might share some because there is pleasure in the other person's enjoyment, and because it increases the prospect of reciprocal sharing in the future.

We have seen how the legal system tends to lag behind social consensus on ethics and establish a minimum of acceptable behavior. For example, though you may have a legal right to kill in self-defense, you may deem it unethical to kill another person for any reason. Likewise, despite having a legal right to collect your share of a settlement in a class action lawsuit, you might deem it unethical that plaintiff attorneys were able to pursue a claim on behalf of individuals who neither sought nor consented to litigation.

23.7 Action versus Consequences-Based Ethics

Further complicating personal, social, and legal ethical determinations are two competing theories of ethics, one based on actions and the other on consequences. Action-based ethics (ethical formalism) holds that an action is either ethical or not based on the action itself, regardless of its consequences. Consequence-based ethics (utilitarianism) holds that the ends justify the means. Under the former theory, killing one innocent person to save 1000 is wrong. Under the latter, possibly so (depending on how one weighs the particular consequences).

Both theories find their adherents in the law, as they do in society – sometimes leading to vehement controversy. For example, Rule 403 in Federal Rules of Evidence[1] states that "[t]he court may exclude relevant evidence if its probative value is substantially outweighed by a danger of one or more of the following: unfair prejudice, confusing the issues, misleading the jury, undue delay, wasting time, or needlessly presenting cumulative evidence."

Balancing the interests, also known as proportionality, runs throughout the law, especially in constitutional law. Applications include "fair use" under copyright, due process of law and "cruel and unusual punishment" under the Fifth and Eighth Amendments, and restrictions on individual property rights under the Takings Clause.

More controversially, the US Supreme Court applied a balancing test in *Roe vs Wade* (1993) to determine that a woman had the right to terminate her abortion during the entirety of the pregnancy, but state interests could be balanced against this during the second and third trimesters.

Presumably, this type of reasoning would pass muster with an ethical utilitarian, though he or she might differ on the relevant interests and which way the balance tips. An ethical formalist might hold that it is wrong to take the life of the fetus for any reason, or that it is wrong to interfere with a woman's autonomy regarding her body. One's choice on the personal autonomy question would also guide whether one feels it should be legal to commit suicide or assist in it, and whether either act is morally wrong. Likewise for the ethics and legality of taking drugs. Individual and social opinions on these issues and the associated sanctions as expressed in the law are similarly in flux.

23.8 Dilemmas As Ethical Mismatches

Expressing choice of ethics as a continuum allows one to think of ethical dilemmas as a mismatch between ethical choices. These mismatches come in several flavors:

- Between the ethics you are tempted to apply versus the ethics you might like to apply
- Between your chosen ethics and those of another person
- Between your ethical choices and those expressed in the law.

We'll take each in turn.

Consider first the mismatch between the ethics you are applying and those you might like to apply. These are often a matter of short-term gain (putting you closer to the origin on the ethical continuum) versus a longer-term gain (greater happiness and possible future reciprocal treatment from heading "north" and "east" on the continuum). Lying is often convenient in the short term, but causes greater unhappiness to yourself and others in the longer term.

Likewise, an ethical dilemma is common when ethical choices you are trying to follow are different than those another person is applying. The perhaps easier cases are when someone is trying to do something to you commonly accepted as wrong (hurt, steal, take advantage of) and you are trying to figure out how to respond without doing something unethical yourself, often with little to no time for consideration. You may just consider you need to defend yourself in an appropriate way and save non-violence (what Gandhi described as "the highest form of courage") for another day when more people have signed up for roughly close-ish ethical choices. Even then, would you harm another person to protect yourself? And, if you did, how would you feel about it afterwards?

The harder cases are when something is being asked of you that is widely accepted (telling "white lies," following accepted organizational rules you don't agree with, etc.). Here, there are often long-term consequences in terms of lower-level needs (your own success and prosperity) from prioritizing the higher-level self-actualization needs of feeling good by doing good.

Possibly the most difficult conflicts arise when your personal ethical choices differ from those mandated in the law. Although the law often expresses a minimum ethical choice with freedom to make a higher choice (e.g., there is an option but not a mandate to kill in self-defense), the law sometimes describes a maximum. For example, a lawyer is required to keep a client's secrets confidential regardless of his or her opinion of the matter in question (with some exceptions).

For example, early in 2016 Apple opposed an order by the FBI to create a backdoor in the iOS that would allow the FBI to decrypt the contents of an iPhone recovered in connection with the terrorist attack in San Bernardino. The FBI took the position that it needed the information on the phone both to investigate the attack and to prevent possible future attacks. This would appear to be application of utilitarian ethics: any possible violation of the rights of innocent iOS users was justified by the ends.

Apple opposed the order on several grounds, including an allegedly unprecedented application of the All Writs Act of 1789. Apple CEO Tim Cook concluded in his letter to Apple customers, "ultimately, we fear that this demand would undermine the very freedoms and liberty our government is meant to protect" (Cook, 2016).

The FBI clearly thought it was acting legally, ethically, and in accordance with the law. Apple contested the order on all those grounds. Both parties thought they were following the demands of ethics and the law, but differed on what those required. There was also an element of consequences versus action-based ethics.

In the end, a third party proposed to the FBI a different way to unlock the phone and, when the method worked, the FBI withdrew the request.

Similar matters are raised in the case of Edward Snowden. Clearly, Snowden broke the law by revealing government secrets. It appears Snowden felt compelled to disclose those secrets to stop the government bulk collection of data on anyone anywhere, most of it on Americans. Collecting that data seems under legal precedent to constitute a search. Americans are specifically protected against search and seizure by the Fourth Amendment to the US Constitution:

> The right of the people to be secure in their persons, houses, papers, and effects, against unreasonable searches and seizures, shall not be violated, and no warrants shall issue, but upon probable cause, supported by oath or affirmation, and particularly describing the place to be searched, and the persons or things to be seized.

Both sides felt ethically justified in the actions they were taking, and a conflict between utilitarian and action-based ethics seems again to have been at issue. These two episodes illustrate how differing choices of ethics, often under cover of law, lead to some of the most serious conflicts in society. We could go on with examples (*Korematsu vs United States*, 1944).

With choice of ethics seen as a continuum stretching across species, history, societies, and even your own life, one sees that the ethical dilemmas stemming from different ethical choices are not just occasional matters. Rather, they will be constant throughout your own life and other people's. Hopefully, your views are evolving and growing as you ponder these questions and, perhaps, on a very good day, you can help someone else progress in their own struggles with these constant battles we all face.

Possibly there are truly enlightened people in the world who do not experience these difficulties, and I may have even met some. I'm not sure I would know one when I met one. Maybe, even for a truly enlightened person, there is a whole new set of dilemmas I'm not presently even aware of. That would truly make ethics a continuous journey and not a destination.

23.9 Implications for Engineering a Better Society

The perspective we have considered is that choice of ethics is a continuum extending across species, history, societies, and one's own life. Ethical dilemmas arise when different alternatives are preferred depending on the choice of ethics. The alternative choice of ethics may be posed internally (depending on which level of ethics you choose) or externally (when your choice of ethics is different than the one chosen by another person, society, or the law).

As an engineer and attorney, I've faced ethical dilemmas in both capacities.

The implication for engineering a better society is that, in engineering a solution, one needs to consider the incentives it presents and what effect those incentives may have on the ethical choices of people operating within the system. People may not be consistently rational and narrowly self-interested agents (*homo economicus*), but they sure do respond pretty well to incentives and rules most of the time.

Discussions of this sort often cite Nazi Germany and sometimes Philip Zimbardo's Stanford prison experiment. As one commentary noted in comparing Zimbardo's experiment with a similar but deliberately varied recreation conducted by the documentary unit of the BBC:

> [t]aken together, these two studies don't suggest that we all have an innate capacity for tyranny or victimhood. Instead, they suggest that our behavior largely conforms to our preconceived expectations. All else being equal, we act as we think we're expected to act – especially if that expectation comes from above ... The lesson of Stanford isn't that any random human being is capable of descending into sadism and tyranny. It's that certain institutions and environments demand those behaviors – and, perhaps, can change them.
>
> (Konnikova, 2015, pp. 16–19)

In engineering any sort of solution, we need to consider what behaviors the solution, institution, or environment being created will prompt and the choice of ethics accompanying those behaviors. Are people being encouraged to move "southwest" or "northeast" in the continuum of ethical choices?

This consideration may perhaps happen at two levels: the effects on participants in (operators of) whatever the solution is, and on the solution designers themselves. What incentives are you responding to in designing a solution that is "better" as evaluated by the person or organization presenting the task or problem? Is your solution helping yourself and the users to become better or worse versions of themselves?

These kinds of issues frequently arise in designing compensation systems for organizations. The tension is between rewarding individual achievement versus team or collective achievement. If a system rewards individual achievement, it encourages those achievements and "lone wolf" behavior like the hoarding of leads, customers, contracts, and so on. If the system rewards collective achievement, it also fosters charges of people not pulling their fair share of the load. In addition, compensation systems are commonly gamed, such as by ensuring that incentive compensation goals are met with metrics that can be manipulated, or by setting goals with certainty of achievement. Most law and management consulting firms that "blow up" do so as a result of compensation issues. The behavior in such cases is not pretty.

However, they potentially arise in the design or analysis of any system with a human component. In one project, I was a junior consultant engaged to analyze the competitive advantages and organizational structure of a very large research organization. It turned out the motivation behind the project was our client trying to force the large and independent software division to report to him. Not only did the project fail, but that turned out to be the only consulting project I've worked on where the client didn't pay the bill. In hindsight, I suspect the cause was a combination of unsavory motives on the part of the client and a senior partner on our side desperate to do the project to meet a compensation target. The senior partner was "encouraged" to leave the firm not long afterwards. In fairness to the partner, he was a brilliant scientist and consultant rather than a salesman, though selling projects is what the compensation system rewarded.

Accordingly, engineers need to be sensitive to what they are being asked to do, why, and what the incentives will be for the behaviors of the people operating in or acted upon by the system. Are you helping people to live up to their potentially better selves, or promoting unsavory behavior? An ethically sensitive engineer needs to ask her or himself these questions.

23.10 Ethical Rules Governing Attorneys

Different professions have varying degrees of formality in their ethical requirements. The ethical rules for attorneys are extensive and formal. In the United States, attorneys are licensed and regulated state by state, and the ethical rules governing attorneys are called Rules of Professional Responsibility. All states except California have adopted the Model Rules of Professional Conduct developed by the American Bar Association (ABA) (ABA, 2018).

Still, the complete set of ethical rules relevant to attorneys is vast. In addition to the state codes of professional responsibility, there are ethics opinions issued by state bar associations, disciplinary proceedings in each state, case law (state by state and federal), and the various codes of judicial conduct (Duke Law, n.d.). Add in the various bodies of rules in different countries governing legal ethics and an entire library could be comprised entirely of ethical rules governing attorneys in various jurisdictions.

As one might guess, it requires a fair amount of effort and study to gain and maintain familiarity with the rules. A course on professional responsibility is typically one semester in a six-semester, three-year law school curriculum. In addition, professional responsibility is tested on bar exams and the continuing education requirements to remain an active member of the bar association (able to practice law) include an ethics component.

The rules are complex and nuanced. For example, the California and ABA model rules on client confidentiality and when an attorney may reveal confidential information differ subtly. The ABA rule allows (but does not require) an attorney to reveal information relating to the representation of the client to prevent reasonably certain death or substantial bodily harm (see Appendix A). The California rules requires a criminal act before allowing (but not requiring) the attorney to reveal confidential information to prevent death or substantial bodily harm to an individual (see Appendix B).

The California and rest-of-the-US rules also differ on whether an attorney may have a sexual relationship with a client. The California rule only forbids such relationships when the attorney coerces the client or requires the relationship as a condition of performing the legal services (see Appendix C). The ABA rule forbids such relationships unless they already existed when the attorney–client relationship began (see Appendix D).

The complete rules of professional conduct alone are quite extensive. The California rules cover thirty single-spaced pages. The ABA model rules are a similar length. Begin to add in the other aforementioned relevant sources and one quickly gets to the library-sized collection.

Discipline for violations of these rules of professional conduct ranges from private criticism to disbarment. First-time offenders typically receive either a private or public reproval. More serious sanctions include probation with monitoring by another attorney. Disbarred attorneys usually have committed a "very serious violation" (like perjury or stealing client funds) or have a history of misconduct.

23.11 Dealing with Ethical Dilemmas for Attorneys in Litigation

In this Section I will first address possible ethical dilemmas in litigation for attorneys, then cover non-attorneys (clients or other parties to litigation) in section 23.12.

For attorneys, we need to separate avoiding violations of the Rules of Professional Responsibilities from other ethical dilemmas.

Of course, a start at avoiding violations of the Rules of Professional Responsibility is some familiarity with what they cover. Making a choice of ethics at a fairly low-value set of coordinates on the ethics continuum would do a lot.

Which failings actually result in disciplinary actions against attorneys? Here's a thought from Cydney Batchelor, who is a long-time prosecutor of discipline violations for the California State Bar.

> After 15 years as a State Bar of California prosecutor, I have become completely convinced that the discipline imposed against attorneys by their licensing boards arises at least 80 percent to 85 percent of the time from the failure of attorneys to document the work they do, their marginal business skills, and their failure to respond appropriately when a disciplinary complaint is lodged against them. Only a very small percentage of legitimate complaints arise from intentional malfeasance by the attorney – there are easier ways to steal money than going to law school and passing the bar exam.
>
> (Batchelor, 2006)

Ms. Batchelor's primary suggestion to attorneys on avoiding a disciplinary filing? "Respond to every telephone call within 48 hours. This is the number-one reason that clients complain to our state bar" (Batchelor, 2006).

Possibly this gives a different impression than what one might guess at how attorneys can best avoid formal ethics rules violations.

Suppose then, you're an attorney who checks the boxes just described to avoid, at the least, a formal ethics disciplinary action against you by the state bar association. What about the matter of law practice within the formal rules that violates your own ethical standards? This is not a particularly easy matter to track down since most written on the subject focuses on avoiding being charged with a violation of the rules of professional responsibility (Thompson, n.d.).

Although I have been an active member of the California Bar Association since 1991, my focus has always been on providing decision analysis consulting to attorneys and their clients, acting as a consultant rather than as an attorney. I restrict my role to my area of expertise: litigation risk analysis and strategy. This approach is recommended by many others: limit your practice to your area of specialty. Attempting to provide services in an area that "is not your day job" is a recipe for trouble. At the very least, you may get into rules trouble for charging clients to get up to speed in an area you don't normally practice. I likewise consult a variety of attorneys whenever I need legal advice in a particular area, whether it be estate planning or business contracts or whatever.

My best thoughts at avoiding ethical dilemmas that violate your personal choice of ethics is as follows:

1. Pick your area of practice carefully
2. Pick your clients carefully
3. Withdraw from representation quickly when necessary.

We'll tackle each of these in turn.

The choice of area of law is a critical one. A colleague from law school started his career as a public defender and, after a very few years, switched to working as a prosecutor, which he continues to this day. The reason? The reality is that, under our criminal justice system, for the most part people taken to trial in criminal matters have a long record of other offenses for which charges were not pressed or a plea bargain agreement was reached. Many of the cases going to trial are against defendants who have such a history of other offenses or a strong case of serious charges in the case that the defendant won't agree to the plea bargain on offer.

My colleague didn't personally feel ethically comfortable defending mostly guilty people – although such defendants are clearly entitled to a defense under our legal system and attorneys are certainly obligated to provide such a defense under the rules of professional responsibility when they have accepted the case. This is a case where your personal choice of ethics may conflict with an alternate choice that is both entirely legal and in your best interest financially. Mafia lawyers make a very good living. Whether they can sleep soundly at night is another matter.

Hence the choice of client is also key. If a matter "smells fishy" at the outset, that smell is likely to only get worse. These dilemmas often pose the kind of internal conflict already discussed between a lower-coordinate choice of ethics (one that's good for short-term financial interests) and a higher-coordinate choice (one that won't trouble your conscience or create other negative consequences in your life).

If, despite your best efforts to pick a law practice area and clients that fit your ethics choice, you find yourself in a dilemma, the best course of action is perhaps to withdraw from the case and the client as soon as possible. This may well have negative consequences for lower-coordinate values. And this is not especially easy for attorneys to do. For example, permission may be required from the court or the client, and actions will need to be taken to ensure that your withdrawal does not foreseeably prejudice the rights of the client. A sample set of requirements can be found in California Rule 3-700.

In short, do your best to avoid ethical dilemmas by your choice of practice area and clients. Then, if you are nonetheless faced with a dilemma between the ethical choice you would like to make and the one you could make, I can't come up with an easy way to resolve this. Talk to your loved ones and other trusted attorneys and do your best to do the right thing.

If you are instead an in-house attorney (working for a company rather than a law firm), it is likewise helpful in avoiding ethical dilemmas to pick a company whose business area and practices are largely consistent with your personal choice of ethics. For example, when I was Senior Director of Advanced Risk Analytics at Stanford Healthcare, one of my responsibilities was applying decision analysis to all the lawsuits, claims, and matters faced by Stanford Hospital, Stanford Children's Hospital, and the Stanford School of Medicine (Celona, 2017). The analysis and its results were used to plan case defense and negotiation strategy, including possible settlement offers. (Stanford was the defendant in all the suits I worked on.)

What kept this work consistent with my personal choice of ethics was Stanford's Process for Early Assessment and Resolution of Loss (PEARL) (Stanford Children's Health, n.d.). In the event of an unanticipated and preventable adverse patient outcome, Stanford would disclose, apologize, implement measures to prevent future recurrences, and make an offer of compensation.

This meant I was not working to get caregivers off the hook in cases where they had screwed up. I was helping Stanford figure out the best defense and resolution where staff had done everything they could and should have and something still went wrong. In cases where there was a preventable adverse outcome, my work went to figuring out what some kind of a reasonable offer of compensation might be to go along with the apology and remedial measures.

In contrast, to avoid ethical dilemmas I have needed to be very careful in my choice of consulting work in the area of patent litigation. Patents are a government-granted monopoly unlikely to have arisen via a free market mechanism. Unlike other types of property, with intellectual property (patents, copyright, trademarks, trade secrets, trade dress, etc.), when someone "steals" your property, you are not deprived of possession and use of it. The limits of this monopoly are set by law according to a balancing of competing interests. Those limits are a matter of continuing controversy and progressive change. Further muddying the waters, examples abound of patent monopolies granted for surprisingly trivial "inventions." The flood of patents applied for and granted has, in particular, been used by non-practicing entities (NPEs), who do not use the inventions for any commercial activity or public benefit at all, but simply purchase them to assert claims of compensation against other entities who do use them.

My personal choice of ethics would be troubled in supporting clear abuse of a government-granted monopoly. This dilemma is possibly made more acute because such work can be highly lucrative. Accordingly, I have avoided working for non-practicing entities, though I know many people who have taken that route. I am honored to have worked to help defendants against NPEs, such as in helping to conceive and set up the Allied Security Trust (AST).[2]

Lending perhaps some hope to the idea that individuals and societies can move "northeast" in their choices on the ethical continuum, the law governing patents in the United States has changed significantly since I began working in this area. For example, the patent assertion in the early 2000s by NTP, Inc. against Research in Motion (RIM), which almost led to a shutdown of the Blackberry email system before RIM agreed in 2006 to a payment of $612.5 million would be very different today. The law has shifted the balance of patent power between patent holders and technologies users significantly so there is much less potential for abuse.

23.12 Dealing with Ethical Dilemmas in Litigation for Clients or Other Parties

The ethical dilemmas faced in litigation by clients or other parties to the litigation are in some ways similar to those faced by attorneys: a choice between alternative ethics at lower versus higher coordinates on the ethical continuum. These choices often have consequences of shorter-term, self-regarding objectives versus longer-term, others-considering objectives (which in turn have higher-level benefits for oneself).

In my experience, one of the main differences driving how litigants versus attorneys face and resolve ethical dilemmas in litigation is the emotional state of the litigants. For attorneys, handling a case is one's job. There are impacts on income, professional success, and personal self-worth, but these are present in any professional and pecuniary endeavor.

For clients and other litigants, it is a rather different matter. A litigation is a dispute, only arrived at because other efforts to resolve the dispute have failed. People are angry. They feel they have been wronged and want their side of the matter proven correct and their asserted rights vindicated. They want to win. This applies to both plaintiffs and defendants.

This emotional state colors perceptions and actions of the parties. It can lead people to act very differently than they would unless less stressful circumstances. Further, because the legal system furnishes only a minimum-agreed upon set of standards for the use of force, it can be used by parties to commit entirely legal acts they would consider unethical in calmer times.

Accordingly, to help litigants avoid and resolve ethical dilemmas in litigation, we recommend they:

1. Consider the ethics versus the legality of the case
2. Mind the emotions and merits of the case on both sides
3. Know the value and risks of the case
4. Remember that almost all cases settle. They will need to reach a deal with the other side at some point.

We will cover each in turn.

As discussed in Section 23.11 on attorneys, there are many cases and areas of the law where a claim may be pursued entirely legally, yet violate the ethical choices one would like to make. This temptation to gain is furthered in the United States by the general rule that, absent a statute to the contrary, each party bears their legal fees and costs. Thus, plaintiffs are not generally at risk for paying the defendant's legal fees and costs if the case is not successful. Further, attorneys can reduce a plaintiff's risk even more by taking a case on a contingent fee in which the attorney's only payment is a portion of any amount recovered by a defendant. (The plaintiff remains at risk for the damages portion of any counterclaim by the defendant).

This system has been criticized for encouraging excessive litigation. The abuses are perhaps most evident in the area of class action lawsuits. These are cases in which attorneys seek to "represent" the damages done to many similarly situated defendants – even though the defendants have never complained of the asserted harm, taken any action, or hired an attorney. An attorney representing hundreds or thousands of "harmed" defendants can potentially recover many millions of dollars as their portion of the damages, while the damages actually paid to individual defendants amount to a few dollars each. All this can proceed with absolutely no action by the individual defendants who, to the contrary, must affirmatively choose to opt out of a class once certified. I, for example, once received in the mail a gift certificate for $50 towards the purchase of a Swarovski crystal item as settlement of my "damages" in a class action suit for some wrong Swarovski had committed. I have no idea what the case was about or how many Ferraris the plaintiffs were able to purchase with their portion of the proceeds.

In contrast, under the English (as in "England") rule, attorneys' fees and costs are generally recoverable. This rule prompts one to think much harder about pursuing a case – you might be on the hook for the defendant's legal fees!

Accordingly, even though an individual may be entirely legal in pursuing a particular claim, he or she must carefully consider how doing so squares with the ethical choices they would like to make. I'll offer one more personal example.

I was once struck by a car while commuting to work via bicycle. The driver was clearly at fault: he drove right into me while distracted by talking to his young daughter he was taking to school. He was also distraught at what he had done and apologized profusely, as well as giving me a ride to work when I advised that my injuries (scrapes and bruises) did not require an ambulance or medical attention.

Clearly, I had a slam dunk lawsuit against the driver. However, it was more important to me that the driver sincerely regretted what he had done, and that a good turn to him might actually make him a champion of looking out for bicyclists in the future. I offered to settle the matter if the driver would pay for the repairs to my bicycle and purchase me a new helmet. He gratefully agreed. Possibly it helped that I was an attorney working at the Supreme Court, State of Hawai'i.

I've had no contact with the driver since then, but often wonder what the lasting impact may have been on his life by the attorney-bicyclist who didn't sue him. That is perhaps often the nature of these ethical choices: one tries to create future higher-level ethical choices by others, though they often may or may not produce results one ever becomes aware of. But what a great world it would be if everyone did the same! In facing my own ethical dilemmas, it is helpful to recount the instances in which I have and haven't lived up to the ethical choices I would like to.

Accordingly, before pursuing or responding to a legal claim, I would urge every potential plaintiff or defendant to consider the ethics versus the legality of the case, and how that squares with where they would like to be in the ethical continuum. In that consideration, it is helpful to mind how the rules of professional responsibility governing attorneys prompt or restrict their actions and ethical choices.

The second point is to mind the emotions and merits of the case on both sides. Angry people want to be right and want to win, and this blinds them to the merits in the position of the other side. I have found that there are three sides to most cases: the plaintiff's, the defendant's, and the truth or fair outcome of the case. In the American adversarial system, attorneys on both sides are sworn both to pursue their client's interests and to uphold the law and justice. This is usually interpreted to require attorneys to zealously pursue a client's claim if at all colorable, and it is extremely rare for attorneys to be disciplined for pursuing a bad-faith legal claim. A very good attorney will advise their client of the shortcomings and issues in their case and the merits of the other side, but this is not required under the Rules of Professional Responsibility.

Minding the emotions and merits of the case on both sides is a key step to understanding the value and risks of the case. Another great tool for doing so is decision analysis (Celona, 2016). Breaking a case down into the possibilities, probabilities, and values is a very effective means of getting beyond the emotions and motivations in the case to what's really at issue and what the values actually are.

A quantified understanding of the case also greatly enables effectively negoti-ating a settlement to case. Almost all cases settle at some point. It's just a question of when the parties decide to cease litigating and sign a deal. Even if a case goes all the way to trial and verdict (as very few cases do), that simply unleashes a nearly endless process of appeal if the parties wish to continue fighting.

The purpose of these four suggestions is to help litigants move beyond the "fog of war" in litigation to really consider what they are doing and why, including the choice of ethics in that choice. A clearer understanding may help to enable people to avoid ethical dilemmas in litigation and resolve them when they do arise. The ethical continuum could help to clarify the alternative ethical choices and the trade-offs between them.

23.13 Ethical Challenges of the Future

As long as people are following different ethical choices, I would expect the ethical challenges discussed here to continue. The tension between more self-regarding versus more other-regarding ethics seems to extend all the way back to lower species. Throughout one's life and career, the tension between helping others and looking out for oneself can be frequent and vexing. It's hard to be "successful" by being nice.

Likewise, the conflict between utilitarian and action-based ethics was present at the founding of the United States and remains to this day. Do the ends justify the means? Answers vary. This debate is not looking anywhere close to resolution.

Does greater technology fundamentally change the issues? I'm not sure how to make an ethical distinction between use of a spear and use of a drone, or how the challenges presented by online social media are fundamentally different than living in a small village.

Maybe, in the long view of history, ethical progress has only ever been one individual at a time. Let's hope we keep nibbling away at this.

23.14 Conclusion

The ethics exhibited by various species is a characteristic that has continuously evolved along with other behavioral and physical characteristics. A key milestone in the emergence of ethics is the development of social, other-regarding behavior. The two dimensions suggested for characterizing this continuous process of development are level of need being met (along the lines of Maslow's hierarchy) and the scope of others considered (self only, family, etc.).

With the continuous nature of ethics development, there are many possible ethical standards. As a minimum ethical level of behavior develops in a society (human or not), it is enforced by social sanctions and, in human societies, also by legal sanctions. The minimum ethical level in a society, as expressed in social and legal sanctions, changes over time. An individual's ethical choices change over the course of his or her life.

Ethical conflicts result when an individual's ethical, prudential, or legal interests conflict, or when individuals are following different ethical choices. Ethical conflicts are further complicated by some individuals and systems (including the law) following utilitarian, consequences-based ethical reasoning, while others follow action-based ethical reasoning.

Because of the trade-offs, ethical conflicts are hard to resolve. Thinking ahead of time about what ethical choices you like to make and why (including possibly why you would value acting according to higher-level needs and ethics) may help to resolve ethical dilemmas when they arise.

It is perhaps easier to avoid ethical dilemmas than to resolve them when they arise. In litigation, attorneys may avoid ethical dilemmas by:

1. Picking your area of practice carefully
2. Picking your clients carefully
3. Withdrawing from representation quickly when necessary.

Clients and other parties to litigation can avoid and better resolve ethical dilemmas by:

1. Considering the ethics versus the legality of the case
2. Minding the emotions and merits of the case on both sides
3. Knowing the value and risks of the case
4. Remembering that your case will likely need to reach a negotiated, agreed on settlement at some point.

People's behavior, including the choice of ethics they act upon, is highly influenced by the signals and incentives in the system they are working in. In engineering and implementing solutions, engineers need to keep in mind how the incentives and feedback they set up will influence the ethical choices and behaviors of those operating in the system. Designing system feedback and incentives to help people move "northeast" rather than "southwest" in their ethical choices may be helpful in engineering a better society.

References

American Bar Association (ABA). (2018, August 16). Rule 1.6: Confidentiality of Information. Model Rules of Professional Conduct. Retrieved from www.americanbar.org/groups/ professional_responsibility/publications/model_rules_of_professional_conduct/rule_1_6_ confidentiality_of_information/

ABA. (2018, August 16). Rule 1.8: Current Clients: Specific Rules. Model Rules of Professional Conduct. Retrieved from www.americanbar.org/groups/professional_ responsibility/publications/model_rules_of_professional_conduct/rule_1_8_current_ clients_specific_rules/

ABA. (2018, December 4). Model Rules of Professional Conduct: Table of Contents. Retrieved from www.americanbar.org/groups/professional_responsibility/publica tions/model_rules_of_professional_conduct/model_rules_of_professional_conduct_ table_of_contents/

ABA. (n.d.). Rule 3-100: Confidential Information of a Client. California Rules of Professional Conduct. Retrieved from www.calbar.ca.gov/Attorneys/Conduct-Discipline/ Rules/Rules-of-Professional-Conduct/Current-Rules/Rule-3-100

ABA. (n.d.). Rule 3-120: Sexual Relations with Client. California Rules of Professional Conduct. Retrieved from www.calbar.ca.gov/Attorneys/Conduct-Discipline/Rules/ Rules-of-Professional-Conduct/Current-Rules/Rule-3-120

Batchelor, C. (2006, October/November). Disciplinary actions: When bad things happen to good lawyers. *GPSolo Magazine*. Retrieved from www.americanbar.org/newsletter/ publications/gp_solo_magazine_home/gp_solo_magazine_index/disciplinaryactions/

Beckoff, M., & Pierce, J. (2009). *Wild justice: The moral lives of animals*. London, UK: The University of Chicago Press, Ltd.

Celona, J. (2016). *Winning at litigation through decision analysis*. Switzerland: Springer International Publishing.

Celona, J. (2017). Applying decision analysis to human factors in decision making at Stanford University Medical Center. In J. I. Kantola et al. (Eds.), *Advances in human factors, business management, training and education*. Advances in intelligent systems and computing 498, DOI 10.1007/978-3-319-42070-7_39. Switzerland: Springer International Publishing.

Cook, T. (2016, February 16). A Message to Our Customers. Retrieved from www.apple .com/customer-letter/

Darwin, C. (1981) *The descent of man, and selection in relation to sex*. Princeton, NJ: Princeton University Press.

Howard, R. A., & Abbas, A. E. (2016). *Foundations of decision analysis*. London, UK: Pearson Education, Inc.

Howard, R. A., & Matheson, J. E. (Eds.) (1983). *Readings on the principles and applications of decision analysis*. Menlo Park, CA: Strategic Decisions Group.

Konnikova, M. (2015, June 12). The real lesson of the Stanford Prison Experiment. *The New Yorker*. Retrieved from www.newyorker.com/science/maria-konnikova/the-real-lesson-of-the-stanford-prison-experiment

Korematsu vs United States, 323 US 214 (1944) (L. Ed.).

Duke Law. (n.d.) Legal Ethics. Duke Law. Retrieved from law.duke.edu/lib/research guides/legale/

McNamee, P. C., & Celona, J. N. (2007). *Decision analysis for the professional*. 4th ed., rev. Menlo Park, CA: SmartOrg.

Roe v Wade, 410 U.S. 113 (1973). (L. Ed.)

Stanford Children's Health. (n.d.) PEARL: The process for early assessment and resolution of loss. Retrieved from www.stanfordchildrens.org/en/patient-family-resources/pearl

Press, Eyal. (2018, June 13). The wounds of the drone warrior. *The New York Times*. Retrieved from www.nytimes.com/2018/06/13/magazine/veterans-ptsd-drone-warrior-wounds.html

Oxford English Dictionary (n.d.). System (para 1). *Oxford English Dictionary* Retrieved from https://en.oxforddictionaries.com/definition/system

Thompson, K. (n.d.) Hanging out your shingle without hanging yourself out to dry – 10 quick and easy ethics tips for new lawyers. American Bar Association. Retrieved from www.americanbar.org/content/dam/aba/administrative/professional_responsibil ity/hanging_out_your_shingle.authcheckdam.pdf

Endnotes

[1] www.law.cornell.edu/rules/fre/rule_403

[2] www.ast.com. Note for decision analysis practitioners: coming up with a short and catchy name is an important part of crafting alternative strategies. The strategy resulting in creation of AST was described in a detailed strategy table, but the short name later leading to AST was "Create an IP NATO."

Appendix A

Rule 1.6 Confidentiality of Information

Client–Lawyer Relationship

(a) A lawyer shall not reveal information relating to the representation of a client unless the client gives informed consent, the disclosure is impliedly authorized in order to carry out the representation or the disclosure is permitted by paragraph (b).

(b) A lawyer may reveal information relating to the representation of a client to the extent the lawyer reasonably believes necessary:

    (1) to prevent reasonably certain death or substantial bodily harm;

    (2) to prevent the client from committing a crime or fraud that is reasonably certain to result in substantial injury to the financial interests or property of another and in furtherance of which the client has used or is using the lawyer's services;

    (3) to prevent, mitigate or rectify substantial injury to the financial interests or property of another that is reasonably certain to result or has resulted from the client's commission of a crime or fraud in furtherance of which the client has used the lawyer's services;

    (4) to secure legal advice about the lawyer's compliance with these Rules;

    (5) to establish a claim or defense on behalf of the lawyer in a controversy between the lawyer and the client, to establish a defense to a criminal charge or civil claim against the lawyer based upon conduct in which the client was involved, or to respond to allegations in any proceeding concerning the lawyer's representation of the client;

    (6) to comply with other law or a court order; or

    (7) to detect and resolve conflicts of interest arising from the lawyer's change of employment or from changes in the composition or ownership of a firm, but only if the revealed information would not compromise the attorney-client privilege or otherwise prejudice the client.

(c) A lawyer shall make reasonable efforts to prevent the inadvertent or unauthorized disclosure of, or unauthorized access to, information relating to the representation of a client.

Appendix B

Rule 3-100 Confidential Information of a Client

(A) A member shall not reveal information protected from disclosure by Business and Professions Code section 6068, subdivision (e)(1) without the informed consent of the client, or as provided in paragraph (B) of this rule.

(B) A member may, but is not required to, reveal confidential information relating to the representation of a client to the extent that the member reasonably believes the disclosure is necessary to prevent a criminal act that the member reasonably believes is likely to result in death of, or substantial bodily harm to, an individual.

(C) Before revealing confidential information to prevent a criminal act as provided in paragraph (B), a member shall, if reasonable under the circumstances:

  (1) make a good faith effort to persuade the client: (i) not to commit or to continue the criminal act or (ii) to pursue a course of conduct that will prevent the threatened death or substantial bodily harm; or do both (i) and (ii); and

  (2) inform the client, at an appropriate time, of the member's ability or decision to reveal information as provided in paragraph (B).

(D) In revealing confidential information as provided in paragraph (B), the member's disclosure must be no more than is necessary to prevent the criminal act, given the information known to the member at the time of the disclosure.

(E) A member who does not reveal information permitted by paragraph (B) does not violate this rule.

Appendix C

Rule 3-120 Sexual Relations with Client

(A) For purposes of this rule, "sexual relations" means sexual intercourse or the touching of an intimate part of another person for the purpose of sexual arousal, gratification, or abuse.

(B) A member shall not:

    (1) Require or demand sexual relations with a client incident to or as a condition of any professional representation; or

    (2) Employ coercion, intimidation, or undue influence in entering into sexual relations with a client; or

    (3) Continue representation of a client with whom the member has sexual relations if such sexual relations cause the member to perform legal services incompetently in violation of rule 3-110.

(C) Paragraph (B) shall not apply to sexual relations between members and their spouses or to ongoing consensual sexual relationships which predate the initiation of the lawyer-client relationship.

(D) Where a lawyer in a firm has sexual relations with a client but does not participate in the representation of that client, the lawyers in the firm shall not be subject to discipline under this rule solely because of the occurrence of such sexual relations.

Appendix D
Rule 1.8 Current Clients: Specific Rules

Client–Lawyer Relationship

. . .

(j) A lawyer shall not have sexual relations with a client unless a consensual sexual relationship existed between them when the client-lawyer relationship commenced.

24

Topics in Next-Generation Medical Ethics

The Art in the Art of Medicine

Josh C. Hyatt

24.1 Introduction

Medicine has a dichotomous personality, some of it is science and some of it is art. The science of medicine focuses on the technical skills and proficiency; whereas the art of medicine examines the ethical decision-making, professionalism, and relationships we foster to provide care to patients, comfort to families, and compassion to colleagues. It is often referred to as bedside manner, but it extends beyond that. It is communication, honesty, and respect.

In addition to this complex interplay, healthcare is arguably the most regulated industry in the country and is fraught with the most personal of experiences, and thus ethical and moral crossroads. This chapter will focus on the foundation of medical ethics and its fundamental principles and decision-making, and then apply these concepts to three principle conditions providers and patients face daily: moral conditions, human conditions, and technological conditions.

These three conditions hold the keys to the past, present, and future of medical ethical dilemmas and decision-making. Moral conditions look at social inequities and health disparities, complex end-of-life decisions, and the effects on providers and their decision-making when they are impacted with these difficult issues. Human conditions explore the roles of communication, professionalism, and how personal biases impact care. Technological conditions explore the present and ongoing future ethical concerns of human interaction being replaced by technology, our over-reliance on technology even in the face of overwhelming physical evidence, and dangers on technology such as hacking into personal medical devices and ransomware.

24.1.1 Moral Philosophy

Ethics is the branch of philosophy that studies the nature of and the justification for general principles governing correct conduct. Ethics provides a means to bring to the conscious level ideal behaviors. Medical ethics and the relevant

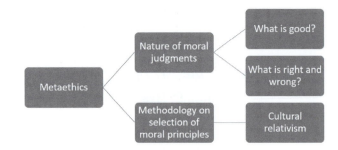

Figure 24.1 *The branches and content associated with metaethics*

Figure 24.2 *The branches and content associated with normative ethics*

decision-making that occurs in medicine can be analyzed within the framework of moral philosophy. Specifically, both metaethics and normative ethics can be applied to the study of ethics in the medical context, which forms the basis of bioethics.

Metaethics, in the medical field, principally applies to professional responsibility. It poses the question of what is right versus what is wrong and can be broken down into two components – namely, the nature of moral judgments and the methodology used to select moral principles (Figure 24.1). The nature of moral judgments stem from an understanding of what is good and the ability to distinguish between right and wrong. The methodology that allows you to select moral principles, however, is largely subject to cultural exposure. In other words, because we view things morally relative, those things that are socially accepted within our culture will influence our concept of morality and thus what is right and wrong. Accordingly, different cultures can disagree over the ethics of specific behaviors. For instance, some cultures find it acceptable to eat meat from a cow, whereas others do not. This relativism can also extend to specific seemingly similar actions. In the United States, for example, though it is socially acceptable to process and eat cow meat, it is not socially acceptable to do the same with dog meat.

Normative ethics, rather than questioning the morality associated with specific actions, is more interested in higher level principles around how we ought to live our lives. Normative ethics can be subcategorized into theory and applied normative ethics (Figure 24.2). Normative theory addresses the basics of right and wrong to enable the construction of general moral principles and asks questions such as "What makes someone a just person?" Applied normative ethics employs normative theory to study the morality of certain complex ethical dilemmas that humans face, such as abortion, physician-assisted suicide, or "designer babies" based on genetic manipulation. Ethics serves little purpose outside of academia if it does not apply to real world situations; therefore, applied normative theory has significant value in both medical and non-medical settings.

24.1.2 Scientific Methodology and Bioethics

Strong similarities can be found between the scientific and bioethical decision-making models. The scientific model searches for answers through explanation and includes: (1) questioning; (2) hypothesis development and testing; (3) theory; (4) explanation; and (5) predictability. According to Beauchamp & Walters (1994), the bioethical model searches for answers through moral justification and includes: (1) questioning (something that challenges our moral beliefs); (2) moral value judgment (something is right or wrong); (3) rule (a code that tells the individual what is right or wrong); (4) principle (basic foundations, i.e., philosophical, religious, cultural, etc.); and (5) moral justification (belief that something is right or wrong is morally justified). The scientific method is formed based on absolutes; whereas bioethics, though using a similar thought structure, is much less absolute in its process or outcome due to the complexities of human factors and belief structures. Consequently, predictability is difficult, if not impossible, to achieve given the variability in circumstance.

24.2 Medical Ethics Principles

Using metaethics, normative theory, and applied normative ethics as the basis, four principles emerged that are generally associated with medical ethics: autonomy, beneficence, non-maleficence, and justice. Each of these principles can stand alone but often work in concert with each other when facing complex medical issues and professionalism concerns.

24.2.1 Autonomy

Autonomy is a guiding principle for patient preference, and ethically following the principle of autonomy requires a respect for each patient's right to accept or reject recommendations made by a physician. Autonomous patients are ultimately the Consones who choose the course of medical action to take. This foundational principle is the center point of discussion when addressing issues such as informed consent and patients refusing medical treatment on personal or moral grounds.

Autonomy stands in contrast to physician paternalism, which suggests that physicians should use only their medical judgment in determining the medical action plans for their patients. Physician paternalism ignores patient preferences and assumes that only the physician can make a reasonable choice about what medical plans to pursue. Respecting autonomy allows for patient-centered medicine where physicians and patients work together to determine the best personalized plan to address the patients' health.

24.2.2 Beneficence

Beneficence is concerned with the duty to attempt to improve the capability of medicine to improve physical and psychological health to diagnose, treat, and heal. Beneficence has implications for both medical indications and quality of life. The fundamental principle is that the provider has a duty to help others by doing what is best for them. Beneficence is usually discussed in the context of medical futility and termination of non-beneficial care.

24.2.3 Non-Maleficence

Non-maleficence has implications for these same concepts and deals with approaching the practice of medicine in a manner that prevents or reduces the risk of further injury or damage. It is the principle from which "do no harm" is most closely associated. The basis of this principle is that the medical provider has a duty not to inflect evil, harm, or risk of harm onto others and is often cited in discussions related to physician-assisted suicide and abortion.

24.2.4 Justice

Justice, in the context of medicine, often deals with the concept of equal distribution and ensuring that resources are equitably allocated. Thus, healthcare providers have a responsibility to ensure that benefits and burdens are not disproportionately appropriated. Organ distribution, insurance coverage and access, healthcare reform, and mandated healthcare coverage are common threads to a discussion on justice in the medical setting.

24.3 The Art in the Art of Medicine

Though medical training tends to focus on curing and lifesaving as the priority, clinical ethics dictates that cures may occur sometimes, but it is more important to relieve and comfort. Following these goals is complicated by the number of players in medical decisions that can constrain the options available to healthcare providers and patients. For instance, administrative issues, financing, the community, and the family can all affect access to healthcare options.

In each clinical ethics situation, Jonsen et al. (2010) indicated are several things that should be examined: medical indications, patient preferences, quality of life, contextual features, and paradigm cases. Medical indications are diagnostic or therapeutic interventions used to evaluate and treat the medical problem. Patient preferences refer to the choices of the patient or those authorized to speak for the patient. Quality of life, which is often a contentious topic, requires considering features of the patient's life both prior to and after treatment. Contextual features are the familial, social, institutional, financial, and legal settings within which the case takes place. The ethical principles most relevant for contextual features are justice and fairness. Finally, paradigm cases are those that have already been thoughtfully considered and perhaps adjudicated that may provide guidance for the current case.

24.3.1 Medical Decision-Making

Understanding how medical decisions are made provides a window into the complexities surrounding ethical decision-making in a clinical setting. A principle focus for an ethicist is understanding what the goals of treatment are and if they are realistic. The goals of medicine are generally to cure, establish an acceptable quality of life for the patient when you cannot cure, or provide comfort when an acceptable quality of life cannot be achieved. Medical ethicists often grapple with issues such as providing care that is non-beneficial; maintaining the physiological status of someone in a persisted vegetative state; procedures or treatments that have limited or minimal curative effect; prolonging of pain and suffering of an individual with a significantly limited life expectancy; and procedures or treatments that will likely result in the patient not returning to an acceptable quality of life.

Thus, we often see conflicts between and within providers, as well as patients and families, surrounding the goals of treatment and how those goals are appropriately communicated. In a survey of 912 surgeons, 43 percent reported conflicts regarding the postoperative goals of care with intensive care clinicians and nurses (Olsen, Basel, Redmann, Alexander, & Schwarze, 2013). These are the unfortunate realities of medical care in today's medical model. It is apparent in the dismal rates that physicians discuss end-of-life choices with dying patients; over-aggressive and painful treatments for chronic diseases for patients at the end of life (most commonly seen with chemotherapy for cancer for patients in stages three and four lung cancer getting aggressive chemotherapy up to three weeks before the end of their life); and an under-utilization of palliative care options.

These conflicts are also prevalently seen within the context of the physician's specialty. A friend of mine once told me a comparison that is apropos to this concept. When a patient dies, doctors ask the physician "What happened?" and they ask the surgeon "What did you do?" Joan Cassell (2005), in her book *Life and Death in Intensive Care*, compared this to moral economies. In her study of intensive cares, she concluded that that surgeons and intensivists/nurses have different moral economies. For surgeons, death is the enemy, and for intensivists and nurses, suffering is the enemy. Consequently, there are special kinds of relationships and perspectives that are specific to physicians, surgeons, and the particular subspecialties to each. This can be referred to as specialty group think. Ethicists can see this play out in a number of ways, including nephrologists that want to dialyze comatose patients with multiple systems failures; surgeons not wanting patients to be DNR during surgery; intensivists using fear-invoking and coercive language to get a patient to have a treatment she does not want; cardiac surgeons who want to place a pace-maker in elderly patients; or oncologists that do not explain to a patient in a clinical trial that he is the subject of an experiment and not actually getting treatment. These are just a few examples, but this can be seen throughout medicine.

Additionally, complicating factors in analyzing ethical situations is that the ethical principles can be in conflict, obfuscating the right action. For instance, the wishes of surrogates may not be aligned with those of the patients. It is important to consider the duties and obligations of each party, as well as all the available clinical options and their short-term and long-term consequences. From this initial analysis, it should be practical to then identify which options appear to be justified, and actions can be selected.

24.3.2 Bioethics, Biomedical Ethics, and Clinical Ethics

The field of bioethics did not formally exist before 1970 because the medical profession was managed mostly though the privacy of the doctor–patient relationship. However, advances in medicine that fundamentally changed the role physicians traditionally played – making them more responsible for life and death and quality of life decisions, as well as patient access to newer, faster information and technology – brought new dimensions to medical decision-making. These dimensions formally structured both the study and application of biomedical and clinical ethics.

Biomedical ethics explores the philosophical rights and wrongs related to medicine and science outside of the context of direct patient care and focuses on modern biological sciences, pharmacology, healthcare systems, and medical research.

Clinical ethics is focused on the ability to identify and analyze an ethical question and to reach a reasonable conclusion and recommendation for action when applied to direct patient care. Clinical ethics is a critical area of study due to the moral and ethical complexity that frequently arises in clinical scenarios. Many

Some basic questions that clinical ethics seeks to answer include:
Are we providing ethical care to the patient? And from whose perspective?
Do we ask about whether patients felt as if they were treated ethically?
How do we or can we quantify ethical behavior?
Do we have ethical decision-making process in our organization?
Do we have competencies in our institution that evaluate ethical decision-making?

Figure 24.3 *Clinical ethics questions*

clinical actions, from taking the professional oath through the choices made at the bedside, have ethical and legal implications on patient care.

Clinical ethics is often treated as an ordered consultation by a treating physician when complex ethical issues arise during the course of treatment. It aims to apply ethical judgment to medical situations to guide practice and does so through a combination of metaethics, normative theory, and applied normative ethics. In the context of clinical care, metaethics can be used to analyze the implications of the oaths (i.e., Hippocratic, Nightingale, etc.), personal beliefs of the healthcare provider, and the influence of their communities. Normative theory can help address professional licensure expectations and community standards of care, and applied normative ethics can enable the assessment of potential bedside actions (Figure 24.3).

Although clinical ethics focuses more on appropriateness of medical interventions, respecting patient preferences and autonomy, and the values of the patient related to their quality of life, medical decisions are not just self-contained conversations as they once were. These conversations are now structure by outside factors, social convention, and public policy. Some of these elements include professional organizations, administration, state and federal agencies, families, professional and community standards, financing, access to healthcare, and research.

In practice, clinical ethics should focus on demonstrating moral courage, compassion for all involved (patients, families, and providers), collaboration (shared information and messaging to make the best decision possible), being prepared for managing complexity, and supportive services for all involved. It should never be used as a bully pulpit for personal morality or vindictiveness, a platform to promulgate religious or political beliefs that are not in alignment with the values of the patient, or to override the treatment and care set forth by the attending physician. These acts often undermine the important work a clinical ethicist sets out to do and reduce the likelihood that these services would be sought out in the future when they are needed.

24.3.3 Ethics and the Law

Because of complexities in ethical decision-making related to personal conflicts, cultural conflicts, medical science, and liability, bioethics and law are often intrinsically interlocked. "The moral conscience is a precursor to the development of legal rules for social order. Law and medical ethics thus share the goal of creating and maintaining social good" (Annas, 1993).

Though laws are often formed with an ethical basis in mind and as a result of joint opinions on the social contract, law and ethics are not equivalent. Rather, law is one specific perspective that provides guidelines for socially acceptable behavior and gives an expression of social value through rule. The law identifies how social value is experienced through the prisms of rule. Ethics, on the other hand, provides a method of proper and humane practice. Whereas ethics is concerned with what we ought to do, law is concerned with what we must do if we want to avoid criminal behavior. Ethics have therefore been described as beginning where the law ends, as principle predicates law.

24.4 Moral Factors

There are numerous moral factors that contribute to ethical decision-making in general and specifically to ethical medical decision-making. Both macro-ethics and micro-ethics are important to consider when thinking about ethical decision-making. Macro-ethics approaches ethics from a big-picture viewpoint and considers what is right and wrong on a global level. Micro-ethics, on the other hand, refers to the way we approach ethics from our own personal experiences (Pozgar, 2012, p.2). The combination of macro-ethics and micro-ethics results in our specific ethical behaviors.

Belief systems also contribute critically to our ethical decision-making and are shaped both by our own attitudes and personal philosophies, as well as by our sociocultural experiences with ethics. While healthcare providers often have much of the same knowledge and are educated on proper standards of care and relevant regulations, they, like everyone else, are influenced by their own values and beliefs. Thus, the care patients receive is subject not only to the rules and information endowed to healthcare providers but also to the individual differences in perspective that are embodied by a diverse array of medical personnel.

Additionally, there are many sociocultural influencers that impact the moral factors of ethics in the medical setting, which are the underpinnings of a culture that either supports or inhibits an ethically supportive environment. If the institution emphasizes doing the right thing as the fundamental management principle, this can support and encourage a culture of organizational ethics. Individuals and institutions must take care and have appropriate systems in place to address critical issues that can quickly undermine this culture of ethics such as being permissive of behaviors that undermine a culture of safety, conflicts of interest,

A Catholic registered nurse who works in an emergency room made a request upon hire that she not be involved with any abortions, even if they are medically necessary. This was placed in writing, was agreed to by the hiring director, and filed in the personnel file. Several years and a couple of directors later, the nurse is faced with a situation where she was requested to assist a physician in an emergency procedure that would result in the death of a fetus in its fifteenth week. The procedure is to save the life of the mother, who will die if the procedure is not performed. The emergency room is busy that there are no other nurses available to assist. She refuses and is told to comply or she would be terminated and reported to the state board of nursing for patient abandonment.

Questions:
1. Should an employee that has repeatedly expressed personal values concerns about abortion, or any other procedure type, be required to assist, even if it is within her scope of practice?
2. Was it ethical for her employer to threaten her with termination if she did not comply?
3. Should an employer enforce that an employee do something that morally offends them or should employees not accept position that they know may significantly violate their morals?
4. If there are guidelines to protect the employee from this event by the employer, who and where do these boundaries get drawn?

Figure 24.4 *Professionalism case study*

privacy and disclosure issues, unjust allocation and utilization of services, and the focus of revenue over safety and justice.

For ethics to practically work, enough people must be morally courageous to challenge what is morally questionable and follow a path to resolution. Thoughts, personal ethics, and behavior are all important components of moral courage, and where these three entities meet is where moral courage occurs (Figure 24.4).

Many virtues are associated with moral courage. For instance, displaying strength in the face of fear, understanding that your beliefs are sacred to you, and having the capacity to identify personal biases and proactively manage them are virtues that make it more likely that one will have moral courage.

For those who want to behave ethically but find that identifying the correct course of action is challenging, Peter Singer (pp. 4–5) suggests four specific steps. First, gather all the available facts and information. Second, identify what information is relevant. Third, assess the information based on your basic moral positions. Finally, address and eliminate personal bias.

24.5 Human Factors

According to a 2012 Gallup Poll, nurses (at 85 percent), pharmacists (at 75 percent), and medical doctors (at 70 percent) are ranked as the top one, two, and three highest-rated ethical professionals. This list is rounded out at the bottom with Members of Congress (at 10 percent) and car salespeople (8 percent). This demonstrates a unique commitment to the application of ethical principles in the medical setting. Anecdotally, one could conclude that the clear majority of providers go into the medical field to heal and demonstrate compassion for those suffering.

The "meta-principle" that is often used by those engaged in bioethics discussions centering around the medical provider is professional responsibility (Arras & Rhoden, 1989). This principle provides that "Any provider (physician, nurse, etc.), as a professional, has an obligation to observe the rules, principles and moral precepts governing relations with patients, colleagues, the profession as a whole, and the community at large."

As part of their training, healthcare personnel are educated on the regulations and the proper standard of care for treating the public. However, much of this training centers on the technical, or science, aspect of medicine and does not include the role providers' own personal values and beliefs play in how they perceive, provide patient care, and personally respond to the situations they face. There has been research in the last thirty years or so to support the psychological, emotional, and physiological impact and suffering of patient care to providers.

When providers make choices, they impact both other people and themselves. Enduring moral conflicts takes energy and can elicit guilt, apprehension, and regret. In medicine, professionals often experience moral distress from ethical dilemmas, which can lead to compassion fatigue and moral disengagement. This cascade may be detrimental to providers, patients, patients' families, and others in the workplace. This process begins with an ethical dilemma.

24.5.1 Ethical Dilemmas and Moral Distress

In an ethical dilemma, the provider must choose between two desirable or two unsatisfactory alternatives. There is a need to ultimately *act* in deciding (Ganz, Wagner, & Toren, 2015). Comparatively, moral distress is the recognition and expectation to enact ethical mandate or action but *not being able to act* on it due to barriers such as bureaucracies, power structures, lack of time, high caseloads, and so on (Barlem & Ramos, 2015; Musto & Rodney, 2015).

Ethical dilemmas generally occur when there are competing values. They could be personal, institutional, cultural, religious, or other values that have powerful repercussions on the provider, patient, and family. Unfortunately, healthcare providers are often faced with these personal ethical dilemmas daily and it can create tension in the workplace and poor patient outcomes.

These ethical dilemmas result in moral distress, which is found in all levels of medical professionals. "Moral distress arises when one knows the right thing to do, but institutional constraints make it nearly impossible to pursue the right course of action" (Jameton, 1984, p. 6). Moral distress is often expressed indirectly, towards others around the provider, and has ethical consequences such as reduced communication, risks to patient safety, burnout, turnover, and moral disengagement (McCarthy & Gastmans, 2015; Payne, 2011).

Moral Courage

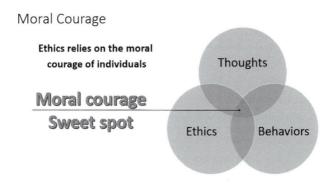

Ethics relies on the moral courage of individuals

Moral courage
Sweet spot

Figure 24.5 *Moral courage sweet spot*

24.5.2 Moral Disengagement

Moral distress can lead to tension or some sort of cognitive dissonance (tension between the codes of ethics and constraints to act ethically) resulting in someone becoming morally numb (Epstein & Delgado, 2010). Moral disengagement is the process in which an individual deactivates their internal self-regulatory mechanism when committing an unethical act to allow their conscience to remain clear and justify the act in order to maintain cognitive consistency (Bandura, 1999; Hinrichs, Wang, Hinrichs, & Romero, 2012).

With moral disengagement, multiple symptoms can be observed. These include affective symptoms (frustration, guilt, depression, anger, resentment, shame, powerlessness, helpless) (Corley, 2002); cognitive symptoms (loss of self-worth, loss of sense of self) (Payne, 2011); physical and somatic symptoms (fatigue, aches, pain, sleeplessness, heart palpitations, nightmares) (McCarthy & Gastmans, 2015; Payne, 2011); and behavioral symptoms (gossip, tardiness, absenteeism, distancing from patients, horizontal violence, avoiding work-related tasks) (Payne, 2011).

When moral disengagement occurs, unethical activity is likely to ensue because the person who is morally disengaged has found ways to justify those types of behaviors. There are three main categories of moral disengagement: sanitizing the act, sanitizing the actor, and blaming the victim (Figure 23.5). Sanitizing the act means that the actor finds a way to frame the act as the only option or the best option. Sanitizing the actor, on the other hand, removes the actor from blame by redirecting the blame elsewhere, often to a policy. Blaming the victim enables the actor to cope with the unethical act by viewing the victim as the perpetrator of, or otherwise responsible for, the act.

Horizontal or lateral violence encompasses a specific type of non-physical act of bullying between two parties in a situation where they perceive they have been oppressed. This occurs frequently in organizations where employees' voices are not heard. Feelings of anger and resentment are internalized and then expressed in behaviors such as insulting, scapegoating, undermining, bickering, criticizing, and so on (Christie & Jones, 2013).

Moral disengagement occurs at both the individual and organizational level (White, Bandura, & Bero, 2009). This is often referred to as collective moral disengagement, which is a network of individuals who behave unethically and vindicate the industry practices (White et al., 2009). White et al. (2009) found the following industry level moral disengagement mechanisms:

Euphemistic labeling – tobacco industry – "establish the minimum dose of smoke nicotine that can provide *pharmacological satisfaction* for the smoker" (White et al., 2009, p. 50).

Advantageous comparison – lead industry – "We have on an average one death each day from *automobile accidents, approximately 300 to 350 each year*, and yet there has been no legislation so far to do away with the automobiles" (White et al., 2009, p. 51).

Moral justification – vinyl chloride industry – "[The industry] should cite the *benefits to mankind through chemicals ... Feeding the world will depend on the use of chemicals... Chemicals are important for both protection and production of food*" (White et al., 2009, p. 49).

Ultimately, the human condition impacts of moral distress and moral disengagement to the provider are burnout and loss of purpose (Burston & Tuckett, 2013); job dissatisfaction (Lamiani et al., 2017); feeling deadened to moral issues; patients' welfare (McCarthy & Gastmans, 2015); and a sense of feeling demoralized, silenced, and passive (Burston & Tuckett, 2013; McCarthy & Gastmans, 2015). This negatively impacts the effectiveness of an institution ethics perception and patient care/safety. The ethical ramifications to patients are seen in behaviors such as distancing and avoiding patients (Corley, 2002; Wilkinson, 1987); inadequate and inappropriate care (McCarthy & Gastmans, 2015); longer hospital stays (McCarthy & Gastmans, 2015); threats to patient autonomy (Choe et al., 2015); patient coercion (McCarthy & Gastmans, 2015); and higher medication and treatment errors (Howard, 2014).

McCarthy and Gastmans (2015) also identified some benefits of moral distress if used in the proper context and frame of mind. It can help lead to professional growth, foster self-awareness, generate communication and dialogue between providers within the discipline and between different disciplines, and promote critical thinking.

24.6 Technological Factors

Science fiction has provided our culture with glimpses of both biomedical and clinical ethical issues based on advancements in medical research. We are now equipped to perform procedures and intervene physiologically at a level and rate never seen in history or even conceived of fifty years ago. Though it is under-standable that healthcare providers would embrace new technologies, doing so without asking serious questions about the implications of using those technolo-gies can lead to ethical problems. We can, but should we?

As technology progresses, so do the ethical dilemmas that arise. Medicine has learned that once the barn door of technology is opened, it is difficult to close again – and sometimes the medical field's love of new technology exists without thoroughly exploring the appropriateness of its uses from an ethical perspective.

Historically, medicine has been practiced as a relationship between the patient and their doctor. This model was based on a physician paternalist model and evolved into an active communication and autonomy-based model. The model then evolved in institution-based requirements where hospitals, insurance com-panies, and healthcare systems began dictating the model and standard of care. As information becomes easier to acquire and individual expectations rise, the model has begun evolving towards patient-centric care. Patients are more literate in their medical conditions, have clear expectations of what they believe the appropriate course of action should be (whether that is correct or not), and demand their medical information in real time. Consequently, these newer technologies are requiring healthcare to reexamine how medicine is practiced and how medical decision-making is done. This results in ethical conflicts and dilemmas for the provider and the patient that can significantly impact their relationship and the care provided.

The technological influencers that generate the most ethical concerns are generally found in the following areas: life sustaining/prolonging technology; genome testing and modification; reproduction; robotics (implants and in surgery); personalized and personality changing medicine; mobile health options; artificial intelligence (AI); medical information; and access to technology.

These technologies are generally developed specifically to prevent illness and suffering and to increase both longevity and quality of life. It can therefore often seem that defaulting to using these technologies when they may serve some purpose is the best course of action. However, it is worth considering that there are cases by which interfering with or not using technology is the ethical choice.

The technologies often work well independently, which is the designer's frame of reference. However, these technologies do not always communicate with each other efficiently or effectively: often resulting in fragmented care, lack of coordin-ation, and ambiguities in what results mean or how to properly interpret them given other pieces of information.

The ethical question that arises with the use of technology in medicine is, "When is it too much or too little?" This question can be a Gordian Knot for the provider. Attempting to uncouple the patient or family expectations, community standards, professional expectations, and complexities of the situation sometimes feels like odds playing and political negotiation, which sometimes it is. Is not trying the latest and greatest surgery on someone because of their physical condition, underlying medical conditions, and quality of life failing the patient or admitting defeat as a provider?

24.6.1 Communication and Mobile Apps

The increased use of technology has fundamentally changed how medical information is shared and communicated between the provider and patient. From patients' self-diagnosing based on an internet search to mobile apps that track health status that is reviewed and interpreted remotely without human interaction, convenience and costs are the motivating factor in the new moral economy of medicine.

One technological area that has dramatically increased in healthcare and would be largely innocuous is that of mobile health. Though there are more than 92,000 mobile health apps available, many of them suffer from issues of inaccuracy, which can prevent an ideal medical plan from being executed.

The Food and Drug Administration (FDA) is responsible for most mobile health products that perform core medical functions (diagnosis and treatment) and could represent a threat to patient safety. The FDA chooses which of the mobile health products to review and which adverse events to investigate. The FDA has identified nine types of mobile apps: three are regulated and the other six are discretionarily regulated. The two primary devices that are regulated are apps that require you to plug something into a phone (blood pressure, glucose, etc.) and those that ask the phone to give advice. The overall rule of thumb, if it looks like a medical device, then it must be regulated.

Mobile apps have specific advantages, such as being cloud-based, using patient-curated data, and being patient centric. This information can be transmitted to providers for analysis and review. Unfortunately, most healthcare providers and systems are not operationally designed to handle this amount of information and liability for not responding to the data in a timely or appropriate manner. This creates unique ethical and legal dilemmas for the provider.

24.6.2 Implementation and Security of Information

A significant concern related to the design and implementation of new technologies centers around the speed at which they are developed and how they can be appropriately integrated into the current medical systems in place (Ng, 2007). When new technologies are developed and patented, the process for wide-spread integration and adaptation is hindered on factors such as training of providers and staff, experience using the equipment, finding qualified and competent people to use this equipment, and fitting the capabilities into the existing administrative and cost-based models.

In the age of hacked credit card and personal information, hacking medical devices, electronic medical records, protection of data integrity, and securing private medical information is a major concern. Evidence suggests that devices such as IV infusion pumps (which deliver a variety of medications such as morphine and chemotherapy to patients) and blue-tooth-enabled implanted defibrillators (which deliver shocks to patients when their heart stops) can be manipulated by a hacker. Blood types can be changed in electronic records remotely, resulting in hemolytic reactions. Electronic medical records can be hacked to change information or even order medications. CT scans can have altered images and radiation level exposure changed remotely. Medical and laboratory equipment can be "blue screened," causing them to have to be restarted or rebooted, resulting in spoilage or more significant patient injury (Zetter, 2014).

Unfortunately, healthcare providers and institutions are dependent on the infor-mation in their records and are often unaware that these vulnerabilities exist until they occur. Because of patient privacy breaches and the strict federal and state laws surrounding them, more institutions are working to improve data security but are missing device vulnerabilities. One principle concern is the exchange of unauthenticated or unencrypted communication between medical devices (Zetter, 2014).

With all the advances in diagnosis and treatment that technology brings, at least an equal number of ethical concerns arise in response to them. When looking at the impact of technology and its future in medical ethics, it is important to consider how the communication is used and secured, maintaining the fundamen-tal physician–patient relationship, working with the patient and the family to determine which options most closely reflect their values and defined quality of life, how this new technology gets implemented in a system that is not designed to support it (operationally, functionally, or financially), and what the impacts are on the provider.

24.7 Conclusion

Though medical ethics is a critical field that analyzes complex questions concern-ing medical behavior and provides various frameworks for working to answer the dilemmas often faced in the practice of medicine, there are many challenges for the field. The field is not well funded, and there are not an adequate number of trained bioethicists to help bring important principles in medical ethics to practice. As such, there is a serious lack of organized and support ethics programs and

Sanitizing the act

- Cognitive reconstruction
- "It was for the best" or "It had to be done"

Sanitizing the actor

- "It's the policy" or "It is against the policy"

Blaming the victim

- "The family threatened to sue me if I didn't do it."

Figure 24.6 *Three categories of moral disengagement*

therefore a lack of education on both the importance of medical ethics and the utility of ethical models.

There is not always a right answer where ethics is concerned, and there is not a one-size-fits-all, predictable answer to specific scenarios. The continuous process of analysis, questioning, and reevaluation of judgments, rules, principles, theories, and facts is needed to adequately manage ethics. Healthcare teams should therefore integrate this type of work into their operational processes to ensure that the teams can meet ethical standards in an ever-changing and dynamic field.

A Catholic registered nurse who works in an emergency room made a request upon hire that she not be involved with any abortions, even if they are medically necessary. This is placed in writing, was agreed to by the hiring director, and filed in the personnel file. Several years and a couple of directors later, the nurse is faced with a situation when she was requested to assist a physician in an emergency procedure that would result in the death of a fetus in its fifteenth week. The procedure is to save the life of the mother, who will die if the procedure is not performed. The emergency room is busy that there are no other nurses available to assist. She refuses and is told to comply or she would be terminated and reported to the state board of nursing for patient abandonment.

Questions:

1. Should an employee that has repeatedly expressed personal values concerns about abortion, or any other procedure type, be required to assist, even if it is within her scope of practice?
2. Was it ethical for her employer to threaten her with termination if she did not comply?

3. Should an employer enforce that an employee do something that morally offends them or should employees not accept a position that they know may significantly violate their morals?
4. If there are guidelines to protect the employee from this event by the employer, who and where do these boundaries get drawn?

References

Annas, G. (1993). *Standard of care: The Law of American Bioethics*. New York, NY: Oxford University Press.

Arras, J. & Rhoden, N. (1989). *Ethical issues in modern medicine* (3rd ed.). Mountain View, CA: Mayfield Publishing.

Bandura, A. (1999). Moral disengagement in the perpetration of inhumanities. *Personality and Social Psychology Review*, *3*, 193–209.

Barlem, E. L. D. & Ramos, F. R. S. (2015). Constructing a theoretical model of moral distress. *Nursing Ethics*, *22*(5), 608–615.

Beauchamp, T. & Walters, L. (Eds.). (1994). *Contemporary issues in bioethics* (4th ed.) Belmont, CA: Wadsworth Publishing.

Burston, A. S. & Tuckett, A. G. (2013). Moral distress in nursing: Contributing factors, outcomes and interventions. *Nursing Ethics*, *20*(3), 312–324.

Cassell, J. (2005). *Life and death in intensive care*. New York, NY: Temple University Press.

Choe, K., Kang, Y., & Park. Y. (2015). Moral distress in critical care nurses: A phenomenological study. *Journal of Advanced Nursing*, *71*(7), 1684–1693.

Christie, W., & Jones, S. (2013, December 9). Lateral violence in nursing and the theory of the nurse as wounded healer. *OJIN: The Online Journal of Issues in Nursing*, *19*(1).

Corley, M. C. (2002). Nurse moral distress: A proposed theory and research agenda. *Nursing Ethics*, *9*(6), 636–650.

Epstein, E. G., & Delgado, S. (2010, September 30). Understanding and addressing moral distress. *OJIN: The Online Journal of Issues in Nursing*, *15*(3), manuscript 1.

Gallup. (2012, November). Honesty/ethics in professions. Retrieved from www.gallup.com/poll/1654/honesty-ethics-professions.aspx#1.

Ganz, F. D., Wagner, N., & Toren, O. (2015). Nurse middle manager ethical dilemmas and moral distress. *Nursing Ethics*, *22*(1), 43–51.

Hinrichs, K. T., Wang, L., Hinrichs, A. T., & Romero, E. J. (2012). Moral disengagement through displacement of responsibility: The role of leadership beliefs. *Journal of Applied Social Psychology*, *42*(1), 62–80.

Howard, C. (2014). Moral distress in healthcare. *Ethics and Medics*, *39*(12), 1–2.

Jameton A. (1984). *Nursing practice: the ethical issues*. Englewood Cliffs, NJ: Prentice Hall.

Jonsen, A. R., Siegler, M., & Winslade, W. J. (2010). *Clinical ethics: A practical approach to ethical decisions in clinical medicine* (7th ed.) New York, NY: McGraw Hill Medical.

Lamiani, G., Borghi, L., & Argentero, P. (2017). When healthcare professionals cannot do the right thing: A systematic review of moral distress and its correlates. *Journal of Health Psychology*, *22*(1), 51–67.

McCarthy, J. & Gastmans, C. (2015). Moral distress: A review of the argument-based nursing ethics literature. *Nursing Ethics*, *22*(1), 131–152.

Musto, L. C. & Rodney, P. A. (2015). Toward interventions to address moral distress: Navigating structure and agency. *Nursing Ethics*, *22*(1), 91–102.

Ng, T. (2007). Ethics in the age of medical device technologies. *AMA Journal of Ethics*, 9 (2), 83–85.

Olsen, T. J., Brasel, K. J., Redmann, A. J., Alexander, G. C., & Schwarze, M. L. (2013). Surgeon-reported conflict with intensivists about postoperative goals of care. *JAMA Surgery.* 148 (1), 29–35.

Payne, K. (2011). Ethics empowerment: Deal with moral distress. *Tennessee Nurse / Tennessee Nurses Association*, *74*(1), 1.

Pozgar, G. D. (2012). *Legal and ethical issues for health professionals.* (3rd edition). Burlington, MA: Jones and Bartlett.

Singer, P. (2000). *Writings on an ethical life.* New York: HarperCollins.

White, J., Bandura, A., & Bero, L. A. (2009). Moral disengagements in the corporate world. *Accountability in Research*, *16*(1), 41–74.

Wilkinson, J. (1987). Moral distress in nursing practice: Experience and effect. *Nursing Forum*, *23*(1), 16–29.

Zetter, K. (2014). It's insanely easy to hack hospital equipment. *Wired Magazine.* Retrieved from www.wired.com/2014/04/hospital-equipment-vulnerable/

25

Next-Generation Ethical Development of Medical Devices

Considering Harms, Benefits, Fairness, and Freedom

Andrew O. Brightman, Jonathan Beever, and Michael C. Hiles

25.1 Introduction

Each year hundreds of new biomedical devices and therapies are developed to attempt to solve unmet medical needs. However, many fail due to unforeseen challenges of complex ethical, regulatory, and societal issues. We propose that a number of these issues can be effectively transformed into drivers of innovation for medical solutions if ethical analysis is considered early, iteratively, and comprehensively in the research and development process.

Such an approach has not been widely adopted in the medical device industry or by education programs training the next generation of biomedical engineers. Thus, the ethical dilemma facing both industry and academia is that, on the one hand, a comprehensive ethical analysis is necessary alongside biomedical device development to stave off failures due to ethical and societal challenges; and on the other hand, design and development engineers are not adequately prepared to make effective ethical decisions in the face of the complex context of medical device development.

In this chapter we discuss the insufficiency of relying on professional codes of ethics, regulatory oversight, or training in responsible conduct of research to provide the necessary comprehensive ethical analysis. We argue that even together these approaches will not bring about the understanding needed to deal directly and innovatively with the rapidly changing ethical and societal issues facing design, development, and delivery of biomedical devices that are safely and effectively meeting the needs of patients.

Rapid changes in societal values, norms, and perspectives introduce novel ethical conflicts for research, development, and design that have not yet been considered within the scope of established professional codes of ethics. Radical technological advances in related fields such as robotics, bionanotechnology, sustainable manufacturing, and imaging and communication technology for medicine are challenging the ability of regulatory efforts to protect the public. Together these changes are creating complex new ethical concerns for research and development engineers that far surpass any training in responsible conduct of research. Thus, there is a demand for an effective method of ethical analysis and decision-making at the level of the individual engineer as well as for medical device companies.

In this chapter we discuss these limitations and consider several alternative strategies for comprehensive ethical analysis. Finally, we explore how a version of biomedical principlism can provide the needed framework for effective ethical analysis for device innovation and development and throughout the product life cycle for the next generation of medical devices. We end the chapter with additional support and examination of these claims with a brief example ethical analysis applying reflexive principlism to an emerging field of medical technology: neuromodulation.

25.2 The Ethical Challenges of Including Ethical Analysis in Product Life Cycle Management

Medical device development is governed by a whole host of regulations and codes, best practices and guidelines, guidance and standards, yet the ethical framework in which these specific directives work is primarily unwritten and ethereal in most, if not all, professional work settings (Pennell, Hirst, Sedrakyan, & McCulloch, 2016). The focus of this chapter is to consider an ethical analysis framework for the next-generation development of medical devices that would be effective in the entirety of product life cycle management (PLM).

For simplicity PLM can be divided into pre-market, market, and post-market phases with subparts in each. As examples, device design and development (including most clinical trials) are part of the pre-market phase; and device surveillance and complaint resolution (including product recalls or terminations) are part of the post-market phase. Although ethical decisions arise in all aspects of PLM, it is most often in four areas – design, development, surveillance, and resolution – where the most obvious, or perhaps impactful, decisions occur.

Ethical decisions in PLM are typically guided by the important codes of ethics and regulations that represent the current wisdom developed by industry and government from years of practical experience. However, the emerging science and rapidly changing values and perspectives on social impact of next-generation technologies regularly create gray area situations where black and white ethical decisions based on codes and regulations are not applicable. In these situations a framework for ethical analysis is critically needed. We propose that an ethical analysis based on principles of common morality, or principlism, could serve as an effective approach for the next-generation medical devices. Principlism begins with a set of mid-level, ethical guidelines (principles). They are considered mid-level because they function between the higher-order ethical theories of morality in the abstract and the particular and contextual ethical rules of conduct that deal with the details of specific contexts of individual cases. We argue, in more detail in Section 25.10, that reflexive principlism (RP) – a version of biomedical principlism that emphasizes the iterative practice of reflective analysis between ethical codes, principles, and case studies (Beever & Brightman 2016) – would be a particularly effective approach for analysis of ethical situations in medical device PLM. The four principles from biomedical ethics are justice, respect for autonomy, beneficence, and non-maleficence. These are fundamental principles from a common morality to be considered in biomedical ethical analysis as "general guidelines for the formulation of more specific rules" (Beauchamp & Childress 2013, p. 13).[1] But where do we start to apply these principles in a reflexive way in the context of biomedical devices? We believe it begins with stakeholder identification and perspective taking within each of the subparts of PLM.

Although perhaps not immediately obvious to the young engineer working on their first (or even twentieth) device design, the stakeholders with legitimate interest in device design and performance often change through the subparts of PLM. For example, one group of stakeholders that could be quite forefront in the mind of the engineer (or at least should be!) during pre-market design is the manufacturing personnel, yet this stakeholder has little relevance in the post-market phase. Similarly, a stakeholder that might come to the fore in post-market (but we hope not!) is the liability lawyer investigating device performance issues. Thus, a chemical used in the manufacture of a device may be hazardous to the manufacturing personnel and violate the principle of non-maleficence from their perspective but have no effect on the final product's performance in the market or in the patient. Similarly, a choice of material in the earliest of design processes for an implantable surgical device might be the source of late-term tissue erosions or rejections and tip the balance away from true beneficence to society (risk of harm over benefit) from the perspective of the liability lawyer even though that material may have been one of the easiest to use in manufacture. Therefore, the exercise of stakeholder identification and perspective taking at all phases of PLM should be considered central to an ethical analysis process for the next generation of medical devices.

25.3 How Have We Missed the Target?

Giving examples post-hoc of how a principle-based approach to ethical analysis might have helped in PLM may not be the best support for real-time application. However, shedding light on how some past medical device mishaps, or outright failures, could be avoided through effective ethical analysis can be instructive for future applications.

One very high-profile, broadly-litigated, and heftily priced device failure that hit an entire category of medical products (and medical device manufacturers) is the recent class action taken against synthetic mesh-based surgical implants for pelvic organ prolapse and incontinence mitigation in women (Kuhlmann-Capek et al. 2015; Brown et al. 2016). In brief (and perhaps over-simplified for our purposes here) these implants, many months to years after implantation, eroded through adjacent soft tissues and allegedly caused late-term pain, infections, and follow-up reconstructive surgeries to be needed in many patients. Tens of millions of dollars were awarded to many plaintiffs based on their pain and suffering and claims of negligence by the manufacturers (not the doctors or hospitals or payers, mind you, but more on this shortly).

Could this "black eye" on the medical device industry have been avoided with ethical analysis implemented early and often throughout the entire PLM? Consider the early design engineering team selecting synthetic polymer meshes already in widespread use in medicine for other purposes. They would think it both logical, from a supply and manufacturing perspective, to choose one of these meshes and reasonable, from the perspective of the patient, that the proven biocompatibility and non-immunogenicity of these meshes would be something they, the patients, would see as a benefit (principle of beneficence). Had this same design team considered the principle of non-maleficence more thoroughly, could they not have sought perspectives of both patients and surgeons on what failure modes might be unacceptable? What frequency of those failure modes, if any, would be considered tolerable? And what different design criteria, implantation technique, or patient selection criteria might have mitigated some of these risks? Could the design team, considering the principle of respect for patient autonomy, not have required that all their pelvic organ prolapse products be distributed with a patient-directed information brochure about the risks of these products in these surgeries? Could the design team, focused on justice for society, not have delved deeper into the history of medical implants to see that erosion and infection in this anatomical location is not only well-described for other surgical implants since removed from the market but also had a history of being particularly damaging to the patient?

Let's consider the perspective of the surgeons in these cases. They understand the anatomy of this location and how the physiology is supposed to work, but do they think they have been adequately trained (respect for autonomy) in the implantation of foreign objects in this part of the anatomy? Or fully trained on the materials within a particular device or possible quirks of the implantation procedure specific to the device they selected? If they practice in a hospital where device selection is limited (based on cost or other considerations), do they feel they or their patients are being justly served by only having one or two devices to choose from for this particular purpose? In parallel, does the surgeon feel that his or her experience with device A would be much more beneficial for that patient than using device B but acquiesces to the payer for that patient who will only pay for device B?

Although many other stakeholders could be examined, let's finally consider in this case the perspective of the company's post-market follow-up and complaint handling team. Rules and regulations in many countries are very clear that complaints must be broadly and openly accepted, actively investigated, and appropriately reported to the regulatory bodies. Yet it is becoming increasingly expected and even required that complaints be folded back into review of product design, product risk, and potential design changes that may be justified base on real-world feedback. Thus, could the post-market team have furthered the examination of patient beneficence by periodic recalculation of risk versus benefit to patients and perhaps informed the design team earlier that these failures were a problem? Could they not have considered risk to the company (in terms of respect for autonomy or non-maleficence) more thoroughly and started a process to warn patients or surgeons more proactively? Could they not have suggested to the clinical team, based on the principle of justice or beneficence, that a study be undertaken to better define the patient cohort likely to have the best outcomes?[2] This example is a late-stage problem for a medical device that potentially could have been avoided, and there are also many cases where early stage failures, often in the form of not bringing a device to market, could have been avoided and made a real difference in patients' lives.

An example is the hypothetical case of tissue-engineered, pediatric heart valves as described by Merryman (2008). In this case study, the design team has the option of offering a less expensive, higher failure rate, more widely available valve design or a more expensive, extremely low failure rate, very exclusive design. Business, legal, and even regulatory arguments can be made for which design to select, but from the more holistic point of view of the four ethical principles, which valve is the right one? Based on the constraints presented in this case, one possible argument might be that the more widely available one could positively impact the lives of many more children, and its beneficence outweighs its potential maleficence. Yet with today's changing societal norms trending towards more and more risk-aversion in medical care, the balance in this case may be tipped towards the more exclusive design that can at least treat a few wealthy or well-insured kids. This concept of societal norms affecting ethics choices is the next part of this discussion.

25.4 How Do Societal Changes Influence Next-Generation Medical Device PLM?

We live in a rapidly evolving technological society wherein our expectations of "quality of life" are constantly changing, yet we all expect that healthcare will be allocated in a just way. Societal pressures in the form of population growth, technological advancement, and fiscal cost containment (among others) create an ever-changing environment in which ethical engineers and medical device companies must work.

The very nature of the Information Age has brought our society an overwhelming glut of data. We can track our fitness and activity data, exact food and caloric intake, physical health and testing parameters (such as blood glucose monitoring), and even get personal genetic testing done. Medical devices often play a key role in obtaining, analyzing, and reporting these data. Patients can benefit immensely from such new technologies, and they have the potential to add immense utility to society as a whole. Yet each of these personal information sources has the potential to be abused in such ways as sedentary lifestyle stratification by insurers, body habitus screening by potential employers, or genetic discrimination by government program managers. Thus, medical device designers must consider that if their devices generate data from the patients they are used on or in, how might that data be used? What controls will be designed in to better assure data privacy? What options will the patient, the doctor, or the hospital have for capturing, modifying, deleting, or disseminating such data? Furthermore, it is often in the purview of device designers to not only answer these questions for the device design itself, but also determine how best to train or educate the users, patients, and other stakeholders that might have access to these data.

The very nature of training on *how* to use a medical device, rather than *what* function the device performs, is often the source of subsequent litigation around medical devices, and public perceptions about risk tolerance and who is at fault can and do change with time (*Consumer Reports*, 2012). A common example is what is known as off-label use of a medical device. Doctors, under the protection of the "practice of medicine," are freely permitted to choose to use a hernia repair material for closure of the dura mater around the brain, even though the two applications have very different design requirements and the subsequently designed devices for each application are typically dramatically different. If the patient who received this misused device suffers a severe adverse event, who is at fault? Who does the family sue for pain and suffering? In the past, the doctor was often perceived as infallible, or nearly so, and nowadays the hospital or even the device manufacturer might be found at fault, especially if the use can be linked to some form of off-label promotion to the doctor, patient, or both by either party. Although this is an almost absurdly stark example of device misuse, consider the less obvious but otherwise similar case of a hernia repair device designed for an adult used as a hernia repair device in a child. This is often the norm today, but it is becoming clearer that regulators, payers, and litigators alike are more often considering pediatric use as off-label use (if the device wasn't specifically designed and tested as such). Further, geriatric use and use in the surgical oncology patient or use in the infected field patient are all examples of where patient cohort or demographic may be used to stratify on-label versus off-label designations. Thus, the medical device designer must consider all the beneficence and non-maleficence aspects of device designs as well as their likely potential off-label uses with the justice to society that might suffer if no devices are available for pediatric use or the autonomy of the doctor that is often reduced by label restrictions.

Another societal aspect of healthcare change is cost containment, and the device designer must consider how to balance reasonable costs for a medical device versus broad access of the device to patients in need. When drug-eluting stents for coronary artery disease first came on the market, there was a race to get them into the hands of physicians to treat patients almost irrespective of cost. Today it is fairly clear that the small differences in efficacy between device types don't often offset the differences in cost, and the product that can provide the best "overall value" is the one chosen by providers. In fact, "providers" in the form of hospital buying groups via contracts or "providers" in the form of third-party payers via coverage decisions quite often narrow the scope of device choice for physicians and patients alike. Once again, medical device designers must question the true beneficence of a device (besides its economic viability for the company) if no one can get it.

25.5 Bringing Ethical Innovation to the Fore

Perhaps two of the most important aspects of ethical innovation for next generation of medical devices involve (1) balancing marketing claims about what a device should do (or is anticipated to do) in terms of harms and benefits with actual device design and (2) balancing what society and medical practitioners want to pay for a therapy or diagnostic with reasonable design implementations. The former is predominantly about effectiveness and respect for autonomy, while the latter is mostly about efficiency and justice.

Designing a device and getting regulatory approval for it are often long, arduous processes that include clinical trials and bench testing studies. These studies have to be well designed to provide evidence to support claims to be made about a device's utility. Ultimately, this evidence is needed to convince doctors to use and payers to pay for a product; but more than that, it is needed to respect the autonomy of these stakeholders to make their own decisions about what is right for the patient. The marketing function of a company tries to position the product in the minds of the customers in a way that makes them desire to have it for their patients, yet it is only just that the claims marketing is making are based in truth and can be supported from the evidence available. Thus, it ultimately falls back on the design team to validate that their design not only meets design inputs but also their process for gaining market approval collects all the most important aspects of evidence for communicating to the stakeholders.

Designing a device to be cost-effective means making sure that materials selected, manufacturing processes used, clinical trial lengths and patient numbers collected, and markets chosen for deployment all align with what the medical system expects to pay for a "disease solution." In fact it is often competing devices or other disease solutions that dictate the economic boundaries that are acceptable. A recent example is the drug–device combination product called

Epi-Pen that is in the news for questions about the manufacturer's pricing practices. Without introducing details about this particular case, it is worth discussing
that companies often get tied up in pricing a product based on "what the market
will bear" versus pricing it for a reasonable profit. Clearly the latter approach is
more consistent with the principle of justice for more stakeholders involved
and allows the treatment of patients while keeping a product on the market.

As society appears to become more risk-averse and regulations seem to become
more arduous, it is also worth emphasizing that these things drive up costs of
development and push solutions to diseases for smaller markets further from
reality. In fact, the medical system as a whole needs to address incentives through
legislative or regulatory channels to encourage companies to develop products
that will meet the needs (provide medical justice) of some of these under-served
populations; and they can still do so with some assurance that the system will
actually buy the product, if proven reasonably effective. In their post-market
phase of device PLM, companies can make the effort to communicate how these
things might be achieved to the regulatory bodies and their legislative communication channels so that next-generation products can benefit. A coherent and
comprehensive approach to ethical analysis applied early and iteratively throughout the process of design and development will facilitate a transformation for
effective and ethical innovation.

25.6 Paradigms of Practice, Education, and Training in Engineering Ethics

If the goal of medical device design, development, and delivery is ethical (safe,
effective, and fair) innovation for improved patient care, then the complexity of
ethical issues surrounding medical device PLM demands an effort towards ethical
analysis that is much more robust and sustained. Safe and effective is clearly an
inadequately low bar for ethical innovation. Of course, ethical innovation is not
the only goal of medical device PLM and, perhaps, not even the primary goal.
Therefore, a wider set of stakeholder values must be considered as essential to the
process and a more comprehensive and rigorous training in ethics analysis
implemented for a significant transformation of ethical innovation and PLM.

Stakeholder values are the normative commitments and perspectives of all
those involved in the complex processes of achieving clinical implementation
of medical devices. These varied values and perspectives reflect a multitude of
distinct lenses through which problems, processes, and outcomes are viewed. Yet
leaders in these processes tend to rely on a narrow set of tools, including codes of
ethics, regulatory frameworks, responsible conduct of research guidelines, and
good manufacturing protocols, as sufficient controls for ethical innovation.
Clearly these paradigms and protocols are not sufficient. Even less so are the

training approaches dependent on these limited paradigms or the traditional philosophical ethical theories approaches despite being each widely adopted in academic training programs. So it is not surprising that the medical device industry has continued to experience significant and costly failures due not only to the external pressures of efficiency, access to resources, and insufficient analysis, but also often to insufficient approaches to ethical analysis in PLM.

25.7 Insufficiency of Codes of Ethics

For example, codes of ethics are regularly developed and implemented by professionals whose experience and placement as leaders in the profession put them in a position to oversee ethical innovation and implementation. However, in the medical device industry perhaps there are only four codes that have any direct relevance to PLM in the field, from the following societies: the Advanced Medical Technology Association (AdvaMed), the Medical Device Manufacturers Association (MDMA), the International Medical Device Manufacturers Association (IMEDA), and the Biomedical Engineering Society (BMES). And although there is some guidance for creating a code of ethics provided by Regulatory Affairs Professional Society consultants (Van Buskirk & Andresen, 2008) the checklist fails to provide any insights into the level of comprehensive and rigorous ethical analysis necessary for ethical innovation and implementation in the full PLM. Further, relevant codes that *do* exist are relevant to a specific context of profession and time. As such, they are prone to becoming static – reactive to ethical concerns out of which they were developed in the first place rather than proactive to the developing and potentially novel ethical contexts in which the members of that profession work. Still, knowledge of one's current professional code of ethics is an essential starting place and has practical appeal. Especially for those new to the profession, codes of ethics offer guidelines by which to identify what really matters to the profession. They are, as such, signposts by which the new professional can orient their decisions and behavior. Alignment with the values and best practices described by codes of ethics identifies the individual as a member of the professional organization.

Engineering ethicist Michael Davis has voiced the importance of codes of ethics as conventions for engineering professionals (Davis, 1991, p. 153). Yet he also recognizes the limitations of codes of ethics: the engineer has "professional responsibilities" that extend beyond that code (Davis, 1991, p. 166). Codes of ethics play that important framing role, but are easily overwhelmed either by competing pressures to act against them or by higher normative standards set by other value frameworks. To the former claim, Spielthenner (2015) has recently argued that there are only a few reasons to adhere to a code of ethics that hold up to critique: sanction-based reasons (p. 199), fairness-based reasons (p. 199), and promise-based reasons (p. 200). So, "there *are* reasons for *complying* with an ethical code, even though they may, on occasion, be rather weak and easily overridden by reasons for deviating from it" (p. 202). Yet even in these cases, he argues, "ethical codes do not inevitably yield reasons for action" (p. 201). To the latter claim, Davis identifies the position codes of ethics play in the broader landscape of value commitments and notes: "But the code would, of course, have to be examined to see whether it actually set standards higher than law, market, and morality would otherwise require" (Davis, 2001a, p. 383). Thus, codes of ethics are limited as normative standards and as guides to actual action in complex situations: not a strong start.

And beyond these problems threatening the useful work of codes of ethics, the very nature of rules and guidelines mark additional concerns. Geoffrey Rush's character Captain Barbossa in Pirates of the Caribbean (2003), said it best after Elizabeth Turner cites the Code of the Order of the Brethren in an effort to be returned to shore: "the code is more what you'd call 'guidelines' than actual rules." The nature of guidelines is peculiar: while many take codes of ethics to offer rules for action, they instead offer "guidelines" in Barbossa's sense.

As Davis noted in an essay about myths concerning codes of ethics, "One feature all three myths seem to have in common is a failure to acknowledge how central interpretation is to the use of codes of ethics. Why this failure? The answer, it seems to me, is that those who rely on these myths lack training in a discipline in which interpretation of rules is a central activity, as it is in law and certain religious vocations" (Davis, 2001b, p. 22). Such myths are still evident in recent literature. A recent response article by Özdemire et al. (2015) voices three complaints about a code of ethics for ethicists: (1) that it might transform ethical practice into a mere "check-the-box" exercise; (2) that it creates a false sense of security for practitioners; and (3) that it isolates practitioners from broader moral obligations" (p. 64). Here, explicitly, are examples of failures to acknowledge the role of interpretation.

Indeed, Davis believes that this confusion about the nature of guidelines (namely, that they mark out actionable rules rather than interpretable guidelines) is the reason many engineering ethics educators ultimately reject codes-based approaches (Davis, 2001b, p. 11). But, then, if we accept the necessity of interpretation of codes of ethics, they lose some of the conceptual solidity and actionability that have set them up as potential guides to ethical analysis within the PLM process. Such limitations make codes of ethics insufficient tools on which to rely when making ethical decisions about complex problems like those found in the context of biomedical device PLM.

25.7.1 Insufficiency of Regulations

Regulatory oversight is an essential strategy regularly employed to guide both ethical decision-making and ethical action in medical device PLM. Yet, like code-based approaches, reliance on regulatory oversight is likewise insufficient for making ethical decisions in many of the complex scenarios of actual medical product development and clinical implementation. Thinking otherwise – that regulatory oversight is sufficient to guide ethical practice – is tantamount to passing the buck: shifting the focus of responsibility from the wide range of decision-makers to the regulatory entities. Indeed, making ethical analysis part of one's professional responsibility is made perhaps more difficult by the existence of oversight structures like federal regulation.

The Medical Device R&D Handbook includes a one-page caveat against taking ethical shortcuts, admonishing the entrepreneur to "fly coach on business trips, but ensure that you are always flying first class when it comes to ethics" (Kucklick, 2012, p. 456). That page of advice goes on to suggest avoiding actions that you might not want to defend in front of a hostile reporter on *60 Minutes* or that may make for a good parody on *The Simpsons*. It concludes that further good advice on maintaining an ethical image can be garnered from angel investor groups and industry conferences (Kucklick, 2012, p. 456). Evident in this seemingly naive advice is that ethics is the sort of thing that, without caution, can bind you up in the otherwise unconstrained process of device design and implementation. Avoid upsetting regulators or offending a hostile public, and you're doing ethical work. Regulations – on some views, like codes – are the sorts of external, in this case legal, constraints one must avoid in an otherwise anything-goes arena of entrepreneurial activity. That arena of entrepreneurship is driven by economic values. Economic concerns (like avoiding risk and maximizing return on investment) might easily trump ethical concerns, given the size and strength of external forces pushing on the ability of the device designer to think and act critically – and ethically.

Considering these legal and economic constraints, regulatory oversight faces many of the same additional challenges to sufficiency as do codes of ethics. At one end of a spectrum, regulations are developed and enacted as responses to already-existing ethical challenges. And at the other end of the spectrum, regulations *ought* to be developed to fend off further negative consequences of design, development, and delivery in emerging contexts. Regulation of stem cell-related research is a good example of the reactive end of the spectrum. While stem cells were first used therapeutically in bone marrow transplants in 1968 (Halme & Kessler, 2006, p. 1730), Food and Drug Administration (FDA) regulation of research involving stem cells was initialized only in the early 2000s (Halme & Kessler, 2006, p. 1735 citations). Growing societal concerns about manipulation and ownership of human cellular materials alongside technological advances in the scientist's ability to make those manipulations realities drove this regulation.

An example at the other end of the spectrum is the recent call for regulations to be developed to certify or control the development of healthcare apps as medical devices, of which there are currently more than 40,000 on the market with little quality control or oversight in place to protect consumers or patients (Boulos et al., 2014). Another example is the relatively recent interest in the FDA to recognize and regulate software in and as a medical device (Fries 2012, p. 118). For contemporary emerging issues like healthcare apps or device software, regulation lags behind and is insufficient as a guide to making related ethical decisions. Further, regulation of devices in the United States has focused on the quality of the device itself but has neglected, in large measure, issues of the interface between device and patient (Banta & van Beekum, 1990) – another potential shortcoming.

25.7.2 Insufficiency of Responsible Conduct of Research Rules

Much of the early stage of medical device life cycle management has its origins in the world of academia, a world with its own value perspective and frameworks to guide ethical decisions. Novel technology research, design, and development for potential clinical applications often have origins in interdisciplinary and frequently entrepreneurial academic teams. These activities and individuals are governed at the institutional level by frameworks for ethical practice described as responsible conduct of research (RCR) practices. The frameworks of RCR scaffolds with regulatory and code-based approaches to further weaken the capacity of device designers to sustain ethical innovation – as will now be shown.

RCR practices are a set of clearly defined areas in which ethical (or unethical) action might occur in research settings. The federal Office of Research Integrity outlines these areas in terms of the stages of research practice: planning research, conducting research, and reporting research (Steneck, 2007). In each stage of the research process, from planning, to conducting, to reporting, ethical issues arise. Each of the central areas of RCR is ethically rich: there are better and worse ways we can uphold them and both ethical and unethical actions we might take in regard to them. Regulations intersect with and, indeed, define RCR practices for any federally funded research. The origins of these federal regulations are egregious cases of research misconduct (Steneck, 2007). The work of specification of the meaning of these responsible conduct practices is done at disciplinary levels: even within the various engineering subdisciplines engaged in biomedical device design and development, these meanings might vary. RCR adds an ethical perspective on top of existing procedural components of scientific research (Tuana, 2013, p. 1961): a band-aid over the injuries of unethical practice without addressing the underlying conditions. Efforts to overcome problems of abstraction and inadequacy have driven contemporary RCR research to greater and greater levels of codification. As Stankovic and Stankovic argue, "Through the medium of research misconduct, the institutions of science are being driven toward a more rigid and formal structure reflecting that of legal institutions. The result of this profound and foreign formalization will likely alter the conduct of research – and the practice of medicine – forever" (2014, p. 541).

More generally, practical and normative conflicts among value perspectives involved in device design and development challenge effective communication regarding complex ethical decisions. Thus, mixed-mode strategies of ethical analysis have been proposed for their apparent ability to identify and communicate diverse positions and normative perspectives, asking students to take the perspectives of members of professional, regulatory, academic, and industry stakeholders (see Martin, Rayne, Kemp, Hart, & Diller, 2005). Yet, such approaches also are prone to failure specifically because biomedical engineers have neither the expertise nor the time to develop the expertise to sufficiently take on those diverse perspectives. For example, offering an overview of regulatory issues involving stem cells in one section of a single lecture is hardly sufficient to develop relevant expertise for ethical analysis (Martin et al., 2005, p. 265). Perspective taking is important for identification of ethical issues, but insufficient for making decisions regarding them.

The innovative design and clinical implementation of medical devices takes place within a complex landscape of divergent value perspectives. All those involved in PLM strategies to design and implement in an ethically responsible manner must understand and negotiate this complex value landscape carefully. Thus, given this complexity, an effective approach to ethical analysis has not been widely adopted in the medical device industry or by programs training the next generation of medical device engineers.

25.8 Considering Ethical Analysis Methods As Potential Tools for Medical Device PLM

As we have emphasized and as some clinicians have recently reminded us, there is still a significant "gap in the safeguards and protections for and oversight of patients involved in the innovative procedures and implementation of medical devices" (Geiger & Hirschl, 2015, p. 117) Despite the urging of agencies in the United States and European Union to technology innovators to involve a broader set of potential stakeholders, including the general public, in the process of ethically developing new technologies, Beekman and Brom (2007) recognized almost ten years ago that methods to consider critical ethical concerns and effectively dialogue were not available. Since then a number of methods for deliberately enhancing ethical analysis have been under development and several are compared here. If we are to consider these methods for use in medical device PLM then on what basis can we compare these various methods to determine if they are in fact *safe, effective, and just* themselves?

One view is that the methods of analysis of ethical issues in technology innovation, development, and implementation should "act as deliberative structures for systematic engagement with ethical issues" (Beekman & Brom, 2007,

p. 3). These methods or tools should support effective ethical analysis by including multiple aspects of analysis. Two critical aspects are:

1. Effective identification of, engagement with, and explicit and clear communication about the diverse and divergent values and perspectives of all stakeholders
2. Systematic and thorough reflection and reasoning about these complex issues.

Reasoning about ethics issues in medical device development cannot be solely about the impact or consequences of implementation but rather needs to evaluate ethical considerations at all stages of product life cycle, including the earliest stages of initial conceptual design and market analysis, to determine the ethics of the various pathways to innovation or even the decision to innovate at all in a particular market space. Effective methods of ethics analysis of medical device development will support deep deliberation that requires recognizing and regarding the diverse and often divergent value perspectives of a pluralistic global society. Therefore, identifying, specifying, and balancing divergent values must be part of an effective method of ethics analysis, reasoning, and eventual decision-making. Finally, it is desired that effective methods would be tested and demonstrated to be safe; for example, to reduce the bias and tunnel vision often found in "innovation ignorance" that can lead to such epic failures as described early in the chapter. While such ignorance can be "a powerful stimulant for creativity and innovation" (Tjan, 2010), it rarely leads directly to successful and ethical medical device development. Rather, the intense creativity must be further enhanced by the essential ethical design and development constraints that become drivers of even greater innovation. The methods of ethics analysis that elucidate current and potential future complexities and challenges should provide innovators and device developers with clear understanding of these drivers.

25.9 Considering Ethical Analysis Frameworks and Methods from Other Fields

In 2000 Mepham proposed a framework for ethical analysis within the agricultural biotechnology innovation space that has been applied more broadly in recent years. The Ethical Matrix method is a tool to evaluate intersection of three normative principles – respect for well-being, autonomy, and justice – with four relevant stakeholder interest groups – the treated organisms, producers, consumers, and biota or environment (Mepham, 2000). The applicability to medical device development could be imagined with application of the same important principles to the relevant stakeholder interest groups of patients, medical device companies, clinicians, and hospitals; and the environment of regulatory, economic, sustainability, and societal concerns and agencies.[3]

In 2007 Millar and colleagues published their application of the classic Delphi Method to ethics analysis as a tool for use in the debates in the European Union about innovations of food biotechnology (Millar et al., 2007). Tools for ethics analysis such as the Ethical Dephi were being developed in order to support broad-based dialogue and particularly effective policy debates that were attempting to guide ethical and effective implementation of novel biotechnologies. More recently in the European Union, philosophers, technology innovators, and consultants have been working together to develop a number of new methods for assessing the social and ethical impact of developing technologies (Wright, 2011; Boenink, Cuijpers, van der Laan, van Lente, & Moors, 2011; Brey, 2012). Wright (2011) has presented a framework for assessment of ethical impact in the emerging information technology space that has special considerations for ethical issues of privacy and data security, both of which are now central concerns in the medical device industry as well. Wright's Ethical Impact Assessment (EAI) method is a complex analysis process based on established questions for introducing consideration under five categories of issues defined by the four principles of biomedical principlism and the addition of privacy and data protection as a separate category. The method then suggests application of a series of other tools for ethics analysis as procedures for additional value appraisal. These include: consultations and surveys, expert workshops, citizen panels, and consensus conference, along with the aforementioned Ethical Matrix and Ethical Dephi tools.

The assessment process of Boenink and colleagues (2011) expanded the list of potential methods for analyzing the social impact of biotechnology innovations particularly in the medical realm. They proposed three steps to assess such potential social and ethical impacts:

1. Analyzing all the underlying concepts inherent in the technology
2. I Imagining a range of possible scenarios involving implantation of the technology
3. Deliberating with a wide range of relevant stakeholders about their perspectives on the technology in light of these concepts and scenarios.

This three-step assessment could have important applications in medical device development especially with completely novel technologies in very early stages of design conceptualization.

Brey (2012) builds on this idea of imagining and anticipating ethical issues with a new method for ethics analysis of new technology development and early introduction. Anticipatory Technology Ethics (ATE) is designed to use forecasting as a tool to deal with the inherent problem of uncertainty in technology development, especially during the research and early development stages. This forecasting approach is intended to surpass the more standard ethics analysis of generic issues that have been previously identified as critical to the development of certain types and genres of technologies. While such analysis is essential for successful and ethical introduction of a new technology, it tends to be more conservative and limited, and thus can often miss critical ethical and social impact issues that are unanticipated or emergent with the novel technology. Such unanticipated ethical impacts have often caused novel technologies to fail after widespread market deployment. Brey's ATE approach involves consideration of potential future uses and impacts with a broader scope that is more liberal and imaginative. The method attempts to surpass the weaknesses he finds in prior methodologies by expanding the ethical analysis through distinguishing three levels: technology, artifact, and application (Brey, 2010, 2012). Brey proposes that discrimination of three levels for ethical analysis is more comprehensive and that identifying *normative* ethical issues that *should be* relevant to the future concerns rather than *potential* ethical concerns that *would likely be* relevant should make this method more effective than previous ethical forecasting methods. However, how do we determine which if any of these widely varying methods and tools for ethics assessment and reasoning are best suited to the practices of medical device development and PLM?

In the realm of health technologies, Saarni, Braunack-Mayer, Hofmann, and van der Wilt (2011) have compared several methods for ethics analysis and evaluated their effectiveness on the basis of the range of arguments identified by each method. In this empirical study four methods or frameworks for ethics analysis – casuistry, axiology, principlism, and a new health technology assessment (HTA) model from the EU called EUnetHTA – were applied to the emerging medical technology of bariatric surgery for obesity and compared. Bariatric surgery, while shown to be effective in reducing obesity for individuals, does not resolve the underlying causes of obesity on either an individual or societal level and thus presents several ethical complexities for wide adoption. Each ethics analysis method was applied by a researcher experienced with the specific approach and the results compared. The study by Saarni et al. concluded that the different methods all were successful in identifying the key thematic issues and a range of relevant stakeholders related to implementation of the technology. However, based on the number of specific arguments provided by each method the axiological and EUnetHTA models provided a larger number, while casuistry and principlism focused on a deeper analysis of the most critical arguments. While we would agree with the conclusion of these authors that "the systematic and transparent use of some method of ethics [analysis] appears more important than the choice of the exact method" (Saarni et al., 2011, p. 305) we would argue that establishing an effective method of choice, or a combination of several, that can be widely and consistently utilized in the medical device industry is necessary for engineering more safe, effective, and ethical devices for the future and thus engineering a better society.

As new methods and specific tools have been developed for ethical analysis it has become clear that no single method is likely to be most effective for "a full assessment of the whole range of divergent ethical issues involved in the introduction and application of new technologies" (Beekman & Brom, 2007, p. 8). So perhaps an ideal practice for a medical device company is to make available and encourage the use of several effective methods in a toolbox of techniques for ethics analysis. Medical device innovators and developers can be trained on all the methods and encouraged to select the most appropriate depending on the focus of the analysis. We propose that RP is one of those effective methods of ethics analysis that aligns especially well with the practice of medical device PLM. We discuss this method as a process for effective ethical deliberation and decision-making and its alignment in more detail in Section 25.10.

25.10 Considering the Approach of RP

RP is an approach to ethics education and training that has been developed, applied, and tested specifically with biomedical engineers (Kisselburgh et al., 2014). RP utilizes the ethical analysis framework of biomedical principlism based on four principles of common morality: *beneficence, non-maleficence, respect for autonomy*, and *justice*.[4] The approach of principle-based ethics, in contrast to theory-based or case-based approaches to ethical analysis, starts from that set of common, mid-level, ethical guidelines (principles). These principles, which are not limited by reference to any particular case or theoretical constraint, are then examined *in situ* within the particular context of an ethical analysis in order to fully explore the reasoning space of the complex ethical issues involved. RP complements this foundational framework of core principles with a staged and iterative process of ethical analysis that includes identification, specification, balancing, justification, and coherence in a continued process of reflective inquiry between codes and cases (Beever & Brightman, 2016). Thus, *reflective* inquiry and analysis becomes *reflexive* through repeated practice with multiple applications to a set of complex cases of ethical consideration in specific contexts. The framework of four principles and the structured, scaffolded, and staged process with a set of multiple example cases has been shown to be a powerful tool to develop rich dialogue among diverse stakeholder perspectives for a more thorough analysis and more effective training for skill in ethical analysis.

The four principles framework central to the ethical analysis approach of RP covers a broad scope of common moral concerns relevant to the process of medical device development, and especially to the engineering aspects. The primary goal of common morality, "to promote human flourishing by counteracting conditions that cause the quality of people's lives to worsen" (Beauchamp, 2007, p. 7), aligns well with the goals and intents of the medical device industry. The primary goal of common morality also fits well with statements of the goals of the practice and profession of engineering – for example, "Engineering is the creative application of scientific principles used to plan, build, direct, guide, manage, or work on systems to maintain and improve our daily lives" (NSPE.org, 2014). In addition, this framework of four principles is situated in a reflective process that allows the particular rules and potential practical guides for action to be derived and refined over time from those shared higher-order principles as the medical device industry and the society it aims to serve continue to change.

Starting from these shared moral principles, decision-makers in medical device PLM can more accurately assess and consider the values and perspectives of a broad range of stakeholders relevant to the ethical issues and complexities. The four principles can be specified by the details of a particular case through direct or indirect or even imagined interactions with various diverse value perspectives. Beauchamp describes this function of specification as a process that "adds content to abstract principles, ridding them of their indeterminateness and providing action-guiding content for the purpose of coping with complex cases" (Beauchamp, 2011, p. 301). The process involves narrowing the scope of applicability and placing the principle within the constraints of a specific context (e.g., What does justice mean in this case? And to whom does it have relevant impact? To what extent does it apply?). These context-specific applications of moral principles may differ between professions and among unique cases. However, this level of ethical understanding with specific contextual application has been shown to enhance the ethical sensitivity and judgment of professionals about appropriate ethical action in novel cases (Rest, Narvaez, Bebeau, & Thoma, 1999).

The process of continued reflection is centrally important to the approach of principlism. Seen as an ongoing process of inquiry, principles-based ethical analysis requires each individual agent, either working alone or together in design and decision-making teams, to engage in iterative stages of reflection about the specification of norms, their relationships, and the outcomes they prescribe. This iterative reflective approach to analyzing ethics concerns clearly has applicability to engineering ethics; since the professional practice and ethic of the engineer is tied to the specifics of a particular situation or design and development problem. The principlist approach helps us work together to more clearly define and then apply insights of reason, balanced judgments, and common intuitions as necessary components of ethical analysis in the engineering context. As the engineering team gains expertise through repeated practice of this process, some of this reflection will become intuitive, or reflexive. Thus, our goal is a *reflexive* not merely *reflective* principlism.

The principles-based methodology to ethical analysis in ethics aligns well with the analytic processes and ethical needs of the professional engineering ethics; much like it does with professional biomedical ethics, helping justify, cohere, and expand ethical concepts already at work like public health, safety, and welfare. To get at this point about the role of process-based thinking, here is a short video to share with you: https://youtu.be/oaEgOwDDYB0. RP can also play an important role in helping medical device engineers dialogue and debate complex ethical issues with a diverse range of stakeholders – from those on their development teams with differing disciplines and backgrounds, to those external constituents who play a large role in determining the applicability and eventual approval and adoption of a new technology. Using the four principles of common morality as shared points of reference should allow deeper and more meaningful dialogue across a broader range of participants in the conversation around the social impact and ethical viability of innovations. The shared reference points should allow and encourage all stakeholders to engage more fully and contribute more clearly to the critical process of specification of the important ethical issues. This should open space for engineers to better understand the complexity of ethical issues that arise both directly and indirectly from their medical device development work. Thus, RP could offer a means of responsible and effective communication about professional ethics in the face of emerging new ethical issues and a growing spectrum of stakeholders with diverse and divergent value perspectives. This approach to ethical analysis has broad potential for application to both new and emerging technologies in medical device industry. We believe that the RP approach would elucidate broader and more effective reasoning in such areas as novel approaches to robotic surgery (Geiger & Hirschl, 2015) and Tissue Engineered Constructs (Lu et al., 2015). A new area of medical device technology where such an approach has been considered is human cognitive enhancement (HCE) and neuroethics.

25.11 Applying RP to an Emerging Area of Medical Devices: Neuromodulation Technologies

An example for application of ethical analysis with a principlism framework is explored here with the potential of novel technologies for neuromodulation of the human brain that are being rapidly developed. A range of electrical stimulation and measurement technologies are being improved for a wider range of applications to diagnosing and treating mental illnesses and to analyzing and stimulating different mental states. Herein, the potential for serious ethical challenges are rising. Neuroscientists and neuroengineers are creating an advanced ability to alter both the functional and phenomenal properties of the human brain. This advanced ability to study and manipulate in a fine-grained systematic approach is gaining us access to altering human experience. As we better understand the neural correlates of experience and thus the content of consciousness and mental states researchers must consider in parallel the ethical issues related to such potential for control (*respect for autonomy and beneficence*) and commercialization (*non-maleficence and justice*) that go well beyond the concerns for safety and effectiveness.

The possibility that new neurotechnologies will provide the ability to alter or even create sensory as well as emotional experiences is already at hand (see papers at Open Mind Project, http://open-mind.net/, in particular Singer, 2015). It appears that the ability to alter higher level properties of the human consciousness such as experiences of agency and will are not far off. Once these minimally sufficient correlates of human experiential states are identified and the potential for neuromodulation proven, there will be a demand to exploit them on a clinical or even commercial level. Developing and distributing these technological abilities would have direct implications for respect for autonomy and for non-maleficence. However, a coherent and common understanding of consciousness, agency, and will are not yet readily forthcoming and thus ethical analysis of these issues in neuroethics has been limited. Such coherence of understanding might not be possible at the deepest philosophical levels; however, some coherence will be necessary for neuroscientists and neuroengineers to grapple with the ethical implications and impact of their research and potential translation of technologies.

We suggest that analyzing the potential for new risks and harms from manipulating the content of consciousness (state, experience, agency, and will) is imperative. We also propose that utilizing a framework of the four principles would provide for an effective process and dialogue between the researchers, engineers, clinicians, and other non-technical stakeholders that are essential to ethical progress in research, development, and clinical practice of such emerging and novel neuromodulation technologies. Hofmann (2017) reported on an attempt to develop an effective method for analyzing the ethical issues related to HCE technologies. He emphasized that there remains a critical need "to expose and elucidate the relevant ethical issues" related to such emerging technologies. We agree and argue that there is also a critical need to carry out these processes in dialogue with a wide range of relevant stakeholders with diverse and often divergent value perspectives in order to fully expose and elucidate the issues. Principlism provides an effective framework for such dialogic analyses by focusing on specification of the mid-level normative principles of common morality as starting points. However strong the potential for success appears in theory and in testing, real-world testing of the ethical analysis framework and process of RP within actual medical device development and PLM needs to occur. Validation of this tool as effective and safe within the intended use arena of medical device development awaits the reports of successful application from further testing in industry. We invite this testing and especially the subsequent critical feedback to engineering educators for modifications that will improve the effectiveness of training of new engineers in ethical professional practice.

25.12 Conclusion

The medical device industry and the engineering colleges that supply it with new engineers is facing a dilemma between the need for integrated ethical analysis to stave off failure and the often insufficient preparation of engineers working within that design and development process. Currently, ethical analysis and decision-making in PLM are primarily guided by the industry codes of ethics and federal regulations that represent the wisdom gathered by industry and government from years of practical experience. However, emerging technologies being developed and rapidly changing values perspectives on those next-generation technologies are creating challenging situations where ethical analysis based on codes and regulations are not adequate for decision-making. In this situation, we have argued, an effective framework for ethical analysis is critically needed. We proposed that ethical analysis based on the process of RP could serve as an effective guide to decision-making for development of the next-generation medical devices.

We conclude that real-world testing of the ethical analysis framework and process of RP for actual cases of medical device development and PLM needs to occur to offer empirical support for our argument here. Such a successful process validation could ensure that RP can indeed help enable safe and effective medical device development. With this in mind the authors invite testing of our proposal by medical device companies. We also encourage these industry partners to provide critical feedback about potential modifications to RP that will improve the effectiveness of training of new engineers in ethical professional practice.

References

AdvaMed.org. (2016). Code of Ethics. Retrieved from www.advamed.org/issues/code-ethics/code-ethics.

Banta, H. D., & van Beekum, W. T. (1990). The regulation of medical devices and quality of medical care. *Quality Assurance in Health Care. 2*(2), 127–136.

Beauchamp, T. L., & Childress, J. F. (2013[1979]). *Principles of biomedical ethics, Seventh Edition*. New York, NY: Oxford University Press.

Beauchamp, T. L. (2011). Making principlism practical: A commentary on Gordon, Rauprich, and Vollman. *Bioethics 25*(6), 301–303.

Beauchamp, T. L. (2007). The four principles approach to health care ethics. In R. E. Ashcroft, A. Dawson, H. Draper, & J. R. McMillan (Eds.), *Principles of health care ethics* (2nd edition, pp.3–10. New York, NY: Wiley.

Beekman, V., Brom, & F. W. (2007). Ethical tools to support systematic public deliberations about the ethical aspects of agricultural biotechnologies. *Journal of Agricultural and Environmental Ethics, 20*(1), 3–12.

Beever, J., & Brightman, A. O. (2016). Reflexive principlism as an effective approach for developing ethical reasoning in engineering. *Science and Engineering Ethics, 22*(1), 275–291.

Boenink, M., Cuijpers, Y., van der Laan, A. L., van Lente, H., & Moors, E. (2011). Assessing the sociocultural impacts of emerging molecular technologies for the early diagnosis of Alzheimer's disease. *International Journal of Alzheimer's Disease*, Article ID# 184298, 1–9.

Boulos, M., Kamel, N., Brewer, A. C., Karimkhani, C., Buller, D. B., & Dellavalle, R. P. (2014). Mobile medical and health apps: State of the art, concerns, regulatory control and certification. *Online Journal of Public Health Informatics, 5*(3), p. e229.

Brey, P. A. E. (2010). Values in technology and disclosive computer ethics. In Luciano
     Floridi (Ed.), *The Cambridge handbook of information and computer ethics*
     (pp. 41–58). Cambridge, MA: Cambridge University Press.

Brey, P. A. E. (2012). Anticipatory ethics for emerging technologies. *Nanoethics* 691), 1–13.

Brown, E. T., Cohn, J. A., Kaufman, M. R., Reynolds, W. S., & Dmochowski, R. R.
     (2016). Lessons learned from mesh litigation for prolapse and incontinence. *Current
     Bladder Dysfunction Report, 11*(1), 73–78.

Consumer Reports. (2012). Dangerous medical implants and devices. *Consumer Reports.*
     Retrieved from www.consumerreports.org/cro/magazine/2012/04/cr-investigates-dan
     gerous-medical-devices/index.htm

Davis, M. (1991). Thinking like an engineer: The place of a code of ethics in the practice of
     a profession. *Philosophy & Public Affairs, 20*(2), 150–167.

Davis, M. (2001). The professional approach to engineering ethics: Five research ques-
     tions. *Science and Engineering Ethics, 7*(3), 379–390.

Davis, M. (2001b). Three myths about codes of engineering eEthics. *IEEE Technology and
     Society Magazine, 20*(3), 8–14.

Fries, R. C. (2012). *Reliable design of medical devices.* Boca Raton, FL: CRC Press.

Geiger, J. D, & Hirschl. R. B. (2015). Innovation in surgical technology and techniques:
     Challenges and ethical issues. *Seminars in Pediatric Surgery, 24*(3), 115–121.

Halme, D. G., & Kessler, D. A. (2006). FDA regulation of stem-cell-based therapies.
     New England Journal of Medicine, 355(1), 1730–1735.

HHS.gov. (1979). The Belmont Report. Retrieved from www.hhs.gov/ohrp/regulations-
     and-policy/belmont-report/

Hofmann, B. (2017). Toward a method for exposing and elucidating ethical issues with
     human cognitive enhancement technologies. *Science and Engineering Ethics, 23*(2),
     413–429.

IMEDA. (2013). International Medical Device Manufacturers Association Code of Ethical
     Conduct for Interactions with Healthcare Professionals. Retrieved from http://cocir.org/
     fileadmin/4.1_Business_and_Innovation/Code_of_Conduct/IMEDA_Code_of_Ethics_
     NEW_01_09_2013.pdf. (Accessed 9.8.16).

Kisselburgh, L. et al.(2014). Effectively engaging engineers in ethical reasoning about
     emerging technologies: A cyber-enabled framework of scaffolded, integrated, and
     reflexive analysis of cases. *Proceedings of the 121st ASEE Annual Conference &
     Exposition, Indianapolis, IN, June 2014* (pp. 1561–1563).

Kucklick, T. R. (2012). *The medical device R&D handbook* (2nd edition). Boca Raton, FL:
     CRC Press.

Kuhlmann-Capek, M. J. et al. (2015). Enmeshed in controversy: Use of vaginal mesh in the
     current medicolegal environment. *Female pelvic medicine and reconstructive surgery,
     21*(5), 241–243.

Lu, L., ARbit, H. M., Herrick, J. L., Segovis, S. G., Maran, A., & Taszemski, M. J. (2015).
     Tissue engineered constructs: Perspectives on clinical translation. *Annuls of Biomed-
     ical Engineering, 43*(3), 796–804.

Martin, T., Rayne, K., Kemp, N. J., Hart, J., & Diller, K. R. (2005). Teaching for adaptive
     expertise in biomedical engineering ethics. *Science and Engineering Ethics, 11*(2),
     257–276.

Medical Device Manufacturers Association. (2009). Medical Device Manufacturers Asso-
     ciation Revised Code of Conduct on Interactions with Healthcare Providers. Retrieved

from https://c.ymcdn.com/sites/www.medicaldevices.org/resource/resmgr/Docs/MDMA_Code_July09.pdf.

Mepham, B. (2000). A framework for the ethical analysis of novel foods: The ethical matrix. *Journal of Agricultural and Environmental Ethics*, *12*(2), 165–176.

Merryman, W. D. (2008). Development of a tissue engineered heart valve for pediatrics: A case study in bioengineering ethics. *Science and Engineering Ethics*, *14*(1), 93–101.

Millar, K., Thorstensen, E., Tomkins, S., Mepham, B., & Kaiser, M. (2007). Developing the Ethical Delphi. *Journal of Agricultural and Environmental Ethics*, *20*(1), 53–63.

NSPE.org. (2014). Frequently asked questions about engineering. Retrieved from www.nspe.org/resources/press-room/resources/frequently-asked-questions-about-engineering.

NSPE.org. (2007). Code of ethics for engineers. Retrieved from www.nspe.org/sites/default/files/resources/pdfs/Ethics/CodeofEthics/Code-2007-July.pdf.

Özdemir, V. et al. (2015). A Code of Ethics for Ethicists: What would Pierre Bourdieu Say? "Do Not Misuse Social Capital in the Age of Consortia Ethics." *The American Journal of Bioethics*, *15*(5), 64–67.

Pennell, C. P., Hirst, A., Sedrakyan, A., &McCulloch, P. G. (2016). Adapting the IDEAL framework and recommendations for medical device evaluation: A modified Delphi survey. *International Journal of Surgery*, *28*(2016), 141–148.

Pirates of the Caribbean: Curse of the Black Pearl. (2003). Dir. Verbinski, G. Perfs. Depp, J., Rush, G., Bloom, O., Knightley, K., et al. Walt Disney Pictures, DVD.

Rawls, J. (1972). *A theory of justice* (pp. 41–82). Oxford: Oxford University Press.

RAPS.org. (2016). Code of ethics for regulatory affairs professionals. Retrieved from www.raps.org/ethics.

Rest, J. R., Narvaez, D., Bebeau, M. J., & Thoma, S. J. (1999). *Postconventional moral thinking: A Neo-Kohlbergian approach*. Mahwah, NJ: Lawrence Erlbaum Associates, Inc.

Saarni, S. I., Braunack-Mayer, A., Hofmann, B.,& van der Wilt, G. J. (2011). Different methods for ethical analysis in health technology assessment: An empirical study. *International Journal of Technology Assessment in Health Care*, *27*(4), 305–312.

Singer, W. (2015). The ongoing search for the neuronal correlate of consciousness. *Open MIND*, *36*(T). Ed.

T. Metzinger & J. M. Windt. Frankfurt am Main: MIND group. doi: 10.15502/9783958570344

Spielthenner, G. (2015). Why comply with a code of ethics? *Medical Health Care and Philosophy*, *18*92), 195–202.

Stankovic, B. & Stankovic, M. (2014). Educating about biomedical research ethics. *Medical Health Care and Philosophy*, *17*(4), 541–548.

Steneck, N. H. (2007). Introduction to the responsible conduct of research. Washington, DC: Office of Research Integrity.

Tjan, A. K. (2010, August 9). The power of ignorance. *Harvard Business Review*. Retrieved from https://hbr.org/2010/08/the-power-of-ignorance. (Accessed 9.8.16).

Tuana, N. (2013). Embedding philosophers in the practices of science: Bringing humanities to the sciences. *Synthese*, *190*(11), 1955–1973.

Van Buskirk, G. E. & Andresen, M. C. (2008). Creating a code of conduct for a medical device company. Retrieved from www.raps.org/WorkArea/DownloadAsset.aspx?id=4027. (Accessed 9.8.16).

Wright, D. (2011). A framework for the ethical impact assessment of information technology. *Ethics and Information Technology*, *13*(3), 199–226.

Endnotes

[1] Beauchamp and Childress are clear that the set of four principles they endorse is drawn from "the common morality to formulate the principles *of biomedical ethics*" and do not claim that these principles "exhaust the norms in the common morality" (2013, p. 421).

[2] To the authors' knowledge, none of these hypothetical actions by these stakeholders actually occurred. They may have but the examples here still are valid.

[3] Mepham's tool for reasoning about ethics was developed with the early insights of John Rawls (1972) in mind and was also influenced by the expanded application of such *prima facie* ethical principles by Beauchamp and Childress in the field of medical ethics (Beauchamp & Childress 1994).

[4] Principlism has been most fully developed within the applied field of biomedical ethics (Beauchamp & Childress 2013). The development of biomedical principlism as an approach for ethical analysis, in this context, arose indirectly from the Tuskegee Study of Untreated Syphilis and directly from The Belmont Report as a means by which to protect the moral value of human subjects in medical research. The Report, released in 1979, outlined three core principles that "are relevant to research involving human subjects" (HHS.gov, 1979): respect for persons, beneficence, and justice. These three principles were "stated at a level of generalization that should assist scientists, subjects, reviewers and interested citizens to understand the ethical issues inherent in research involving human subjects" (HHS.gov, 1979). Importantly, the authors understood these principles to be "among those generally accepted in our cultural tradition" (HHS.gov, 1979). Through the work of bioethicists Tom Beauchamp and James Childress – both contributors to the Belmont Report – principlism within bioethics came to be identified with a further specified set of those ethical principles: respect for autonomy, beneficence, nonmaleficence, and justice that form a "common morality" – that is, a set of mid-level moral norms that apply more universally, even when particular moralities and historical theories about morality might not.

26

Looking Back to Go Forward: The Ethics of Journalism in a Social Media Age

Glenda N. Cooper

26.1 Introduction

In recent times, both journalism and *who* is defined as a journalist have undergone significant change. With the growth of the internet, and the subsequent ability of anyone with a smartphone camera and a web connection to publish, the business model of journalism that had remained stable for decades has been declared broken and the public service model of journalism under threat. Meanwhile, a US president communicates via Twitter; Facebook Live spreads news while the mainstream media scramble to keep up.

The question scholars therefore have to address is how can mainstream media function ethically in this challenging environment? Journalists have traditionally adopted a normative framework defined by professional constructs, in particular the values of accountability, autonomy, and authenticity (Hayes, 2007). With a media cycle that has been transformed to the "1440-minute news cycle" (Bruno, 2011), some academics have suggested a whole new ethical approach needs to be developed for next-generation journalism. This chapter, however, will argue that these changes in the business model and in technology actually strengthen the call to return to *traditional* ethical approaches to journalism. The news may be coming to us livestreamed or via an app rather than on the printed page or beamed through a cathode ray but for those who consider themselves journalists, an ethical framework that considers public service, privacy, verification, and sensitivity around graphic imagery remains hugely pertinent.

This chapter draws on academic research and original interviews. It is structured as follows. Section 22.2 introduces in more detail the concept of what journalism is and who journalists are in a world where anyone can publish, while Section 22.3 looks at the increasing problem around fake news. The following three sections focus in on specific ethical issues. Section 22.4 looks at how livestreaming has altered the type of content we are exposed to, in particular the use of death imagery. Section 22.5 argues that privacy is more of a pressing concern than ever in a world of porous information boundaries. Section 22.6 looks at the need for crediting and copyright to be taken seriously as mainstream media appropriate content for their own profit. Finally, as consequence of the ethical issues highlighted, Section 22.7 discusses how the mainstream media can work to regain trust given the questions over practices discussed so far and the need to return to an idea of public service journalism.

26.2 Defining Journalism and Journalists Today

Every day in the United States, around ninety-three fatal shootings occur (Everytownresearch, 2017). Most of them will not command much notice, except from grieving relatives, and the courts, if necessary. Yet between July 5 and 7, 2016, three separate events occurred in the United States that did grab worldwide attention.

The first was the shooting of Alton Sterling by police in Baton Rouge; the second that of Philando Castile by police in Falcon Heights, Minnesota; the third the deaths of five police officers in a bloody shoot-out in Dallas.[1]

All three events were controversial. But what made these three incidents particularly unusual was that they were all captured on mobile phone videos, and either rapidly broadcast or distributed via Facebook – and then in various forms by the mainstream media – raising ethical questions right at the heart of journalism at the moment.

These are troubled times for journalists and media organizations who have seen their industry changed out of all recognition in recent years. As Emily Bell, Director of the Tow Centre for Digital Journalism, describes it:

> Our news ecosystem has changed more dramatically in the past five years than perhaps at any time in the past five hundred. We are seeing huge leaps in technical capability – virtual reality, live video, artificially intelligent news bots, instant messaging, and chat apps. We are seeing massive changes in control, and finance, putting the future of our publishing ecosystem into the hands of a few, who now control the destiny of many.
>
> (Bell, 2016)

In the past, news stories used to be journalist-only spaces where ordinary people appeared merely as archetypes in narratives, or sources for comments – the outraged passerby, the grieving widow(er), the "vox pop." Journalists acted as gatekeepers – controlling what we the public were told, or not told. Those journalists who acted ethically (and of course, not all did) protected their sources, fact-checked, and at least paid lip service to the principles of objectivity, impartiality, and balance.

But in the past two decades the advent of the Internet, and particularly that of social media, has challenged mainstream media. The very way we consume news has changed. "It's happened in the past ten years," says Alan Rusbridger, former editor-in-chief of *The Guardian* who pioneered the online version of the newspaper, during an interview with the author. "The concept of the 'front page' died – and content was divorced from context."

Meanwhile journalists are no longer gatekeepers – they are gate*watchers* (Bruns, 2008). Their role is not just as gatherers of information anymore, but as curators of user-generated content (UGC).[2]

Ethically, this raises two main challenges. First, creators of this content are not trained as journalists and subject to the norms that journalists themselves adhere to, which means very different kind of material is shared. Second, how journalists themselves go on to reuse that content is often more reminiscent of a smash and grab raid than careful considerations around privacy, taste, decency, and copyright that they would be expected to give to material created by professionals.

During an interview with the author, Dr. Claire Wardle, Director of Research and Strategy at *First Draft News*, a non-profit that looks at the challenges around trust and truth in a digital age, says, "In newsrooms, the competition is fierce, UGC is cheap, easy to access and audiences like the authenticity of such content." "And for those who take the moral high ground," she continues, "they're faced with the digital equivalent of audiences slowing down to watch a traffic accident."

The "turning point," as Dan Gillmor of the Walter Cronkite School of Journalism and Mass Communication puts it, was the Indian Ocean tsunami. On December 26, 2004 when it struck, none of *Reuters'* 2300 journalists or 1000 stringers were on the beaches. "For the first 24 hours," Tom Glocer, the former head of Reuters pointed out, "the best and the only photos and video came from tourists armed with telephones, digital cameras and camcorders. And if you didn't have those pictures, you weren't on the story" (Glocer, 2006).

What seems almost quaint now is that, at the time, there was no way for people to share these dramatic images easily. Some managed to share via blogs – one website, waveofdestruction.org, put up by Australian blogger Geoffrey Huntley had more than 682,000 unique visitors in just four days (Cooper, 2007). But many others simply went home – only to be met by journalists at the airports, desperate to get hold of their footage (Burrell, 2005).

Today, however, if you see something interesting you can snap a picture or take a video on a cellphone – then share it via social media sites such as Instagram, YouTube, Twitter, or Snapchat, or closed messaging apps like WhatsApp. You can even broadcast it live via Periscope or Facebook Live, which has been pushed relentlessly by the social media giant. Mark Zuckerberg was apparently so impressed with how much time people spent watching video online that he put 100 of his company's top engineers on lockdown for two months to come up with a tool (Dwoskin & Timberg, 2017).

This content can greatly add to how we understand what is happening in the world. Ordinary people can alert the wider community to stories that would not have been covered otherwise – especially in an era of cutbacks and budget squeezes amongst media organizations. It allows different points of view to be heard. Those who watch it or read it often praise the authenticity of the content – first person, raw, and subjective; which can bring alive what impact a story has had on a community.

26.3 The Growing Problem of Fake News and Distortion

But there are problems too, most notably faking. In the early days of UGC it was seen as more authentic and free from the biases of the mainstream media. However, this was not the case. While many posts, pictures, and tweets allowed the world a first-hand glimpse into a breaking news story, things were not always what they seemed. The "shark" pictures from Hurricane Sandy[3] might have caused amusement but in a country like Syria where many journalists are unable to get access, our understanding has often heavily depended on UGC, which may be created by activists with their own agendas.

Places like the BBC's UGC Hub in London have highly trained journalists who work to verify such content – identifying the creator, checking location, language, even assessing if the weather or clothing is correct for where the event is said to be taking place. But ordinary people looking at content online are unlikely to be skilled enough to spot these giveaway clues.

And this has recently gone much further than the odd Photoshopped picture or manipulated video. "Fake" news (or what I would call the deliberate spread of misinformation) has sparked what could be dubbed a moral panic (Cohen, 2002) and gone beyond user-generated content to embrace the media generally. This was exacerbated in the wake of scandals such as that of the UK phone hacking, which saw the *News of the World* newspaper be closed down in its wake (Keeble & Mair, 2012).

This has become such an ever-present problem that in the 2016 US election the most popular fake news stories were shared more widely on Facebook than the favorite mainstream stories, with the two most popular being fake claims that the Pope had endorsed Donald Trump and Hillary Clinton had sold weapons to ISIS (Silverman, 2016). Researchers Hunt Allcot and Matthew Gentzkow state that they cannot conclusively say that fake news swung the election. But they estimate that the average US voter read and recalled at least one or perhaps several fake news article during the election period, with higher exposure to pro-Trump than pro-Clinton articles (Allcot & Gentzhow, 2017).

As a result of the growing concern about exposure to fake news, Facebook announced in December 2016 that it was introducing a tool to allow readers to flag possible fake stories, which the social media giant would then send to fact checkers to verify (Jamieson & Solon, 2016). Ahead of the 2017 UK election Facebook also placed full page advertisements in newspapers in order to alert readers to signs of fake news on its site (Murgia, 2017).

Other problems with UGC can be that it can potentially distort focus even if it is not "faking." UGC may skew the definition of news even more towards the unexpected, the spectacular visual event, with the result that the less photogenic but equally important one can get pushed out – the chronic famine ignored in favor of the dramatic earthquake. As Tom Sutcliffe, of the *Independent* newspaper once put it: "The problem with citizen journalists – just like all us citizens – is that they are incorrigible sensationalists" (Sutcliffe, 2007).

26.4 Livestreaming and its Consequences

In January 2016, as many as 20,000 people watched the unremarkable sight of pedestrians trying to negotiate a large puddle in Newcastle, England (Cresci & Halliday, 2016). But this – and the viral "Chewbacca Mom" Facebook Live video – have become subsumed in questions over the more controversial broadcasts that Facebook Live has become associated with. Diamond Reynolds' filming of the aftermath of the fatal shooting of her boyfriend Philando Castile was seen by millions. She started the video with the words "Stay with me" before panning to Castile whose shirt was soaked with blood, and going on to document her interactions with the authorities for as long as ten minutes after the shooting. The video was shared by Black Lives Matter activists and a succession of protests and vigils were held as a result.

But not all, like Reynolds, only start filming after the violence has occurred. Suicides, murders, and terrorist attacks have all been Facebook Live "events." In 2017, four people in Chicago were charged with hate crimes, kidnapping, and battery after a Facebook Live video showed them beating a disabled man (Levin & Jamieson, 2017). A year earlier in 2016 a double murder of police employees in Paris was broadcast with ISIS claiming responsibility (Toor, 2016).

Showing a death as it happened was not something that journalists traditionally shared with their readers and viewers. Zelizer (2010) writes persuasively that journalists do not show the moment of death – instead they show the moments before or after, thinking that their readership would not want to see this (what British newspaper editors like to call the "breakfast test"[4]). But this has been challenged by UGC:

> Journalists often avoid depicting what they think is most problematic, but as recent events involving citizen journalists show, non-journalists may have no such reticence. When people other than journalists can exploit the porousness of images of impending death and distribute them at will, decisions about what to show can be taken in journalism's name but without journalism's sanction to varying effect.
>
> (Zelizer, 2010, p. 266)

Experiencing such events live can often expose people to incredibly distressing sights. When the Bangkok bomb blast happened in 2015, a Periscope user Derek van Pelt filmed the aftermath live. Numerous viewers praised the authenticity of what he was filming. But live streaming apps exposed some viewers to traumatic images they may not have wished to see. At one stage the camera focused on what turned out to be body parts. Comments read, "That's a body? Wow, just a hat and meat left … OMG I can't ever unsee that." Van Pelt's response showed how difficult it can be to avoid live broadcasting of graphic content – he revealed that he didn't know what the object was before filming (Brown, 2015).

Sometimes people do know what they are filming – but in such a stressful situation do not think through clearly enough whether they should be sharing such material. When journalists then take such footage and broadcast it, this may go far wider than the creator ever intended – and can become the responsibility of the broadcaster. This was seen in the use of Jordi Mir's footage in the aftermath of the attacks on the Charlie Hebdo offices in Paris.

Mir had filmed the attackers Cherif and Said Kouachi in the act of killing a police officer, Ahmed Merabet, and uploaded the video onto Facebook, before realizing the potential consequences and deleting it fifteen minutes later (Satter, 2015). By then, however, it was too late – he had lost control of the film. It had been uploaded to YouTube and widely used. Merabet's brother later said they were traumatized by the continual reuse of the footage and attacked journalists, saying:

> How dare you take that video and broadcast it? I heard his voice. I recognized him. I saw him get slaughtered and I hear him get slaughtered every day.
>
> (Alexander, 2015)

Mir, who later said his decision to upload had been a "stupid reflex reaction," turned down offers of payment, while authorizing some media organizations to use the film as long as they cut the moment of death. Some, he said, continued to run it without permission (Satter, 2015; Sargent, 2015).

For Claire Wardle, the wider distribution of such content by journalists is a key ethical issue and there needs to be much more training in newsrooms to use such content in the right way. "Managers and editors really need to think about what the boundaries are," she says during an interview with the author. "If there is a livestream, do you embed it or do you provide a link to it? If you livestream it, what are you going to do about the comments? For example, in the livestream of the Dallas shooting, people were making comments that they knew who the guy was and where he lived."

26.5 Privacy

This raises another pertinent issue. Not all content shared and used by journalists may be as graphic as the aforementioned examples. But it may be picturing people in places and situations they do not want – or ever expect – to be broadcast to the wider world. The privacy theorist Helen Nissenbaum says the fundamental problem here is a breakdown in what she calls "contextual integrity" (Nissenbaum, 2004, p. 138).

For Nissenbaum, privacy can mean different things in different situations, and that it is violated when people do not respect two types of contextual norms – those of appropriateness (what information may be shared) and those of flow and distribution (with whom the information is shared). Grimmelmann (2009) calls this a "flattening" of relationships – the erosion of the fine divisions in social relationships that there are in real life. When material is pilfered from social networking sites by the media, then this transgression of contextual norms is taken even further.

In the most extreme cases, this can result in widespread vilification and even loss of a job and social status, as in the case of Lindsey Stone. Her bad-taste photograph in which she pretended to shout and swear in front of a sign asking for silence and "respect" at the Arlington National Cemetery, led to her being "trolled" and then fired after it was shared widely online and in the media (Ronson, 2015).

Meanwhile, Peterson cites the example of the *Daily Mail*, which published dozens of photos of drunk girls. The photos had been lifted from a Facebook group called "30 Reasons Girls Should Call It A Night." One of the students pictured, taken by surprise as she had not posted the photos herself, then found herself besieged by calls from overseas organizations offering her money for sexually explicit interviews. A Google search of the student's name returned the *Daily Mail* article as the first result (Peterson, 2010, p. 11).

For those who are not even part of the story – but end up being photographed by a random onlooker, there may also be consequences. During the Westminster terror attack of March 2017, there was a striking photo shared of a woman wearing a brown hijab and looking at her phone as she walked across Westminster Bridge, seemingly unaware of people gathered round an injured victim lying on the sidewalk nearby.

This photo went on to be widely shared on Twitter and anti-Islam blogs, and then in the mainstream media. One social media user even posted it alongside a photo of the Conservative MP Tobias Ellwood trying to resuscitate a police officer wounded by the attacker with the inflammatory caption "the main difference between Muslims and Christians" (Hunt and Pegg, 2017).

This picture, however, had been taken out of context. It was one photograph in a sequence that made clear the woman was visibly distressed. Such was the vitriol, however, that the woman eventually had to release a statement through TellMAMA, a group that logs anti-Muslim incidents, but was not named in order to protect her identity. She said:

> I'm shocked and totally dismayed at how a picture of me is being circulated on social media. To those individuals who have interpreted and commented on what my thoughts were in that horrific and distressful moment, I would like to say not only have I been devastated by witnessing the aftermath of a shocking and numbing terror attack, I've also had to deal with the shock of finding my picture plastered all over social media by those who could not look beyond my attire, who draw conclusions based on hate and xenophobia.
>
> (TellMAMA, 2017)

Clearly there is often a mismatch between what the general public may expect when they put a photograph or comment into social media, and what the media think is acceptable. Those who tweet a picture or put it up on Facebook may have little idea of the consequences not only for themselves, but those who are involved in their content. When these pictures are then shared more widely, particularly by the mainstream media, it can be devastating.

Some media organizations have taken this on board. The BBC, as a public service broadcaster, was one of the first in its guidelines to reflect on how material from social networking sites should be used. It comments:

> Whilst some in the media might argue that, once an individual has begun a declarative lifestyle . . . they cannot expect to be able to set limits on that, people making content for the BBC should ask themselves whether a door that is only ajar can justifiably be pushed further open . . . Use of social media content by the BBC often brings that content to a much wider public.
>
> (BBC, 2014)

Many others, however, still see any content in the public domain as "fair game." Yet these reporters would often simultaneously sign up to journalistic norms of protecting sources, respecting the feelings of those whom they report on if it had been them taking the picture or writing the story instead.

26.6 Crediting

One of the other ethical issues that is raised by the use of such content is copyright. Often journalists take content – words, photos, or video – and reproduce it without naming the creator or giving them any money for the use of their work. Again, journalists should ask themselves whether they would use another professional's content in such a way – and if not, why should they use ordinary people's? Journalists who utilize other people's video, photographs, or tweets should certainly be asking themselves the following questions:

Who was the author, and who is the rightful owner?
Is it copyright protected?
What possible problems with reuse and linking might there be?

Can UGC be copyright protected? Copyright law, certainly in Europe, often focuses on the *expression* of an idea rather than the idea itself, and does not concern itself with the quality or merit of a piece of work. So a hurried picture, video, or blog could be seen as copyrightable. In fact the main problem may be establishing authorship – both for creators claiming ownership and mainstream media looking for permissions in fast-moving news events. This goes further than copyright and also embraces moral rights as well (i.e., rights of attribution, the right to have it published anonymously or pseudonymously, and the integrity of the work).

The 2016 Brussels terror attacks saw a case in point. Anna Ahronheim, a defense correspondent with a Middle East TV channel, shared a video on Twitter of the explosions at the airport (https://twitter.com/AAhronheim/status/712177856768569344). It was retweeted nearly 27,000 times and Ahronheim was commonly credited with it – despite having merely taken the video from a WhatsApp group. Even after the social news agency Storyful tracked down the real creator, Pinchas Kopferstein, and Ahronheim tweeted "Just FYI, this is NOT my video. Im [sic] not in **#Brussels**. It was shared with me on whatsapp.I dont have a name for credit but please DONT use mine" (https://twitter.com/AAhron heim/status/712270155208912896),[5] she was still commonly credited (Cobben, 2016).

David Clinch, of the social media agency Storyful concluded that journalists should approach how to establish ownership of content differently:

> Instead of asking "can we use it?" journalists need to ask: where does this video come from, where were you when this happened? Do you have any other images to show that you were there?

> (quoted in Cobben, 2016)

Journalists should also be sensitive to the idea that not everyone may want to be credited for their work. This is a particular problem when mainstream media websites embed tweets, which can reveal to a much wider audience who took a particular picture or video – and can lead to trolling. After the Moore tornado of 2013, one eyewitness, a security guard, took Vine videos[6] and shared them on Twitter. He was subsequently overwhelmed by the media attention with journalists asking permission for his six-second clips to be reused, but it also brought him to the unwelcome attention of trolls, who attacked him (erroneously) saying that he was making money out of a disaster. This distressed him so much that he took down all his video clips and even removed himself from social media temporarily to try to get away from all the attention (Cooper, 2018).

"I do think it's the crediting aspect is important because if you embed something elsewhere then it's been taken out of context," says Wardle during an interview with the author.

> For example, if someone posts a picture on Instagram of their kid in an Easter Bunny costume that they expected 50 friends to see, then what happens if a mainstream media organisation embeds their post and name in their site? Or what if you happened to take some important footage of the Westminster attacks but you weren't meant to be there, or don't want to be a target of trolls. It's about seeking people's permission and respecting their wishes.

> (Wardle, during an interview with the author)

26.7 Regaining Trust

The impact that social media and the Internet have had on journalism is undeniable. This chapter so far has dealt with the content and the impact that has had on how journalists report the news. But with the whole business model broken, editors chasing viral videos and hits, the whole public service model of journalism has come under threat.

"I suppose the classic defence of what we [journalists] do is that we are there to oil wheels of democracy, let citizens make better informed decisions and to hold power to account," says Alan Rusbridger during an interview with the author. "That is the argument why journalism deserves to survive and why it matters but I think the economic model for that is really challenged."

The economic model that journalism had existed on for around 150 years – a combination of advertising and circulation – means that public service journalism has always been subsidized in some way. The Internet cannot be held solely to blame for journalism's current woes – newspaper circulations in the United States and the United Kingdom have been in decline since the 1950s (Campbell, 2011) – but the way that it disrupted the traditional classified advertising sector resulted in the print sector hemorrhaging money.

"Public interest journalism is not a going concern," says Aidan White, director of the Ethical Journalism Network, during an interview with the author. "The question arises whether we need it and whether democracy requires pluralism of information to operate and be credible. But we need to work out who is going to pay for it and how do we define new business models. But so far no has one come up with sustainable answers."

There have been various attempts to come up with solutions. Some include a philanthropic approach to public service journalism where foundations or individuals step in and fund. This includes, for example, the non-profit ProPublica, which was set up as a public service journalism site and initially funded by the Sandler Foundation and then others. Bill and Melinda Gates's foundation has funded *The Guardian*'s Global Development site and partially funded NPR's global development and health beat.

This has not been without controversy. For example, when the Open Society Institute founded by George Soros (who also put money into ProPublica) gave $1.8 million to NPR back in 2010, there was criticism from both right and left about whether one person should have that much influence (Meares, 2011).

There have also been other inventive ways to fund public service journalism on a smaller scale. *De Correspondent* launched as a digital-only news website in the Netherlands in 2013, crowdfunded by 20,000 backers and raising $1.7 million to get it off the ground. It now has more than 50,000 subscribers and its explicit mission is to:

> cover stories that tend to escape the mainstream media's radar because they don't fit neatly into the drama of the 24-hour news cycle. De Correspondent provides *an antidote to the daily news grind* – shifting the focus from the sensational to the foundational, and from the attention-grabbing headline to the constructive insight. We refuse to speculate about the latest scare or breaking story, but work instead to uncover the underlying forces that shape our world.

(https://thecorrespondent.com/)

The NYU professor and new media expert Jay Rosen worked with *De Corres-pondent* to bring an equivalent to the United States, which should start publishing in late 2019.

Meanwhile, Alan Rusbridger was also editor-in-chief of *The Guardian* when it attempted to improve its finances by creating what he calls a "mutualization" project – where readers paid a membership fee, not only to get benefits but to explicitly support *The Guardian*'s journalism. There is currently a three-tier system – supporter, partner, or patron – each with a different tier of payment per month, and with different rewards for doing so.

There are currently around 50,000 paying members and, despite cutbacks, David Pemsel, Chief Executive of Guardian Media Group (GMG) told the Digital Media Strategies 2016 seminar that GMG aimed to make its membership scheme account for a third of overall revenues within three years (Cole, 2017).

Rusbridger, who did not take up his seat as the chairman of *The Guardian*'s Scott Trust[7] after divisions with his successor as editor, says that this model is something that would be difficult to replicate elsewhere. In an interview with the author, he states:

> This [*The Guardian*] is a brand for which the consumers are so proprietorial, so that's why we did it … There's a strong almost philanthropic tinge to it. We want to keep journalism out in the world rather than behind a paywall, and if you believe in public service, that's a public good.

26.8 Conclusion

"There's no difference from how we have always worked – what we do in 2017 compared to the year 2000," says Mark Frankel, Social Media Editor of the BBC, during an interview with the author.

> The only difference is the propensity of social media channels to amplify these stories and the audience are also able to access that information in way they couldn't in 15–20 years ago. But in terms of what we present back to our audience, our approach to journalism hasn't changed – we need to put news in context and not merely present a raw and unfiltered way into the internet.

In the days following the death of her boyfriend Philando Castile, Diamond Reynolds found herself continually pressed for information by the media. In one interview with CNN's Chris Cuomo, she retorted:

> I'm grieving the loss of a loved one, of a best friend, of a role model, and father figure to my child…You guys constantly keep asking me all of these disturbing questions, and I've already made my statement. I don't want to keep reliving this moment.
> (Horowitz Satlin, 2016)

Did Diamond Reynolds put herself in that position by posting a video on Facebook? Should she be treated in a more cavalier way because she put herself in the public domain? In fact the ethical problems that journalists are facing today are, as Mark Frankel said, very similar to those that they have always grappled with. How do they deal with the privacy of someone caught up in a tragic event? If they use pictures or videos that someone else has created should that person not be paid and/or credited for it? What remains within the bounds of taste and decency – and what should not be shared?

The ethical debate may focus on new technologies but the questions remain the same as they have ever been. Journalists should respect privacy, credit other people for their own work, think carefully before releasing violent content rather than allowing it to circulate, and not propagate fake news.

But the real problem for journalists is that public service journalism and defense of such has found itself under threat thanks to the proliferation of raw, subjective reporting by citizen journalists, the growth of fake news, and the collapse of the economic model in journalism. So in the end, the ethical questions are less about the tactics – how and when to use social media – because any journalist who abides by longstanding journalistic norms should be able to judge what is best to do. The real ethical crisis is whether the public and journalists themselves can mount a sufficiently robust defense of public service journalism for it to continue. As Aidan White put it during an interview with the author:

> The first thing young journalists need to reconnect with is a fundamental understanding of what journalism is – and how it is distinct from free expression. When we talk about journalism, it is not about free expression, it is about constrained expression within a framework of values, and in particular the idea of independent journalism as a public good, with a responsibility to provide sources and information and to scrutinise both political and corporate power.

Note

The interviews with Mark Frankel, Alan Rusbridger, Dr. Claire Wardle, and Aidan White were conducted via telephone and Skype for this piece in February–April 2017.

References

Alexander, H. (2015, January 11). Funeral for French policeman Ahmed Merabet held in Paris. *Daily Telegraph*. Retrieved from www.telegraph.co.uk/news/world news/europe/france/11338404/Funeral-for-French-policeman-Ahmed-Merabet-held-in-Paris.html [Accessed April 18, 2016].

Allcot, H. & Gentzhow, M. (2017). Social media and fake news in the 2016 election. *Journal of Economic Perspectives*, *31*(2), 211–236. Retrieved from https://web.stanford.edu/~gentzkow/research/fakenews.pdf [Accessed May 8, 2017]

BBC. (2014). Editorial Guidelines: Privacy. BBC. Retrieved from www.bbc.co.uk/guide lines/editorialguidelines/edguide/privacy/reportingsuffer.shtml [Accessed: 18 April 2016]

Brown, P. (2015). OMG I can't ever unsee that. Eyewitness Media Hub August 25, 2015. Retrieved from https://medium.com/1st-draft/omg-i-can-t-ever-unsee-that-what-happened-when-the-aftermath-of-the-bangkok-bomb-blast-was-7a3f39ee2b0 [Accessed May 4, 2017]

Bruno, N. (2011). Tweet first, verify later. Oxford: Reuters Institute for the Study of Journalism.

Bruns, A. (2008). 3.1. The active audience: Transforming journalism from gatekeeping to gatewatching. Retrieved from http://snurb.info/files/The%20Active%20Audience.pdf [Accessed April 15, 2016]

Burrell, I. (2005). On the front line. *The Independent*. Retrieved from www.independent.co.uk/news/media/on-the-front-line-15131.html [Accessed January 8, 2015].

Campbell, D. (2011). Sixty years of daily newspaper circulation trends. *Communic@tions Management Inc* discussion paper. Retrieved from www.david-campbell.org/wp-con tent/documents/CMI_NewspaperCirculationTrends_6May11.pdf [Accessed May 8, 2017].

Cobben, I. (2016). Mass misattribution of viral Brussels video. *World News Publishing Focus*. Retrieved from http://blog.wan-ifra.org/2016/03/24/mass-misattribution-of-viral-brussels-video [Accessed April 8, 2016].

Cohen, S. (2002). *Folk devils and moral panics: the creation of the Mods and Rockers* (3rd edition). London: Routledge.

Cooper, G. (2007). *Anyone here survived a wave, speak English and got a mobile? Aid agencies, the media and reporting disasters since the tsunami.* Oxford: Nuffield College.

Cooper, G. (2018). *Reporting humanitarian disasters in a social media age.* New York, NY: Routledge.

Cresci, E. & Halliday, J. (2016, January 6). How a puddle in Newcastle became a national talking point. *The Guardian.* Retrieved from www.theguardian.com/technology/2016/jan/06/the-internet-cant-stop-watching-this-livestream-of-people-trying-to-cross-a-puddle [Accessed May 3, 2017].

Dwoskin, E. & Timberg, C. (2017, April 17) Facebook wanted "visceral" live video. It's getting livestreaming killers and suicides. *The Washington Post.* Retrieved from www.washingtonpost.com/business/technology/facebook-wanted-visceral-live-video-its-getting-suicides-and-live-streaming-killers/2017/04/17/a6705662-239c-11e7-a1b3-faf f0034e2de_story.html?utm_term=.bb44e90317f3 [Accessed May 4, 2017].

Everytownresearch. (2017). Gun Violence by the Numbers. Everytownresearch.org. Retrieved from https://everytownresearch.org/gun-violence-by-the-numbers/#Daily Deaths [Accessed August 8, 2017]

Glocer, T. (2006). We media Speech. *Tom Glocer.* Retrieved from www.tomglocer.com/2006/10/11/we-media-speech-3/ [Accessed April 18, 2016].

Grimmelmann, J. (2009). *Saving Facebook* NYLS legal studies research paper No. 08/09-7. *Iowa Law Review.* *94*, 1137.

Hayes, A. S., Singer, J. B., & Ceppos, J. (2007). 'Shifting roles, enduring values: The credible journalist in a digital age.' *Journal of Mass Media Ethics*, 22(4), 262–279.

Horowitz Satlin, A. (2016, July 8). Diamond Reynolds nails what's wrong with media coverage of Philando Castile. *Huffington Post*. Retrieved from www.huffingtonpost.com/entry/diamond-reynolds-cnn_us_577f9f7be4b0c590f7e8df83 [Accessed May 9, 2017].

Hunt, E., & Pegg, D. (2017, March 24). Woman photographed in hijab on Westminster Bridge responds to online abuse. *The Guardian*. Retrieved from www.theguardian.com/uk-news/2017/mar/24/woman-hijab-westminster-bridge-attack-victim-photo-misappropriated

Jamieson, A. & Solon, O. (2016, December 15). Facebook to begin flagging fake news in response to criticism. *The Guardian*. Retrieved from www.theguardian.com/technol ogy/2016/dec/15/facebook-flag-fake-news-fact-check [Accessed May 8, 2017].

Keeble, R. L. & Mair, J. (2012). *The phone hacking scandal: Journalism on trial*. Bury St Edmunds, UK: Abramis.

Levin, S. & Jamieson, A. (2017, January 5). *The Guardian*. Retrieved from www.theguardian.com/us-news/2017/jan/05/facebook-live-beating-anti-donald-trump [Accessed May 3, 2017].

Meares, J. (2011). A Soros problem at NPR. *Columbia Journalism Review*. Retrieved from http://archives.cjr.org/campaign_desk/a_soros_problem_at_npr.php [Accessed May 9, 2017].

Murgia, M. (2017, May 8). Facebook campaigns against fake news in UK ahead of election. *Financial Times*. Retrieved from www.ft.com/content/3b9700ce-31ad-11e7-9555-23ef563ecf9a [Accessed May 8, 2017].

Nissenbaum, H. (2004). Privacy as contextual integrity. *Washington Law Review*, 79(1), 119–158.

OECD. (2007). *Participative Web: User-Created Content - DSTI/ICCP/IE(2006)7/FINAL 12*. OECD. Retrieved from www.oecd.org/sti/38393115.pdf (Accessed: 12 May, 2015).

Peterson, C. (2010). *Losing Face: An Environmental Analysis of Privacy on Facebook*. Retrieved from http://ssrn.com/abstract=1550211 [Accessed April 15, 2016].

Ronson, J. (2015). *So you've been publicly shamed*. London: Picador

Sargent, J. (2015). Respecting the eyewitness; learning lessons from the Paris Shootings. *First Draft*. Retrieved from https://medium.com/1st-draft/respecting-the-eyewitness-learning-lessons-from-the-paris-shootings-a1391a7cbe23#.xllxvz5lc [Accessed April 18, 2016].

Satter, R. (2015). Witness to Paris officer's death regrets video. *Associated Press*. Retrieved from http://bigstory.ap.org/article/5e1ee93021b941629186882f03f1bb79/ ap-exclusive-witness-paris-officers-death-regrets-video [Accessed November 2, 2015].

Silverman, C. (2016, November 16). This analysis shows how viral fake election news stories outperformed real news on Facebook. Buzzfeed. Retrieved from www.buzzfeed.com/craigsilverman/viral-fake-election-news-outperformed-real-news-on-facebook?utm_term=.icpYLlBBEQ#.tbgKvJyyN3 [Accessed May 8, 2017].

Sutcliffe, T. (2007, January 2). Ethics aside, citizen journalists get scoops. *The Independent*.

TellMAMA. (2017, March 24). The truth behind the picture of the Muslim woman on Westminster bridge. TellMAMA. Retrieved from https://tellmamauk.org/the-truth-behind-the-photo-of-the-muslim-woman-on-westminster-bridge/ [Accessed May 8, 2017].

Toor, A. (2016, June 14). The Verge. Retrieved from www.theverge.com/2016/6/14/ 11930916/france-terrorist-larossi-abballa-facebook-live-video [Accessed May 3, 2017].

Zelizer, B. (2010). *About to Die*. Oxford: Oxford University Press.

Endnotes

[1] As of May 3, 2017, the US Justice Department has decided to bring no charges against two white officers in the case of Alton Sterling. In November 2016, police officer Jeronimo Yanez was charged with second degree manslaughter in the case of Philando Castile. Micah Xavier Johnson who shot the Dallas officers was killed by a bomb disposal remote controlled vehicle.

[2] The term "user-generated content" is highly contested – with many alternatives being suggested, including "citizen journalism," "citizen witnessing," and "accidental journalism" – but it is generally accepted as the least bad option. In this context I am using as a basis the OECD's definition – that it requires some kind of creative effort, publication and it is created outside normal professional routines and practices – i.e., it is produced by non-professionals, "without expectation of profit or remuneration but the primary goals being to connect with peers, level of fame and desire to express oneself" (OECD, 2007).

[3] See, for example, http://mashable.com/2012/10/29/fake-hurricane-sandy-photos/

[4] Meaning what a reader/viewer could face seeing while eating their breakfast, and not be put off.

[5] This second tweet was retweeted ten times in comparison by April 8, 2016.

[6] Vine was a video-sharing service on Twitter. It closed down in October 2016.

[7] The Scott Trust was set up in 1936 to ensure *The Guardian*'s financial and editorial independence in perpetuity. See www.theguardian.com/the-scott-trust/2015/jul/26/the-scott-trust

27

Social Media Ethics 2.0

Jeremy H. Lipschultz

27.1 Introduction

The development and popularity of computer-mediated communication (CMC), social network sites (SNSs), and social media communication (SMC) sparked twenty-first-century ethical dilemmas (Patching & Hirst, 2014; Barnes, 2003). At the heart of social media ethical concerns are data privacy and ownership. The fallout from the Cambridge Analytica data breach on Facebook, which followed a class action settlement in 2012 over the Beacon program, offers clear evidence that lack of user consent over gathering and disseminating information is a long-standing problem (Terelli, Jr. & Splichal, 2018). Facebook appears to have made the problem worse by allowing user data access to outside, third-party program applications ("apps"), and granting user friends the ability to further weaken privacy (Stratton, 2014).

From an engineering perspective, SNSs are disruptive in that they prosper by empowering individuals to use and abuse SMC technologies. At the same time, the powerful – governments, spy agencies, corporations, political parties, and others – quickly learned to use and abuse large and granular data. From surveillance to manipulation, SMC paradoxically extends Internet freedom at the same time that it threatens it through authoritarian practices. Developers, however, may be focused on the "coolness" of new SNS products without fully taking into consideration the implications of the power of the apps for society and culture. For example, it was not until 2018 that former and current Facebook employees were reported to express concerns about obvious invasion of individual privacy rights. The ambiguity of US privacy law application to corporations and individuals perhaps plays some role in the widespread apathy by the developer community. In the fast-paced race to outsmart other Silicon Valley startups, SNSs and their businesses tend to respond to the market without regard to deep thinking about the need for ethical privacy boundaries.

As with other areas in this book, SMC offers a fluid technological space in which harm to individual privacy must be considered. While SNSs open us to exciting networked interaction and online community building, the social exchange appears to be loss of data privacy to those profiting from the data. Facebook, for example, also owns Instagram and continues to amass private data from more than one billion global users. Never in human history has there been such a massive store of behavioral data for nearly one-quarter of the world's population. If data are power, and they clearly are, then Facebook represents growing un-elected control of our personal lives. In response, we can examine ethical requirements, such as transparency and independence, in order to offer alternative models for ethical data use and privacy.

SMC ethical concerns reside within a broader context of Internet of Things (IoTs), as explored in Chapter 3. From self-driving cars to use of technologies in all areas of the public sphere, SMC ethics involve communicating moral reasoning and decision-making based upon key variables: transparency *and* independence (Ward, 2013a). From journalist arguments about the definition of "fake news" to public relations (PR) best practices, ethics are being transformed by new communication technologies and the realities of a SMC age. Traditional mass media ethical concerns over access to information and publication of private facts pale in comparison to digital data collection, storage, and use. Power computing enables those collecting "big data" to search, filter, and target groups, as well as individuals.

The European Union demands user privacy based upon the concept of human dignity that is built into international law, but US practitioners continue to resist ethical structures constraining corporate behavior. At the same time, the United States has a particular dilemma of balancing ethical practices against First Amendment freedom. Beginning with Reno v. American Civil Liberties Union (ACLU, 1997), the US Supreme Court granted broad and deep publisher freedom to Internet service providers (ISPs), and this right extends to SNSs. The purpose of this chapter is to bring a SMC perspective to the discussion of engineering freedom and responsibility, and relate this to SNS law and ethics.

27.2 Global Media Ethics

Within the global context of rising nationalism and growing fears about terror attacks, governments and the private sector seek to manage and even control SMC – even as individuals extend their social capital and influence through electronic word of mouth (eWOM), social media engagement best practices, social marketing campaigns, and personal branding efforts (Lipschultz, 2018). SMC, then, involves a paradigm of risk and economic opportunity. Ethical issues exist because there are higher global legal standards of human dignity, which rise above current expectations of, for example, privacy law in the United States and elsewhere (Mills, 2015). Privacy began in the United States as a nineteenth-century legal theory, expanded under tort law, and is distinguishable from Fourth

Amendment constitutional rights. Mills (2015) articulates "informational autonomy" as an argument for data control:

> Personal information in this sense could mean anything from social security number
> and bank account information to cell phone data, records of consumer purchases, and
> photographs taken of or by a person. It could also refer to information contained in e-
> mail, online profiles, or other sources. Personal control may have a basis in the personal
> nature of the information, the ownership of the information, and the privileged nature of
> information shared in certain relationships.
>
> (pp. 19–20)

Mills seeks to contextualize information in determining intent for resolving
legal conflicts over intrusion and public disclosure of private facts. From a legal
perspective, conflicting national and international law. For Mills, there are cases
in which the European Union and others have it correct in protecting reputation –
including truthful, private facts – because human dignity demands a need for
"drawing the blinds" from public view: "The European Union and others will
look at the disclosure of truthful information and weigh the public good of the
disclosure against the individual harm" (Mills, 2015, p. 177).

The EU model leads to regulation, such as a "right to be forgotten." However, it
is unclear that such rights serve the long-term best interests of society. While there
are calls for new US laws, these proposals must be offered within a competing
entrepreneurial business mindset that fosters innovation and communication
openness through transparency (Guo, 2016). Technological and legal responses,
such as Facebook's response following the Cambridge Analytica data "scandal,"
tend to fall short of ideals found within broader ethical frameworks. Social media
ethics may begin with simplistic calls for transparency, but they tend to strive for
greater mutual respect among individuals.

27.3 Conceptual Clarity of Social Media Ethics

Ward (2013b) offered that a focus on transparency alone was conceptually weak
by failing to distinguish conceptual distinctions within new media ethics. Post-
modernism, for example, would suggest the need to accept "multiple truths . . .
acknowledge uncertainty, understanding of alternate perceptions, and awareness
of publics' increasing wariness of 'organizational truth,' as promoted in managed
PR messaging" (Caldiero, 2016, p. 28). The National Opinion Research Center
(NORC, 2016) and Edelman Trust Barometer (Edelman, 2017) for many years
have registered a decline in public support for all forms of authority – from social
institutions to various professional occupations. Edelman views the steady fall in
global trust as reason for concern:

> With the fall of trust, the majority of respondents now lack full belief that the overall
> system is working for them. In this climate, people's societal and economic concerns,

including globalization, the pace of innovation and eroding social values, turn into fears, spurring the rise of populist actions now playing out in several Western-style democracies.

(Edelman, 2017, para. 2)

Consider the NORC GSS question asked in twenty-six of the past thirty years: "Generally speaking, would you say that most people can be trusted or that you can't be too careful in dealing with people?" In 1972, 738 (47.9 percent) respondents said most people can be trusted, while 803 (52.1 percent) said you cannot be too careful. By 2014 the split had tilted away with less than one-third trusting — 519 (32.5 percent) to 1076 (67.5 percent). The patterns are reflected in social institutions, such as confidence in the press. By 2014 only 8.2 percent of respondents had a great deal of confidence in the press, compared to 47.0 percent with only some, and 44.8 percent hardly any (GSS Data Explorer, n.d.). The skepticism is similar for financial institutions, government, and law enforcement. These data suggest a crisis, which may be related to a lack of perceived ethics in the public sphere.

Ward's (2013) response is for media ethics that go beyond transparency to editorial independence and responsible publication within media and social media. The challenge, of course, is that professional gatekeepers have lost influence within social media spaces that allow anyone – regardless of media training – to publish. In the wake of the US 2016 election cycle, it became clear that those having an interest in political outcomes shared popular social media information. Ward calls this by the traditional term of "propaganda" or in modern terms "narrow advocacy" (paras. 29–30).

Another consideration is the speed of distribution and diffusion, which favors being first with the latest information instead of verifying facts and data. In the world of professional journalism, truth may be found through the values of verification and fairness (Mathewson, 2014). These norms, though, fail to recognize a far more complex and fluid environment for the making of real-time meanings in social media spaces, such as Twitter and Facebook (Caldiero, 2016). At issue is whether or not truth is singularly objective or defined through a plurality of voices and opinions. In early 2017, for example, the Trump administration clashed with traditional journalists seeking evidence of assertion of widespread voter fraud. Instead of data, Trump and his spokespersons tended to respond with an "everyone knows" assertion of opinion – a popular social media tactic had jumped the shark. Like "fake news," fact checking matters in an ethical sense (Sullivan, 2017). This is because provable facts are the basis for forming reasoned and ethical opinions. Just as the legal system requires courts to first determine facts before rendering application of precedent under the law, ethics similarly must rest upon first examining source and message credibility. This is a much different process from those of partisan interests seeking to shape opinion to appear to be factual.

New media organizations, such as Wikileaks and Buzzfeed, have contributed to the lack of conceptual clarity in social media ethics by making an argument that complete disclosure of all allegations would allow audience members to decide for themselves. This is a different model from the historic Pentagon Papers publication, for example, in which elite newspapers published complete government documents that were verified. New media activists, though, use unverified private emails or investigative reports as tools to make a particular case against political opponents. Rumors may take on the properties of facts or solid data through the art of illusion that resonates through subcultures. Eventually, by "going viral" the social media magician may invade the broader culture of ideas, as traditional media amplify influence.

27.4 Limitations of Transparency and Issues of Independence

Digital blurring happens when traditional news organizations, which value independence and fact checking, enter the murky world of Twitter and Facebook and reside within the news feed alongside of propagandists. Similarly, advocates with interests in power attract large numbers of followers and use social capital to appear to be credible sources of information for the press and public. The idea of conflict of interest becomes lost within social media that provides cover for the current president and his followers. Of course, the same was true for many of his opponents who lost power after being in the previous administration for eight years. What is lost, then, is a higher ethical concern for what became known in the law as public interest.

A social media "thought leader" first and foremost must be concerned with building follower lists through virtual, often in research terms *imagined*, communities. A lack of independence on the part of a political advocate means that journalists are left to do their media storytelling by accumulating large numbers of conflicting sources (Mathewson, 2014). This is an opening for advocates willing to express outrageous views, inflame political debate, and give rise to conflict – a news value that plays to the fundamental interest in building and maintaining large audiences.

Media ethics traditionally used the Potter Box as a way to think about morality within "a systematic process" (Christians, Rotzoll, & Fackler, 1991, p. 2). Such moral was built upon the logic of definition, values, principles, and loyalties. Under the paradigm, truth would be published even in the face of possible harm within balancing between extremes, morality, utility, and vulnerability – frequently grounded in Judeo–Christian beliefs. A global context of the Internet, though, quickly challenges such norms because of the diverse religious and other values (Ward & Wasserman, 2010). Global citizens rather than media professionals define right and wrong in "peer-to-peer ethics," as well as "accountability" through social media engagement (p. 286). In Habermas, Ward and Wasserman (2010) found that "reasoning should aim at an ideal mode of inclusive and equal discourse" (p. 288). This would employ cultural sensitivity (Motlagh, Hassan,

Bolong, & Osman, 2013), as well as trustworthy roles (Chung & Nah, 2013). We may advance a social media ethics idea that involves agreed upon credibility standards through crowdsourcing behavior.

27.4.1 Legal Analysis

Bloggers and micro-bloggers add to the social media ethical confusion because they punch through social media noise and directly compete with the practices of journalism and traditional media gatekeepers (Patching & Hirst, 2014). At the corporate level, the legal obligation is to maximize profit for stockholders, and this has a negative effect on PR practices. Corporate social responsibility (CSR) within PR is negotiated through best practices of reputation management (Pompper, 2015). In the early days of social media, respected PR firms offered hidden payments to bloggers, but the Federal Trade Commission (FTC) later moved to require disclosure of financial interests. The regulation involves challenging enforcement issues.

In the Matter of Lord & Taylor (2016), the FTC (2016) approved a final consent order with the retailer based upon a claim that it failed to properly disclose paid native advertising and online product endorsements. Among the complaints, the company created an Instagram post for the Nylon publication's account without disclosing that it was a paid promotion of its clothing line. The FTC also claimed that Lord & Taylor had paid fifty online fashion influencers thousands of dollars each to post Instagram photographs wearing a new dress given to them. The FTC agreement required that the company stop its misrepresentations and demand public disclosure in future influencer posts. Clearly, FTC regulation seeks to use existing law to require ethical behavior on social media sites. However, requiring transparency and disclosure of economic interests barely scratch the surface of social media ethical concerns. Use of an #ad or #sponsored hashtag in a post does not address data behind the media storytelling content.

To begin with, Wikileaks publication of private emails or National Security Agency (NSA) collection and use of data attack any presumption of digital human dignity. Little by little, social norms shift away from an expectation of data privacy. Rapid diffusion of new technologies does not offer time to absorb and process the implication of these profound changes. Mobile apps track location and movement, and this alone should be alarming given the linkage to our data stored within cloud computing spaces. As China and India recently passed the United States in number of Internet users, the ownership of private data rises to the level of global crisis.

Top US sites Google and Facebook offer policies addressing the harm associated with, for example, hate speech. While deleting content deemed offensive, these global giants guard their right to collect and maintain user private data.

The US Supreme Court has yet to address the heart of digital privacy issues. Instead, case-by-case decisions fall short. Beginning with Smith v. Maryland (1979), the Court found no constitutional right to hide telephone numbers already available to phone companies. In Reno v. ACLU (1979), the Court found unconstitutional provisions of the Communications Decency Act and Telecommunications Act of 1996 and left Internet publishers free to operate within other law. In general, courts are responsive to the need to assist parents in protecting their children from adult content, but not when this restricts adult access. Zoning the online content to adult spaces seemed to be a workable solution in balancing interests.

Employees have limited rights when online at work. When an employer owns equipment and states clear policies, the Supreme Court has narrowly protected a right to review online messages (Ontario v. Quon, *2010*). Of course, most employees now have access to privately owned smartphones, but employers may limit use to breaks from work time. For social media sites, such as Facebook, users agree to extensive Terms of Service (ToS) agreements. These are essentially contracts between users and the company. When it comes to workers covered under collective bargaining agreements and labor law, the National Labor Relations Board (NLRB) has initially ruled that employees may use social media sites to share relevant information (Kroger Co. of Mich. v. Granger, *2014*). In that case, a grocery store chain enacted social media policies that violated employee rights by requiring post disclaimers that might chill free speech rights.

At the same time, the Supreme Court has recognized the importance of social media in finding that states "must exercise extreme caution before suggesting that the First Amendment provides scant protection for access to vast networks in that medium" (Packingham v. North Carolina, *2017*, p. 1736). In that case, registered sex offenders could not be summarily denied complete Internet access to "the modern public square." In another case, the Court was sympathetic to the need to assess state of mind before finding Facebook posts about an estranged spouse and former employer to be "true threats" under criminal law (Elonis v. United States, *2015*, p. 2001). Under the pseudonym "Tone Dougie," Anthony Elonis claimed he was posting rap lyrics when he attached a protection order: "Is it thick enough to stop a bullet?" Clearly, such posts violated the privacy and human dignity of family and former co-workers, yet the US constitutional system offered some deference to the value of free speech.

First Amendment rights, however, may be restricted in extreme cases of privacy invasion. For example, Terry Bollea, known as Hulk Hogan, won an initial $140 million jury verdict against Gawker.com, after the site published a sex tape. While Bollea eventually settled for a $31 million award, the case spun the celebrity tabloid publication into bankruptcy. This case highlights the need for a delicate balance between individual privacy rights and press freedom. "There is no question digital technology, the Internet, social media and mobile are all affecting societal expectations and legal doctrines regarding privacy" (Terilli, Jr. & Splichal, 2018, p. 287). From the EU right to be forgotten to Google Street View, privacy invasion can take on many new forms – including intrusion through the use of various new technologies. From hidden cameras to enhanced vision, it has become increasingly difficult for individuals to know that they are surreptitiously being recorded. Without this knowledge, the traditional requirement of consent is lost. Beyond ubiquitous government-controlled audio and video equipment, individuals now have access to inexpensive, high quality video cameras, drones, and other robotics that offer technological agility. These devices collect streaming data that may be linked to, for example, facial recognition and other systems that accurately identify individuals.

In the wake of the Cambridge Analytica data breach, Facebook's Mark Zuckerberg was called to testify before US House and Senate committees investigating the need for privacy regulation. In response to concerns expressed by senators, Zuckerberg acknowledged personal responsibility for the "big mistake."

> It's not enough to just connect people. We have to make sure that those connections are positive. It's not enough to just give people a voice. We need to make sure that people aren't using it to harm other people or to spread misinformation. And it's not enough to just give people control over their information. We need to make sure that the developers they share it with protect their information, too.
>
> https://www.washingtonpost.com/news/the-switch/wp/2018/04/10/
> transcript-of-mark-zuckerbergs-senate-hearing/

Zuckerberg also responded to a question about the massive amount of data collected by Facebook and other third-party apps about individual users:

> To your broader point about the privacy policy, this gets into an – an issue that I – I think we and others in the tech industry have found challenging, which is that long privacy policies are very confusing. And if you make it long and spell out all the detail, then you're probably going to reduce the percent of people who read it and make it accessible to them.
>
> So, one of the things that – that we've struggled with over time is to make something that is as simple as possible so people can understand it, as well as giving them controls in line in the product in the context of when they're trying to actually use them, taking into account that we don't expect that most people will want to go through and read a full legal document.

Zuckerberg appeared to fall back to simple transparency for users rather than addressing the deeper legal and ethical concerns. Although he and Facebook expressed responsibility for the data breach mistake, it was clear that users also were blamed: "Actually, at – the first line of our Terms of Service say," Zuckerberg added, "that you control and own the information and content that you put on Facebook." It is not clear, though, how users take control of the data that Facebook and other third-party apps collect. At times even deleting old photographs and other posts has been difficult under the Facebook architecture. In order to fully control social media data, the only sure solution is to not post. Even then, friends and other may tag photographs and connect non-users to data. Recently, it was disclosed that Facebook tracks non-users across commercial websites. There was no disclosure or opt-in for these users. So, it is difficult to see Zuckerberg's public statements as anything more than crisis communication, damage control, and PR manipulation. Free from many US regulatory constraints, SMC companies may or may not treat their individual users in an ethical manner.

27.5 Ethical Conclusions

Social media ethics as a topic of debate is natural within democratic thinking. There are clear concerns about how platforms may be utilized to promote dangerous political extremism. Rhetoric of hate, for example, runs counter to the ideals of freedom. Social media engagement should have an ethical foundation: "Without it, you risk falling victim to social media's relentless and unforgiving nature of real-time relevance or irrelevance" (Solis, 2014, p. xvi). Impression management within social media may become manipulative, if not based upon the ethics of transparency and independence. Therein lies the problem of social media marketing, which uses advocacy to spark conversion of conversation into the sale of products and services. The communication may or may not be clear about interests. The typical social media marketing funnel begins with increasing awareness, and quickly move to sparking engagement through eWOM with an intent to sell consumers products or services. The granular nature of mobile geo-location data through the position of cell towers, Wi-Fi spots, and Bluetooth suggests that individuals potentially have lost all personal privacy to data tracking. Further, triangulation of mobile data through sharing from one company to another means that by using Starbucks or airport free wireless, an individual also may be sharing personal data with a retailer. Mobile data companies, such as Phunware, sell the value of personal data:

> Everything consumers do with their smartphone, tablet or laptop contributes to a daily digital trail that can tell brands who they are, where they have been, their preferences and even where they're likely to go next. It's all valuable information that users naturally share and mobile devices naturally collect.
>
> https://www.phunware.com/

Describing and predicting data trails happens without regard to philosophical notions of ethics and personal privacy. Instead, the market is being served by sophisticated technologies now being enhanced through audio, video, and robotics.

At the same time, truth, independence, and minimization of harm may be viewed as idealistic given the realities of digital spaces. The marketplace is more likely to view information and data as commodities to be bought and sold. Online community engagement may magnify or hide political motivation and viewpoints (McBride & Rosenstiel, 2014; Shirky, 2014). Thus, consumers become open to the assertion of facts without empirical evidence. Shirky's view is that normative coordination by institutions has been lost, and with it goes definition of objective truth. Audience members may process media storytelling within their own experiences, but power may be negotiated through audience interaction (Huang, 2014). Hidden behind the content are data structures and data trails. Data companies and brands know the rules of engagement, but consumers most likely remain oblivious to the business game. They know they are being sold ideas, goods, and services, but they may not know *why* a brand knew to target them in a particular place or at a specific time. Social media listening provides streaming of real-time data that offer pinpoint accuracy in branding opportunities. Much of the branding happens through creative social media storytelling and influence peddling.

27.6 Narrative, Crowdsourcing, and Moral Development

Narrative crowdsourcing of the stories we tell each other and come to believe assumes that they are the product of developed ethics – cultivated moral developmental principles, rules, codes, and processes of interpersonal and small group communication (Roberts, 2012). The gap between ideal and practical expectation fails to be closed by professional codes of ethics, but instead represents values, such as "universalism" (i.e., "tolerating") and "benevolence" (i.e., "enhancing the welfare") concerning "tradition" (i.e., "commitment"), "security," and "conformity" (Roberts, 2012, pp. 117–118). Social media Return on Investment (ROI), however, is a matter of money and results. If content leads to increased sales, then social media managers are considered to have been effective in doing their jobs. The boundaries, then, are more regulatory than ethical. As long as the FTC defines the problem as one of disclosure and transparency, then the social media industry has no need or interest in delving into deeper ethical discussion.

Transparency of communication within social media has a dimension of trust found in Bowen's (2013) values list: fairness; avoiding deception; dignity and respect; eschewing secrecy; reversibility; viewpoint identification; rationality; clarity; disclosure; verification; responsibility; intention; community good; and consistency (p. 126). The desire for information consistency is likely grounded in psychological cognition, and it also may help explain institutional distrust (Himelboim, Lariscy, Tinkham, & Sweetser, 2012). At a time when survey data show steady decline in public trust of most social institutions and authority, social business is more about sales conversion than trust building. SMC may be a function of outgoing freedom of expression rather than incoming evaluation of trust. Thus, there could be a sort of disassociation from personal ethics. This may be related to CMC perception of anonymity (Leonard & Toller, 2012), which offers one explanation for a lack of ethics in the corporate use of fake blogs or "flogs" (Bowen, 2013). "Deliberately concealing sponsorship, astroturfing, and flogging are practices that violate the moral duty communicators have to society to be universally honest, to communicate with dignity and respect, and act with good will" (Bowen, 2013, p. 127). The use of unethical "ghost blogging and ghost commenting" (Gallicano, Bivens & Cho, 2014, p. 21), Facebook page "impression management" (DiStaso, 2014, p. 44), and skepticism (Waters, 2014) suggest a complex SMC environment rather than consistent application of ethics.

In one case study, a Yelp employee published an open letter that was critical of the CEO about low pay and struggling employees (Winchel, 2016). Social media may offer the opportunity for employee voice, but agency is limited within existing corporate structure. In another case, tweets represented social media attacks and bullying (Gettys, 2015). However, it is difficult to identify normative boundaries in social media spaces that would limit or sanction those who bully others. Similarly, while cyberbullies launched a constant attack on female sportswriters and announcers in Chicago and women launched a responsive campaign (Lipschultz, 2016), there is no evidence that online communication became more civil. There are cases of clearly unethical social media behavior – typically by users hiding behind accounts with cloaked identities. Bullying or hate speech seems to have become the norm on sites such as Twitter, which struggle to ban offenders. This represents a disrespectful and mutual orientation toward the human dignity of others. In these cases, a discussion of social media ethics must address harm to victims of abusive communication.

27.7 Natural Law and Harm

Harm is fundamental, yet sometimes problematic when assessing reputation damage (Bowen, 2013). Harm has more clarity when it comes to online predator behavior or other illegal action (James et al., 2010). Privacy and ownership are among the legal and ethical concerns from a "good play" perspective of technological literacy, value-based thinking, and monitored online communities that address "transgressions" plus understanding "why, how, and where good play happens" (James et al., 2010, p. 226). One can imagine emergence of SNSs that cater to those seeking civil interaction and engagement instead of unbridled free speech. Importantly, however, ethical rights and responsibilities do not depend on perception of others (D'Arcy & Young, 2012). Thus, ethics presumes an objective standard for moral online behavior. It is a tall order to agree on standardization in an increasingly fractured and politicized society.

From reported "suppression" of conservative stories on Facebook newsfeeds during the last election (Nunez, 2016, para. 1) to investigation into company practices (Owen, 2016; King, 2016; Dinan, 2016; Pegoraro, 2016), the lack of journalistic gatekeeping placed new ethical pressures on others. Facebook has struggled with ethics in the application of its filtering algorithms. The company frequently fails the ethical test of transparency *and* independence. The advertising model that funds Facebook profits means that independence is lost. As long as users do not pay subscriber fees, they take a back seat to advertisers and their needs to target consumers. The ideals related to freedom and social responsibility within a democratic context (Christians, Rotzoll, & Fackler, 1995) begin with a desire to avoid harm to others, but Facebook and other social media companies lack ethical accountability. Business interests and stockholder responsibilities amount to a conflict of interest when cultivating the Facebook community (Ward, 2019). If public interest were applied, content rules would be clearly articulated in advance. The ethical communication paradigm would require that Facebook and other SNSs clearly tell users the rules of the business, along with providing opt-in procedures.

The lack of ethics within social media suggest that manipulation could be a threat to sovereignty through technological imperialism. The broader context of urbanization, anonymous "mistrust," (Lowery & DeFleur, 1995, p. 10), and media dependency are troubling. Facebook is but one very large new media company that embraces the interests of wealth and power – namely, advertisers (Fiss, 1996; Smolla, 1992). These forces may distort the social media marketplace of ideas (Fraleigh & Tuman, 1997). The problem of social media ethics, then, is fundamental. A search for "equality" or "justice" is quite subjective (Stevenson, 1995, p. 208). Corporate interests tend to be hidden (Schiller, 1989), which helps explain why ToS policies at Facebook and other sites are obscured by legal language. Site architecture also reshapes cultural commonalty (Carey, 1992), as it forces us to search for privacy. In the end, users do not demand data privacy because they have no way of knowing how to begin the process. The brand that is Facebook emerges as benevolent dictator with absolute control over data painting nearly every waking moment of site users.

27.8 Return to Social Media Ethics

The startup economy and its stories does not favor ethical behavior because, "Every company has to do something crazy or unorthodox when it's young" (Guo, 2016, p. 2). For Mills this translates into serious concerns about how one protects a right of privacy. "For global companies that traffic in digital data – Google, Facebook, and Amazon – the challenges of adhering to a patchwork of localized regulations concerning one's right to be forgotten will be considerable unless we enact global standards" (Mills, 2015, p. 26). In the failing of law to do so, we are left with a willingness to incorporate ethics into company behaviors.

Whether we speak of social media news or information sharing, the public must "engage with this growing debate" because the search for truth is likely to be "messy and chaotic" (McBride & Rosenstiel, 2014, p. 219). In the area of PR campaigns, for example, research, data gathering, and the campaign itself all raise concerns about "ethicality," as "the new 'tools' and unprecedented access to target publics and audiences" must increase CSR (Bowen & Stacks, 2014, p. 232). Rising levels of complexity do not diminish the fundamental need to exercise processes of moral reasoning (Christians, Rotzoll, & Fackler, 1995).

One journalistic view is that, "Secrecy is the enemy of public interest" (Patching & Hirst, 2014, p. 231). Data privacy laws may be designed for "the rich and famous" rather than people without resources to pay for protection:

> The lives of ordinary people will still be subject to detailed scrutiny; physical and electronic surveillance will continue to expand behind the veil of 'information privacy'. 'Big Data' is already here, gathering millions of bits of information about who we are. Privacy laws will not stop that from happening.
>
> (Patching & Hirst, 2014, pp. 231–232)

In this sense, social media ethics remains a problem of media literacy. "The notion of agency places the media literate individual at the center of a more connected, responsible, and diverse landscape" (Mihailidis, 2014, p. 155).

The idea is that we each have at least some freedom to make choices about social media use and apply moral reasoning. Ethical decision-making happens when there are stated boundaries on social media consumption behaviors, and the focus shifts to promotion of identity and interaction that cultivates online community citizenship. There is a need for media literacy education that would begin at the earliest use of SMC devices and sites. Users need to learn to deconstruct media storytelling content and the motivation of commercial interests. There is no absolute model for social media ethics, and no clear path to find it given the complexities of ever-changing media technologies.

References

Barnes, S. A. (2003). *Computer-Mediated communication: Human-to-Human communication across the Internet*. Boston, MA: Allyn & Bacon.

Bowen, S. A. (2013). Using classic social media cases to distill ethical guidelines for digital engagement. *Journal of Mass Media Ethics, 28*(1), 119–133.

Bowen, S. A., & Stacks, D. W. (2014). Understanding the ethical and research implications of social media. In M. W. DiStaso & D. S. Bortree (Eds.), *Ethical practice of social media in public relations* (pp. 217–234). New York, NY: Routledge.

Caldiero, C. (2016). *Neo-PR, public relations in a postmodern world*. New York, NY: Peter Lang.

Carey, J. W. (1992). *Communication as culture: Essays on media and society*. New York, NY: Routledge.

Christians, C. G., Rotzoll, K. B., & Fackler, M. (1995, 1991). *Media ethics, case & moral reasoning, third and fourth editions*. New York, NY: Longman.

Chung, D. S. & Nah, S. (2013). Media credibility and journalistic role conceptions: Views on citizen and professional journalists among citizen contributors. *Journal of Mass Media Ethics, 28*(4), 271–288.

D'Arcy, A. & Young, T. M. (2012). Ethics and social media: Implications for sociolinguistics in the networked public. *Journal of Sociolinguistics, 16*(4), 532–546.

Dinan, S. (2016, May 10). Senate begins probe into Facebook over conservative censorship allegations. *Washington Times*. Retrieved from www.washingtontimes.com/news/2016/may/10/senate-begins-probe-facebook-censorship-allegation/

DiStaso, M. W. (2014). Bank of America's Facebook engagement challenges its claims of "high ethical standards." In M. W. DiStaso & D. S. Bortree (Eds.), *Ethical practice of social media in public relations* (pp. 21–32). New York, NY: Routledge.

Edelman (2017). 2017 Edelman Trust Barometer, Global Annual Study. Retrieved from www.edelman.com/trust2017/

Elonis v. United States, 135 S.Ct. 2001 (2015).

Federal Trade Commission (2016, May 23). *In the Matter of Lord & Taylor, LLC.* C-4576. Retrieved from www.ftc.gov/enforcement/cases-proceedings/152-3181/lord-taylor-llc-matter

Fraleigh, D. M., & Tuman, J. S. (1997). *Freedom of speech in the marketplace of ideas.* New York, NY: St. Martin's Press.

Fiss, O. M. (1996). *Liberalism divided.* Boulder, CO: Westview.

Gallicano, T. D., Bivens, T. H., & Cho, Y. Y. (2014). Considerations regarding ghost blogging and ghost commenting. In M. W. DiStaso and D. S. Bortree (Eds.), *Ethical practice of social media in public relations* (pp. 21–32). New York, NY: Routledge.

Gettys, T. (2015, April 2). "Proud of yourself sweeties?": Trolls attack reporter who quoted anti-LGBT pizza shop owner. *Raw Story.* Retrieved from www.rawstory.com/2015/04/proud-of-yourself-sweetie-trolls-attack-reporter-who-quoted-anti-lgbt-pizza-shop-owner/

GSS Data Explorer. (n.d.). NORC GSS compress variable. Retrieved from https://gssdataexplorer.norc.org/variables/454/vshow

Guo, C. (2016). *Unscalable, unorthodox startup growth stories.* San Francisco, CA: Inkshares.

Himelboim, I., Lariscy, R. W., Tinkham, S. F., & Sweetser, K. D. (2012). Social media and online political communication: The role of interpersonal informational trust and openness. *Journal of Broadcasting & Electronic Media, 56*(1), 92–115.

Hochberg, A. (2014). Centers of investigative reporting. In K. McBride & T. Rosenstiel (Eds.), *The new ethics of journalism* (pp. 123–135). Los Angeles, CA: Sage.

Huang, T. (2014). Centers of investigative reporting. In K. McBride & T. Rosenstiel (Eds.), *The new ethics of journalism* (pp. 39–59). Los Angeles, CA: Sage.

James, C., Davis, K., Flores, A., Francis, J., Pettingill, L., Rundle, M., & Gardner, H. (2010). Young people, ethics, and the new digital media. *Contemporary Readings in Law and Social Justice, 2*(2), 215–284.

King, H. (2016, May 12). Zuckerberg wants to meet with conservatives amid Facebook bias allegations. CNN Money. Retrieved from http://money.cnn.com/2016/05/12/technology/facebook-trending-guidelines/

Kroger Co. of Mich. v. Granger, NLRB, No. 07-CA-098566 (April 22, 2014).

Leonard, L. G. & Toller, P. (2012). Speaking Ill of the dead: Anonymity and communication about suicide on MyDeathSpace.com. *Communication Studies, 63*(4), 387–404.

Lipschultz, J. H. (2018). *Social media communication: Concepts, practices, data, law and ethics* (2nd edition). London: Routledge.

Lipschultz, J. H. (2016, November 11). Dealing with social media bullies. *The Huffington Post.* Retrieved from www.huffingtonpost.com/entry/dealing-with-social-media-bullies_us_582615b3e4b02b1f5257a113

Lipton, E., Sanger, D. E., & Shane, S. (2016, December 13). The perfect weapon: How Russian cyberpower invaded the U.S. *The New York Times.* Retrieved from www.nytimes.com/2016/12/13/us/politics/russia-hack-election-dnc.html

Lowery, S. A., & DeFleur, M. L. (1995). *Milestones in mass communication research, media effects* (3rd edition). White Plains, NY: Longman.

Mathewson, J. (2014). *Law and ethics for today's journalist: A concise guide.* Armonk, NY: M. E. Sharpe.

McBride, K. & Rosenstiel, T. (Eds.) (2014). *The new ethics of journalism, principles for the 21st century.* Los Angeles, CA: SAGE.

Mihailidis, P. (2014). *Media literacy and the emerging citizen: Youth, engagement and participation in digital culture.* New York, NY: Peter Lang.

Mills, Jon L. (2015). *Privacy in the new media age.* Gainesville, FL: University Press of Florida.

Motlagh, N. E., Hassan, M. S. B. H., Bolong, J. B., & Osman, M. N. (2013). Role of journalists' gender, work experience and education in ethical decision making. *Asian Social Science, 9*(9), 1–10.

National Opinion Research Center (2016). NORC General Social Survey (GSS). http://gss.norc.org/

Nunez, M. (2016, May 9). Former Facebook workers: We routinely suppressed conservative news. *Gizmodo.* http://gizmodo.com/former-facebook-workers-we-routinely-suppressed-conser-1775461006

Ontario v. Quon, 560 U.S. 746 (2010).

Owen, L. H. (2016, May 10). Facebook: "No evidence" that contractors "manipulated trending topics" or suppressed conservative viewpoints. Nieman Lab. www.niemanlab.org/2016/05/facebook-no-evidence-that-contractors-manipulated-trending-topics-or-suppressed-conservative-viewpoints/

Packingham v. North Carolina, 137 S.Ct. 1730, 1736 (2017).

Patching, R. & Hirst, M. (2014). *Journalism ethics, arguments and cases for the twenty-first century.* London, UK: Routledge.

Pegoraro, R. (2016, May 11). There are worse things than manipulated 'trending' story lists. Yahoo! Finance. http://finance.yahoo.com/news/the-only-thing-worse-than-a-manipulated-%E2%80%9Ctrending%E2%80%9D-list–an-unfiltered-on-162716282.html

Pompper (2015). *Corporate social responsibility, sustainability and public relations: Negotiating multiple complex challenges.* London, UK: Routledge.

Reno v. American Civil Liberties Union, 521. U.S. 844 (1997).

Roberts, C. (2012). Identifying and defining values in media codes of ethics. *Journal of Media Ethics, 27*(2), 115–129.

Schiller, H. (1989). *Culture, Inc.* New York, NY: Oxford University Press.

Shirky, C. (2014). Truth without scarcity, ethics without force. In K. McBride & T. Rosenstiel (Eds.), *The new ethics of journalism* (pp. 9–24). Los Angeles, CA: Sage.

Smith v. Maryland. 442 U.S. 735 (1979).

Smolla, R. A. (1992). *Free speech in an open society.* New York, NY: Alfred A. Knopf.

Solis, B. (2014). Forward: Social media is lost without a social compass. In M. W. DiStaso & D. S. Bortree (Eds.), *Ethical practice of social media in public relations* (pp. xv–xxiv). New York: Routledge.

Stevenson, N. (1995). *Understanding media cultures, social theory and mass communication.* London: Sage.

Stratton, S. E. (2014). Password please: Rethinking the constitutional right to information privacy in the context of social media. *Hastings Constitutional Law Quarterly, 41,* 649–679.

Sullivan, M. (2017, January 8). It's time to retire the tainted term "fake news." *The Washington Post*. www.washingtonpost.com/lifestyle/style/its-time-to-retire-the-tainted-term-fake-news/2017/01/06/a5a7516c-d375-11e6-945a-76f69a399dd5_story.html

Terilli, Jr., S. A. & Splichal, S. (2018). Privacy rights in an open and changing society. In W. Wat Hopkins (ed.), *Communication and the law 2018 edition* (pp. 287–314). Northport, AL: Vision Press.

Ward, S. J. A. (2019). *Disrupting Journalism Ethics, Radical Change on the Frontier of Digital Media*. London and New York: Routledge.

Ward, S. J. A. (2013a, November 4). Why hyping transparency distorts journalism ethics. *PBS Media Shift*. www.pbs.org/mediashift/2013/11/why-hyping-transparency-distorts-journalism-ethics/

Ward, S. J. A. (2013b, August 19). Why we need radical change for media ethics, not a return to basics. *PBS Media Shift*. www.pbs.org/mediashift/2013/08/why-we-need-radical-change-for-media-ethics-not-a-return-to-basics/

Ward, S. J. A. & Wasserman, H. (2010). Towards an open ethics: Implications of new media platforms for global ethics discourse. *Journal of Mass Media Ethics*, *25*, 275–292.

Waters, R. D. (2014). Openness and disclosure in social media efforts, a frank discussion with Fortune 500 and Philanthropy 400 communication leaders. In M. W. DiStaso & D. S. Bortree (Eds.), *Ethical practice of social media in public relations* (pp. 3–20). New York: Routledge.

Winchel, B. (2016, February 23). Yelp employee's angry open letter to CEO starts online firestorm. *PR Daily*. www.prdaily.com/Main/Articles/Yelp_employees_angry_open_letter_to_CEO_starts_onl_20213.aspx

28

Artificial Intelligence, People, and Society

Eric Horvitz

Editorial

In an essay about his science fiction, Isaac Asimov reflected that "it became very common ... to picture robots as dangerous devices that invariably destroyed their creators." He rejected this view and formulated the "laws of robotics," aimed at ensuring the safety and benevolence of robotic systems. Asimov's stories about the relationship between people and robots were only a few years old when the phrase "artificial intelligence" (AI) was used for the first time in a 1955 proposal for a study on using computers to "solve kinds of problems now reserved for humans." Over the half-century since that study, AI has matured into sub-disciplines that have yielded a constellation of methods that enable perception, learning, reasoning, and natural language understanding.

Growing exuberance about AI has come in the wake of surprising jumps in the accuracy of machine pattern recognition using methods referred to as "deep learning." The advances have put new capabilities in the hands of consumers, including speech-to-speech translation and semi-autonomous driving. Yet, many hard challenges persist – and AI scientists remain mystified by numerous capabilities of human intellect.

Excitement about AI has been tempered by concerns about potential downsides. Some fear the rise of super-intelligences and the loss of control of AI systems, echoing themes from age-old stories. Others have focused on nearer-term issues, highlighting potential adverse outcomes. For example, data-fueled classifiers used to guide high-stakes decisions in healthcare and criminal justice may be influenced by biases buried deep in data sets, leading to unfair and inaccurate inferences. Other imminent concerns include legal and ethical issues regarding decisions made by autonomous systems, difficulties with explaining inferences, threats to civil liberties through new forms of surveillance, precision manipulation aimed at persuasion, criminal uses of AI, destabilizing influences in

Horvitz, E. (2017, July 7). "AI, People and Society." *Science*. 357(6346), pp. 7. DOI: 10.1126/science.aao2466.

military applications, and the potential to displace workers from jobs and to amplify inequities in wealth.

As we push AI science forward, it will be critical to address the influences of AI on people and society, on short- and long-term scales. Valuable assessments and guidance can be developed through focused studies, monitoring, and analysis. The broad reach of AI's influences requires engagement with interdisciplinary groups, including computer scientists, social scientists, psychologists, economists, and lawyers. On longer-term issues, conversations are needed to bridge differences of opinion about the possibilities of superintelligence and malevolent AI. Promising directions include working to specify trajectories and outcomes, and engaging computer scientists and engineers with expertise in software verification, security, and principles of failsafe design.

The good news is that studies, programs, and projects have been organized. In 2008, a multi-month study on long-term AI futures was hosted by the Association for the Advancement of Artificial Intelligence, culminating in a meeting in Asilomar, California. That meeting inspired the One Hundred Year Study on AI at Stanford University, a project charged with organizing similar studies every five years for a century and beyond (the first report was re- leased last year). Other recent efforts include workshops and studies hosted by the US National Academies. In April 2018, a report was published on influences of automation on the US workforce following a two-year study. Early in 2019, representatives from industry, academia, and civil society formed a nonprofit organization called the Partnership on AI, aimed at recommending best practices for developing and fielding AI technologies.

Asimov (1956) concludes in his essay, "I could not bring my- self to believe that if knowledge presented danger, the solution was ignorance. To me, it always seemed that the solution had to be wisdom. You did not refuse to look at danger, rather you learned how to handle it safely." Indeed, the path forward for AI should be guided by intellectual curiosity, care, and collaboration.

References

Asimov, I. (1956). *The naked sun* (p. 8). New York, NY: Bantam Books.

29

Ethics in Cyberspace: Freedom, Rights, and Cybersecurity

Richard A. Spinello

29.1 Introduction

The study of cyberethics represents an evolution of computer ethics. When the computer first appeared it was seen as a "revolutionary machine," because of the scale of its activities and its capability to "solve" certain problems with the help of sophisticated software. Attention was soon focused on the disruptive potential of databases, vexing questions about software ownership, and the "hacker ethic." Traditional moral concepts and values such as responsibility, privacy, and freedom had to be creatively adapted to this new reality (Johnson & Nissenbaum, 1995).

In a classic paper, Jim Moor (1985) presented a rationale for why this branch of applied ethics was so essential. The computer was "logically malleable" a highly versatile tool that could be manipulated in many different ways, and those manipulations created complex ethical challenges. Problems arose when there was a "policy vacuum" or a "conceptual muddle" about how technology should be properly used. Moor argued that conventional applied ethics could not easily accommodate the normative issues generated by information technology. Hence the need for a systematic computer ethics. Thanks to the work of Moor and his colleagues, computer ethics soon flourished as an independent discipline.

The information technology revolution was propelled forward by the invention of the Internet and networked technologies. The Internet's use rapidly spread not only throughout the developed world but also in emerging economies. There are currently over 560 million Internet users in China alone. When the World Wide Web first appeared, personal computing and networking technologies converged to create a new social space. As Abbate (1999) points out, the web fundamentally changed the Internet: it was no longer regarded as a research tool or conduit for online communications but as "an entertainment media, a shop window, and a vehicle for presenting one's persona to the world."

Of course, like the digital computer, the Internet and network technologies are characterized by a certain plasticity. This is evident in the recent development of mobile platforms, cloud computing, and the phenomenon of social media. The

444

dynamic and evolving nature of this technical infrastructure gave rise to a whole new set of ethical challenges. There are good reasons why the network has been referred to as a "technology of freedom" (de Sola Pool, 1984). But the freedom to manipulate information sometimes undermines intellectual property protection. Some methods of exploiting the Internet's web-like structure are in conflict with traditional intellectual property (IP) rights. Thus, ethical protocols have been proposed for the prudent use of peer-to-peer networks, information sharing, and music streaming.

In addition, early apprehensions about the Internet's encroachment on privacy rights were not unwarranted. Architectures like cookies and beacons combined with data mining techniques opened the way for surreptitious online surveillance and subtle forms of domination and control. The amount of information collected online about individuals has grown exponentially, and privacy issues cast a long shadow over the utility of social media. Major technology companies like Amazon, Facebook, and Google benefit from a loose privacy enforcement regime in the United States as they constantly seek to monetize information flows and turn them into profits (Cohen, 2016).

This "technology of freedom" has undoubtedly made it easier to distribute information and express ideas to a global audience. But this enhanced freedom to communicate often collides with new laws and technologies designed to curb online speech. While some want to further liberate the tools of expression, others actively seek to constrain them. Of special interest has been the fringe of Internet communication such as hate speech, online threats or libel, and pornography. Finally, the Internet's highly decentralized structure makes it vulnerable to viruses and other forms of malicious code, and this greatly complicates security issues. Connectivity increases vulnerability. Many private and public organizations have had their networked systems hacked or experienced serious data breaches. Hackers steal sensitive data, gain control of computer systems for nefarious purposes, or simply disrupt online operations through costly denial of access attacks.

Regulators and others dealing with these complex issues are also faced with a different reality about regulation and control: norms, laws, and the market are not the only regulatory mechanisms in cyberspace. As Lessig (1999) has astutely pointed out, "code" is also a regulatory force, and quite often "the code is the law." What Lessig has in mind is not the code at its most basic level of Internet exchange such as the transmission control protocol (TCP) and IP protocols, but the multiple software and hardware applications that implement these protocols. These programs, often referred to as the "architectures" of cyberspace, can easily limit and constrict our activities just as laws do. Software such as DRM systems lock up digital content (i.e., DVDs or music) with the help of encryption technologies. They represent new modalities of copyright enforcement that can regulate information flows far more effectively than actual laws. However, technology's full regulatory impact is often occluded, buried in these lines of proprietary source code. With opaque regulations embedded into technological tools we are confronted with a "new form of necessity" whereby "logical constraints" now assume the form of social constraints (Bourdieu, 1998).

In summary, there are four principal issues that have emerged in the area of cyberethics, which are managed through the market, code, laws, and norms. Those issues are free speech, IP protection, privacy, and security. The goal of this essay is to present some informed reflection on these four themes with special attention paid to the interconnection between privacy and cybersecurity. When privacy is secured by strong encryption, it can endanger public safety and social welfare if the user is a criminal or terrorist. This acute conflict between safety and privacy became manifest in the confrontation between Apple and the FBI over the utilization of encryption code to ensure unbreakable data privacy for Apple's iPhone customers. That controversial case illustrates the intricacy of the moral dilemmas that so often arise in the cyberspace. How can companies like Apple protect customer privacy without shirking their responsibilities to society for the public's safety? The key question is whether or not diminished privacy rights are sometimes necessary for a safer environment, especially in the age of terrorism. But we begin with a brief review of free speech issues.

29.2 Free Speech in Cyberspace

The Internet has clearly expanded the potential for individuals to exercise their right to freedom of expression. Internet users can host their own blogs, publish electronic newsletters, or disseminate information from a home page on the web. As the Supreme Court has reminded us so eloquently in its Reno v. ACLU (1997) decision, the Internet enables an ordinary citizen to become "a pamphleteer, . . . a town crier with a voice that resonates farther than it could from any soapbox." Moreover, the early architecture of the Internet clearly favored broad and uninhibited free expression: users could communicate their ideas across the vast network with little interference from government or private censors.

What is the social value of this amplified opportunity for free expression? According to Balkin (2005), digital and network technologies greatly enrich the cultural and "participatory features" of free speech. They promote semiotic democracy, that is, a more democratic culture in which more people have an opportunity to participate in different forms of meaning creation and consumption. Technology drastically lowers the cost of copying and distributing information. In addition, thanks to the Internet's global reach, it is considerably easier to distribute content across different cultures and geographical borders.

Social media has also had a positive impact on opportunities for free expression and the formation of online communities. Facebook, Twitter, LinkedIn, and other social media venues help facilitate the sharing of many different types of information and the cultivation of certain bold and novel formats of civil discourse.

However, along with civil discourse and welcome forms of online expression, many problematic forms of speech have also proliferated in cyberspace. The widespread use of the Internet and social media, especially among more vulnerable segments of the population such as young children, has prompted many attempts to restrict online speech. Pornography, hate speech, virtual threats, harassment, bullying, and even the nuisance speech known as spam have all been targeted by private and public regulators.

Hate speech, for example, has found a new forum in the fragmented and undisciplined world of social media. Social media platforms have had to contend with abusive and offensive speech, which has challenged the tolerance of Facebook and Twitter users. Both companies have struggled to monitor users' content for forbidden expression such as threats, racist comments, or online harassment. Libel and defamation have also been a common sight on these platforms. Social media companies should be sensitive to extreme speech, but they must also walk a fine line between censorship and the protection of users' free speech rights.

Many national sovereignties have intervened to censor the Internet, and their laws typically reflect their own political or social agendas. It was once thought that states would have a difficult time enforcing their sovereignty in cyberspace but, thanks to code such as filtering software, freedom of expression is threatened by state power often assisted by private companies. But states are boldly reasserting their authority and demanding that Internet companies and gatekeepers (such as Google) comply with the host country law. As a result, the Internet has lost some of its "generative" potential as a viable force for semiotic democracy (Zittrain, 2003).

In the United States there were numerous futile attempts to regulate pornographic speech in cyberspace such as the ill-fated Communications Decency Act. Filtering technologies, however, have helped to fill this policy vacuum. While the United States has been preoccupied with pornography, Europe has focused more intently on controlling hate speech. Given the legacy of World War II government regulators along with the courts sought to ban anti-Semitic speech or virulent neo-Nazi propaganda. In the famous case of *Yahoo v. LICRA,* a French court ordered Yahoo to remove Nazi memorabilia from auction web sites despite the fact that the company's servers were located in the United States. Yahoo reluctantly complied. Those bringing the suit against Yahoo claimed that the company violated local French law. But to what extent should these global and borderless network technologies be subjected to local laws or standards?

Perhaps the most troubling forms of censorship have occurred in non-democratic countries such as China. With the help of its "great firewall" the Chinese government blocks all "sensitive" political content from ever reaching the computer screens of its users. Chinese authorities are especially anxious to stifle online expressions of discontent or dissidence that might provoke anti-government demonstrations. China has transformed the Internet into a "giant cage," and the cage metaphor suggests the extent to which the Chinese government has infused regulatory controls into the Internet's architectures and processes. As Schmidt and Cohen (2013) point out, "China is the world's most active and enthusiastic filterer of information." Routers equipped with sophisticated content filters are successfully deployed to this end. In this way the architectures of freedom yield to the architectures of control. The firewalls and filtering mechanisms used for this purpose are far from foolproof but they make it much more difficult for Internet users to retrieve sought after information. According to Mitchell (1995), control of code is power, and we might add that control of code is control of content. Code is designed to structure what we see and read in cyberspace and it can thereby easily advance the work of the censor.

Unfortunately, gatekeeper companies like Google, Yahoo, and Microsoft, which influence and control Internet access, have cooperated in these efforts. In 2002, Yahoo signed a pledge to accommodate the government's attempts to censor content for the sake of social stability. And when Google entered China to compete with Baidu, the Chinese search engine, it hesitantly agreed to censor its search results to comply with China's restrictive rules. This self-censorship was abruptly halted in 2010 as Google pulled back from its aggressive China strategy. On the other hand, some social media platforms such as LinkedIn, whose mission is to connect the world's professionals, believe it is their destiny to have a presence in China. But in order to accomplish its mission LinkedIn has agreed to censor objectionable content rather than commit to free expression. Thus, all links to blacklisted web sites are disabled, and any user posts that represent "prohibited expression" are not seen in China.

These cases suggest that the optimal scope of free speech rights in cyberspace requires more careful deliberation. Much has been written about problems like cyberporn, spam, and online threats along with the proper use of content controls and filtering technologies (Spinello, 2017). But very little has been written about free speech and communication as an intercultural issue. Those who advocate for ethical pluralism typically avoid addressing specific thorny issues like guidelines for permissible "hate speech" or China's restrictive policies, let alone review the moral liability of gatekeepers who directly cooperate with authoritarian governments. Ethicists must carefully consider the perils of allowing countries like China to decide the parameters of free expression in cyberspace. Suppression of free speech rights typically leads to an ill-informed public and other adverse consequences. There must also be more thorough reflection on whether the right to free expression is contingent on culture and history or whether it is a universal right. Is there sufficient philosophical warrant for the claim that *everyone* has a broad right to freedom of expression? There is little doubt that prudent public and corporate policy will depend on how that question is answered.

29.3 Intellectual Property Rights

The properties of digital information seem to change all the rules about IP protection, especially copyrights and software patents. A motto adopted by many legal scholars and civil libertarians is that "information should be free." It should no longer be enclosed by law or by physical containers. According to one perspective, information and networked technologies "have paved the way for the total undoing of copyright" (Koepsell & Inglott, 2016).

To be sure, the ability to reduce all forms of information into a digital format means that it is possible to make limitless, perfect copies of books, videos, and music, and to distribute those products easily and quickly across the borderless web. As a result, violations of IP rights have become commonplace and are not always taken seriously in legal venues. Moreover, certain excesses have worked their way into IP law. Thanks to laws like the Copyright Term Extension Act, the breadth and duration of copyright entitlements has been extended for questionable purposes. The scope of patent protection has also been unreasonably expanded to include minor innovations such as Amazon's "one click" payment method. Such abuses have ignited anti-property rhetoric and calls for the undoing of copyrights. But is IP really an anachronism? Has the copyright, which dates back to the Statute of Anne in early eighteenth-century England, outlived its usefulness in this dynamic digital era? Or are such rights still necessary for the purpose of stimulating innovation and rewarding authors?

These new dissemination technologies do not alter the reality that a creative work still requires an investment of time and money (Merges, 2011). Hence there remains much to be said for the intelligibility of IP rights even in this digital era. Intellectual property rights, which include patents, trademarks, and copyright, are still essential to protect the interests of the creators of IP goods. IP law incorporates both economic rights and authors' rights (Couto, 2008; Wilson, 2009). The former safeguard the financial interests of authors and those intermediaries that publish their works. Authors' rights protect their non-economic interests, which include the right to be properly credited along with the right to control the meaning of their work at least for a limited amount of time. As Hughes (1999) has observed, the push for "recoding freedom" ignores the positive utilities that are derived from the stability of social meaning.

In addition, the normative insights of liberal philosophers like John Locke are still valid. According to Locke, purposeful labor engenders a limited property right so long as certain conditions are met and the granting of that property right causes no harm. Thus, creators too deserve a property right in their original works. An author or inventor who invests his or her time, energy, skill, and personality in a creative, original project surely has an abiding and "morally significant" interest in the end result (Himma, 2007). This entitlement is a simple matter of fairness. If we accept the argument that the creator has a morally significant interest in his or her work, it should logically follow that the creator has a presumptive claim to ownership, so long is no one else is injured by the recognition of this claim.

Property rights are protected by law, but code also has a unique role to play. Digital technologies such as digital rights management (DRM) systems and encryption software can enclose this copyrighted information such as a song or movie more tightly than ever before. But code that protects IP is ill-suited to allow for the extraction of "fair use" excerpts as allowed by copyright law. As a result, "The information infrastructure has as well the potential to demolish a careful balancing of public good and private interest that has emerged from the evolution of U.S. intellectual property law over the past 200 years" (National Research Council, 2000).

Also, code is often buttressed by specific laws to give it even greater force. Consider the Digital Millennium Copyright Act (DMCA) of 1998, which forbids circumventing technological measures (such as a DRM) that protect copyrighted material. It also prohibits making or "trafficking in" anti-circumvention devices. In this case, law and technology work together as a potent constraint in order to protect online digital content. There is valid concern that the DMCA undermines the balance in IP law between content creators and consumers. Thanks to code in the form of digital rights architectures, it is now possible to control or enclose digital information to a degree never before possible. When reinforced by laws such as the DMCA, the digital content becomes hermetically sealed. Rights management systems give content providers the ability to define what rights users will have to use, copy, or edit a work that they have purchased. Code becomes the new enforcer of property rights and that code need not honor copyright's internal safety valves such as fair use or first sale.

But the answer to these problems is not to dismantle institutional arrangements that vindicate the rights of authors. Rather, it is to concentrate on finding the proper equilibrium, to recalibrate the requisite measure of legal and technological protection so that authors and creators are justly rewarded and future innovation stimulated, without impediments to the vitality of the intellectual commons or the free flow of knowledge and information. Boundaries need to be reconfigured without making copyright so thin that authors cannot control the meaning of their works nor appropriate their economic value.

29.4 Privacy

Computer and networking technologies have created enormous new opportunities for both suppliers and consumers of information. Every organization has at its disposal vast computerized resources for processing its many functional activities. As a result of the revolutionary technology of digitization, data have become a commodity to be mined and monetized as much as possible. Pieces of data can also be easily aggregated or recombined to create revealing profiles of consumers. Thanks to new "big data" techniques, behavioral and transactional data can easily transform information flows into valuable knowledge.

At the same time, monitoring technologies and the Internet's open architecture allow for the careful tracking of a person's movements both in cyberspace and in the physical world. Technologies like mobile telephony also provide ample opportunities for such surveillance. There was considerable consternation when people learned that the National Security Agency (NSA) had collected phone records of every US citizen along with the Internet browsing records of foreign citizens.

The preservation of privacy is especially challenging for online consumers who must provide certain information when they make a purchase or engage in other Internet activities. Thanks to the proliferation of cybertechnologies, every move a consumer makes leaves behind a digital imprint that can be captured, stored "forever" in a data base, and recombined with other data. This assembly of data into comprehensive databases enables the creation of "digital dossiers," which include a sequence of records on almost every aspect of a person's life. These data systems, however, are typically easy prey for hackers so this information, including credit card numbers, is often misappropriated.

Almost all web site vendors track the browsing activities of their customers through the use of cookies – small data files that are written and stored on the user's hard disk drive by a web site such as Amazon.com when the user visits that site. These cookies enable the monitoring of a user's movements while on that web site. Did this customer browse through history books or was she more interested in romantic novels? Did she seem to favor any one particular author? Did she put any books into her shopping cart? And did she look at any other items besides books? All of this "cookie data" provides Amazon with important feedback.

Why do companies commit resources to all of this data collection, aggregation, and profiling? The principal objective is targeted marketing and advertising. Internet companies like Amazon use these profiles to personalize the ads or promotions they show to consumers. Most corporations are convinced that the more detailed information they acquire about the consumer, the greater their ability to successfully tailor their marketing efforts. Targeted campaigns minimize risk and increase the likelihood of a positive response by the consumer. Companies see a correlation between the prediction of consumer preferences and increased revenues. As social philosopher Albert Borgman (1992) has observed, "the distinctive discourse of modernity is one of prediction and control."

In addition to online consumers, users of social networks like Facebook are also at risk for the erosion of privacy rights. Facebook often knows the most intimate details of a person's life. Social media users derive many benefits and pleasures from sharing personal information within their network of "friends" and associates. But sometimes that information is shared too widely when users inadvertently make some Facebook settings public. Social media sites typically rely on "opt-in" privacy controls. Worrisome policies by social network platforms include the availability of user's data to third parties for marketing purposes, data mining, research, and surveillance by law enforcement authorities. Also of concern is the use of cookies to track online user activities after they have departed from a social media site (Vallor, 2015).

A more recent test for privacy is the shift to cloud computing where Internet companies become caretakers of consumer data. Old emails, messages, photos, documents, and other data are stored in the cloud and become a commodity for the Internet companies that mine and monetize that data. Cloud data is often mundane but it can include sensitive behavioral information such as personal preferences, browsing history, geolocation data, and so forth. Putting this data into the hands of Apple or Google creates new tensions and obstacles for users seeking to restrict access to their information (O'Brien, et al., 2016).

As Cohen (2013) points out, when weighed against other imperatives such as national security or even the progress of knowledge and technology, privacy is often the loser. But there are certain costs to living in a "surveillance society," that must be taken seriously. The loss of privacy is often a loss of freedom and security. Trading privacy away could ultimately undermine the great promise and potential of networked technologies.

29.5 Cybersecurity

In the last decade the issue of cybersecurity has taken center stage thanks to many high-profile security breaches. Consumers are targeted by clever schemes that can compromise their online accounts or their personal computers. Corporations have had their networks disrupted and assets stolen. Many government agencies have also suffered serious data breaches. Often hackers are looking for consumer or employee data such as credit card numbers or social security numbers. Sometimes hacking is done as revenge. In 2014 Sony Pictures' network was hacked in retribution for a critical film about North Korea that the Studio planned to show. In that same year, 56 million credit card records were pilfered from Home Depot in a massive security breach (O'Brien, et al., 2016). In the fall of 2016 Yahoo revealed that hackers had penetrated its systems and stolen the personal data of more than 500 million users. The pilfered data included email addresses, dates of birth, telephone numbers, and encrypted passwords. And in September 2017 the credit-monitoring firm Equifax disclosed that a massive cyberattack had put at risk personal information of 143 million Americans. The Equifax hacking crisis exposed the company's lax security policies. Outside experts claimed that serious vulnerabilities were obvious in Equifax's security systems months before the hacker attack (Andriotis, 2017).

Thanks to its open architecture, the Internet is particularly susceptible to viruses, self-replicating programs usually hidden away in another host program or file. Macro viruses, which exploit programs called macros included in many applications like Microsoft Word, are particularly insidious. The biggest fear is that terrorists will use a worm or virus to disrupt vital services controlled by computer technology. Use of this malware is not confined to terrorists or black hackers. Some government apparently unleashed the destructive Stuxnet virus into Iran's computer system to thwart some of its nuclear capabilities.

Software code is often especially vulnerable to sabotage and to outside attacks by hackers. Flaws embedded in that code can be exploited by hackers to intrude on to a networked computer system. Browsers can pick up malware such as a virus from an infected web site. Moreover, as more devices and things come online the network's "attack surface" grows to dangerous new levels. One vulnerable component such as a TV or game box can jeopardize many other connections (O'Brien, et al., 2016).

What can be done to guard against these various threats; to safeguard the Internet and make it a more secure environment? A sound security scheme should begin with protecting the perimeter usually by means of a firewall. A firewall consists of hardware and/or software that is positioned between an organization's internal network and the Internet. Its goal is to insulate a companiy's private network from intrusions by trapping any external threat such as a virus before it can penetrate and damage an information system. Antivirus software is obviously another critical element of any sound security architecture. This software is programmed to scan a computer system for malicious code and deletes that code once it has been found.

A more complicated problem is securing information that is being transmitted from one Internet user to another over this open network. It is particularly important to ensure reliable security for online payments and other financial transactions. The optimal way to secure this data is through encryption – encoding the transmitted information so it can only be read by an authorized recipient with a proper key that decodes the information. Through the use of encryption, this information can be protected against interception and tampering. All major Internet companies now use highly dependable public key encryption, an asymmetric system that uses both public and private keys to encrypt and decrypt data. Both Secure Socket Layer (SSL) and Transport Layer Security (TLS) have become industry standards.

But the use of strong encryption is not without controversy. For several years Apple has used unbreakable, "end-to-end" encryption to protect customer communications through its iMessage and FaceTime services. This led to protests from law enforcement officials since only the sender and the intended recipient possessed the keys to access their messages. Encryption can be used not only to protect data being transmitted across the Internet but also data "at rest." When Apple chose to encrypt user data on its iPhone with very strong encryption code, the protests grew louder and culminated in its recent confrontation with the FBI. Do privacy rights reinforced by encryption trump public safety as Apple's policies imply? We turn to that question in Section 29.6.

29.6 Going Dark: Apple versus the FBI

On December 2, 2015 a young married couple, Syed Rizwan Farook and Tashfeen Malik, who were allegedly followers of the ISIS terrorist group, opened fire at a festive Christmas party in San Bernardino, California. The San Bernardino

County Department of Public Health was hosting that party along with a training event in a banquet room. Fourteen innocent people were killed and twenty-two others were severely injured. Most of these individuals worked for the county. Farook was also a health department employee. The motive behind the shooting has remained somewhat obscure though authorities suspect that there were workplace tensions.

Farook, a man of Pakistani descent, was born in the United States. He and Malik began plotting this terror attack before they were engaged to be married and before Malik moved to the United States from Pakistan in 2014. This horrific and unprovoked assault came only a month after a shocking terrorist attack in Paris. In that incident, 120 people were killed in a series of bomb explosions throughout the city of Paris. These acts heightened security concerns throughout the United States and the entire world.

After the San Bernadino episode, the FBI rapidly moved into action. Its investigators were able to recover one of the murderer's iPhones among his or her belongings. The Bureau's agents sought access to the iPhone's hard drive for leads and clues among the messages, photos, or other data. They were anxious to learn whether the couple worked with any collaborators and whether there were plans for future terrorist attacks. The phone was locked, however, and it was not possible to break through the robust encryption that protected its data. Despite appeals from the FBI, Apple refused to give the FBI any technical assistance that might have helped them to access the encrypted data. But the FBI persisted in its refusal to back down, and the stage was set for a titanic struggle between an icon of Silicon Valley and the Federal Government.

The origins of this controversy can be traced back to a critical strategic decision made by Apple, Inc. when it built its newest operating system for its popular iPhone, called the iOS 8. This operating system, unlike its predecessors, incorporated full disk encryption, which means that everything on the iPhone – messages, email, photos, calendar, and contacts – is locked up tight. A decryption key is linked to the user's passcode; that key is stored on the phone and nowhere else. Apple no longer retained the master key to unlock the content on these phones. Therefore, only the phone's user could access the data by means of his or her passcode. The same holds true for the iOS 9. When Apple first released this new operating system it issued the following statement: "For all devices running iOS 8 and later versions, Apple will not perform iOS data extractions in response to government search warrants because the files to be extracted [including photos, messages (including attachments), and email] are protected by an encryption key that is tied to the user's passcode, which Apple does not possess" (Apple, 2015).

Some data such as incoming and outgoing phone numbers and lengths of conversation are saved by wireless carriers. SMS texts are also stored by wireless carriers. If data such as messages, notes, contacts, video, and photos were backed up to Apple's iCloud service, they too would have been available outside the phone itself.

Since the San Bernardino assailant's iPhone ran iOS 9, the encrypted phone data could not be accessed by the FBI as part of its investigation into these horrific shootings. The last iCloud backup was October 19. This meant that subsequent photos, notes, contacts, messages, and video resided only on the device. Since the shooting happened on December 2, forty-four days of information was only on the phone (Nicas & McMillan, 2016). And, by design, Apple did not have the key to decrypt the encrypted disk. Thus, Apple could not comply with the FBI's request to provide this evidence even though the Bureau had a valid warrant. Accordingly, the FBI beseeched Apple to create new software that would simply overcome the phone's built-in hyper security. The FBI did not ask Apple to relinquish its security keys or construct a master key. Rather, its request was quite specific: an alternative operating system for this one phone that would allow its investigators to break into this device. But Apple refused because it was concerned such software, which bluntly overrode the iOS 9, could be used on other devices. This tool might also be misappropriated and fall into the wrong hands. Apple argued that while the FBI's request might seem quite narrow, that was not the case (Benner, 2016).

Apple was also concerned that by giving into this request pressure would mount for some type of back door access to handle these situations in the future. The company believed that it was compelled to stake out an unequivocal position. For Apple, this was a matter of principle: to protect user privacy in the fullest way possible the company did not construct a "back door" into its newest iPhones and it would refuse to do so. Apple was supported by many other companies in Silicon Valley including Facebook, which maintained that weakening digital security by means of backdoor access was not the way to combat crime and terrorism.

The FBI, on the other hand, took its case to the public where it often received a sympathetic hearing. Prior to the San Bernardino case, the Bureau had already been vocal about the perils of strong device encryption, and it was joined by other Washington agencies such as the CIA and the NSA. Their message was simple: use of this encryption without a backdoor key will hinder efforts to investigate or stop terrorist attacks. According to FBI Director James Comey:

> Unfortunately, the law hasn't kept pace with technology, and this disconnect has created a significant public safety problem. We call it "Going Dark," and what it means is this: Those charged with protecting our people aren't always able to access the evidence we need to prosecute crime and prevent terrorism even with lawful authority. We have the legal authority to intercept and access communications and information pursuant to court order, but we often lack the technical ability to do so.
>
> (Comey, 2014)

The FBI continued to pressure Apple, but the company remained steadfast in its refusal to cooperate in getting at this evidence. Tim Cook maintained that the FBI's request for new software that would allow access to the encrypted data was unprecedented. According to Cook, "We can find no precedent for an American company being forced to expose its customers to greater risk of attack" (Mims,

2016). Both sides geared up for a protracted battle in the courts. However, the FBI subsequently uncovered a different method to unlock the phone, and the court showdown was avoided, at least temporarily.

Nonetheless, this watershed case raises many provocative ethical issues about how to calibrate the proper balance between privacy and public safety. Law enforcement officials certainly have a valid interest in preventing criminals and terrorists from "going dark," planning out crimes or terror plots on their encrypted devices that are inaccessible to law enforcement agencies. Those agencies regard strong encryption in the wrong hands as a tool that impedes their investigations of kidnapping, child pornography, gang activities, and terrorism. One solution is to cooperate with authorities on an ad hoc basis. Another is to create a master key for encrypted software or devices that could be held in escrow (perhaps with a government agency) and made available with a court order to law enforcement authorities. However, the key held in escrow would surely become a favorite target for those "bad actors" who roam about in cyberspace. Also, as Cohn (2015) points out, if the FBI is given a key for backdoor access when they present Apple with a warrant, won't other governments make similar demands. Can other countries necessarily be trusted in these matters?

But is it morally proper for Apple to defy this legal request, a valid court order for a one-time tool that will unlock this terrorist's iPhone? What about Apple's moral obligation to help the US government learn more vital facts about vicious crimes or terrorist attacks such as the one in San Bernardino? Does this take precedence over its duty to protect the privacy rights of its customers? If Apple refuses to assist law enforcement, isn't it potentially shielding terrorists by hindering this investigation? Also, Apple's resistance could have economic ramifications. The company has to consider how its policies could affect its economic mission and the interests of its shareholders.

On the other hand, Apple is justifiably worried that compliance with the FBI's demands could set a bad legal precedent and lead to many future requests for data on their customers' phones that are far less compelling. And who will determine the criteria for granting those requests – Apple or the courts? Moreover, Apple's CEO, Tim Cook, operates this company based on certain values, and a betrayal of those values could erode customer trust. But is absolute privacy encoded in its products the *right* value for Apple to champion? Is it hyperbole to suggest that complying with the court order to help the FBI would threaten everyone's civil liberties? And is there any room for compromise? All of these questions should be thoughtfully considered before rushing to judgment about who's right and who's wrong when criminals and terrorists "go dark" (Sorkin, 2016).

29.7 Conclusion

Within the limited narrow compass of these few pages we have reviewed the key themes of cyberethics. Despite shifting technical infrastructures, four moral challenges – free expression, IP rights, privacy, and cybersecurity – continue to persist in the realm of cyberspace. We have relied upon Lessig's helpful taxonomy to explore some of the normative and technological implications of these issues. The debates about the optimal scope of online speech rights, control of information flows, or "information freedom" are far from over. One dominant issue today for Internet companies is how to balance strong data privacy for customers with public safety. As we have seen, Apple has been a leader in fending off government incursions into user data, even when those users might be terrorists or criminals. However, whether this is a prudent policy is certainly debatable. Also debatable is whether technology companies should be more trustworthy than sovereign nations in guaranteeing personal security and privacy.

The broader challenge in the digital world is how to balance information access, security, freedom, and reasonable property rights. How do we write and promote code that gives ordinary citizens the tools to truly enhance their own autonomy and well-being?

References

Abbate, J. (1999). *Inventing the internet.* Cambridge, MA: MIT Press.

Andriotis, A. (2017, September 27). Equifax chief quits amid hacking crisis. *The Wall Street Journal*, A1–2.

Apple. (2015). Privacy. Retrieved from www.apple.com./privacy/government-information-requests

Balkin, J. (2005). Digital speech and democratic culture. In A. Moore (Ed.), *Information ethics: Privacy, property, and power* (pp. 297–354). Seattle, WA: University of Washington Press.

Benner, K. (2016, February 23). Narrow focus may aid FBI in Apple case. *The New York Times*, B1, B6.

Borgmann, A. (1992). *Crossing the postmodern divide.* Chicago, IL: University of Chicago Press.

Bourdieu, P. (1998). *Practical reason: On the theory of action.* Stanford, CA: Stanford University Press.

Cohen, J. (2016). Between truth and power. In M. Hildebrandt (Ed.). *Information, freedom, and property* (pp. 57–80) New York, NY: Routledge.

Cohen, J. (2013). What is privacy for? *Harvard Law Review*, 126, 1904.

Cohn, C. (2015, December 24). The Debate over encryption. *The Wall Street Journal*, A11.

Comey, J. (2014). Going dark: Are technology, privacy and public safety on a collision course? Retrieved from www.fbi.gov/news/speeches/going-dark

Couto, A. (2008). Copyright and freedom of expression: A philosophical map. In A. Gossieres & A. Strowel (Eds.), *Intellectual property and theories of justice* (pp. 33–51). New York, NY: MacMillan Palgrave.

De Sola Pool, I. (1984). *Technologies of freedom.* Cambridge, MA: Harvard University Press.

Himma, K. (2007). Justifying property protection: Why the interests of content creators usually win over everyone else's. In E. Rooksby & J. Weckert (Eds.), *Information technology and social justice* (pp. 47–68). Hershey, PA: Idea Group.

Hughes, J. (1999). Recoding intellectual property and overlooked audience interests. *Texas Law Review*, 77, 923.

Johnson, D. & Nissenbaum H. (1995). *Introduction, 1–12 computer ethics and social values*. Englewood Cliffs, NJ: Prentice-Hall.

Koepsell, D. & P. Inglott (2016). ICT's architecture of freedom. In M. Hildebrandt & B. van den Berg (Eds.), *Information, Freedom, and Property: The philosophy of law meets the philosophy of technology* (pp. 109–132). New York, NY: Routledge.

Lessig, L. (1999). *Code and other laws of cyberspace*. New York, NY: Basic Books.

Merges, R. (2011). *Justifying intellectual property*. Cambridge, MA: Harvard University Press.

Mims, C. (2016, February 18). Apple CEO Cook's risky encryption strategy, *The Wall Street Journal*, B1.

Mitchell, W. (1995). *City of bits: Space, place and infobahn*. Cambridge, MA: MIT Press

Moor, J. (1985). What is computer ethics? *Metaphilosophy*, *16*(4), 266–275.

Reno v. ACLU (1997). 521 U.S. 844.

National Research Council (2000). The digital dilemma: Intellectual property in the information age. Washington, DC: National Research Council.

Nicas, J. & McMillan, R. (2016, February 18). Newer phones aren't easy to crack. *The Wall Street Journal*, A6.

O'Brien, D., et al. (2016, September). Privacy and cybersecurity research briefing. Networked policy series, Cambridge, MA: Berkman Klein Center.

Schmidt, E. & Cohen, J. (2013). *The new digital age*. New York, NY: Knopf.

Sorkin, A. (2016, February 23). When the moral high ground lacks clear boundaries. *The New York Times*, B1, B6.

Spinello, R. A. (2017). *Cyberethics: Morality and law in cyberspace* (6th edition). Sudbury, MA: Jones and Bartlett Publishers.

Vallor, S. (2015). Social networking and ethics. *Stanford Encyclopedia of Philosophy*. Center for the Study of Language and Information.

Wilson, J. (2009). Could there be a right to own intellectual property? *Law and Philosophy*, *28*(4), 393–427.

Yahoo v. LICRA 169 F. Supp 2d 1181 (N.D. Cal. 2001).

Zittrain, J. (2003). Internet points of control. *Boston College Law Review*, 44, 653.

30

Next-Generation Religion and Ethics

Varun Soni

30.1 Introduction

Over the last decade, I have served as the Dean of Religious Life at the University of Southern California (USC), where I oversee more than ninety student religious groups and more than fifty campus chaplains on campus; collectively representing all the world's great religious traditions and many humanist, spiritual, and denominational perspectives as well. I also have the great privilege to do this work on a campus with more international students than almost any other university in the United States, in the heart of Los Angeles, the most religiously diverse city in human history (Loskota, 2015). As a result, the opportunities to think deeply about geo-religious diversity, interfaith engagement, and global ethics are unparalleled at USC (Mayhew, Rockenbach, & Bowman, 2016).

As Dean of Religious Life, I have the extraordinary privilege to walk alongside our students during the most ecstatic and agonizing times of their lives, during their most intense times of triumph and tragedy (For a comprehensive study on college students and their religious tendencies, see Astin, Astin, & Lindholm, 2011). My work fully engages the interplay of shadow and light that animates a student's university experience, and every week I see the full range of human emotions through my confidential work in pastoral care and spiritual counseling (Lartey, 2003). Accordingly, the way I imagine the future of religion and ethics is rooted in my experiences working with millennials and post-millennials – or Generation Y and Generation Z – as they engage religion and ethics in their lives.

The United States is in the midst of a historic transformation of national religious identity. As a deeply Protestant country since its inception, Protestant-ism has historically been the majority religion of the United States – a country where most people are religiously affiliated and a national culture that has been shaped and molded by public Protestantism (Putnam, 2007). But for the first time in its history, the United States is now no longer a majority Protestant country and will likely never be one again.

The composition of the US Supreme Court highlights this shifting national religious identity. During its early history, Supreme Court Justices were Protestants. Eventually there was a Catholic seat on the Supreme Court, and then a Jewish seat, but it was still majority Protestant.[1] But today, there are no Protestants on the Supreme Court. All the Justices are Catholic or Jewish, and so one of the most visible centers of American power in a historically Protestant country has no Protestant representation.

The decline in public Protestantism reflects a larger generational trend that is one of the most significant stories in American religious history – the dramatic rise of those with no formal religious affiliation at all, a group referred to as "nones." In 1950, 2 percent of Americans were not formally affiliated with religion. Today, more than 20 percent of Americans are not formally affiliated with religion, and nones make up the fastest growing religious demographic in the country (Lipka, 2015).

For Generation Y and Generation Z, nearly 40 percent are not affiliated with religion (Lipka, 2016), marking a dramatic increase in non-affiliation over several generations. At USC, 43 percent of our first-year students are not affiliated with religion, and almost 70 percent of our students describe themselves as more spiritual than religious, or spiritual but not religious – a group referred to as "SBNRs" (spiritual but not religious) (for more information on the distinction between "spiritual" and "religious," see Hatch, 1991; Fuller, 2018). In so many ways, the exponential rise of "nones" and "SBNRs" among people under the age of thirty will fundamentally reshape the future of religion in the United State and in the world, at a time when more than half of the world is under the thirty: more than 60 percent of the Muslim world is under the age of thirty (Statistics, 2013), and more than 60 percent of Indians and Chinese are under the age of thirty (Central Intelligence Agency, 2017). More than three billion people are below the age of thirty, and they will collectively write the story that is the future of religion and ethics.

Religion has historically been the predominant location where the intergenerational transmission of ethics and values occur for most people in the world. It has traditionally provided a framework for the majority of human beings worldwide to think about their moral responsibilities and spiritual pursuits. Religion has historically been the primary source of identity and community for most of the world's population; the most important place for human beings to reflect upon the ultimate questions of meaning and purpose, of significance and authenticity in their lives. And religion has historically offered leadership, counseling, care, and prophetic wisdom for the majority of people in the world.

In the age of the non-affiliated, and at a time when most young people in the United States consider themselves more spiritual than religious, what is the future of religious community, religious leadership, religious practice, religious teachings, and religion? Is this the end of religion as we know it? This chapter discusses two megatrends that are emerging in America today, and provides reflections on interfaith and religion in the next generation.

30.2　Two Emerging Megatrends in American Religion

Scholars have predicted the demise of God for a long time now. From Friedrich Hegel to Friedrich Nietzsche, from Sigmund Freud to Karl Marx to the "secularization thesis," scholars have long sounded the alarm that religion is about to end. But religion endures, evolves, and engages. Accordingly, this profound historical moment does not mark the end of religion or the "death of God," because despite a rise in the number of young people not affiliated with formal religion, when individuals walk away from religion, they don't necessarily walk away from faith, God, meaning, purpose, transcendence, community, service, ritual, or prayer. Rather, they interpret those things in a different way that makes sense for them. That is why religion will continue, albeit in a different form, as a location for the transmission of values, community, and leadership; and it will do so through two megatrends that are emerging in American religion today.

The first is the movement away from organized religion toward personal spirituality – away from institutions toward individuals. In terms of religious leadership, religious institutions will no longer exclusively produce the faith and moral leaders of tomorrow as they have done in the past. How could they when 75 percent of mainline American Protestant churches are on the verge of closure because of dwindling attendance, an aging demographic, and limited financial resources? As a result, the United States will likely lose 200,000 Protestant churches in over the next twenty years (Finke & Stark, 1997). Two-thirds of American divinity schools and theological seminaries are about to close because they cannot generate enough tuition to remain financially viable due to the lack of student interest in religious vocations and ordination traditions (Association of Theological Schools, 2015). And even though evangelicals have long been a powerful political, social, and cultural force in American public life, 65 percent of American evangelicals will leave their church before they turn thirty-five, and most will never return (Cooper, Cox, Lienesch, & Jones, 2016).

Accordingly, future spiritual leaders will be rooted in a universal spirituality that connects people between and within faith traditions. This shift is apparent when analyzing national spiritual leadership. For example, over the last several decades, the innovative Billy Graham has been the most influential American spiritual leader, for he was the most popular Christian minister in a majority Christian country (see Lee & Sinitiere, 2009).

But who is the national spiritual leader in the age of nones and SBNRs? I believe the nation's most important spiritual leader is Oprah Winfrey because she challenges us to think deeply about the enduring human questions in our lives, the spiritual questions of meaning, purpose, and identity (see Lofton, 2011). She is a prophetic voice for compassion, reconciliation, empowerment, forgiveness, and justice – themes that are central to all religious faiths. Because she has no formal religious training, she can cross over traditional divides of religion, nationality, race, and gender. She has legitimacy for many people precisely because she is not ordained; she is not formally affiliated with any specific religious tradition; and she speaks from both a humanist and a theistic prospective. Indeed, the passing of the mantle from Billy Graham to Oprah Winfrey is emblematic of the national demographic shift from a predominantly Protestant nation to one that is increasingly non-affiliated with formal religion at all but rather invested in personal spiritual questions and pursuits.

I experienced a similar phenomenon when I was appointed Dean of Religious Life at USC. At that time, all the other deans of religious life and university chaplains around the country were ordained Protestant ministers. I, however, was a non-ordained Hindu attorney, so USC really thought outside the box! Therefore, I don't have a traditional chaplaincy background in the way that my colleagues across the country do. Accordingly, when *Trojan Family Magazine* did a story on me, they called it "The Unchaplain" (Krieger, 2011). The intent was to show that my lack of a traditional chaplaincy background gave me a different perspective, and therefore a different legitimacy to the spiritual lives of students.

But in no other profession would this work. Imagine this scenario happening in either medicine or law. "Here's your surgeon. We call him the non-physician. He has no medical training whatsoever." "Here's your attorney, the un-attorney, who has never been to law school and never tried a case." It could never work in those fields. But somehow, the "Unchaplain" can be framed as a positive and progressive idea; and that is only possible because Americans now recognize religious leadership that is outside the traditional mold. That means that our future leaders will not just be clerics, but they will be other professionals as well. They will be physicians and educators, artists and activists, musicians and athletes, community organizers and nonprofit leaders. They will be leaders who speak directly to the human condition in a way that resonates with others across the faith spectrum and inspires them to action around shared beliefs, values, and aspirations.

The second megatrend we see with religion in the United States is the evolution of an interfaith consciousness. With the rise of nones and SBNRs" and with the increased religious diversity in the United States beyond the Abrahamic traditions through immigrant religions that are now firmly planted in the United States – like Hinduism, Buddhism, Sikhism, Jainism, Taoism, and the Baha'i faith – we are now at a unique moment in American religious history, when young people know more about each other's faiths than ever before (Smith, 2002). Indeed, one-third of all marriages in the United States are now interfaith marriages (Wormald, 2015), and that number actually starts at one-half but over time, one partner will convert to the tradition of their spouse.

Accordingly, young people's families look like the Parliament of the World's Religions.[2] It's not just that young people know someone of a different faith; now they are probably related to someone of a different faith. As a result, young people are more comfortable with differences and diversity. They know and love people from across the faith spectrum, and they fully embrace new hybridized and fusion religious identities. For example, on the USC Student Interfaith Council, we have students who identify as members of all the major world religions.[3] We have students who identify as secular humanists, Pagan, and Wiccan. We have a student who is a member of the Church of the Jedi. Some students call themselves "Zen Christians," part Buddhist and part Christian; others are "Hin-Jews," who come from Hindu and Jewish backgrounds. We have a student who self-identifies as "Sushi" – mother is Sunni and father is Shia. And we have students who call themselves transpiritual.

30.3 Interfaith and Religion in the Next Generation

More than any other sector in American society, higher education is the location where interfaith engagement and religious reconciliation happen. In 2011, the Obama White House launched a national campaign to get college and university students to devote one year to interfaith community service as a way of commemorating the tenth anniversary of 9/11.[4] The planning team expected that several dozen colleges and universities would participate because it involved a lengthy application process, project proposal, and the approval of the college or university president. But more than 200 institutions participated that first year, including community colleges, military and law enforcement academies, and seminaries.

President Obama's Interfaith and Community Service Campus Challenge did not create an interfaith consciousness at American colleges and universities; rather, it revealed that consciousness. It legitimized and celebrated it. It brought it into the public's eye. But that interfaith consciousness is deeply rooted in the values of diversity and inclusion, and those values are very much in the DNA of most colleges and universities in the United States.

As Dean of Religious Life at USC, I have been inspired by student leaders who are greatly invested in the powerful idea that their faith traditions can be part of a solution to the world's great crises and not part of the problem. For example, as USC's response to President Obama's challenge, students created the Ansar Service Partnership, the first Muslim interfaith community organization in the United States. Ansar meets every month and leads interfaith community service initiatives within a ten-mile radius of campus. Every year they also host the Fastathon, an event that embodies the power of interfaith community service.[5]

For Fastathon, Muslim students fast with non-Muslim students, and local businesses sponsor the students as they fast. Each year, the students end their fast together at USC's Caruso Catholic Center in an event that is also sponsored by the Muslim Student Union, Hillel, the Hindu Student Organization, and the USC Interfaith Council. Accordingly, Fastathon raises several thousands of dollars each year for the Intellect, Love, Mercy (ILM) Foundation, which provides much needed services that combat hunger and homelessness in Los Angeles.[6] This type of deep engagement across fundamental differences that implicates the hard work of translating values into action, and of connecting the global and the local, can only happen at a research university like ours. Accordingly, research universities are the location where the next generation of religious reconciliation occurs because they are where the world's next leaders meet, grow, and form deep relationships with each other.

I was reminded of this after the terrorist attacks in Mumbai in 2008 when hundreds of USC students from India and Pakistan came together for an interfaith memorial service. These students read from each other's holy books, lit candles with one another, and embraced each other in solidarity and support. These students would likely never have met in India or Pakistan, but they met at USC, shared a powerful interfaith encounter and experience, and returned to their home countries with a new interfaith consciousness. Since then, I have seen students from Israel and Palestine and students from China and Japan work together on common goals and aspirations. Students who come from regions and countries that are historically antagonistic toward each other, meet right here at USC and they grow friendships, hereby proving that our campuses are unique and powerful locations for reconciliation and engagement.

30.4 Conclusion

So, what does this all mean for religion and ethics for the next generation? I believe that what emerges from a new generation of spiritual leaders with an interfaith consciousness, is a universal ethic predicated on inclusion and shared responsibility; that engages both secularism and science; that demands that religion help solve the world's great crises; that is predicated on well-being, self-care, and flourishing; that challenges all of us to translate our faith into action and our values into service; and that ultimately imagines compassion not as a noun, but as a verb.

Acknowledgment

I am very grateful to Jem Jebbia, a Ph.D. student in Religious Studies at Stanford University, for her research support and suggestions.

References

Association of Theological Schools. (2017). Annual Data Tables. The Association of Theological Schools – The Commission on Accrediting. Retrieved from www.ats.edu/resources/institutional-data/annual-data-tables

Astin, A. W., Astin, H. S., & Lindholm, J. A. (2011). *Cultivating the spirit: How college can enhance students' inner lives*. San Francisco, CA: Jossey-Bass.

Central Intelligence Agency. (2017). Age Structure. Retrieved from www.cia.gov/library/ publications/the-world-factbook/fields/2010.html

Cooper, B., Cox, D. PhD, Lienesch, R., & Jones, R. PhD. (2016). Exodus: Why Americans are leaving religion-and why they're unlikely to come back. PRRI. 2016. Retrieved from www.prri.org/research/prri-rns-poll-nones-atheist-leaving-religion/

Eck, D. L. (2002). *Introduction to a new religious America: How a "Christian country" has now become the world's most religiously diverse nation* (pp. 1–25). New York, NY: Harper One.

Finke, R. & Stark, R. (1997). The churching of America: 1776–1990: Winners and losers in our religious economy *(p. 246)*. New Brunswick, NJ: Rutgers Univ. Press,

Fuller, R. C. (2018). Spiritual but not religious: A brief introduction. In W. B. Parsons (Ed.), *Introduction to being spiritual but not religious: Past, present, future(s)* (pp. 15–29). Abingdon, UK: Routledge.

Hatch, N. O. (1991). Democratization of American Christianity (pp. 4–5). New Haven, CT: Yale University Press.

Krieger, D. (2011). The unchaplain. *Trojan Family Magazine*. pp. 18–21.

Lartey, E. Y. (2003). *In living color an intercultural approach to pastoral care and counseling*. London, U.K.: Jessica Kingsley Publishers, 21.

Lee, S. & Sinitiere, P. L. (2009). *Holy mavericks: Evangelical innovators and the spiritual marketplace* (pp. 1–10). New York, NY: New York University Press.

Lipka, M. (2015, May 13). A closer look at America's rapidly growing religious "nones." Pew Research Center. Retrieved from www.pewresearch.org/fact-tank/2015/05/13/a-closer-look-at-americas-rapidly-growing-religious-nones/

Lipka, M. (2016, August 24). Why America's "nones" left religion behind. Pew Research Center. Retrieved from www.pewresearch.org/fact-tank/2016/08/24/why-americas-nones-left-religion-behind/

Liu, J. (2011, January 27). The future of the global Muslim population. Pew Research Center's Religion & Public Life Project. Retrieved from www.pewforum.org/2011/01/27/the-future-of-the-global-muslim-population/

Lofton, K. (2011). *Oprah: The Gospel of an icon*. Oakland, CA: University of California Press.

Loskota, B. (2015, February 3). Mile of miracles: A microcosm of L.A.'s religious diversity. San Diego County Center for Religion and Civic Culture, Retrieved from https:// crcc.usc.edu/miles-of-miracles-a-microcosm-of-las-religious-diversity/

Mayhew, M. J., Rockenbach, A. N., & Bowman, N. A. (2016, May 1). The connection between interfaith engagement and self-authored worldview commitment. *Journal of College Student Development 57*(4), 363. doi:10.1353/csd.2016.0046.

Putnam, R. D. (2007). *Bowling alone: The collapse and revival of American community* (pp. 65–66). New York, NY: Simon & Schuster..

Smith, T. W. (2002, December 17). Religious diversity in America: The emergence of Muslims, Buddhists, Hindus, and others. *Journal for the Scientific Study of Religion* **41**(3), 577–85. doi:10.1111/1468-5906.00138

UNESCO. (2013). Statistics on Youth | United Nations Educational, Scientific and Cultural Organization. Retrieved from www.unesco.org/new/en/unesco/events/prizes-and-cele brations/celebrations/international-days/world-radio-day-2013/statistics-on-youth/

Wormald, B. (2015, May 12). Chapter 2: Religious switching and intermarriage. Pew Research Center's Religion & Public Life Project. Retrieved from www.pewforum.org/2015/05/12/ chapter-2-religious-switching-and-intermarriage/

Endnotes

[1] The first Catholic was appointed in 1836, Edward Douglass White, while the first Jewish justice, Louis Brandeis, was appointed in 1916.

[2] "About Us." Our Mission. https://parliamentofreligions.org/about/mission

[3] The Interfaith Council (IFC) Mission Statement is as follows: "The Interfaith Council (IFC) is a vibrant community where students can learn and share about different religious and non-religious worldviews, and faith traditions. IFC works to foster respect, friendship, and appreciation through the sharing of personal experiences, visiting local sacred spaces, expanding religious literacy, and participating in service projects, among other events. In collaboration with the USC Office of Religious Life, IFC hopes that through mutual understanding, students will be strengthened and inspired to actively engage in building a just and peaceful world."

[4] The President's Interfaith and Community Service Campus Challenge. National Archives and Records Administration. https://obamawhitehouse.archives.gov/administration/eop/ofbnp/interfaithservice

[5] "Ansar Service Partnership." Ansar Service Partnership. www.uscasp.org/#who-we-are

[6] "Mission and Vision." ILM Foundation. www.humanitarianday.com/ilm-foundation/mission-vision-values/

Index

467